D1188659

# TUNGUSKA:
# CAULDRON OF HELL

*A Star Original*

It happened seventeen minutes and eleven seconds after midnight on the last day of June 1908. Suddenly – like the Sun falling from the sky – a monster 'invaded' our planet. A monster that ripped into the atmosphere and exploded with the appalling fury of a thirty-megaton nuclear bomb that could be heard 750 miles away. The colossal shock wave that followed reverberated twice round the world and was clearly recorded in Britain.

Also by Jack Stoneley and A. T. Lawton in *Star*

IS ANYONE OUT THERE?
C.E.T.I.

# TUNGUSKA: CAULDRON OF HELL

Jack Stoneley

*Scientific Editor*
A. T. Lawton, FRAS

**A STAR BOOK**
*published by*
the Paperback Division of
W. H. ALLEN & Co. Ltd

A Star Book
Published in 1977
by the Paperback Division of W. H. Allen & Co. Ltd
A Howard and Wyndham Company
123 King Street, London W6 9JG

Copyright © Jack Stoneley 1977

Printed in Great Britain by
Hazell Watson & Viney Ltd, Aylesbury, Bucks

ISBN 0 352 39619 9

# LIST OF ILLUSTRATIONS

## CONTENTS

# INTRODUCTION

It happened seventeen minutes and eleven seconds after midnight* on the last day of June 1908. Suddenly – like the Sun falling from the sky – a monster 'invaded' our planet. A monster that ripped into the atmosphere and exploded with the appalling fury of a thirty-megaton nuclear bomb that could be heard 750 miles away. The colossal shock wave that followed reverberated twice round the world and was clearly recorded in Britain.

And yet no one had the remotest idea what had happened. No one, that is, except a few terrified peasants in an isolated region of Central Siberia, who crossed themselves and were convinced it was the end of the world.

For it was here, in the uninhabited upper reaches of the River Podkamennaya (Stony) Tunguska, that the thing from outer space – still unidentified almost seventy years later – shattered itself into eternity and flattened nearly 800 square miles of forest like a gale raging through a cornfield, contemptuously wrenching out mighty tree trunks by their roots.

It was here that this cosmic vandal thundered and roared and coughed out fearful gases and radiation in a scorching wind that seared vast areas of earth and swept great sheets of water from the rivers. Herds of reindeer were consumed and scattered about as charred corpses. Even forty miles away men were thrown into the air and one horror-stricken herdsman was left speechless for seven years. And it was from this same god-forsaken outpost, 2200 miles from Moscow, that millions of tons of mysterious silvery dust fanned half across the globe suddenly turning night into day.

One particularly frightening aspect of the monster's assault is that had its course varied by only a few degrees it would have exploded over the very heart of bustling Edwardian London.

* Greenwich Mean Time

9

Yet it was to be thirteen years before the first news filtered through to the West that something 'out of this world' had taken place in 1908. The Imperial Tsarist government of Nicholas II sneeringly dismissed Siberian newspaper reports as irresponsible hearsay. Peasants who talked to correspondents were written off as imbeciles.

Even now, after numerous expeditions by Russian researchers, the Tunguska Event is still one of the world's most intriguing unsolved mysteries. For, whatever it was that caused this incredible explosion no evidence of its original form has ever been found. It came, it destroyed and it vanished. It left no fragments, nor is there any sign of a crater.

Modern scientific techniques are revealing other strange phenomena. One is now being investigated by a Russian expedition that went to Tunguska in the summer of 1976. Layers of moss, calculated to have grown in 1908, have been found to contain particles, the composition of which is unknown anywhere else on this Earth.

Even more remarkable are the bizarre biological changes taking place. The rate of genetic mutation of flowers and trees there has speeded up an astounding twelvefold. There is now a flourishing coniferous forest in the stricken area.

What *is* the hidden secret of Tunguska? For years experts had assumed it was a giant meteorite that fell, like the one that blasted a three-quarters-of-a-mile crater in Arizona. But, if this were so, what happened to it? There is no mighty scar of impact at Tunguska. There are no meteorite fragments. And why were some trees right in the centre of it all left almost untouched?

This book tells the whole gripping story, right from the moment the monster struck to the many conflicting theories that are still being argued over today. Part One contains the dramatic eye-witness reports and graphic accounts of courageous bands of dedicated men who searched this forbidding region in the 1920s and 1930s. Part Two discusses some of the terrifying forces of nature that scientists have put forward as possible answers – such as exploding comets, fearsome 'Black Holes' and the uncanny 'antimatter' of outer space.

The final section poses the most intriguing question of all. Could the source of this diabolical power have been artificial? Could it conceivably have been created by an exploding artifact from some other world beyond our own Solar System? Could it, in fact, have been an alien counterpart of the NASA Viking probes that touched down on Mars in July and September 1976? And, if so, could unexplained signals picked up by Russian scientists since 1973 be originating from a replacement satellite still orbiting our Earth?

Every possible known phenomena is excitingly dealt with. For, even today, no one's sure *what* it was – any more than they can be sure it will not strike again, perhaps next time over the crowded streets of London, New York or Moscow.

# PART ONE

CHAPTER ONE

# DAY OF THE FIREBALL

It is 30 June 1908. Stifled passengers on the dusty trans-Siberian railway train are still trying to doze after a clammy, restless night on the hard carriage seats. Others stare in bleary-eyed silence through the thick black smoke that coughs rhythmically from the engine up front, occasionally curling in throat-searching whiffs through the door cracks.

The view through the streaky grime of the compartment windows does little to break the monotony of a gruelling journey. It is raw, untamed land. Mile after rugged mile of naked plains, mountain ranges and gaunt regiments of forest trees.

A red-eyed man loosening a coarse and sticky shirt collar wonders what in hell's name convinced him to come out here. But he knows there's no turning back now. Like many of the other grey-faced passengers, he is travelling on a one-way ticket. He's one of the Tsarist Empire's twentieth-century pioneers. For, like the earlier covered wagon trails of the wild American west, the trans-Siberian railway is the 4000-mile Russian artery to the East that will pump life-blood into the deadest place on Earth.

Already, only two years after its completion in 1906, a million hardy settlers have joined this soulless trek into a lost world which, for centuries, had been nature's 'dungeon' for the Tsar's political prisoners to sweat out their sentences in the mines or to freeze in the mighty forests. Later Bolshevik leaders like Lenin and Stalin were to have their bitter taste of exile. For Siberia sprawls like a giant corpse over four-and-a-half million square miles, from Vladivostok to the Urals, and from China to the Arctic Ocean. It is half as big again as the United States.

Before the inauguration of the trans-Siberian railway, hordes of banished humanity rattled their chains of bondage

15

in pitiful marches across the Urals. Assassins, murderers, bandits and those who had incurred the displeasure of some ruthless Government official. Wretched individuals from all classes of nineteenth-century Russian society had spent the last miserable years of their lives deep beneath the ground or in the purgatory of solitary confinement. Even the gilded carriages of pampered notables of the aristocracy, personally deported by the Tsar, joined the pathetic procession, often with their wives and children, their servants and what few family treasures they had been able to salvage.

Many of the new pioneering families will not survive the long and merciless Siberian winters when the temperature can vary fifty degrees fahrenheit on the same day; when the earth freezes like granite and the rivers become tentacles of solid ice for eight long, weary months of the year. When a man's breath solidifies into crystals of ice and birds drop frozen stiff out of the sky. Only the fittest will survive in a callous wilderness where there is one doctor for every 8000 square miles. Some of the less robust immigrants will even perish on the journey to this harsh new world. But to most of them, unalluring as it is, Siberia presents a personal challenge. To those willing and able to come to accept its rugged terms of survival, there is land, mineral wealth – and a kind of freedom they have not known under the insatiable Tsarist exploitation of European Russia.

Now a few trans-Siberian passengers are glancing at their watches. It's a little after 7.15 a.m.* They'll soon be rumbling into dreary little Filimonovo Junction. At least they can get out here and stretch their legs.

The sun is up. There is no cloud. Nothing stirs out there. It's like trundling across the desolate surface of the Moon.

And it is then that they see it . . . streaking across the blue sky like a bolt out of hell. An immense, searing ball of fire that dims even the blinding rays of the sun. Seconds later a towering tongue of flame licks the horizon and a thunderous explosion shakes the astounded passengers to their feet.

As the heavy coaches tremble on the metal track, the engine driver is convinced some of them have been derailed.

* Local time

16

He jams on the brakes hard. The train grinds fiercely to a juddering halt as the travellers lurch forward, shake themselves and then scamper out on to the track.

For a few moments they listen to dull thuds and distant rumblings. Then nothing more. The air is still again. The mean, uninviting territory stretches lifelessly about them. They shudder, wondering what kind of Satanic land they're venturing into.

But if those frightened travellers on the trans-Siberian railway had been 350 miles to the North, at the lonely little trading station of Vanavara huddled on the banks of the Stony Tunguska River, they would most certainly have taken the next train back to civilization.

Here, where the hunting tribes of the nomadic Evenki people come to barter their furs for provisions, the sky itself appears to rip apart and burst into flame. The earth shakes with appalling violence. A searing blast of radiation scorches the handful of inhabitants, hurls men into the air, wrenches doors from their stout log cabins and shatters heavy iron stoves. In the fields a tent is lifted high into the air together with the Evenki hunters sheltering inside it. All around them cattle stampede and startled horses gallop off in all directions dragging their ploughs behind them.

And yet the place where the monster struck is still thirty-seven miles away – deep in the mighty uninhabited Yenisei forest in the basin of the Tunguska river. Here the devastation is unbelievable.

Whatever it is that unleashes its awesome power tears up tree trunks by the roots, tossing them into heaps like spilled matchsticks, severing others as cleanly as a lawn mower ploughing through grass. And over an area almost the size of Surrey its hot breath belches forth, scorching everything before it for hundreds of square miles.

All wildlife in its relentless path, including herds of reindeer, are wiped out in those few disastrous moments. Had the centre of the catastrophe been heavily populated the death role would have been phenomenal.

And yet it is to be twenty years before Western civilization learns the incredible things that have taken place deep in the no man's land of Central Siberia on this hot summer morning in 1908, and to wonder at some of the uncanny phenomena that are to make it one of history's most intriguing unsolved mysteries. For the more searchingly scientists seek the elusive truth of the Tunguska holocaust, the stranger it is to become . . .

It is 5.30 a.m., Greenwich Mean Time, on 30 June 1908 . . . almost five and a quarter hours after the Tunguska disaster. Three thousand seven hundred miles away most of Edwardian London is still sleeping. But at three of the city's meteorological stations – Westminster, South Kensington and Shepherds Bush – the sensitive microbarographs suddenly begin picking up strange aerial shock waves. The same thing is happening at Cambridge, Leighton (Bedfordshire) and Petersfield in Hampshire.

The recordings last for just under two minutes. The waves have in fact, encircled the Earth twice before being picked up on their second journey. But they arouse little interest. No one bothers to find out from where they have originated. The most urgent truly British concern on this sunny Tuesday morning is to accurately forecast the weather for King Edward's visit to Newmarket races. Then there are of course the lawn-tennis championships at Wimbledon and the all-important social event of the year, the Henley Regatta. A mass meeting of women suffragettes is planned at Caxton Hall, with a public rally in Parliament Square. They'll want to know if it's going to be a nice day too.

A record of the anomalous seismic wave is nonchalantly filed away and forgotten, later to be catalogued merely as no. 1536 on the list of earthquakes for the year 1908.

But that night something very odd happens. It is abnormally light. The candy-floss sky over London is tinted with a peculiar bright red glow, and late West-End revellers jogging home in their hansom cabs are amazed to find they can actually read the small print in their newspapers at midnight. Not that they find any reference to the incredible Tunguska incident – the actual cause of the phenomena.

18

The only tit-bit of news from Russia that catches their eyes that morning is *The Times* headline: 'Fatal Duel in St Petersburg', telling how 'Count Nicholas Sumaroff was shot in an encounter with Count Mantenffel of the Horse Guards' in a squabble over a woman.

Many other places also experience the strange 'white night' of 30 June to 1 July. In Glasgow, between 11 p.m. and 3 a.m., it is so light that all but the brightest stars are invisible. As in London, people can read clearly in the streets. At 10 p.m. throughout Germany groups of curious observers watch an unfamiliar greenish twilight which dramatically changes to a glowing red rim along the horizon at midnight. And everywhere the clouds are shining like silver.

In Antwerp and other Belgian cities reports describe the ruddy glow of a huge fire rising above the horizon that makes it possible to see the seconds hand of a watch. And in some places there is no night at all. A student from Kazan University on vacation 300 miles east of Moscow, is astounded to find he can take excellent photographs in the streets at midnight. These are published in the magazine *Metoritika*. From Saratov on the River Volga passing ships are clearly visible from nearly two miles away.

The following brief items appear in the monolithic columns of, *The Times* on Friday 3 July. They receive the same prominence as the court report of a motor cyclist driving without lights 'at a furious pace, from 15 to 25 miles an hour'.

British Astronomical Association – At the monthly meeting held on Wednesday evening at Sion College, Victoria embankment, Mr G. J. Newbegin drew attention to the disturbed state of the solar atmosphere, showing a drawing and giving a description of a very large prominence that he had observed and measured in the morning of that day (1 July), and that showed unusual changes of form. Allusion was made by Mr E. W. Maunder and Mr H. P. Hollis (both of the Royal Observatory) to the long-lasting aurora of the previous evening.

## Curious Sun Effects at Night

To the Editor of *The Times*

Sir, – Struck with the unusual brightness of the heavens, the band of golfers staying here strolled towards the links at 11 o'clock last evening in order that they might obtain an uninterrupted view of the phenomenon. Looking northwards across the sea they found that the sky had the appearance of a dying sunset of exquisite beauty. This not only lasted but actually grew both in extent and intensity till 2.30 this morning, when driving clouds from the east obliterated the gorgeous colouring. I myself was aroused from sleep at 1.15 a.m., and so strong was the light at this hour, that I could read a book by it in my chamber quite comfortably. At 1.45 a.m. the whole sky, N. and N.E., was a delicate salmon pink, and the birds began their matutinal song. No doubt others will have noticed this phenomenon, but as Brancaster holds an almost unique position in facing north to the sea, we who are staying here had the best possible view of it.

Yours faithfully,
Holcombe Ingleby,

Dormy House Club, Brancaster, 1 July.


On 4 July, a leader article in *The Times* goes into the phenomena more deeply.

### *The Recent Nocturnal Glows*

The remarkable ruddy glows which have been seen on many nights lately have attracted much attention and have been seen over an area as far as Berlin. There is considerable difference of opinion as to their nature. Some hold that they are auroral; their colour is quite consistent with this view, and there is also the fact that Professor Fowler of South Kensington predicted auroral displays at this time from his observations, which showed great disturbances in the sun's prominences. There was a slight, but plainly marked disturbance of the magnets on Tuesday night, and this materially strengthened the auroral theory, as the two phenomena are very closely correlated. However, this was shaken on the following night, when the glow was quite as strong, but the magnets were exceptionally quiet.

This convinced many who had before been inclined to the auroral theory, that the phenomenon was an abnormal twilight glow . . . It is only necessary to suppose that some temporary condition of the atmosphere made this twilight much brighter and redder than usual.

The article then goes on to compare the phenomenon with that witnessed after the enormous Krakatoa Volcano eruption in the East Indies a quarter of a century before, when abnormal sunset glows continued for months. This furious holocaust blasted a column of fiery dust thirty-three miles high, and scattered rocks like mammoth hailstones for fifty miles. The volcano collapsed into a six-hundred-foot sea crater, causing 36,000 people and nearly 300 towns to be destroyed in the tidal wave that followed (see chapter 10).

We may recall the circumstances of the wonderful glows which were seen in this country in the autumn of 1883, and which were due to the dust scattered in the upper atmosphere by the terrific outburst at Krakatoa at the end of August. These glows had many points in common with the recent ones; the deep, lurid colour suggesting a distant conflagration (many were for some time doubtful whether Tuesday's glow was not due to this cause), and both glows were seen at a much longer interval after sunset than ordinary sunset glows, and the latter had already faded before the abnormal glow began. This indicated an extraordinary height for the dust causing the glow, and consequently the extreme fineness of the latter.

By charting the places and dates of the first visibility of the glows in 1883, it was found that the dust was carried westward by a previously unknown upper current at a speed of some 80 miles an hour. It did not reach the British Isles till its third circuit of the globe, each circuit having a wider range in latitude. We thus see that distance is no obstacle in vast cosmical phenomena of this kind, which are absolutely world-embracing.

No volcanic outburst of abnormal violence has been reported lately; there have, however, been some moderate outbursts in the Pacific during the spring, and it is possible that the dust may have reached us from these, or from some unreported eruption in some little-known region of the world.

By 5 July, the news of the strange white nights reaches the *New York Times* from their man in London.

Like Dawn at Midnight, *runs the headline.*

London sees Sky Blue and Clouds tipped with Pink at the Hour.

London, 4 July: Several nights throughout the week were marked by strange atmospheric effects which Dr Norman Lockyer of the South Kensington Solar Physics Laboratory, believes to be a display of the *aurora borealis*. Following sunsets of exceptional beauty and twilight effects remarkable even for England, the northern sky at midnight became light blue, as if the dawn were breaking, and the clouds were touched with pink in so marked a fashion that police headquarters was rung up by several people who believed a big fire was raging in the north of London.

(For the following two months the Northern hemisphere continued to have brighter nights than normal. However, it was not until 1930 that this phenomenon, together with the hitherto unaccountable' seismic recordings were directly linked to the mysterious Tunguska Event. It was then that the eminent English meteorologist C. J. P. Cave realized that the dates coincided. Dr F. J. W. Whipple, then superintendent of Kew Observatory, also noted that the Tunguska district lay approximately in a direct line with Cambridge and Petersfield where the seismic waves had been picked up. Later research concluded that, as the giant fireball had thundered towards the Earth, several million tons of pulverized material had scattered in the atmosphere and acted as a huge reflector to the rays of the Sun, out of sight below the Northern horizon. Though exactly what this material was remained a mystery.)

Within days of the Tunguska invader's dramatic descent, eye-witness reports begin to appear in a number of Siberian newspapers, though nothing is yet known of the incredible havoc that resulted. The nearest inhabited place from where the interviews come is the village of Kenzma – still 130 miles from the object's deadly point of impact. It is from here that the newspaper *Krasnoyarets* receives the following comprehensive report, published on 13 July:

An extraordinary atmospheric phenomenon was noticed in this region. A noise as from a strong wind was heard, followed immediately by a fearful crash, accompanied by a subterranean shock which caused buildings to tremble. One had the impression that some huge beam or heavy stone had struck the buildings. This was followed by two equally forceful blows and an extraordinary underground roar like the sound of a number of trains passing simultaneously over rails. Then followed a sound like artillery fire . . . between fifty and sixty bangs, becoming gradually fainter.

Eye witnesses relate that, before the first bangs were heard, a heavenly body of a fiery appearance cut across the sky. Neither its size nor shape could be made out owing to its speed and unexpectedness. However many people in different villages distinctly saw that, when the flying object touched the horizon, a huge flame shot up that cut the sky in two.

Bangs were heard as soon as the tongue of flame disappeared. On the island opposite the village, horses began to whinny and cows to low and run wildly about. One had the impression that the Earth was about to gape open and everything would be swallowed up in the abyss. Fearful bangs resounded from somewhere, shaking the

Earth, and the invisibility of the source inspired a kind of superstitious terror. People were literally dumbfounded.

One of the first news stories, in the Irkutsk paper *Sibir*, is from the village of Nizhne-Karelinsk, more than 200 miles from the Tunguska Basin and dated 2 July. The correspondent writes:

In the North West, quite high above the horizon, the peasants saw a body shining very brightly (too bright for the naked eye) with a bluish-white light . . . The body was in the form of a cylinder.

The sky was cloudless, except that low down on the horizon in the direction in which this glowing body was observed, a small dark cloud was noticed . . . It was hot and dry and when the shining body approached the ground it seemed to be pulverized, and in its place a huge cloud of black smoke was formed and a loud crash, not like thunder, but as if from the fall of large stones or from gunfire, was heard.

All the buildings shook and, at the same time, a forked tongue of flame broke through the cloud. All the inhabitants of the village ran out into the street in panic. The old women wept and everyone thought the end of the world was approaching.

Some of these early reports of the happening are rather haphazard and conflicting. No one seems to know exactly where the object has landed. Many newspapers quickly dismiss the whole thing as local gossip.

One sceptical editor sends a reporter 350 miles to the town of Kansk where he has been told a meteorite has fallen. Needless to say, as the town is nearly 400 miles from the disaster zone, the investigator doesn't get very much of a story. The following contemptuous item appears in the newspaper on 4 July:

The noise was considerable but no stone fell. All the details of the fall of a meteorite here should be ascribed to the over-active imagination of impressionable people.

There is no doubt that a meteorite fell, probably some distance away, but its huge mass and so on are very doubtful.

End message.

Other local editors continue to carry brief references. On 14 August, the newspaper *Sibirskaya Zhizn* tells of the frightening effects the explosion has had on men working in a goldmine 150 miles away.

Everyone felt a trembling of the ground accompanied by a loud roar as though from thunder, followed immediately by two fainter crashes and then by at least ten more still fainter ones. The mine buildings creaked and groaned, the gold-washing machines quivered, and people ran out in fear on to the street. The horses fell on their knees.

By the autumn of 1908 reports in the press dry up altogether. The cruel Siberian winter isolates the tiny hamlets and villages from even their closest neighbours. And a forbidding blanket of snow and ice covers the devilish handiwork of the Tunguska monster.

In the world outside, the distant babblings of a few superstitious peasants are quickly forgotten. To the hierarchy at St Petersburg – capital of the Tsarist regime 3000 miles away – whatever was seen and heard in Tunguska concerns them no more than if it had been in the remote Scottish Highlands or the wild Australian outback. They have far more pressing problems to worry about ... like the distant rumblings of a political volcano that could shatter their vast empire far more alarmingly than any mythical fireball from the sky. They have far more to fear from the growing wrath of the proletariat than from that of the gods.

The most tortuous and bitter years in Russia's harsh history are to follow. From 1914 to 1920 the straggling country is to be ravaged by war, first in the marathon struggle against Germany and then three brutal, agonizing years of internal bleeding for civil turmoil. It all claims a sickening twelve-and-a-half million lives – almost 8 per cent of the Russian people. Three million more of them are to perish in a cataclysm of human suffering through starvation and disease. Little wonder that in 1921, few people bother themselves about vague, thirteen-year-old rumours from the boggy pine forests of Tunguska.

But one man does. His name . . . Leonid A. Kulik.

## CHAPTER TWO

## MAN WITH A MISSION

A bearded man in his late thirties hugs the astrakhan collar of a greatcoat over his ears and listens to the clatter of heavy train wheels over the points of yet another desolate little railway junction strung along the trans-Siberian railway. It reminds him of the death rattle of machine-gun fire, so familiar to this young revolutionary during the long, savage years of war. But it is now mid-September 1921. The killing is over. There is time for men like Leonid Kulik to think of other things. And in the searching mind of this restless scientist, one objective dominates. The Tunguska monster.

To Leonid Kulik from the Mineralogical Museum of St Petersburg (now re-named Petrograd) the mysterious fireball of 1908 has become an obsession. Whatever it was, he is determined to seek it out.

For the countless time he thumbs through a file of fraying newspaper clippings – those first vague reports of the strange affair. He wonders if the word of a handful of uneducated peasants so long ago really justifies him making this punishing journey into the cold heart of Central Siberia.

Actually the original motive for the visit here had nothing to do with the Tunguska phenomenon. He hadn't even heard of it when he had been commissioned by the Russian Academy of Sciences to collect general information about meteorite falls. But, before his party of researchers left Petrograd, a diligent Soviet researcher called Svyatsky had handed him a sheet ripped from a 1910 calendar. Pasted to the back of it was part of an article from the newspaper *Sibirskaya* printed in 1908.

It described that trans-Siberian journey on the morning of 30 June, thirteen years ago, when the passengers at Fili-monovo Junction had watched the fireball streak by. According to *this* report, later found to be incorrect, the

27

driver and the passengers had found a red-hot meteorite that had cooled into a huge white stone block almost entirely buried in the ground.

This account had urged him to search the back numbers of other Siberian newspapers. The fearful stories – conflicting as many of them were – intrigued him. He had to find out what really happened.

Unfortunately this particularly ferocious winter of 1921 closes in early. By the time Leonid Kulik has calculated where the object struck, its violent secret is guarded by a vast impregnable fortress of ice and snow. But he doesn't waste those first precious months in Siberia. Instead he probes the still-vivid memories of many people in the towns, cities and villages in the populated areas of Kansk and Tomsk with persistent interviews and by distributing 2500 searching questionaires.

But, back in Petrograd – like those original newspaper accounts of 1908 – the scientific fraternity soon forgets them. It is to be yet another six years before Kulik can pursuade the Russian Academy of Sciences to send his team out there again.

What finally does convince them is a succession of startling reports from other researchers working on various projects in the Tunguska region. They pass on stories told to them by the wandering Evenki (Tungus) people who were camped within twenty-five miles of the explosion. Stories of a thousand reindeer being wiped out, great forests being utterly destroyed and 'water gushing up from the earth'. One report comes from a geologist named Sobolev, employed by the Krasnoyarsk Museum near Kansk who was working in the Tunguska area in the summer of 1923. There he met a man called Ilya Potapovich.

Fifteen years ago, reads the geologist's account, Ilya Potapovich's brother lived on the River Chambé. One day a terrible explosion occurred, the force of which was so great that the forest was flattened for many miles along both banks of the river.

His brother's hut was flattened to the ground, its roof

was carried away by the wind and most of his reindeer fled in fright. The noise deafened his brother and the shock caused him to suffer a long illness. In the flattened forest at one spot a pit was formed from which a stream flowed into the River Chambé. The Tunguska road had previously crossed this place but it was now abandoned because it was blocked, impassable, and moreover the place aroused terror among the Tungusi people. From the Podkamennaya Tunguska River to this place and back was a three-day journey by reindeer.

In 1924 another geologist, S. V. Obruchev, also interviews Ilya Potapovich who tells how his brother was 'deprived of speech for several years' after the experience. Ilya, himself, was to be one of the guides for later expeditions by Kulik.

More fascinating eye-witness accounts are passed on to the Academy of Sciences by a member of the Russian Geographical Society, ethnographer I. M. Suslov who, in March 1926, was working at the windswept little trading stations of Vanavara and Teterya on the Tunguska River. He too has closely interrogated the Evenki people. One of them is a woman called Akulina, the widow of Ilya Potapovich's brother. She describes the night of the great fireball like this:

'Early in the morning when everyone was asleep in the tent, it was blown up into the air, together with the occupants. When they fell back to earth the whole family suffered bruises.' She and her husband lost consciousness. When they came round they 'heard a great deal of noise and saw the forest blazing around them and much of it devastated.'

An old man who was living with them at the time adds: 'The ground shook and incredibly long pronounced roaring was heard. Everything round about was shrouded in smoke and fog from the burning falling trees.'

Suslov also talked to sixty other Evenki people at the trading stations in June 1926. All agreed that, when the fireball fell, it 'burned the trees, killed the dogs and the reindeer, injured people and flattened the *taiga* (forest)'.

29

An engineer called Gundobin sends Kulik this story from Ivan Vasilyevich Kokorin, helmsman of a boat navigating the turbulent River Angora at the time:

In the north flashed up a bluish light and there passed in the sky (from the south) a fiery ball, considerably larger than the sun, which left behind it a wide luminous streak. Thereupon there occurred such a cannonade that all the labourers that were in the boat rushed to hide themselves in the cabin, having forgotten about the danger which threatened from the rapids. The strength of the sounds was so great that the oarsmen were entirely demoralized and it took great efforts to return them to their places in the boat.

Early in 1927 new research is also published in the magazine *Mirovedeniye* by the former Director of the Irkutsk Magnetic and Meteorological Observatory, A. V. Voznesensky, who estimates that the thunderous explosion from Tunguska had been heard over 380 000 square miles ... four times the area of the United Kingdom.

Like Kulik, he believes the intruder was a meteorite. But, as there were a number of explosions, he concludes that it must have shattered into smaller bodies before landing. It is highly probable, he claims, that future investigators will find a mass of fragments.

Backed by this later information, together with warnings that the object might be destroyed by atmospheric corrosion, Kulik is eventually able to convince the academy that a further expedition to find the Tunguska monster is now justified. And so, in February 1927, Leonid Kulik finds himself back on the trans-Siberian express to continue the incredible mission that is to dominate the rest of his life.

It is early spring in Central Siberia, but still agonizingly cold as Kulik and his assistant Gyulikh load horse-drawn sledges with supplies of food and equipment at Taishet station, some one hundred miles East of Kansk.

Their next objective is the Vanavara trading station 350

miles to the north. They travel through the village of Kezhma where they replenish their supplies and struggle on for three exhausting days into wild, uncharted country, finally staggering into Vanavara on 25 March. It's like a miniature Dodge City before the prospectors came. Just a few log cabins and one or two primitive wooden buildings line the 'streets' of ankle-deep mud.

Kulik finds Ilya Potapovich at the trading station who agrees to guide them on horseback into the mighty *taiga* the following day. But the weary animals just can't make headway through the huge snowdrifts and they have to turn back to Vanavara.

For the next few days Kulik gets to know some of the rugged residents of the outpost as well as the tough Evenki hunters who come to the settlement to trade their furs.

They discuss with dread the day they saw the sky 'open to the ground and fire pour out ... fire brighter than the Sun', and of the ground trembling and earth thundering down on to their roofs.

One man called Kosolapov describes how 'a fierce heat scorched my ears'. Another, Semenov, claims 'a hot wind as if from a cannon' seemed to burn the shirt from his back as he sat in the porch of his house at the trading station.

I saw a huge fireball that covered an enormous part of the sky. Afterwards it became dark and at the same time I felt an explosion that threw me several feet from the porch. I lost consciousness for a few moments and, when I came to, I heard a noise that shook the whole house and nearly moved it off its foundations. The glass and the framing in the house shattered and, in the middle of the area where the hut stands, a strip of ground split apart.

It all makes Kulik even more eager to penetrate the gaunt forest to find the thing that still strikes terror into so many Tunguskan hearts. He urges Ilya Potapovich to help them try again. The dubious man reluctantly agrees.

The staunch little party sets off, stumbling blindly through soggy, infection-ridden marshland, until they reach the last tiny outpost before what Kulik is told is the fringe of the

31

stricken region. It is the cabin of a Tungusi called Okhchen, perched on the side of the Chambé River. Here they are given a night's shelter and reindeer to carry their belongings the rest of the way.

Two days later, on 13 April, they cross the murky Makirta River that sweeps into the Chambé and, suddenly, the crippling hardships of the journey are forgotten.

A shattered but elated Leonid Kulik stands in awed silence on the river bank and gazes out across a nightmare of utter devastation. It is something quite beyond his wildest expectations. Something sinister and unreal. He shudders in the thin icy air.

There, scattered like the huge gnarled bodies of a fallen army of giants, regiments of burly pines that had withstood centuries of violence from the most brutal climate in the world, now lie flat and lifeless on the frozen ground.

As he stares about him, Kulik can only wonder what kind of monstrous vandal could conceivably have caused such outrageous havoc. What unbelievable force must have raged across this once-proud forest nineteen years ago, stripping its majestic trees as naked as telegraph poles. What demonic fury had torn these deep unyielding roots from the grasping earth and laid them bare?

The party push on for several days and reach the top of the high Khladni ridge from where they can see for many miles across the ravaged landscape. From here it is even more breathtaking. Kulik scribbles his first dramatic impressions in his diary:

I cannot really take in the whole majestic picture, he writes. A very hilly, almost mountainous region stretches away tens of miles towards the northern horizon. In the north, the distant hills along the River Khushmo are covered with a white shroud of snow half a yard thick. From our observation point no sign of forest can be seen, for everything has been devastated and burned, and around the edge of this dead area the young, twenty-year-old forest growth has moved forward furiously, seeking sunshine and life. One has an uncanny feeling when one

32

sees twenty to thirty-inch thick giant trees snapped across like twigs, and their tops hurled many yards away.

Kulik cannot wait to go on into this astounding graveyard, littered with its rotting corpses, the stumps of their amputated limbs groping out of the snow. For there, he is sure he will find the monster.

But an unexpected problem crops up. Ilya Potapovich and Okhchen have had enough. They adamantly refuse to go any further. They are convinced something supernatural still lurks in the shadows of the great dead *taiga*. Something whose wrath they have no wish to incite.

For Kulik it is a bitter blow. He has travelled more than 3000 miles. He is now so close to the very heart of this whole fantastic mission into the unknown. But he realizes it would be suicidal to risk continuing through the region with only his assistant Gyulikh. The treacherous spring floods are due soon and they are a long way from the safety of the trading station. He has no choice, therefore, but to return to Vanavara.

Fortunately, back here he meets some bold Evenki hunters who are willing to take over as guides for a second attempt, which begins on 30 April. The snow is still thick on the ground, but, three days later, they reach the River Chambé and make camp.

The ice is now beginning to thaw and break up into thick chunky slabs that swirl in the perilous rapids of the *taiga* rivers. Despite this, Kulik decides to penetrate the devastated forest area by sailing rafts along the Chambé and into the River Khushmo.

On 19 May, the rafts are ready and the slow, tortuous cruise begins. Time and again they find the route blocked by massive ice floes. The water is rising alarmingly and surging over the river banks. A raft loaded with equipment rips from its overnight mooring and is waltzed downstream as easily as a fallen leaf in a rippling English stream. But, four days and twenty-five miles later, the party reach the Khushmo, and, by 22 May, they are well into the devastation area.

Now they have to hack a way through great masses of

33

uprooted trees blocking the river and sprawling together in macabre embrace along the banks.

It is 30 May. The weary expedition has reached the mouth of the ill-tempered little River Churgima. Here, in the deep valley, they pitch their tents. Kulik senses he is within striking distance of the very centre of the impact zone. He makes daily reconnaissances and finally decides that his objective lies beyond a barrier of ridges to the north. He pushes eagerly on.

Suddenly, spread out before him, is a gigantic amphitheatre of hills, surrounding a huge marshy basin. The Evenkis know it as the legend-ridden Southern Swamp. To Kulik it resembles a mammoth cauldron, and this is what he will call it from now on. The Great Cauldron of Tunguska. It is the most stimulating experience of this dedicated young scientist's life. For, somewhere inside it, he is convinced he will find the burial ground of the cosmic brute that went beserk in this same month of June nineteen years ago.

Leonid Kulik's jubilation is expressed in his own notes after making a preliminary survey.

There can be no doubt I had circled the centre of the fall. With a fiery stream of hot gases and cold solid bodies, the meteorite had struck the cauldron with its hills, tundra and swamp and, as a stream of water striking a flat surface splashes spray in all directions, the stream of hot gases with the swarm of bodies penetrated the earth, and both directly and with explosive recoil, wrought all this mighty havoc.

In the Cauldron there are hills, ridges, isolated summits and flat tundras, marsh, lakes and streams. The *taiga*, both in the Cauldron and outside it, has been practically destroyed by being completely flattened. All the former vegetation of the Cauldron, of the surrounding mountains and of a zone of several miles around them, bears characteristic traces of uniformly continuous scorching, unlike the traces of an ordinary conflagration. The area with scorch marks is estimated to be tens of miles across.

As Kulik encircles the Cauldron, he is fascinated to find that the rolling carpet of decapitated and uprooted trees have been scattered outwards from the centre, like the tangled spokes of a wheel – their exposed roots pointing to the hub, the tops facing outwards in the direction they were flung in the incredible blast.

Another remarkable discovery is that trees on the lower ground, which he is certain was the epicentre of the blast, are still standing. The further he goes up the hillsides, the more severe the damage. It's as though a giant scythe has been swept in a circle from the centre. On the lower slopes only the tips of the trees are missing. Higher up the trunks are severed off – the remaining stumps gradually getting shorter and shorter until, at the summits, the trees are completely uprooted. Later studies are to show that only an explosion *above the ground* could have caused this pattern of devastation.

Kulik is still convinced the object that caused it all was a meteorite, especially when he finds numbers of flat holes of different sizes pock-marking the peat bogs like small lunar craters. He assumes the body split up before landing, each fragment forming its own scar. But, after much later research he has to concede that these are naturally-formed depressions in the earth caused by the thawing of the permafrost. No actual meteorite crater is found. Nor is one ever to be found.

But, whatever it was that pounded from the sky had thrust the earth into strangely deformed folds – like a carpet that rumples up on a polished floor. Kulik is overwhelmed by it all. There is so much more research he'd like to do. But, with enough food left for less than a week, he reluctantly leads his intrepid little group back to Vanavara. He staggers up to the trading station nine days later, exhausted, ravenously hungry but glowing with satisfaction. Leonid Kulik has found what he came for. He has walked in the Cauldron of Hell. Soon he must come back to find the thing that created it. He is not to know that the secret will still be hidden long after his death. For what he has done in the summer of 1927 is to present the scientific world with the riddle of the century.

CHAPTER THREE

# THE WORLD TAKES NOTICE

The mysterious Tunguska monster suddenly hits the headlines. Newspaper and magazine editors throughout the world begin poring over large-scale maps of Central Siberia, prodding their fingers at faraway places they've never heard of until now. They rummage through their files. They call in their science writers. Why has it taken nearly twenty years to get on to this remarkable story?

The post-revolutionary hierarchy of Russia – eager to impress the West with a new progressive image – are now more than willing to listen to Leonid Kulik, who wastes no time in urging the Academy of Sciences to sponsor a further expedition. In December 1927, he submits his estimates, together with a letter to the Presidium of the Academy.

The results of even a cursory examination exceeded all the tales of eye witnesses and my wildest expectations. The devastation can only have been caused by an air wave of tremendous power.

He then goes on firmly:

For seven years I have been holding the view that since this fall occurred on the territory of the Soviet Union, we are in duty bound to study it. If the matter was delayed until last year on the pretext that it was all pure fancy, this objection has now been swept away since the positive results of my expedition are irrefutable. Their unique scientific significance, like the significance of the Tunguska fall itself, will be fully appreciated only in history, and it is necessary to record all the remaining traces of this fall for posterity.

There are few objections to a new expedition. The scientific fraternity, sceptical for so many years, is now eager for more news. And so, on 12 April 1928, Kulik is back in Siberia.

The notorious spring floods are at their height when he arrives with zoologist V. Sytin at Vanavara trading station thirteen days later. Here they are joined by a movie camera-man from Moscow named Strukov who is to give the out-side world its first dramatic glimpse of the rape of Tunguska. He almost records Kulik's death too.

When the party reaches the mouth of the River Chambé they have to travel upstream in boats towed by a pair of horses. Here the rapids are particularly treacherous, swirling and pounding the huge boulders that jut menacingly from the narrow river bed.

Suddenly Kulik's boat overturns. He is flung headlong into the icy water. The powerful current thumps him against the rocks. Then, miraculously, as he is about to be swept helplessly downstream, his leg gets entangled in a mooring rope that has wrapped itself about a rock. He is able to struggle, gasping, to the surface and frantically grabs the side of the boat. Eventually he drags himself to the bank as the news-minded photographer calmly shoots the whole incident. Kulik – despite the ordeal – is still wearing his spectacles.

After building a temporary camp on the River Khushmo, near the mouth of the Churgima stream, with a shed perched on stilts to be out of reach of marauding wolves and bears, they finally settle in the heart of the Cauldron itself on 23 June.

Kulik's main concern is to probe the small round holes dotted about the area. He is still convinced they have been caused by meteorite fragments and he's determined to find them. He digs deeply into the earth but finds nothing. In fact little new is to emerge from this 1928 visit. Its purpose is mainly to prepare the way for a later, and far better equipped expedition. However cameraman Strukov gets the first exclusive pictures that are to astound the world, and help Kulik to get all the backing he needs for more really extensive research.

Meanwhile in the United States, Harvey H. Nininger of

the Colorado Museum of Natural History, and one of the country's foremost authorities on meteorites, tries to get the leading scientific societies there to finance a super equipped American expedition to Tunguska to secure, as he puts it 'what is yet available of this greatest message from the depths of space that has ever reached our planet'. All his efforts fail. In his book *Our Stone-Pelted Planet* he remarks:

> It is a sad comment on the mental alertness of the scientific world that even until now there has been no adequate effort put forth to collect the great fund of information which awaits any well-equipped expedition into these parts.
>
> Meanwhile, these same societies spend enormous sums studying volcanoes and other phenomena which are always with us, and worthy as are these studies, they could be pursued any time and indefinitely, while here is an event the like of which was never before witnessed in man's recorded history, year by year losing from its hidden store of information, and no effort is made for its acquisition.

Leonid Kulik's third, and largest expedition, financed jointly by the Academy of Sciences and the Scientific Department of Sovnarkom, heads again for Siberia on 24 February 1929. It is to last a gruelling twenty months, including a nightmare winter in the lonely Southern Swamp region with temperatures plummeting to a merciless minus fifty degrees centigrade ($-58°$ Fahrenheit).

Here Kulik and his team of experts drill and excavate deep into the frozen crater-like pits and the massive peat formations, still hoping to find some evidence of a giant meteorite. One particularly large depression is drained by a forty-yard trench. Kulik is confident this is the object's grave. But when its base is finally cleared of dense moss, a tree stump is found firmly rooted in the centre. It could not possibly have remained there if the hole had indeed been the original crater.

The team continue to work so strenuously that three of its exhausted members have to leave the expedition. Another

38

man lies for several days unconscious and delirious from acute appendicitis before he can be moved for treatment.

Kulik's deputy is Evgenii Leonidovich Krinov, another brilliant authority on meteoritics, who keeps meticulous records of the expedition. As he moves around the Southern Swamp he finds it inexplicable that, though this has been calculated as the very centre of the explosion, there are parts of it with absolutely no trace of devastation. Yet, in a massive radius around it, the trees are flattened and scorched, and uprooted stumps lay where they have been blasted great distances.

On 18 November Kulik sends Krinov and another member of the team back to Vanavara with scientific samples to be forwarded to the Academy of Sciences. It is a grim journey. The rough track is now hidden beneath waist-deep snowdrifts. Krinov describes his experience in *Giant Meteorites*, one of a number of books he is to write on the Tunguska Event.

Late at night we arrived at the expedition's winter hut on the River Chambé, our clothes wet with snow and sweat, and our leggings soaked through from crossing the *taiga* streams and pools. After spending the night on the Chambé, feeding the horse and drying our clothes, we continued our journey the next morning. It was a cold, frosty day and towards evening the temperature fell to forty degrees below zero. Our leather-lined leggings, which had not dried completely, froze, and our feet began to suffer from frostbite.

After two days, covering nearly sixty miles through deep snow, we were almost completely exhausted and literally dragged ourselves to Vanavara with frozen feet. There was a great danger of gangrene setting in, so it was essential to travel at once to Kezhma for medical treatment.

After sending off urgent supplies to Kulik, Krinov and his companion spend a further six painful days travelling to Kezhma on horses obtained from some Evenki hunters at the trading station. Here Krinov is forced to remain in hospital until mid-February and one of his toes has to be amputated. He is not to know that vital soil samples he has risked his life to send on to the Academy of Sciences are to lie forgotten in someone's desk for 28 years before being analysed.

By the summer of 1930, the expedition's funds are exhausted and they arrive home in the autumn. It has been a long, frustrating ordeal of sweaty, mosquito-ridden summer and unbelievably bitter winter, completely cut off from the outside world. And they have found nothing that can even begin to answer the niggling enigma of Tunguska.

In the 1930s scientists can think of only one cosmic warhead that could conceivably have scorched and bulldozed the mighty *taiga* so savagely. It *has* to be a giant meteorite. Somewhere, they persist, there *has* to be a crater, or a mass of them if it had shattered. But, despite three exhaustive expeditions, followed in 1938, by searching aerial photographs, the only relevant holes that show up are those in the meteorite theory itself.

Certainly the pre-impact phenomena witnessed in 1908 is very consistent with the falling of meteorites. These *do* appear as brilliant, rapidly-moving fireballs and they *can* make terrifying sounds as their chunky masses of stone and iron power-dive into the Earth's atmosphere at anything up to forty miles a second.

Like the description of the Siberian object, they have often been likened to 'fast moving stars', and the blazing light from those seen during the daytime have been compared with that of the Sun. They also have huge, luminous dust and gas clouds in their wake that can be hundreds of yards across. The dazzling colours of meteoric fireballs are also consistent with most eye witnesses of the Tunguska event. According to the speed at which they are streaking by, they can vary from white, at their hottest, through blue, green, yellow, orange and finally red as they decelerate. However this incandescence, caused by temperatures reaching some thousands of degrees, occurs with any object entering

Earth's atmosphere – including our own returning space vehicles.

The kind of awesome noises, described by witnesses in 1908, are also emited by a falling meteorite as a powerful compression wave builds up ahead of it, causing a supersonic boom like that of a high-speed aircraft. Witnesses accounts of 'artillery fire and boulders falling from the sky' can be produced when a meteorite breaks up, each fragment detonating individually. Before impact there are often hissing or rustling sounds. One witness interviewed at Kansk in 1921 said he heard 'something like the fluttering wings of a frightened bird'.

For a human or animal anywhere near the area of a meteorite fall the experience is quite shattering. When one dropped on England in 1965, an eye witness compared it with a war-time dive-bomber attack, and suffered severe shock for some time after.

Fireballs have been petrifying people for centuries. It is interesting to compare the following excerpts from an eye witness account of a meteorite fall far back in November 1662 in the Russian village of Novyre Ergi. It was recorded by a priest named Ivanishch and might well have been referring to the Tunguska Event.

Many people saw in the clouds a terrible apparition. The Sun had barely set when there suddenly arose a great star (fireball) which looked like lightning in the sky. The sky was cleared into two parts . . . and there was indescribable light, like fire. Afterwards a small cloud appeared where the image had been. The sky seemed to close and fire fell upon the earth. Then it rose into a cloud and from this cloud poured forth noise and smoke like thunder or like a great terrible storm. For a long time the earth and houses shook and many people fell to the ground in terror. All animals crowded together, choking on their fodder, their heads raised towards the sky, bellowing each in its own fashion.

But similarities to the Tunguska phenomena no longer

apply once we consider what happens *after* impact. As Ivanishch goes on:

> Stones started falling, shining bright, large and small ones, all hot. They fell upon the fields and streets ... some of the larger ones bored into the ground and froze.

More than three centuries later, in March 1976, what is claimed to be the greatest shower of meteorites in recorded history peppered 260 square miles near the outskirts of Kirin in China. Here, too, there is plenty of material evidence of the fall – more than a hundred pieces of stone weighing up to $1\frac{3}{4}$ tons that pounded their craters in the frozen soil. Witnesses describe seeing a large fireball before the meteorite exploded, flinging slabs of earth hundreds of feet into the air.

Another recent fireball, in the Dallas area of Texas in September 1971, was seen by thousands of Saturday-night patrons at drive-in movie shows. The pictures vanished in a blinding light 'as bright as the Sun'. The meteorite, believed to have originally weighed many tons, left an ionized trail that blacked out television screens. As in other normal meteorite falls fragments were found over a four-mile area.

There is, of course, a remote possibility that the Evenkis *did* find something after the catastrophe which they hid from the outside world during those twenty years before Kulik's first expedition. They were a superstitious race. Perhaps any remnants of such a heavenly body were considered sacred – some timely omen from the gods. The ancient Egyptians are known to have worshipped meteorites and a necklace of beads made from pieces of one was found in a pyramid dating back more than 5000 years and is still preserved.

Generations of devout pilgrims have kissed the famous Black Stone meteorite at Mecca which is regarded as holy in the Moslem world. Another found in India was anointed and decorated with flowers for many years. The Japanese revered a meteorite in one of their temples as recently as the nineteenth century, when, even in the Western world few people would believe that anything larger than a hailstone could actually drop from the sky. In 1807 the trustees of the

British Museum were highly dubious that four meteorites presented to them were anything more exotic than ordinary earthbound rocks.

It is easy to imagine, therefore, that among the remote and backward communities of Tunguska, anything they found would have supernatural significance, especially in a land that already abounded with legends of monsters and ancient vengeful gods. The camping site of one Evenki group who lost twenty reindeer in the scorching blast was in a region of the Ognija River – a place considered accursed following an earthquake there. When the geologist Obruchev first questioned the Evenkis near Vanavara trading station in 1924, they denied the fall altogether. Obruchev wrote in the magazine *Mirovedeniye*: 'In the eyes of the Tungusi people, the meteorite is apparently sacred and they carefully conceal the place where it fell.'

Voznesensky of the Irkutsk Observatory, also wrote in the same magazine:

The Indians of Arizona still preserve the legend that their ancestors saw a fiery chariot fall from the sky and penetrate the spot where the crater is. The present-day Tungusi people have a similar legend about a new fiery stone. This stone they stubbornly refused to show to the interested Russians who were investigating the matter.

It is extremely doubtful, however, that after so many expeditions to the devastation area over the last half century, such hidden evidence would have remained undetected. It must now be accepted that whatever hit Siberia left no trace of its origin. Never before or since has a recorded meteorite fall failed to leave solid evidence in the form of either fragments or craters. And if the Tunguska monster *had* been a meteorite it could have weighed millions of tons when it entered the atmosphere.

Certainly some of these mighty cosmic cannonballs that have been bombarding the Solar System since the beginning of time, are quite capable of vandalism on the Tunguska scale. Over the unruly centuries the face of the Earth has been thumped like that of a punch-drunk heavyweight – and it's got plenty of nasty scars to show for it.

In fact, some scientists now believe that more than three-and-a-half billion years ago one mighty blow virtually cracked its skull. A monumental meteorite, slightly smaller than the Moon, pounded head-on, they claim, smack in the middle of a vast primeval land area. The massive fracture it caused in the Earth's solid outer crust started sections of it moving apart and resulted in what we now know as the Continental Drift.

There are plenty of lesser battle-scars too. Like the huge Barringer Crater at Canyon Diabalo in Arizona. The belligerent brute that caused it seared through the atmosphere and blasted four hundred million tons of rock out of the desert, leaving posterity to ogle at a natural amphitheatre three-quarters of a mile across and 570 feet deep. All but a tiny fraction of its original bulk – estimated at between 100 000 and a million tons – is believed to have been vapourized in the explosion.

It has been estimated that, on average, a meteorite or asteroid capable of producing a crater of this size batters into Earth every 50 000 years. *The Arizona Crater is reckoned to be 50 000* years old. It would seem we're about due for another! But, even this is dwarfed by the Bosumtwi crater in Ghana. It is a breathtaking eight miles in diameter.

Scientist Robert Dietz, formerly an oceanographer at the US Navy Electronics Laboratory in San Diego, California, has taken geological tests on a raised area of granite in South Africa called the Vredefort Ring. It is twenty-five miles across and is surrounded by a further pattern of rock folds 130 miles in diameter. He is now convinced this massive landmark was originally caused by a small pre-historic asteroid about a mile in diameter that blasted a crater ten miles deep. This brute, he says, could have released the explosive equivalent of a million megaton bomb – enough to make the entire Earth itself shudder in its orbit round the Sun. Dietz believes the granite below the crater reacted to the removal of this great weight of earth by welling up to fill the hole and to bulge into a dome, as it now is.

Exactly where meteorites come from is a question scientists still argue over. Most are now convinced they are the airborne debris from our own Solar System that frequently career off-course. One theory is that they originate from the swarm of asteroids – those chunks of rock up to 480 miles in diameter that swirl between Mars and Jupiter.

Astronomers in the past have suggested the asteroids are the result of a disintegrating planet that either exploded or collided with another. One fascinating, but unlikely embellishment is that some ancient race of intelligent beings that once populated this hypothetical world, either blew it to bits through their own nuclear experiments or were involved in a Wellsian war of the worlds with some superpower from elsewhere in the galaxy.

The fragmented planet idea however is not widely accepted. Although some fifty or sixty thousand asteroids orbit within observable range at sometime, their total mass – even including the meteorites that have fallen over the years – would have been far less than even the mass of the Moon. There certainly does not seem to have been enough material to have formed a planet of any reasonable size.

The larger asteroids are now believed to have been created from left-over material in the early stages of the Solar System's formation. Meteorites could be the chippings from these bodies or from the planets themselves.

A number of asteroids have orbits that reach out as far as the Earth. One, called Eros, is twenty miles long and passed close to us in 1975. Consider what havoc a collision with that could cause.

In 1976 the American astronomer Eleanor Helin at Palomar Observatory discovered an asteroid only twelve million miles away. Astro-geologist Eugen Shoemaker says it would be 'one of the easiest places to get to in our Solar System, aside from the Moon'. Its Earth-crossing orbit is uncomfortably close. If it hit us at twelves miles a second it would produce a crater twenty-five miles across, even though it is the smallest asteroid ever actually measured.

Some researchers are now convinced that really super-meteorites in the distant past were responsible for many famous missing chunks of land area, like Hudson Bay and the Gulf of Mexico. The pock-marked face of the Moon is certainly the surrealist handiwork of countless meteoric raids in its adolescent years. From rock samples brought back by the Apollo astronauts it now seems quite feasible that – like Earth's Continental Drift – the vast Lunar depression known, ironically, as the Sea of Tranquillity, might too have been caused by a mighty meteorite attack billions of years ago that spewed out molten rock from deep inside the Moon. Work on the surveys of Mars, Mercury and Venus by Mariner spacecraft show that here, too, there are craters up to a hundred miles wide, gouged from the desolate planets like a scooped-out Stilton cheese.

But even demolition of this magnitude cannot explain the extraordinary behaviour of the phenomenal force that deformed Tunguska . . . a force quite unknown on our own planet. Why, for instance, do trees remain standing and virtually unscathed at the very centre of the explosion? There were no natural land formations to shield them from the blast. Similarly in other parts of the Cauldron, small islands of proud, undamaged larches still stand firm in the midst of utter devastation.

In his book *Giant Meteorites*, Krinov writes:
The impression is that the explosive wave acted in a very irregular fashion around the place of fall, and that it was not only the relief of the area that provided shelter. The explosive wave seems to have selected individual areas of forest for complete devastation . . .

Aerial photographs of the area round the mouth of the Churgima, i.e. two to three miles to the south of the Cauldron, also show clusters of preserved trees still growing . . . A striking fact is that these trees have not only remained standing but are not even broken or scorched, although they were unprotected as a direct effect of the explosive wave. Moreover here . . . clusters of undamaged trees, dead trees still standing and those completely uprooted, are found together. In these same places along the bank of the Khushmo other areas are found in which the trees, though still standing, have lost their tops, and which Kulik called 'telegraph poles'.

At the junction of the rivers Khushmo and Ukhagitta, twelve to fifteen miles from the Cauldron, Krinov describes how 'the flattened trees lie in a solid carpet, their roots sticking up into the air and facing the Cauldron, with here and there new growth showing through'.

The curious way the *taiga* has been scorched cannot be explained either. It bears no resemblance to that caused by any ordinary forest blaze. At the tip of every snapped-off branch is a charred cinder. In every case the fracture itself runs obliquely downwards, resembling, as Kulik describes, 'a bird's claw'. At the top of the trees, both thick and thin branches alike have been guillotined in this way with cindered tips. This could only have been caused by a sudden momentary burst of tremendously high temperature. In a normal fire the slender, flimsy twigs would have been completely burned away by the kind of heat sufficient to char the tips of the thick ones.

Still faced with these baffling questions, Kulik spends a further six weeks in Siberia in the summer of 1939. Now the journey is far less hazardous. A small airstrip has been constructed near Vanavara and a thirty-five mile road cleared through the forest leading to a camp site not far from the Southern Swamp area.

It is to be his last visit. All research is suddenly suspended indefinitely. Russia, like most of the world, now has a war on her hands. On 22 June 1941, the Germans attack. Kulik, though he is fifty-eight years old, volunteers for the Soviet Militia – the ill-trained, middle-aged 'Dad's Army' in Russia's desperate all-out defence of Moscow. In October he is wounded and captured. And, on 14 April 1942, stricken with disease, the courageous Leonid Kulik – like three million other Russians – dies in the humiliation of a Nazi prison camp. For him the fanatical search for the Tunguska monster is over.

## CHAPTER FOUR

# ANOTHER 'CAULDRON OF HELL'

It is shortly after 8 o'clock on the morning of 6 August 1945. The war with Germany is over. And so are the lives of eighteen million Russians. As happened over Tunguska thirty-seven years before, something is about to fall from the sky. And this is *certainly* no meteorite.

*Enola Gay*, an American B-29, is completing the deadliest mission in the long, tortuous history of man's inhumanity to man. Like the Tunguska object, the thing it is to release will leave no trace of itself. Neither will there be any craters. But its fury will bear the same diabolical characteristics ... complete and utter devastation.

This time, however, the impact zone 30 000 feet below is not a forest of gaunt trees in Central Siberia, but a tightly-packed mosaic of buildings and streets that throb with life. And the creatures that move down there are not scattered herds of reindeer, but streaming masses of men, women and children. For the 320 000 inhabitants of Hiroshima in Japan it's the start of another busy day.

The workers are already in the factories. The shops are opening up and the kids are on their way to school. The Japanese early warning radar net has spotted the aircraft above, but it's probably just a reconnaissance flight, they say. No one bothers to take cover.

The weather over Hiroshima is sultry but reasonably clear. At 8.11 a.m., Colonel Paul Tibbets, pilot of the *Enola Gay*, swings round for the run-in. He nods significantly to his bombardier, Tom Ferebe. The thing the US Air Force has nick-named *Thin Boy*, plummets earthwards. Inside it is Uranium-235. For this is the world's first atomic bomb to be detonated in anger.

In the central section of the city below a blinding white flash is all that many people see before they are blown to bits, ripped apart by flying fragments, or grilled to charcoal by the wave of searing heat that rushes out from the explosion. A dense forbidding cloud of smoke and dust chokes the city into darkness. Through it all grope the survivors, stumbling over a carpet of corpses in blind agony and confusion.

*Enola Gay* swings away and heads back to base. For a while the crew say nothing. Then the tail-gunner's voice whispers through the intercom: 'Oh, my God . . . what have we done? What have we done?'

President Harry S. Truman is having lunch on board the United States cruiser *Augusta* when he hears the mission is a 'complete success'. His prepared press release tells America that the 'important army base' of Hiroshima has been atom-bombed. And for those who are not too sure what this means, the joyous statement proclaims: 'It is harnessing the basic power of the Universe. The force from which the Sun draws its power has been loosed against those who brought war to the Far East.'

Meanwhile the mushroom-shaped shroud clears from over Hiroshima to reveal the most gruesome aftermath in the annals of warfare. In a moving documentary of the rape of Hiroshima, author and researcher Robert Jungk writes in *Children of the Ashes*:

It was no quick and total death, no heart attack of a whole city, no sudden, agonizing ending that struck Hiroshima. A mercifully quick release, such as is granted even to the vilest criminals, was denied to the men, women and children of Hiroshima. They were condemned to long drawn-out agonies, to mutilation, to endless sickness. No, neither during the first hours nor in the days that followed was Hiroshima a silent 'graveyard', filled solely with the mute protest of the ruins, as misleading photographs imply; rather was it the sight of movements repeated a hundred thousand times, of a million agonies that filled morning, noon and night with groans, screams, whimperings, and of crowds of cripples. All who could still run, walk, hobble or even drag themselves along the ground were searching for something, for a few drops of water, for food, for medicine, for a doctor, for the pitiful relics of their possessions, for shelter. Or searching for the uncountable thousands who need no longer suffer . . . for the dead.

Soon after the explosion, researchers like Professor Shogo Nagaoka, a geologist from the city's university, rummage through the mountains of ash. They come up with some macabre specimens. The intense heat has even melted stone and rock and twisted bottles like the handiwork of an insane glassblower. Rotting corpses shimmer as swarms of gnats and flies cover them over with a living shroud of black. A skinless hand, grotesquely fused into a motor car engine, must have been that of the mechanic who'd been repairing it when the bomb went off.

At 11 a.m., on 9 August, another atom bomb falls on Nagasaki. This one contains plutonium, and they call it *Fat Boy*. The target should have been the town of Kokura, but it was too cloudy over there. Nagasaki is the next option on the pilot's list.

It is not to be until 1976 that the full horrific implications of these two bombs are to be made known, when a group of Japanese scientists prepare a special report for the General Secretary of the United Nations in an effort to urge the world to outlaw nuclear weapons. These new statistics show that the total number of deaths as a direct result of the raids actually reaches a sickening quarter of a million. Even now victims are dying at double the rate of the general population.

At Hiroshima, over 80 per cent of people living within half a mile of the impact centre, and 60 per cent of those up to a mile away, were slaughtered. Out of 76 000 buildings 70 000 were totally burned.

And yet the force of this bomb – equivalent to 20 000 tons of TNT – was only a fraction that of the Tunguska monster which is estimated to have released the shattering energy of thirty *million* tons of high explosives. Devastation in Siberia was not confined to one mile, but twenty!

However, despite the vast difference in the power of the two explosions, some Russian researchers who visit Japan in the 1940s are intrigued at the many similar features.

One of them is Alexander Kazantsev. He is convinced the kind of force that razed Hiroshima and Nagasaki also flattened the forests of Siberia. For surely the atom bomb answered so many questions that had stumped Leonid Kulik in the 1930s. Here in the rubble is the same kind of blast damage. The same radial scorching. There are no craters. There are no fragments of the brute that caused it. There is even the same uncanny phenomena of a few bare tree trunks still standing in the very midst of the cataclysm.

The Japanese bombs didn't explode on the ground. They burst 1800 feet above it. In a paper on his expedition findings written in the 1930s, Kulik noted: 'The whole central region of the blown-down woods, to judge by the remaining dead trees, has been scorched from *above*.' The height is later estimated to have been between three and five miles.

The scorching effects at Tunguska are particularly consistent with the Japanese explosions. When the atom bombs were detonated, one third of the explosive yield was emitted as a pulse of radiant thermal energy. The heat flash lasted only a millionth of a second. And yet at ground zero, solid materials were grilled to some 3500 degrees centigrade. The appalling results of this massive thermal radiation were the gruesome 'flash burns' that accounted for a third of the total deaths.

In 1927 – even thirty-five miles away from the Tunguska impact centre – witness Semenov had told Leonid Kulik:

The sky split in two and high above the forest the whole northern sky appeared to be covered with fire. A hot wind, as from a cannon, blew past the huts from the north. At that moment I felt great heat as if my shirt had caught fire.

Another witness had described how 'a fierce heat scorched my ears'.

The 'heat' Semenov referred to was caused by the radiant energy from the explosion. The 'hot wind' was the blast that had swept through Vanavara. But witnesses much further away also felt the effects of the blast. A man called Bryu-khanov, who was 125 miles away from the impact in a village near Kezhma, told Kulik in 1938:

When I sat down to have my breakfast beside my plough, I heard sudden bangs, as if from gunfire. My horse fell on to its knees. From the north side above the forest a flame shot up. Then I saw that the fir forest had been bent over by the wind and I thought of a hurricane. I seized hold of my plough with both hands so that it would not be carried away. The wind was so strong that it carried off some of the soil from the surface of the ground, and then the hurricane drove a wall of water up the Angora.

Even people near Kirensk, 300 miles away, claimed they felt a strong wind. One man wrote in a letter the day after the fall: 'trees were bent over and their leaves quivered. At the time the sky was clear and peaceful, the water did not show a ripple, and no damage was noticed.'

There is the similarity of the mushroom clouds over Japan and that seen over Siberia. In a letter to Kulik, the Director of Kirensk Meteorological Station reported one of a number of eye-witness accounts of 'a pillar of fire in the shape of a spear' and a dense cloud appearing over the spot.

Another remarkable phenomena at Hiroshima, also discovered at Tunguska, is that flowers and vegetation never seen in the city before the bomb, suddenly begin to flourish. Fresh lotus flowers in the ornamental pond of Hiroshima castle suddenly burst forth anew from those that have been blackened and scorched. Grasses and weeds sprout everywhere. The radiation that is to kill so many more humans is a vibrant stimulus to the genetic make-up of plant life.

In the Southern Swamp area of Central Siberia trees and vegetation are also reported to be growing at a phenomenal rate with a luxuriance not known before 1908 (see chapter 5).

The abnormally light nights that persisted over Europe and Russia following the Tunguska blast are also reported to a less marked degree after atom explosion tests.

All these similarities convince Kazantsev and others that

it was a nuclear explosion which shattered the blue sky over Siberia. They are to be even more convinced some years later when scientists at the impact zone report excessive traces of radiation. But, as there were certainly no man-made atom bombs in 1908, Kazantsev comes to the mind-boggling conclusion that something from outside Earth must have brought it. This intriguing possibility is fully discussed in chapter 11.

Life for most of Russia in the first few post-war years is an economic nightmare. The nation is exhausted. Its industrial machinery, its railways, its power stations – all, like its men and women, driven far beyond normal tolerance in the dogged struggle to survive – is now about as efficient as a worn-out, second-hand car. Agricultural losses have been immense. As the Germans retreated they had systematically destroyed the harvests, burned down the villages and slaughtered livestock. Now food is desperately short. The 1945 harvest is a bad one. The next year's is catastrophic in an exceptionally dry season. Food prices treble and thousands of Russians starve to death.

Raw materials are now urgently needed if the Soviet Union is to survive the peace and recover its strength. For this reason Stalin gives the go-ahead for scientific exploration in ore-rich Siberia. He is also anxious to find uranium there in his anxiety to match the West in atomic power.

Interest in the Tunguska mystery begins to revive too, and a group of scientists are able to convince the government that another expedition there is worth funding. However, at 10.38 on the morning of 12 February 1947, another monster from outer space screams across Siberia. The first spectacular characteristics appear the same. Thousands see the dazzling fireball, the brilliant fiery tail spitting out sparks like a rocket, the great track of swirling smoke curling from horizon to zenith that hovers for several hours after the object pounds into the Sikhote-Alin mountain range near the Chinese border.

Again there are those same fearful sounds. The thunderous rumblings, the rapid cracking like artillery fire. Talking to eye witnesses is like listening to the stories of the Evenki people told to Kulik more than twenty years before.

One man, N. F. Kushnarev, who was only five miles south of the fall, tells of a 'great flash, brighter than the Sun' that hurt his eyes. He then saw a dense black streak of smoke in the sky followed by an explosion that caused houses to tremor and a series of crackles 'like a machine-gun salvo'.

Others talk of doors being blown open, windows blasted out and plaster showering down from ceilings. Two pilots, Firtsikov and Ageev, at a nearby airfield, describe the fireball as being 'as large as the Moon' as it disappeared over the hills. Horses and cows whinnied and lowed in terror, broke free and bolted about in all directions. Dogs howled and fled into the forest. A mechanic, V. I. Esteev, who was working on a telephone pole at the time, felt a severe electric shock from the wires, even though the line was disconnected.

After the first reports the investigators waste no time in scurrying to the fall area. Here, at last, could be the elusive answer to the riddle of Tunguska. A hurriedly-assembled team of geologists are despatched by air.

But, instead of solving the riddle, the expedition findings merely make it even more confusing. For, here at Sikhote-Alin, the evidence of a normal meteorite bombardment is obvious. There are 122 rusty-coloured craters, some up to thirty feet deep and eighty feet wide pock-marking the snow. Meteoric iron is abundant on the mountain slopes and lying among the rocks. But there are no traces of blast and scorching. None of the explosive phenomena found in 1908. In fact the meteorite's impact was not even registered by the sensitive instruments of the nearest seismic station 300 miles away at Vladivostok. It all strengthens the view that the Tunguska invader was no ordinary meteorite. Unfortunately the Sikhote-Alin fall is to dominate meteorite research by the Academy of Sciences for the next three years, during which time it sends four expeditions there. Again the Tunguska mystery has to be shelved.

However, in 1957, the specimens of soil brought back by Leonid Kulik which had lain forgotten at the Academy for more than a quarter of a century, are finally unearthed and analysed with the more sophisticated apparatus now available. Some samples appear to contain tiny iron dust fragments, possibly meteoric in origin.

The Academy, therefore, launches its largest expedition to Tunguska to settle the matter once and for all. It is equipped with the very latest instruments and aerial maps and its leader is Professor Kirill P. Florensky, one of Russia's most respected geo-chemists who flew over the impact region in 1954. For Florensky and his scientific team in June 1958, there are to be none of the hardships Leonid Kulik had been forced to endure. No crippling weeks driving primitive horse-drawn wagons over hundreds of treacherous miles of uncharted country. For Florensky, getting to Vanavara means merely a few hours flight on a comfy aircraft from Kezhma. The derelict little trading station of Kulik's time is now a bustling centre in full radio contact with the outside world. It has its own airport, hospital and school. Neither is there to be the tortuous struggle against the floods and rapids of the river journey into the *taiga*. Instead fast and powerful motor boats are waiting to transport the tons of valuable new equipment.

And yet, after thirty-four days in which they search 500 miles of forest, the team still finds no sign of meteorite craters or fragments. In fact, they discover that those small iron 'meteoric' particles analysed in Moscow before they left, are artificial and of terrestrial origin. They came from various metal instruments such as bores and spades that had been used in the earliest expeditions.

# PART TWO

## CHAPTER FIVE

# THE MONSTER THAT MAKES THINGS GROW

By the late 1950s – despite five major expeditions and dramatic development in all fields of technology – the world's scientists are still unable to uncover the secret of the Southern Swamp. It is now half a century since the monster struck. Vast new forest growth veils the whole area just as age veils the memory of those original eye witnesses still alive.

Basically all that the researchers can confidently state is that nothing else like it has ever been recorded; that, whatever it was, pulverized itself in mid-air and did not strike the ground; and that the only known force approaching its ferociousness is that of a nuclear explosion.

The radiation from a nuclear explosion, too, could account for the incredibly high mutation rates being reported in the Southern Swamp region.

In 1959, Dr Gennady Plekhanov of the Betatron Laboratory of the Tomsk Medical Institute, tests 300 soil samples and 100 plants from the area. He claims his analyses clearly show that 'in the centre of the catastrophe radioactivity is one and a half to two times higher than that found 20 to 25 miles away.' Other analyses show the level to be six times above normal.

Researchers are finding that, since 1908, trees in the impact region have grown at a fantastic rate. Those that have sprouted since that date are twice the normal height and their trunks three times as thick. Some plant growth is reported to have been stepped up twelvefold.

Examinations of the growth rings in older trees shows that, from the time of the explosion, cell production has increased dramatically, causing the rings to be broader. Traces of the radioactive isotope cesium 137 is also claimed by some researchers to be present in the ring structures.

Even in 1931, Kulik had remarked on 'the surface of the swamp being luxuriantly overgrown with sphagnum (bog-moss) whose age does not exceed twenty years'. And one Evenki had told him: 'How overgrown it has become. It was not like this before.' It appears that the high radiation level in the swamp area is acting as a stimulus to all forms of vegetation growth.

(In 1975 a series of scientific papers concluded that there was also a mutant effect in the tree population along the trajectory taken by the Tunguska object. The publication is by the Meteorite and Cosmic Dust Commission of the Academy of Sciences and is edited by Academician V. S. Sobolev, leading authority on current research into the Tunguska Event. The book title *The Problematic Meteorite* emphasizes the mystery that still surrounds it.)

Though no evidence exists of any mutations affecting the animal life there, these could conceivably have taken place. Kulik's earlier expeditions would not have been looking for such abnormalities and by now these could have been obliterated in the normal course of natural evolution. In most animal groups, weak or deformed members do not normally live for long. If they cannot feed themselves they starve to death. If they are a burden on the rest of the group they are killed. There is little chance of them reproducing further mutants. In the case of a deformed male reindeer, for example, it would most likely be killed off by its competitors during the mating season. Nature is extremely selective. Only the fittest survive.

Another probability is that, if any malformed animals had roamed the *taiga*, the Evenkis would have slaughtered them. They were a highly superstitious people. Such strange afflictions in their herds could well have been interpreted as bad omens. They would have been reluctant to tell strangers about them for fear of aggravating the gods.

However, the large-scale mutation in the vegetation could eventually lead to changing animal species as their feeding habits become adapted to the new varieties of growth. This would, of course, take many generations.

There have certainly been no reported cases of human

beings suffering from mutation effects, though, here again, if any child *had* been born with a deformity, those same primitive beliefs might have induced the Evenkis to hide the offspring.

Among some Siberian tribes even the feebleness of old age was considered a reason for eliminating a man or woman no longer able to keep up with the rugged life of the nomadic community. A person believing themselves to be a burden would ask their nearest relatives to kill them. At a special ceremony the self-condemned person would then kneel down, surrounded by his family and friends, and allow the noose of a rope to be tightened round his neck. After his death, all 'imperfections' would then be cut from his body with a knife. If he had suffered from tuberculosis, for example, the lungs would be removed. Defective limbs would be hacked from those who were disabled and a mentally deficient's body would be completely cut to pieces. The corpse was normally left for the wolves.

Let's consider briefly how radiation causes mutation. Our physical characteristics are dependent on the genetic coding in our cellular make-up. This coding is in turn passed on to our children. If, for any reason, this pattern is broken, a genetic change takes place. This can be brought about by severe chemical stimulus. But the most rapid cause is for part of the genetic structure – which, after all, is molecular and atomic – to be destroyed by radiation. If the exposure is particularly drastic, the individual's characteristics will be affected. It has been found that fruit flies exposed to radiation rapidly breed others with such mutations as deformed legs and no wings.

Recently Britain's National Radiological Protection Board and the Department of Health began a two-year nationwide survey to find if medical X-rays were causing genetic harm. One of the potential dangers of X-rays is that they can damage chromosomes which carry the genetic code. Doctors are warned not to X-ray pregnant women. Dr Stewart Rae, assistant director of the board, is quoted as saying: 'We want to find out just what sort of genetic burden we are imposing on future generations.'

Apart from radioactivity, soil tests taken at Tunguska in the late 1950s also reveal strange globules composed of magnetite and silicate. They are either spherical or in the form of droplets measuring only a few thousandths of a millimetre across. Some are hollow and completely transparent, and one striking feature is that some of these 'cosmic ball-bearings' are coalesced or fused into solid masses – an indication that they must have been subjected to tremendous heat (see Appendix I).

Krinov sees all this as more evidence for the comet theory. He writes:

Meteoric bodies when moving through Earth's atmosphere, are destroyed by fragmentation and by the melting of their surface layers. The molten layer is blown off by the air currents encountered and sends out a spray of minute droplets that are scattered in the atmosphere. Because of their small size these droplets harden to form tiny globules. Such globules form the dust trails which are observed for some time after the bolide (fireball) flashes across the sky and a meteorite falls. Research has proved that when meteoric bodies composed of iron are destroyed, they form globules of magnetite, i.e. the globules differ in composition from the meteorite body from which they originated, due to oxidization of the molten droplets of iron by the air.

When meteorite bodies of the achondrite or the chladnite types, i.e. consisting almost entirely of the snow-white mineral enstatite, and with practically no intrusion of nickeliferous iron, are destroyed, transparent or white silicate (glass) globules are formed . . .

A whole series of fact . . . the appearance of an anomolous optical phenomena in the atmosphere after the fall, the high initial speed of the meteoric body, the explosion in the atmosphere, and finally the discovery of the globules of different composition, lead to the conclusion that the Tunguska meteorite was a comet.

In samples from the fall area taken in 1953 globules were also found to contain small amounts of nickel, cobalt, copper and germanium– combinations of which do not occur in natural ores on Earth.

But there are still unanswered questions. Russian analysts now claim that the particles from Tunguska differ from any found in normal meteorites. The iron traces there are not substantially higher than the normal accumulation of meteoric dust from the sky that is slowly deposited all over the world. Even Krinov admits *'it will take many years before the remarkable phenomena of Tunguska can be regarded as fully investigated and explained'*.

The nearest natural explanation that anyone comes up with in the 1950s is the comet theory. It is suggested that the nucleus of a very small one plunged into the atmosphere at such a high speed that the heat generated caused it to explode. Already American astrophysicist Fred Whipple had suggested the pulverized tail of a comet caused the phenomena of the bright nights recorded in many parts of the world. The tail, directed away from the sun (then in the south east) would have stretched over Europe where it was captured by the upper layers of the atmosphere.

A number of eye-witness reports were consistent with comets. In 1935 a letter from one of them to Leonid Kulik describes the Tunguska fireball as a 'brilliant white mass in the form of a ball of cloud with a diameter far greater than the Moon'. On 1 July 1770, Lexell's Comet, passing closer to the Earth than any other is known to have done before or since, appeared over two degrees, 30 minutes in diameter – or five times the apparent diameter of the Moon. And many centuries before the fireball of 1908 terrified the Evenki people, observers were describing comets in similar terms. One report, recorded on a stone tablet in Babylon and dated 1140 BC, reads: 'a comet arose whose body was bright like the day, while from its luminous body a tail extended like the sting of a scorpion'.

Another record, from Syria in 146 BC, describes 'a comet as large as the Sun. Its disc was at first red, and like fire, spreading sufficient light to dissipate the darkness of the night.'

Comets can vary right through the range of colours reported by witnesses in Siberia. In forty-nine sightings recorded by the Chinese, twenty-three were white, twenty bluish, four red or reddish-yellow and two greenish.

However no description of the Evenkis could surely match this lurid one by Ambroise Paré, a distinguished French surgeon of the sixteenth century:

> This comet was so horrible and so frightful and it produced such terror in the vulgar that some died of fear and others fell sick. It appeared to be of excessive length and was the colour of blood. At the summit of it was seen the figure of a bent arm, holding in its hand a great sword, as if about to strike. On both sides of the rays of this comet were seen a great number of axes, knives and blood-coloured swords among which were a great number of hideous human faces with beards and bristling hair.

Hardly what you might term a 'heavenly body'.

But then most of our ancestors regarded comets with dread and suspicion. They have been interpreted as celestial messengers of the most unsavoury warnings, like death, destruction and disease, war and famine, the dethronement of monarchs, the fall of empires – and even the end of the world. They were said to have predicted such shattering events as Nero's death, the Great Plague of 1665, the fire of London, and believe it or not, the dividing of the Red Sea during the Israelites' exodus from Egypt! The arrival of Halley's Comet has been associated with a number of historical highlights. In 1066 it was the Norman Conquest and in 1696 a church minister suggested it had caused Noah's flood. When it returned in 1910 some people in the Middle East are reported to have committed suicide. It is due to visit us again in 1985.

So what exactly is a comet? The remarkable thing is that, even today, no one's quite sure, even though some 300 new ones are identified every century and it has been estimated that there could be as many as five million in existence.

We know they travel in orbits round the Sun, just like the

solar planets, and occasionally pass very close to Earth. We know some of them appear at regular intervals ranging from a few years to many centuries depending on how long it takes them to encircle the Sun. We know they consist of a bright, star-like centre, or nucleus, surrounded by a cloudy head (the coma) which blends into a long, luminous tail that can be one of the most spectacular sights in the sky.

But precisely what the nucleus is made of is still debatable. There are three principal theories.

1. It is loosely-packed ice and frozen gases like ammonia, methane and carbon dioxide in which are embedded minute particles of solid matter. Recent spectroscopic analysis shows that sodium, nickel, chromium, silicon, calcium and magnesium can also be present.

2. It is made up of large chunks of solid matter, some up to a mile or more in diameter and is surrounded by gas and dust. The famous Kohoutek Comet, last seen in 1973, is thought to have been composed of a tough, stony silicate outer surface protecting volatile gases inside.

3. The nucleus and surrounding coma is a great cloud of gas molecules and dust particles.

Whatever it is made of, its actual mass seems to be very small. For although the entire nucleus can be thousands of miles across, its average density is believed to be a mere half an ounce per cubic mile compared with five million tons of air per cubic mile on Earth's surface.

A great deal of research is now being done to find out the chemical and physical processes that occur in comets. In 1970 the Orbiting Astronomical Observatory (OAO 2) was able to study the Comet Tago-Sato-Kosaka from beyond the Earth's atmosphere. Using an ultra-violet telescope it found that the comet itself was enveloped in a huge cloud of hydrogen vaster than the diameter of the Sun. The same year, the Orbiting Geophysical Observatory (OGO 5) found the brilliant Comet Bennet was surrounded by a similar cloud an enormous eight million miles across. But even these were long-distance observations. Now scientists hope to despatch space probes to fly by a comet – or even to attempt a sensational soft-landing on the actual nucleus.

The return of Halley's Comet could be a heaven-sent opportunity.

No one really knows where comets come from either. The most common theories are the following:

1. They are formed from gaseous matter ejected from the Sun which somehow escapes into space and is prevented from falling back to the Sun again by the gravitational pull of the giant solar planets.

2. They are material from the giant planets themselves, perhaps blasted into space from huge volcanic eruptions.

3. They are bits of a planet that was once part of the Solar System and disintegrated in some catastrophic explosion or collision – like the chunky belt of asteroids that orbit the Sun between Mars and Jupiter.

4. They are the left-over debris from the time the Solar System was first formed.

5. They are from a huge belt of frozen materials called Oort's Ring that orbits the Sun at 18 billion miles.

When a comet's material begins to break up, tiny fragments of it splay off into their own slightly different orbits, forming a belt along the comet's path. If the earth passes through them, they can enter its atmosphere to produce meteor showers (shooting stars). Those that don't entirely burn away in the process arrive here as solid meteorites. We are well aware of the havoc that even a giant meteorite can cause. But, supposing the entire nucleus of a comet careered off-course and pounded to Earth. Perhaps its lethal potential might even be as awesome as that calculated by a French mathematician named Maupertuis, back in the eighteenth century who wrote:

> there are some comets so small that collisions with Earth would destroy only a few kingdoms without shattering its mass, but there are others the contact of which might be fatal to every living thing on the globe.

The comet theory, incidentally, does not rule out the possibility of the Tunguska devastation having been caused by a nuclear blast. All such explosions need not be man-made.

66

Let us assume that in 1908 a comet nucleus with a stony outer shell, like that of Kohoutek, enters the Earth's atmosphere at something like twenty-five miles a second. The only heating it has experienced on its long journey through free space has been that from the normal radiation of the Sun. Now it suddenly begins to glow at far greater temperatures, enough to begin stripping away the stony protective layer until the highly volatile gases inside – originally frozen – heat up drastically and try to escape through the stony shell. But they are held back by the brute force of the shock wave that has formed in front of the comet. Finally, however, they produce an almighty armour-piercing blast which bursts through the shock wave. This process immediately heats up the gases, largely hydrogen, to the critical limits of temperature and pressure when they are transformed into helium. What we now have is the basis for a natural nuclear 'bomb' explosion – the kind that takes place continuously inside the Sun itself.

Such a thermo-nuclear reaction could conceivably occur a few miles above the ground, which might cause the kind of devastation found around the Southern Swamp and also be consistent with the blast pattern at Hiroshima.

Writing in the Special Supplement of the *Moscow News* in September 1976, Igor Zotkin, a research associate of the Committee of Meteorites, USSR Academy of Sciences, supports the comet theory. Zotkin, who works with Academician V. Fesenkov and who has studied the Tunguska phenomena for many years, writes:

Some 500 papers and as many popular science articles have been written about the Tunguska enigma, and interest in this problem persists both among scientists and with the public. Like any scientific puzzle, it has drawn a flow of hypotheses. I doubt if there is any recent discovery that has not been called on to explain the Tunguska enigma.

The hypothesis that fits best with the information available is that the Tunguska body was a loose and not very strong aggregation containing a lot of volatile substances, as in the nuclei of comets . . .

Suppose on 30 June 1908, Earth did collide with a small comet. Its nucleus was several dozen yards in diameter and its mass some hundreds of thousands of tons. Unlike meteorites, comets may have a collision velocity up to twenty-five miles per second. According to eye witnesses, it was moving in from the Sun, i.e. no one could see it coming.

Having entered the dense layers of the atmosphere at space velocity, this ice (or snow) meteorite was seen in Siberia as a powerful bolide. Its tail would have been over Europe.

When a body is flying at supersonic velocities in the lower atmosphere, it produces a ballistic shock wave. Eye witnesses on Earth will take it for a blast wave, as in the case of a supersonic aircraft. Compressed by the meteor body, the air is heated to tens of thousands of degrees, the body evaporates vigorously and emits bright light. This emission could be sufficient to produce a forest fire. At the altitude of three to six miles, air resistance and the heat reach such proportions that a loose, unsolid body is bound to disintegrate. It turns into dust or vapour. The cross section of the body increases greatly in both cases. On hitting the air it would brake instantly, the enormous energy of its motion turning into a shock wave.

This would hit the forest from above like a blast wave and fell the trees in a ring around the epicentre, and would account for the extraordinary radial felling of the forest. Some time later small pellets of molten meteoric matter settled on the ground and were found in the Tunguska marshes.

What was decisive in the explosion of the Tunguska comet – fragmentation or evaporation – is still not certain. Academician V. Fesenkov and I came to the conclusion several years ago that it was fragmentation. We hold that the nucleus of a comet was literally pancaked by an aerodynamic force of 30 tons per square cm (nearly 200 tons per square inch).

The year before last (1974), however, Academician G. Petrov and his associates calculated that under a very low density of the comet matter, evaporation, too, can be very swift. In a few seconds the whole mass could turn into a cloud of vapour which would brake immediately.

Whichever it was, the comet hypothesis of the Tunguska body helps explain the catastrophic phenomena at the end of its flight.

However, if the object *was* a comet, it is the only recorded instance of one reaching the Earth, despite the vast number that streak through the Solar System. The closest any is known to have approached in modern times is three-and-a-half million miles.

(Note: A fuller, revised version on an exploding comet head is given in Appendix II.)

But there are many other cosmic forces even more inexplicable and ferocious than comets and meteorites. And so, in the Fifties, while men like Professor Florensky are still desperately trying to dig up the past from the mud of the Southern Swamp, others are looking far beyond Earth itself for the answers. That's where the monster came from. Surely that's the place to look. For somewhere out there could be its celestial breeding ground. Somewhere out there could be many others of its kind.

It is a good time for such a search. Man is taking the first timid steps into space. Already, in 1957, he has sent an inquisitive little satellite called Sputnik I scurrying round the globe. For the first time everyone *knows* there is life in space – even though it's only a Russian dog. Four years later man tries it himself. By 1969 two Americans are actually leaving footprints in the Lunar dust. By the 1970s satellites are busy monitoring the remotest corners of the world while spaceships infiltrate the Solar System and even land robots on the planets.

From it all is emerging a fascinating and far-reaching new technology. No longer is mankind confined to grovelling about his own terrestrial backyard for the relics of the facts of life. Now space research is giving him a fresh and exciting vision into not only his own creation but that of the Universe itself.

If any fading vestige of the thing that created the Cauldron of Hell still remains, what hope is there of exhuming it now after the searching ravages of atmospheric decay, the churning geological unrest and the everchanging shroud of prolific vegetation? On the other hand, though seventy years may be an Earthly life-span, in astronomical terms they compose but a fleeting moment in time. Out of erosive reach of those ageing, withering influences of our own environment, life can be sterilized for eternity and gauged not in decades but in billions of years.

And so we shall now continue to investigate possible answers to Tunguska far beyond the *taiga* of Central Siberia – even beyond our own Solar System. For among the strange and inexplicable predators that lurk in this endless cosmic jungle could well be the counterpart of the thing that left its abrupt reminder in 1908 that this Earth of ours is far from invulnerable.

## CHAPTER SIX

# FURY OF THE BLACK HOLE

Could the unprecedented force that lashed Tunguska and vibrated round the Earth in 1908 have been compressed into a body the size of a speck of dust?

Inconceivable though this may seem, it has been put forward by two highly-qualified scientists from the Center for Relativity Theory at the University of Texas. And in September 1973, their findings were published in *Nature* – one of the world's most respected and fastidious scientific journals. The object, they say, was a 'Black Hole' (see Appendix III).

In considering such a possibility we must now smash through all normal barriers of credibility. We must peer far beyond the limits of our own logic, conception and experience. A Black Hole in the Cauldron of Hell! Could anything sound more forbidding? But, remember, we are now infringing on a new and bizarre region of space research where science fact is emerging as even stranger than science fiction.

We are also attempting to unravel a happening that every known and tested avenue of man's scientific scrutiny has failed to classify. As Krinov wrote in 1966: 'The effects associated with the immense explosion which occurred on 30 June 1908, are unlike those reported for any other natural or man-made phenomena.' And an assessment of the Black Hole Theory published in the *Royal Astronomical Society Journal* in November 1975, states:

The apparent uniqueness of the event requires that all possible explanations must be seriously considered and no explanation can be discarded merely because it has a low possibility of occurring.

A Black Hole is virtually the celestial phantom of a star

originally many times bigger than our own Sun. It acquires this macabre state when its matter collapses in on itself and shrinks beyond a point of no return. In condensing to merely a few miles in diameter, its phenomenal power of gravity remains to dominate every other force. It devours its own body and everything about it. Nothing we know of appears able to withstand its frightening ferocity.

We can't see Black Holes because even the light from their own tiny white-hot nucleii is dragged back before it can escape the irresistible embrace of this super-gravity that develops. We only know they exist because they have been found to even affect the movement of mighty stars in their vicinity.

It is now believed that gigantic Black Holes could be at the centres of entire galaxies of stars causing them to gather in clusters as they do. Such is their overwhelming power.

In April 1976, researchers at the Cambridge Institute of Astronomy suggested that a Black Hole with the mass of ten million Suns, could be the source of intense X-rays being picked up from the galaxy known as Centaurus A. The nucleus of this galaxy emits nearly as much X-ray power as do all the 150 billion stars in the Milky Way (our own galaxy). It is thought that this Black Hole was originally a supermassive star or a dense cluster of stars that is now compacted within a radius less than fifty times that of the Sun.

Actually the X-rays would be originating from stray matter the Black Hole is drawing into itself like an enormous vacuum cleaner, which is being heated to temperatures of hundreds of million of degrees. A Black Hole of this dimension could be systematically devouring nearby stars that venture too close. For, like any other predator, the Black Hole must go on seeking new prey in order to survive. In astronomical terms their life-expectancy is not great. If they don't ingest sufficient material they literally starve to death.

Cygnus X, an insatiable Black Hole discovered in our own galaxy, is sucking huge clouds of hot gas from the atmosphere of a large, visible star around which Cygnus X is in orbit. Eventually the entire star could be swallowed up into the Black Hole leaving no trace of its former existence.

Consider then, the appalling result of our own Earth finding itself anywhere within clutching distance of such an horrific force. Nothing could stop it being ruthlessly torn apart bit by bit.

As an example of how this gravity build-up takes place, imagine that our Earth, which has a gravitational pull of 1 g, could be reduced to a quarter of its present size (i.e. a diameter of only 2000 miles), but somehow retain its present mass. The gravity field on our highly-compressed planet would then become 16 g. If the diameter were reduced even further, to 500 miles, the inward pull would be 256 g – a force that would crush the human frame.

Based on this fixed square law relationship between the size of a body, its mass and the gravitational field it exerts, by the time the Earth was compressed to a mere mile in diameter, the force field would be an incredible 64 million g.

After such massive shrinkage the very basic characteristics of the atoms themselves, of which the planet is composed, would collapse. To compress Earth beyond this point would produce a critical limit at which no known structure could support the force field produced. Nothing could then stop the collapse to a pin-point. The planet would then be a small Black Hole. A similar object hitting our world would destroy it as utterly as if we had collided head-on with Venus. And the tiny, invisible vandal would merely continue on its way.

To produce merely the kind of energy release that violated Tunguska would require a Black Hole tinier than a speck of dust. Yet it would be so dense it would weigh an astounding ten thousand million tons!

A. A. Jackson and Michael P. Ryan of Texas University suggest that such an object hit Siberia, drilled its way right through the Earth and emerged from a point in the North Atlantic. They write:

We suggest that a Black Hole of substellar mass . . . could explain many of the mysteries associated with the event.

The Tunguska meteorite left a visible fiery trail accompanied by thermal radiation and a blast wave that levelled forest over several hundred square miles. No crater and no meteoric material that can unambiguously be associated with the event have ever been found.

These characteristics they claim, are consistent with the impact of a Black Hole entering the surface of the Earth. Such an object approaching our planet would draw in constituents of the atmosphere from a wide area around itself. Its temperature would rise to between 30 000 and 300 000 degrees centigrade and the ultra-violet radiation would produce a plasma column that would appear as deep blue in colour. Jackson and Ryan continue:

These results agree well with eye-witness reports of the event and with measurements of the pattern of throwdown of trees at the site. Eye-witness reports of flash burning, descriptions of the object as a bright blue 'tube' and searing of trees at the site indicate a compatible temperature.

Since the Black Hole would leave no crater or material residue, it explains the mystery of the Tunguska Event. It would enter the Earth and the rigidity of rock would allow no underground shock wave. Because of its high velocity and because it loses only a small fraction of its energy in passing through the Earth, the Black Hole should very nearly follow a straight line through the Earth, entering at 30 degrees to the horizon and leaving through the North Atlantic in the region of 40 to 50 degrees N, 30 to 40 degrees W.

However there are a number of holes (other than black ones) in the Jackson and Ryan theory. Firstly, their geographical co-ordinates mean the object, after melting a tunnel through the rocks of the Earth, should have emerged to the north east of the deep Atlantic Ridge roughly in an area known as the Flemish Cap. From here, the nearest land area is St Johns, Newfoundland, approximately 800 miles away. About 1500 miles to the west is the busy port of

Lisbon on the Iberian Peninsular. Here the enormous tidal wave such a disturbance must have caused would most certainly have been recorded, even in 1908. We are dealing with a concentrated energy release up to one hundred thousand times greater than that of the largest known earthquakes. And even these can produce tidal waves of thirty feet. As far as is known no exceptional ones were reported at the time of the Tunguska Event.

A force such as that of even the minutest Black Hole passing so close to the North Atlantic Ridge – a major crustal scar in the sea bed – could have torn open the 'wound' sending a massive split along the ridge, causing colossal volcanic eruptions. Such a cataclysm could not possibly go unnoticed.

Jackson and Ryan suggested that microbarograph records should be checked for evidence of shock waves from the emerging Black Hole. Two other researchers at Texas University, William Beasley and Brian Tinsley, did this, and their findings were published in *Nature* in August 1974.

They estimated that the object would have taken ten to fifteen minutes to pass through the Earth, causing an explosion at the place of exit similar to the one that occurred at Tunguska. They point out that it took the Siberian waves five hours to reach meteorological stations in London. So similar waves from the North Atlantic should have arrived there too – some three hours earlier.

'We have examined copies of the English microbarograph records,' they say, 'but have been unable to find any sign of waves from the suggested exit explosion.' Not only should these have been recorded, but they should also have been stronger. They would not have had so far to travel.

Further objections to the Black Hole theory are also contained in a paper published in the *Royal Astronomical Society Journal* in 1975. The authors are Jack Burns, George Greenstein and Kenneth Verusub of the Universities of Indiana, Amherst (Massachussetts) and California. They claim that the point where the Black Hole entered the Earth should be marked by a patch of melted and resolidified rock of diameter a quarter to two-and-a-half miles, overlain by fused soil of comparable extent. As the hole entered the soil it would have vaporized the water, oxidized the organic matter and fused the residual material such as quartz, feldspar and mica ... The point of impact should therefore be marked by a depression.

But Burns, Greenstein and Verusub have to agree that there *is* in fact a depression at Tunguska. The Southern Swamp. However, they add: 'This depression may predate the Tunguska Event and is not inconsistent with other explanations.'

Once inside the Earth, a Black Hole would be expected to cause drastic stress changes in the surrounding rock, resulting in large-scale earthquakes. But the seismograms that registered the Siberian blast showed it to be consistent with a *surface* wave and not with extraordinarily violent shocks underground.

However, until we know far more about the behaviour of these super-charged monstrosities from outer space – and many scientists now believe them to be scattered in vast numbers throughout the Universe – it is difficult to entirely rule out the possibility, however remote, that one of them was just 'passing through' on a visit here in 1908. There is not a scrap of recorded evidence showing exactly what such an impact would cause. They may have been here before. Like the detonations of comet heads or the fall of gigantic meteorites, Black Holes too might well have sculptured the very face of our planet in its early history.

## CHAPTER SEVEN

# ANTIMATTER – THE ULTIMATE FORCE

During the early 1930s when Leonid Kulik was still firmly convinced the Cauldron of Hell was the brutal handiwork of a meteorite, another scientist made an astounding discovery that could yet prove him right. For, according to the remarkable findings of P. A. M. Dirac, the brilliant British physicist and Nobel Prize winner, there could be a form of meteorite infinitely more fearful than the kind for which Kulik was searching – one that could have produced most of the Tunguska phenomena and still left no crater or any tell-tale fragments of itself. It could also have accounted for those unusual flash burns. And it would not have had to weigh a million tons. Or even one ton. It need have been no larger than a cube of sugar. For this meteorite could have been composed of the most potentially violent explosive material in the Universe . . . *antimatter*.

The instant antimatter encounters ordinary matter there is complete and utter annihilation. The energy released is greater than that from any other source known to science. Six cubic inches of antimatter pounding into our Earth could produce a blast capable of flattening the British Isles.

Quite simply this remarkable material from the exotic world of high-energy physics, is composed of atoms identical in every respect to those in ordinary material . . . except that everything is constructed in reverse.

To appreciate this, first consider the make-up of normal atoms, of which everything on Earth, including ourselves, is formed. A hydrogen atom has a positively-charged nucleus called a proton. Around it, a negatively-charged particle called an electron spins in dizzy orbits at the inconceivable rate of 4 billion circuits a second. The opposing charges cancel each other out so that the entire atom itself has *zero charge*.

A similar atom of antimatter would be constructed in precisely the same way. It would be the same size, the same weight. But, in this case, the electrical charges would be *reversed*. In other words, the central proton would have the *negative* charge. The 'satellite' electron would have the *positive* charge. One atom, in fact, would be a mirror image of the other (see Appendix IV).

If these two atoms meet, the positive charge of the ordinary proton annihilates the negative charge of the anti-proton. At the same time the negative charge of the ordinary electron is annihilated by the positive charge of the anti-electron (known as a positron). The nett result is that they vanish in a tiny, but intense flash of gamma radiation. This belligerent alliance produces the highest known energy yield.

Most people are vaguely aware that today's physicists are able to tap the enormous energy trapped in the whirling maelstrom of electrons and nuclei that form the atoms of normal matter. They see the results in nuclear-driven submarines, aircraft carriers, ice-breakers and tankers. So awesome is the source of their power that the tankers have been barred from entering some of the world's harbours.

But just how do we obtain and harness this basic energy of the atom? What *is* nuclear power. What makes an atom or thermonuclear bomb? And what is 'fission' and 'fusion'?

The power within an atom lies purely and simply in its mass. If we cause this to change, we obtain *energy*. This stems directly from Einstein's famous equation: $E=mc^2$ (where $E$ is called 'rest mass energy', $m$ is the mass of the material and $c$ is the velocity of light).

What this means in layman's terms is this: *If we destroy the mass, we get pure energy in the form of radiant light.* And there is only one way of *totally destroying* a mass of matter (whether it's iron, lead, water or anything else), and that is by combining it with an equal mass of antimatter. The result is that tremendous blast of gamma rays – a form of 'light' that we cannot see, but is capable of penetrating solid objects which are even opaque to X-rays. This is called *annihilation energy*.

Up to the present time scientists have discovered no way of safely harnessing such total energy. But they *are* able to produce a fraction of it through 'fission' and 'fusion'. Nuclear *fission* is the energy obtained by the splitting up of large heavyweight atoms. Nuclear *fusion* is the combining of very light atoms to form heavier ones. We know the catastrophic results of these processes in the A-bomb and its more powerful successor, the H-bomb. Yet these are infinitely less lethal than the total annihilation energy produced from mixing matter with antimatter (see Appendix V).

The energy release in an A-bomb is produced by the loss of only 0.4 per cent of its original mass. A startling example of this is the Hiroshima bomb whose initial total explosive size was roughly that of a standard can of baked beans. The actual quantity of matter consumed to *produce* the explosion that devastated the city would have been about the size of a grain of birdseed!

Scientists can observe the behaviour of antimatter particles by sophisticated laboratory techniques. But they require colossal amounts of energy and extremely powerful instruments to produce them in even the most minute quantities. Even then they only survive until they combine with normal particles – a matter of a millionth of a second. Only the complicated equipment of the high-energy physicist can record the traces of radiation that are produced.

What is more mind-boggling, is that for every particle of ordinary matter there is believed to be an anti-matter counterpart. This means that there could be regions in the unpredictable realms of outer space where *everything* is composed of antimatter – even entire galaxies, populated by antimatter stars and planets. There is no way we could distinguish them from normal heavenly bodies. The light generated by the stars would be exactly the same as that from any in our own galaxy. If any of these planets were inhabited by intelligent life, that, like everything else around it, would be fashioned in antimatter. They would be quite unaware that any other kind of material existed. Unless, of course, they happened to 'bump into *us*'.

In that case the first historic meeting between man and 'anti-man' would produce the most devastating handshake in the history of community relationship.

Research is still going on into the intriguing possibility that antimatter did, in fact, cause the Siberian blast, when a mass of it exploded soon after entering the Earth's atmosphere. There are a number of consistencies. The brilliant blue streak described by many eye witnesses in 1908 is precisely the visual effect a chunk of antimatter would produce as it drove towards Earth and began to react with small scraps of ordinary material in the atmosphere. The nearer it got to us, the denser would be the atmosphere and the more violent the reaction.

Though actual impact with Earth would seem the most likely cause of a final full-scale explosion, it is conceivable that a powerful shock wave occurred in front of the falling body that pre-detonated it, resulting in a mid-air blast. This would cause the same radial destruction and flash burns found at Tunguska.

Williard F. Libby, ex-member of the Atomic Energy Commission whose discovery of radio active carbon dating won him a Nobel Prize, has suggested that the nuclear processes resulting from the annihilation of a meteorite of antimatter would have increased the content of carbon 14 in the atmosphere. Had this happened, he said, trees all over the world soon after the explosion should have absorbed abnormally large traces of it.

The carbon-14 content was therefore measured in the rings of a three-centuries old fir tree in Arizona and an ancient oak near Los Angeles. Remarkably enough, the highest levels were found to have been absorbed in 1909 – *the year following the Tunguska Event*. However this evidence is not accepted as conclusive. Carbon 14 can build up through normal processes. It is produced at a fairly regular rate by the bombardment of cosmic rays from space. Libby believes a meteorite entirely composed of antimatter would have resulted in even bigger increases in carbon 14 than those actually detected.

Dr Hall Crannell of the Catholic University of America in

Washington, writing in *Nature* in 1974, suggested there could be other materials whose presence at Tunguska in any considerable quantities would indicate a matter–antimatter explosion having taken place. One of them is the radio-active isotope Aluminium-26 which could be traced by counters. These tests have not so far been carried out (see Appendix VI).

There is one obvious loophole in the antimatter meteorite theory as applied to Tunguska. It is unlikely that many of these frightening little cosmic warheads retain their lethal power for long once they encounter the ordinary interstellar matter of a galaxy such as our own. They certainly couldn't have originated in the Milky Way, which means they would have had to endure incredibly long journeys over many billions of years.

Even if some of them began their marathon flights as gigantic hunks of rock, they would inevitably be whittled down by countless minor explosive impacts with interstellar particles of ordinary matter on the way. And the sniping would be even more concentrated once they streaked into the dusty, gas-laden regions of the Solar System itself.

In addition, the objects would have to negotiate an end-less gauntlet of various suns and planets long before they got here, and somehow avoid being dragged towards them by the individual forces of gravity.

However, like the Black Hole, the antimatter meteorite cannot be entirely ruled out as the Tunguska monster. Here again there are so many unknown factors; so many questions our scientists must still answer in an unfamiliar field of research of which, as yet, we are only on the fringe. Antimatter may have somehow found ways through to us many times in the past. There are other unaccountable depressions dotted about the world similar to the Southern Swamp.

One intriguing theory is that ball lightning – that strange will-o'-the-wisp phenomenon frequently witnessed all over the world – could be caused by tiny fragments of meteoric antimatter from the upper atmosphere (see Appendix III).

David Ashby and Colin Whitehead of the Atomic Energy

Research Establishment at Harwell, England, suggest that a 'hypothetical barrier' exists between matter and anti-matter. A minute particle of antimatter might, therefore, be comparatively stable if it was travelling at a low speed, whereby colliding air molecules would be unable to get through this 'barrier'. During thunderstorms they may acquire enough energy to annihilate with ordinary matter, resulting in an energy release that would form a luminous ball. Ashby and Whitehead have actually observed several short bursts of gamma rays, a phenomenon also associated with matter–antimatter annihilation.

About 70 per cent of ball lightning outbreaks appear to occur during periods of thunderstorms, and these are particularly prevalent and violent in Siberia during the summer months.

Some years ago the Soviet authorities were baffled by frequent and unaccountable disappearances of aircraft on long-distance flights from Vladivostok to Moscow. Often the last radiomessages from aircrews described 'brilliantly glowing balls' moving towards them. Days later the mangled wreckage of the aircraft would be found scattered over some desolate area. There were never any survivors to tell exactly what had happened.

It was Academician Peter Kapitsa, at one time head of the Academy of Sciences and a specialist in high-energy electrical discharges, who insisted that the disasters were caused by ball lightning. This eerie phenomenon takes the form of rapidly-spinning balls that glow vivid blue, violet, pink or green according to the spectra of the dust that is contained in them, skipping briskly about the sky, like Peter Pan's fairy Tinkerbell – but infinitely more lethal. Without warning, and within seconds or minutes of appearing, they often explode violently. If one of these little horrors forms inside a building they can cause extensive damage.

Kapitsa actually produced ball lightning in the high-voltage laboratories of Moscow University. It was almost a Doctor Frankenstein operation. To simulate even the tiniest specimens, he had to momentarily short-circuit the entire electrical power grid of the city during the early hours of the morning. For a few millionths of a second, thousands of megawatts were released into enormous lightning sparks. This produced a very small ball that bobbed about the vicinity of the spark, disappearing a few seconds later with a loud, sharp explosion. Had the ball been as large as some created under natural conditions, the entire laboratory would have been devastated.

There have been many hair-raising eye-witness reports of ball lightning. One was seen by terror-stricken airliner passengers. It is claimed to have actually formed *inside* the craft where it silently floated along the gangway like a luminous phantom, eventually seeming to vanish right through the structure of the plane. A red lightning ball about two feet in diameter is claimed to have dug a trench a hundred yards long and more than a yard deep in soft soil near a stream, and then tear away a further 25 yards of the bank. There have been reports of others shattering logs, cutting metal cables and causing other damage requiring surprisingly large amounts of power.

In April 1976, the scientific journal *Nature* described how a glowing purple-coloured sphere with a halo of flame suddenly appeared over the gas cooker of a startled housewife in Staffordshire, England. Physicist Mark Stenhoff of the Royal Holloway College, Surrey, who investigated the incident, says the object was about the size of a tennis ball and had emitted a peculiar rattling sound and a singeing smell. It had moved towards the woman who instinctively brushed it away. Almost simultaneously the ball exploded. It burned a three-inch hole in her dress and left her hand red and swollen.

It has been estimated that the fireball generated a temperature of 200 degrees centigrade. When the hole in the dress was laboratory-tested, the central portion had vanished and the gap was surrounded by an area in which the pattern had faded and the fabric was shrivelled.

Other eye-witness accounts of ball lightning were quoted by Neil Charman, a lecturer at the University of Manchester Institute of Science and Technology, in the magazine *New Scientist* in February 1976. One man from Norwich describes how a glowing orange ball about two inches across once drifted through his scullery window and hovered by the down-wire of an electric light. It suddenly vanished 'with a loud pop'.

Another man recalls how, many years ago, while sheltering from a violent thunderstorm, he watched a glowing sphere the size of a football enter an empty stationary tramcar, glide through it, and emerge at the other end where it exploded on the ground outside. The witness says he later found large holes blasted through the front and rear panels of the tram. Charman estimates that the ball must have dissipated at least a million joules during its destructive passage through the vehicle.

One couple claim that, following an intense lightning flash over Lake Geneva, they watched a ball 'the colour and size of the Sun at noon' suddenly appear a few hundred feet in the air. 'The edges were slightly fuzzy,' they say. 'It was about three miles away and drifting with a smooth, non-rotating motion like a balloon for about half a mile ... and then vanished.'

From hundreds of eye-witness reports Dr Charman lists the following properties of a 'typical' lightning ball, or *Kugelblitz* as it is often called.

They are generally spherical or pear-shaped with fuzzy edges, ranging in diameter from an inch to a yard. They come in a wide range of colours, red, orange and yellow being the commonest. Their life-time usually ranges from one second to over one minute. They can either move horizontally or vertically or just remain stationary. Many balls appear to spin. In some cases their sudden disappearance liberates heat. Some lightning balls show an affinity for metal objects and may move along conductors such as wires or metal fences. Others appear inside buildings 'passing through closed doors and windows with curious ease. Chimneys, fireplaces and ovens appear to be favoured haunts of these exotic objects.' They can vanish silently or explosively, often leaving odours resembling ozone, burning sulphur or nitrogen oxide, and perhaps a faint mist or residue.

In 1936 a correspondent to the *Daily Mail* told how a large 'red hot' ball fell from the sky, struck a house, cut the telephone wire, burned a window frame, then submerged itself in a four-gallon tub of water. The water boiled for some minutes after. The witness could find nothing in the tub when he searched it. The implied energy of the ball was about $10^9$ joules.

Recently, after researchers scrutinized more than a hundred thousand records of lightning strokes, they found six photographs of strokes, ending above the ground, with balls at the end which appeared to be floating to the ground.

Though no one really knows what lightning balls are, these frivolous objects appear to exist either through some energy source within themselves or by some external energy source that somehow sustains them throughout their brief lives. In most recorded instances their explosive force corresponds roughly to that of between 2.5 and 25 lbs., of TNT.

One theory is that they might be a nuclear phenomenon. M. D. Atshuler and other researchers at the High Altitude Observatory in Colorado, suggested they could be caused by reactions involving the production of radioactive elements from the oxygen and nitrogen of the air. However, if this were so, that Staffordshire housewife who brushed one from her dress would probably have received a sufficient radioactive dosage to have caused radiation sickness.

Similarly, if *Kugelblitz*, or ball lightning is caused by minute traces of antimatter, anyone in its vicinity would be expected to suffer burns from the release of gamma radiation. No evidence of this has been found, despite tests carried out by researchers from Oxford University.

A. T. Lawton, scientific editor of this book, suggests this bewildering phenomenon might even be a micro Black Hole – possibly created by the tremendous energy of a particularly violent flash of lightning. Lightning itself is an enormous spark or pulse of electrical energy that generates a colossal magnetic field. This field envelopes the spark and compresses it like a vice. In most cases nothing unusual results from this pressure. But there could be instances where a super-intense lightning flash, lasting for a far longer period than normal, might crush the ionized oxygen and nitrogen atoms to a point where they pass the Schwarzschild Limit* and collapse into themselves to form miniscule Black Holes.

The smaller the Black Hole the shorter its life-span. One that could exist for only a few moments would be less than the diameter of a hydrogen atom. One such as this could produce an explosion similar to those reported during instances of ball lightning. A Black Hole of such incredibly small dimensions would account for ball lightning being seen to pass through the walls of buildings and the fuselages of aircraft. To such a tiny entity the pores in stone or metal would be like wide open 'windows'.

The micro Black Hole would also explain other characteristics of ball lightning. By ionizing the surrounding air with its tremendous gravitational field it would create the familiar glow and possibly produce the crackling and hissing sounds as particles of matter are sucked in and then blasted out again at extreme velocities. Since the ionization radius would be much larger than the nucleus, the glowing mass would literally float on air in exactly the way ball lightning does.

*So could some particularly massive form of ball lightning conceivably be associated with the Tunguska Event?*

Lawton calculates that, to cause such devastation, would require a specimen of *Kugelblitz* 3700 feet in diameter. In fact this is very close indeed to the estimated size of the Tunguska fireball. From eye-witness reports early researchers reckoned it to be about 3300 feet. This is so close that we cannot dismiss the possibility that the Siberian monster might have been a giant *Kugelblitz*.

But is it possible for ball lightning to attain such immense proportions? The most common ones are merely a few inches across. Lawton maintains it is, provided it is com-

---

* In 1916 Karl Schwarzschild, a brilliant German mathematician, deduced that light could not escape from a body that was creating a sufficiently powerful field, but would bend back to its surface. This effect is known as the Schwarzschild Radius or Limit.

posed in a particular way. He suggests that if the fireball is made up from dust particles bound tightly together by an electrical charge, it could achieve these huge dimensions. One 3300 feet across entering Earth's atmosphere might disintegrate in a gigantic electrical flash that would produce the scorching radiant energy and searing shock wave associated with Tunguska and with nuclear explosions. (Full details of Lawton's calculations are in Appendix III.)

## CHAPTER EIGHT

## NATURE'S DEADLY ROULETTE

There is no reason whatever why a similar visitation should not fall at any moment upon a more populous region. Had this meteorite fallen in Central Belgium there would have been no living creature left in the whole country ... Had it fallen on New York, Philadelphia (nearly a hundred miles away) might have escaped with only its windows shattered ... But all life in the central area of the meteor's impact would have been blotted out instantaneously.

That, according to one of Leonid Kulik's lectures in Moscow, is the horrifying significance of the thing that struck Central Siberia in 1908. The only reason it did not perpetrate one of the most appalling massacres in human history was simply the 'luck of the draw'. Like a flaming ball of fortune, the object just happened to slot itself into the spinning roulette wheel of Earth at a spot completely devoid of humanity. Had its timing been slightly different, its trajectory a few degrees either way, the Cauldron of Hell could have been the centre of London, Moscow or New York. It is estimated, for example, that had it arrived four hours and forty-seven minutes later it would have crushed the mighty city of Leningrad.

Tunguska therefore gives us little ground for complacency. We don't know what the monster was. We don't know if others of its awesome ancestors visited us in the past. We don't know if and when its successors will strike again. All we *do* know is that it was capable of more destruction than anything man's most devious ingenuity has so far created.

How many of its kind have pounded into the vast oblivion of the sea? How many have blasted tidal waves of sand across the empty deserts? How could we know, after the camouflaging winds of centuries have long since repaired their imprints?

And let's face it, if it hadn't been for the natural moat of atmosphere that envelopes Earth, the bombardment of extra-terrestrial missiles would have smashed our tiny fortress to bits long ago. Even those objects we know – the giant meteorites – could have pulverized us time and again. Imagine, for instance, the gargantuan dimensions of the one that left its moon-like scar in Arizona. It exploded with the violence of many nuclear bombs, even though a vast proportion of its original bulk must have been gnawed away by the hungry heat of its fierce atmospheric encounter. Its pre-entry weight must have been many millions of tons.

The fact that the outer defences of our planetary environment was unable to ward off the Tunguska invader is particularly disturbing. The sudden and unheralded return of another in today's uneasy world could have even more far-reaching repercussions.

At a symposium in 1964, James R. Arnold of the University of California remarked: 'Let us hope that the next such impact occurs during a period of relaxed international relations. For it would closely resemble the explosion of an H-bomb.'

It is not difficult to foresee the dreadful chain reaction if it happened to fall at a time when the major powers were squaring up to one another with their itchy fingers poised over the red alert buttons.

In fact on 10 August 1972, our planet had one of the luckiest escapes in its recorded history. A blazing bluey-white ball of fire, looking like a giant welder's torch, seared over the Western United States and Canada at more than nine miles a second, leaving a sinister smoke trail in its wake. It was a thirteen-foot meteor and weighed a thousand tons.

It was first spotted over Utah. One-and-a-half minutes later it was a thousand miles away over Alberta. Its lowest trajectory occurred as it swept over Salt Lake City. The kinetic energy of this object has been estimated at twenty kilotons. In other words it had the lethal punch of the atom bomb that destroyed Hiroshima. Even so, by giant meteorite standards, it was comparatively small, its mass being only about 2 per cent of the Arizona meteor.

The startling thing is that, after finding its way here across billions of miles of space, it missed hitting us by a mere thirty five . . . and it was virtually a miracle that prevented it devastating a crowded American city. For, instead of hitting the Earth – as almost 99 per cent of meteorites would have done – it literally richochetted off the atmosphere and flew on harmlessly into space again.

Fortunately the Aerospace Corporation of Los Angeles had a satellite-borne near-infrared radiometer in orbit over the United States at the time which identified the intruder as a meteor. But had it not been spotted and, in fact, landed, the immediate assumption might well have been that it constituted a nuclear attack. By the time its correct classification had been confirmed by the White House, retaliatory warheads might have been on their way east.

The news of this frightening near-miss was considered so unsettling that details of it were kept secret from the public for nearly two years. They were not released until February 1974, when a short scientific announcement by R. D. Rawcliffe and others from the Aerospace Corporation appeared in *Nature*.

A further disturbing comment in the same issue pointed out that calculations have shown that meteorites of this mass should cross the Earth's orbit, and therefore collide with it, an average of once *every ten or twenty years*. And remember, only one in a hundred of them 'bounce' clear like that in 1972.

One would like to assume that, during periods of East–West detente, neither side would take instinctive nuclear action over the sudden detonation of one of these stray cosmic bombs on their territory. But supposing some delicate state of international 'call my bluff' was simmering at the time. Supposing the American president was poised over the threat of another Cuban-style incident, or the Kremlin was seething about another possible Vietnam. What then?

Would there still be the time and inclination for cool, calm reflection?

It seems unlikely that anything could prevent a major confrontation if the intruding object happened to fall on one of two countries – allied to the East and West – already engaged in active warfare. It is chilling to contemplate such a dramatic incident taking place on Arab or Israeli territory at the height of a Middle East War. By the time the true cause was discovered it would most certainly be too late. Nuclear warheads could be criss-crossing the world like scheduled international airway flights.

One of Britain's near-misses from 'NFOs' – Natural Flying Objects – is thought to have occurred millions of years ago in the rugged Shetland Islands, creating what is known as St Magnus Bay. The bay, which is the most prominent feature of the islands, is ten miles across and 540 feet deep in the centre – an unprecedented depth for coastal waters in this region.

Admiralty charts show that the ridge around it continues beneath the sea to form a complete and almost perfect circle. Scientists from the University of Liverpool suggest it was excavated by a two-million ton meteorite more than a thousand feet in diameter that struck the Shetland Islands at a velocity of 25 miles a second. They believe it exploded, sending pulverized material high into the stratosphere in the form of a giant mushroom cloud. The rocks in which St Magnus Bay is formed were once joined to the Canadian Shield, in which geologists have traced some thirty impact scars since 1950.

Ironically enough the Tunguska Event itself might well have taken place here, even though the islands are nearly 4000 miles away from the Southern Swamp of Central Siberia. For, if the monster had arrived in the vicinity of Earth some hours later, it could have splashed down just off the Shetlands.

An even more startling possibility, however, is that had its course changed very slightly in longitude and been depressed by 10 degrees in latitude (a very small variance) it would have exploded at latitude 51.5 degrees at shortly after 7 a.m., Greenwich Mean Time. Its target ... the centre of London.

Consider how slight this variance would have needed to be. The simple reason the monster exploded over the stony Tunguska region was because *that* particular part of the world just happened to be in its line of flight at the time.

The Earth makes one complete revolution every twenty-four hours. This corresponds to fifteen degrees of turn in one hour. Tunguska is situated at Longitude 101 degrees east. Greenwich is at longitude zero degrees. To move those vital 101 degrees, the Earth takes six hours forty-four minutes. So had the monster arrived from outer space that much later, it would have struck at longitude zero.

It exploded over Siberia at seventeen minutes and eleven seconds after midnight (GMT). Had it done so at seven hours, one minute and eleven seconds instead, it would have been slap on the Greenwich meridian. On the latitude corresponding to Tunguska, this would have placed it slightly north of the Shetlands.

But let's assume it had steepened its trajectory by a mere ten degrees (or ricocheted off the atmosphere like the meteorite did over the United States in 1972 – but in this case dropped back towards earth). It would then have exploded at latitude 51.5 degrees north and longitude zero. Only one point on the globe corresponds to these two co-ordinates ... *London*. These same co-ordinates fed into the automatic pilot device of any long-range missile would steer it to no other target but Britain's capital city.

Had the fireball followed the southwest to north-east course plotted by Kulik and others, it would have been first seen over Toulouse and Bordeaux. Had it taken the south-east–north-west course suggested by Krinov, it would have passed directly over Paris with a thundering roar like continuous gunfire. Some fifteen minutes later people in the French capital would have been terrified by a rumbling explosion and tremors shaking buildings all around them. As they gazed along the horizon they would witness the billowing 'tombstone' of smoke and dust towering in a fifty-mile mushroom cloud from the other side of the Channel. It would also have been visible from other major North European cities such as Copenhagen, Amsterdam, Oslo, Frankfurt and Berlin.

## CHAPTER NINE

# LATITUDE 51.5 ... DESTINATION LONDON

*Had the monster arrived at the Earth six hours and forty-four minutes later than it did and on a slightly varied course, it would have exploded over latitude 51.5 degrees at about seven a.m., Greenwich Mean Time.*

Seven a.m., 30 June 1908. It is clammy and airless as the stifled passengers on a local train steaming into Frankfurt fan themselves with rolled-up newspapers and shuffle uneasily on the hard carriage seats. They are early starters in what is obviously going to be a long, hot working day in the dusty city.

The sun is up. There is no cloud. A few travellers glance at their watches. One minute past seven.*

And then they see it ... streaking across the blue sky like a bolt out of hell. An immense, searing ball of fire. The train grinds to a halt and the passengers scamper out on to the track. For a few moments they listen to distant rumblings. Then nothing more. The air is still again.

Like the passengers at Filimonovo Junction on the trans-Siberian railway, they are nearly four hundred miles from the place the monster has struck ... the *centre of Edwardian London*.

Here, at 7 a.m. on this sticky Tuesday morning, the busiest city in the world is already rustling itself awake. In the stables of the elegant mansion houses coachmen in shiny black top-boots prepare high-stepping greys for their lordships' first summons of the day, as a few ankle-hugging skirts already flap side-saddle along Rotten Row.

In the suburbs, the well-to-do middleclass are still lingering over the family breakfast, ceremoniously laid out on heavy mahogany sideboards – mixed grills under

* Greenwich Mean Time

silver-plated domes and precisely-timed boiled eggs nestling beneath hand-painted china covers.

In less-affluent Battersea, overworked, underpaid clerks have already left the tidy rows of lace-curtained terraces to the fussy indulgence of mob-capped wives who dust rooms littered like pawnshops with bric-à-brac and family heirlooms.

But in the city centre itself the streets echo to the impatient clatter of racy little hansoms, gigs, dog-carts and lumbering drays. The walrus-moustached drivers of horse-drawn omnibuses – bright red and packed inside and out with bowler-hatted city workers – nuzzle their panting steeds past new-fangled electric tramcars, cursing the arrogance of overtaking motor cars that honk pompously like flocks of frustrated geese.

In prosperous Piccadilly, blue-aproned lackies are already polishing up the brass-door opulence of palatial offices and high-class restaurants in readiness for the clients whose business deals over coffee and brandy will influence the capitals of Europe. Breakfast is being served at the newly-opened Ritz Hotel. The cleaners are dusting between the rows of red plush seats at Drury Lane, the Gaiety, Her Majesty's and the lively little Tivoli where Marie Lloyd and George Robey titilated packed houses the night before.

There's a sale starting at Harrods. The window-dressers are busily arranging opera cloaks at fifty shillings, real ostrich boas at fifty-nine and six and 'unrepeatable' ladies' chemises at seven and elevenpence. Billingsgate market has been alive as cockles for three hours, its cobbled approaches crammed with fishcarts and cursing costermongers. So has the tangy-smelling Covent Garden market where the porters balance leaning towers of round wicker baskets on their heads as they step gingerly through a swamp of flattened oranges and slimy cabbage leaves.

*Big Ben stops at one minute and eleven seconds past seven.* A blinding split-second flash of hell incinerates the city. The whole of Greater London is suddenly grilled and pulverized out of existence. It is literally torn from the map. The intense Sun-like heat of the monster's breath of fire melts the very stone of the city's mighty edifices. Within seconds the innards of the metropolis are ruthlessly ripped apart and then sucked up into the fearsome vacuum that results. The vapourized debris of the most noble buildings in the world – the Houses of Parliament, St Pauls, Westminster Abbey, Buckingham Palace and the rest – is whirlpooled high into the sky to hover in a bellowing mushroom-shaped cloud.

Shock wave follows shock wave. Destruction within a twenty-five mile radius is total. Death is instant. Charred bodies in their thousands are frozen like waxwork figures in the final postures of life . . . rigid in the micro-second of blind, instinctive flight or joined with others in the last erotic contortions of embrace. The macabre bleaching effect of the blast has left the tortured silhouettes of others on the surfaces of walls still standing, like a grim mural record of the worst holocaust in the history of the human race.

The sickening scenery of death in the crowded streets is horrific. Countless thousands of dismembered corpses – limbs amputated by their roots like the trees now strewn about Hyde Park – smoulder among an angry sea of ruins. The city is a crematorium, where animate and inanimate life is welded together in the vast melting pot the monster has created. An omnibus, its passengers, and the horses that strained between the shafts a few moments ago, are all fused into one shapeless hulk of indeterminate matter. There are no broad streets any more. Just furrows in the devastation. The mansions of Mayfair and the slums of Whitechapel and Bethnal Green have merged into an indistinguishable jungle of molten rubble where those still bewilderedly alive can only stare blankly into the face of death.

Thirty-six miles from London (the same distance as Vanavara from the Southern Swamp) is Henley-on-Thames. It is the first day of the world-renowned regatta. Scores of little craft, bobbing about in readiness for the first of the events that have attracted thousands of visitors, are suddenly swept from the river as the hot gale-like blast wave sears through the town, burning and ripping away the roofs of picturesque little cottages and fragmenting the fine old stained-glass windows of its centuries-old churches. Even here the casualties are high as a mammoth tidal wave also lashes up the river claiming its own helpless victims.

Crystal Palace – that exotic showplace of Europe – vanishes in a hail of fragments. In an area around it scores of people lay dead or dying, their bodies pierced by arrow-like splinters from nearly a million square feet of shattered glass.

The rigid skeleton of this once-glorious construction is composed of brittle cast iron. It doesn't bend to pressure like steel. It disintegrates into fearsome razor-sharp shrapnel that explodes in all directions, guillotining the living in its gory path. Many who momentarily survive the original flash of hell are immediately cut down by these lashing sabres that sweep indiscriminately over a three-mile radius.

The carnage from this murderous kind of fragmentation also occurs at London's main glass-domed railway terminals like Euston and Paddington. Like so many other Victorian buildings their very components – stone, brick, cement, cast-iron and glass – literally burst apart in the blast.

All is silent now. And strangely still. There are no nightingales in Berkeley Square. No pigeons peck at the stub that's left of Nelson's shattered column. The River Thames boils. Giant tidal waves have lashed scores of boats clean out of the water. Their twisted wreckage litters the embankment and the only things left to float beneath Tower Bridge are the corpses.

A charred copy of the day's *Times* ripples away from the hand that clutched it. 'The King and Queen arrived back at Buckingham Palace yesterday after a visit to Lord and Lady Pembroke at Salisbury,' reads one item. Now Edward VII is dead. So is Prime Minister Asquith. So are most cabinet ministers and members of the government. And so is the seat of an empire . . .

Though none of this nightmare *really* happened to London it is only by such a reconstruction that one can remotely grasp the magnitude of the force that was unleased at Tunguska. A few degrees variance in course, a few hours difference in time. That's all it would have required to make that lurid report authentic. So let us now consider the monstrous aftermath of such a disaster.

What we must try to visualize is a major capital city – the most influential in Europe – attempting to cope with a nuclear explosion 1500 times more furious than that at Hiroshima in 1945, at a time when it was unequipped to deal with even a traditional bomb attack. Even one of to-day's international capitals, well aware of the lurking spectre of a nuclear war, would take decades to recover from the sudden death blow of those awesome dimensions. But we are considering a city at the turn of the century, complacently assured of its impregnability so long as England ruled the waves and the guards went on changing at Buckingham Palace. A densely-packed metropolis whose only answer to a thirty-megaton holocaust would have been a fire-fighting force that still relied on horses to trundle it around, and a primitive medical service that knew nothing of the appalling after-effects of blast and radiation.

Ironically enough, the shape and area of total devastation around Siberia's Southern Swamp is almost precisely that of Greater London.

*This* Cauldron of Hell would have formed an elliptical ring of death reaching areas as far from the city centre as Willesden, Finchley, Walthamstowe, Woolwich and Kingston-upon-Thames. There would have been little anyone could have done for those pathetic survivors left to scavenge a few more days of life from the ruination and the festering decay all around them. Little anyone outside this gangrenous open graveyard could do as the gruesome symptoms of radiation sickness began to whittle down the white blood corpuscles and gnaw at vital internal organs.

Within days central London would have become a crude, lawless jungle, its crippled, its dying and its hopelessly insane, cowering like wild animals among the carnage. For those able to ward off death it would have been a ruthless battle of survival. Food supplies would rapidly putrify in the hot days and nights that followed. The strongest might loot and murder to exist a few more weeks. For many of the weakest the only relief would have been the already corpse-ridden waters of the Thames. There could have been few vestiges of human dignity left in this once proud and powerful city.

Some of those people on the fringes of the cauldron might have dragged themselves into safer areas outside. But even here they would find little consolation or help. The chaos and suffering would still be on a frightful scale. They might have been forced back like lepers by those neighbouring communities determined to preserve for themselves what paltry remnants of survival remained.

It must be appreciated that a nuclear explosion, or super-blast, is vastly different from that produced by conventional bombs – such as the type used in the Second World War containing from 500 to 5000 pounds of high explosive. These created straightforward shockwaves that travelled *outwards* at the speed of sound, lasting for a few seconds. With the smaller range of bombs, damage was mainly confined to windows and doors which were usually blown inwards – though some objects might then have been sucked outwards by a secondary shock wave.

Flash burns from these conventional bombs were negligible. Casualties were mostly the victims of flying glass and other debris, bomb fragments, crumbling masonry from buildings receiving direct hits, or the outbreaks of fire that swept through the wreckage later. Grim though these war-time attacks were, few people were actually killed by the blast itself.

But consider the appalling effects of a mid-air nuclear superblast taking place a few miles above a major city (say at around 20 000 feet). Initially there would be a blinding flash instantly burning any object it enveloped *due to radia-*

*tion energy alone*. Any living thing within a few miles radius of ground zero would be vapourized or incinerated beyond recognition. Most human beings outside that immediate zone, but still within the radiation's deadly embrace, would still die from dreadful burns. Ironically the victims in these areas could be reckoned the lucky ones. Death would be ugly, but mercifully quick.

It would not be so for those in regions adjoining the fringes of total annihilation . . . in the nightmare zone of the 'half-dead'. Here would be mile upon mile of dismembered, screwed-up humanity.

In the outer areas people *inside* buildings might survive the initial blast, provided their bodies were not exposed to radiation through windows and other apertures.

But, so far, we have only considered the casualties resulting *immediately the explosion occurs*. The most brutal part of a superblast would be yet to come. This is the enormous shock wave it generates. Assuming the explosion took place at 20 000 feet, this wave – travelling at the speed of sound or roughly one thousand feet a second – would reach ground level in about twenty seconds.

But, during that sinister lull following the initial death flash, thousands of temporary survivors from inside buildings would instinctively rush headlong into the open. This is when the new scorching shock wave of white hot compressed air would strike, claiming countless more victims with its kiss of death.

Remarkably enough, though everything would be devastated or burned within a concentrated area of the blasts, one tiny region would be preserved – as happened at Tunguska and Hiroshima. This would be a spot directly below the explosion, where the shock wave fronts would be cancelled out by the reflected waves from the ground. Here would be a tiny protected haven virtually unscathed by it all.

Even the two types of blast so far described are not the end of a superblast's fury. There is still what is known as 'negative pressure effect' (NPE) – a force that can be perhaps the most devastating of all in built-up districts surrounding the central area. What happens is that the blast wave now reverses its direction to form a partial vacuum. This literally bursts apart buildings that are already cracked and weakened. They all explode simultaneously in one almighty upheaval. Those earlier survivors would almost certainly be caught up in this final outburst as rubble and fragments showered down on the molten and flaming debris left by the first two killer blasts.

This negative pressure is caused by the rising columns of hot air which spouts skywards to form the familiar billowing purple-brown mushroom cloud. The macabre constituents of this cloud would include not only the pulverized remains of buildings, but also those of humans and animals.

So the carnage from a superblast is in three parts. First, the flash burning from radiant energy. Next the burns and blast from the *outward-moving* superheated shock wave. And finally the explosive effects of the *inward-moving* negative pressure wave. These same effects must have occurred at Tunguska. It would have been the final NPE wave that tore away the surface of the *taiga* and spread the resulting dust over a large part of the Earth's atmosphere causing those brilliant sunsets referred to in chapter 1.

It is not easy to estimate the total death toll for which the monster would have finally been responsible had it blown up over London in 1908. It would have been many days, or even weeks, before anyone could have penetrated the central area of the city, and months before any meaningful estimate could have been made of the staggering number of casualties. The true figure might never have been known. Somerset House, with its exclusive records of Britain's population census would, of course, no longer exist. Only by years of painstaking research through the relatives of missing persons could even the roughest estimate be obtained.

If another Tunguska Event was to occur over present-day London, the total number of fatalities – directly or indirectly caused by the explosion – might be something like twenty millions, which is even greater than the number of Russian men, women and children estimated to have perished in the Second World War. The toll of lives in and around

Edwardian London might have been between six and eight million, if we consider the overall British population as being roughly a third of what it is today. In other words the nation's death rate would have been a grim one in three.

In those days too it would have been a considerable time before information reached the rest of the country. Though, even then, the world's most sophisticated city had a rapidly-developing private and commercial telephone service (it had been the National Telephone Company since 1906), all exchanges in and around London would have been destroyed. A further phenomenon would have disrupted communications. It is one now associated with all nuclear detonations and is called 'electromagnetic pulse' effects (EMP). This takes the form of a huge electrical surge that is produced at the same instant as the initial flash of radiation. The power released is stupendous – about 50 000 volts per yard of air, which is ionized in the immediate vicinity of the blast. It is also accompanied by blinding flashes of lightning. Most, if not all, of the telephone and telegraph instruments up to at least a hundred miles away would have been fused and put out of action.

The fact that communication cables in the early part of the century would be above ground would have meant that virtually every telephone would have been destroyed by the intense wave of electricity passing through the cables, including those linking Britain with countries abroad. Marconi's recently established 'Wireless Telegram' service too would have ceased to function in an ionosphere so drastically disturbed that any SOS messages would have been undetectable.

Even today this powerful EMP force (many of its side-effects have 'top secret' military classification), would destroy every transistor radio for miles. The ionospheric disturbance would make short-wave broadcasting impossible for several days. Only the defence communication networks, specifically designed to cope with EMP, would survive.

An example of EMP was actually recorded at the time of the Sikhote-Alin meteorite fall in 1947 (see chapter 4), when

An artist's impression of the Viking Mars lander as it prepares for touchdown on the Martian surface after its 440 million mile journey from Earth. (The Associated Press Ltd)

The almost total devastation of the city of Hiroshima after the explosion of the first atom bomb on 6th August 1945. (The Associated Press Ltd)

An old larch with young suckers growing around it in the north-west peat bog area of the cauldron. (Pergamon Press Ltd)

Continuous forest devastation near the bank of the river Khushmo, to the south of the cauldron. May 1929. (Pergamon Press Ltd)

The Evenok Il'ya Potapovich Petrov (Lyuchetkan), eye-witness of the fall of the Tunguska meteorite, and one of the guides of Kulik's expeditions. (Pergamon Press Ltd)

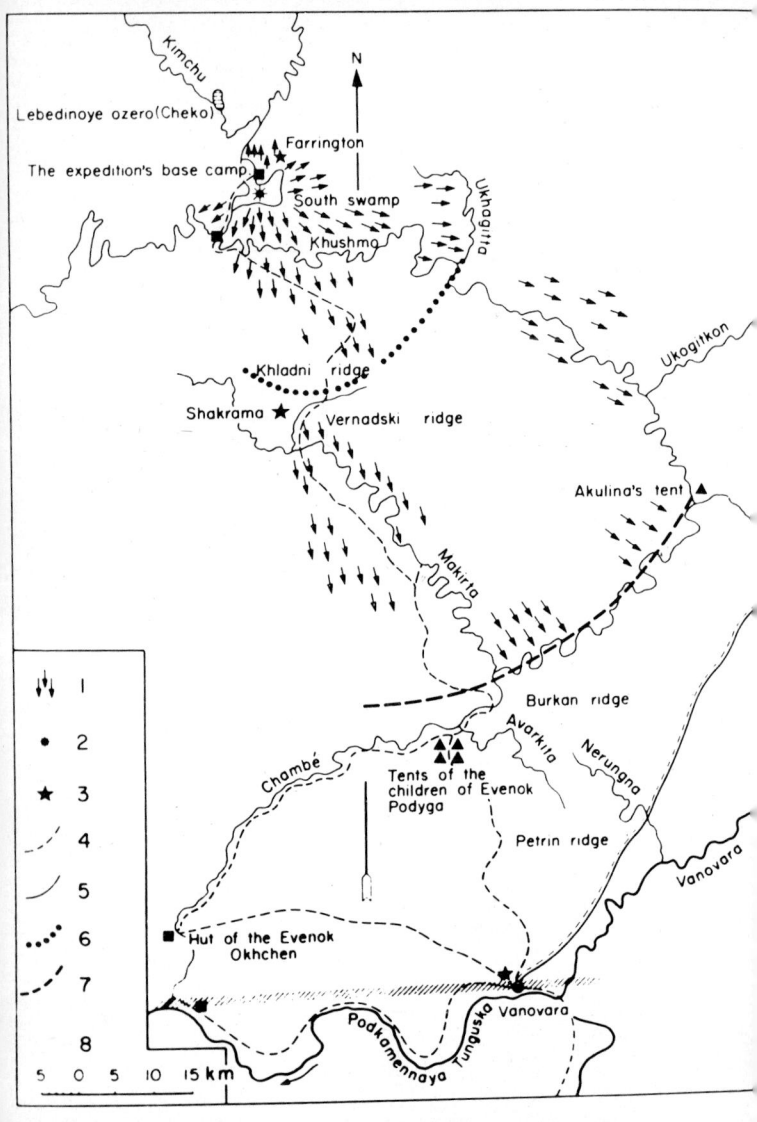

A map of the region where the Tunguska meteorite fell. 1 devastated forest;
2 place where meteor fell; 3 astro-radio survey points; 4 tracks; 5 road to the Strelka
trading station; 6 limit of scorched area; 7 limit of forest devastation; 8 limit of the
effect of the explosive wave.

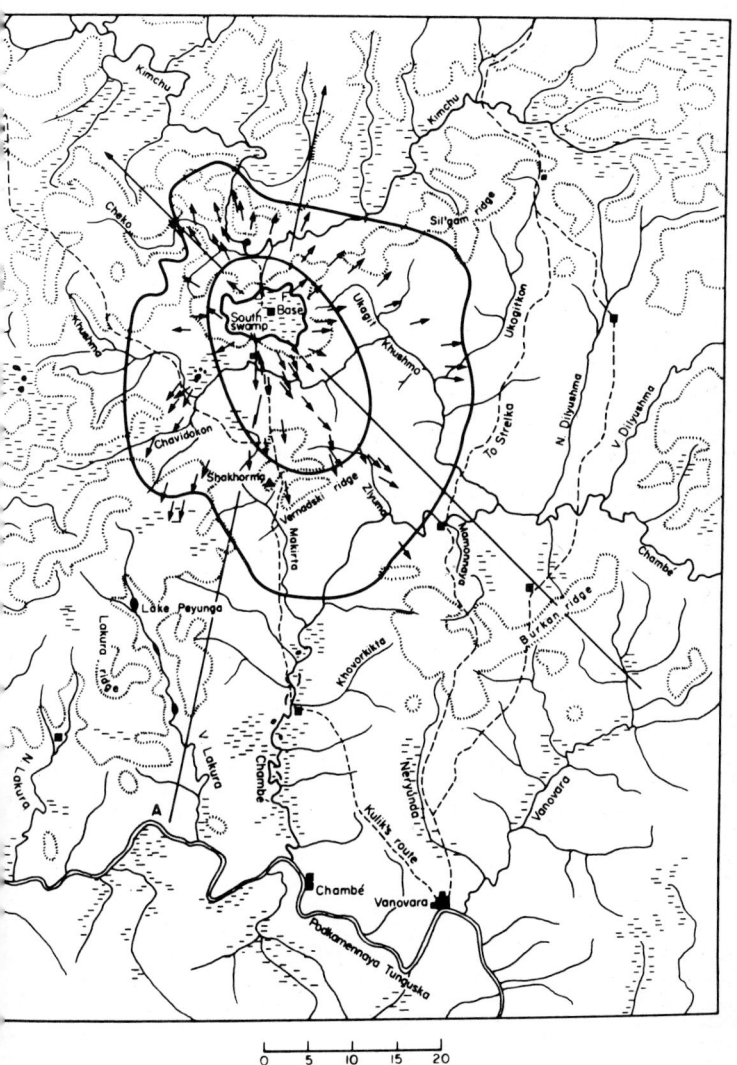

A 1958 map of the Tunguska region summarizing most of the data available at that time about the blast. The shape of the explosion wave and two different trajectories are shown, according to A: I. S. Astapovich and K: E. L. Krinov. (Pergamon Press Ltd)

A stony-iron meteorite from the Desert of Atacana in Chile. (Institute of Geological Sciences)

0 CMS 15

A polished and etched piece of the Canyon Diablo meteorite. (Institute of Geological Sciences)

A piece of the Canyon Diablo meteorite. (Institute of Geological Sciences)

5 centimetres

A fragment of the Barwell meteorite ('stone'). (Institute of Geological Sciences)

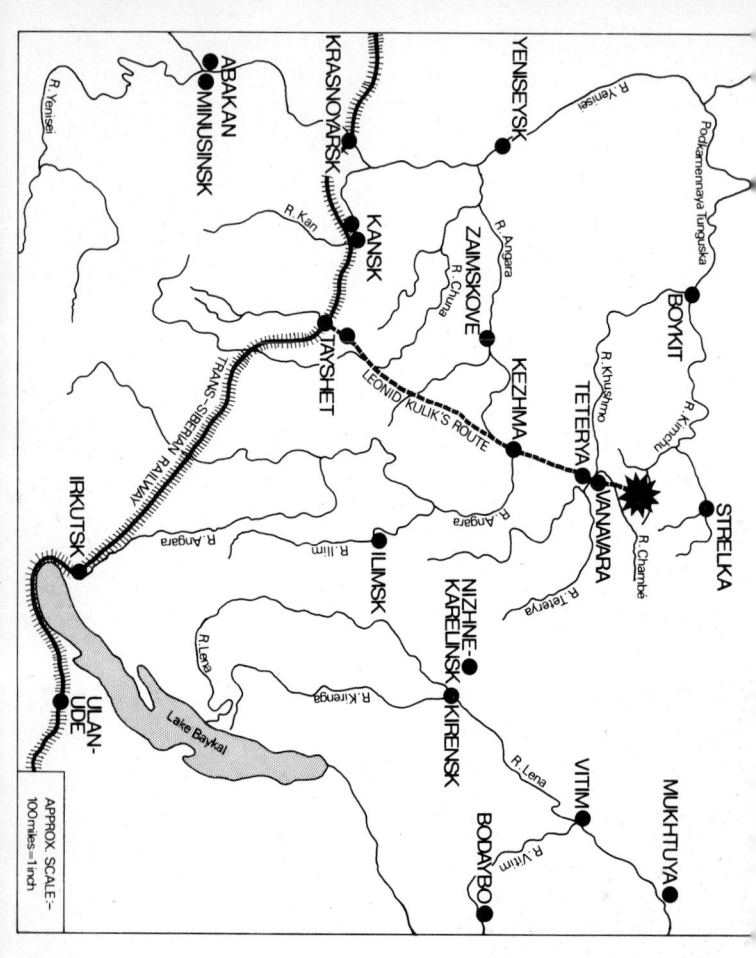

The Tunguska region in Siberia where the explosion (marked by a star) took place.

a mechanic working on a telephone pole felt a severe electric shock from wires that were disconnected.

The only means of getting news out of a stricken London in 1908 would have been by word of mouth. Even when the rest of Britain heard the sickening facts, there would have been little immediate relief work that could have been done. The only movement in and out of the disaster area would have been on foot or horseback. Hundreds of miles of railway track, curled like well-grilled bacon rind in the heat flash, would have been utterly unserviceable. No roads would have been passable.

In fact the great city of London may have been as desolate as the Siberian wilderness for years. It is unlikely the Edwardians could have accomplished anything like the kind of rapid restoration that took place in Hiroshima and Nagasaki after the Second World War. And remember, those atomic bombs were 1500 times less powerful than the force we are considering.

Apart from the immediate massacre from the blast, the devastated sewage and waste disposal system of those days would have produced waves of epidemics unsurpassed since the Great Plague of 1665. The city would rapidly have been infested with multitudes of rats, flourishing unrestrained among the countless tons of rotting human and other remains. Some time later grotesque mutations could have been expected to break out in these animals, caused by the gamma radiation of the explosion. They might then have completely overrun huge areas of southern England.

But the disastrous consequences of it all would not have been confined to London. A political and economic shock wave would have reverberated round the globe that could have changed the whole course of twentieth-century history.

Consider Britain's lofty place in world affairs at that period. The Empire was at its peak. Edward VII – one of Europe's principal peace-makers – would have died, along with most important members of the Royal Family and the government, and those civil and military chiefs responsible for running not only their own country but many other parts of the Earth still under its flag.

In today's nuclear age, governments have emergency plans for any similar man-made catastrophe. The carefully-monitored climate of international relationship would probably allow time for a nation to evacuate its principal citizens, its offices, wealth and documentation, to areas of safety before disaster struck. But in 1908 there would have been no such warning. Suddenly the central government would cease to exist. The gold that then constituted the foundation of Britain's economy would have melted into the rubble and dust of what had been the financial fortress of the Bank of England. The diamond market of Hatton Gardens, the priceless wealth of the art galleries, the museums and many other public and private strongholds of our heritage would have been lost forever.

With the nation in a helpless state of chaos and confusion the Army would no doubt have taken over government and inflicted rigid martial law on the entire country. A new temporary capital city would have had to be established, perhaps at Manchester, Liverpool or some other region even further north. But Britain would have ceased to exist as a world power. She could no longer have controlled the wealth and resources of her vast commonwealth, where opposing factions might well have seized this unexpected opportunity to stake their claims with violence and bloodshed. With Britain immobilized it is almost certain that Germany would have hesitated no longer in her move to dominate Europe. It had always been King Edward who kept his ambitious nephew Kaiser Wilhelm II in check; with Edward's sudden death there is little doubt that the First World War would have started years before it actually did.

All this, and so many other drastic reshuffles of events at that time, whose repercussions would even be influencing the world today, could have been the final outcome of that one event on the morning in June 1908.

In fact all that London suffered were phenomenal thunderstorms now thought to be due to atmospheric disturbances caused by the Siberian blast. The following is part of a news article that appeared in *The Times* on 6 July:

In London (on Saturday 4 July) the storms raged with great severity in most districts. Buildings were struck ... torrential rain fell ... the thunder was frequent and the lightning of the most vivid and alarming description.

The report then describes how many buildings were struck by lightning, some being destroyed or set alight; of flagstaffs and roof beams being split to pieces, coping stones crashing into the streets, railway track demolished and animals killed on the spot. One man had his clothes set alight and another was temporarily paralysed. One house was said to have been 'filled with blue flame'.

At a manor house near Newmarket, a rector and his family described how 'a terrific shock appeared to shake the whole house, temporarily stunning them'. *The Times* report goes on:

The building seemed incandescent. Realizing that something series had happened, the rector rushed upstairs to the bedroom where the youngest child was sleeping. He found the passages full of sulphurous fumes. He then went to the assistance of the cook who was lying stunned in the passage. (She had been struck by falling masonry.) She was in a state of collapse and the other servants stated that they had been blown into the passage by some terrific force ... A huge gap showed that a large portion of one end of the rectory had been demolished. Masses of stonework were distributed about the ground outside over a considerable radius.

So it seems that even from nearly 4000 miles away, Britain did not *entirely* escape the wrath of the Siberian monster.

## CHAPTER TEN

## THE ANGRY EARTH ·

Though the Tunguska Event is unique in recorded history, we can compare its effects with a known energy force that does not come from the heavens, but from the very bowels of 'hell' – deep below the crust of the Earth.

It is the latent ferocity of the volcano – ever-poised to burst open and engulf all those who dare to live in its shadow of death. Man can never entirely trust these dormant brutes, simmering and slumbering on the face of our crowded planet.

Six years before the Tunguska Event, such a force of nature went berserk on the sun-drenched little island of Martinique in the clear, blue tropical waters of the Carribbean. It was almost 8 o'clock on 8 May 1902. Saint-Pierre, a bustling port with its picture-postcard maze of narrow twisting streets and quaint multi-coloured stone houses, was still rubbing the sleep from its eyes.

Suddenly a series of ear-splitting explosions ripped through the still morning air. Six miles away a small volcanic mountain called Pelée tore itself apart. A gigantic blast furnace of superheated gases burst through the side of the mountain and seared across the terror-stricken city with the fury of a tornado. Three minutes later Saint-Pierre was a blazing shambles and all but two of its 30,000 inhabitants were dead or dying.

The following is part of an eye-witness report by the assistant purser on board the *Roraima*, one of the ships steaming towards the port:

As we approached Saint-Pierre we could distinguish the rolling and leaping of red flames that belched from the mountain in huge volumes and gushed into the sky. Enormous clouds of black smoke hung over the volcano ...

There was a constant muffled roar. It was like the biggest oil refinery in the world burning up on the mountain top. There was a tremendous explosion about 7.45 a.m., soon after we got in. The mountain was blown to pieces. There was no warning. The side of the volcano was ripped out and there was hurled straight towards us a solid wall of flame. It sounded like a thousand cannon.

The wave of fire was on us and over us like a flash of lightning. It was like a hurricane of fire. I saw it strike the cable steamship *Grappler* broadside on and capsize her. From end to end she burst into flames and then sank. The fire rolled in mass straight down upon Saint-Pierre and the shipping. The town vanished before our eyes.

The air grew stifling hot and we were in the thick of it. Wherever the mass of fire struck the sea, the water boiled and sent up vast columns of steam. The sea was torn into huge whirlpools that careened toward the open sea. One of these horrible, hot whirlpools swung under the *Roraima* and pulled her down on her beam end with the suction. She careened away over to port, and then the fire hurricane from the volcano smashed her and over she went on the opposite side. The fire wave swept off the masts and smokestacks as if they were cut by a knife.

The ship's captain was the only person on deck not killed outright, but he fell overboard from the bridge. The purser goes on:

The blast of fire from the volcano lasted only a few minutes but it shrivelled and set fire to everything it touched. Thousands of casks of rum were stored in Saint-Pierre and these were exploded by the terrific heat. The burning rum ran in streams down every street and out into the sea. This blazing rum set fire to the *Roraima* several times. Before the volcano burst, the landings of Saint-Pierre were covered with people. After the explosion not one living soul was seen on the land.

Many of the fearsome blast effects reported at Saint-Pierre that day bore remarkable similarities to those that were to sweep Tunguska and Hiroshima. Although the phenomenal heat completely carbonized many objects in its path, others, like some of the trees in the Southern Swamp, were left completely unscorched. Glass was melted and heavy iron bars distorted, yet quite nearby delicate chinaware remained unbroken. Among groups of people swept by instant death, some had been stripped naked while others remained fully clothed. A box of unignited matches were found right next to a man's cremated body.

Léon Compère-Leandre, a Negro, was one of the city's only two survivors. There is no explicable reason why he should have escaped. All those around him died. His account of the blast effects is remarkably comparable with that given to Leonid Kulik by the Evenki Semenov at Vanavara (see chapter Two). He says:

On 8 May about 8 o'clock in the morning, I was seated on the doorstep of my house, which was in the south-east part of the city. All of a sudden I felt a terrible wind blowing, the earth began to tremble, and the sky suddenly became dark. I turned to go into the house, made with great difficulty the three or four steps that separated me from my room, and felt my arms and legs burning, also my body. I dropped upon the table.

The rest of his account concerns the appalling deaths of the other members of the household:

At this moment four others sought refuge in my room, crying and writhing in pain, although their garments showed no sign of having been touched by the flames. At the end of ten seconds one of these, the young Delavaud girl, aged ten, fell dead ... Then I got up and went into another room, where I found the father Delavaud, still clothed and lying on the bed, dead. He was purple and inflated, but the clothing was intact. I went out and found in the court two corpses interlocked; they were the bodies of the two young men who had been with me in the room.

The only other survivor of the awful Saint-Pierre catastrophe was in the prison dungeons, another Negro called Auguste Ciparis, though he was badly burned.

The explosive eruption of Pelée completely devastated an area of ten square miles, compared to eight hundred square miles at Tunguska. And yet it claimed that staggering death-toll of 30,000. The reason is that this particular type of outburst, known as a Peleéan eruption, is the most deadly of all volcanic activity. Instead of spewing out the familiar lava flow, the vent of the volcano becomes blocked by solidified magma. There is no way out for the volatiles and molten materials inside. So they begin to create an enormous pocket of pressure below the vent. Eventually the towering fury can be held back no longer. It blasts through the weakest part of the mountain's geological structure. Mount Pelée suddenly gaped open at one side and the hurricane of searing gases and particles blasted out at more than a hundred miles an hour across the built-up area of Saint-Pierre.

In June 1912, sensational volcanic eruptions ripped the earth apart in a wilderness now known as the Valley of Ten Thousand Smokes on the southern coast of the Alaskan Peninsula. Their booming anger could be heard nearly a thousand miles away. More than 30,000 million tons of rock and other debris were scattered over fifty square miles reaching depths of up to 700 feet.

Fortunately the nearest inhabited settlements were fifty miles from the outbursts. Yet even here buildings were crushed by the ten-foot high drifts of dust and ash that had risen in an enormous cloud, turning day into night. Rainfall, condensing into sulphurous vapours, burned holes in clothing and scarred the skin. Fish died in the rivers and birds dropped dead from the sky.

It was four years after the eruptions that the first scientific expedition went to the valley. It was sponsored by the National Geographical Society and was led by Dr Robert F. Griggs, who wrote:

The whole valley as far as the eye could reach, was full of hundreds, no thousands – literally tens of thousands of smokes curling up from its fissured floor. It was as though all the steam engines of the world, assembled together, had popped their safety valves at once and were letting off steam in concert.

If such an event had happened near a packed town or city nothing could have possibly survived. Dr Griggs, in one of his accounts, says that if it had taken place on Manhattan Island in the United States, the explosions would have been heard in Chicago, the fumes would have swept over all states east of the Rocky Mountains and acid raindrops would have caused burns as far away as Toronto. 'Ash would accumulate in Philadelphia a foot deep,' he says.

As for the horrors that could be enacted along the lower Hudson, no detailed picture may be drawn. There would be no occasion for rescue work, for there would be no survivors. The whole of Manhattan Island, and an equal area besides, would open in great yawning chasms, and fiery fountains of molten lava would issue from every crack. This, disrupted by the escaping gases, would be changed into red hot sand, which, consuming everything it touched, would run like wildfire through the town. The flow of incandescent sand would effectually destroy all evidence of the former city. In its deepest parts, the near-molten sand would probably overtop the tallest skyscrapers, though the top of the Woolworth Tower might protrude if its steel supports could endure the fiery furnace surrounding them. It is doubtful, indeed, if there would be any considerable ruins left behind to mark the site of the great city.

There are some ways in which the devastation in the Valley of Ten Thousand Smokes can be compared with the Tunguska Cauldron of Hell, though obviously the source could not have been the same. Not a single life was lost. Trees for some miles around were flattened. And for months after the eruptions brilliant coloured sunrises and sunsets were reported over a wide area.

Twenty-five years before the Tunguska Event, a sleeping

monster suddenly reawakened after two centuries of peaceful slumber and devoured an entire island. Between 5.30 and 11 a.m., on 27 August 1883, four monumental explosions tore apart Krakatoa, situated in the Sunda Strait between Java and Sumatra. Its thunderous rejuvenation set up towering fifty-foot tidal waves in the Indian Ocean that smashed through towns and villages along the coastlines. On that single day more than 36,000 people died as they groped blindly in pitch darkness.

Krakatoa's ear-shattering roars were heard more than 2000 miles away. The vibrations of its wrath cracked the walls of buildings 150 miles from the outburst. And, as happened following the Tunguska Event, people in many parts of the world gazed in wonder at phenomenally brilliant risings and settings of the Sun.

There was no reason to expect Krakatoa to go insane the way it did. There had been no eruptions anywhere in the region since 1680. But, in May 1883, the pretty little group of tropical islands began to feel the first shudderings of the reviving dragon in their midst. A few sightseers peered in casual curiosity over the rim of its gaping mouth – like Sunday afternoon visitors at a zoo. They listened to it roar and stared into its deep, hot throat as it belched out steam. But no one was particularly alarmed.

By the middle of August however the ferocious symptoms of its fitful awakening began to increase alarmingly. And on 26 August, a series of terrifying detonations were heard all over Java. Pumice began to rain down on towns and villages from a sky ripped by fierce flashes of volcanic lightning. No one slept that night, and a strange shower of phosphorescent mud covered the decks, masts and rigging of ships up to fifty miles away from Krakatoa so that they resembled floating phantoms in the gloom.

On the sinister morning of 27 August, the island of Krakatoa began to disintegrate as four titanic blasts spat debris fifty miles into the air. Some 200 000 million cubic feet of rock vanished into the sea. Houses were shaken 200 miles away. In Burma – nearly 1500 miles from the eruptions – people heard what sounded like heavy gunfire. Even in

111

South Australia the explosions and vibrations kept people awake.

Back in the vicinty of the Sunda Strait vast numbers of people stumbled helplessly through the black pall of deadly ash that suddenly enveloped them, as mammoth tidal waves lashed angrily through their towns and villages – leaving a pitiful trail of human flotsam in their wake. Ships were washed two miles inland and stranded thirty feet above the water level. An enormous cloud of volcanic material rose fifty miles into the sky and began to spread over the world. By the end of the month it was billowing over the Atlantic. Five days later it was reported over the Hawaiian Islands. By 9 September, it had completely encircled the globe. Like a rainbow after a storm, it picked out the spectrum of the Sun and painted the sky in breathtaking masterpieces of colour. In India the Sun was seen as greenish-blue. In Sydney, Australia, the ever-changing hue of the sky merged through yellow, purple, crimson, pink and brown. The Sun appeared green, blue, silver and coppery from other widely-separated regions. The atmospheric effects of the dust cloud were seen in Britain on its third circuit of the Earth.

Devastating though the Krakatoa eruption was, a force estimated to have been five times as powerful is thought to have wiped out an entire civilization in ancient times. And some scientists now believe this Mediterranean land mass that was sucked into the sea, was the site of Plato's legendary Island of Atlantis.

Nearly three and a half thousand years ago Crete and its string of little islands were inhabited by one of the richest, most highly intelligent and sensitive people on Earth ... the Minoans. Their majestic cities contained palaces and luxurious, air-conditioned homes in an age when Britain was still uncivilized. They produced breath taking works of art and were superb ocean navigators.

Without warning a 5000-feet volcanic mountain on the beautiful island of Thera unleashed its unprecedented savagery with the ruthlessness of several hundred hydrogen bombs. The centre of Thera vanished with tens of thousands of people into a sea-filled trough 1300 feet deep. The segments that remained are now known as the Santorini Islands. The tidal wave from this unimaginable holocaust are estimated to have loomed 700 feet. They radiated in all directions surging on to the Greek mainland and even reaching the African coast.

On Thera itself, a flourishing, densely-populated metropolis with its dazzling white marble palaces that symbolized the elegance of the Minoan race, was bulldozed out of existence. Sixty miles to the north the inhabitants of Crete perished in the same kind of cataclysm that was to engulf those residents of Java and Sumatra in 1883. Great 200-foot waves must have surged up the mountain sides leaving hordes of corpses scattered like seaweed on a shore.

In the 1960s a team led by Professor Angelos Galanopoulos of the Athens Seismological Institute, excavated part of the stricken Minoan city that had not been claimed by the sea. This was followed by further diggings by a party from American institutions headed by Professor Spyridon Marinatos of the University of Athens. Much of the city was still preserved – the tastefully frescoed walls of palatial relics, the rooms and passages of well-built houses, solid stone bases of once-lofty columns, superbly fashioned pottery in colours as gay as they were the day they were painted, cooking utensils and precious goblets.

Galanopoulos was intrigued to discover remarkable comparisons between this shattered Aegean island and the legendary Atlantis described by the Greek philosopher Plato more than 2000 years ago. Now he, and other researchers, are convinced the two islands are one and the same.

Galanopoulos even believes that the Minoan catastrophe could also have accounted for the ten biblical plagues that swept Egypt, more than 400 miles away. The estimated dates of Exodus coincide with the destruction of Thera. The description of 'water turning to blood', speculates this Greek scientist, might have been the deposit of rose-coloured pumice from the eruption. The 'plague of frogs' could also have been caused by pumice driving them out of the water to die on shore. He offers explanations for the plagues of 'lice, flies,

113

boils, pestilence and locusts' as possible environmental aftermaths of the volcanic outburst. The 'hail, thunder, fire and darkness' mentioned in the Bible were all the kind of phenomena widely recorded after the Krakatoa explosion and would also have taken place at Thera.

It is thought that the few scattered refugees from the doomed Minoan empire – possibly those who were absent on sea voyages at the time – fled to the Greek mainland to escape the deadly volcanic fall-out. Here they could have passed on much of their culture to the Greeks and provided the basis for their science, mathematics and architectural techniques.

Those volcanoes considered utterly extinct have been known to produce the most catastrophic revivals. Inside their gigantic 'combustion chambers' alarming pressures can slowly build up for centuries or even thousands of years. Generations may have farmed and grazed their herds over the rich, florid slopes. Then suddenly comes the monstrous resurrection.

Vesuvius had been long 'dead' when the solidified lava that had belched into the Bay of Naples in prehistoric times was confidently chosen as a site for the vigorous city of Pompeii. Yet, in AD 79 the entire city was entombed in a matter of a few hours beneath a steaming ocean of cinders and lapilli. And there it remained hidden until researchers began its remarkable disinterment 1700 years later.

It was like opening up an Egyptian pyramid. Inside were the 'mummified' casts of many of the city's 20 000 inhabitants, frozen in the last instant of life like stark tableaux depicting the agony of that fatal day. The terror, the contortion, the very expressions of fear and despair on their faces, had all been preserved ... encased in the timeless vacuum of moulds of volcanic ash that had been soaked and then dried and hardened in deathly embrace about its victims. As bodies had decomposed, their detailed impressions remained within the stony tombs. Some were huddled in doorways, or petrified in the desperate actions of flight. Others were clasped in someone's arms or still clutching valued possessions. There was the form of a dog still frantically biting at its chain. Sixty gladiators were found dead in their barracks, two still manacled in their cell. A richly-dressed woman was also found alongside them.

But from this incredible graveyard – still being excavated to this day – is a unique record of the life of a thriving commercial city exactly as it was nearly 2000 years ago. There are the colourful, airy suburban villas with their loggias and terraces and the luxurious houses of the wealthy merchants, enhanced with exquisite murals and mosaics. There are the theatres, the baths, the mighty forum, the temples. Lining streets that still bear the deep wheel-tracks of Roman chariots, are the shop counters, some still bearing the eggs and loaves on sale that day; the roughly-plastered inns, the stifling cubicles of the harlots. The walls still bear the revealing graffiti of everyday city life. Snatches from favourite poets, salacious slogans and caricatures, obscenities and threats, the names of gladiatorial idols and the touching pledges of devotion to someone who may never have had time to be loved.

The sprawling hunk of Mount Vesuvius still reminds us of its occasional virility. Its minor, bilious spasms may be more predictable to today's scientists. But, as we've said before, you can never entirely trust a volcano . . . any more than the many other aspects of nature's restless moods.

# PART THREE

## CHAPTER ELEVEN

# THE ALIEN QUESTION

There is still one chilling question we *must* ask in searching for the source of the mysterious force that was unleashed over Central Siberia.

Suppose the Tunguska monster wasn't a *natural* object at all. Suppose it was *not* something conceived and aborted from the vast womb of outer space, like a comet or a Black Hole. Not some cosmic 'gall-stone' like a meteorite or a chunk of anti-matter wrenched from the innards of a distant star system. *But that it was, in fact, artificial* . . . created by some form of intelligence.

We know that no human agency at that time was remotely capable of producing a device of such multi-megaton fury. And even if there were, there is no plausible reason how or why it was unleashed over the desolation of Central Siberia.

One must, therefore, ask the second startling question: If it *was* artificial, could it have been brought here by some form of interstellar space vehicle from a planet millions of miles beyond our own Solar System . . . by an artifact that was pulverized in the split-second inferno that seared the *taiga* and perhaps committed the alien souls of a crew of highly-intelligent beings to the Cauldron of Hell?

The idea is not a new one. Russian engineer and science-writer Alexander N. Kazantsev has been fervently advocating this astounding concept since 1946 – soon after the atom bombs fell on Hiroshima and Nagasaki he was convinced that the Tunguska explosion was nuclear. He postulates that the atomic-powered engine of a fully-manned alien craft, attempting to land on Earth, blew up over Siberia. Such a dramatic event, he insists, would have been entirely consistent with the many strange phenomena witnessed, and since investigated, at Tunguska.

Over the years, as each new expedition publishes its findings, Kazantsev slots them neatly and ingeniously into his spaceship theory. When globules of metallic iron from the impact zone were found to contain traces of nickel, cobalt, copper and germanium, he explained that the nickel and cobalt originated from a splinter blasted from the outer shell of the spacecraft. The copper and germanium, he declared, were from the electrical wiring, semi-conductors and highly-sophisticated instruments on board.

Among his other arguments is that a spaceship exploding in mid-air would leave no crater. It would also explain the radial scorching and the undamaged trees at the very centre of the blast. The fiery pillars and the billowing dust clouds, too, were consistent with the 'mushroom' formations of Hiroshima and other nuclear explosions. He describes the effects of a shattering spaceship as follows:

The explosion wave rushed downwards, and the trees directly below the point of explosion remained standing, having lost only their crowns and branches. The wave burned the points of those breaks on the trees, and hit the permafrost, splitting it. Underground waters, responding to the tremendous pressure of the blow, gushed up as those fountains seen by natives after the explosion. But where the explosion wave struck at an angle, trees were felled in a fanlike pattern.

At the moment of the explosion, temperatures rose to tens of millions of degrees. Elements, even those not involved in the explosion directly, were vapourized and, in part, carried into the upper strata of the atmosphere where, continuing their radioactive disintegration, they caused that luminescent air. In part, these elements fell to the ground as precipitation, with radioactive effects.

He even believes that this radiation may have caused the deaths of curious tribesmen who ventured too close to the Southern Swamp soon after the blast. At the time a few superstitious Evenkis were spreading a rumour that Ogda, their legendary god of fire, was behind the whole thing and that some people had been burned and killed. There has never been any actual evidence of such fatalities.

In 1959, Professor Felix Zigel, an aerodynamics expert at the Moscow Aviation Institute, agreed that the Tunguska explosion must have been nuclear. 'At the present time,' he wrote in the publication *Znanie-Sila* 'like it or not, A. N. Kazantsev's hypothesis is the only realistic one in so far as it explains the absence of a meteorite crater and the explosion of a cosmic body in the air.' But, at that stage, he couldn't quite see eye to eye with Kazantsev's spaceship theory – especially as the latter was suggesting it came from one of the planets in our own Solar System. However, as space research advanced dramatically in the 1960s and more and more hard-headed scientists accepted the high probability of intelligent life existing in many parts of the galaxy, Zigel was more ready to believe in alien spaceships.

In fact, in July 1975, Professor Zigel, now fifty-five and having helped train many of the Soviet cosmonauts, told the American newspaper *National Enquirer*: 'Based on hundreds of sightings reported by respected people and actual evidence taken to our laboratories, there is no doubt that extraterrestrial probes have been reconnoitering Russia.'

Kazentsev interprets research by a Soviet aircraft designer, A. Y. Manotskov, as further evidence that the Tunguska invader was under intelligent control. Manotskov produced a detailed chart of the object's movements which he presented to Boris Laipunov, a Russian rocket expert and another spaceship advocate. They both agreed that the object slowed down as it neared the Earth to 0.7 kilometres per second, or about 1500 miles an hour. As the average meteorite hits the ground at many times this velocity, could this indicate the object was attempting to land?

Kazantsev also claims that, travelling at this slow speed, a meteorite capable of causing the Tunguska devastation, would have had to be so vast ('more than one kilometre in diameter') it would have covered most of the sky. Therefore, he insists, it must have been a relatively small body – the size of a spaceship.

Professor Felix Zigel adds further intriguing speculation on the spaceship theory. This is that the Tunguska object made a deliberate 'manoeuvre' and actually changed its course during descent. He and his scientific disciples base this conclusion on the conflicting flight paths calculated by experts from the varying descriptions of eye witnesses.

Voznesensky and Kulik had both fixed the trajectory as running from south-south-west to north-north-east. Later however Krinov and Florensky reckoned it was from south-east to north-west. Zigel concludes that the object was, in fact, seen to move in *both* these trajectories and had described an arc of some 375 miles in extent (in azimuth) – a performance, he says, that could have been achieved only by something under intelligent control.

Dr Aleksei Zolotov, another scientist who visited Tunguska in 1960, attributes the oval shape of the blast area, shown in aerial photographs, to explosive material being encased in a shell. He reminds sceptics of the original eye-witness reports of 'a body in the form of a pipe or cylinder' and 'an elongated body narrowing towards the end'.

In 1975, Zolotov, head of a Soviet team still studying the Tunguska phenomena, embellished the theory by suggesting the explosion was not an accident. It was, he suggests, deliberately detonated by a highly advanced civilization simply wanting to let us know of their existence. They chose the lonely Siberian site so that no human lives would be lost. A similar blast, he warns, 'can be expected somewhere on Earth at any time'.

The doctor's startling diagnosis is based on the type of blast damage, and on such things as 'evidence of the radio-active isotope cesium-137 in the ring structures of trees at the site'.

In 1964, two Russian writers suggested that the Tunguska event was the dramatic result of a super-concentrated laser beam having been directed at Earth by an advanced intelligence occupying a planet in the star system of 61 Cygni – eleven light years away.* Genrikh Altov and Valentina Zhuravleva, in a lengthy article published by the magazine *Zvezda* and summarized by the Soviet news agency Tass, say

* A light year is the distance light travels in one year at a velocity of 186,272 miles per second. The distance of 61 Cygni is, therefore, 66 million million miles.

the laser beams were intended as signals and were sent here on three occasions – 1882, 1894 and 1908.

Evidence given for the first signal are the sightings of long, green, sausage-shaped 'balloons' of light and large greenish clouds, particularly prominent over London and south-east England in 1882. The second laser signal, in 1894, produced similar phenomena, they claim, which were reported at the time in the magazine *Nature*. The third beam – powerful enough to devastate Tunguska when it struck the ground – was apparently sent in reply to what the alien astro-physicists thought was a man-made signal from Earth. This 'signal' was, in fact, the mighty volcanic eruption at Krakatoa in August 1883, and the distance of eleven light years between their planet and ours would have accounted for the delay of twenty-five years between signals.

Altov and Zhuravleva suggest that material from the Krakatoa catastrophe, flung high into the air, reacted with the upper ionosphere and could have emitted a strong radio beam and light signal far out into space.

The reason the two Russians selected 61 Cygni as the source of the laser beams is that one of its two stars is be-lieved to be orbited by a very large planet, about ten times the mass of Jupiter. In 1964, it was the only system known to have a planet of this size. Other nearer stars have since been found to also have what appear to be planets. Barnard's Star, only six light years away, is calculated to have three orbiting bodies as big as Jupiter and the nearest system to Earth – Alpha Centaurus at four-and-a-half light years – has a star identical to our own Sun, extremely well suited to support an Earth-type world.

However, fascinating though Altov and Zhuravleva's theory may be, it is inconceivable that a laser beam could produce a mid-air explosion – certainly not one on the scale that flattened the Siberian *taiga*. If one actually struck our planet it would probably drill a hole in the Earth, more like those caused by normal meteorites. But, instead of leaving the familiar untidy gap littered with shattered rock frag-ments, a laser beam scar would be smooth where high tem-peratures had melted the rock. In any case you would get none of the pre-explosion 'fireball' phenomena and streaks of brilliant light quoted by observers in 1908. The laser would pass through the atmosphere without trace until the solid surface of the Earth blocked its beam of energy and caused it to explode.

It would also have to be an unbelievably strong laser to cause such damage after travelling billions of miles, requiring an energy output many times higher than that of the Sun itself. There is, of course, the remote possibility that an intense beam released from a spacecraft quite near to Earth could have created havoc. Though our own scientists are only on the fringe of laser technology, some American researchers say they will have the means of 'wiping out an entire forest' by 1980. Already under laboratory conditions, high-energy rays have burned through steel plate, and the canopy of a high-altitude aircraft is said to have been blasted away by a laser directed at it from the ground – though convincing evidence of the latter claim is not available at present.

Vast sums of money are being allocated for laser development in both America and Russia in the race to perfect the first operational 'death rays', which, among other uses, would instantly destroy guided-missile warheads. The US 1976 budget for laser experiments was 170 million dollars.

But, if an alien society wished to communicate with us, why should they use destructive laser beams? That's no way to begin a lasting interstellar friendship.

Mind you, should the intention of an alien race be to demonstrate its superiority with an initial show of strength, there are plenty of methods they could adopt. Apart from the use of their own sophisticated armoury, one would expect they would be well able to harness the latent forces of our own geophysical environment in a number of devious ways.

Man himself is already learning to do this. In 1976 the Stockholm International Peace Research Institute (SIPRI) gave frightening details of possible warfare techniques for artificially modifying the weather and for triggering off earthquakes and other natural phenomena as a means of inflicting death and destruction. The previous year Leonid

Brezhnev, secretary of the Soviet Communist Party, warned the world: 'The level of contemporary science and technology is such that a serious danger arises that a weapon may be evolved even more terrible than nuclear arms.' And the Russians have called on the United Nations to ban the 'deliberate manipulation of natural processes of the earth, oceans and atmosphere'.

The earliest of what are now termed 'environmental and weather weapons' was used by the US Air Force to 'seed' rainclouds with silver iodide over the Ho Chi Minh Trail so as to stimulate torrential rainfall – though their available technique at that time was not very effective. They also created 'Tunguska-type' destruction in the forests of Vietnam with herbicides and defoliants and by blasting huge tracts with 'instant jungle clearance bombs'.

Russia claims that America is now experimenting with ways of inducing artificial earthquakes and volcanic eruptions by underground nuclear explosions, and of creating man-made floods, tornadoes and lightning. It is quite likely that a society of aliens whose technology is thousands of years ahead of ours could have perfected these, and even far more appalling environmental weapons.

Two possible means of mass destruction now said to be occupying the minds of modern army strategists would seem to come straight from the realms of science-fiction. One is to melt the Polar ice-cap to create massive tidal waves. The other is to blast great gaps in the ozone layer of Earth. This would allow through the Sun's deadly unfiltered ultra-violet rays which could destroy vast numbers of people either through burning or skin cancer. The main drawback to both these hair-raising techniques is that it would be difficult to confine their horrific effects to a particular 'target area'. Other parts of the world could be drastically affected too. But, of course, a belligerent extra-terrestrial intelligence would not be concerned about distinguishing between one nation and another. We'd all be the same to them.

One unsavoury field of experimentation now causing concern to some UN delegates is the possible use of devices for producing *sounds* that can cause suffering and death. Tests with extreme low-frequency and infrasonic sound have been taking place in France for some years.

Italian scientists are said to have killed laboratory animals by exposing them to high-frequency sounds. They found that each species was sensitive only to its own particular frequency.

There might be a number of ways in which an alien aggressor could effectively poison our atmosphere or even drain it of oxygen so that vast populations would suffocate. The North Vietnamese Foreign Ministry claims that 'oxygen-sucking asphyxiation bombs' were used by the South Vietnamese on the outskirts of Saigon. During the Second World War many citizens in German cities suffocated when intensive incendiary attacks drained the air of oxygen. Gases that attack the nervous system so that victims have no control of their body functions are also in the pipelines of the major military powers.

One particularly morbid form of mass subjugation an advanced intelligence might possibly exploit would be to use the natural wave-guide between the ionosphere and Earth to propagate very low frequency radiation in a way that would effect the electrical behaviour of the human brain activity. 'It might become hypothetically possible to impair the performance of a large group of people in selected areas over extended periods' says a SIPRI publication.

Immediately one considers the possibility of the Tunguska catastrophe being inspired by a 'super-race', there must surely be any number of ways, far beyond the realms of our own modest technology, by which this could have been brought about.

Let us now discuss 'evidence' for the space-ship theory as submitted by Kazantsev, Zigel and others.

First, the description of the Tunguska object as 'a small body' does not fit that of any credible *fully-manned* spacecraft propelled by normal nuclear reaction. To be capable of getting to our Solar System from even the closest star (Alpha Centauri) such a craft, equipped with sufficient supplies and fuel for a two-way journey, would be massive – probably in the order of a hundred thousand tons. Remember that, even travelling at the unlikely speed of light, a startrek from Alpha Centauri would take four-and-a-half years plus time for acceleration and deceleration. Travelling at a more feasible velocity, say a third that of light, would involve some sixteen years. For such a journey a full compliment of maintenance and scientific personnel would be expected to total perhaps twenty aliens. The materials from which the vessel would have to be composed to withstand the rigours of such a trip through space could not be flimsy. One would expect it to be constructed of steel, titanium, ceramic or other such substances and deliberately designed to cope with immense stress, dramatically high temperatures and extreme radiation over long periods.

A ship of such rugged construction is unlikely to have been entirely vapourized by any internal explosion. The hefty shielding necessary to protect the crew from the radiation produced in the reaction chamber is unlikely to have disintegrated. Fragments of it should still have been found in an area which has now been combed more thoroughly over the years than any other region in the world.

However, a really massive, sturdily-built space vehicle such as this would account for it being seen and heard from places nearly four hundred miles away. And such an object *would* cause the brilliant tube-like streak described by eye-witnesses as it glowed in the atmosphere. The sonic boom as it plunged through would also explain noises like 'artillery fire and thunderclaps'.

This 'tube-like' spectacle – described as being various colours by different witnesses – is consistent with the re-entry effects of our own spacecraft. A. T. Lawton, in an interview with Rusty Schweickart – command pilot of the Apollo 13 capsule involved in a dramatic NASA rescue operation – asked precisely what impression of the re-entry an astronaut gets from inside the capsule.

It is fascinating [said Schweickart]. First faint violet tongues of flame appear round the edge of what seems to be a long blazing tunnel of light. At the end of it is just a jet black patch of space. The flame becomes brighter then glows first yellow, then brilliant green. It becomes so bright you cannot bear to look at it, and you are warned not to do so in case of eye damage. As entry proceeds the colour of the flame changes to red and finally dies out as you slow down to the speed of sound and the parachutes burst open soon after.

However it is not only spacecraft that produce these phenomena. A giant meteorite would do the same. In fact, one large enough to get through the atmosphere and retain sufficient bulk to cause serious damage – such as the one that pounded into Arizona – would create an entry tube several miles across and scores of miles long.

The 'cylinder shape' a number of observers described could have been the entry tube of any rapidly-moving body. Kazantsev and others suggest this was the actual shape of the spaceship. But the body could have been round or conical and still have produced a similar appearance.

It seems highly unlikely that an extra-terrestrial crew would have been aboard a spacecraft travelling anywhere near Earth, as Kazantsev assumes. An unmanned 'survey vessel' might have been despatched, but it is probable the mother ship would have been orbiting a considerable distance away. No sane commander – human or alien – would be likely to attempt to land the main ship on a strange, inhabited planet.

What *are* the chances of an out-of-control spaceship blowing itself to bits? For one driven by *conventional atomic power* they are extremely slim.

At the present time, the British Interplanetary Society is preparing 'Project Daedalus' – a remarkable blueprint for man's first nuclear-powered starship. This breathtaking concept is designed for travel to Barnards Star system, six light years away, at some 15 per cent of the speed of light, or 28,000 miles a second. Even at this staggering speed it is scheduled to take forty-seven years to reach its target. The journey would take a conventional chemical rocket around 135 000 years!

Daedalus would be gigantic – five times the length of a Saturn rocket, nearly twice the height of America's Empire State Building – with an overall weight of nearly 70 000 tons. The propulsion would be by a nuclear pulse fusion system. In simple terms this would involve detonating thermonuclear pellets, or 'bombs' – each the size of a tennis ball and each equivalent to a Hiroshima-type bomb – 250 times every second. The colossal shock waves produced would thrust against a massive, flexible molybdenum mirror. This bowl-shaped reflector would then spring back, so transmitting the enormous thrust towards the main structure of the vehicle. The mirror itself, built to withstand white hot temperatures of 1300 degrees centigrade, would, in fact, collect all the force of the explosion, projecting it in the right direction for the maximum propelling force. The nuclear fuel would be a mixture of deuterium and helium-3. A spaceship of this kind – and bear in mind it is designed for only a one-way, unmanned mission – would require 40 000 tons of fuel.*

True enough, contained in such a monster as this would be enough potential nuclear energy to blow up the whole of Siberia. In fact if the complete second-stage of a Daedalus 'fly-by' type spaceship hit the Earth the results would be diabolically more devastating than the Tunguska Event. Weighing some 1000 tons on its arrival and travelling at 15 per cent the speed of light, the energy released in its collision would be 67,500 times greater! It would punch a giant gap in the Earth's crust producing the worst series of earthquakes ever known and a sea of molten lava twenty-five miles across. The Tunguska Event however, appears to have been the airburst of a fairly slow-moving object.

The chances of an uncontrolled blast on board Daedalus are virtually nil – just as they are with a conventional aircraft carrying nuclear bombs. There is no way in which these lethal pellets can be made to explode, except by feeding them separately into the centre of the ship's powerful detonating

* Full details and specifications of the Daedalus Project are given in *CETI – Communication with Extra-Terrestrial Intelligence*, by the authors of this book.

field and firing them with specialized gear. It is impossible for the rest of the fuel to be detonated spontaneously even if the spaceship crashed. One has to assume that any really advanced intelligence capable of bringing such a craft into our Solar System would have ensured it was equally accident-proof.

We cannot know, of course, the particular type of propulsion system any alien technologists might have developed. It could be very different from our own. But certainly, if the fuel content of a spaceship driven by *conventional atomic means* had exploded over Tunguska, hundreds of tons of uranium-235 would have saturated the area and been detectable in vast quantities. If the fuel had been plutonium the amount would have been somewhat less. But this material, one of the most poisonous elements known, would have had disastrous and long-term effects on human and animal life over a very large fall-out region. Such appalling consequences could not have been overlooked.

We can calculate the amount of plutonium or uranium that would have been aboard an exploding nuclear-powered spacecraft to produce the equivalent thirty-megaton bomb energy that blasted Tunguska. The atom bombs used against Japan to end the Second World War contained about twelve pounds of plutonium or thirty-five pounds of uranium-235. A thirty-megaton bomb would contain nine *tons* of plutonium or twenty-seven tons of uranium. However, to produce this energy release from a ship driven by reactors or piles, the quantities of plutonium and uranium would be about tenfold – i.e. 90 and 270 tons respectively. Such quantities of these materials would still be easily traceable in Siberia today. There is no record of such obvious evidence being found.

Here again an accident resulting in the kind of devastation at Tunguska is difficult to imagine. Every precaution would obviously have been taken in the construction of a spaceship needing to contain so much highly-lethal material. It would certainly have been stored in many small, self-contained sections, each heavily shielded from the rest. Had an accidental explosion occurred in one of these compartments it is unlikely to have reached the rest of the system. And even if it did, this would not result in a catastrophic chain reaction. The vehicle would be more likely to melt under the intense temperatures produced, but a high proportion of the craft would fall to Earth intact. Large fragments, or even complete sections of it, should have been found at the impact site.

Kazantsev claims that traces of nickel, cobalt, copper and germanium found during expeditions were from a spaceship's instruments. But all these materials can be found in normal meteorites, nickel and cobalt being the most common ingredients (see Appendix I).

The reported presence of the radioactive isotope cesium-137 in the ring structures of trees cannot be accepted as evidence of a deliberately-detonated nuclear explosion as Zolotov has suggested. It is true the isotope can only be produced by atomic fission. But this could have occurred naturally in such an object as a comet head at the correct critical temperatures (see Appendix II).

Finally we shall consider Professor Zigel's suggestion that the object actually 'manoeuvred' and changed its course during descent. There is no solid aeronautical evidence that it did. The theory is based merely on conflicting estimates of its trajectory from unqualified eye witnesses in different areas.

But, even if Zigel is correct; even if it *did* make such manoeuvres, this does not prove his contention that they could only have been carried out by an intelligent navigator. A comet could have done the same thing. They have frequently been observed to change course many times in distant flight. If a comet head composed of gasses enclosed in ice had heated up on driving through the Earth's atmosphere, it could have burst on either side causing a jet of gas forceful enough to push the object off course. The comet would then have described an arc for as long as the jet provided sufficient thrust. Comet Bennet was recently seen to break up as it approached the Sun. Sections of it appeared to steer themselves about the sky due to this release of high-pressure pockets of gas acting like course-changing jets of a space vehicle. The gases released as a comet head dissolved could also produce a reverse thrust that would slow it down to the speed of sound.

*However, despite all the uncertainties, until positive scientific evidence identifies the Tunguska monster beyond doubt, it would be unjustifiably dogmatic to entirely rule out the possibility of some form of spaceship having caused the devastation.* The fact that such a bizarre event has never been recorded before or since, or is beyond our terrestrial comprehension, are insufficient grounds for dismissing the concept out of hand. If we do, then we must also dismiss all the natural explanations put forward so far ... for none capable of creating the same phenomena has ever been recorded either. Even those who persist in the exploding comet theory – admittedly the most likely natural cause – can turn up no records of other such happenings.

So what are the chances of such a visit from aliens? From all the evidence they seem to be extremely high, as we show in the next chapter.

## CHAPTER TWELVE

## THE LIVING UNIVERSE

Since the installation of vast radio, radar and television networks throughout the world, the possibility of a visit from some extra-terrestrial intelligence *must* have increased. Any such intelligence within a fifty-light year radius of Earth should now be capable of eavesdropping on our transmissions. And the further these penetrate the galaxy the more new alien star systems come into range.

In November 1974, a three-minute message, specifically intended for any receptive aliens, was transmitted from the massive radio-telescope at Arecibo in Puerto Rico, modified to operate on wavelengths advanced intelligences are thought likely to be using. The message, in an easily deciphered binary code, is a potted biography of the human race that also pinpoints our precise location in the galaxy. It has been beamed towards a cluster of 300 000 stars called Messier 13 in the constellation of Hercules. Though the signals, travelling at the speed of light, will take 24 000 years to reach this mini-galaxy, there is still the fascinating possibility that one of countless stellar communities nearer Earth, but directly in the path of the transmission, might pick it up far sooner than we expect.

Carl Sagan of the Centre for Radiophysics and Space Research at Cornell University, told British television viewers in July, 1976:

Though no one can be sure, it is beginning to look as if there are an enormous number of advanced technical civilizations out there in the Universe. We have, for the first time in our history, the tools to find out.

At Algonquin in Ontario, Canada, astronomers are using a 150-foot radio-telescope for a systematic search of stars thought suitable for sustaining planets with intelligent life, in the hope of picking up signals. Russia, too, is well in the hunt for alien messages with her gigantic 1800-foot reflector based in the Northern Caucasus.

By the early 1980s NASA hopes to launch a 120-inch optical telescope into orbit round the Earth. Clear of atmospheric distortion, this 300-million dollar watchdog of space, powered by direct energy from the Sun, will probe galaxies of stars a hundred times fainter than those detectable by the largest ground-based equipment. There is also a specialized committee, set up by the International Academy of Astronautics in 1974, to investigate all methods of communicating with extra-terrestrial intelligences, on which A. T. Lawton represents Britain.

It is virtually certain a vast number of these intelligences are already interchanging knowledge and ideas with each other over a far-flung interstellar network, and probably have been doing so long before man arrived on Earth. Their technology could be so far ahead of ours by now that it would be utterly inconceivable to even our most accomplished scientists. The shock of actually discovering such a superior intellectual force anywhere within striking distance of Earth would shatter the complacency of the human race in a way never before experienced.

If any of those signals we are pumping into outer space *do* get a response, it must be treated with the utmost tolerance and respect. Alien minds could be quite impossible for us to comprehend. Their logic could be founded on quite different fundamentals than ours. Our philosophy and moral code may make no sense at all to them. The way they love, tolerate, or hate would have been influenced by emotional development tailored to cope with their own pattern of survival – just as their technology would have evolved according to the particular order of their enlightenment.

The manner in which they communicate may be based on vastly different principles to man's. Language, for instance may be telepathic, visual or through some other medium rather than the spoken word. Their dominant senses would have developed in tune with their own environment – perhaps like the sonar senses of bats and other creatures on our Earth.

Man's concept of a friendly gesture might be interpreted by alien logic as a direct challenge. Our physical appearance might seem as aggressive to them as theirs to us. A really advanced race might have already had disastrous encounters with other aliens before contacting humans, which could make them instinctively distrustful of any uncustomary move we made. The last time they shook something's hand it may have clobbered them!

For these, and many other reasons, man's first response to any extra-terrestrial signal or approach would have to be guided by psychological rather than political instinct. For aliens to have been able to make contact in the first place would be a likely indication of their superiority. It would be suicidal to take chances with a super-power that might well be equipped to display their displeasure with sophisticated warheads lethal enough to blast us – and the entire Solar System – out of existence.

The amount of caution necessary in the way we responded to any aliens would depend a great deal on how far away they were. Signals originating from a star merely a few light years distance would demand the utmost diplomacy. The consequences of inciting the wrath of a super-race could be far more horrific than the force that struck Tunguska. George Wald, Harvard biologist and Nobel Laureate, is very uneasy about mankind making extra-terrestrial contact. It would, he says 'be the most highly classified and exploited military information in the history of the Earth'. It is quite likely the general public would not be told.

Dr Nikolai Kardashev – the eminent Russian astrophysicist at present searching the galaxy for alien signals at the Radio Institute at Gorky – has graded extra-terrestrial life into three categories according to the level of their technology. He puts humans in almost the Grade I group – that is, among those societies advanced only sufficiently to utilize the resources of their own planet. His Grade II societies are those able to harness the total energy of a star, or sun. Finally there are the elite of the Universe ... the god-like races in Grade III who would command the unbelievable power resources of an entire galaxy ... in control of millions of stars focused into a technology utterly beyond our wildest dreams.

The Universe itself is a living thing. Sensuous, hot-blooded and promiscuous. The intercourse of masses of plasma is continuous. Its pregnancy perpetual – thrusting vibrant new suns into the galaxies so that they, in their turn, can nurture their own little families of planets. True, many of their offsprings may be stillborn. Like the barren outposts of our own Solar System they may be too far away to be breast-fed through the vital energy of their mother Sun. But surely vast numbers of others will flourish into adolescence like Earth. Surely they too will have been safely nursed in a cotton-wool blanket of cloud, their steaming little bodies bathed by the cooling rain of centuries, their birthmarks topped up to become vast oceans. And surely nothing can then have stopped the molecules of organic life taking shape.

In the Milky Way galaxy alone there are some 150 billion stars – suns greater or smaller, hotter or cooler than ours. Most are now believed to have planets bustling around them. And there are at least 100 billion other *galaxies*, each with as many stars or suns of their own. To realize the Earth's infinitesimal part in all this, consider that to make a one-way flight to one of the *nearest stars* by our fastest Saturn rocket would take an incredible 160 000 years. For even *light* to reach Earth from the most distant stars in our galaxy (travelling at 186 thousand miles a second) takes 160 000 years. From the furthest known galaxies it takes ten *billion* years!

The total number of stars within range of our telescopes alone is estimated at $10^{28}$. To appreciate the immensity of that figure, write down 10 and add twenty-eight noughts after it. And our observers could only yet have penetrated the fringe of the Universe. It is only to be expected if those foregoing statistics are just too enormous to grasp. The human mind cannot do so. They are quite beyond its true comprehension.

Is it, therefore, in any way logical that all this cosmic matter, energy and fertility should have been created exclusively for the benefit or *one* race of moderately intelligent beings on *one* tiny planet? The purpose of life is to procreate. The Universe is life itself. Its very elements are those of which every one of us is composed. So why should not those same elements have also combined into an endless array of other intelligent forms? It is arrogant and intolerant in the extreme to assume that the same biological evolution that culminated in intelligence on this Earth should not have found equal opportunity to flourish on other worlds. Even in the tenuous atmosphere of Mars, the NASA Viking spacecraft detected a small percentage of nitrogen, one of the necessary elements in the creation of biological organisms.

For some years scientists have been able to simulate in their own laboratories the natural process of producing life by the simple interaction of certain basic chemicals. A gas mixture of methane and ammonia over water is subjected to radiated energy at levels believed to have existed on Earth in primeval times. The products resulting from these reactions are found to contain the very biochemicals required by our bodies for part of our metabolic process. Surely similar conditions and ingredients will stimulate the same life-producing reactions elsewhere in the Universe.

It is now known that life forms can survive in the most outrageous conditions. Bacteria have been found flourishing in the hot springs of Yellowstone Park. Microbes, discovered in Antarctica core samples taken from thousands of feet below the surface, have been thawed out and revived after half a million years in suspended animation. Certain fish in the polar regions are endowed with 'antifreeze' elements in their blood. Microbes can live in acid and bats in Mongolia exist on infinitesimal amounts of water. Why should extraterrestrials not flourish merely because conditions may not suit the cosy environment of delicate warm-blooded humans? Nature has the most miraculous ways of teaching all living things to adapt to the surroundings she creates.

At the time of going to press, the momentous question 'Is there life on Mars?' was still unanswered – though almost certainly the ingredients seemed to be there for flourishing life forms to have existed in its earlier history.

The first pictures Viking I radioed back to Earth were breathtaking. Engineers and scientists at the Jet Propulsion Laboratory in Pasadena were enraptured. Here, 200 million miles away, was a scene that might well have been in the Arizona desert ... a rock-strewn plain stretching to hills gloriously silhouetted against a dazzling pink sky. Dr Noel Hinners, the normally impassive NASA associate administrator for space science, told an emotional press conference: 'I'm almost speechless. Really I can't think about science right now. My heart's beating fast and I had tears in my eyes this morning for the first time, I guess, since I got married.'

The first biological tests by Viking I on the Martian soil created a sensation. It was found to be giving off incredibly large amounts of carbon dioxide and oxygen – a reaction normally associated with the presence of micro-organisms. However, it seemed just too much of a good thing. So the NASA scientists began to consider other *chemical* actions that might have caused these startling results. But they could not rule out the biological possibility.

On 3 September Viking II landed to cheers, hugs and the pop of champagne corks at mission control. Three weeks later it was reporting that the Martian North Pole was composed not of frozen carbon dioxide as scientists had previously believed, but of frozen *water*. Dr Barney Farmer, in charge of the search for water on the planet, told the Press: 'It looks as if Mars not only had seas and rivers, but had seasonal rains at one time.'

In fact, it was beginning to look as though Mars is a sleeping planet, locked in a deep Ice Age, that may one day burst into life again.

The success of the Vikings must inevitably be followed by mobile probe vehicles that can explore vast areas of the Red Planet. Already Soviet scientists are developing a grotesque insect-like robot with a laser 'eye'. It is called the 'Cockroach', and is designed to roam the valleys of Mars like some science-fiction monstrosity, searching for life. The planners are also adapting a special, armoured version to explore the sizzling surface of Venus.

The robot explorer will be able to 'think' for itself. Its laser eye will help to keep it out of trouble by continually scanning ahead. When this encounters an obstacle, the Cockroach will stop automatically at a safe distance and feed details of the problem to its brain, which will immediately work out a way around it. If it can't solve it alone, it will signal Earth for further instructions.

Already a six-legged prototype of Cockroach has been put through its routines at the Soviet Institute of Problems of Information Communications.

Meanwhile American scientists are developing a robot with metal arms and hands, a visual system of two television cameras and a laser, and wheels instead of legs. Thousands of instructions will be programmed into its computer brain when it is ready to trundle across Mars by the 1980s, by which time all its 'vital organs' will be miniaturized.

The versatile Vikings are only the vanguard of an advancing army of Earth-sent robot infiltrators that will soon be intruding upon the privacy of the Solar planets. For, whatever else the Vikings discover, most scientists agree that they have already justified the eight years and one billion dollars spent on their construction. Whether they actually find living organisms or not, no other mission has so strengthened the argument that prolific life exists in the Universe. For if a static probe on another planet in our own Solar System indicates suitable ingredients, the chances of countless worlds in countless galaxies of stars nurturing intelligent species is overwhelming.

As Robert F. Freitag, the man responsible for planning NASA's future manned space flight programme, says: 'Today many scientists, if not the majority, agree that extraterrestrial life must surely exist, and possibly in enormous abundance. The question now is no longer so much one of "if" as of "where"?'

The one question no one can answer is in what form intelligent aliens have developed. The permutations are endless. Each species will be synchronized with its own particu-

139

lar environment – just as we are with ours. Their skeletal structures will have developed to cope with the territory and gravity of their own worlds. On a tiny planet the dominant life-form might literally be 'angels' ... light, willowy creatures adapted to fly over their low-gravity world, whereas great lumbering monstrosities might be the intelligent species that crawl sloth-like across the face of a world whose powerful gravity would crush the human frame.

At the National Air and Space Museum in Washington, USA, are models of imaginary creatures from other planets. One – created to suit a high-gravity world – is a monstrous herbivore with eight legs, a large mouth in its chest, two eyes on a stalk and ears along the side of its body. Its weight – 30 000 lbs! Another, designed for a planet like Jupiter, is a great beast with a hydrogen-filled balloon on top of its head enabling it to float in the atmosphere.

Some of the really extreme genetic masterpieces of life in distant outer space would no doubt seem far more grotesque to us than even the most hideous creations from the fertile minds of the most outrageous writers of science-fiction. The instinctive nausea and revulsion man could well experience when he meets his first aliens would be one of the most difficult psychological barriers to overcome. It would not be easy for him to disregard what, by his standards, is horrific far beyond his most tortured nightmares, and to accept such manifestations for their superb intelligence alone. It would not be easy to find himself exchanging information with, say, a loathsome, shapeless mass of protoplasm. *Somewhere* out there, may be creatures similar in appearance to ourselves, but the odds against us meeting them must be enormous.

Even man himself might eventually change as technology influences his environment. One group of scientists have predicted we may develope larger heads and smaller bodies. Increasingly efficient computers and labour-saving devices might result in smaller limbs and our teeth might not be so conspicuous as we devour less and less solid food. Dr James E. Harris, chairman of the Department of Orthodontics at the University of Michigan, has been studying the changing face of humans. He is convinced we'll eventually look different than we do at present. Our lower jaws, he says, will get smaller, eventually receding to a point where we have practically no chin.

British astronomer and author Patrick Moore raises the fascinating possibility that, when we begin to colonize the Moon and Mars, a new race of humanoids might develop to suit these unusual environments. Writing in the *Daily Telegraph Magazine* in September 1976, he says:

There will undoubtedly be both men and women in the lunar and Martian colonies, so that children are inevitable. We are entitled to ask: 'What will happen to them – and how will they develop?'

The gravitational pull of the Moon is much less than that of the Earth, and the weight of a man (or woman) is reduced to one-sixth of its terrestrial value. A baby born on the Moon and growing up on the Moon would develop under this relatively weak force, and coming back to Earth could present major physical problems. It might even prove to be impossible.

No doubt the problem will be side-stepped in the early days by returning 'lunar babies' to Earth before they have started to grow, but even so there may be all kinds of unforeseen complications. With Mars, where the gravity is admittedly greater than that of the Moon but still only one-third that on the surface of the Earth, babies will certainly stay with their parents for a time at least, and there must be cases in which their spell on Mars turns out to be permanent.

Consider a 'Martian' boy or girl aged, say, fourteen. Muscles will have adapted to the weak gravity, and the pull of Earth would, presumably, put an intolerable strain on them. If these young people in turn marry and produce offspring, we will be well on the road towards a genuine separation of species, and after several generations the 'Martians' might be expected to develop physical characteristics which would at once single them out from their Earth ancestors. Whether mentality would also change is something which we do not know.

But whatever form we humanoids eventually take, our aesthetic values will be adjusted along with our features. We will still consider ourselves to be as handsome as ever, just as the most repulsive alien we could ever imagine would be firmly convinced he was the god's gift to the Universe. The adage that 'beauty is in the eye of the beholder' could not be more applicable than it is in any comparison of alien life-forms.

For a moment try to imagine an alien's-eye view of late twentieth-century humanity. We shall assume 'he' is from a small, low-gravity planet and is a million years more technically advanced than ourselves. As we cannot possibly know what he would look like, we shall make him shapeless ... just a delicate, pliable, blob of near-transparent matter something like a huge jelly-fish. On his world anything that did not have his own unblemished streamlined form would be unnatural and grotesque. Heads, torso, limbs would be repulsively unfamiliar.

To him, humans would be strange, ungainly creatures. The face of a beautiful woman would be nothing more than a contorted oval-shaped chunk of protoplasm, hairy at the top, with two sockets and a flabby, red-rimmed hole that emitted peculiar grating sounds as it continuously opened and closed. Her elegant 36-21-36 inch figure would be an ugly, mis-shapen bulk with long, thin tentacle-like attachments which she occasionally wrapped around other slightly-less malformed creatures of the opposite sex.

Nothing in the general behaviour of this curious species would be in any way logical to an alien mind that had formed in entirely different evolutionary channels. Human habits could appear disgusting and obscene ... The way we eat and drink, the way we move, the way we make love.

Such an alien might belong to a highly-organized community existing in a secure, Utopian state of global togetherness that may have long-since outlawed war, poverty and disease. Greed, suspicion and all social segregation through wealth, politics, religion and colour might no longer fetter the unilateral progress of their planet. Human standards, ethics, values and loyalties could not possibly make sense to them. Nothing in the concept of their own clinical, finely-adjusted logic could justify a single, dominant and reasonably intelligent species cowering in their incompatible warrens of philosophy and tradition – in most cases incapable of even understanding each other's languages, let alone their emotions and points of view.

The physical, moral and intellectual differences between aliens and humans could be as vast as the chasms of space between their planets. In view of such unpredictability, in any sudden confrontation it would, therefore, be far better for friendly interstellar relationship if preliminary long-distance communication were first established so that each community could become mentally attuned and prepared for the kind of unfamiliar life-form they could later expect to encounter.

## CHAPTER THIRTEEN

# THE INTRUDERS

In considering the exploding spaceship theory in the search for the answer to the Tunguska Event, one must inevitably bring in the tantalizing controversy of Unidentified Flying Objects that has raged all over the world for decades.

All those vivid descriptions of the Siberian fireball streaking across the sky can be found somewhere among the bulging files of UFO researchers. The 'bluish-white light in the form of a cylinder' reported in the Irkutsk newspaper *Siber*, for instance, might be compared with the 'hissing, cigar-shaped UFO . . . a brilliant blue-white glow surrounding it', claimed to have been spotted by a Police Sergeant Lester Shell at Tennessee in October 1973. However there have been so many variations in the descriptions of 'flying saucers' over the years, they could be made to account for just about everything that's ever been seen in the sky.

Though nothing on the scale of Tunguska has ever been associated with the activity of UFOs, there have been many accounts of ground being scorched, crops incinerated and odd indentations in the earth, sometimes attributed to spacecraft landing and taking off. In 1973 a farmer in Clarion, Ohio, found a forty-foot wide area of his bean patch scorched with holes a foot across at each corner. The previous year a similar discovery was made fourteen miles away by a farmer in Goldfield, where UFO watchers claimed an unusually large number of sightings in 1972. But such 'evidence' as this would have been quite easy to set up by practical jokers – and there have been many of these responsible for 'flying saucers'.

But it isn't so easy to explain away reports of a 'mini-Tunguska' from the village of Montauroux in the South of France in October 1972. This was the account published in the British *Sunday Express*.

Last Sunday (8 October) M. Rene Merle, a local peasant, went along to his woods for a little rough shooting, and was flabbergasted to find that 330 square yards of ground among the pines and white oaks had been 'flattened'.

Fragments, of a section of dry stone wall had exploded in all directions, lacerating the bark of many trees. One tree stump, previously so firmly embedded that it could not be moved by man alone, had been uprooted and hurled several yards. Pine tree trunks, 18 inches thick, were coiled up as if by some gigantic centrifugal force, some twisted in a clockwise direction, others the reverse way.

A line of pine trees were sectioned as if by a blade in a cut rising progressively from 18 inches to 6 feet above ground level. On his dry wall, M. Merle detected traces of rubbing but no fragments of metal. The police, from the local gendarmes to Riviera headquarters, have confessed they are baffled. The wildest rumours are circulating this quiet corner of Provence.

Montauroux villagers are convinced that only a flying saucer could have wreaked such havoc to M. Merle's land which is more than 100 yards from the nearest forest track and bears no marks of a heavy military or other vehicle.


The newspaper report adds that a fireball was seen shortly before the discovery of the havoc by several witnesses. The fire brigade had been called out but had found no outbreak.

A chill early morning mist shrouded the woods when Guy Turco, Professor of Mineralogy at the Faculty of Sciences at Nice University arrived to study the phenomenon two days later. Souvenir hunters had already trodden and ransacked the area. He wanted to salvage whatever evidence might still have remained before a fresh horde of sightseers stormed in. After closely examining rocks and soil in the area, he told the newspaper *Nice-Matin*:

I was searching for just a crumb. I didn't find it. I have nothing in my store of knowledge which allows me to explain the phenomena. I had come to verify the hypothesis of a meteorite. I found nothing which can confirm it.

Could the damage have been caused by a tornado, a whirlwind or, perhaps, lightning? Meteorological experts who later visited the site ruled out these possibilities. The trees had been twisted in different directions. A whirlwind always turns in the same direction, and it is unlikely such a force would have limited the damage to one circular area as had happened at Montouroux. 'A whirlwind,' explained one researcher 'always has a definite trajectory. It does not begin and end in the same place. There would have been a trench, not a circle.'

Lightning was also ruled out by visiting scientists. They discovered no signs of burning. Though lightning can create devastating energy they did not believe it could uproot tree stumps so deeply embedded in the ground, or twist pine trees in that manner.

Among the investigators at Montouroux was a biologist from Cogolin, Alain Histarry. He claimed that, directly over the stricken spot, his compass 'went mad'. Instead of pointing magnetic north the needle swung firmly to due west. Professor Turco, however, could find no evidence of disturbance in the local magnetic field and there were no anomalous amounts of radioactivity.

Within a week or so of the Montouroux incident little of the debris remained. Some fanatical collectors even took away the largest uprooted tree stump and later sold it to a local antique dealer!

Although these reports suggest nothing remotely as fierce as the Tunguska event, the characteristics of the phenomena – the fireball, the flattened and uprooted trees, the angled slicing effect of the pines and the absence of fragments from any cosmic object – seem to come straight from the notes of Leonid Kulik more than thirty years before.

Since the 1950s Dr Felix Zigel of the Moscow Aviation Institute has been studying the many reported sightings of UFOs over the Soviet Union. One of the most extraordinary dates back to April 1961. Twenty-five witnesses claim to

146

have seen a bluish-green, oval-shaped object the size of an airliner travelling at tremendous speed over Lake Onega, north-east of Leningrad. A team led by scientist Fyodor Denidov investigated.

Some eye witnesses claimed the object then flew so low that it seemed to scrape the ground, yet still continued on its course without slowing down. Major Anton Kopeikin, an army engineer who was also on the investigation team, reported that it left a trench in the earth fifty feet long and ten feet deep as well as two other smaller trenches.

Kopeikin told an American newspaper in July 1975:

> The ice on the lake had broken up. The underside of the ice floes was bright green. Sample pieces of the ice, when melted, left a residue of magnesium, aluminium, calcium, barium and titanium.
>
> Also found were a strange piece of metal and tiny black grains of exact geometrical form consisting of iron, silicon, lithium, titanium and aluminium. The grains were resistant to acid and high temperatures.

Dr Vladimir Sharanov, a Soviet geophysicist and member of the Leningrad Technological Institute, examined Kopeikin's findings. He is quoted as saying:

> The black grains are unexplainable at the present time – but they are clearly of artificial origin. This object couldn't have been a meteor. As for the possibility that it was a plane, technical experts claim a plane couldn't withstand so heavy an impact against the frozen ground.

Among the case histories of UFOs in Zigel's file are reports of strange substances he calls 'angel's hair' said to have been left floating in the air following some sightings. He explains:

> It's usually like a glassy, cotton cobweb. Witnesses say it has a bad odour and dissipates quickly. The secretary of the Committee for the Geophysical Year, N. V. Shebalin, has received several reports of angel's hair drifting through the atmosphere over the Voronezh region, south of Mos-

cow. From the samples we've analysed our scientists have not yet identified the substance with anything that exists on Earth – natural or man-made.

Similar material was claimed to have been found in the United States in 1974. Police departments in the Denver, Colorado area received a flood of calls on the evening of 16 October that three UFOs (also tracked by radar at the International Airport) were hovering over a one-hundred-foot radio tower. At daybreak the following morning police claimed they found 'strange, silvery cobweb-like strands' on the tower, which eventually blew away in the wind.

Zigel talks of another form of UFO 'left-over' found by geophysicist Alexander Zayekin at Tambov, south of Moscow. He calls it 'space tumbleweed' and claims it contained 'intertwining metal needles each about five to eight centimetres long and half a millimetre in diameter'.

'The needles,' he goes on, 'were of an unknown brittle, grey-coloured metal.'

The discovery of such needles is intriguing. These could constitute tiny aerials whose length corresponds to a quarter wavelength of *an actual transmission frequency*. Strips of metal and needles of this type were used to confuse enemy radar installations in the Second World War. They act as signal reflectors and can sabotage attempts to identify aircraft. As they drift over a wide area they produce a confusion of echoes which makes it extremely difficult to trace the actual aircraft echo.

The fascinating thing about the needles Zigel says were found at Tambov, is that those measuring five centimetres in length would correspond to a transmission wavelength of 20 centimetres. This is very close indeed to the 'universal' wavelength of 21 centimetres, corresponding to a frequency of 1420 mHz. And this is one of the frequencies now being closely checked by astronomers all over the world in their search for possible signals from extra-terrestrial intelligences. *It is a frequency scientists consider they could be using.*

Needles measuring eight centimetres, also mentioned by Zigel, correspond to a wavelength of 32 centimetres, or a frequency of 938 mHz. This frequency does not fit any known *natural* molecular absorption frequency.

There are therefore two alternative explanations for the presence of these needles at Tambov. They are either man-made and designed to correspond to frequencies used by the Russians in some of their military exercises, or there is the fascinating possibility that they are extra-terrestrial. A. T. Lawton explains:

> If this were indeed the case, these needles might represent a riddle *and* the key to solving it, combined in one very neatly arranged package. The 5-centimetre needles (or 5.25 centimetres, to be precise) could be recognizable as the clue to the 21-centimetre 'universal wavelength'. The 8-centimetre, needles might then represent a frequency which could be used by an extra-terrestrial group. They may wish to communicate on 32 centimetres, or 938 mHz to avoid radio pollution at the more general frequency of 1420 mHz. In other words, though 938 mHz, is a totally unnatural or illogical frequency to use for interstellar communication, it has all the advantages of freedom from atmospheric and ionospheric interference and distortion.

Using this hidden clue or key by deliberately mixing 5- and 8-centimetre needles might possibly be an alien's way of testing the ingenuity of the human mind and to ensure that it is sufficiently advanced to make further communication justifiable.

In most UFO sightings scientists are able to offer logical explanations. These include such things as unusual atmospheric phenomena, reflections from artificial lighting, heat mirages, high-powered xenon arc lamps on aircraft, Earth-launched satellites, weather balloons, and ordinary aircraft shimmering in the sunlight. Other causes can be hallucinations brought on by fatigue or mental stress, and strange effects on the human brain stimulated by electrical or magnetic field activity.

A twenty-three-year-old pilot who claimed to have been surrounded by UFOs on a flight to Mexico City in May 1975, was thought later to have been suffering from hypoxia, or lack of oxygen – a condition that might have stimulated hallucinations. Images and visions have actually been deliberately produced in the human brain by feeding slight electric currents into it. Certain people have also been found to be affected in similar ways by electrical, magnetic or radio fields such as those generated by lightning, overhead high-voltage cables or even intense sun-spot activity.

The US Air Force UFO investigation team can quote scores of other natural phenomena that can produce flying saucer effects. They still admit, however, that about 2.5 per cent of the thousand sightings a year that they scrutinized could *not* be explained by any of these phenomena.

However, if serious researchers in Siberia ever *do* find acceptable evidence that a spaceship blew up over Tunguska, it would certainly be the greatest-ever boost for UFO enthusiasts throughout the world.

## CHAPTER FOURTEEN

# THE INCREDIBLE ANSWER?

Though all the explanations discussed so far in the 'exploding spaceship' theory contain serious loopholes, there is one that would still account for every phenomena recorded at Tunguska.

The hypothesis however is dependent on one vital factor ... evidence for the presence of antimatter (see Appendix VI). If this *is* found the possibility of it being *artificial* are overwhelming. For one cannot conceive how a piece of *natural* antimatter could survive long enough in our own galaxy to ever reach Earth. Only with some sophisticated form of protective shielding could such material be transported through the barrier of normal matter that makes up the environment of our Solar System. And the most functional way in which this could take place would be in the form of fuel for a spacecraft powered by that devastating mixture of matter and antimatter.

In July 1976, a special NASA study into the prospects for future interstellar space flight came to the following conclusion:

There are those who speculate on the possibility of creating and containing antimatter. This would indeed represent the most efficient energy storage system of which we can conceive, permitting the total conversion of mass to energy. If such systems could actually be operated as rocket engines, the flight time to a star might be cut down to a matter of decades.

However we are not likely to see such engines before the year 2000. Although it is possible to create antimatter in high-energy accelerators, no one as yet has any idea of how to store it in such a way that it could be made available as an energy source for a rocket engine. What is required is not simply further development along an established line of research, but a completely new breakthrough or invention. If this new invention – the storing of antimatter – were to come along in the next decade, then it might be technically feasible to build an antimatter reaction rocket motor by the turn of the century.

A really advanced alien technology could well have acquired the delicately-balanced technique of combining matter and antimatter in such a way that they could harness the awesome energy this would release. Basically there would have to be some form of reaction chamber where these two belligerent forces could be safely allowed to annihilate each other without blasting their surroundings out of existence too.

The only kind of 'reaction chamber' capable of containing such a highly-lethal combination would be some powerful magnetic force field which would also focus the released gamma radiation in the correct way for maximum thrust. The efficiency of such a propulsion system would be quite staggering and could drive a spaceship at enormous velocities exceeding 90 per cent the speed of light. The antimatter fuel itself could not, of course, be allowed to make contact with any type of conventional container constructed of ordinary matter. So, here again, a magnetic field system would have to be devised within which the antimatter could be safely isolated or suspended until it was required to be reacted explosively with the fuel of normal matter inside the reaction chamber.

The fearsome energy output from combining merely one pound of matter and one pound of antimatter would be equal to that produced by burning nine million tons of coal ... enough to keep an average power station going for between five and eight years.

If the Tunguska event *were* caused by a spaceship, the matter–antimatter drive model would seem the most feasible. If somehow the magnetic field isolating the antimatter fuel collapsed, this fuel would then make that fatal, uncontrolled contact with its ordinary matter surroundings. At the same time the power supplies controlling the other force fields would be cut off. The entire structure of the ship would be instantly vapourized without trace in a catastrophic explosion that could certainly have produced the type of devastation found around the Southern Swamp region. In fact, if such a spacecraft was intending to return to its own planet, the quantity of fuel remaining on board would have been lethal enough to have gouged out the entire Asian continent. It would require only a relatively small amount of antimatter to create the thirty-megaton blast over Tunguska.

This would indicate that the spaceship was never scheduled to return from its mission. Could it therefore have been manned by a small 'kamikazi' group of scientists and technicians prepared to sacrifice themselves to the cause of interstellar research? If the explosion was accidental, were they intending to land when the force field suddenly broke down? Had they specifically chosen the uninhabited region of Siberia as a favourable location to set up base before making their first cautious contact with the human race?

A more likely alternative would be that the visitor was an *unmanned* vehicle. In this case its computers could have been programmed to move it into a safe survey orbit round the Earth, but not to enter the atmosphere. Something might have gone irrevocably wrong during the complex manoeuvres. The quantity of antimatter fuel retained to power an unmanned observation satellite of this kind would probably have been about the right amount to cause that thirty-megaton explosion.

Another possibility is that the satellite was damaged in collision with some particularly formidable hunk of solar-space debris, or that a vital system on board was drastically affected by a natural phenomenon closer to Earth.

Whatever it was, once that force field containing the antimatter fuel broke up, nothing could have saved it from utter destruction.

The odds *against* a visiting spaceship from another star system containing living aliens are overwhelming. Why should it, when highly sophisticated, computerized satellites can do the job more efficiently? NASA did not send astronauts to seek for life on Mars in 1976. They sent those auto-mated Viking orbiters and landers. The Russians didn't risk *their* highly-trained space crews when they, too, attempted to investigate the mysterious Red Planet ... which was rather fortunate because their 'Mars-3' lander was instantly knocked 'senseless' by a fearsome 200-mile-an-hour gale that suddenly lashed it across the rugged surface, putting its delicate instruments out of action.

No space authority would commit human beings to the searing hell-hole of Venus. But unmanned probes go there. In fact two sent back dramatic pictures of the scalding planet while they were being slowly barbecued by its lethal atmosphere.

If *we* can explore the Solar System with these inquisitive little 'private eyes', there is every reason to believe that really advanced extra-terrestrial intelligences are well capable of sending them far vaster distances. By the next century our own space programme should be including these interstellar 'messengers' that will feed back to Mankind an unimaginable wealth of knowledge. From their lonely orbits around won-derful new worlds they will seek out vital clues to intelligent life, perhaps even intercepting alien radio signals. They will be telling us, too, which of those worlds might one day be suitable for the overspill settlements of the human race.

Starship Daedalus is designed to be equipped with auto-mated probes to investigate the planetary system of Bar-nard's Star. These would collect masses of data and send it to their mother ship for re-transmission back to Earth. But there would be no question of risking the lives of a living crew on these initial surveys of hostile planets.

Of course, had an extra-terrestrial intelligence *already* sent probes to Earth and was now entirely satisfied their own kind could survive here, then a 'manned' expedition might be justified. There is the remote possibility that these earlier surveys found that human life was so primitive that the super-beings from their own planet could colonize it without serious risk.

But the ratio of manned to unmanned space vehicles likely to be operating in the galaxy makes such a situation highly improbable. We might roughly calculate the odds from the breakdown of American and Russian missions to date. Of these (excluding military satellite launches) only 1 to 2 per cent have so far been manned. On this basis, the odds against *interstellar* missions being manned would be much higher ... possibly ten thousand to one. The enormous expense, the risk, the time element and the unwieldy size of a fully-crewed starship, all make unmanned exploration the obvious choice.

In the early part of this century a really advanced race might have been turning out assembly-line probes, infinitely more efficient than the NASA Vikings at the same time as the Americans were producing Model-T Fords. And, despite their sophistication, just as cheaply.

In July 1975, an interstellar exploration project submitted to the Committee on Science and Technology of the United States House of Representatives, and which now forms the basis for part of NASA's space programme for the rest of this century, strongly advocated the use of automated probes to investigate nearby star systems. Among the findings, compiled by senior scientist Robert L. Forward of the Hughes Research Laboratories of California, are papers on alien planet detection by A. T. Lawton.

In his introduction to the project, Dr Forward writes:

The initial goal is to send sophisticated autonomous probes to the nearest stellar systems before the century is out. The interstellar probes would use advanced computer micro-miniaturization techniques to achieve unrivalled orbital surveillance capability, combined with almost human intelligence, in a few pounds of payload.

So could the Tunguska object, in fact, have been the counterpart of those Viking spacecraft NASA sent to Mars? ... its mission – to seek out life *here* on Earth? With matter–antimatter propulsion power it could have streaked across a vast area of the galaxy at an incredible velocity. Once its highly-developed computers had fed back their information to its own star system, the satellite would have been disposable. It might even have been programmed to destroy itself by deliberately collapsing the force-field containing the last remnants of its antimatter fuel. Alternatively some unforeseen system breakdown could have occurred that was beyond the ability of the computer 'brain' to correct.

It might have ventured too close to Earth. Perhaps its auto-pilot system misjudged the height of the atmosphere and caused it to make entry. Here such a probe could not function. Its multitude of antennae, power-dissipating fins and other accessories sprouting from the main structure, would have been designed specifically for the frictionless tranquillity of outer space. Once in the dense, restrictive atmosphere of Earth this vital equipment could have been torn away as the probe glowed like a giant multi-coloured fireball. It would be completely out of control. Like the reentry of man-made satellites, this searing atmospheric friction would consume the probe – its framework, motors, fuel tanks and everything else.

In this situation a probe powered by matter–antimatter fuel *could* explode spontaneously. If the structure disintegrated in this way the antimatter fuel would be exposed and then be free to combine with ordinary matter.

One might even speculate on the type of fuel such a probe would carry. For various reasons it would probably be a liquid, a good conductor of electricity and preferably very dense so that it could be contained in a conveniently small area. Mercury would fit these requirements very well. Two and a half pounds of anti-mercury could be contained in a tank about the size of a small thermos flask. This mini-tank would have an intense multi-phase AC magnetic field surrounding it, thus suspending the fuel in a swirling mass in the centre of the tank, safely isolated from the inner walls of the casing. Secondary fields at either end would hold the anti-mercury in a kind of 'magnetic bottle'. By adjusting the strength of the field force at one end, the fuel could be induced to enter a reaction chamber where it could be mixed with ordinary matter (again, probably mercury).

If, in an accident of some kind, the magnetic field to the anti-mercury was cut off, the fuel would splatter the container walls in a flat 'puddle'. This would be more than adequate to trigger off an annihilation explosion.

Actually about $2\frac{1}{2}$ pounds of mercury–antimercury would produce an explosion far greater than that of a thirty-megaton bomb. So, if a craft of this kind *did* destroy itself over Siberia the fuel content might have been less. This, however, is quite feasible, as it would require only a very small quantity to slow down a moderately-sized unmanned vehicle and to slot it into an orbit round Earth. The bulk of the fuel, of course, would have already been used up on the vast journey from its home planet.

Since matter–antimatter annihilation is the most powerful and efficient method of obtaining energy, it is highly likely that a technically advanced race would be using it. As stated previously, in view of the insurmountable hazards of anti-matter reaching our Solar System in a natural and unpro-tected form, any traces of its original existence found at Tunguska by current or future investigations would be powerful evidence of the alien artifact theory.

A satellite, well equipped to transmit detailed information over vast distances to its own world, may have been pro-grammed to communicate with Earth had man's radio tech-niques been sufficiently advanced. But, of course, in 1908 they were not. Any attempt to create such a link-up would have been pointless. Realizing this, might have been sufficient reason for the computer to release the order to 'self-destruct'.

Until now, advocates of the exploding space-ship theory have assumed the vehicle to have been a massive one, driven by conventional nuclear power. A recent book *The Fire Came By* written by Thomas Atkins and John Baxter, follows the popular reasoning that it must have had 'a mass of thousands of tons' propelled by 'nuclear fire'. A small matter-anti-matter fuelled probe such as we have described, is a far more functional vehicle for aliens to use in any investigation of our Solar System.

A number of scientists believe it quite feasible that alien probes such as this are exploring planets in many parts of the Universe and could, at some stage, have orbited Earth. Certainly if such an object arrived here *now* our astro-physicists would be well able to set up a system of communication. A tremendous amount of research has been done in the last decade to cope with any kind of extra-terrestrial signals that may suddenly arrive here.

One of the foremost advocates of the alien space probe theory is Professor Ronald Bracewell of Stanford University in California who is one of the world's leading radio astronomers. In an article published in 1975 by *Mercury*, the official journal of the Astronomical Society of the Pacific (adapted from his book *The Galactic Club*) Professor Bracewell writes:

It is clearly possible in principle to pack an enormous amount of information into a modest interstellar probe and to send it into the vicinity of a likely star. When the probe arrives, it fires a rocket and goes into circular orbit about the star in the middle of the habitable zone and in the star's equatorial plane – the plane where planets will be situated ... the probe then begins a programme of investigation, supplementing its internal power source with stellar power in a way similar to, or better than, the scheme that has been so successful on Skylab and other solar-powered spacecraft.

It is quite possible that a probe arrived in our Solar System when our radio transmissions had not yet begun. It would therefore be desirable for the probe to continue listening. We are sensitive to this point, because the Earth could have been the target of a messenger probe as recently as a few decades ago, but even then we did not have commercial broadcast transmitters in operation.

We would have a great deal to learn from such a probe. In fact it could profoundly change our entire philosophy, uproot our religions and certainly destroy our chauvinism. But, as Professor Bracewell goes on:

Knowledge of our language will enable the probe to tell us many fascinating things; the physics and chemistry of the next hundred years, wonders of astrophysics yet unknown to man, beautiful mathematics. After a while it may supply us with astounding breakthroughs in biology and medicine. But first we will have to tell it a lot bout out biological makeup. Perhaps it will write poetry or discuss philosophy. Perhaps the messenger knows how the Universe started, whether it will end, and what will happen then. Maybe the probe knows what it all means.

If an orbiting satellite *had* come to grief over Siberia, it could, like the Vikings, have been attempting to actually set a life-seeking 'lander' unit on to the surface of the Earth? Did it deliberately choose this barren, uninhabited area so that painstaking analysis of soil organisms and other ground-level research could go on undisturbed? In the Martian-like seclusion of the Southern Swamp it might have remained undetected for years, feeding masses of vital information to the computer 'brain' of its orbiter which, in turn, would have transmitted this to the planet of the alien star system from which it originated.

Though there could be many similarities in the self-sustaining functions of the Vikings and those of an interstellar satellite, the differences in the journeys they made would be vast. The first Viking took more than ten months to make the 200-million-mile trip to Mars before landing on the 'Plain of Gold' on the sunny morning of 20 July 1976. A matter–antimatter driven craft could cover the distance in about twenty minutes.

If therefore (and this is not inconceivable even within our own technological trends) a sophisticated matter–antimatter version of the Viking spacecraft was orbiting Earth in June 1908, let us now imagine the last moments of its fascinating mission . . .

## CHAPTER FIFTEEN

# THE BRAIN

The Brain moves in silence. A multitude of delicate sensors feeds a perpetual flow of information to the millions of micro computer cells that forms its membrane. Twenty-five thousand miles below, a pale blue bauble is suspended among countless fairly lights in the endless blackness of space. It is the planet Earth.

The Brain's orders are to find life. They have been programmed into it by a supremely advanced intelligence somewhere out in the galaxy. It has come a long way. The incredible journey has taken many years. But its remarkable memory banks have been packed with masses of precise navigation data, geared to the changing positions of numerous star systems. Its artificial mind – so extensively programmed it can now think and act for itself – has been carefully shielded from the radiation and debris of outer space.

Six months ago it automatically swung into an orbit around the Sun. Its sensors then systematically 'interrogated' the solar planets for signs of those vital elements that could sustain life. They had soon selected Earth. Here was water and oxygen in abundance. The Brain had, therefore, made another manoeuvre and moved in for a closer probe, finally settling itself in a new orbit around this promising world.

The phenomenal energy force that has brought it here has been created by the awesome blending of matter and antimatter. Though almost all of this lethal fuel has been expended on its mammoth trek across space, sufficient remains safely isolated in powerful magnetic force fields for any movements it might wish to make in our Solar System.

Already the Brain has transmitted a detailed report on

Earth to its own planet, though it will take many years to get there. It has analysed the rich composition of the atmosphere. But there is no evidence of an advanced technology. If intelligent beings exist they are a comparatively backward race. There is no evidence of powerful radio signals, so there is little point in attempting long-distance contact. The amount of energy under their control is minimal. There are no indications of any exploitation of nuclear power.

The Brain considers all the relevant data. It has little to fear in making an even closer survey of the planet. It decides to despatch a research lander on to the Earth's surface, so it prepares to move into a tighter orbit. The calculations must be infallible, every movement precise. Already matching the Earth's orbital speed, the Brain now orders that little extra boost to overtake it and to nudge itself into its new 'parking area'.

Below sweeps the wrinkled face of Earth's ragged land forms, puckered and rutted and flaking into the vast blue oceans like multi-coloured peeling coats of paint that have been blistered and ravaged by its turbulent adolescence. It passes over the icing sugar of the North Pole that merge. into the nooks and crannies of the frozen Canadian wastes Now it is a soap-bubble world as all the Brain 'sees' is the enormous water expanse of the Pacific.

One area dominates the attention of the geological and biological analysis cells in the Brain. It is the middle of Earth's greatest land mass. Central eastern Europe. Sprawling in all directions is the whole range of the planet's surface structure. Here is where intelligent life might flourish. This is the region on which the investigation must be concentrated. It moves in closer. Too close. It is entering the dense buffeting atmosphere of the Earth.

The first indications of a malfunction in this masterpiece of astro-engineering is a 'red alert' to the Brain, originating from the auxiliary fuel areas alongside the combustion chamber of the craft. The magnetic force-field is breaking up. An instantaneous series of system checks are fed through the computer cells. Rapid counter-measures are

161

put into operation. They have no effect. The force-field continues to collapse.

The Brain battles with every permutation in its vast programme to control its flight path. But now it is streaking deeper into the quagmire of the clawing atmosphere. Its outer shell ignites like a fireball a thousand times its real size. At any moment the deadly antimatter fuel will make suicidal contact with the ordinary matter of the surrounding fuel chamber. The power supplies controlling the other force fields die.

The moment of annihilation occurs at seventeen minutes and eleven seconds after midnight (GMT) five miles above the dense *taiga* of Central Siberia. In an almighty flash of gamma rays an explosion vapourizes the spacecraft in one dreadful microsecond of fury. Destruction is absolute. No vestige of it remains. 'Mission Earth' is over.

Nearly four hundred miles away to the south a train on the trans-Siberian railway that snakes across the desolate land below grinds to a halt. The passengers scamper on to the track . . . For a few moments they listen to dull thuds and distant rumblings. Then nothing more. The air is still again . . .

If, in fact, this fascinating scenario *did* occur in 1908, it would have been some years before the Brain's last dramatic message reached the intelligence that had despatched it. Even if it had come from a planet of the nearest star, Alpha Centauri, the radio 'news flash' of its destruction would have taken more than four years to cover the journey across space. But, however long it took, the probe would have already transmitted enough pictures and data for an advanced intelligence to know that Earth was an ideal world to sustain life . . . that it was a place well worth further investigation. It is almost certain, therefore, that it would decide to send a second probe to carry on the interrogation started by its luckless predecessor.

But this time there would be no mistakes. The frantic stream of information on its failure that the Brain would have pumped out in those final dying seconds as it plunged Earthwards, would enable the alien scientists to produce a more sophisticated probe that would be programmed to cope with any similar emergencies.

So has a replacement probe already been sent here? Could it in fact be orbiting Earth at this very moment? It is at this point that the whole situation becomes *really* intriguing. Because in October 1973, the Russian astro-physicist Dr Nikolai Kardashev and two other scientists at the Gorky Radio Institute – Academician Samuil Kaplan and Professor Vsevlod Troitsky – claimed they had actually picked up sequences of radio signals from space that *could* have originated from an alien intelligence. *And they appeared to be coming from somewhere without our own Solar System,* which could only mean they were being transmitted by an extra-terrestrial probe.

The signals, claimed the Russian newsagency Tass, occurred in 'trains of pulses after definite lapses of time and are repeated over a wide range of wavelengths'. Kardashev was later quoted in the American press as saying: 'The character of the signals, their consistent pattern and their regular transmissions, leave us in no doubt that they are of artificial origin – that is, they are not natural signals.' Troitsky was reported as saying they were 'definitely calls signs from an extra-terrestrial civilization'.

These signals are said to have been detected simultaneously from widely separated areas of Russia, which completely eliminates local sources. The wavelengths on which they were transmitted are those that scientists would expect aliens to use if they were attempting to make contact. They were those that would not be unduly distorted by ionospheric disturbances. The sequence in which they were transmitted – specific trains of pulses each lasting a few minutes – is precisely the kind an orbiting probe would be likely to adopt.

No further confirmation or denials of these startling announcements by the Russians have been received by Western scientists. In July 1976, the Soviet press agency, Novosti, had still been sent nothing further on the signals despite their requests for information. We do not know if they were successfully decoded or whether others have been received since. We *do* know however that the search for extra-terrestrial signals at Gorky and other places in the USSR has intensified since.

So, if these signals *were* alien – if they were not emanating from a runaway man-made satellite or some unidentified natural source – could they be coming from a probe sent to replace the one that exploded over Tunguska? For *this* time, a computerized satellite would have no doubt the world is inhabited by intelligent beings. There is now unquestionable evidence of this from the intense output of powerful radio signals transmitted into space from innumerable sources every moment of the day.

So the next question must be: Where could these probes have come from? There are 150 billion stars in our galaxy alone. How can we possibly begin to pick out the right one? Oddly enough, the task is not all that formidable. We can reduce the candidates to a very small number. From 1908, when we shall assume the original probe was destroyed over Siberia, to 1973, when Kardashev announced he had picked up artificial signals, is sixty-five years. *Theoretically* this means that the furthest possible distance the planet could be from Earth is thirty-two and a half light years. This allows thirty-two and a half years for the distress signal to get back from the *first* probe, and a further thirty-two and a half years for a *second* probe to reach the Earth travelling at the speed of light.

But, in *practice*, the maximum distance is considerably less. It is unlikely a spaceship would travel at the speed of light. It would be extremely risky and uneconomical. The highest velocity an advanced race would be likely to consider for such a comparatively short interstellar journey is about half the speed of light. This would drastically cut down the amount of fuel, (and consequently the space vehicle's original size), and also reduce the damaging effects of interstellar matter that might put vital and sensitive life-seeking instruments out of action, rendering the entire mission useless.

Travelling at this more logical velocity narrows the choice

of possible star systems to a twenty light-year radius of Earth. This restricts us to eighty-one visible stars (see Appendix VII). But we can reduce this figure even further. For various reasons it is highly unlikely that the majority of these eighty-one stars are suitable to encourage the evolution of any kind of life-form that we can conceive. However, within this twenty light-year limit, are *nine* star systems that certainly could be. And a number of these stars are known to have planets orbiting them. Some, too, are almost exactly like our own Sun. This means that any form of intelligent life might be very similar to our own. Their systems could be based on carbon, water and oxygen. This does not necessarily mean they would *look* like we do. Like automobiles, you can produce a vast range of conflicting designs, but their basic functions are the same. Communication and some acceptable level of compatibility would, therefore, be feasible. So let us now do a run-down on those nine star systems that would appear to have life-sustaining characteristics.

The nearest is the binary (double) system of Alpha Centaurus, 4.3 light years away. It consists of two stars, Alpha Centauri A and B. Centauri A is virtually a twin of our own Sun. It is in the same spectral class and 1.3 times as luminous. Its companion star, Centauri B, is about as close as the solar planet Saturn is to Earth. A Pioneer-type space vehicle could shuffle between the stars quite comfortably.

We can consider Alpha Centauri A for an example of how a man-made probe mission from Earth might work out. If the spaceship transporting it there accelerated at one Earth gravity (1g) for one year, it would reach a speed of more than 90 per cent that of light in a distance of half a light year. It would then coast at this speed for another three years. *Deceleration* would then take a further one year, so that it would arrive in the region of Alpha Centauri in about five years. A radio signal travelling back to Earth at the speed of light announcing its arrival would take 4.3 years, making a minimum total mission time of a little over nine years.

If the probe moved through space at *half* the speed of light, it would reach Alpha Centauri in eleven years. Add the 4.3 years for its arrival message to get back to Earth, and we get a total mission duration of roughly fifteen years. This compares with a twenty-year mission time at 30 per cent the speed of light and forty-eight years at 10 per cent.

An obvious question, if we consider Alpha Centaurus as the star system sending an Earth-bound probe, is why they would bother to do so when they are so close they could have been picking up our radio signals for nearly half a century? A possible answer is that they might wish to know far more about us through secret orbital surveys before rushing blindly ahead with direct communication. It is a basic instinct of all known life-forms to approach any unfamiliar species with caution – learning as much about the other as they can before announcing their presence. Similarly, an alien race might want to know how advanced we were and whether we were the type of society that could be a threat to them in any way.

The next nearest star system worth considering is Epsilon Eridani, 10.69 light years from our Sun. This is one of the two stars on which Dr Frank Drake, now director of the National Astronomy and Ionospheric Centre at Arecibo, Puerto Rico, concentrated his search for extra-terrestrial signals during 'Project Ozma' in the early 1960s. Epsilon Eridani also appears to have planets. We can't *see* them, but astronomers can detect their presence by the slight 'wobbly' movement of the star caused by the gravitational pull of large planets orbiting it. Epsilon Eridani is believed to have at least one giant planet, about eight times the mass of Jupiter.

A little over eleven light years from Earth is Epsilon Indi. Here life is just about credible, though the star is only 13 per cent as brilliant as the Sun. About the same distance is Tau Ceti – the second star chosen for examination during Project Ozma. It is a very good candidate indeed for intelligent life. Half as bright as the Sun, any planet orbiting it at about the distance of Venus (65 million miles) would produce ideal Earth-like conditions.

A satellite probe travelling to Tau Ceti from Earth would take twenty-six years cruising at half the speed of light.

Allowing almost another twelve years for an arrival signal to get back, would make a total mission time of thirty-eight years. This would increase to fifty-five years moving at 30 per cent the speed of light and 133 years at 10 per cent.

At almost seventeen light years distance is the star system called 70 Ophiuchi, suspected of having planets, and, at eighteen light years, 36 Ophiuchi – twin stars with light outputs one quarter that of the Sun and appearing to be quite capable of supporting Earth-like planets. In the same range are two other likely stars, Sigma Draconis and Delta Pavonis – the latter, like Alpha Centauri A, having a light output almost exactly that of the Sun.

We now come to the final, and most exciting, star in the twenty-light-year radius for possible sources of probes since 1908. It is called Eta Cassiopeiae A – 19.2 light years away. In every respect it is virtually an identical twin of our Sun. Its mass is similar, its light output is almost the same, and its companion star is known to have planets moving around it. This being the case it is reasonably certain that Cassiopeiae A has planets too, which would have been created from the same residual material when both these stars were first formed. It is so Sun-like that, as explained earlier, a form of intelligent life could well be similar in many respects to our own. It could, therefore, well wish to investigate us.

Another striking factor is that its life-time is comparable to that of the Sun, and it is very slightly brighter. This would produce a higher degree of radiation which might result in a greater mutation rate than that which occurs on our own Earth. This being so, one would expect any intelligent beings there to have developed at a slightly faster rate. They would therefore be technically more advanced than mankind, and would be expected to be far better equipped in the field of interstellar travel and communication.

In every aspect Cassiopeiae A must be considered the most likely source of advanced intelligent life within twenty light years of Earth. And the remarkable thing is that this star fits precisely into our time scale of sixty-five years (the period from the Tunguska explosion in 1908 to the first report of those Russian signals in 1973) if we are to consider a logical mission project.

This is how such a mission could have progressed:

*June 1908:* Probe explodes over Siberia and transmits final radio message back to Eta Cassiopeiae, 19.2 light years away.

*Mid-September 1927:* Message received. It is apparent from the probe's earlier data that Earth is suitable for life. A second probe is justified. This takes between one and two years to plan, construct, test and launch.

*1929:* A spaceship carrying probe number two blasts off from Eta Cassiopeiae. It is designed to travel at half the speed of light – the most logical choice of velocity to cover the journey in a reasonable time and to give an acceptably efficient consumption of propulsion energy. To travel those 19.2 light years – allowing five years for acceleration at launch and deceleration into the Solar System – takes a total of 43.4 years.

*1972:* The probe settles in an orbit around the Earth and begins transmitting signals. These are picked up by Kardashev at Gorky and the first news is released by the news-agency Tass in October 1973.

# CONCLUSION

30 June 1908, is a lifetime ago. Bustling new cities and sprawling industrial networks now grope across the once forlorn wilderness of Siberia – frisking its copious pockets of mineral wealth. Flourishing young communities are taking root where only the *taiga* grew. And armies of fresh young scientists regularly pound along the concrete routes that long-since covered Kulik's pioneering tracks. All eager to pay homage at the overgrown graveyard of the monster that nature never fails to garnish with her continually-replenished wreaths of botanical abundance.

Like surgeons they prod and cut away the earth and amputate the trees, then scurry off back to space-age laboratories equipped with every conceivable technological refinement. Still hoping that, somewhere from these endless post-mortems, the true secret of the Southern Swamp will suddenly emerge.

Yet, despite the most searching techniques; despite a mighty reservoir of evidence and specimens that has accrued from half a century of exploration, analysis and debate, *some* gaping loophole, some flaw in an otherwise air-tight solution inevitably shows up. Still the mystery remains officially listed 'unclassified'. Nothing, it seems, in the continually widening field of known natural phenomena can fully explain what really happened.

With each passing decade, the chances of solving the riddle diminish. Even from the first soil samples taken half a century ago, it is extremely difficult to identify any tell-tale explosion materials from those that accumulated naturally in the earth. In any case the vast proportion of any chemical evidence would have vanished in the explosion and been lifted and dispersed into the stratosphere as dust, producing those bright skies over many parts of the world in July 1908. What was left in the ground offers few clues either. The intense heat of the blast melted the separate grains of sand and clay to form those small balls or spherules of glass. It is virtually impossible now for scientists to classify these.

As men continue to scoop up the soil of Tunguska, NASA's mechanical Viking probe is doing precisely the same thing on the boulder-strewn surface of Mars. It is ironical that, though these computerized invaders millions of miles from home are already sending us back the secrets of a planet we have never even set foot on, our most brilliant scientists still cannot unravel a mystery right here on our own Earth. But perhaps, indirectly, Viking is also offering the clue to Tunguska. Perhaps it was also such a self-disciplined satellite that contained the appalling power to devastate the taiga and all evidence of itself in the awesome process.

But, whatever caused the Siberian Event, there is the inevitable question: where and when will it happen again? Certainly it must make us all aware of just how vulnerable this tiny world of ours really is in the turbulent Universe. For how can we take even the most familiar forces of nature for granted – let alone the many unknown ones that lurk out there beyond the flimsy barrier of our atmosphere? That seemingly empty space about us can be ruthlessly unpredictable. We can never tell when some friendly little glow in the night sky might once again suddenly become the most destructive missile man has ever encountered.

On 20 October 1976, one such missile nearly collided with Earth. It was one of the nearest misses ever recorded. The object was an asteroid. Had it struck a populated area the results would most certainly have been catastrophic. The asteroid, hundreds of yards across, passed 750,000 miles from our planet. That sounds a long way off. In astronomical terms it is frighteningly close. Astronomers coded it '1976 UA' and it was photographed at Mount Palomar as it sped by in its orbit round the Sun. It will be centuries before this missile comes as close again. But, remember, there are countless others where it came from.

Even our own Sun – the very furnace of life – will one day reduce everything it has created to ashes. It will die. And in its tortuous death throes it will transform into an enormous 'Red Giant', 250 times its normal diameter, slowly incinerating its entire family of planets. But that may not happen for billions of years. Perhaps the most immediate threat to life on this Earth is the unpredictability of man himself. For though no-one knows what the thing that ravaged Tunguska really was, *everyone* knows of a brute that could cause the same kind of insane devastation. For man has already created his own Siberian monsters ... enough of them to reduce the entire civilized world to one gigantic Cauldron of Hell. Caged in the nuclear reservations of the major powers, they are breeding at an alarming rate.

*Perhaps the Tunguska Event is a timely message to us all.*

# APPENDICES

# APPENDIX I

*Analysis of Tunguska peat samples* (see chapter 5)

In 1971 the leading Soviet scientific journal *Doklady Akademii Nauk USSR* published the results of tests on peat at Tunguska by Dr Yuri Dolgov and a team from the Meteorite and Cosmic Dust Commission of the Academy of Sciences. Dolgov dug samples to depths of eleven to fourteen inches. They included peat dating from 1908 containing residual material from the explosion. When this was isolated from the normal material by washing and burning the peat, it was found to consist of tiny glass-like spherules of various sizes. The largest were 1.4 mm (about one twentieth of an inch) in diameter. The smallest were 10 to 180 micro millimetres (about 4 to 80 micro inches). The largest were mostly transparent or colourless; the smaller ones were a variety of colours including blue and green. Some were black.

Their composition was unlike that of surrounding rocks and stones of the Podkamennaya Tunguska region. Neither did they have a make-up resembling Moon rock samples. The closest comparisons the Russians could make for these spherules were to tektites – flat-shaped discs found in parts of Australia, South-East Asia, Texas, the Ivory Coast and Czechoslovakia. These are mostly of a silica-rich glass (about 75 per cent silica) with a composition close to granite. The true origin of tektites is unknown, but some scientists believe they may be the products of impacts by comets or giant meteorites on the Earth's surface. However the resemblance was not entirely the same and the Tunguska material was richer in sodium and potassium. Concentrations of aluminium, silicon, calcium, magnesium and iron were present in both.

The Russians also analysed *soil* at the Tunguska site which would contain traces of normal meteoritic and cosmic dust. These were not the same as the material found in the samples preserved in the peat. The soil had been contaminated by industrial products whereas the peat samples remained uncontaminated, having been sealed between the original moss and that growing over it since 1908.

There is no mention in Dolgov's report of germanium – a material claimed to have been found in earlier analyses, and one that has been associated with the possible remains of a spaceship's semi-conductors and transistors. In any case germanium can be found in ordinary meteorites. In the late 1960s, Drs A. V. Jain and M. E. Lipschutz of Purdue University, La Fayette, Indiana, found evidence of germanium in 117 samples of meteorites from different areas. The amounts were within a narrow margin of about twenty parts per million.

Jain and Lipschutz believe most of their samples came from the Apollo family of asteroids whose closest approach to the Sun lies between Earth and Venus. Hermes and Adonis are two such 'mini-planets'. For each of these larger objects there are thousands more smaller ones, some merely a few feet across. Asteroids from this family are believed to have collided with Earth in the past and will certainly do so in the future. The result of a substantial one falling on a populous city would be catastrophic.

# APPENDIX II

*'Natural nuclear bombs'* (see chapter 5)

Given the right ingredients and conditions, Nature herself can produce 'H-bombs'. It happens on an enormous scale in stars like our own Sun, which throws off four million tons as light every second. A nuclear-type explosion might take place in the head of a comet by what could be termed 'superfuels'. These are perhaps a hundred times more powerful than ordinary petrol or coal. They are not in themselves 'nuclear', and do not directly produce nuclear explosions. But under extreme build up of heat in a comet head entering Earth's atmosphere, they may do so.

This would be caused by the compression of the air building up in front of the comet, which acts as a brake on the fast-moving body. The air becomes white hot and superdense in the process. Anything trapped inside the comet cannot get out except by bursting the outer shell.

In one theory, comets are believed to be composed of solid frozen gases locked up in a strong stony outer casing. The Tunguska object might have been such a comet, its core consisting of frozen hydrogen and ammonia and mixed with liquid helium, in what is called a 'triplet' state. Helium in this condition stores energy which is about ten to a hundred times more powerful than ordinary explosives. In addition it changes state and attempts to form ordinary gaseous helium at very high temperature (40 000 degrees centigrade at ordinary atmospheric pressure). If the pressure is raised to 125 atmospheres (1800 lbs per square inch), the temperature approaches that required to detonate heavy hydrogen (about five million degrees centigrade). If the pressure rises to double this (3600 lbs per square inch), the temperature produced by the triplet helium suddenly changing state, may be enough to detonate ordinary hydrogen.

The thick stony shell could possibly contain this pressure

before it burst. Meanwhile the white-hot atmosphere would burn away the outer layer of the shell at the front where the shock waves were fiercest.

The sequence of events can, therefore, be summarized as follows: The comet enters the atmosphere and the heat generated starts to 'cook' the inside of the core and also to wear away the shell which disappears as a cloud of dust trailing behind. Eventually the tightly-packed core reaches a critical temperature where the trapped gases try to change state. They cannot, because the thick shell prevents this. Up goes the temperature caused by the explosively-changing state of the internally trapped gases. If the outer shell can hold together up to the correct critical pressure, then the temperature is forced to a point where any trapped hydrogen detonates or fuses to form helium, as in a normal H-Bomb. The amount of hydrogen needed to produce a thirty megaton explosion is not large (about 2000 lbs), for a proportion of the energy will come from the other parts of the pent-up gases being released.

The detonation, of course, would destroy most of the stony shell, though some of it might be melted into silicate spherules. Those found at Tunguska are said to have some resemblance to tektites (see Appendix I). These are a rocky glass material similar to Earth granite. Some forms of granite might be tough enough to form a shell able to contain up to 3600 lbs per square inch pressure.

# APPENDIX III

*Black Holes and ball lightning* (see chapters 6 and 7)

Dr Steven Hawking (*Nature*, vol. 248, 1974) has produced a general formula for small black holes showing that, below a critical limit of half the Earth's mass, a hole cannot sustain itself and will exist for only a geologically short time (a million years at the most). Smaller holes have shorter lives. This is a serious flaw in associating the phenomena with the Tunguska Event. For such an encounter with Earth, the black hole must be expected to have been in existence for a reasonably long period. If so, it would be at or near Hawking's limit. In this case it would demolish the Earth on impact.

When considering the possibility of 'micro black holes' being created by the action of lightning, it is possible to estimate the size such a hole would have to be to correspond with the lifetime of only a few minutes or seconds.

Professor John Taylor of King's College, in his book *Black Holes*, calculates that the energy obtainable from a single black hole has a theoretical upper limit of 30 per cent of the total rest mass. In other words $E = \dfrac{mc^2}{3}$. This is at least one hundred times more efficient than fusion energy. But, let us assume that a micro black hole lightning ball extracts only 5 to 10 per cent of the energy of the mass. We can then calculate the mass of a black hole sufficiently explosive to demolish an average-sized room. This would roughly correspond to an explosive charge of one to ten kilograms (2.5 to 25 lbs) of TNT. So how much matter is required to produce this force when used at an efficiency of 10 per cent?

Scientists use a unit called the 'erg' when relating mass and energy. In the case of the Tunguska explosion we are dealing with $10^{24}$ ergs of energy, producing the equivalent of thirty megatons of TNT. If we scale this down, we get the reduced comparison of one kilogram of TNT explosive being equal to $5 \times 10^{13}$ ergs. Ten kilograms of TNT will equal $5 \times 10^{14}$ ergs. We can now work out the equivalent mass of a micro black hole.

The rest mass energy of 1 kg of any matter is $10^{24}$ ergs. To get $5 \times 10^{13}$ ergs, we require only $5 \times 10^{-11}$ kg if we have 100 per cent efficiency. But we are assuming the micro black hole is only 5 to 10 per cent efficient in obtaining energy. The mass is therefore larger (about $10^{-9}$ kg).

A tiny fraction of matter compressed into a micro black hole produces the explosion of ball lightning. The mass involved is one billionth of a kilogram, or roughly half a billionth of a pound of mass. Since this mass would be tremendously compressed, the diameter of the sphere into which it is contained works out at $4 \times 10^{-27}$ metres, which is smaller than the diameter of a hydrogen atom.

It can be estimated that a one foot-wide lightning ball or *Kugelblitz* has a total energy force of ten million joules of which it dissipates some 20 per cent, or two million joules. A joule is equal to $10^7$ ergs. Two million joules equals $2 \times 10^{13}$ ergs. Lawton now estimates the size of a *Kugelblitz* capable of causing the Tunguska devastation. Assuming that the energy is proportional to the volume of the explosive (whatever that was), then the volume of the Siberian object would be larger by the ratio of $10^{24}$ divided by $2 \times 10^{13}$ ... or $5 \times 10^{10}$ larger. The volume of a sphere is proportional to the cube of its diameter, so the diameter of the sphere would be the cube root of $5 \times 10^{10}$ larger than the one-foot *Kugelblitz*. This works out at 3700 feet, or a little over one kilometre.

It has been suggested that ball lightning is composed of dust bound tightly together by an electrical charge. Professor Lyttleton of the Mathematics Department at Cambridge University firmly believes that comets, too, are large dust balls. A likely force in space that might bind the dust into a ball could be electrostatic charges. These could be generated by the solar wind particles 'rubbing' the outer layers of the dust and debris. The wind particles are small and, in the outer parts of the Solar System, are not intense enough to disrupt the comet as may happen when it sweeps towards the Sun. The 'rubbing' process produces similar effects to those from polishing a piece of amber, causing it to attract dust or bits of paper.

The electrical charge in a comet cloud can be enormous – literally billions of volts. There is no way for the charge to leak away in the insulation of space. If a one kilometre electrostatically-charged *Kugelblitz* entered the Earth's atmosphere, it is just possible it would disintegrate in a giant electrical flash. This could produce the scorching radiant energy, the searing shock waves and the negative pressure effect (NPE) referred to in chapter 9.

# APPENDIX IV

*Notes on antimatter* (see chapter 7)

The simplest possible atom, that of hydrogen, consists of a central core or nucleus with only one proton. Around this central core spins a single electron, much like a lone star with only one planet orbiting it. Traditionally, the electron is associated with a negative electrical charge, which means that the proton must have an equal and opposite positive charge if the atom itself has zero charge. In other words, the opposing charges of the proton and the electron cancel each other out.

In 1933 it was suggested that there should be 'anti-particles' which were mirror images of the conventional ones, the central proton being *negative* and the electron positive, thus still preserving an overall zero charge as in the case with ordinary material. This speculation was confirmed when the 'positive electron' or 'positron' was discovered in 1934. Since then a number of other anti-particles have been recognized – such as anti-protons (sometimes called negative protons), anti-neutrons, anti-neutrinos, etc. – as higher and higher energies are used to smash up atoms and their flying debris examined.

The following list is the atomic composition of a few well-known materials referred to in the main body of this book, together with their antimatter counterparts. In each case the number of protons, neutrons and electrons contained in the normal matter are equal to the negative protons, anti-neutrons and positrons of the antimatter. For example: carbon has 6 protons, 6 neutrons and 6 electrons. Anti-carbon, therefore, has 6 negative protons, 6 anti-neutrons and 6 positrons.

Other combinations are: oxygen and anti-oxygen (8,6,8); silicon and anti-silicon (16,16,16); uranium U235 and anti-U235 (92,143,92); plutonium 242 and anti-plutonium 242

(94,148,94). Hydrogen has only one proton and one electron giving anti-hydrogen one negative proton and one positron.

If we attempt to mix any of the above pairs – or indeed any other material with its *exact* mirror image – it would invariably result in the same enormous release of gamma-ray energy. But what would happen if we mixed *different* types of matter–antimatter elements – for example silicon with anti-carbon? (silicon has 16 protons, 16 neutrons and 16 electrons whereas anti-carbon has only 6 negative protons, 6 anti-neutrons and six positrons). After the initial gamma flash we would theoretically be left with a material that had 10 protons, 10 neutrons and 10 electrons. No such material exists. Instead the residue would sort itself out so that some of the protons would swiftly change into neutrons, the positrons given off decaying in gamma radiation by meeting stray electrons.

A likely material remaining would be ordinary carbon (6 protons, 6 neutrons, 6 electrons), leaving 4 protons, 4 neutrons and 4 electrons over, which conveniently splits into two atoms of deuterium (heavy hydrogen) ... i.e. two sets of 2 electrons, 2 neutrons and 2 protons. We would, in fact, have lost the antimatter in the energy flash and produced a residue of ordinary matter which may or may not be similar to the original. In the above example we would be left with ordinary carbon and ordinary heavy hydrogen, more correctly termed deuterium.

## APPENDIX V

### *Nuclear reaction notes* (see chapter 7)

The nuclear physicist looks for processes which involve a loss of mass between elements at the start of the process and those left at the finish. The classical case is that of U235 which splits up naturally and of its own accord. In doing so, the massive uranium atom splits into two unequal parts. One part is the metal barium of mass 139; the other is the metal molybdenum of mass 95. Therefore the mass left over is 234/235 or 0.996 of the original. This means that the tremendous explosion release in an atom bomb is caused by the loss of only 0.4 per cent of the mass.

When dealing with nuclear reactors, the reaction rate is slowed down and the explosive chain reaction kept to a continuous but controlled heat. In early reactors the temperature was nearly 400 degrees centigrade (black heat), but in later models the working temperatures are much higher. The total amounts of working material in some of these reactors is large, but the actual matter destroyed is still extremely small (about 0.05 to 0.2 per cent of the original weight). In practical terms, the size of a block of uranium used to drive a nuclear submarine round the world is roughly equal to half a house-brick. We would be left with a mixture of barium and molybdenum metals whose size would be slightly smaller than the original block of uranium. But the amount of actual matter that had vanished would be roughly equivalent to a couple of sugar lumps.

### *Definition of 'half life'* (See Appendix VI)

Half life is a term used by the nuclear physicist to determine how long a radioactive material may exist. Most of the 92 natural elements in the Periodic Table are stable, but a few of them are naturally radioactive. This means they decay by giving off particles or rays and transform into different elements. For example, uranium U235, the metal normally associated with nuclear bombs, will, if left to itself, gradually decompose to form lead. Therefore if, at the present time, we have 1 lb of U235, then at some time in the far distant future we should have slightly less than 1 lb of lead. The balance of weight lost will have disappeared as energy. But how long will we have to wait?

U235 has a half life of 71 million years. This means that after that period we would have lost half our original weight of uranium (i.e. half a pound). In a further 71 million years we would have lost another quarter of a pound, then a further one-eighth of a pound, and so on. In 213 million years, 7/8 of the U235 would have turned to lead and, after another 213 million years, 63/64 of it would be lead.

It should be noted that U235 (unless stacked in large quantities) is not *violently* radioactive material. However radium, the element discovered by Pierre and Marie Curie, is an extremely radioactive element. It can assume a variety of forms, the most active of which is radium 224 that quickly decays to thorium in just over three-and-a-half days. The variety discovered by the Curies and used for the treatment of cancer, is radium 226, which has a half life of 1600 years. Even so, this is short, and accounts for the struggle the Curies had in obtaining this rare and valuable element.

From a ton of crude pitchblende ore they obtained a few micrograms of radium – enough to discolour the bottom of the dish holding it. But the radioactive glow from the stain lit up their laboratory and badly burned the hands of Marie Curie and other pioneer radiologists, making them the first radiation 'victims'.

Some materials have half lives in millionths or billionths of a second, others in billions of years. However, they are still radioactive and must not be confused with the entirely stable elements that will last indefinitely.

# APPENDIX VI

*Test for antimatter at Tunguska* (see chapters 7 and 14)

Dr Hall Crannell (*Nature*, vol. 248, pp. 396, 397) points out that a matter–antimatter explosion should produce aluminium 26 (symbol $^{26}$Al) by interaction with silicon. The most common form of silicon is silicon 28 (symbol $^{28}$Si). In such an explosion, a proton and an anti-proton annihilate and produce an average of four charged pions (pi-mesons) and two neutral pions. If the silicon 28 absorbs *one* charged pion, it will become ordinary aluminium 27, which is not radioactive and not detectable. However, if it absorbed *two* pions (and there would be plenty around in such an explosion), it would then become aluminium 26 which *is* radioactive and, therefore, can be detected.

Dr Crannell goes on to illustrate the type of counter system that could be used, and then shows that, with aluminium 26 having a radioactive half life of 750 000 years (see Appendix V), and the number of aluminium 26 atoms in the Tunguska site centre estimated as $2 \times 10^9$ per lb of rock, there should be an extremely good chance of finding such material should a matter–antimatter explosion have occurred. Crannell estimates that in such an explosion the dosage concentration of $^{26}$Al should be 15 per cent higher than the normal background dosage received by the surrounding area in one million years. Since his counter system can detect an increase as small as a few per cent (say less than five), he feels confident that this test could confirm whether the explosion was due to antimatter.

His test has not yet been carried out, but we have been able to examine the results of the mineral composition of small silicate spherules obtained from the impact area. The composition is quite different from that of normal rock. Crannell considered his average rock as having 29 per cent silicon and 8 per cent aluminium, but our information shows that the Tunguska material has a silicon content of approximately 25 per cent and an aluminium content of 2 per cent, the balance largely being oxygen and traces of iron and manganese. With silicon/aluminium ratios much higher than Earth rocks, it is highly probable that the aluminium *will* have a high per centage of $^{26}Al$ should it be the residue of a matter–antimatter explosion.

The current (1976) expedition despatched by the USSR Academy of Sciences, will almost certainly collect rock and soil samples from the impact area. If they subject these to the Crannell test and *do* find high levels of $^{26}Al$ (in which case the antimatter theory is acceptable), then the most likely source of the material would be *artificial* rather than natural (see chapter 14). Natural antimatter would have great difficulty in surviving contact with dense particles in the Solar System. The Sun, too, emits a continuous stream of solar wind particles and is itself enveloped in a cloud of dust which reaches out beyond the asteroid belt and shows as the Zodiacal Light. This dust and gas is relatively harmless to ordinary objects (including our own spacecraft), but if an antimatter object entered the Solar System, it would be continuously attacked and gradually eroded in a tremendous outpour of energy. This would produce the bright blue 'tube' seen by witnesses in Siberia.

If anti-rock did reach the ground and bury itself, there would be the most frightful explosion, certainly capable of causing the damage recorded. However a ground explosion would leave a crater several miles across and seismographs in various parts of the world would have recorded appropriate *crustal* earthquake shock, not the surface waves which were reported.

## Antimatter used as rocket fuel (see chapter 14)

Antimatter material used as a rocket fuel would be reacted with ordinary matter to form pure radiant energy. If this was focused in some way not as yet developed by our technology, the most conceivably efficient interstellar propulsion system would result. With a matter–antimatter rocket capable of travelling at 90 per cent the speed of light, every ton of payload would require 34 tons of fuel, i.e. an equal amount of matter and antimatter. A Saturn rocket has to carry 1200 tons of conventional fuel for every ton of payload to attain a speed of only 25 000 miles an hour.

# APPENDIX VII

*Nearest stellar targets for automated probes and the use of
antimatter energized propulsion* (see chapter 15)

(Excerpts from 'A national space programme for interstellar
exploration', by Dr L. Forward, Hughes Research Laboratories, Malibu, California. Submitted at the invitation of the
Subcommittee on Space Science and Applications, Committee on Science and Technology, United States House of
Representatives, July 1975).

Within twenty light years of the Sun there are fifty-nine
stellar systems containing eighty-one visible stars. These
include forty-one single stars, fifteen binary and three
triple systems.

First-generation probes will search for planets existing
in a temperature zone roughly equivalent to the Venus–
Jupiter zone in the Solar System. This includes not only
planets in single-star systems, but also small satellites of
large Jovian-type planets orbiting within the correct temperature zone of the primary, and those planets in binary
(and triple) systems whose total incident energy flux
raises surface temperatures to the correct levels. Also
included are those planets with highly eccentric orbits,
which spend only part of their orbital period within the
correct zone.

Since one star, our Sun, is positively known to possess
a planetary system, it can only be assumed that stars
similar to the Sun in spectral type, mass, radius and
luminosity also have some possibility of possessing a
planetary system. By using a star's similarity to the Sun
as a selection criterion, we hopefully will be choosing
target stellar systems not only for their potential planetary
systems but also on their ability to support life.

The Sun is a GO-type star with an effective temperature

of ∼5900 degrees K. Unfortunately there is only one other G0 star (Alpha Centauri A) and a total of only four G-type stars within 20 light years. The selection criterion can be extended to include all the cooler K-type stars. Below these lie the red dwarfs (M-type), generally regarded as being too small and cool to supply the required amount of energy for life to any planet, except one in an extremely close orbit. This has led many to eliminate red dwarf stars as prospective targets for interstellar probes. However, we know that red dwarfs have planets (six of the eight stars known to have planets are red dwarfs) and until we are sure that a system has no planet within its life-supporting zone, we should not eliminate it from consideration as a potential target for an interstellar probe.

Since more than 25 per cent of the stellar systems under consideration are multiple, the possibility of a planet occurring in a stable orbit and a temperature zone conducive to life in a multiple system must be considered. For a while it was thought that in most multiple systems the formation of several stars simultaneously prevented the formation of a planetary system. However, at least two binary systems, 61 Cygni and Eta Cassiopeiae, are known to have planetary companions.

For missions to the nearby stars, we do not need vehicle velocities very close to that of light, so we do not need the exhaust velocity to be that of light. A more efficient method is to use a small amount of antimatter to energize a much larger amount of regular matter.

An optimized engineering study of an interstellar propulsion system using antimatter has yet to be done, but some approximate numbers can be estimated now. If we assume the development of a very lightweight (10 kg) interstellar exploration probe design, and an antimatter propulsion system optimized for a probe coast velocity of one-third the speed of light, then the minimum in the mass ratio of each propulsion stage occurs at a mass ratio of 4, and the antimatter mass required is 1/10th of the burnout mass, or 2 per cent of the initial mass. The interstellar probe at launch would consist of a 51-kilogram second stage, 200 kilograms of propellant and 5 kilograms of antimatter. This would suffice to accelerate the second stage to one third the velocity of light. The 51-kilogram second stage would consist of the 10-kilogram exploration probe payload, 40 kilograms of propellant and 1 kilogram of antimatter which would be used to decelerate the probe at the target star.

Besides the obvious engineering problems that remain to be solved in the design of an engine that can effectively convert the antimatter energy into directed thrust of the propellant, there is a real question of the obtainability and control of the antimatter.

The containment and control, once made, should not be too difficult since we have a number of ways of applying forces to the antimatter without touching it. Electric fields, magnetic fields, rf fields and laser beams are all used in present-day technology to levitate and control small amounts of regular matter that we do not want to contaminate. These would all be equally effective on antimatter.

The generation of appreciable amounts of antimatter is the primary engineering problem that should be addressed early in any investigation of the feasibility of using antimatter for interstellar propulsion. We already destroy hundreds of kilograms of regular matter each year in our electric generating plants and convert it to electricity. All we need to do is to develop efficient methods of turning that energy back into antimatter instead of regular matter.

The present methods for producing antimatter involve the use of large linear accelerators which can produce a proton beam of $10^{15}$ protons per second. When such a beam collides with a target, antiprotons are produced as part of the debris. The anti-proton yield is independent of beam energy and is of the order of 1 per cent. Factors such as limitation in the number of anti-protons which can be captured by an applied magnetic field and optimum size of the target in order to avoid collisions of anti-protons with target nuclei reduce further the production of anti-protons by two orders of magnitude. Hence, the rate of anti-proton production is of the order of $10^{11}$ anti-protons per second. Based on this number, the estimated time to produce one kilogram of antiprotons from one machine is $10^8$ years. This number has led some people to the conclusion that the use of antimatter for propulsion purposes is not feasible.

However, the presently used methods are not designed for antimatter production, but rather for studies in the physics of elementary particles. A study to investigate the possibility of increasing antimatter production rates to the level required for propulsion applications would be one of the critical technology areas that should be studied in the initial phases of an interstellar exploration programme. The problems of antimatter storage, annihilation rate control and development of practical propulsion schemes are also those on which future studies should be focused.

# BIBLIOGRAPHY

Altshuler, M. D., House, L. L. and Hilder, E., 'Is ball lightning a nuclear phenomenon?', *Nature*, vol. 228, p. 545, 1970.

Ambartsumyan, V., *Soviet Sputniks*, Soviet New Booklet, No. 25.

Astapovich, I. S., *Soviet Astron.*, vol. 10, p. 465, 1933.

Astapovich, I. S., 'More about the night of 30 June 1908', *Mirovedeniye*, 1926.

Astapovich, I. S., 'Air waves caused by the fall of the meteorite of 30 June 1908 in Central Siberia', *Quart. Jnl Royal Met. Soc.*, 1934, no. 2.

Beasley, W. H. and Tinsley, B. A., 'Tunguska Event was not caused by a Black Hole', *Nature*, vol. 250, pp. 555–6, 1974.

Boyarkina, A. P. and Bronsten, I. S., 'Ob. energii vzryva Tungusskogo meteorita i uchete neodnorodnosti atmosfery', *Astronomicheskii vestnik*, vol. 8, no. 3, pp. 172–7, 1975 (English abstract).

Brown, P. L., *Comets, Meteorites and Men*, Robert Hale, 1973.

Burns, J. O., Greenstein, G. and Verosub, K. L., 'The Tunguska Event as a small Black Hole', *Monthly Notices, R.A.S.*, vol. 175, p. 355–7, 1976.

— 'Centaurus-A powered by a massive Black Hole', *New Scientist*, 29 April 1976.

Charman, N., 'Ball lightning photographed', *New Scientist*, 26 February 1976.

Charman, N., 'The enigma of ball lightning', *New Scientist*, 14 December 1972.

*Comets*, Ash & Grant, 1973.

Crammer, J. L. and Peierls, R. E., *Atomic Energy*, Penguin, 1950.

Crannell, H., 'Experiments to measure the antimatter content of the Tunguska meteorite', *Nature*, vol. 248, pp. 396–8.

Dole, S. and Asimov, I., *Planets for Man*, Rand Corporation, 1964.

Dolgov, Yu. A., Vasil'ev, N. V., L'vov Yu. A., *et al.*, 'Chemical composition of silicate spherules in peats of the Tunguska meteorite fall region', *Akad. Nauk USSR, Doklady*, vol. 200, no. 1, pp. 201–4, 1971.

Feis, H., *The Atomic Bomb and the End of World War II*, Princeton University Press, 1966.

Fesenkov, V. G., 'The nature of the Tunguska Meteorite', *Meteoritika*, 20, pp. 27–31, 1961.

Fleming, S. J. and Aitken, M. J., 'Radiation dosage associated with ball lightning', *Nature*, vol. 252, pp. 220–21, 1974.

Florensky, K. P., 'Preliminary results from the 1961 combined Tunguska Meteorite Expedition', *Meteoritika*, vol. 23, pp. 3–29, 1963.

Galanopoulos, A. G., 'Die ägyptischen Plagen und der Auszug Isreals ans geologischer Sicht', *Das Altertum*, vol. 10, 1964.

Gass, I. G., *Understanding the Earth*, 1972.

Glasstone, S., *Nuclear Reactor Engineering*, Macmillan, 1956.

Glasstone, S., *The Effects of Nuclear Weapons*, US Atomic Energy Commission 1962.

Gregory, J. S., *Russian Land Soviet People*, Harrap, 1968.

Griggs, R. F., 'The Valley of Ten Thousand Smokes', *National Geographical Society*, 1922.

Heilprin, A., *Mount Pelée and the Tragedy of Martinique*, Lippincott, 1903.

Hibbert, C., *London: The Biography of a City*, Longman 1969.

Hindley, K., 'Comets in perspective', *New Scientist*, 17 April 1976.

Hirschfeld, B., *A Cloud over Hiroshima*, Bailey & Swinfen, 1974.

Hughes, D. W., 'Earth: an interplanetary dustbin', *New Scientist*, 8 July 1976.

Ince, M., 'A meteorite crater in Britain', *Hermes*, July 1972.

— 'Invitations from outer space', *Daily Telegraph*, 21 March 1964.

Jackson, A. A. and Ryan, M., 'Was the Tunguska Event due to a Black Hole?' *Nature*, vol. 245, pp. 88–9, 1973.

Jordan, E. C., *Electromagnetic Waves and Radiating Systems*, Prentice-Hall, 1970.

Jungk, R., *Children of the Ashes*, Heinemann, 1961.

Kardashev, N. S., 'Transmission of information by extra-terrestrial civilizations', *Astronomical Journal*, vol. 41, 1964.

Kennan, G., *The Tragedy of Pelée*, Outlook Co., 1902.

Krinov, E. L., 'The Tunguska meteorite', *Publ. Acad. Sciences USSR*, p. 196, 1949.

Krinov, E. L., 'The Siberian meteorite fall of February 1947', *Sky and Telescope*, vol. 15, no. 7, 1956.

Krinov, E. L., 'Der Tungusker Meteorite', *Chemie der Erde*, vol. 20, no. 3, 1958.

Krinov, E. L., *Giant Meteorites*, Pergamon, 1966.

Krinov, E. L., *Principles of Meteorites*, Pergamon, 1960.

Kulik, L. A., 'Account of meteorite expedition', *Journal of the Russian Academy of Sciences*, 1922.

Kulik, L. A., 'On the history of the bolide of 30 June 1908', *Journal of the Russian Academy of Sciences*, 1927.

Kulik, L. A., 'Preliminary results of the meteorite expeditions made in the decade 1921–31', *Works of the Lomonossoff Institute of the Russian Academy of Sciences*, part II, pp. 73–80, 1933.

Kulik, L. A., *Mirovedeniye*, vol. 11, no. 2, pp. 143–4, 1922.

Lawton, A. T., 'Interstellar communication – antenna or artifact', *Journal BIS*, April 1974.

Lawton, A. T., 'The interpretation of signals from space', *Spaceflight*, vol. 15, 1973.

— 'Le mystère de Montauroux', *Nice-Matin*, 11 October 1972.

McCall, G. J., *Meteorites and their Origins*, David & Charles, 1973.

Marinatos, S., 'The volcanic destruction of Minoan Crete', *Antiquity*, 1939.

— 'Massive meteorite blast in Siberia really nuclear explosion?', *National Enquirer*, 13 May 1975.

Mattinson, H. R., 'Project Daedalus: astronomical data on

nearby stellar systems', *Journal of the British Interplanetary Society*, vol. 29, no. 2, 1976.

Mavor, J. W., Jnr, *Voyage to Atlantis*, Putnam, 1969.

— 'Meteorites which bounce off the Earth', *Nature*, vol. 247, p. 423, 1974.

Millman, P. M., *Meteorite Research*, Dordrecht, 1969.

— 'Montauroux', *Nice-Matin*, 12 October, 1972.

— 'Mutation mystery', *Sunday Times*, 4 April 1976.

— 'Newest merchandise of doom', *Daily Telegraph Magazine*, July 1976.

— 'NASA on interstellar flight', *Spaceflight*, July 1976.

— 'New Japanese report registers grim atom bomb toll', *New Scientist*, 15 April 1976.

Moore, P., 'Little Green Men', *Daily Telegraph Magazine*, September 1976.

Obruchev, S. V., 'Concerning the place of the fall of the large Khatanga meteorite of 1908', *Works of the Lomonossoff Institute of the Russian Academy of Sciences*, vol. 10, no. 1, p. 40, 1921.

Parry, A., *Russian Rockets and Missiles*, Macmillan, 1961.

Petrov, G. I. and Stulov, V. P., 'Novaya gipoteza a Tunguskum meteorite', *Zemlya i Vselennava*, no. 4, pp. 74–5, 1975.

Polkanov, A. A., 'Phenomena accompanying the fall of the Tunguska meteorite', *Meteoritika*, vol. 3, p. 69, 1946.

*Pompeii, the Rediscovered City*, Instituto Geografico de Agostini, Novara, 1969.

*Project Daedalus*, Interim Report of the BIS Starship Study.

Rawcliffe, R. D., 'Meteor of 10 August 1972', *Nature*, vol. 247, pp. 449–50, 1974.

Ricketts, A., *Fundamentals of Nuclear Hardening of Electronic Equipment*, Wiley 1972.

Rondière, P., *Siberia Land of Promise*, Constable, 1962.

— 'Secret evidence shows UFOs come from other worlds', *National Enquirer*, 15 July 1975.

Sobolev, V. S., *The Problematic Meteorite*, USSR Academy of Sciences, 1975.

Sorlin, P., *The Soviet People and their Society*, Pall Mall Press, 1968.

Stern, D. K., 'First contact with non-human cultures', *Mercury (Journal Astr. Socty of the Pacific)*, Sept/Oct., 1975, pp. 14–17.

Stewart, W., *Characters of Bygone London*, Harrap, 1960.

Stoneley, J. and Lawton, A. T., *Is Anyone Out There?*, Warner Books, 1974, W. H. Allen, 1975.

Stoneley, J. and Lawton, A. T., *CETI: Communication with Extra-terrestrial Intelligence*, Warner Books, 1976, W. H. Allen, 1976.

Sullivan, W., 'A hole in the sky', *New York Times Magazine*, 14 July 1974.

Sullivan, W., *We Are Not Alone*, Hodder & Stoughton, 1965.

Suslov, I. M., 'In search of the great meteorite of 1908', *Mirovedeni*, vol. 16, 1927.

Symons, G. T., 'The eruption of Krakatoa and subsequent phenomena', *Krakatoa Committee of the Royal Society*, London, 1888.

— *The Amazing World of Nature*, Readers Digest, 1969.

— *The Times*, 29 June–10 July 1908.

Tompkins, D. R. and Rodney, P. F., 'Photographic observation of ball lightning', *Soviet Physics JETP Letters*, vol. 18, p. 114.

Troitsky, V. S. and Kaplan, S. A., Reported work, *Tass*, 16 October 1973.

Troitsky, V. S. and Kaplan, S. A., Reported work, *Novosti Bulletin*, October 1973.

Valèry, N., 'The shape of war to come', *New Scientist*, 17 June 1976.

Vasil'ev, N. V., Ivanova, G. M., L'vov, Yu., 'New data on the composition of the Tunguska Meteorite', *Prirodo*, no. 7, pp. 99–101, 1973.

Vasil'ev, N. V., L'vov, Yu., *et al.*, 'Silicate spherules in peats of the Tunguska meteorite fall region', *Akad. Nauk USSR Doklady*, vol. 199, no. 6, pp. 1400–1402, 1971.

Voznesensky, A. V., 'The fall of the meteorite of 30 June 1908, on the upper part of the River Khatanga', *Works of the Lomonossoff Institute of the Russian Academy of Sciences*, vol. 1, no. 14, 1925.

Whipple, F. J. W., *Q.J.R. Meteor. Soc.*, vol. 16, p. 287, 1930.

Wick, G. L. and Isaacs, J. D., 'Tunguska Event revisited', *Nature*, vol. 247, p. 139, 1974.

Wilcoxson, K., *Volcanoes*, Cassell, 1966.

— 'World's largest stone meteorite falls on China', *New Scientist*, 6 May 1976.

Yavnel, A. A., 'Meteoritic matter from the place where the Tunguska meteorite fell', *Astron. J.*, vol. 34, pp. 794–6.

Zigel, F., 'Nuclear explosion over the taiga', *Znaniya-Sila*, vol. 12, 1961.

Zolotov, V., *Soviet Phys. Doklady*, vol. 12, p. 108, 1967.

Zotkin, I., 'Tunguska catastrophe: a black hole? A comet?', *Special Supplement Moscow News*, vol. 37, issue 2713, 11 September 1976.

# COSMOLOGY (NF)

| 0352 | | Star | |
|---|---|---|---|

Adi-Kent Thomas Jeffrey
| | 398280 | **THE BERMUDA TRIANGLE** | 50p* |
| | 398620 | **THEY DARED THE DEVIL'S TRIANGLE** | 50p* |

Jack Stoneley & A.T. Lawton
| | 300604 | **IS ANYONE OUT THERE?** | 55p* |

# COSMOLOGY (NF)

| 0426 | | Tandem | |
|---|---|---|---|

P. Moore & I. Nicholson
| | 088387 | **BLACK HOLES IN SPACE** | 40p |

Elizabeth Nichols
| | 162994 | **THE DEVIL'S SEA** | 40p |

Ivan T. Sanderson
| | 138805 | **INVISIBLE RESIDENTS** | 40p* |
| | 138724 | **UNINVITED VISITORS** | 40p* |

Arthur Shuttlewood
| | 169263 | **THE WARMINSTER MYSTERY** | 50p |

Brad Steiger and Joan Whritenour
| | 163281 | **FLYING SAUCERS ARE HOSTILE** | 40p* |
| | 134427 | **THE NEW U.F.O. BREAKTHROUGH** | 35p* |
| | 163362 | **STRANGERS FROM THE SKIES** | 40p* |

Paul Thomas
| | 127226 | **FLYING SAUCERS THROUGH THE AGES** | 35p* |

B. Le Poer Trench
| | 134508 | **OPERATION EARTH** | 35p* |

Jacques Vallée
| | 130715 | **ANATOMY OF A PHENOMENON** | 35p* |
| | 157397 | **PASSPORT TO MAGONIA** | 45p* |

*Not for sale in Canada

# THRILLERS

| 0352 | | Star | |
|------|--------|------|------|
| | | Georges Arnaud | |
| | 397012 | **THE WAGES OF FEAR** | 50p |
| | | Niven Busch | |
| | 300167 | **THE TAKEOVER** | 50p* |
| | | Max Caulfield | |
| | 398361 | **BRUCE LEE LIVES?** | 45p |
| | | Henry Denker | |
| | 300523 | **A PLACE FOR THE MIGHTY** | 75p* |
| | | Robert Flood | |
| | 300337 | **THE HIT MAN** | 65p* |
| | | Robert Hawkes | |
| | 398906 | **NARC: THE DELGADO KILLINGS** | 50p* |
| | 398213 | **NARC: THE DEATH LIST** | 50p* |
| | 398558 | **NARC: THE DEATH OF A COURIER** | 50p* |
| | | Burt Hirschfeld | |
| | 398590 | **MOMENT OF POWER** | 75p* |
| | | William Woolfolk | |
| | 300914 | **THE OVERLORDS** | 75p* |

# THRILLERS

| 0426 | | Tandem | |
|------|--------|------|------|
| | | R. L. Brent | |
| | 141709 | **LIQUIDATOR 1** | 30p* |
| | 145844 | **LIQUIDATOR 2: CONTRACT FOR A KILLING** | 35p* |
| | 150503 | **LIQUIDATOR 3: THE COCAINE CONNECTION** | 35p* |
| | | Nick Carter | |
| | 143493 | **AGENT COUNTER-AGENT** | 35p* |
| | 173473 | **ASSAULT ON ENGLAND** | 50p* |
| | 168976 | **AZTEC AVENGER** | 45p* |
| | 173635 | **BERLIN** | 50p* |
| | 125622 | **A BULLET FOR FIDEL** | 40p* |
| | 17304X | **CAIRO** | 50p* |
| | 173554 | **THE COBRA KILL** | 50p* |
| | 169182 | **DEATH OF THE FALCON** | 45p* |
| | 174003 | **THE DEATH STRAIN** | 50p* |

*Not for sale in Canada

## SOCIOLOGY (NF)

| 0352 | | Star | |
|------|--------|------|-----|
| | 398310 | Derek Bowskill<br>**SWINGERS AND SWAPPERS** | 60p |
| | 300302 | G. L. Simons<br>**THE SIMONS BOOK OF SEXUAL RECORDS** | 75p |

## SOCIOLOGY

| 0426 | | Tandem | |
|------|--------|------|-----|
| | 163958 | Robert Chartham<br>**MAINLY FOR WOMEN** | 45p |
| | 086279 | **YOUR SEXUAL FUTURE** | 75p |
| | 086198 | Ellen Peck<br>**THE BABY TRAP** | 75p* |
| | 146050 | Joy Warren<br>**HOW TO BE AN EROTIC WOMAN** | 35p* |
| | 145925 | Roger Warren<br>**HOW TO BE AN EROTIC MAN** | 35p* |
| | 141970 | Erna Wright<br>**THE NEW CHILDBRITH** | 50p* |
| | 060318 | **THE WOMANLY ART OF BREASTFEEDING** | 40p* |

*Not for sale in Canada

## FILMS & TV

*Not for sale in Canada

# HISTORICAL

| 0342 | | Star | |
|------|--------|------|------|
| | 397098 | Mary Ann Ashe<br>**ALAS, FOR HER THAT<br>MET ME!** | 50p |
| | 300094 | Robin Maugham<br>**THE LAST ENCOUNTER** | 40p |
| | 398345 | Rosemary Anne Sisson<br>**THE STRATFORD STORY** | 60p |

# HISTORICAL

| 0426 | | Tandem | | |
|------|--------|------|------|------|
| | 123190 | **THE CONQUERING FAMILY<br>1135-1216** | (NF) | 80p* |
| | 123433 | Thomas B. Costain<br>**THE LAST PLANTAGENETS<br>1377-1485** | (NF) | 95p* |
| | 123271 | **THE MAGNIFICENT CENTURY<br>1216-1272** | (NF) | 80p* |
| | 123352 | **THE THREE EDWARDS<br>1272-1377** | (NF) | 95p* |
| | 171608 | Catherine Darby<br>**A FALCON FOR A WITCH** | | 60p* |
| | 171365 | Clare Darcy<br>**CECILY** | | 50p* |
| | 148088 | **GEORGINA** | | 50p* |
| | 156919 | Marceline Gobineau<br>**STEPHANIE — THE PASSIONS<br>OF SPRING** | | 50p* |
| | 168380 | **STEPHANIE — SNOWS OF<br>SEBASTOPOL** | | 55p* |
| | 171527 | Magdalen King Hall<br>**THE WICKED LADY** | | 50p |
| | 165551 | Edith Pargeter<br>**THE GREEN BRANCH** | | 55p |
| | 165713 | **THE HEAVEN TREE** | | 60p |
| | 165632 | **THE SCARLET SEED** | | 55p |
| | 167902 | **SUNRISE IN THE WEST** | | 60p |
| | 152107 | V. A. Stuart<br>**CAPTAIN OF CAVALRY** | | 50p* |
| | 167317 | **MASSACRE AT CAWNPORE** | | 50p* |
| | 069552 | Jill Tattersall<br>**ENCHANTER'S CASTLE** | | 30p* |
| | 132823 | **LADY INGRAM'S RETREAT** | | 30p* |
| | 069048 | **LYONESSE ABBEY** | | 30p* |
| | 060822 | **THE MIDNIGHT OAK** | | 30p* |
| | 071735 | **A TIME AT TARRAGON** | | 30p* |

*Not for sale in Canada

Wyndham Books are available from many booksellers and newsagents. If you have any difficulty please send purchase price plus postage on the scale below to:

Wyndham Cash Sales,
123 King Street,
London W6 9JG

Whilst every effort is made to keep prices low, it is sometimes necessary to increase prices at short notice. Wyndham Books reserve the right to show new retail prices on covers which may differ from those advertised in the text or elsewhere.

*UK AND EIRE*
One book: 15p plus 7p per copy for each additional book ordered to a maximum charge of 57p.

*OTHER COUNTRIES*
Rates available on request.

NB These charges are subject to Post Office charge fluctuations.

Grantly Dick-Read, M.D.                    *Prager*

# FIFTH EDITION

# Childbirth
## Without Fear

The Original Approach
to Natural Childbirth

## GRANTLY DICK-READ, M.D.

Revised and Edited by
HELEN WESSEL and
HARLAN F. ELLIS, M.D.

**PERENNIAL LIBRARY**

Harper & Row, Publishers, New York
Grand Rapids, Philadelphia, St. Louis, San Francisco
London, Singapore, Sydney, Tokyo, Toronto

Grateful acknowledgment is made for permission to reprint:

Excerpt from *Tight Corners in Pastoral Counselling* by Dr. Frank Lake; copyright 1981 by Darton, Longman and Todd Limited, London, reprinted by permission of the publishers.

Excerpt from *Prisoners of Pain* by Arthur Janov (Doubleday & Co., Inc.); reprinted by permission of the author.

Excerpt from *The Secret Life of the Unborn Child* by Thomas Verny and John Kelly (Summit Books, a Division of Simon & Schuster, Inc., 1981); reprinted by permission.

A hardcover edition of this book is published by Harper & Row, Publishers, Inc.

First PERENNIAL LIBRARY edition published 1985. Reissued in this format in 1987.

Library of Congress Cataloging-in-Publication Data

Dick-Read, Grantly, 1890–1959.
   Childbirth without fear.

   "Perennial Library."
   Bibliography: p.
   Includes index.
   1. Natural childbirth.   I. Wessel, Helen, 1924–
II. Ellis, Harlan F.   III. Title.   [DNLM: 1. Natural
childbirth.   WQ 150 D547r]
RG661.D55   1987        618.4′5        83-48340
ISBN 0-06-080870-5 (pbk.)

90 91 OPM 10 9 8 7 6 5 4 3 2

*This edition is gratefully dedicated by the editors to*

*JESSICA DICK-READ BENNETT*

*whose invaluable support of her late husband, Grantly Dick-Read, helped make his teaching available, and who was the first to establish childbirth education classes, an example now followed all over the world.*

# Contents

# Acknowledgments

Our special thanks are given to the following for their cooperation in the preparation of this edition:

*Jessica Dick-Read Bennett* for her encouragement, and for her help in obtaining copies of Dr. Dick-Read's other books and manuscripts;

*The central California couples* who so willingly served as models for the pictures, both while in training for their own natural childbirth babies and at the time of birth;

*The Visalia Community Hospital staff,* for their full cooperation in developing a natural childbirth program, and for their patience with all the extra photography needed for this book.

The *Sierra Medical Group of Visalia*—Dr. Claude H. Kleyn, Dr. Joseph S. Manuele, Dr. James C. Long, Dr. Ronald Marconi, Dr. Fred Ozawa, Dr. Joseph P. Manuele, and Dr. John Moran—who have supported, participated in, and financed this natural childbirth program. *Dr. Long, Dr. Moran, Dr. Ozawa,* and *Dr. Marconi* are especially appreciated for their participation and assistance in directing parts of this program. The office and teaching staff also are an invaluable inspiration and help, without whom the program could not continue;

*Helen Moore* for her help and patience in working out the many details involved in this project;

*Our long-suffering spouses, Joan Ellis* and *Walter Wessel,* who patiently accepted the many intrusions into the normal household routine that a book such as this involves.

HARLAN F. ELLIS, M.D.
HELEN WESSEL

# Foreword

Mention is long overdue of the invaluable aid given to Grantly Dick-Read by his beloved wife Jessica. She was the one who rescued his manuscript from the flames when, thoroughly discouraged by the opposition he encountered from the medical profession, he intended to destroy it. She was the one who accompanied him to South Africa when pressures from the British medical profession caused him to leave England in despair. She was the one who introduced him to the Marymount maternity home in Johannesburg where his success in natural childbirth became a model for the world.

It was Jessica who first set up prenatal classes in which expectant mothers could learn in small groups how to prepare for natural birth. She wrote the curriculum, trained the personnel, and supervised the classes. Up until this time Dr. Dick-Read had attempted to teach his patients individually, but at Marymount his practice became so large this was no longer possible. Today nearly every hospital in the United States, as well as in other parts of the world, has some form of childbirth education. Few, if any, realize that their thanks are due to Jessica Dick-Read for this creative innovation in preparing for childbirth.

Jessica had the courage to have a natural birth after a cesarean section, having full confidence in Dick-Read's teaching in the earlier years of his practice. It is only recently that the medical profession has begun to question the dictum, "Once a cesarean, always a cesarean," and to promote vaginal birth after cesarean in carefully selected cases.

It is for these reasons, and more, that this edition of *Childbirth Without Fear* is dedicated to Grantly Dick-Read's widow.

It has been nearly seventy years since Grantly Dick-Read (1890–1959) first prepared a monograph on his carefully developed philosophy of childbirth. At that time, the concept of childbirth as a positive experience, free from suffering, was a shocking and revolutionary idea, unacceptable to many, for almost all women in labor were delivered under deep anesthesia.

But he was not to be deterred from the truth he had discovered, and the intervening years have proven the validity of his teaching. In the 1920s he not only defied tradition by educating his women patients for labor and birth, but even set up classes for their husbands as well. Today the concept of prenatal education for both husbands and wives, no longer controversial, is widely adopted.

Grantly Dick-Read was a man out of step with his time in many other important ways, in addition to his approach to childbearing. He was one of those who set the pace for succeeding generations, and in the years since his death social changes in the world have brought to public attention the importance of many of the things he was advocating during his lifetime.

Among his "heretical" ideas were his outspokenness against environmental pollution, as well as against the "pollution" of people's minds by false fears and their bodies by drugs. His approach to obstetrics was fastidiously scientific, but he also brought to bear upon it an interdisciplinary interest, relating psychology, sociology, and anthropology to his studies in physiology and the natural sciences. He continually emphasized the importance of treating the patient as a whole person, and not just concentrating upon a physical mechanism within her body.

In order to limit his practice to obstetrics, he entered group practice at a time when it was such a new concept that it created an outcry. He shocked many people with his proposals that teen-agers should be taught about such important matters as sex, reproduction, and family life in the schools.

He was a man "against the establishment," not opposing it arbitrarily, but continually questioning the maintenance of the status quo at the expense of creativity and truth. He spoke out against the futility of cold scientism, materialism, and social prestige at the expense of an awareness of human relationships and metaphysical realities.

He was vocal in expressing the equality of the black person as a human being, and the need the white person has to learn from the lore of black history and wisdom.

None of these views made him popular with many of his contemporaries!

Then, at the height of his successful obstetric practice, at forty years of age, Grantly Dick-Read wrote a book in 1930 that was to change the course of obstetric history. He had proven from his own experiences as a physician his belief that childbirth is a natural physiological process not meant to be painful, and because he had built his teaching around a study of the "laws of nature," he chose for his book the title *Natural Childbirth*. He had not the faintest notion that this book title would be taken as a "name" for this kind of childbirth experience. Indeed, though often misunderstood, the term became a household word everywhere, for when the book was finally published, in 1933, Grantly Dick-Read rose from the relative obscurity of a local medical practice into a target for the ire or praise of people all over the world. The rest of his life followed the course of such great medical pioneers as Simpson, Semmelweis, Lister, Pasteur, and many others who were rejected by their contemporaries but whose teachings nevertheless became the foundation stones for future medical progress.

Grantly Dick-Read did not envision his teaching on childbirth as an "end" to discovery, but as a true foundation from which many further discoveries could be made. He was not afraid to challenge tradition by asking the disturbing question, "Why?" If he were here today, he would encourage young people to keep on asking questions, to keep on challenging tradition, to keep on testing current medical practices and theories, including his own, for validity. All those who share his faith in the consistency and orderliness of natural law, which we disregard at our own peril, will continue in the search for truth.

This fifth edition of *Childbirth Without Fear* includes some new discoveries which validate the principles he taught. This new material is incorporated into his writings in Part I; Part II presents his basic philosophy of natural childbirth and its physiological rationale; Part III is his autobiography. The best of his teachings have been gathered from all his writings, extracting the most vital, timeless portions for this edition.

HELEN WESSEL

# Preface

This Preface first appeared in the original edition of *Natural Childbirth* in 1933 (London: Heinemann). The editors include portions of it here because its accuracy and relevancy after more than fifty years is most remarkable.

There has been no subject during recent years that has claimed so much attention as obstetrics. Learned societies have invited lectures and discussions upon its practice and teaching, and committees have been set up by the government for the purpose of investigating maternal and infant mortality. Medical journals have published a vast amount of literature concerning the abnormalities and complications of childbirth, while the lay press rarely misses an opportunity to bring before the public any information upon the subject that can be gleaned from the transactions of the societies and associations of the medical profession. Vast improvement has resulted in both knowledge and technique, but, unhappily, statistics have not shown a relatively pronounced advance upon those of ten or fifteen years ago.

An effort has been made in the following pages to regard childbirth from a different angle. A large percentage of the dangers and complications can be avoided by careful prenatal observation and instruction. An exact knowledge of the shape and size of the pelvis, and of the position and development of the fetus, prevents problems because such knowledge leads to the application of correct treatment.

But it is generally agreed that one of the most important factors in the production of complicated labor, and therefore of maternal and infant mortality, is the inability of obstetricians to stand by and allow the natural and uninterrupted course of labor. It may be an excess of zeal, or anxiety born of ignorance, but it is an unquestionable fact that interference is still one of the greatest dangers with which both mother and child have to contend.

It is not fully realized that the majority of "pelvic" invalids suffer from the mistaken application of human sympathy. But it is equally obvious that *if there is suffering, it should be allayed.* Therefore the problem arises: How can prolonged suffering be prevented or stopped without the risk of injury to the mother or child? For which is the greater immorality, to allow an agonizing labor or to injure mother, child, or both?

It becomes clear that the solution to this problem lies in an investigation of pain. In certain chapters that follow, the various influences to which cultured women are subjected have been considered, and the whole question of pain reviewed.

A new attitude toward childbirth has been evolved, and deductions upon which treatment is based made from the premises of experience, and the results have been gratifying.

It must not be presumed that a full understanding is obtained by simply recognizing the principles; their application will require greater patience from the scientist and the academically minded physician than from those whose conception of this doctoring is unhampered by the ever-present bugbear of abnormality.

Had it not been for the enthusiasm of those who have accepted this teaching, these pages would not have appeared in print. It must not be presumed that any claim is made to invariable success: where there are anatomical abnormalities, the operative procedure of modern obstetrics is unhesitatingly resorted to; and again, abnormal conditions of the mother's mind may impair its sensibility and receptivity.

The first and most obvious benefit that results from the care of the mother psychical as well as the mother physical is the natural perfection of labor, and the almost complete absence of many of the complications of the second and third stages.

Perhaps a feature that is even more pleasing is the happiness of motherhood, and the manner in which both mother and baby thrive following the birth.

If, in spite of all, there is pain, it should be immediately overcome. Painless labor is the greatest gift that our profession can make to humanity, but if painless labor is obtained at the cost of the integrity of the function, it becomes a choice between two evils.

Childbirth is the perfection of womanhood, and the beautifying of the maternal conscience is one of its most acceptable rewards, not only for the mother herself, but for her home, the community, and the nation. Thousands of women today have their babies born under what are known as modern humanitarian conditions—they are the first to disclaim any knowledge of the beauties of childbirth, they are the first to tell the doctor how easy it is for a man to be enthusiastic —but those who have known all and suffered little are not slow to sympathize with mere man in that he can never know the joy that is the reward of natural reproduction.

1933                                    GRANTLY DICK-READ, M.D.

# Introduction

I would like to encourage every medical student, physician, or birth attendant unfamiliar with the principles of natural childbirth to review the basic tenets of Grantly Dick-Read's principles. They have stood the test of over fifty years, and have yet to be disproved. We may not accept every statement or criticism he has made of our specialty, but this must not allow us to be deterred from exploring this physiological and therefore most valuable way to handle pregnancy and the birth of a child.

If we believe that a physiological process, namely, normal childbirth, must by its very nature represent suffering and severe pain, then we must review the following facts:

1. In no other animal species is the process of birth apparently associated with any suffering, pain, or agony except when pathology exists or in an unnatural state such as captivity.

2. There are certain "primitive cultures" in which childbirth is looked forward to with joy and anticipation as something good. Here one finds little evidence of suffering, pain, or agony, again except when pathology is present.

3. There is no other physiological process in our body that is painful under normal conditions except when complicated by pathology, including fear and tension.

4. Experience shows that when a woman can be prepared so

that fear and tension are prevented from occurring in labor, there is minimal or no suffering, pain, or agony.

5. When no physical pathology is present clinically, pain appears directly related to the amount of fear and tension present.

6. Childbirth education programs can be found in almost every American community today. Although some more effectively teach the principles of natural childbirth than others, stories of good experiences are spreading by word of mouth. The result is that increasing numbers of women are discovering that natural childbirth is a more exciting and rewarding way to have a baby.

In the mid-1950s I gave one of my first professional papers at a national meeting of physicians. I had just finished my specialty training. That is a special time because one knows everything! I felt I knew all the answers and knew I could answer any question. I showed some colored slides which I had had made up. The subject was obstetrical anesthesia and forceps, and I was really proud of my slides and my record because I reported 87 percent of my patients in a particular year as having complete obstetric anesthesia. Eighty-two percent had forceps, of which I reported that 15 percent had a mid-forceps and about a third of those were classified as a high mid-forceps.

Looking back now, I realize how foolish I was. How little I really knew and how little I understood about birth and bonding—"the delivery," as we called it at that time. The principles of natural childbirth had already been recorded and the importance of imprinting was in the literature (the forerunner of human bonding). I had failed to study these things, although they were available. During this period of time between the 1950s and the 1980s I've had the opportunity to attend over seven thousand births and to be part of an evolution in obstetrics. I think many obstetricians who have not had the chance to witness this evolution really don't appreciate how special births can be today.

If we look at the period from the 1950s to the 1980s, we have moved from deliveries to births. In the fifties we did something to a woman; in the eighties a woman accomplishes something. In the fifties we talked about delivery rooms; now we talk about birth rooms. In the fifties we had a labor room, moved the patient onto a gurney, then moved her into the delivery room onto a delivery table. And we did all this right in the middle of transition and second-stage labor, the worst possible time! Today we have birthing rooms where the patient labors and gives birth in the same bed.

In the fifties we tried to give everybody a full anesthesia except for those fortunate enough to give birth precipitously in the labor room; today we rarely use a full anesthesia. In the fifties we tried to use forceps in every delivery, and gave glowing reports on its use; today we rarely see a need for forceps. In the fifties we hydrated patients unphysiologically with IVs; today we hydrate patients with oral fluids. In the fifties we dealt with the "pains" of labor; today we deal with the contractions of labor. In the fifties we shaved their perineums and gave them enemas. I shudder to think how we even held women down, strapping their arms and legs and covering their faces. All this was not given up until the early sixties when we started our own program.

During the fifties we completely separated the mother and baby; today we think of nonseparation. Then we hadn't even heard of the term "bonding"; today we not only think of bonding the mother and father with the newborn, but want any siblings there to bond also, not as something nice to do but as something important. In those days it didn't seem to matter whether a woman breastfed or not; if she did want to breastfeed, she was not allowed to do so until twenty-four hours later. She might have had a brief glance at her baby, but that was the only contact during those first twenty-four hours. Today we expect, and encourage, every woman to breastfeed her infant, and we want her to start breastfeeding even before the cord is cut.

In the fifties a woman breastfed for maybe two or three months and thought that was great. Today we're talking about a woman totally breastfeeding for a full nine months, with no water, no supplements, nothing else for nine months, in the best interests of the newborn (this of course when no pathology of the newborn exists).

We used to talk about cesarean deliveries where today we talk about cesarean births. In the fifties we didn't think there was any place but the waiting room for a husband during a cesarean delivery, since it is a surgical procedure. Today in our hospital, he has a specific, tremendously important role. If it is a vaginal birth, we expect the father to support his wife in newborn bonding; in a cesarean birth, we expect the father to bond with the newborn while his wife is being cared for.

During the fifties we started using hypnosis, which was kind of a fad at the time. Hypnosis really increased our incidence of spontaneous nonmedicated births, and we needed that. But it takes a lot of work. The physician has to work with the patient, to be there throughout labor, and when he or she begins to receive many patients it's just not possible. So we began using tape recorders with these large numbers of patients. We taught them about pain and how to control it through relaxation. The tape would hypnotize them to a certain point, and I've actually performed a cesarean under hypnosis. But the support person for the patient in labor was a mechanical tape recorder, even on the delivery table! It worked all right for a time; after a while, though, the tapes would break, or somebody knocked the tape recorder off the stand right in the middle of a birth, and everything fell apart. With the tape recorder going, a woman's husband often sat in a corner reading the paper!

In the late fifties I began teaching husbands hypnosis, so they could work with their wives throughout labor and birth, and that was an improvement. During that time I was also teaching at the University of California, Irvine, and at the Los Angeles County Hospital. I delivered a lot of students' wives, interns' wives, residents' and staff members' wives, and these husbands were permitted to observe the labor and birth (no other husbands were permitted at that time in our hospitals). But I discovered that the further along students were in their training, the worse they were in supporting their wives. They were interested only in the clinical aspects of the birth, when they should have been helping their wives. They didn't know how. It wasn't until we finally said, "Now, look, you're going to have to go to childbirth classes just like the other expectant parents," that the whole picture changed.

It was in the mid-fifties that I was introduced to the writings of Grantly Dick-Read by Dr. Charles Mount III, under whom I trained and who first taught me the dictum: "Tense doctor = tense patient = tense cervix = pain." Later I was encouraged by Dr. Robert Bradley to involve the husbands. In 1959 we began our first classes for support people, usually the husband. We learned a lot about their value. Early in this endeavor they were there to watch; today they're present to work. In the late fifties they were permitted to be there; in the eighties they're *required* to be there, if we're to accept the care of the patients. In the fifties we thought the patient would fall in love with her obstetrician. Today we expect the patient to fall more in love with her husband.

In California the central nursery for all babies is still a frequent practice. The babies are wrapped in blankets because it's thought that this produces warmth and security. In our hospital we don't even have a well-baby nursery: the newborn should get warmth and security from skin-to-skin contact with its mother, not from blankets. Mothers and babies go home without ever having been separated.

Then we started rooming in; now I'm against it. In rooming in, the baby is right next to the mother in the little bassinet. That's not good enough! What we want is *bedding* in. The baby sleeps right next to the mother, and we want *full* skin-to-skin contact for the baby for the first twenty-four hours. We expect that first twenty-four-hour experience to set in motion a type of closeness in the next nine months that is contrary to the usual closeness found in this country.

My experience in learning and applying the natural childbirth philosophy has been most satisfying and rewarding. In our particular setting, we have a rather large obstetrical practice. We (three obstetricians) have twenty-six childbirth educators working for us, not all full time. They take each new couple who comes to us and first sit down for a 45-minute interview, exploring their attitudes toward pregnancy, childbirth, the newborn, and related topics. We also want to know about their own early experiences. This review helps establish a rapport at the very outset, then we build on that, spending more time as necessary on certain areas, depending on their attitudes.

Natural childbirth, of course, does not correct all obstetrical problems; we will still have many of those. Natural childbirth does, however, offer an opportunity for a high percentage of simple, easy, nonmedicated vaginal births. The essence of what we are doing was discussed and outlined by Grantly Dick-Read in his early writing some fifty years ago. The only thing that time has done has been to prove his basic principles of natural childbirth, and what these principles mean to the patient, her baby, and her husband, and therefore to the family and society in general. For the magnanimous contributions that these natural childbirth programs have thereby made to happier childbirth, the art of obstetrics is truly indebted.

HARLAN F. ELLIS, M.D.

This book is not intended to instruct women in matters that are the special province of medical advisers. The proper diagnosis and therapy for all symptoms connected with pregnancy and the postpartum period require the advice of a qualified specialist.

# P A R T  I

# Natural
# Childbirth
# in
# Perspective

In all his writings, Grantly Dick-Read spoke not of a "method" of childbirth, but of a philosophy of life, of which birth is just a part, although a most essential part. He believed that the quality of a birth experience influenced (for good or ill) not only the child, but the family into which he or she was born. He stated that the childbirth practices of a nation were reflections of that nation's beliefs concerning the integrity and dignity of life, and influenced that nation for good or ill, and that ultimately the world itself is affected.

He not only believed that the manner of birth and subsequent period had its influence, but that the fetus *in utero* was affected by the moods and circumstances of its mother. He wrote:

> We are beginning to learn that the fantasy of folklore is not so funny as we thought, particularly in relation to the unborn child.
>
> We have come to realize that a child is nourished in the womb through its mother's blood, and that any emotional variations of the mother, in spite of constants, may in some way affect the nutrition and metabolism of the unborn child. I don't believe in biochemical constants; I don't believe even genes are constant. I believe there is something that flows in the mother's blood that varies according to her temperament. These substances, which come from the internal secreting glands and other structures that secrete or exude, vary as the physical and emotional state of the mother varies and are poured into the bloodstream that nourishes the baby. Thus the baby undoubtedly has its constitutional variants. We know today that by altering the emotional state of the mother we can record the concomitant changes in the pulse of the baby. We know that as the mother is, so at least is the baby directed in its development, *particularly in its emotional development.* *

Research during the years since Dick-Read's death has led to the development of prenatal and perinatal psychology as a science, in which Dick-Read's assumptions are verified with remarkable evidence. Thus in the following chapters childbirth will be presented as a continuum, from conception through birth and the several months following birth, in its psychological as well as its physical components for the infant as well as the mother.

---

* Italics ed.

## CHAPTER 1

# The Child Within

**C**hildbirth is but one part of a continuum, from conception to birth, from birth through infancy, from infancy to adulthood, and from one generation to the next. None of us can escape the consequences of our life in the womb, the manner in which we were born, or our experiences in the subsequent months. The first eighteen months, from conception through nine months of age, with its prenatal, natal, and postnatal influences on each of us, have lasting effects. In this chapter we will explore these influences on the physical, mental, and emotional development of the child in the womb.

## DEVELOPMENT OF THE HUMAN BABY

Nearly all animals, including human beings, have much the same principles of breeding. The female makes eggs and the male produces sperm. Eggs have to be fertilized by the sperm before they can grow into babies. Nature makes the process of fertilization pleasant to experience, because each race must go on reproducing itself or it will die out.

The female reproductive organs are located in the lower abdomen, below the level of the hip bones. In the center of these is the *uterus,* or womb, which in its nonpregnant state is about two and a half inches by one and a half inches by one-half inch. A small, muscular organ that weighs about one and a half ounces, the uterus is shaped rather like a pear with the narrow end pointing downward, where it is attached to the upper end of the vagina. The lower, narrow end of the uterus is closed by circular muscular tissue called the *cervix,* through which a narrow passage opens into the uterus.

At the upper end of the uterus are two narrow tubes that extend out from each side, rather like arms extending out from the shoulders. Each tube is three or four inches long, and opens at the end furthest from the uterus into a shallow bell shape. Underneath each of these two bell-shaped structures is a small, oval organ called an *ovary.* Each of the two ovaries contains *ova,* or egg-forming tissue.

An egg *(ovum)* is developed and sent on its way by one of the ovaries each month, about ten days after menstruation. The ovum travels down the narrow tube from the ovary to the uterus, while the uterus prepares a lining of tissue to make a good "nest" to receive it. If the egg is not fertilized by a male sperm, it passes on through the uterus and is cast off. About two weeks later the lining of the uterus is also thrown off, and a new lining prepared for the next egg. The flow of cast-off, unused material is called *menstruation.*

A male child is born with testicles which, shortly before birth, have moved down from the abdomen into the scrotum, outside the body. In these organs *spermatozoa* are produced. It is estimated that each testicle contains over one mile of sperm-producing tubules, from the walls of which a healthy man may produce at each ejaculation over two hundred million spermatozoa.

The male sperm is ejaculated from the penis into the vagina of the female at the culmination of mating, or *coitus.* The mature sperm cell has a long, thin tail, which enables it to move toward the opening in the cervix of the uterus. It travels at the rate of about one inch in ten minutes. Considerable numbers find their way through the uterus into the tubes and engage in what might be described as a race for the ovum. As soon as a sperm penetrates an ovum, making it fertile, the ovum undergoes an immediate change, which prevents any further penetration by another sperm.

The fertile egg moves on through the tube, becomes embedded in the wall of the uterus, and starts to grow. The lining of the uterus alters its character, developing the *placenta,* through which the mother nourishes her child. The placental site rapidly expands, its blood vessels and nerve fibrils bring vitality to the egg, and the growth of the *fetus,* the developing baby, begins.

Very shortly after the ovum is fertilized, it starts to develop cells that are differentiated to form the various organs and structures of the body. Some of these become the mother cells of spermatozoa and ova, so that quite early in fetal life the sex of the child is determined.

During its growing life, the baby is protected by a "bag of waters," in which it lives. This protects the baby from injury if the mother is bumped or falls, keeps its body at a constant temperature, and provides space for it to move about freely until the later months of growth.

The fetus grows very fast. At four weeks it is one sixth of an inch long, lying in a fluidlike sack about the size of a pigeon's egg. At the end of the second month it is about one and one-sixth inches long, and the arms, legs, and head are clearly distinguishable. By this time it has its own circulation of blood and its own nervous system.

It is now fed through its navel by a tube called the *umbilical cord,* which is attached to the placenta. This wonderful organ, the placenta, is attached to the inside wall of the uterus and filters from the mother's blood the substances necessary for the development of the child. Not only does it have the power of passing on to the child what it requires, but it also has the power of refusing to take from the mother's blood some of the substances that may not be advantageous to the child. By the time the baby is due to be born, the umbilical cord between the placenta and baby may be from one to three feet in length.

At the end of the third month the fetus is about three and a half inches long, weighs approximately an ounce, and at the end of the fourth month it has grown rapidly to about seven inches and weighs about four ounces. Its heart can now be heard beating strongly, and it is possible to tell the sex of the child if it should be born at this stage. By this time the mother will have become conscious of the baby's movements. This is known as *quickening,* and it occurs at about eighteen or nineteen weeks after conception.

At the fifth month of pregnancy the baby is almost ten inches long and weighs about one and one-half pounds. Occasionally one reads in medical literature of babies born at this age who survive. By the end of the seventh month, twenty-eight weeks old, the child is perfected. Although not fully grown or fully nourished, some twenty-eight-week-old children have survived well after birth.

At the eighth month the child is almost seventeen inches long, and has a very good chance of healthy survival. At the ninth month, or thirty-six weeks, the average weight is five to five and one-half pounds. The organs and functions are all well developed, and al-

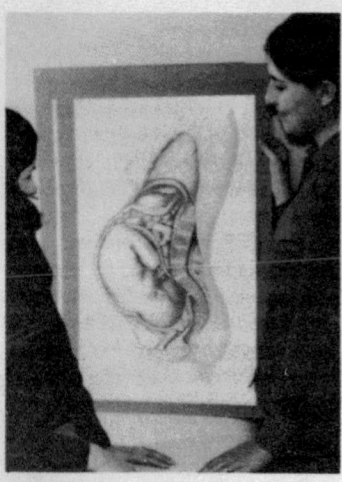

Diagram of baby *in utero*
at full term

though children born now require more care than full-term children, they should survive perfectly well if born at this age.

At the tenth month, forty weeks—which is about the average time a child takes to develop—it should weigh about seven to seven and one-half pounds and be about nineteen inches in length, and it is in this condition that natural birth takes place.

This description of the normal development of the human baby does not take into account the genetic, nutritional, emotional, and environmental factors that may affect the fetus at any point during the months in the womb. Some of these contingencies are beyond individual control, but conscientious parents can do a great deal to provide as optimum an internal environment as possible for their infant. This includes caring for their own health and nutrition *prior* to conceiving, and modifying environmental factors by healthful living during the pregnancy. Even then, the child in the womb *may* fail to thrive physically if the mother is *continually* unhappy throughout the pregnancy. Occasionally this profound unhappiness may even possibly lead to miscarriage or prematurity. It is thought that perhaps the psychological as well as the physical environment has its effect on the normal physiological development of the child within.

## BRAIN DEVELOPMENT

Out of all proportion to the skeletal growth of the baby is the development of its brain. From the earliest weeks, brain substance is present in the fetus. At three and a half weeks the brain can be differentiated into its three main divisions, and between three and five months it develops integrative cerebral function. One month before the baby is born, its brain is perfected.

Our brain is what makes us different from and dominant over all other animals. The most important and critical factor to every pregnant woman in the world is the insurance of adequate brain development for her child, the prevention of injury to that child's brain, and developing its potential from the moment of birth.

The principles of natural childbirth are among the most important factors in reducing brain injury during labor and birth. But the continuum of brain development runs from conception through birth and on through the age of nine months. For example, the brain's tissue size is approximately 60 cubic centimeters at *four months after conception,* 360 cubic centimeters at *birth,* and 850 cubic centimeters at *nine months.* At this time—nine months of age—about 90 percent of brain development is completed.

Neuroanatomists, specialists who study the structure of the nervous system, tell us that once brain tissue is developed, it is there for life. The brain cells, the dendrites, the axons, the ability to produce neurotransmitters, and the potential for brain development are all largely completed by nine months of age. When this brain growth and development follows our genetic and instinctual programming, then we have the best foundation for future development. If that foundation is not good (less than optimum intelligence) or that foundation is faulty (brain injury) or that foundation is not complete (gross defects), we cannot expect the best results in the years to come. This does not mean that the baby who does not have the best brain development by nine months of age cannot be helped or improved. But the better the foundation of brain development, the greater the potential for that child.

Once the brain has been injured, it is most likely injured for life. Thus an awareness of brain growth from conception to nine months of age should be of special interest to all pregnant women and their husbands. This should be taught to *all* pregnant women, not just those who go to various types of childbirth classes. From a societal or cultural viewpoint this type of information may indeed be more important than weight, blood pressure, and urine checks. Physical ease is important; but relatively speaking, care of the brain is more important, and of course abnormal blood pressure and urine may possibly have an effect on the brain.

There are many factors that influence brain growth and development. A most significant and important benefit is preventing brain injuries during pregnancy (pregnancy without fear) and during labor and birth (childbirth without fear). Natural childbirth is one of the most significant "helps" possible in producing the easiest, most spontaneous, most nonmedicated labors and births.

This does not imply natural, unmedicated childbirths "at all costs." There are times when medications, anesthetics, forceps, and cesarean sections can also help to prevent brain damage, in a small percentage of cases. But what a tragedy if through *ignorance* or *indifference,* brain development is less than it might be, as a result of failing to apply some of the principles of prevention known today.

What are some of the factors that affect brain growth and development? A few examples—by no means complete—follow:

### GENETIC PROGRAMMING

This is something over which there is no control after conception. Factors prior to conception are to be considered if there is evidence of some inherited disorder.

### INFECTIONS

Early pregnancy is the most vulnerable time for brain damage as a result of infections such as rubella (German measles), due to the effect of the virus on brain tissue.

### DRUGS

It is well known that certain drugs, including alcohol and tobacco, may cause brain damage. The use of such drugs even *prior* to pregnancy may be of some harm. For example, tobacco has been implicated in defective sperm, and there may be defective genes as a result of either parent having been on drugs. And there is an element of risk in any drugs taken during pregnancy, so that it is wise for the pregnant woman to avoid all over-the-counter drugs—including aspirin, cold remedies, tranquilizers, sleeping pills, and so on. Physicians should prescribe drugs with great caution during pregnancy, and only when the benefits of a particular drug outweigh the risks. This includes the commonly prescribed anti-nausea drug for early pregnancy, Bendectin. Production of Bendectin was halted on June 9, 1983, because it had been the target of hundreds of lawsuits asserting that the drug caused deformities in fetuses.

## NUTRITION

Low-protein diets certainly affect brain growth, as do certain other nutrient deficiencies. Ideally, *both* parents should have had an optimum diet at least a month before conception, and preferably all their lives. It is imperative for the expectant mother and her fetus to be well nourished. (Nutrition is discussed more fully in chapter 3.)

## ANXIETY AND FEAR

Negative emotions have a powerful effect on the body. Anxiety or fear produces biochemical changes in the body which prepare it for fight or flight. If fighting or taking flight is inappropriate, then these changes have a negative effect on the body, as well as potential ill effects on neonatal brain growth and development.

One of these biochemical changes is in the production of catecholamines, which constrict the arterioles, reducing blood flow to the internal organs. During pregnancy, continuous constriction of the tiny blood vessels in the placenta might reasonably restrict the amount of oxygen going to the fetus. Oxygen, of course, is critical to brain development. While the fetus can withstand an occasional fear reaction fairly well, months of anxiety or fear could have an adverse effect. Catecholamines may possibly also inhibit the "health-producing" brain endorphine hormones.

## OXYGENATION IN LABOR AND BIRTH

The more natural and physiological the labor and birth, the better the possibility of good oxygenation. Anything that restricts oxygen to the fetal brain may, if prolonged, damage brain tissue. For example, placental dysfunction might interfere with the oxygen going to the fetus. Compression of the umbilical cord, since it carries oxygen to the fetus, can be a serious problem. Natural childbirth, which normalizes the physiology of labor, helps assure the flow of oxygen to the fetus.

On the other hand, the anxious laboring woman is inadvertently restricting the flow of oxygen to her infant. And the more anxious she is, the more medication she may need, further reducing the flow of oxygen. This may lead to the more potentially dangerous anesthetics and/or instruments, which unless expertly used, have the potential for brain injury. Brain damage of course can occur with certain types of difficult forceps births or in certain types of difficult breech births. Only those with expert training and ability should use forceps or assist the breech birth.

Natural childbirth is not a game. It is not just for fun, nor just so the parents can have an emotionally satisfying experience. It is an extremely important factor in preserving the integrity of the infant's brain.

## BONDING

Bonding is that specific period of time following birth during which a special relationship is developed between the newborn and the parents. This special relationship is accomplished through the five senses: hearing, touching, sight, taste, and smell. Although this special bonding period goes on for nine months in humans, it appears most acute immediately following birth.

Bonding will be discussed later, but it is important to mention it specifically here in regard to brain development. Ashley Montagu has lectured and written for years about the fact that the less animals are touched, the poorer their brain development, if the lack of touching is during their imprinting (bonding) period immediately following birth.[1] And animal studies reveal that the lack of touching during the bonding period results in poor developmental behavior in the adult animal. If newborn monkeys are inadequately touched during their bonding period of two weeks, they appear to be brain-damaged for life. Harry Harlow has shown that the newborn Rhesus female monkey whose first two weeks of separation have been severe will likely have trouble conceiving as an adult, and will most likely abort if she does.[2] The implication is poor brain development.

In humans, although the immediate newborn bonding is extremely important, the bonding period lasts for around nine months. Is it not possible that similar negative effects occur in those infants who suffer separation and received inadequate human touching and affection during their first nine months of life? The consequence may not simply be emotional deprivation, but may also result in failure of the brain to complete its normal development.

## BONDING BEFORE BIRTH

It is within the brain itself that the heritage of parental influence is most readily discovered. The baby's mental development is influenced, not only by heredity, but also by the nature of the mother's emotions during pregnancy. The calmness or anxiety that affects her own nervous system may have an effect on the baby also.

Many women have instinctively felt this to be true. Some cultures have made a practice of attempting to influence the fetus through the mother. For example, some Japanese mothers have attempted to look only at beautiful objects, so that their child might be artistic. Such notions of prenatal influence have been dismissed as "old wives' tales," until recent scientific evidence validating this theory appeared. Now there is growing scientific interest in prenatal and perinatal psychology.

Personal memories of birth experiences have been verified with astonishing accuracy. Otto Rank was among the first in psychiatry to note how often analytic transference in therapy evoked metaphors associated with birth trauma.[3] A Christian psychiatrist in Britain, Dr. Frank Lake, discovered the reality of primal pain in his patients in 1954 and began dealing with it in therapy.[4] A little later Arthur

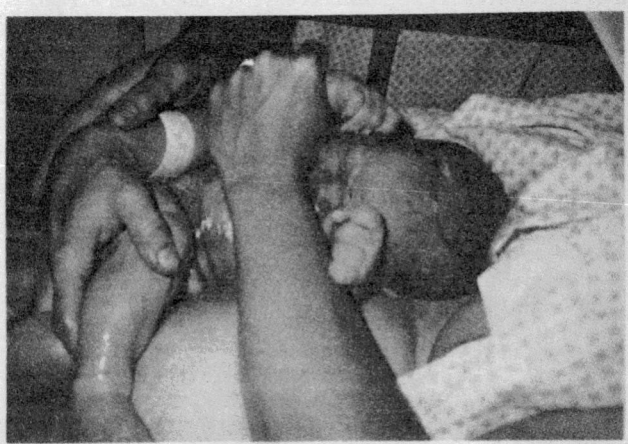

Immediate newborn bonding

Janov's work in primal therapy gained attention.[5] Patients in his program were allowed to regress in therapy to a painful memory. Often the source of extreme pain was memory of their own traumatic births, with sensations of being crushed, threatened by asphyxiation, pulled about, and/or a sense of abandonment following the birth (due to separation from the mother and isolation).

As interest in birth memories grew, an increasing number of clinical and research studies developed which contain valid evidences of psychological and physical damage at or before birth,[6,7] including damage caused by routine professional interventions. Spontaneous flashbacks of birth memory are more common than previously thought, but have generally not been recognized. Hypnosis has been used by some as a means of aiding recall,[8] and in one such recent study of ten mother/child pairs, with mother and child questioned independently, there was a characteristic dovetailing in the separate stories, a single pair showing as many as twenty-two points of correspondence.[9]

Births may also be recalled without hypnosis, under relaxed circumstances.[10] Some of the most astonishing evidence concerning birth memories has come from very young children between the ages of twenty months and three or three and a half years old, when asked open-ended questions about when they were born.[11] Helen Wessel knows of some remarkable incidences of very young children telling of their births.[12] The spontaneous recall of the small child seems clearer if the birth was nontraumatic, perhaps because painful birth memories are repressed and less likely to be recalled.

This is once again a serious reason for the most natural, comfortable birth possible, with a minimum of intervention to disturb the mother's peace and the harmony of the birth. Frederick Leboyer has emphasized the importance of a gentle birth for the baby, who experiences any violence at birth and will correctly identify the thoughts and emotions of the participants.[13] Frank Lake writes:

> However, there has been and still is an obstetrical myth that the baby feels nothing of this pain. . . .
>
> Our now common task of helping people to retrieve repressed experiences to do with their birth, leaves us in no doubt that fear and pain are often experienced, and at once split off from consciousness. The "emergency" was dissociated and prevented by various gating processes from re-entry into full, contextualized awareness. Those who are, in this way, able to remember events, before, during, and after birth, recall with specific accuracy the

bodily sensations, the accompanying emotions, and a detailed sense of the environmental pressures or deficiencies, with a vividness which has etched them forever on the recording cells of the organism.[14]

Psychiatrists and psychologists discovering that birth memories can often be recalled have made another astounding discovery—the life experienced in the womb can often also be recalled. Thomas Verney details this remarkable discovery in a recent book. He says:

> What emerges from new reports is a picture of a human intrauterine bonding system at least as complex, graded and subtle as the bonding that occurs after birth. Indeed, they are part of the same vital continuum: What happens after birth is an elaboration of, and depends on, what happened prior to it.
>
> This realization explains the source of the newborn's surprisingly accomplished post-birth performance. His ability to respond to his mother's hugs, stroking, looks and other cues is based on his long acquaintance with her prior to birth.[15]

From the moment of conception, mother and baby enter into continual interaction. Far from being a passive recipient of nutrients, the baby in the uterus is more likely to kick, squirm, and be restless when the mother is upset. Her stress triggers her sympathetic nervous system and the release of adrenaline. Catecholemines cross the placental barrier and the baby responds to the stress the mother is feeling.

Conversely, when the mother is calmly going about her work, the baby is rocked and soothed and lies quietly or sleeps. When she lies down and the "rocking" stops, the baby may wake up and let her know it wants to be "rocked" some more! One reason babies love to be "walked" after birth is that it is a familiar motion they remember, and enjoy. Unborn children adjust their rhythms to their mothers' with as much precision as newborns can. Bonding after birth is simply a continuation of the process.

It is understandable that conscious memory can occur by the sixth month *in utero,* for the cortex of the baby's brain is able to receive and retain messages by this time. What is more astonishing is that there appears to be memory that goes all the way back to conception. Stanislaus Grof began discovering this in the mid-1950s,[16] as has Dr. Lake with his patients over a period of years. Their work has led to a definition of the maternal-fetal-distress-syndrome, recognizing that the fetus is invaded by the mother's complex emotions, to which the fetus responds in predictable ways.[17] But how can memory occur in the fetus before the full development of the fetal cortex of the brain? Dr. Lake comments:

> What processes could subserve learning and memory in the zygote and blastocyst before and after implantation? We ask this because our patients so consistently produce them. It seems that there may be structures in the protein molecule of the single cell which can do this. . . . The principle of *multilevel redundancy* provides for the reduplication of the genetic material in the original zygote into the nucleus of every cell in the body. Could there be reduplication and transfer of memory also in the cytoplasm? Apparently so.[18]

Dr. Lake mentions the work of the embryologist Richard Dryden[19] as evidence of this possibility, and goes on to say: "The 'implicate order' opens up possibilities of micro-storage, inconceivable until recent years. My interest in the possible biological bases of pre-verbal memories is not to demonstrate the legitimate existence of our findings but to indicate their biological feasibility, and to guard against dismissive criticism based on antiquated neurology when they are reviewed."[20]

The implication of these new findings is clear: that good prenatal bonding between mother and infant is important to the child's physical, mental, and psychological health. But before some leap to the conclusion that this is just one more instance in which a woman is "blamed" for anything that happens to her child, another factor must be mentioned.

> Every kind of social distress, at whatever level, in the family, the neighborhood, the local community, and on to the national and global systems, impinges on the woman. The message of these surroundings penetrates her spirit and whole person, an influx of emotion and contextual sense which she shares with the foetus embedded in her.
>
> Every item of distress operating against full humanness and caring within the community inevitably feeds through into the pregnant woman. This happens first at the intimate level of her marriage. Active brutality on the part of the husband may be uncommon, but she may suffer from a perhaps crueller neglect, should he ignore the naturally stronger needs of the newly-pregnant woman for more assured protection and closer-drawing intimacy. . . . If the husband stands closer to his wife, to share the added strain, the pregnancy experience becomes what Hans Selye

called "eustress," good stress, growth-promoting stress, the opposite of distress. . . . The unsuccoured wife is bound to undergo immense turmoil, bitter disappointment and perhaps outbursts, or more likely, "inbursts" of justifiable anger. She may regress, actually or emotionally, running back home, rejecting the husband and the marriage. These violent emotions, whether yearnings or revulsions, as all our present researches show, pass, in some as yet unfathomed way, into the placental circulation, entering the foetus through the umbilical cord.[21]

## PRENATAL BONDING AND THE HUSBAND

Not many decades ago, in England and the United States, the idea of a husband being no more than proudly, but distantly, interested in the pregnancy of his wife was generally accepted, and in the mid-Victorian era women retired from public life as soon as they became "obviously with child." The relationship of the father to the family was less intimately companionable than it is today. But there is a change, and it is noticeable that as early as the 1940s husbands have demanded to know more about childbirth. In many other countries, however, the cooperation of the husband in pregnancy has long been recognized as one of the first essentials of family life.

In the 1920s I started a series of lectures for men's organizations because of requests I had received to instruct groups of young and expectant fathers in what I considered should be their attitude and behavior during the pregnancy of their wives. These talks were given almost entirely to the working classes of the suburbs around London, and one of the main features at such meetings was that, after I had spoken, an hour should be set aside for questions and discussions.

It soon became obvious that the ignorance of the average man in the street about childbirth was incredible. At that time I had the advantage of being the father of a growing family of young children and was closely interested in the question of the husband's role during both pregnancy and the early months of infancy of his offspring.

Some of the men whose wives had to work, whether they were pregnant or not, expressed very strongly the view that the local nursing associations should organize what they called "mother's helpers," who would be responsible for many of the domestic duties that normally fell upon the shoulders of their wives. They were concerned for the health of the prospective mother but at the same time expressed no desire to take upon themselves some of the extra duties that they considered were too much for a pregnant woman.

Others made it clear that the woman of the house was responsible for the provision of food and comfort that they enjoyed when they came home after a strenuous day's work, but many broke down the natural reticence of the Englishman and stated quite plainly what they thought, in some such terms as these: "I love my wife—she's got to have all the trouble and pain of giving me a child. My job is to go on earning a living to keep the home together while she is ill, but I want to do more than that and I don't know how to be of any help to her."

That attitude of the husband toward the wife was very prevalent, and I have no doubt that it was prompted by a deep affection and concern for her welfare. The general trend of my talks was to elaborate this aspect of the husband-wife relationship by giving the men a simple explanation of what went on during pregnancy, how the child develops, and the changes that occur during pregnancy in a woman's mind, particularly toward her husband.

During pregnancy a woman's activities, thoughts, and behavior need careful understanding and considerable tolerance and unselfishness on the part of the husband. There is, in return for this small burden that he must bear, a change in his own attitude, for pregnancy often intensifies his love for his wife. It creates in him an ardent desire to take care of her and attend to her needs and wishes with tenderness and consideration.

The importance of the husband's attitude toward, and understanding of, childbirth cannot be exaggerated. His words and actions, and even the atmosphere in the house that he may create in silence, have a profound effect upon his wife. Her health and happiness during pregnancy, and certainly her approach to labor, will be influenced for better or for worse by harmony or discord that she feels in her husband's mind.

The real joy of childbirth is most frequently experienced when husband and wife have mutual confidence, affection, and understanding, and have worked together in preparation for the arrival of their baby.

A man who knows nothing about these things will often sublimate his ignorance in irritability—preferring to succumb to the latter rather than disclose the former. He may even state dogmatically what is sense and what is nonsense. His urge to take care of his wife, whom he loves very dearly, easily develops into a rigid military-type discipline. Men often formulate domestic principles during their wife's pregnancy, and demand that they be meticulously carried out. Rest, diet, exercise, recreation, and even personal hygiene are matters in which they suddenly become expert without absorbing any authoritative teaching on the subject. If the doctor does not agree— the doctor is wrong.

This is, of course, a manifestation of conflict in a man's mind. Pride, anxiety, and tenderness get horribly mixed up, and that is one of the main reasons why some husbands suffer so much in childbirth. They need preparation and understanding just as do their wives. The surest way of being of assistance in the cause of peace and confidence, both in the home and elsewhere, is to urge, with quiet but kindly-stern authority, that the husband learn with his wife the phenomena and common sense of this natural human function.

During the last several years I have been gratified to find that the majority of husbands accept this advice—and what a difference it makes to obstetrics!

Let us, insofar as possible, give a few wide generalizations of the signs and symptoms of pregnancy, both physical and emotional, that will become apparent to an observant and attentive husband.

Conception is a supreme event in a woman's life—it is the beginning of that phase which represents the achievement of her physiological purpose. Conscious and unconscious experiences of her childhood and early maturity flood the vista of her future while being strongly influenced by the fantasies of the past. Every impression that she has received of childbirth shapes her acceptance of pregnancy. Each stress or strain that has caused her doubts or fears during those years when the small girl rehearses to her secret self what motherhood must be finds a place in her mind. As women vary in nature so do these psychological manifestations, but even more important are the different aspects of parenthood that arise from such considerations as: Is the baby wanted or unwanted? Was it planned or accidental? Is she longing for a child but her husband disappointed that she is pregnant?

Women develop, very early after conception, an acuteness of mind and thought that intensifies their appreciation of the words and feelings of their husbands. Although it is not necessary to explore more deeply the actual psychological basis for her reactions, it should be recognized that these are not just whims and moods but real mental states based upon sound psychological deductions.

Herein lies the responsibility of a husband to his unborn child.

Happily, some men seem to have the inborn understanding of a woman's thoughts and needs at that time, and others wish to learn how they can be of service to the woman they love and admire. Husbands should take part in the intrauterine development of their children, learn and practice the important role of father. It is the most crucial phase in the life of a human being, for as the miracle of the child's construction progresses, the changing tissues, utilized in making the perfect form, may be deflected from the natural course. Therefore, the health of the mother is the responsibility of the father of the child and may thereby directly affect the quality of the baby.

There is so much more we need to learn of all these things. We know today that some of the things that happen during pregnancy may be attributed to superstitions that are not true (e.g., the child whose mother saw a horse stumble gets a wart on his neck!), but there may be something valid in some of the "old wives' tales." We are very unwise if we turn them down without a very discriminating investigation, especially those ideas which have stood the test of time.

Let this postulate be examined in simple common sense. A pregnant woman's health has certain manifestations, but first and foremost she must be *happy*. This demands companionship and interest in her baby and all that concerns it. She can be happy if her husband shares her hopes and anxieties, her laughter, and her waves of fear. He can be the safety valve of her unpredictable emotions and accept unmoved the explosions of her love, hate, fear, jealousy, and anger. The storms are usually followed by warm sunshine. But if she is alone and feels, justly or unjustly, that the baby she longs for has robbed her of her husband's love, serious temperamental and emotional states can occur that may set up local and sometimes general reactions within her body. A disturbed mind will upset the circulation of blood to certain organs of the body,[22] perhaps causing a serious deprivation of the oxygen supply within the body that is essential for the well-being of the small fetus in the womb.

Therefore, throughout pregnancy the husband's part develops with the wife's. He reads and learns with her the dignity, the beauty, and the spiritual advantages of family union. To understand he must learn, and to be the pillar of strength his wife desires takes time; but nothing can be of greater or more lasting value to each member of the family unit.

It becomes obvious that it is the pregnant *couple* that are to be nurtured by a caring community. Early pregnancy classes have great value—the husband can learn the profoundly important role he has to play for his unborn child's welfare. The husband can respond to his wife's emotional needs more fully as the community responds to his, allowing him to be freely involved from the outset. We are all responsible for assuring the happiness and welfare of the expectant couples among us, for the sake of our nation's unborn children.

The couple themselves can learn to nurture their child before birth,[23] not only by working toward harmony in their relationship and avoiding stress as much as possible within the home (including the stresses of changing jobs, moving into a larger home, etc.). They can learn to nurture their child in the womb, stroking it, singing and talking to it, reassuring it of their love. The pressure of loving touch, the sound of their voices directed *to* the infant, provides a sense of being recognized and accepted. The child can bond to the voices of both the mother and the father during the pregnancy, and thus bond more easily and quickly in the moments just after birth.

CHAPTER 2

# Birth with Dignity

**B**irth with dignity implies that a newborn arrives into a situation in which there is every consideration for the human aspects of birthing. Any necessary clinical care is carried out in an unobtrusive manner, with the mother's desires responded to respectfully. The presence of the baby's father is considered a valuable asset. The birth attendants interact with courtesy and human kindness not only with the parents, but with each other as well. The baby arrives in an atmosphere of peace and dignity, and receives immediate human touch and affirmation. The goal is the healthiest, best baby possible, and the most comfortable birth for the mother. All this is compatible with safe obstetrics. In fact, it is the safest way to have a baby. It is natural childbirth at its best.

## WHAT IS NATURAL CHILDBIRTH?

Natural childbirth is one part of a continuum of normal physiological events representing and illustrating the two basic laws of the continuance of a species, namely, the law of reproduction and the law of maintenance of the species. Natural childbirth means normal physiological childbirth. When childbirth becomes associated with varying degrees of fear and therefore varying degrees of tension, it becomes in varying degrees unphysiological or pathological.

Natural childbirth as originally stated never meant that every woman will have a completely painless childbirth, although it frequently produces no more discomfort than that which any woman herself wishes to experience, or is able to control by natural childbirth principles. Natural childbirth does not indicate that analgesics and/or anesthetics could never be used. Anesthetics should always be available if required, for no woman should be allowed to suffer pain needlessly.

The term "natural childbirth" has left a bad impression on many doctors because while in training at many teaching hospitals throughout our Western culture they frequently saw numerous examples of young women suffering through labor and birth with inadequate relief, which process was called, although incorrectly, "natural childbirth"; they seldom saw truly physiological childbirth during any of their medical training days, and, as a result, natural childbirth was synonymous with suffering and pain. Indeed, to many doctors, and to the general public as well, natural childbirth meant —and still means—simply childbirth without anesthetics or any kind of pain relief.

The suffering they continuously witnessed in childbirth so affected them that long before completing specialty training in medical school, internship, and three or four years of exposure in a residency they became dedicated to the principle that when they had their own private patients they would never let them suffer in birth, believing that without medication pain was inevitable. They determined that each and every one of their private patients would be entitled to some type of pain relief. And so, after a number of years of using pain relief for birth, too few have had the opportunity of seeing a truly physiological or natural childbirth.

Natural childbirth is a physiological birth, and when childbirth is not accompanied by fear and tension, or other pathological conditions, there seldom will be more discomfort than any woman wishes to experience. *The problem is that it is not always a simple matter to have her enter the labor suite completely relaxed, calm, and competent.* Each woman is different, and each one may require varying amounts of preparation time and effort in order for her to arrive at this most advantageous condition. The rewards—for the patient, for the newborn, for the husband, and for the family as a unit—are great. The principles are correct, and they do work clinically.

Throughout this book there are numerous instances where preventive medicine can be applied, not only in the interest of the baby, but in that of the mother, the father, and possibly even the society into which the baby enters. There is a message here for those in obstetrics, that they can significantly contribute, not only another birth to our already overcrowded population, but a certain amount of quality in the birth process that may aid in some small way—or perhaps great way—our society in general. And they should always remember that childbirth to many couples is a very private event, and that to others it is also deeply spiritual.

## NATURAL CHILDBIRTH AND PAIN

As stated above, natural childbirth does not necessarily mean painless childbirth. In the past, textbooks in obstetrics have used the word "pain" to mean "normal uterine contractions" so often that doctors began to believe that the pains of labor are the same as normal uterine contractions. Indeed, in the most current textbook on obstetrics, the word "pain" is used for contractions. Pain hurts; normal uterine contractions do not. In fact, uterine contractions will seldom give rise to any pain whatsoever if unassociated with fear and tension. Fear, of course, is followed by tension, and when cervical tension occurs in labor, the previously normal uterine contractions

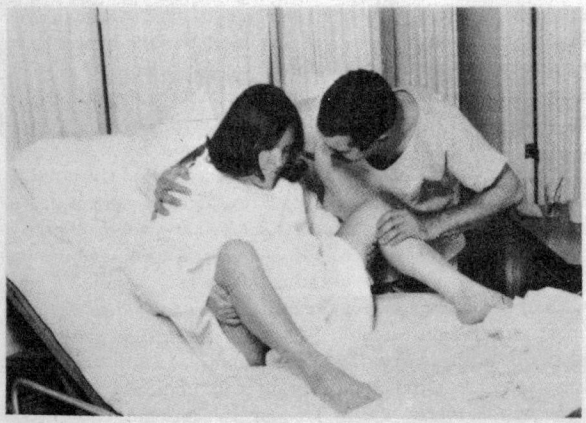

Position for overcoming backache in late transition and early second stage

Husband learning to use heel of hand for backache in labor

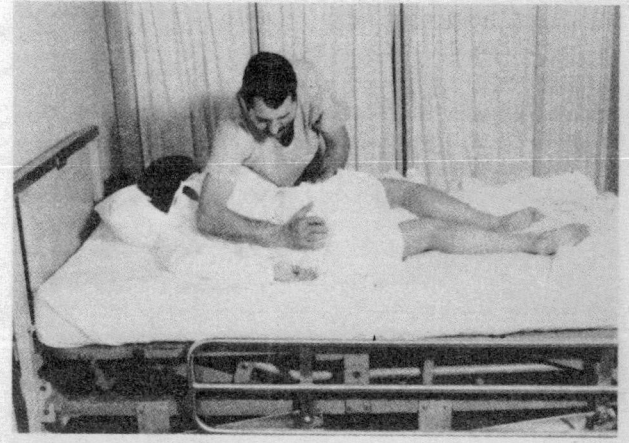

Husband massaging and applying pressure with heel of hand in labor

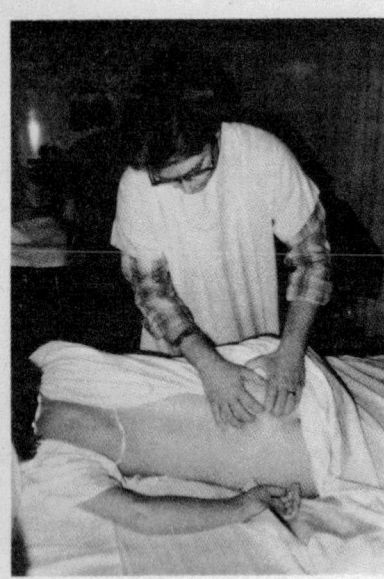

Husband digging in with
fingertips for backache
in labor

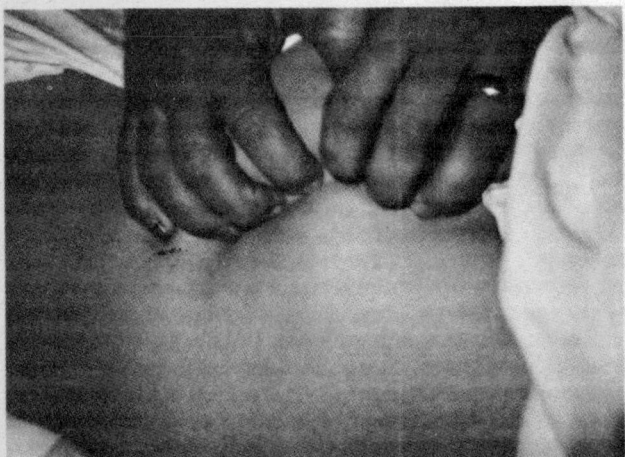

Intense fingertip pressure on sacrum for backache in labor

must overcome it. In their turn the uterine contractions get stronger, frequently to the point of producing varying amounts of pain, at which point they become pathological—that is, unphysiological—contractions.

As was said in 1920 by Rudyard Kipling, the *words* one uses are more powerful than any drug known to mankind. Thus it is important to realize the power of words upon the suggestibility of an obstetrical patient.

When we speak of fear or tension in connection with painful uterine contractions, we are talking about pathology. We are also talking about pathology when we speak of an *abruptio placenta* during a contraction; any degree of placental abruption, although minimal, causes pain. Another source of pathological pain during childbirth is contracting muscles fed by an inadequate supply of oxygen, as in angina pectoris. Such a condition can be caused by incorrect breathing. This demonstrates the importance of the natural childbirth principle of correct breathing during labor to prevent pain.

Still another area is involved in pain during labor, and that is the back. A back pain is most common with the first pregnancy, particularly toward the end of the first stage of labor. Note we are talking about pain *in the back*—the feeling a parturient patient has in the lower part of her back, usually over the sacral area—not about uterine contractions. In some this merely means a mild ache; in others it means more than mere discomfort; in still others it is severe pain. This discomfort can frequently be relieved adequately for many women by rubbing, for others by strong pressure from the heel of the hand or fingers of a prepared and trained husband. Other patients may require a change in position to overcome the problem. Others again may get into a "pelvic rocking" position for a short period of time, possibly aiding in the spontaneous rotation of a *posterior occiput* position. Still others may require analgesics or anesthetics of varying amounts for relief.

Another source of pain is the pubic area, and, while such discomfort occurs near the end of the first stage of labor, as is also true of pain in the back, the pubic area usually does not produce as much discomfort as the back. Too, a patient does not usually experience both the back discomfort and the pubic discomfort at the same time. Gentle massaging of the area, changing to a semisitting position with her knees raised, and breathing techniques are all that a woman requires to control this type of temporary discomfort.

Physicians have used anesthetics basically for pain at the actual birth because they felt this must be the most severe pain of the entire event. Indeed, a woman unprepared for natural childbirth can have severe pain at this time. She tightly contracts the pelvic floor in fear of the oncoming head, and this leads to severe pain as the baby emerges. With this type of unnatural birth, all of us would offer the appropriate amount of anesthetic. This, again, is not natural childbirth.

For the prepared patient, the birth itself usually means feelings of stretching, deep pressure, and, for some, discomfort—although seldom does a well-prepared patient feel any more discomfort at this time than she wishes to handle herself in order not to lose the more positive sensations of birth. But when the prepared woman who has just experienced natural childbirth is asked: "What is the most difficult part you experienced?" she doesn't mention the actual birth! She invariably replies: "The most difficult time came just before pushing," usually adding something like, "That back pain was really getting to me, but not the birth. The birth was exciting and I wouldn't have missed it for anything!" She felt the birth, yes, but, as an amazingly high number of women do, talks about it as a satisfying, exciting, good, thrilling experience. Even when asked in detail about the back pain, and why she would not accept anesthetics, she frequently replies: "Oh, it actually wasn't that bad," and adds: "Besides, I didn't want to take a chance on missing the experience of the birth."

When a woman complains of pain, it isn't psychological. It isn't emotional. It isn't "just in her head." If a woman has pain, she has pain, and her complaint should be taken at face value and her specific complaint responded to as effectively as possible. It is frequently said that in natural childbirth one has to "stand the pain"—have a high pain threshold. This is not so. It is very common for a woman who has a so-called low pain threshold to have an easy vaginal birth, if she is well prepared.

## STRESS RELIEVED

Fortunately, there is a proven way to prevent contraction pain from occurring. This is by applying complete muscular relaxation throughout the body. Anxiety or fear exerts a deleterious effect on uterine motility and cervical dilatation. But a woman who has the ability to relax at will can anticipate an easy labor and birth.

A tense doctor or attendant makes a tense patient and, in turn, a tense cervix. Tension of the cervix during an apparently normal uterine contraction produces an obstruction, which the uterine contraction must become stronger to overcome, producing more discomfort. When the cervical tension is severe, the uterine contractions become more powerful still—and certainly they are painful. Every woman should practice and learn complete muscular relaxation as if the ease of her childbirth depended on it, because it does!

*The ability to relax during a normal uterine contraction is a basic principle in natural childbirth.* For most women this must be learned, but for many the learning comes easily.

Relaxation performs many benefits during pregnancy, labor, birth, and during the immediate newborn period, but its opposites, tension and anxiety, as Cannon[1] and others have described in detail, produce many alterations of normal physiological processes throughout the body and work nothing but harm. If there is one characteristic that stands out above all others in an easy, non-medicated spontaneous birth, it is the characteristic of muscular relaxation. But in most labor wards where the principles of natural childbirth are not practiced, exactly the opposite is obvious: patients hang on during a contraction, brace themselves, tense against each oncoming one. A patient preparing for a comfortable childbirth experience *must* learn relaxation.

The woman in labor should be under *no* stress other than that of being in labor. Her surroundings, attendants, the procedures, her expectations of those procedures, must all be planned to keep stress at an absolute minimum. Any stress to the mother stimulates the adrenal glands to pour out *catecholemines.* As a result, muscle sphincters tighten down, making uterine contractions less effective and sending blood away from the uterus to the arms and legs, because stress and tension prepare the body for fight or flight. All this prevents an adequate supply of oxygen to the big contracting muscle —the uterus. No wonder it becomes painful—the uterus itself becomes painful!

On the other hand, anything which aids peace of mind and relaxation of the body stimulates the brain into producing *endorphines,* which are nature's own painkillers. There are at least seven different kinds of endorphines, some of which have analgesic actions analogous to externally injected morphine[2] (a potent and dangerous form of pain relief seldom used in pregnancy or birth because of its danger to the baby).

The lack of stress and muscular relaxation does not mean that the laboring woman has to be lying down all the time. It is far better for her to stay out of the labor bed as long as possible. She can sit in a rocking chair comfortably; the upright position and slight activity of rocking are good for the labor, and she can still relax completely during contractions. She can walk around as much as is comfortable, go to the bathroom, stroll up and down the halls. When she is in bed, she can relax comfortably on her left side (to aid blood flow to the uterus and the baby) or in the reclining chair position.

## SUPPORT PERSONS

Perhaps the most important element in helping to eliminate stress and promote proper birthing is the loving attention of a support person in whom the woman has complete confidence. Klaus and Kennell have reported on a study of several hundred births in Guatemala, in which the presence of a *doula* (supportive person) shortened labors by as much as one third.[3]

In the United States, the support person is most often the husband, although this has occurred in some earlier cultures also. Margaret Mead writes of certain healthy Polynesian societies where husbands played active roles in the care of their wives during labor.[4] In some other cultures the husband has actually assumed direction, supervising the birth.[5]

This very special person provides support during pregnancy as well as during birth and bonding. The support person is especially necessary with a high-risk mother, for example in a breech birth, a premature birth, or a cesarean birth. This is not just a "fun" thing, it is *essential* in lowering stress and thus lowering risk. If the husband is not able to be present at the birth, then someone else emotionally close to the woman in labor should be there, her mother or sister or sister-in-law or close friend.

It is important to have some knowledge of the support person and his or her special needs. For example, one husband had recently been caring for his father who was dying of cancer; he visited the father in the hospital every day until the father died. In the meantime, his wife became pregnant. Because of his painful associations, he couldn't bring himself to go near a hospital, so arrangements had to be made for an alternate support person for his wife at the time of birth.

In another instance, the mother was a heroin addict and the husband in jail. The judge made it possible for the husband to come

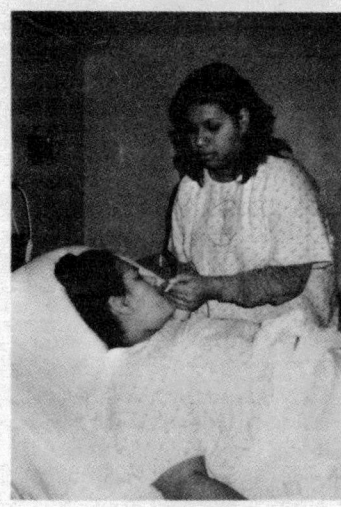

Teenage daughter as support person in labor

to prenatal sessions with his wife, but in handcuffs! He was at the birth with his wife. Hopefully, through the good experience they had with this birth, this child will have some positive impact on their lives.

A diabetic husband supporting his wife may go without eating, or forget his insulin. Thus the staff has to anticipate the special needs of the support person as well as the mother. Each couple is unique, with its own particular history and/or problems.

Those husbands who participate during labor and birth are taught that they are not to be there as an observer to see a birth; they can be shown a film for that. Nor are they there to assist the doctor or the nurse. Each is to be there for the sole purpose of assisting his wife and then sharing her joy in their child's arrival.

Husbands are taught in the preparation classes and in books such as this and others[6,7] that they have specific duties in the labor and birth room. Each is taught, for example, to remain close by the side of his wife, to help her relax; to rub her back and apply pressure if she has back pain; and to give her continual emotional and physical support.

Following the birth, the husband has new responsibilities, not only in relation to his wife, but to his newborn. Husbands are taught that they must not wait until their child is five or six years of age to develop a relationship, but they must do so from the moment of birth. An important part of the husband's new role is to encourage his wife's close relationship with the baby as well, including such factors as skin-to-skin contact and breastfeeding, which are not minor matters but important aspects of the growth and development of the newborn. Indeed, much of the future of the newborn depends on the parents' attitude and relationship to him or her *starting at birth.* [8] A good experience for the husband at the birth of his child won't solve all future problems, of course, but it may provide the stimulus for a close relationship that will endure.

## THE CHILDBIRTH TEAM

The support person is just one member of the childbirth team, which works together for a safe, comfortable birth for mother and baby. The physician is an important member of that team, whether he or she is the one attending the birth or the one providing back-up for certified nurse-midwives or other qualified birth attendants. The obstetrician is one who "stands by," ready to make his or her medical skill available if there is special need, if not the one actually attending the birth.

The childbirth educator(s) have an important role. They provide added support for the husband/wife laboring couple, unobtrusively. If they are working through a physician, they can take calls twenty-four hours a day to answer questions, meet the couple at the hospital or birthing center entrance, and facilitate harmony with the obstetric staff.

*It is the team effort that makes natural childbirth the success it is.* This includes not only the patient and her husband, but the obstetrician, prenatal nurses, and childbirth training personnel. In the hospital or birthing center it includes every individual who comes into contact with the prepared couple, from the admitting, labor, and delivery personnel to the postpartum nurses.

Husbands who are aware of the sincere interest of the hospital staff and obstetrician in observing all the safeguards for their wife and baby have little or no inclination to put blame on the hospital or doctor, even when the outcome is not a healthy, normal child.

When a prepared couple enter a hospital and the first question asked them is "How hard are your pains?" and this by a supposed hospital authority, they are certainly anything but encouraged! What a difference when one says, "How strong are your contractions?" Most sensitive husbands are very quick to pick up an atmosphere of negativity among labor and delivery room personnel, which may cause the experience to end up as a contest—hospital personnel versus husband. Because he is concerned for the welfare of his wife, he wants to protect her from negative influences and from interruptions that may disturb her relaxation and comfort.

It is important that medical students, interns, and obstetrical residents learn that they can tell *more* about the progress of the labor by a detailed observation of three or four uterine contractions than they can by three or four rectal or vaginal examinations. This does not mean that internal examinations are not important, for of course they are, and a certain number need to be done. One can frequently tell the sensitivity of an obstetrician, student, intern, or nurse by the care and expertise with which they do a proper painless vaginal examination.

Hospital personnel, as well as the doctor, must remember that since during a uterine contraction the husband may have his wife completely relaxed, this is not the time to interrupt in order to get a urine specimen or make some other routine examination. And it must also be remembered that there appears to be minimal value to perineal preps or routine enemas, which most women dislike intensely.

During the end of the first stage of labor it is important to give continuous support to both husband and wife. If the woman is to be transferred to the birth room, it should not be during a uterine contraction. There is ample time between. As soon as the second stage of labor has begun and the bearing down starts, it is important that she be propped up adequately in as much of a sitting position as possible.

Natural childbirth backrests are available that fit most birth room tables. These can be elevated to almost any degree, and are indeed very helpful. With the patient prepared for natural childbirth, her husband at her side, the back of the table elevated, and the patient bearing down with each uterine contraction, there appears to be little question that the second stage of labor can be shortened. With such a wide-awake, cooperative patient, there is no need for such things as hands being strapped to the table. While the patient is on the birth table the room must be kept absolutely quiet, so that she can remain deeply relaxed between uterine contractions, with no thoughtless remarks or even irrelevant banter between physician and husband. The laboring mother is to be the respectful center of everyone's loving attention until she has successfully given birth to her baby.

## NATURAL SURROUNDINGS FOR A NATURAL EVENT

How much better for a patient, having completed a natural childbirth training program, to be greeted as she enters the labor room by someone she knows. One of the requirements for an attendant working on the maternity ward should be that he or she should be part of the childbirth education program. If the patient and her husband have visited the hospital labor and birth area enough times to feel comfortable with the surroundings, their entrance at this time will not produce the anxiety and apprehension that is so common when a patient enters strange surroundings and sees personnel she has never met before.

Ideally, a maternity ward should have a waiting room lounge equipped with television, stereo, magazines, and games. This waiting room would not be for husbands, but for *couples* in early labor. How often a patient is "not sure" if labor is under way, particularly if she has been so well trained in natural childbirth that she can feel the contractions even though they are barely perceptible. Too often she arrives at the hospital in early labor, is admitted, put to bed and in a labor room—only to be sent home several hours later when contractions cease, or prove to have been "false labor."

How much better it would be to have a comfortable waiting room lounge where those who think they "might be" in labor could come as guests, without being formally admitted. Husband and wife could then relax, watch television, play games, or read. If labor really proved to be under way, this would be a tremendous advantage—no last-minute "rush" to the hospital would be needed. If not, the couple could return home later without having inconvenienced anyone, and without embarrassment. This lounge could perhaps also serve as the room where childbirth classes are held, and thus be a familiar, comfortable place.

If the patient is definitely in labor, she is taken to a labor room, a room that has all the decor and atmosphere of home—which does not mean it has to lack aseptic conditions. The setting up of such a room may require a little planning and some imagination by interior decorators and architects, but basically it does not need elaborate or expensive equipment.

Many hospitals are providing birthing rooms where the mother may labor, give birth, and spend bonding time all in the same bed, her husband present throughout. Many birthing rooms have a double bed, so that during the night or a slow labor, the husband can lie down beside his wife at any time. It is now recognized that the closeness, touch, and caresses of a loving husband can be a great asset in facilitating labor. Too often the beds even in birthing rooms are too narrow for this to take place, or when the husband is tired he sits in a comfortable chair across the room. How much better if he can lie down beside his wife with his arm around her. She is used to relaxing next to him during the night. Her sense of his warmth and closeness to her is not only relaxing, but relieves her anxiety about his fatigue. When the time for birth approaches, it is a simple matter to slip sterile pads under the mother on the bed, which can be removed after the birth. Both parents can then lie in the bed bonding with their new baby, if birth occurs during the night or it has been a long labor.

Some labor and birthing rooms have beds that are firm, electrically operated, and that can also be used as a guerney to transport the mother in emergency. (A separate guerney is necessary if the bed is a double bed.) Some of the newer labor beds have a triangular attachment, which, when added, allows the patient to turn only about thirty degrees to be in position for the birth, without ever moving her into the birth room. The expense and cost of maternity care is diminished with this type of birth.

Still other birthing rooms have a labor bed that converts into a birthing chair. The foot of the bed drops away and the back raises, so that the mother is in a semisitting position for the birth. During labor, the arm and leg rests are more comfortable for side-lying, which may also help turn babies which are lying in the posterior (face-up) position. It also provides support for the woman giving birth lying on her side.

Rocking chairs should be available for the mothers' use in the labor suite, if not in the birthing room itself, and comfortable chairs for the husbands. It is best for the woman in labor to be up as much as possible; a rocking chair provides activity, while still keeping her in an upright position with its advantages of gravity.

The room should have lights that can be dimmed and a decor

that is comfortable and relaxing, with harmonious colors and a few attractive pictures. Perhaps the day will come when all labor rooms can have this homelike atmosphere. Even for high-risk mothers, where closer supervision and more interventions may be needed, these considerations would aid rather than detract from the comfort and safety of the birth.

The atmosphere of the birthing room should be that of a comfortable room at home. Yet what makes a birthing room effective is not the decor, but the parents' knowledge that the usual interventions will not be imposed against their wishes. IV paraphernalia, fetal monitors, and staff coming in and out to give injections or make frequent vaginal exams will negate the effect of even the most beautiful room. A sign should be on the door: "Knock Before Entering." One of the comforts of home is the right to privacy. The couple should be alone as much—or as little—as they desire, their peace undisturbed, but with staff close by to respond immediately whenever requested.

An alternative to hospital or home birth is the birthing center, which has grown tremendously in popularity in a short period of time. The concept of birthing centers is not new, but is a revival of the "maternity homes" of the past. In 1975 there were only three birthing centers in the United States; by 1981 there were an estimated 125 to 150, and this number is increasing rapidly.[9] About one third of the centers are operated by or utilize nurse-midwives as the primary providers of care expertise. Others are sponsored by physicians and/or lay midwives under the supervision of physicians. All the free-standing birth centers are associated with hospitals.

Regardless of the setting in which the birth occurs the cooperation of the team is essential not only during labor, but during the actual birth as well. A common custom is to hold a baby up by the feet right after birth. This should never be done, for it increases the danger of intracranial pressure and may be harmful. If even minimal hemorrhages had occurred in the brain during birth, permitting the head to be lowered would have a tendency to increase bleeding that the attendants were not aware was taking place.

Instead, the baby is delivered up over the abdomen into its mother's waiting arms and laid on her abdomen for immediate skin-to-skin contact. The cord is long enough for the mother to put her baby to the breast for immediate newborn breastfeeding. The cord is not clamped immediately, nor is it milked in an effort to force an unusual amount of blood into the baby.

The baby remains in the mother's arms until the third stage of labor, the delivery of the placenta, has been completed. The only cleaning of the baby necessary is a gentle washing off of any blood or meconium. The normal *vernix caseosa*—the whitish, cheesy deposit covering the baby's skin at birth—is not removed, nor is to be removed later, since it may be of value in protecting the newborn from skin infections. It is gradually absorbed into the skin.

The one- and five-minute Apgar scores can easily be made while the parents are holding their baby; the child can then be tagged and weighed right in front of the parents' eyes after a few moments, and given back to them. If birth took place in a hospital delivery room, the father should have ample opportunity to hold and bond with his new baby before the mother is returned to her room—or before she returns herself, for in natural childbirth many mothers prefer to get up from the birthing table and walk back to bed. The baby stays with the parents until they are all discharged from the hospital, often within a few hours of the birth.

From all this it is obvious that it takes a team effort. *If any portion of this team breaks down, it can be expected that the accomplishments will be proportionately less.*

## CHILDREN PRESENT AT BIRTH

With the more relaxed atmosphere of a birthing room in the hospital, or a birthing center, some couples like to have other people present at the birth—grandparents, close family members or friends, or their own children. In this case it is helpful to hold an informal class for grandparents, and special classes for siblings of the newborn, in order to prepare them for being present. The parents' decisions about who is to be present at the birth need to be worked out in advance with those who will be responsible for the birth.

More commonly what is encouraged is sibling bonding within minutes following birth. The decision to allow siblings at birth depends on the age of the children, their preparation, and the enthusiasm of the physician and hospital staff. Such a choice should of course be made only when one might expect a *positive* effect on the sibling. It would not be in the best interest of the mother if she felt she had to "perform."

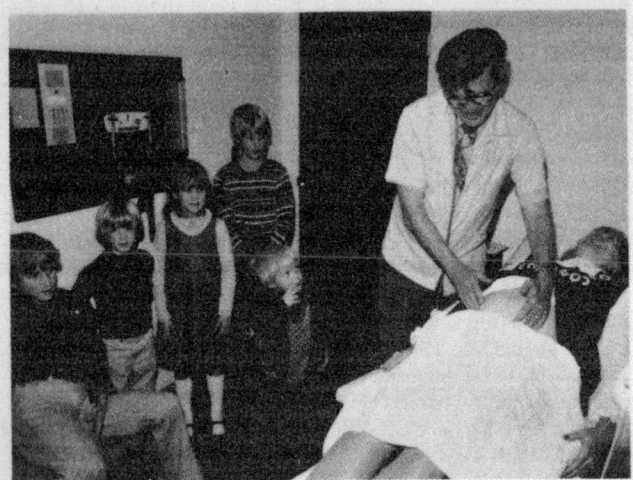

With mother at prenatal visit

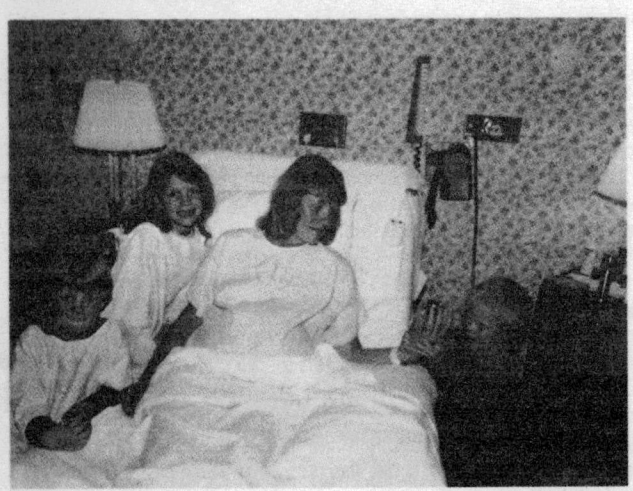

At home in the birthing room

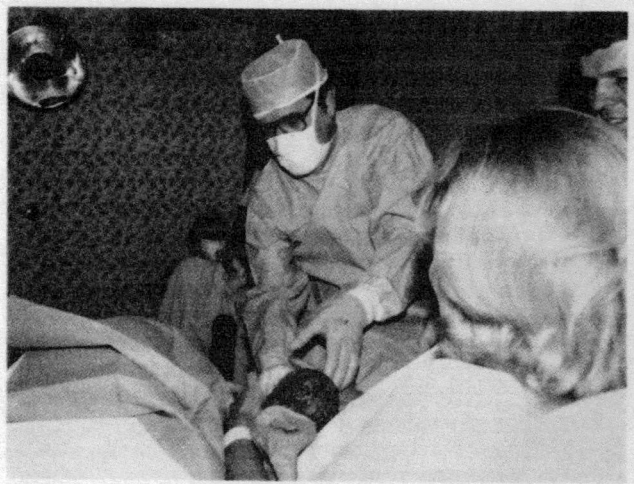

Baby born into mother's waiting hands, little sister watching

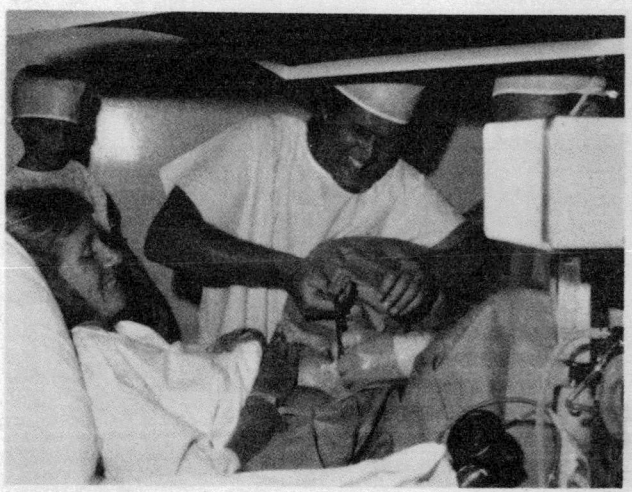

Father cuts the cord

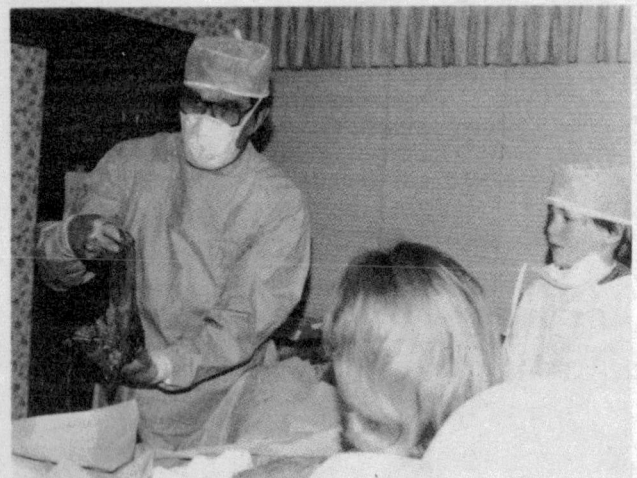

Doctor explaining the placenta and sac to the children

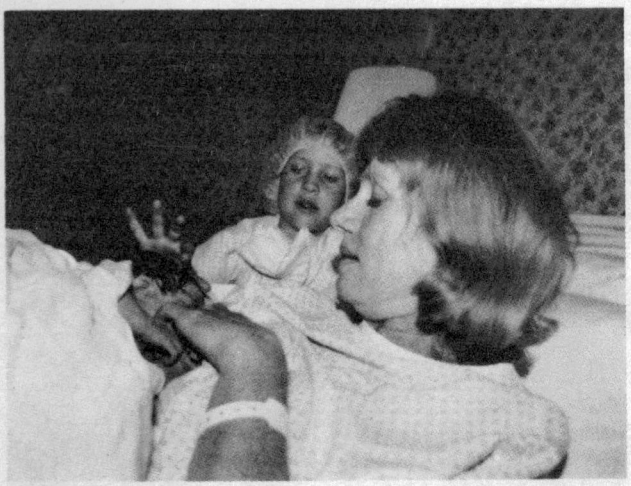

Immediate newborn breastfeeding

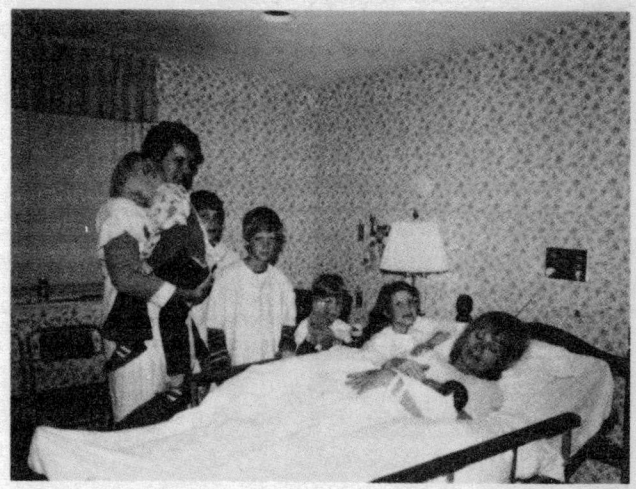

It's been a long night!

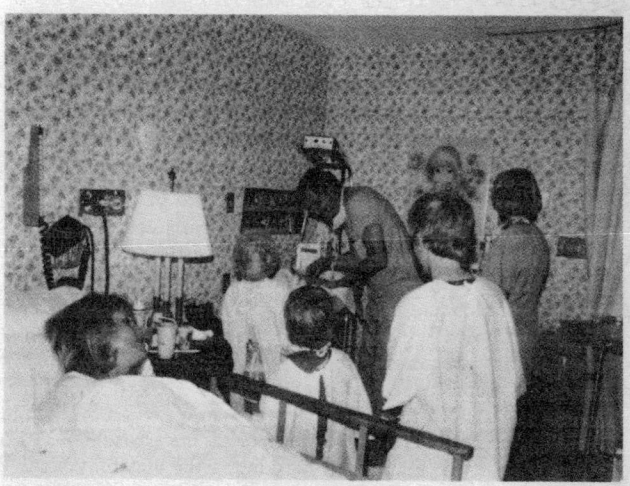

Children watch doctor checking newborn

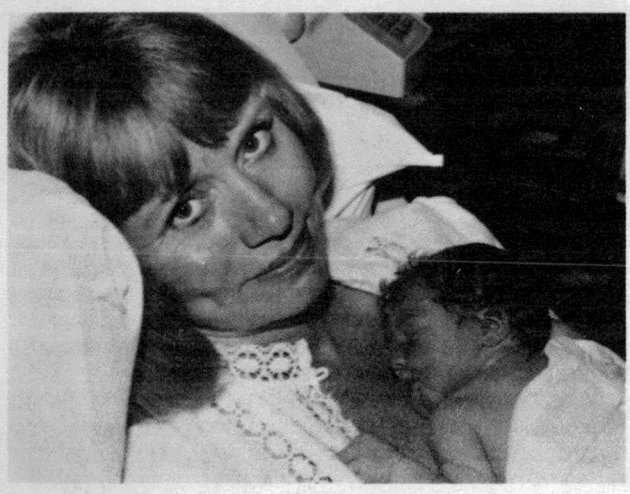

Skin-to-skin with mother first twenty-four hours

## *EDUCATION FOR NATURAL CHILDBIRTH*

If the birth is to be in a hospital, the training program preferably should be given in that hospital by the personnel who will be providing care at the birth, a concept designed to increase the confidence of the patient and also the hospital personnel. If this is not feasible, the couple should have ample opportunity to become familiar with the settings where birth will take place and meet those who will be assisting at the birth. The needs are:

1. A room large enough to train at least fifteen couples at any one time.

2. A movie projector and such films as are available, to aid in childbirth education and training.

3. A blackboard.

4. A library adequately supplied with all types of childbirth education and training material.

5. Charts, such as the birth atlas.

6. Other available audiovisual educational materials.

7. Personnel who are actively working in the maternity ward areas of the hospital, including labor, birth, and postpartum.

In addition, the maternity or birth center personnel should be assisted by the office personnel from the various doctors' offices. In this way all of the personnel who come in contact with the obstetrical patient will be intimately associated with the basic principles of natural childbirth and family-centered maternity care, producing a continuous line of care from the doctor's prenatal office through the labor, birth, and postpartum period, and back to the doctor's office.

Ideally there are four distinct parts to this type of childbirth education:[10] (1) *eight two-hour sessions* to be given in early pregnancy; (2) *eight two-hour sessions* given in late pregnancy (a total of sixteen prenatal classes); (3) *in-service training* given during the hospital postpartum stay; and (4) *four two-hour ABC* (After Baby Comes) *sessions,* a time of discussion, sharing, and support for new mothers and their babies.

## CLASSES IN EARLY PREGNANCY

It is extremely important that childbirth preparation classes begin *early* in pregnancy, at least by the end of the first trimester, so the expectant parents can put into practice all those things that will make for a healthier pregnancy as well as for a happier labor and birth. Conception to birth to nine months of age is presented as a continuum so that couples understand that the birth of the baby is just one important landmark along the way, in the optimum development of the potential of their infant. This concept is discussed at length in the first session, along with a hospital tour. A few exercises (pelvic rock, good posture, tailor sitting), training in relaxation, and some ideas on comfort measures are also introduced.

The second session is devoted to nutrition, the discussion including the quality of foods necessary, as well as the need to avoid refined foods and sugars. The importance of good nutrition is stressed not only for the infant while *in utero,* but as a good foundation for his or her development after birth. There is no better time to educate young couples for good eating than when they are setting a nutritional pattern for their expected child during pregnancy. It is an ideal time for them to evaluate their own nutritional needs and life-long nutritional goals.

Additional early pregnancy classes should include sessions on sexuality; breastfeeding; stimulating the emotional, intellectual, and physical development of the infant from birth through nine months; illness prevention and care of the baby from birth through nine months; emergency care, car safety, and safe-proofing the home; and one session devoted to a "Prenatal Potluck," with the topic being

"Nourishment of the Newborn," in which nutrition during pregnancy and breastfeeding is discussed.

Reading material should always be available to allow the prospective parents to study and investigate any of the subjects covered in more detail. During these early classes relaxation is emphasized, for it takes considerable practice for some patients to learn how to develop muscular relaxation. Others learn more readily. But for those who find it difficult, the additional weeks for practice can be of incalculable benefit during pregnancy as well as during birth. Once muscular relaxation has been adequately learned, it can be utilized for getting to sleep more quickly at night and for gaining much more benefit from short times of rest through the day.

These early classes help awaken the husband's realization that he has a great opportunity to assist his wife during pregnancy, childbirth, and with their newborn child, and to consider the factors affecting the emotional, mental, and physical potential of this child. When this material is given early, the parents have opportunity for further study on their own in the quieter months before the child arrives. Young couples who are expecting for the first time are often excited about the prospect of parenthood and are highly motivated at the outset of pregnancy to learn all they can. These sessions therefore provide an ideal opportunity for pediatricians, psychiatrists, psychologists, sociologists, educators, and members of other disciplines in our society to be on hand for questions and answers.

## CLASSES IN LATE PREGNANCY

These eight sessions are designed to train the couple to work as a team during the birth itself. They should include: (1) introduction and role of the support person, the mechanisms of labor and birth; (2) early first stages of labor, exercises, *relaxation,* breathing techniques, film; (3) discussion of possible problems, such as the need for fetal monitoring, cesarean sections, and the presence of newborn jaundice; (4) late first-stage labor, transition, exercises, techniques for comfort, film; (5) second-stage labor, slides, and hospital tour; (6) review, mock labor "practice," film; (7) parent-infant bonding, postpartum care, hospital stay, film; and (8) guest speaker on parenting.

## IN-HOSPITAL TRAINING

While in the hospital, further guidance is to be given on continued bonding with the newborn. Family planning information should be made available, as well as further guidance on nutrition and breastfeeding. Parents should also be taught how to bathe, diaper, and otherwise care for their babies. And this is an important time for sibling bonding.

### AFTER BABY COMES CLASSES (SOME CALL THIS "AFTER BIRTH CRISES")

These four once-a-week sessions for new mothers and their babies up to three months old explore coping with a host of new experiences—the "advice" of others, nights, crying, sleeping, feeding, and so on. These informal sessions often form friendships between the participants that continue for years to come.

In addition to these four distinct, essential parts of an adequate childbirth education program, some additional classes may be offered. Cesarean birth classes are helpful, for example, for those who know that a cesarean birth will probably be necessary. These classes should include the father's role.

It is helpful to have classes for the brothers and sisters of the new baby, even if they are not to be present at the birth. It is really important to understand how siblings feel and for them to be ready for the coming of the new baby. A little display can be made of how baby grows in the mother's body and how it is born, the teacher sitting down on the floor among the children. The children can chat about this informally and express their ideas and questions. After the session children can draw pictures at home of what they think babies look like, bringing these back to the next session to talk about. A little certificate could be given to them at the end of the series. Children who will be present for the birth will need some additional instruction.

One session for grandparents or others who are to be at the birth is also helpful, to talk informally about natural childbirth, what to expect at the birth, breastfeeding, and so forth, letting them air their questions and feelings from the perspective of their generation.

## CHAPTER 3

# A Healthy Pregnancy

As soon as a woman becomes pregnant, she should seek medical advice. When she does so, she usually attends a prenatal clinic or visits a doctor. She wishes to know that all is well and to be in contact with some person from whom she can get advice upon matters relating to the birth of her child, and through whom she can arrange for a bed in the maternity ward of a hospital.

We overlook, perhaps, the excitement that attends these preliminary arrangements and the disappointment when preparations cannot be made according to plan. During the first pregnancy in particular, the average woman needs considerable support; she requires explanation of unfamiliar occurrences. The doctor, the nurse, and the prenatal clinic are responsible for her attitude toward childbirth, for these people are, in her eyes, experts on the subject.

To a young woman appearance, shape, and gracefulness are matters of serious importance. She is rightly proud of her figure; she demands to retain its beauty; she dislikes the ungainly spectacle of women whom she has seen in the later months of pregnancy; she fears swollen ankles, pigmented patches upon her face, white lines and stretch marks upon her abdomen, and development of the breasts. Attention needs to be given to these matters, along with explanation and care, by one who shows obvious interest in her well-being.

Of course she has her pelvis measured, her blood pressure taken, her abdomen listened to and prodded, the urine examined, blood taken for grouping, Rh factor, type, and complete blood count. But even if all is well, there is still need for a great deal more than just a few hints as to exercise and diet. However complete the prenatal care may be according to all accepted rules, it is lifeless if the mind is not cared for. And however carefully physical conditions are diagnosed and corrected, all these attentions may well be in vain if the emotional influences are abnormal. No woman should arrive at the hospital in labor without adequate preparation from qualified teachers.

Some women attend prenatal classes in hospitals or elsewhere, only to discover when labor begins that they have learned little that is of value to them *in labor*. There is nothing more disconcerting to a woman in labor than to find that she has been misinformed, or misled, concerning the part she must take in the process of childbirth. Untrue statements are worse than no teaching, for they add to the woman's disappointment a complete loss of confidence in her attendants.

We have to beware of those who aspire to teach never having learned! In such instances the approach to childbirth as a natural or physiological function will most likely be misrepresented, and a high percentage of failures earn a bad name for procedures that have been improperly employed. Intellectual information may be given concerning pregnancy and birth, but relaxation and correct breathing may be incompletely taught and their use as *essential* functions of normal labor not explained.

In other cases, a wonderful picture of positive painless achievement may be repeated at each meeting or class. But surely any teacher of experience knows that no one has the right to imply, without some qualifications, an invariable course of labor. A hundred possible variations of physical and emotional phenomena at the time of birth must be anticipated by the good clinician, and any that are harmful or threatening to the comfort or well-being of the mother or her child call for special attention and care.

Women inadequately trained for a natural birth have suffered severe frustration and disappointment when deviation from the absolutely normal has to be corrected by assistance. Others who suffered more discomfort than they were led to understand might occur have hesitated to ask for, and even been unwilling to receive, pain relief, and by their refusal increased their babies' and their own troubles.

Women improperly taught believe that pain relief by injections, drugs, or analgesics is evidence of failure and become morbidly depressed. I have too many reports from others who blame themselves because salutary scientific interference has been clinically indicated and skillfully employed. This is not the woman's fault; had she been properly and understandingly prepared she would have known the possibility that help might be advisable, and that birth can be made easier for both herself and her baby in these circumstances.

No woman unprepared for the possibility of rectifiable difficulty has been accurately taught the natural childbirth principles, for in these that possibility is strongly emphasized, in simple terms, enabling her to understand that modern science can help when trouble arises. Such knowledge gives courage and confidence, not fear.

Reproduction is a natural physiological function, not an illness. Our aim is to ensure good health, both physical and mental, during pregnancy and so minimize the discomforts of labor and the necessity for interference, in order to assure the safe arrival of a healthy baby.

There are five specific objectives a conscientious physician may employ to help achieve these good results:

1. *To observe* the physical condition of pregnant women in order to prevent or diagnose as early as possible any abnormalities or irregularities that may disturb the health of either the mother or child during pregnancy, childbirth, or the postpartum period.

2. *To be forewarned* of physical or mechanical factors predisposing to a difficult labor, in order to avoid as far as possible emergent and unpremeditated interference.

3. *To educate* women concerning pregnancy and childbirth so that the inhibiting influence of fear may be replaced by understanding and confidence.

4. *To instruct* women in each phenomenon of normal labor so that they may be prepared to interpret its varying sensations correctly, and meet its demands with discernment, patience, and self-control, assisting the natural forces rather than resisting them.

5. *To teach* women how to prepare themselves for the birth of the child in a manner that will enable them:

    a. *To relax* when tension will cause resistance and pain, particularly during the contractions of the first stage of labor.

    b. *To breathe* normally and without thought, for when physically relaxed and without fear, breathing will automatically pace itself to the activity of the uterus.

c. *To be physically fit* in order to persist in the expulsive effort of the second stage of labor without undue exhaustion.

The first two objectives are in the province of purely medical attention rather than prenatal education. Therefore I shall not discuss them fully, because they are described in manuals and textbooks of obstetrics for the guidance of students, graduates, and postgraduates. It is numbers 3 through 5, and their application to the physically healthy woman who is well equipped to have her baby normally, that I propose to emphasize, with more details in later chapters.

When a young woman enters the consulting room believing, hoping, or fearing that she is going to have a baby, the physician's first investigations should be to confirm that she is pregnant. This may be ascertained by clinical signs, without an internal or vaginal examination at the first visit. If at thirteen weeks the uterus is not in the correct place and position, a vaginal investigation should be carefully performed for sound clinical reasons.

The doctor should then examine her attitude toward childbirth, both personally and generally. Close observation will unmask the true feelings of the prospective mother. We have all known the apparently indifferent woman, the enthusiastic, the alarmed, the radiantly happy, the angry, and the tearful. From such indications we may well mark out the psychological ground that has to be covered.

It should not be difficult to discuss quite freely any doubts or anxieties arising in the mind of the expectant mother. The attitude of the obstetrician should be that of an impersonal but approachable counselor, and it is for this reason that it is best—in private practice —to arrange a fee inclusive of all visits during pregnancy as well as labor and the weeks following. This kind of arrangement leaves a woman free to see her doctor when and as often as she wishes, which is a great comfort to many. At a chosen moment, it is my practice to point out that I want my patient to know everything she wishes about childbirth, and that any questions in her mind should be put to me until the point is clearly understood: "I am far more concerned that you should have no doubts or fears in your mind than I am about your health. You are a perfectly healthy girl doing a perfectly natural thing. Your body is much less likely to mar your happiness just now than your mind is. If you cannot remember the various things you want to ask me, write them down as they come to your mind. We can probably settle them in a very few minutes. I am here to watch your physical development, to guard you against ignorance and misunderstanding, and to be an adviser upon all subjects directly concerning your baby's arrival in a natural and healthy way."

Not infrequently, if the spirit of the occasion is suitable, I add some phrase to allay self-consciousness on the part of my patient lest I might think some of the questions foolish. Many women do not ask questions because they feel they ought to know the reply, and feel foolish mentioning a simple, but to them perplexing, subject. "Talk to me about it," I have frequently said. "We can say a lot in five minutes, and you are not wasting my time." And that is true. Measurements of blood pressure and hemoglobin, urinalysis, and abdominal examination can be conducted inside fifteen minutes if the consulting room is well organized. In a prenatal clinic, where the work is probably divided, five to ten minutes per patient is the maximum required for full routine examinations. This gives time for conversation, which, if it leads to important matters, can be prolonged.

But it is not the time that matters; it is the personal relationship, the friendliness of greeting, and the gentle care in examination that breaks down the barriers of shyness. Kindness can be dispensed as quickly as first aid, and a good deal more effectively, because its relief is permanent. Sympathetic understanding of troubles, both physical and mental, is an inexpensive remedy that often lifts a load of weariness and worry. Women are receptive at this time, and should be quietly guided to become interested in details.

The prospective mother should be taught how the baby grows in the womb, and how it is born. But she should also be reminded of those basic everyday rules of good health which we all need to enjoy life to the full: good nutrition, correct breathing, good posture and moderate exercise, and conscious control of muscular relaxation. There are no "tricks," no fancy breathings, no difficult, unnatural, or complicated techniques to be learned. But *disciplined application of these few basic principles is essential for a healthy pregnancy, as well as for a happy outcome at birth.*

## NUTRITION

There is little reason why a woman should alter the normal diet with which she has maintained good health. Her body is accustomed to it, and any sudden change may do more harm than good. Skipping meals or going on crash diets to avoid weight gain is foolish, and detrimental to her basic health and vitality.

Vegetarians need not add to or change their food, provided they are receiving enough protein. They generally have less trouble with pregnancy and labor than those who are heavy meat-eaters, because the latter tend to skimp on fresh vegetables and fruits. If a woman is accustomed to eating meat, she would do well to choose liver, fish, and poultry more often·than beef, pork, or lamb, and to balance it with salads rather than potatoes and gravy.

*Fluids* assist in the metabolism of other foods. An adequate amount of *protein* is essential, and is found in lean meat, eggs, milk, peas, beans, and nuts. Wheat germ is an excellent source of added protein and B vitamins. *Fats* are necessary as fuel for heat and energy in the body, and are obtained in cream, butter, cheese, and some of the fat meats. *Carbohydrates* are also energy-making, and should be obtained in their unrefined form in potatoes, milk, unrefined rice, whole grains, unrefined flours, and unrefined natural sugars.

*Iron, calcium, phosphorus, iodine,* and all the *vitamins* and *minerals* are necessary; they are supplied in a well-balanced diet containing fish and liver, milk, grains (100 percent whole wheat, barley, oats, etc.), fresh vegetables, and fresh citrus fruits.

Some physicians advise supplemental vitamins and minerals such as *zinc, folic acid,* and especially *vitamins C* and *E.* Folic acid is a member of the B complex family and received its name from green leafy vegetables, or *foliage;* much of it is destroyed by cooking, canning, processing, and storage. Zinc and vitamin C must be present in the diet for folic acid to be properly utilized. Many Americans have too few fresh, deep green, leafy vegetables in their diet. Inadequate folic acid has been implicated in some premature births and related pregnancy problems.[1]

Alcohol and smoking are unwise. Research on smoking in pregnancy has shown its relationship to: (1) miscarriage and prematurity; (2) smaller babies at birth (hence a smaller, less-developed brain); (3) learning disabilities; (4) respiratory infections; and (5) an increased incidence of sudden infant death syndrome. Smoking causes the blood vessels to constrict, reducing the flow of oxygen and nutrients to all organs, including the uterus, and hence to the baby.

## CORRECT BREATHING

The growth of the baby inside the uterus is maintained through the mother's blood. The wonderful organ known as the placenta, which develops along with the baby, is able to filter from the large blood vessels of the uterus the food required by the baby. This is passed to the baby through the umbilical cord to its navel. Through the cord the waste material of the baby is returned as well, to be disposed of by the mother. So it becomes clear that to have healthy babies it is necessary to eat and drink the right things.

*One of the most important foods is oxygen.* We cannot live without it, and whenever the supply of oxygen to the brain is insufficient for a short period of time, the brain becomes damaged to that degree. Adults breathe in oxygen through their lungs. The baby doesn't use its lungs for breathing, but takes its oxygen from the placenta straight into its bloodstream. Therefore, by breathing correctly, the mother can supply as much oxygen to her baby as it requires. During pregnancy it is of the utmost importance that as much fresh air as possible is taken into her lungs, and with the least effort.

Correct breathing is also essential during labor. The big muscles of the uterus are working to expel the baby, and when big muscles are used they require more fuel, just as a car uses more fuel to go faster or climb a hill. We don't feel our big muscles working if we are healthy, but we do breathe faster and deeper, and that is how they get extra fuel. During labor correct breathing is essential in supplying the necessary oxygen to the working muscles of the uterus. It also helps keeps the baby in good condition while it is being born.

But in order for the breathing to help, the mother must also be *relaxed* enough during labor to allow the blood to circulate more freely through the middle layer of muscles in the uterus, thus replenishing its oxygen supply more quickly and plentifully.

No one can work to the best of her ability either physically or mentally if she does not breathe correctly; indeed, incorrect breathing is *the* bad habit that causes more illness than any other. It is surprising to learn that not one woman in fifty breathes properly.

The secret of correct breathing lies in the *control* of respiration —that is, control of breathing in and also of breathing out. Fresh air is taken into the lungs, which are like a very fine sponge made of minute air spaces and even smaller blood vessels. The walls are so thin that the oxygen from the air passes into the blood and the waste gas from the blood passes into the air spaces. By breathing we take in pure air and get rid of "waste" air.

Most people use less than four fifths of their air space. To maintain a sufficient supply of oxygen, this means that they have to breathe five times for every four breaths taken by the person who breathes correctly. Breathing faster means more work for the muscles concerned with breathing, and more work for the heart to pump the blood around the body. In pregnancy this can become a strain and even a discomfort; the enlarging uterus causes discomfort to many women because they do not maintain good posture and breathe correctly. Therefore, during this time when the oxygen intake is so dependent upon the correctness of breathing, these simple exercises should have priority over all other physical movements.

## BREATHING FOR GOOD HEALTH

Place your hands flat on your lower ribs, with your head up and shoulders back. Open your mouth and fill your chest slowly with air, filling in the upper part of the lungs as well as the lower, clear up under the collarbones. When you have breathed in as much air as possible, then let it out, slowly and completely. Lean slightly forward and force out the last possible breath. This will not cause any harm, so don't be afraid to take these slow, deep breaths.

Spend five or ten minutes each morning and evening breathing in and out, slowly and deeply, in this way. Many women are surprised at how much better they feel after only two weeks of practicing this simple breathing exercise each day. They quickly find themselves able to do more without becoming "out of breath." Rapid progress is made because there is usually so much room for improvement!

## NORMAL BREATHING DURING REST

Breathing can be demonstrated to be either tense or relaxed. If too deep a breath is forced, or breathing is too rapid, certain tensions become apparent in the diaphragm, the ribs, and elsewhere. In relaxed breathing, both breathing in and breathing out should be without tension. "Sleep" breathing—that is, drawing the air into the lower diaphragm rather than the upper chest—aids in achieving relaxation more quickly and deeply. As the person relaxes, the abdominal wall will gently rise and fall. But as relaxation becomes deeper, breathing becomes perfectly smooth and in many cases almost inaudible, for less oxygen is needed during relaxation than when in a state of tension or movement. This quiet breathing is quite adequate to carry on all respiratory functions in labor during the first stage, without any necessity for shortness of breath, panting, or occasional deep breaths or sighs. All these breathing variations are signs of tension and incomplete relaxation.

It is helpful to understand how our bodies automatically adjust our rate of breathing to our rate of activity. While we are sleeping soundly, the rate of breathing is deep and slow, and an observer can see the lower abdomen rising and falling gently. After arising, the pace of breathing quickens to meet the body's need for a greater supply of oxygen. If one were to run several hundred yards, breathing would quicken still further.

It is a great aid in achieving relaxation to attempt *consciously* to slow the breathing rate down to normal "sleep" breathing. In order to observe this relaxed breathing, one can take a slow, deep breath, but not so deep as to fill the upper chest also. As the diaphragm gently expands, the abdomen can be seen rising. Slowly one should let the breath out again, relaxing more completely at the same time. Repeat. After a few such slow, deep breaths, a person often yawns, showing that this conscious effort to slow down the breathing is a real aid to relaxation. As this quiet, slower breathing continues and the person becomes more relaxed, the breathing itself again becomes automatic and continues without further thought.

This relaxed, natural "sleep" breathing is invaluable during pregnancy for falling asleep at night, and is most helpful in achieving relaxation during pregnancy and in labor.

## NORMAL BREATHING DURING ACTIVITY

After a relaxed period of "sleep" breathing, one can sit up for a moment, then stand, then begin moving around. After a few minutes of activity, working around the house, or walking, *the person will notice how the breathing has changed.* One will realize that he or she is breathing more quickly without giving it a single thought because the body has *automatically* adjusted the breathing rate to the extra oxygen needed for less, or more, physical exertion.

## NORMAL BREATHING DURING LABOR

As labor progresses, remember to stay relaxed during contractions, and the breathing will take care of itself. If at any time a mother feels herself becoming tense, a brief, conscious effort to slow down the breathing will help her relax more completely. There is no need to "count" breaths or to "control" breathing in any other way, as this increases tension and may contribute to pain. As the mother stays relaxed and in a comfortable position, the breathing will continue to take care of itself.

**BREATHING DURING THE BIRTH**

Breathing during the second stage will also adapt itself automatically, but the mother should not attempt to hold her breath for long periods of time, and should bear down with her mouth open, taking further breaths during each contraction as desired.

As the head is born, and again during the birth of the shoulders, the attending physician or midwife may ask the mother to pant gently to avoid pushing, so that the birth occurs slowly and under control. This helps prevent any sudden and excessive pressure on the outlet, and thus helps avoid tearing.

## COMFORT AND MOBILITY

Certain movements associated with the mobility and flexibility of the muscles and joints of the pelvis are valuable during labor and delivery. When we visualize the course of normal labor, we realize that *the first stage must be without muscular effort on the part of the woman,* while the second stage may require an hour or two of physical effort, in the case of first labors, to help the uterus expel the infant.

But we must not *exaggerate* the importance of exercises for childbirth. They make the mother feel fit and help improve her daily breathing and relaxation, but a woman with a well-trained mind who knows how to breathe and relax correctly but is unable for some health reason to do any exercises can still have a good birth experience. She will have her baby much more easily than will a woman who has a highly trained athletic body but who knows little or nothing of how to cooperate with nature in giving birth. Indeed, some of the most perfect labors I have witnessed have been of women with groups of muscles partially paralyzed below the waist. They had suffered from accidents or polio, and their crippled bodies, which they swung from the hips on crutches or walking sticks, could not be physically trained.

I am anxious that this be understood, for the exercises described in this chapter are *not to prepare mothers for an athletic event, but for a natural, common-sense experience in which a certain degree of physical fitness has advantages.* These exercises represent the most elementary practice of physical training, but they are enough. Anything more than sufficient has been shown by experience to make *no difference* to the course or comfort of labor. Anything less deprives a woman of advantages she might more easily have enjoyed by being in better health.

## CORRECT POSTURE

Correct posture enables a woman to move gracefully and to breathe freely. A straight line from the ear to a point just in front of the heel on the sole of the foot should be envisaged passing through the center of the shoulder and the hip joint, enabling the muscles of the limbs to work to the best advantage in all directions and retaining the abdominal organs in good position within the pelvic cavity. Holding the head at such an angle avoids round shoulders and the poking forward of the chin, and holding the body in this position makes breathing free, deep, and effortless and gives one a feeling of well-being and cheerfulness, which is important.

A woman can adopt the correct position by standing near a mirror and imagining the straight line just described. Her head should be carried as though slightly above her height. She should check her posture in this way periodically through pregnancy, for the alteration in the shape and weight of the body during pregnancy will unconsciously lead to stooping unless attention is paid to it. There is nothing more attractive than a young pregnant woman moving freely and maintaining her personal appearance in good posture.

### LOOSENING THE SPINE AND PELVIC JOINTS

The pelvis and spine of the human body are not rigid, but flexible. During birth, a baby must make its way down through the pelvic basin, along the sacrum (end of the spine), and out. A baby's head can be molded to fit the shape of its mother's pelvis; but her pelvis is also movable. In the center front of the pelvis is the *symphysis pubis,* which can be felt as a slight depression in the center of the pelvis just above the vulva. It is composed of fibrocartilage, and holds together the two side bones of the pelvis. During pregnancy the symphysis pubis softens and reaches a certain degree of mobility, so that it can spread apart slightly as the baby is being born. The mobility of the symphysis pubis, as well as the mobility and relaxation of the joints of the lower back, can be increased during pregnancy by "rocking" the pelvis, tipping it back and forth. This is a great help to comfort in labor, and works to prevent or overcome backache during pregnancy and back pain during labor.

On hands and knees, place the hands about twelve inches apart and the knees about nine inches apart, keeping the knees directly in line with the hips. Let the back sag, at the same time raising the buttocks as high as possible. Take a deep breath in this position. Slowly raise the back, allowing the breath to be expelled as the

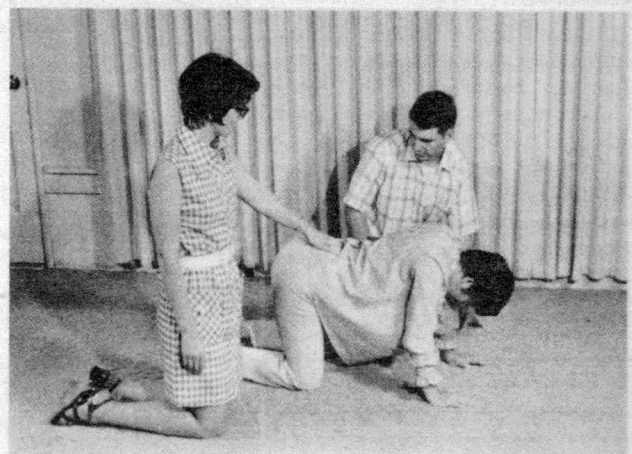

Pelvic rocking. Let back sag, keeping elbows straight, knees directly under hips

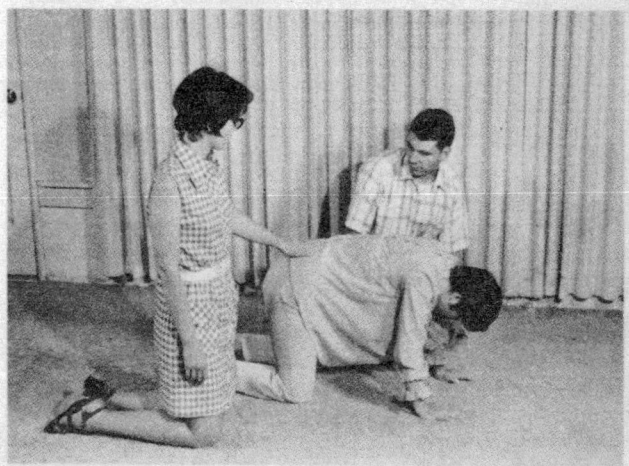

Slowly raise *small* of back, keeping upper legs at right angles to the floor

back arches. At the same time, squeeze together the muscles of the buttocks and pelvic area and tighten the muscles of the upper legs.

Return to the original position and *repeat ten times,* slowly and firmly.

There are other ways to "rock" the pelvis. Stand against the wall, heels about six inches from the wall, and try to touch the wall with the small of the back. Or, lying on bed or floor, try to press the small of your back against it. Notice how this exercise moves the *pelvis,* by putting a hand on your hip bones at each side and feeling the movement. But do this (as well as any other exercise) gently.

### STRETCHING THE MUSCLES OF THE INNER THIGH

During labor, much of the time may be spent with the knees relaxed and apart. The inner thigh muscles need to be stretched so that this position can be maintained comfortably for some time. Practicing this position in pregnancy also loosens the knees and the hip joints and tones up the muscles of the legs. It parallels the best position for birth, for in this position the pelvic diameter is enlarged to its maximum size.

Stand on the toes, and then sink down to a position of squatting or sitting on the heels, still balancing on the toes. Place the palms of the hands on the knees and stretch the legs wide open, keeping the back straight. Rise to a standing position and then lower the heels to the floor. If the balance cannot be maintained, hold on to a support with one hand. *Repeat five times.*

VARIATION A.  For those who find the squatting too difficult or too strenuous, the same exercise can be simulated while lying on the back, with the knees drawn up toward the chest and pressed together. Allow the knees to fall outward, pressing them widely apart with the palms of the hands, the soles of the feet pointing inward. *Repeat five times.*

VARIATION B.  Sit on the floor Indian style, with knees outward, the soles of the feet placed together. Grasp the ankles with each hand, lean forward and place the forearms on the lower legs, then gently press the knees apart with the elbows. *Repeat five times.*

VARIATION C.  Sitting Indian style as in variation B, grasp the ankles but keep the arms straight. Let your husband or an attendant push up against the knees while you try to *push* down against the pressure of his hands. *Repeat five times.*

VARIATION D.  Sit Indian style often during the day for quiet work, reading, sewing, or watching television, ankles crossed. Try

Squat, balancing on toes. Press knees open with hands

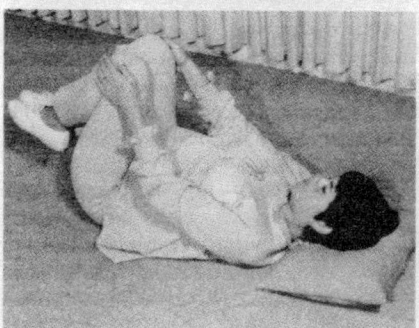

Draw knees up toward chest, press together with hands

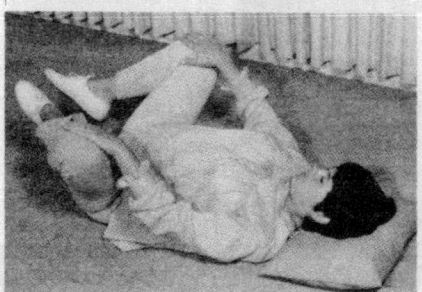

Press knees as far apart as possible with palms of hands

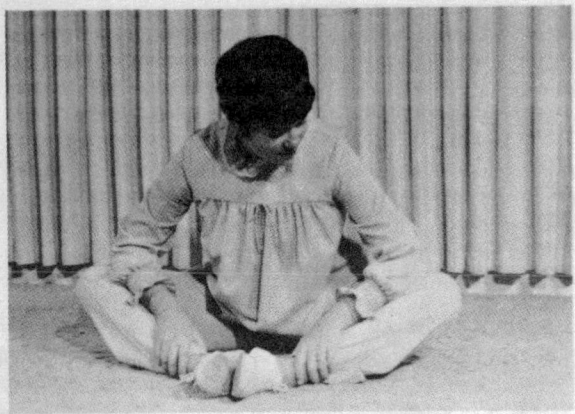

Soles of feet together, press knees apart with elbows, grasping ankles

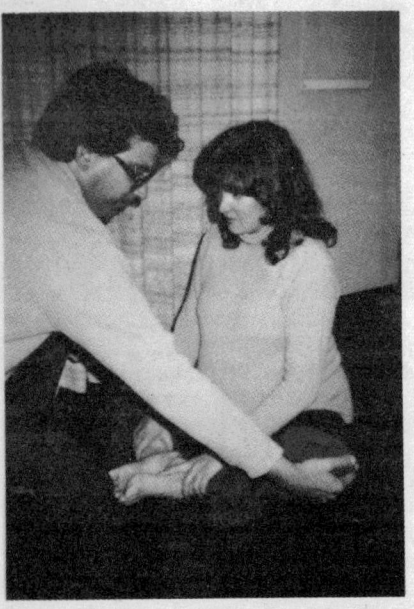

Soles of feet together, press knees down against husband's hands as he resists

relaxing occasionally in this position, letting the elbows rest on the knees, the back sag, and the head drop gently forward, eyes closed.

## CARE OF THE BREASTS

The breasts and nipples may be tender to the touch in early pregnancy, but this soon passes. The nipples should be kept clean with warm water only during the daily bath or shower, with no soap or other product drying to the skin used, as dryness encourages cracked and painful nipples when breastfeeding begins. The softer and more elastic the nipples are kept, the more comfortable the initial breastfeeding will be.

During the last three months of pregnancy a few simple preparations are helpful in preparing for breastfeeding.[2] After bathing, rub each nipple gently with a soft terrycloth towel, then place a thumb and forefinger near the base of the nipple and press gently together. Now gently draw the nipple outward, and turn it up and down. Do this several times with each nipple. If the nipple is slightly retracted and doesn't stand out as it should, call it to the attention of the doctor. In addition to this nipple pulling, he may also advise wearing a breast shield during pregnancy, to help the nipple come forward. Some women like to use a lubricant on their nipples. Any skin cream will do, if it is not perfumed; safflower or other cooking oils are inexpensive choices which work just as well.

During the last ten or twelve weeks of pregnancy the breasts may exude a few drops of a very thick, yellow secretion called *colostrum*. If it cakes on the breasts, warm water will soften it, and if it gets too thick, very gentle pressure at the base of the nipple with the thumb and forefinger will clear the little openings into the breast. This should be gently done. Great care should be taken never to handle the breasts roughly.

Breast massage can be done by cupping a breast in one hand, thumb on one side and fingers on the other. Now circle the breast with an easy massaging motion while pressing gently inward toward the chest wall. Repeat with the other breast.

During lovemaking the husband can fondle the breasts in this way, and draw out the nipples by sucking on them. This is a natural, loving way of preparing the breasts for the nursing baby.

It is of utmost importance that the breasts be supported by well-fitting, rounded cups, without any pressure whatever across the breasts or nipples; they should also be supported by shoulder straps

Exercise for lifting and firming the breasts

that lift them to the correct height. The breasts are larger during both pregnancy and breastfeeding, but proper care will keep them from sagging. After the baby comes, it will be important to hold the infant in such a way while feeding that the breast is not pulled down. The baby is to be held at the level of the breast.

The following exercise helps keep the breasts firm, increases the circulation to the tissues under the breasts, and may help in establishing an adequate milk flow for breastfeeding. It should be continued during lactation after weaning, to lift the breasts and keep them firm on into old age.

Grip each arm firmly behind the wrist and raise the arms to the level of the shoulders. Push the skin of the forearm up, tightening the arm muscles and the muscles of the chest. When done correctly, one can feel the breasts lift. Relax and repeat.

Now take a deep breath, and hold it while doing this exercise *ten times,* taking about ten seconds. Relax. Repeat several times each day.

## FIRMING THE PELVIC FLOOR MUSCLES

This is the most important of all prenatal and postnatal exercises, and requires some explanation in detail.

The anus, vagina, and urethra are the three openings in the female pelvis. The anus is the end of the bowel; the vagina, the end of the birth canal; and the urethra, the end of the urinary bladder. When standing, the force of gravity places an immense strain upon the muscles that support the floor of the pelvis and close the openings.

Contract the anal and vaginal passages firmly and at the same time tighten the buttocks. Close the anus until the sensation of drawing it up into the rectum is felt. There is no need to move the legs or buttocks, as this distracts attention from the important area. When the anal sphincter is completely closed and retracted, the vaginal sphincter, the *levator ani*—a large internal muscle—and the sphincter of the urine outlet are also tensed. Each of these openings is surrounded by fibers of muscle arranged as a double figure eight; therefore all three outlets are closed by what is virtually one muscle. Squeeze these muscles as tightly as possible, hold for a definite pause, and relax *slowly*. By relaxing slowly, one learns how to "let go" tension in these muscles. Do this exercise at least *twelve times, twice a day*. It can be done any time, anywhere.[3] As the uterus grows, the blood vessels multiply in number and increase in size. If the tone of the outlet muscles is below normal standard, control over them is lessened. Urine may leak, particularly during laughing or coughing. Similar defects may arise in the anus, as well as the development of *hemorrhoids,* or *piles*—varicose veins of the anus. If the muscles of the pelvic floor and outlets are exercised and kept in tone, these troubles will occur less frequently.

This exercise also facilitates the restoring of the stretched and dilated openings to normal size and tone after labor, and prevents some of the minor discomforts of aging. The feeling of firmness underneath has a marked influence on a woman; she will move or stand in a more confident posture.

Controlled activity of the vaginal sphincter and the static tension of the pelvic floor are also assets of considerable domestic value. Coitus can be performed satisfactorily for both husband and wife when the wife has learned conscious control of the vaginal sphincter. Rather than the too-frequent complaint that intercourse is uninteresting after a woman has had a baby, this natural marital function may be performed more satisfactorily than before.

This simple exercise is a panacea for many ills and should be taught to and performed habitually by all women—whether pregnant, postparturient, or just woman!

## CHAPTER 4

# Relaxation: The Key to Comfort in Labor

**B**efore we discuss briefly the teaching of relaxation during pregnancy, there are certain other considerations that demand attention. The attitude toward childbearing is variable; as obstetricians we must be conscious of what type or pigeonhole our individual patients fall into, and that is particularly important when we begin to teach them relaxation. Now, strangely enough, there are two types of women who are difficult or impossible to teach. Women who do not want their babies, who are bored by the whole procedure, and who feel they are merely doing a duty and are fed up at having to do it, very often avoid any practice of relaxation and become antagonistic to its teaching. Curiously, the other type is represented by the "plus" women, active, enthusiastic live wires to whom the application of modern science is all important. They are told the benefits of relaxation, but their reply is not infrequently that it would be quite unnecessary to apply it to them, as they will be able to control themselves when the time comes. They are sure that the whole thing should be conducted in a natural way and are preparing themselves along natural lines. Very often these women prefer the physical exercises, avoiding the careful practice of relaxation and assuming understanding, with no willingness to learn what they need to know.

But the majority of women are in the three types that lie between the negative and positive extremes, all of whom willingly submit to being taught relaxation:

1. Those who are mildly negative, who are lazy and casual in the conduct of pregnancy; they have to be kept up to the mark.

2. The real and natural mothers to whom all things to do with motherhood are inborn gifts and who are balanced in the exercise of their instinctive activities. They adjust themselves to the new rules of life without difficulty.

3. The slightly positive woman, who is so keen to do everything really well that she has to be gently restrained and very carefully educated.

Now, I am sure it will be readily appreciated by any experienced physician that a rule-of-thumb method of teaching relaxation is quite impossible under the circumstances. We have to use our discretion; it would be absurd to ask the negative woman to carry out, in exactly the same way, on the same principles, at the same times of day, those practices which we would invite the plus woman to carry out. If we are to get adequate results, we must balance our demands.

What, then, is relaxation in the sense in which we use the term? I suggest that for the purpose of its application in obstetrics, we consider relaxation to be *a condition in which the muscle tone throughout the body is reduced to a minimum.* We must remember that physiological reactions and reflexes vary, both in speed and intensity, with the fluctuations of neuromuscular tension. It is a quality that is susceptible to the moods and modulations of emotion in individuals, and there is *a direct relationship between the emotional state and muscular tone.* In fact, Edmund Jacobson goes so far as to say: "Present results indicate that an emotional state fails to exist in the presence of complete relaxation of the peripheral parts involved."[1]

In applying this to obstetrics, we can say that if the body is completely relaxed, it is impossible to entertain the emotion of fear. This is the important factor, for if fear is absent, then the overruling power of the sympathetic nervous system is absent from the mechanism. I must remind you that this eliminates any excess muscle tone in the circular fibers of the lower uterine segment, the cervix, and the outlet of the birth canal. Complete relaxation, therefore, offers the minimum of resistance to the muscles of expulsion in the birth canal.

Complete general relaxation is the ideal to aspire to, but on the other hand it is astonishing how even imperfect relaxation may alter the whole course of labor. Possibly an expert like Jacobson might feel that some of our patients were not relaxing, according to what he believes to be complete relaxation. But if he saw a patient both before and after she had been asked to relax during labor, he would realize what a marked difference there is even if the performance leaves much to be desired. I have frequently been told how different labor becomes when the body is allowed to be "slack," and if women have tried to learn relaxation and are able to put it into effect, astonishingly gratifying results are obtained, for *the discomforts of labor vary inversely to the woman's ability to relax.*

Instruction in relaxation should begin *early* in pregnancy. Adequate relaxation is not easily applied in labor unless it has been *learned* and diligently practiced in the several months prior to the birth. It aids the pregnancy also, helping to overcome the symptoms of nausea and to prevent undue tiredness.

The husband can do a great deal in encouraging his wife to apply the relaxation she is learning throughout pregnancy. Indeed, he would be wise to learn and apply it himself, for relaxation is not only of value for pregnancy and labor. It lays a foundation for good health also, because when relaxed, the body functions more normally. We all live under considerable stress, and there is more emotional as well as physical weariness than is usually recognized. Such tension undermines both health and happiness in the rush of modern living.

In order to understand how relaxation aids in labor, it helps to know something of the uterine muscles and how they function.

## THE UTERUS DURING PREGNANCY

The duration of pregnancy is counted from the first day of the last menstrual period. Most women suspect that they are pregnant when the expected period does not arrive. They feel perfectly well, unless for any reason they are anxious about pregnancy. When about six or seven weeks pregnant, many women will be conscious of sensitiveness and slight enlargement of the breasts. By this time the pregnant woman should see a doctor, and keep in constant touch with him or her or a clinic throughout the whole of pregnancy, and until at least six weeks after the birth of the baby. These chapters are not intended to instruct mothers in matters that are the special province of medical advisers. There must be someone qualified to whom they can turn for advice upon any subject that creates the slightest doubt in their minds.

With the growth of the fetus the uterus develops in size. The muscle fibers become longer and more numerous. Fluid is secreted into the cavity of the organ, which fills and expands. After two months the pregnant uterus is about the size of a large hen's egg. At the third month it can just be felt, in a thin woman, above the pubic bone. At the fourth month it is halfway between the pubic bone and the navel. At five and a half months it is up to the navel. At eight months it is about halfway between the navel and the lower end of the breastbone.

Between the seventh and eighth month the baby's heart beats loudly enough for the mother to hear it through the doctor's stethoscope, although the doctor, with practiced ear, will have been able to detect it long before this time.

By thirty-five weeks the baby should have taken up its correct position for birth, with its head downward and its back slightly to the right or the left of center. At nine and a half months, or thirty-eight weeks, the uterus reaches its highest point in the abdomen.

At about the thirty-eighth week women who are having their first baby will experience what is known as *lightening*. This is the slipping down of the baby's head into the brim of the pelvis. The baby's chin becomes flexed upon its breastbone, and the back of its head (called the *occiput*) slides downward into the upper portion of the birth canal. The change is often felt in the abdomen. The uterus appears to have lowered, and this often gives the mother added freedom of movement and breathing. Thus at full term, or forty weeks, the uterus has dropped back one to two inches. The actual size of the uterus varies according to the amount of water in it and the size of the baby, but the levels in the abdomen at certain weeks of development do not vary much in different women.

The birth of the child may usually be expected within ten days or two weeks after this lightening occurs. With second and subsequent babies it may not occur, however. Not infrequently, in the easiest births of additional children, the head will remain quite high in the pelvis, or even above it, until well into the second stage of labor.

## THE MUSCLE LAYERS OF THE UTERUS

When the baby is ready to be born, the uterus is a muscular bag about fourteen inches in length and not quite half an inch in thickness. It is well supplied with nerves that stimulate its muscles to contract, and it also has a plentiful supply of blood vessels, which are necessary to take fresh blood to the uterus and to carry away all the waste products of muscular activity. There are three muscle layers in the uterus:

1. The outer layer goes up the back, over the top, and down the front. These long muscle bands are found mainly in the middle and upper part of the uterus.

2. The middle muscle layer is a mass of interwoven muscles in which the big blood vessels lie.

3. The inner muscle layer goes around the uterus in a circular manner, and is found almost entirely in the area of the lower part of the uterus and cervix.

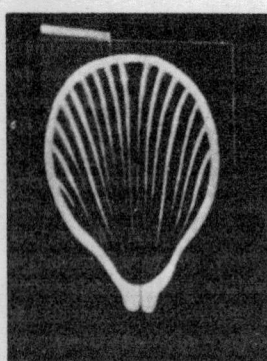

Longitudinal muscle fibers

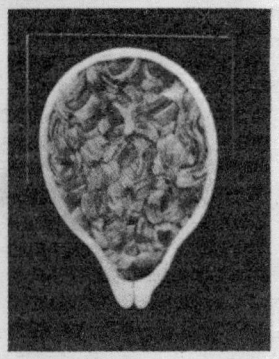

Muscles interwoven with blood vessels

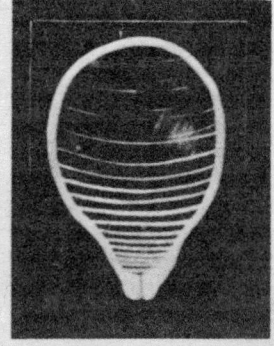

Circular muscle fibers

The outer muscles contract (shorten and tighten) to push the baby down, through, and ultimately out of the uterus. The middle muscles contract to squeeze the blood out of the walls of the uterus, and then relax to allow the blood vessels to fill up again with a fresh supply of blood.

But when the inner, circular muscles contract, they close the outlet, maintaining the uterus in its unemptied shape. Thus these inner, circular muscles *must be loose and relaxed* when the long muscles contract to open the womb and push the baby out. If a woman is frightened during labor, this inner muscle layer contracts. Then the muscles that empty the uterus and the muscles that hold it closed are working against each other.

All through the body one finds examples of the harmony of muscles in polarity. For example, one's biceps relax when the triceps hold out the arm, but the triceps relax when the biceps pull the forearm up to the shoulder. If both sets of muscles are activated at the same time, pain soon results.

Whenever there are two big groups of muscles working against each other they soon begin to hurt, and in a short time the pain becomes very severe. We speak of this as the "fear-tension-pain syndrome" of childbirth, for a woman who is afraid is unconsciously resisting the birth of her baby by tightening the circular fibers, preventing the progress of the birth, and increasing the muscle tension within the walls of the uterus. This causes nearly all the pains and distresses in otherwise normal labor, which describes the labor of about ninety-five women out of a hundred.

## *FEAR-TENSION-PAIN*

This fear-tension-pain series of events is experienced by everybody in circumstances very similar. The bowel is full, the desire to empty is acute, it pushes against our active restraint, but the time and place are not convenient. We are afraid to stop resisting even though it is uncomfortable and becoming painful, until there is the right opportunity to relax the outlet and let the contents be released. Again, we have a strong urge to urinate, but the right place is not available. We dare not relax the muscles that hold the bladder closed because of social and domestic repercussions, so we suffer increasing pain, sometimes agony, until the opportunity comes for the comfort of relaxing the outlet and emptying the distended, contracting organ.

This same principle is at work during the birth of a child. Fear of pain causes resistance to the working muscles of the uterus, increasing tension and causing pain. The muscles of the bowel and bladder are less powerful than those of the uterus, but even they become painful if their efforts to expel are resisted.

Fear is the natural protective emotion without which few of us would remain alive for many days. Its intensity varies from precaution and doubt to uncontrollable terror. Even mild anxiety can make a woman tense, thus causing the circular muscles to resist the expulsive muscles of the uterus. A tense woman has a tense outlet to the uterus, giving rise to the saying "Tense woman—tense cervix." A tense cervix means a long and painful labor in the majority of cases, for the mother is closing the door against the progress of her baby from the uterus.

By contrast, a relaxed woman allows the cervix, the "door" of the uterus, to open easily. If she understands what is taking place, is fully relaxed and confident, then the muscles that held the uterus closed during pregnancy will become loose and easily stretched open, when the long muscles begin their work of expelling the baby. The tension created by resistance to the birth will not be there to cause pain, and the baby will be born more easily and comfortably.

It is necessary for a woman carrying a baby to have a certain amount of rest, even if it is only for half an hour a day. Physical tiredness may become embarrassing in the later stages of pregnancy if the habit of rest is not acquired in the earlier months. Learning to relax properly makes this rest more effective.

Thus relaxation is of great benefit during pregnancy. Half an hour's relaxation is worth more than twice that time in sleep. It releases states of tension that a woman might unconsciously develop, and so helps avoid all manner of aches and pains. It introduces a calmness and helps establish confidence, which, in a state of tension, is practically impossible to do. Tension is caused by anxiety, and relaxation helps overcome anxiety by relieving tension of the mind as well as of the body.

Relaxation is also of the greatest possible assistance to a woman during labor. If she is able to become completely relaxed *during* the contractions of the first stage and *between* the contractions of the second stage, she will find that normal labor has no unbearable discomfort from beginning to end.

As stressed, the teaching of relaxation should be begun *early;* by the time the baby quickens, around the fourth month of pregnancy, the mother should already be obtaining good results. The conscientious practice of relaxation is of value throughout pregnancy for all pregnant women. In addition, relaxation enhances a woman's natural beauty, helps her to feel more poised with friends and strangers and more at ease with her husband, and later with her newborn.

Muscular relaxation brings about changes not only physically, but even in brainwave electrical activity. During normal activity, the *beta waves* of the brain occur in 13 to 25 cycles per second. As a person relaxes, these slow down to *alpha waves* of 8 to 13 cycles per second, as in nonfocused thinking and daydreaming. As relaxation deepens further, the brain electrical activity slows to *theta waves* of 4 to 8 cycles per second. This is a reverie, twilight state, usually experienced just before falling asleep. It is impossible to be anxious about anything at this level.

Muscular relaxation is a condition in which *the muscle tone throughout the body is reduced to a minimum.* When muscular tension is absent, emotional reactions and even thought patterns fade. Thus a completely slack body during labor eliminates any excess of muscle tone in the circular fibers of the lower uterine segment, the cervix, and the outlet of the birth canal. And this is not all. In a state of complete relaxation and mental calm, the sensations of uterine muscle activity during labor are interpreted in their true sense, just as the contraction of the biceps in the arm might be interpreted.

## PREPARATION FOR RELAXATION

Draw the curtains and darken the room slightly—bright sunshine makes relaxation more difficult than shade or soft light. Before starting to relax, eyeglasses and dentures, if any, should be removed. The bladder must be completely empty so that the pelvic muscles can safely be relaxed.

It is important that the person relaxing be in such a comfortable position that she feels no need of support to remain in that position without moving. She should be on a very firm bed or couch or on the floor, with a folded blanket under her on the floor if it seems too hard. Two pillows are needed, one under her head and one under her knees. Her head should fall slightly to one side on the pillow and her arms should lie a few inches from her side, with the elbows half bent outward and the hands half closed. Her knees, supported by a pillow, should be slightly separated, her feet falling outward. It is important to have *all joints in a semiflexed (i.e., slightly bent) position,* for joints as well as muscles must be completely relaxed.

## RECOGNIZING TENSION

When we speak of muscle tension, we are referring to tension in the muscles attached to the bones—the skeletal muscles. These are all under the control of the will. With practice they can be tensed or relaxed when so ordered by the mind. While the involuntary muscles of the intestines, blood vessels, heart, lungs, stomach, uterus, etc., cannot be directly relaxed by the will, they are all profoundly influenced by the complete relaxation of the skeletal muscles, which enables them to carry out their respective functions more efficiently.

One cannot be conscious of muscular relaxation unless one is able to recognize muscle tension. This is usually quickly done. Tell the person to let her arms and legs lie as loosely as she is able to: "Try to avoid moving your toes, and do not wiggle your fingers. Just lie absolutely still and loose. Now let me have your right arm and let me have it *entirely*. Do not try to help me raise it, because any effort you make to help me is going to do more harm than good."

Then take hold of her elbow and wrist and raise her arm just off the couch. I explain that I want her hand to drop so that there is no "life" in it at all. It is astonishing how many people cannot drop their hand! Because of unnecessary muscle tension they slowly lower their hand, and then wiggle a finger or a thumb.

Continue testing the elbow and wrist until complete relaxation of the hand is obtained. Say again, "Now I am going to lift your hand, and I want you to let it drop absolutely as if it had no life in it at all." This sometimes takes quite a long time to do. Then put a finger across the back of her hand and say, "Raise your hand very slowly, and at the same time you will feel my finger pressing it down. When you do that, realize what muscles are trying to raise your hand."

At the first movement of the muscle of the forearm in the effort to raise her hand, say, "Let it go," or "Relax." Do this several times, and point out that it is the muscle of the forearm that is trying to raise the hand. Not infrequently the person observes that as soon as the effort to lift the hand is made, the muscle can be felt tightening.

This instruction is then extended to groups of muscles, allowing them to become slightly tense and then definitely relaxed. It is amazing how quickly the average woman is able to relax her arm, once she understands the muscle tension and the "pull" of the muscle in action, but it takes considerable practice before she becomes expert at *releasing* this tension. Then ask her to do the same thing with her left arm, and on to other parts of her body.

Instruction is to be given in a quiet voice, slowly and clearly. "Take a deep breath through an open mouth; curl up your toes and tense the muscles of one leg." Pause. "Release your breath slowly and relax the whole limb. Compare in your own mind the feelings of tension and relaxation." This is repeated, followed by the same procedure with the other leg.

The instruction is then extended to other groups of muscles throughout the body, allowing them to become alternately tense and relaxed, thus discovering what tension of each muscle feels like, and then how it feels to release that tension and relax the muscle. This applies to the chest, back, and abdominal muscles as well as the arms and legs. When learning to relax the abdominal muscles, particular attention should also be called to tensing and relaxing the muscles of the pelvic openings, the vaginal and anal passages.

*Relaxation of the face is extremely important.* A woman who screws up her face in labor is not sufficiently relaxed in other parts of her body. There are about sixty facial muscles that can be tensed, and a woman must be trained to "let go" this tension. It must be remembered that a woman does not look her best when her face is relaxed. I always point this out and tell her that I have no desire for her to look her best, but I want her to *be* her best. I find that the face is probably the most difficult part of the body for a woman to relax.

But women must be taught to release the tension in muscles around their eyes, cheeks, mouth, and especially the eyelids. After a time she who acquires good relaxation of the face finds it very much easier to eliminate tension from her whole body. Any woman who is capable of relaxing her facial muscles at will can go through labor with the maximum ease that the absence of tension makes possible.

As time passes during a period of relaxing, the weight and heaviness of the limbs will be realized. Only with considerable difficulty can one leg be raised slowly from the bed. Recognition of tension versus relaxation will be assisted if the contraction of muscles in the leg is noticed before the heel is raised from the bed. The thigh muscles and those down the front of the leg will produce a distinct sensation of tension if the movements are made sufficiently slowly. The same may be tried with the arm. From the shoulder start to lift the arm—not the hand, but the whole arm—from the bed. The strain upon the muscles will be felt long before there is sufficient force to raise the limb. These tests must be carried out thoughtfully and *very slowly*. Violent and sudden flinging of the arm or the leg into the air will undoubtedly be easy, but it will teach nothing of the sensations of relaxation and early tension. Having raised the limb one or two inches from the bed, let it fall. In this way a consciousness of muscle tension will be developed, which makes the practice of deep relaxation much easier to recognize and practice.

When a person becomes physically relaxed, the mind takes care of itself. Several patients have told me that it is very difficult for their imaginations to become quiet. All the events of the day are vividly recalled as soon as they try to relax. This is, of course, an indication that their relaxation is incomplete. But they should not be urged to avoid thought in any way, because the attempt to stop thought is one of the most *active* mental exercises! Instead, it must be remembered that no emotional state can be present if there is real relaxation of the muscles of the body. Thought is to be concentrated on relaxing these muscles. As the muscles relax, the mind itself will automatically become quieter, until thoughts fade.

## *PRACTICING RELAXATION*

It is not necessary to tense the muscles of the body each time in order to relax, once one has learned to recognize the *difference* between tension and relaxation in any part of the body. For each practice session, the following procedure may be carried out:

1. The bladder should first be emptied, so that the pelvic muscles can be relaxed with safety. Then stand and stretch the whole body, breathing in deeply through the nose to full lung capacity. Then exhale, allowing the shoulders to drop and the head to fall forward as the lungs become empty.

2. Lie down on a wide couch, the floor, or a hard bed, with a pillow under your head *and the upper part of your shoulders.* Another pillow should be made into a roll and placed under your knees for support, so that both knee and hip joints are slightly bent.

3. The feet should be about six or eight inches apart. Arms should be eight inches to a foot away from the body, with the elbows flexed outward, the hands with palms down and fingers curled slightly inward. The head should be allowed to fall gently to one side on the pillow, with the chin slightly raised as the head falls back.

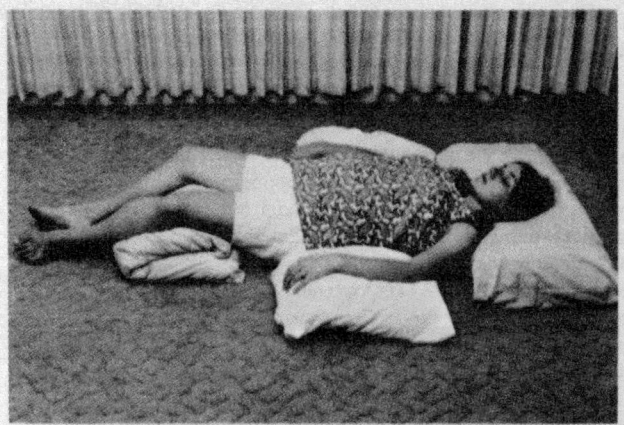

Note the excellent relaxation of legs and feet, knees falling outward, soles inward. Head is incorrectly supported, neck bent forward because the pillow is not also correctly pulled down under neck and shoulders

4. Take three or four slow deep breaths and, on breathing out each time, let every muscle in the body become limp and still. Think of the shoulders as "opening outward." Feel the arms hanging from the shoulders and the hands lying heavily on the bed. Fingers and thumbs must not move. There will be a sensation of sinking into, or even through, the bed. The feet fall outward upon the heels, and the knees are carried outward by the weight of the feet. There must be no movement of the toes.

5. The head and shoulders are to be so completely supported upon the pillow that the muscles of the neck are absolutely loose. Let the eyelids half close of their own weight.

6. Concentrate briefly on each arm without moving or tensing it, to be sure it is not being held stiffly in any part, that the muscles are not twitching or the fingers fidgeting. Do the same with the legs, buttocks, and back. Note carefully the muscles of the back. If they are relaxed, there will be a sensation of pressure upon the bed or floor from the weight of your body.

7. Relax the muscles of the face, the brow, eyelids, cheeks, and the muscles around the mouth. Think of your head as making a dent in the pillow. Particular care must be taken not to blink the eyes or

move the eyeballs within their sockets. The muscles of the face will be felt hanging loosely from the cheekbones, which causes the jaw to drop slightly and hang loose.

8. Release any remaining tension in the abdominal muscles and pelvic floor muscles. Take two or three breaths deeply into the diaphragm, letting the chest and abdominal wall collapse with its own weight slowly as each breath is exhaled. Allow the breath to leave the lungs through the mouth without controlling or impeding it. Do not force it out. After each expiration, pause for two seconds (or until you want a new breath) before inhaling into the diaphragm again, deeply and gently. With each outgoing breath, relax the abdominal wall more fully, and "let go" tension in the pelvic muscles, as if opening up down below. Remember to keep your lips parted and your cheeks and jaw "hanging loose," to help relax the pelvic area. If your mouth is tense, you will be tensing the pelvic area, too. As relaxation deepens, the breathing will become very gentle and quiet, as if you were really asleep.

This perfectly smooth and almost imperceptible breathing is fully adequate to carry on all respiratory functions in labor during the first stage, for less oxygen is needed during relaxation than when in a state of tension or movement. It is not necessary to remain conscious of breathing once full relaxation is achieved.

9. Let all the joints of the body relax a little more with each outgoing breath until they seem to be detached altogether. Note the train of sensations in the limbs—usually heaviness followed by lightness or "floating"; faint, transient pins and needles in the hands; feelings of warmth passing up from the extremities.

10. A pleasant, daydreaming state generally ensues (as in sunbathing) and any tendency to directed thinking should be deliberately diverted into a daydream. Remain in this relaxed state for about half an hour. (The sense of the passage of time is often lost or blunted.) Sleep is not the aim, and for most patients muscular relaxation without falling asleep seems to be more refreshing. But relaxing again in this way at night will help many insomniacs put themselves to sleep.

11. *Get up slowly.* Jumping up suddenly may cause faintness or dizziness. Take two or three deep breaths, bend the knees and arms once or twice, and then slowly sit up. Take two or three more breaths before standing up. Stretch the body once more, and then normal movement may again be safely resumed.

## POSITIONS FOR RELAXATION

1. *On the back.* This position has been described above. However, after eighteen to twenty weeks of pregnancy many women have difficulty being comfortable in this position.

2. *Reclining chair position.* The body rests at an angle of 45 to 50 degrees, the forearms relaxing on the arms of the chair and the knees relaxing on the lower portion of the chair, tilted slightly higher than the hips. The head should be supported and fall slightly to one side, so that the neck muscles are slack and no part of the body requires any muscular effort to remain in its position.

In the hospital, this same position can be attained by raising the head of the bed to the proper angle, and either placing pillows under the knees to elevate them, or raising the bed under the knees, if it has that kind of mechanical flexibility. Pillows should be placed under the elbows to simulate the arms of a chair, and the head and shoulders should be so well supported that the neck muscles are fully relaxed, with the head falling slightly to the side and backward.

3. *Lateral position.* This is a most important position, and should be learned as an alternative to the other positions in early pregnancy, even though it may not be necessary at that time. In the later months, when the uterus is large, it is usually uncomfortable to

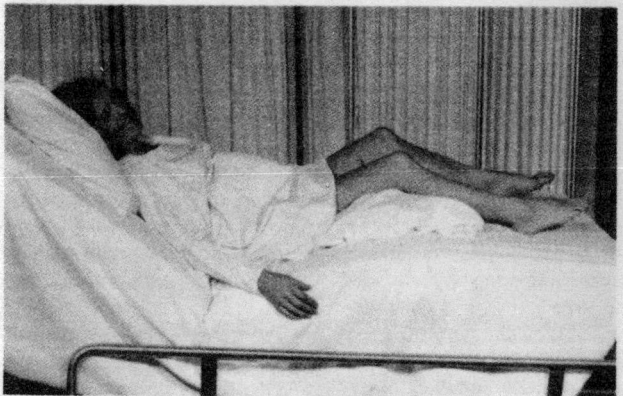

"Reclining-chair" position for relaxation in labor. Pillows under the forearms (not shown) may be helpful in keeping arms limp

Practicing relaxation in left lateral position during pregnancy

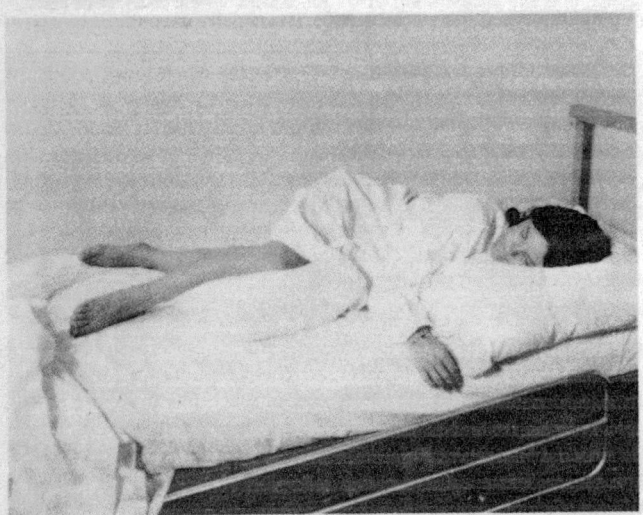

Relaxing in left lateral position during first-stage labor

lie flat on the back, for this interferes with good circulation and, because of the pressure of the uterus within the abdomen, makes breathing difficult. The lateral position is most helpful during labor.

Lie on the bed or floor on the left side, with the left arm behind the back and relaxed alongside the body. The right shoulder should be dropped, or supported by a corner of the pillow, and the right arm flexed slightly at the elbow and resting loosely on the bed alongside the pillow. It is important to either support the right shoulder or make sure it drops forward, as there is a tendency for muscle tension to hold it up. The head should be resting on a pillow, face turned toward the right shoulder, the chin slightly raised to make breathing easier, lips parted, and jaw slack.

The left leg should be stretched out on the bed, but bent slightly at the knee to relax the knee and hip joints, and the right leg should be drawn up until the knee is on a level with the upper abdomen. A large, firm pillow should be placed under the right knee and thigh to give it support, so that the knee and hip joints are fully relaxed and loose, and the muscles of the upper thigh, abdomen, lower back, and pelvic area can hang completely slack.

Two or three deep breaths into the lower diaphragm should be taken, and the whole body made to "let go" more fully with each exhalation. A sense of comfort and support will be felt immediately, if the position is right. The uterus will be supported upon the bed without pressure, taking the strain off the back muscles. Free movement of the diaphragm and abdomen is obtained during breathing.

During early pregnancy this position may also be used while lying on the right side. Relaxation is equally effective while lying on either side, but in later pregnancy, and when in early labor, the *left* lateral position is the best.


## RESIDUAL TENSION

The difference between simply lying still and true neuromuscular relaxation can be recognized, by a competent observer, in indications of residual tension. A rapid pulse rate and certain nervous reactions and reflexes are the result of tension. But the physician can also diagnose tension by listening to the breathing of a woman, for any irregularity in her breathing is evidence of imperfect relaxation. The flicker of an eyelid, moving of her eyeballs in their sockets behind closed lids, shifting of a finger or toe, or swallowing, all demonstrate the presence of residual tension of which the woman herself is not aware. If in the silence of a relaxing class the instructress makes a sudden slight noise, she will notice those who react immediately to this disturbance and those who do not react at all.

The aim should be to train women to relax until all residual tension is eliminated, but at the same time realize that the instruction received at prenatal classes alone is not enough to achieve this desirable state in every woman. Those who do overcome residual tension are usually the perfect obstetric patients, providing they have no disproportion and the baby is lying in the normal position. But every woman benefits by the measure of relaxation she learns, for any lessening of tension in labor lessens discomfort by just that much. The experienced obstetrician will realize that no one can prophesy with certainty the conduct of any woman in labor, although it is possible to detect those who appear likely to do well, and to predict those who are more likely to find relaxing difficult.

Perhaps I may add that the obstetrician would be very well advised to become adept at relaxation. Not only would he or she be more competent to teach the patients or train his or her staff, but such people retain their energy during those long hours of waiting. One's mental acuity and manual dexterity would be more efficient also than in someone who remained tense with anticipation during attendance at the labor.

# Overcoming Doubts and Problems

The human body is not a series of individual organs carrying out their allotted tasks unaffected by their neighbors. Our bodies are unified structures whose components exhibit the most perfect harmony that science has the privilege of investigating. Our organs and purposes are interdependent. No physical strain beyond our ability can be sustained without circulatory or skeletal injury, and no chronic fear or anxiety can be maintained in the human mind without the disruption of the normal physiological balance. The manifestations of such fear or anxiety may be either psychological or physical, for nature rebels against intruders upon its ordered processes.

It is important for women to understand the development of a baby within the uterus, for ignorance of these elementary facts may cause anxieties and doubts that are difficult to overcome, affecting their health adversely. Such complaints of pregnancy as persistent nausea, sickness, constipation, desire for unusual foods, excessive salivation, headaches, backaches, and a general feeling of weariness may often be the physical manifestations of anxiety, which knowledge can help dispel.

## NAUSEA

Many women consider that it is only right and proper that they should suffer certain discomforts in pregnancy. Pregnancy means morning sickness to some—indeed, morning sickness is one of the horrors of pregnancy to women of all classes of society, although when it occurs it frequently occurs in the afternoon! And the knowledge of that state acts as a conditioned reflex; having heard that it is one of the signs of pregnancy, they believe it to be a necessary accompaniment. They therefore start to have nausea and even vomiting as a subconscious justification of their state. It is Pavlov's story all over again—the association has become so definite from hearsay that the thought of pregnancy produces reflexes long conditioned in the mind. On two occasions women whose menstruation was overdue consulted me about their pregnancy because of morning sickness, nausea, and loss of appetite and weight. Neither was pregnant, and their symptoms cleared up as soon as they knew for certain that that was so! Conversely, it is frequently observed that the girl who does not know that she is going to have a baby does not have any of these symptoms.

Of course there is a percentage of women in whom nausea is actually caused by the chemical changes in the body that accompany pregnancy, but there are vast numbers of women who have felt neither sickness nor nausea during pregnancy. Women should be clearly told from the outset that nausea is not physiologically necessary, and that any tendency toward it can be controlled. It should be pointed out that the stomach should neither be empty too long nor overfilled; consequently, small, frequent meals are advisable until all tendency to nausea disappears. Very dry toast, or crackers, or small items for nibbling that can be carried in the purse are helpful. Frequent protein snacks and fruit snacks help prevent undue fatigue. The B vitamins (especially B6) have been found helpful in preventing or controlling nausea.

The capricious changes of taste and smell, and even sight and sound, are a cause of great concern to some. Some women develop a strong dislike for the smell of certain foods and a craving for other foods. These changes—which are found in some cases to be due to a forgotten association—may promote considerable anxiety if they are not discussed and their importance minimized.

## FREQUENCY OF URINATION

At the eleventh to thirteenth week, complaint is often made of frequency of urination. Perhaps the uterus is not quite clear of pressure at the brim of the pelvis; it may be slightly or completely retroverted. Usually this condition corrects itself in a short time.

Toward the end of pregnancy a need to urinate frequently often occurs, due to the pressure of the greatly enlarged uterus, and to the baby's "lightening," that is, moving further down into the pelvis in preparation for birth.

## CONSTIPATION

Constipation need not be a problem if there is adequate fiber and bran in the diet. A glass of hot water, with or without a spoonful of honey stirred into it, helps maintain a daily bowel action when taken first thing in the morning. No other tablets or preparations should be taken unless a doctor so advises.

It is especially important that constipation not be allowed to develop in the final weeks of pregnancy, for hard fecal matter in the lower bowel can cause discomfort during the final moments of birth. If the bowel movements are kept regular and soft, early labor often stimulates evacuation so that no enema is needed.

## TIREDNESS

Many women complain of tiredness in the early weeks of pregnancy, and say they feel like sleeping all the time. The bodily changes a woman is experiencing are reminding her to get more rest, and to modify her schedule in a way that will help her maintain optimum health, both for herself and her baby.

But the physician needs to be alert to one physical condition that is not always given the attention its importance demands. What appears to be tiredness and a poor attitude during pregnancy may be due to iron-deficiency anemia. I am not referring to the *physiological anemia* of pregnancy, that is, the plasma increasing in proportion to the number of red blood cells, which is compatible with good health. Nor do I refer to severe cases of *macrocytic* and *microcytic anemia,* or the "blood diseases," but to a shortness of iron apart from gross blood-cell changes. I have rarely seen a good example of natural labor in women whose hemoglobin has been allowed to remain very low from thirty-three to thirty-four weeks onward. I do not mean that their babies arrive with difficulty, but not infrequently labor is long, exhausting, and painful, with a slow recovery afterward.

The clinical aspect of anemia in relation to pain interpretation deserves some attention, for anemia is another cause of diminished general resistance to painful impressions.[1] Let us think for a moment of a woman who, tired in mind and body, short of hemoglobin, and forced to eat food she does not want, bravely faces what she believes she must endure. Labor begins—and soon she is in pain, a weary, weeping woman. Whether she was tired before she started labor or whether she is tired because of the expenditure of nervous and physical energy at the time is of no consequence. Tiredness of body intensifies pain. An ache becomes a severe pain; the mind is worn out and seeks only peace.

The hemoglobin should be estimated at prenatal visits as a routine; this is simple to do and takes very little time. If it is low, but during pregnancy follows the normal curve of variation—that is, falling slightly at about twenty-eight to thirty-two weeks and then picking up—it does not require special treatment. But if the hemoglobin remains markedly depressed, with increasing tiredness, exhaustion after normal activities, breathlessness without reasonable cause, depression, and an absence of desire for meals also complained of, treatment is indicated. This is not to suggest that the woman feels ill, but she may say, as many do: "I'm feeling fairly well, but get so tired."

The method of treatment will depend upon the diagnosis and judgment of the medical attendant. An iron supplement often works well, and with rising hemoglobin the patient will find new strength, spirits, and appetite, and will quite likely say she has never felt so well in her life. The wise attendant will first explore the eating habits of the mother before prescribing supplements, however. Foods rich in iron include liver, kidney, lean red meats, eggs, green vegetables and carrots, prunes, apricots, and other fresh or dried fruits.

"Tiredness" may not have any physical cause, but be due to the emotional adjustments the woman is making to being pregnant, and to all the changes this will necessitate in the future. If at times she feels like crying, this is wholesome, for tears can provide great release from tension and aid in attaining greater personal calm. Arthur Janov says:

> There is a good deal to be learned in the study of tears, for they have roughly the same ingredients as the blood system without its red cells. We are engaged in a study of the biochemistry of tears of our patients in cooperation with William Frey, biochemist at St. Paul University of Minnesota, Biochemistry Department. Dr. Frey has studied the chemistry of tears and discovered in them

high concentrations of stress hormones. This does not occur in tears resulting from irritants such as onions. Clearly, if there is indeed a release of stress hormones with tears, then the blocking of that release may result in the buildup of stress hormones. We believe that crying is an important biologic function and that the shedding of tears is *central,* not incidental, to the resolution of neurosis. There is no such thing as a "talking cure." The fact of weeping *itself* helps relieve suffering. Tears not only remove toxic substances of the eye, they also have a precise role in the removal of toxic biochemical substances from the entire system.[2]

If the tiredness or weepiness of an expectant mother is more than transitory, it would be wise to ascertain whether or not she has the loving support of persons concerned for her welfare, and a cooperative husband. The value of support persons during pregnancy as well as at the time of birth cannot be overemphasized.

## BLEEDING OR CRAMPING

The physician or midwife should be notified at once of any bleeding or spotting, at any time during the pregnancy. At times there may be some slight spotting following coitus. The doctor or midwife should be informed, but this is almost never significant.

If cramping occurs and is uncomfortable or begins to occur at regular intervals, the doctor or midwife should be notified. For while the uterus contracts all through pregnancy, these normal, occasional uterine contractions—felt as a hardening of the uterus under the abdominal wall—do not hurt, nor do they continue to occur.

The expectant mother should also report at once any persistent headache, dizziness, swelling or puffiness, sudden rapid weight gain, or premature leaking of the bag of waters. These may be signs that prompt treatment is needed to avoid greater problems.

## COITUS DURING PREGNANCY

Many women desire their husbands when pregnant, and in young people the bond of approaching parenthood often stimulates an irresistible affection that results in frequent and delectable copulation. During the early months a gentle performance of the act under the urge of affection is unlikely to be harmful. On occasion the wife may have no desire for it, just as when she is not pregnant. An understanding husband will respect her wishes, knowing that her mood will no doubt change within a few days.

A candid and sympathetic discussion of this subject is often a great relief to the young couple. The only medical contraindication would be in instances where miscarriage or premature birth already threatens to occur, although coitus is not a direct cause of either miscarriage or premature labor.

## SEXUALITY

During pregnancy, if coitus is uncomfortable, there is still a great deal of "lovemaking" that can take place. Both husband and wife can be very responsive to much touching and sexual play.

## FETAL POSITION

Before the baby "quickens," the mother should be warned of it. She should understand that the first faint throbbings or regular tappings are movements of her child exercising its muscles and of its own initiative taking part in the perfection of its development. The child becomes a reality at this stage, and if the fetal heart can be heard clearly one can give the mother a long stethoscope so that, if she wishes, she can hear her child's heartbeat. Explain that the baby is now about ten inches in length and weighs about one half to three quarters of a pound. Some women have complained of a disturbing regular throb in the uterus that goes on for half an hour or even longer; the possibility of the baby having an attack of hiccups interests the mother and gives her a sense of the reality of the child.

As the baby develops, it has ample room to move about freely, cushioned by the waters of the amniotic sac in which it is growing. The baby can thrust its arms and legs, somersault, and so on. But when the baby's size increases, the space within the mother's womb becomes more crowded, so that eventually it settles into the position in which birth may begin.

A mother can usually feel the baby's back, slightly to one side of the uterus or the other. As she follows the line of its back with her hand, she will come to a "hump" which is most likely the baby's bottom. On the opposite side from this hump she will feel the thrusting of the limbs. The head is usually low in the pelvis, felt as a hard lump just above the pubic bone. She may feel the jabbing of the baby's hands against her bladder or sacrum. It is easier to feel the outline of a foot or limb, back and bottom, when the baby kicks and squirms. Most mothers have some idea of the position of their babies.

It is more difficult to determine if the "hump" felt is the baby's bottom or head, but an experienced physician or midwife can tell, so that he or she and the mother can know. (The attendant palpating the mother's abdomen should always explain to the mother what is being felt, to help the mother become familiar with the position of her own baby.) If the "hump" is the bottom, moving it will move the whole body. If it is the head, it will bounce up and down under one's fingers without moving the body as well.

If the baby is in the breech position (buttocks presenting rather than head), the shape of the abdomen will be more like a triangle, and all the limbs felt jabbing higher (not against the bladder or sacrum). If the baby is in the posterior position, that is, with its back of the head against her backbone, the limbs will all be felt more toward the front.

Since the most advantageous position for the baby's birth is with the head down, facing toward the mother's back, it is helpful to try to change the baby to this position in the later weeks of pregnancy. The principle of natural childbirth during pregnancy as well as labor and birth is always to look first for a common-sense, natural, noninterventive way of correcting a problem or potential problem.

The safest way to help a baby change to a more advantageous position for the labor and birth is by changing the center of gravity in its environment. It is safer to "turn the mother" than to try turning the baby. Shifting the center of gravity of the uterus helps the baby move into polarity with that center.

Often at about seven and a half months a baby lies in the breech position; these babies frequently turn themselves into a head-down position in the latter weeks of pregnancy. The baby can be encouraged to turn by reversing the mother's position. Since it is impossible for most (not all!) mothers to stand on their heads, an alternative is to have her raise her hips higher than her head and lie in that position for several minutes every day, or even several times a day, until the baby turns.[3] Twice a day on an empty stomach, such as before lunch and dinner, the expectant mother lies on a hard surface on her back for ten minutes with her hips raised by pillows to a level nine to twelve inches above her head. This can begin by the thirtieth week of pregnancy and continue at least four to six weeks.

The mother can talk to her baby, encouraging it to turn around. (The baby can move by itself; it is not an inanimate object.) The baby may not understand the words, but the soothing tone of voice will ease any anxiety about shifting out of a disadvantageous position.

The same principle applies for a baby lying in the posterior position. It can be encouraged to turn by shifting the center of gravity. The posterior position often causes a longer, more uncomfortable labor with extreme back pain at times. To encourage the baby to turn, during the later weeks of pregnancy the mother should assume the pelvic rock position on hands and knees for ten minutes at a time, several times a day. In this position, she should also rock her pelvis gently up and down, and someone should stroke the baby, gently pushing it.[4] The husband can do this, talking to the baby as before, since it will recognize his soothing voice and may be more willing to try moving.

At night, the mother should avoid lying on her back, but lie on her side or stomach. (Yes, even at full term it is all right to sleep *on* the baby since it is cushioned by the bag of waters.) If she is too uncomfortable lying on her stomach, the side position can be used, lying on the side *toward* which the weight of the baby's body should fall.

During labor, if the baby is still in the posterior or breech position, it is better to labor on hands and knees, using the pelvic rock. (In fact, it has been said that in home births, about a third of the mothers choose to spend at least part of their labor on hands and knees in the pelvic rock position for comfort, regardless of the position of the baby.)

Since this position is tiring for the mother, ways should be found to keep her comfortable and relaxed. A soft footstool on which she can kneel is more comfortable than the hard floor. She can then rest her head on her arms across the bed, so that her upper torso is completely supported. Or she may sit on the edge of a chair, leaning on the bed for support. This position helps the baby rotate more quickly from the posterior position into the normal position for birth.

If the baby is breech, the hands and knees position can be modified to a standing-squat position in second stage—still with the mother's upper body completely supported—so that gravity helps bring the aftercoming shoulders and head down more easily.

## TESTS AND TECHNOLOGY

Every procedure, every course of treatment, should be explained to the expectant woman for her understanding, *and* for her approval or disapproval. Today's woman is no longer the passive "girl" that a woman was in the decades past, expecting the "big daddy" physician to take care of everything for her, if she meekly did as she was told. Women are increasingly well informed not only about the birth, but about the various interventions and techniques that may be used during their pregnancies and labors.[5]

Far from being offended by this, the wise physician will welcome the opportunity for an intelligent expectant woman to share the responsibility of making decisions. Her husband also has a right to this information, and for his opinion to be considered.

In order to give *informed consent,* people need to learn to take responsibility for their own health, and to learn all they can about the advantages and disadvantages of various types of treatment. The increasing *routine* use of medications and/or treatments cannot all be blamed upon the medical profession. People too often expect "something" to be done to solve all their problems. The expectant mother is no exception.

Parents who wish to be informed can read for themselves the uses and abuses of such things as antinausea medication, ultrasound, amniocentesis, X-rays, fetal monitors in labor, glucose IVs, analgesics (including the paracervical and epidural blocks), cesarean sections, and so on. Physicians will be relieved not to be pressured into using these things, so that they along with the parents can agree when the benefits outweigh the risks.

## ANXIETY, FEAR, OR DISTRESS

Fear is not the only cause of tension leading to pain. Fear is a form of emotional *dis*tress, but there are other negative emotions which, to a greater or lesser degree, disrupt the peacefulness of a woman in labor. The causes may change, but the *effects* on the parturient woman are negative. A well-prepared woman, not ignorant of the processes of birth, is still subject to all the common interventions in the hospital environment, much of which places her under unecessary stress and disrupts the *neuromuscular harmony* of her labor.

It is for this reason that thousands of women across the country are staying home to give birth. (Having a baby at home might be a *cause* of anxiety for a woman not well prepared, who would feel "safer" in a hospital environment.) Women are choosing midwives as attendants, and choosing birth centers and birthing rooms, in order to regain the peaceful freedom to "flow with" their own labors without the stress of disruption and intervention. Pictures on the wall and drapes on the window do not mask the fact that a woman is less free to be completely herself in the hospital environment, even in a birthing room. The *possibility* of her being disturbed is still there.

The woman in labor must have NO STRESS placed upon her. She must be free to move about, walk, rock, go to the bathroom by herself, lie on her side or back, squat or kneel, or anything she finds comfortable, without fear of being scolded or embarrassed. Nor is there any need for her to be either "quiet" or "good." What is a "good" patient? One who does whatever she is told—who masks all the stresses she is feeling? Why can she not cry, or laugh, or complain?

When a woman in labor knows that she will not be disturbed, that her questions will be answered honestly and every consideration given her, then she will be better able to relax and give birth with her body's neuromuscular perfection intact. The presence of her loving husband and/or a supportive attendant will add to her feelings of security and peace, so she can center upon the task at hand.

*Any* stress—a slammed door, an attendant asking her to turn on her back for a vaginal check, an injection—disrupts her relaxation and in turn disrupts the harmony of her labor in that same degree. This makes her contractions less effective and the cervix more resistant to dilation, increasing her discomfort.

Further, this disruption, however slight, increases the electrical activity of her brain in direct proportion to the disruption of her relaxation. It also interferes with the production of endorphines, which appear to be the body's own pain-relieving substances. And this disruption stimulates the production of catecholemines, those substances stimulated by the adrenals that appear to increase pain by blocking the action of endorphines and interfering with circulation.

As research continues in the field of neuroendrocrinology, we may someday find ourselves as aghast at today's thoughtless disruptions of the neuromuscular harmony of labor and birth in many hospitals as we are aghast at the unwise use of forceps, deep analgesia, and anesthesia in years past.

Many potential problems in labor can be prevented by keeping all necessary interventions to an absolute minimum, and by carrying them out in as polite and unobstrusive a manner as possible, helping the laboring mother to maintain her dignity as well as her peace.

At no time in the natural childbirth program are we interested in a patient simply being a "good patient" or a "quiet patient." She is not in any way to attempt something because someone else accomplished a certain feat. There is no such thing as failure! When pathology is present, other methods of birth need to be considered, including anesthetics, instruments, and so forth. The principles of natural childbirth still aid in making whatever problem exists less significant. Having a patient relaxed, calm, and cooperative is a significant advantage in the case of an emergency cesarean section or other form of emergency treatment. The essence of educated and prepared childbirth is for any mother to get the very best baby she can in the easiest way for herself.

When such conditions as transient hyperventilation are produced, one can only look to improper methods of preparation. Relaxed, quiet breathing is to be maintained throughout the first stage. High respiratory rates may lead to hyperventilation; persistent hyperventilation has been shown to increase fetal blood pH (acidosis).[6]

Other basic problems in natural childbirth are occasionally caused by the emotional instability of the mother and/or the father. When this is the case, making the birth pathological, it complicates natural childbirth just as physical pathology does. This type of neuropsychiatric pathology takes, if the patient is to have a fairly good natural birth experience, more patience and skill on the part of the physician and his or her assistants than would be required in other forms of childbirth using anesthetics. For in the latter case the husband can be removed and the woman sedated, although these procedures may compound their emotional problems afterward.

There are a number of contributions that natural childbirth can make in the area of preventive medical care today, one of which is in relation to premature labor. Premature labor represents a forerunner of morbidity, such as respiratory distress of the newborn. In addition, immature development of the infant's neurological system is responsible for such pathology as mental retardation and cerebral palsy. In premature labor, how rewarding it is to have a well-prepared woman, calm, cooperative, understanding the process of labor, having an easy, nonmedicated birth. It is the pediatricians who stress the importance of a nonmedicated premature birth, for the potential of the child in question may be at stake relative to the outcome of premature labor. With 300,000 to 400,000 premature births in the United States yearly,[7] childbirth education and preparedness may be the most important aspect of prenatal care for any of these particular pregnancies.

The benefits of a childbirth education program for the unmarried pregnant girl or woman have been reported many times. Each year many babies are born out of wedlock.[8] Childbirth education as part of a natural childbirth program offers a time of education and preparation for the unwed mother-to-be. It appears as well that with this type of program the incidence of repeat unwed pregnancies is decreased. Very valuable emotional and moral support, not given in the past in the usual prenatal care, is provided by natural childbirth instructors, who guide the young women to a new sense of self-worth. To consider the future of any particular conception, we must consider what the environment is going to be like into which that child will be placed. The unwed mother who is to keep her baby needs special preparation in how to raise a child without the influence of a husband. For the unwed mother who intends to give her child up for adoption, it is questionable whether the procedure of "completely" anesthetizing her with a general anesthetic in order to prevent her from ever seeing her child is in either the best interest of the unborn child or helpful to the mother as a person.

For patients who are classified as high-risk pregnancies, natural childbirth offers very special advantages. In a pregnancy complicated by pathology it is important to have a calm, cooperative, understanding patient who knows how to relax correctly and how to breathe to the most advantage for her labor. Because she has learned the value of lying on her left side, there is no problem in keeping her in the correct position during the different stages of labor. As a result, natural childbirth–trained high-risk pregnancies require less analgesic and anesthetic, thus reducing some of the risk for the infant.

## CHAPTER 6

# Labor and Birth

Two hundred and eighty days is an arbitrary figure for the length of pregnancy, calculated from the first day of the last menstrual period. (The average actual length from conception to birth is estimated as 267 days.) But a baby may be full term and quite normal if it arrives at any time between 253 and 281 days. It must not be thought, therefore, that a baby born ten days before the expected date is necessarily premature, or ten days after is postmature. Each pregnancy needs evaluation on its own merits. When a baby is "ripe" and ready, labor will begin.

As soon as a baby is ready for birth, it releases hormones which activate the mother's hormone secretions to set the birth in motion.[1] A mother doesn't just "give" birth. It is an interaction between two human beings, the mother and her baby.

## ONSET OF LABOR

There are three signs that labor is beginning:

1. *Rhythmical contractions of the uterus.* These are felt as sensations of tightness without discomfort in the abdomen. The uterus becomes hard and tightness can be felt all over the organ. The importance of the sign is in the *rhythm* and not the contractions. A pregnant woman may have definite contractions for some weeks

before her baby is due, but if a regular and continuous rhythm is not established, they do not usually indicate the onset of labor. True labor contractions may start once every ten or fifteen minutes, or even at longer intervals, but gradually the interval decreases until they come every three or four minutes. There is no pain as long as the abdomen is relaxed.

2. *Leaking of the waters.* The bag of waters may leak slowly, or it may suddenly burst and the waters flow out in a gush. This occasionally occurs before the uterus starts its rhythmical contractions, but this is true more frequently with subsequent babies than with the first. There is no pain when the bag of waters bursts, though it may be startling. It is wise to notify a doctor or midwife immediately. Rhythmical contractions may begin in an hour or two if they have not begun previously, or they may not begin for two or three days. But it is an indication that labor will soon be under way, so the woman should be under her doctor's advisement.

3. *The show.* A light discharge of blood and mucus, known as "the show," may appear. It usually occurs after uterine contractions have begun to dilate the cervix slightly, thus dislodging the plug of mucus that kept the cervix sealed during pregnancy. This is positive evidence of the onset of labor.

Any one of these three major signs usually makes it easy for a woman to realize that her baby is on the way. She should get in touch with her doctor or midwife, even if there is some doubt in her mind, and follow advice on when to leave for the hospital.

## EARLY FIRST-STAGE LABOR

Once labor has begun and the doctor has been notified, "plenty of time" should be the motto, with no hurry or anxiety unless the hospital is a long distance away. Small chores can be attended to around the house in preparation for leaving. Often there is excitement and relief that the day has come, which gives rise to a flurry of last-minute activity. This distraction helps the uterus settle down to its work without too much attention until labor is steadily under way. The doctor or midwife will advise when to leave for the hospital or birthing center.

Upon arrival, the woman is greeted by a receptionist and taken immediately to a labor room if labor is progressing rapidly. If not, she is identified by her prenatal records and admitted according to the usual obstetric routine.

Once in the labor room, she will be gowned and made ready for an examination by her doctor or midwife. This preparation must be in keeping with the written instructions of her own physician. No enema, perineal shaving, analgesics, amnesics, sedatives, fluids, or oxytocics (which induce or stimulate labor) are to be given orally or intravenously, except on the physician's written orders specifically for her and with her consent. These written orders may also include the request for no routine use of internal or external monitors, and the freedom for her to be up and about and/or to assume any position she finds comfortable, in or out of the bed. It is wise for the written orders from the physician to have been sent to the hospital in advance and it would be well for the couple to bring an extra copy with them, in case the one at the hospital cannot be located. This will help assure cooperation from the staff. The husband can be a great help in explaining his wife's desires to the staff, so that she can proceed with her labor without needing to make any explanations.

If the bag of waters has broken, the mother will need to stay in bed until after being examined, to be sure the baby's head is well engaged and there is no danger of prolapse of the cord. During the medical examination the physician will also determine how far along she is in labor, listen to the baby's heart, and determine its position by palpating her abdomen.

I do not advise that during the first stage of the average labor a woman should be asked to relax the whole time unless she wishes it, unless she has overcome all the difficulties of progressive relaxation and is adept at the art. In the ordinary labor I prefer the woman to be awake to her general condition, able to listen to instruction and learn what is going on, and able to recognize the encouragement given her by those in attendance. *But as soon as there is a sign of a uterine contraction, she must at once apply herself and relax to the very best of her ability.*

A quiet restfulness between contractions is sufficient. Many women prefer to sit in a rocking chair and read during the earlier part of the first stage. Some prefer to walk about, if the waters have not yet broken. Undisturbed peace should characterize the first stage of labor—without mental or physical tension, with every happiness that a woman can be given, and with every encouragement to be confident in the right outcome of her labor.

Sometimes, when labor is slow in making progress, a mild sedative may be beneficial to help her rest peacefully or sleep. A few hours' sleep, particularly at night, during the early dilatation of the cervix evades the weariness of mind and body that causes a woman to begin to interpret any sensation as painful. This therapeutic common sense should not be confused with the use of drugs to relieve pain. No woman should have to go without sleep for fifteen or twenty hours of a slow first stage.

Not infrequently labor begins, the contractions become regular and increasingly stronger, yet when the woman arrives at the hospital they slow down or even stop. This "latent phase" need not make everyone alarmed, injecting pitocin to "stimulate" labor, or having the mother walk up and down the hall for endless hours in an attempt to "hurry it up." Being admitted to the hospital seems to make some attendants and couples alike think that labor should move along at an arbitrary pace and finish in an arbitrary period of time. The stress of thinking labor should progress "faster" actually tends to inhibit its progress, and may even stop it altogether.

It is helpful for hospitals to have a lounge area where mothers in early labor can rest or walk about without being admitted, while waiting to see if labor proceeds. If not, they can return home. When labor again enters an active phase on its own, they return and are admitted. Left at peace, when active labor begins on its own, progress will likely continue more quickly toward full dilatation.

During labor the mother should receive adequate nourishment through liquids such as milk, orange juice, or tea to avoid fatigue and dehydration. Her husband should be brought full meals at every mealtime so that he need not leave her nor become worn out through lack of food.

Once active first-stage labor is well established, *the woman should never be left alone.* Her husband's presence is invaluable, for he not only helps her be relaxed and comfortable during contractions, but his loving caresses stimulate her sexual hormones to make the labor more effective (breast stimulation has been shown to be an effective stimulus to labor),[2] and they also help her to relax the cervix and perineum.

The couple should be allowed as much privacy as they desire, with no one entering the labor room without knocking and requesting permission to enter—a simple courtesy. The physician, midwife, or labor attendant should be close at hand, however, and present as much as the couple desires, to give guidance and reassurance.

As rhythmical contractions of the uterus increase in intensity, gradually dilating the cervix, there is a demand for patience. If the training that has been given in deep, quiet breathing and complete

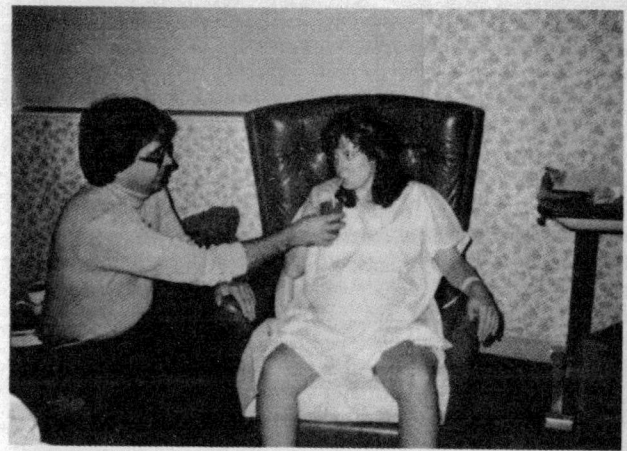

Ample fluids taken orally are needed by the mother throughout labor to avoid dehydration

relaxation is well and truly carried out during contractions, this period of waiting is much less taxing on a woman's patience. The routine of becoming *completely flaccid,* especially in the abdominal and pelvic area during a contraction, will help her improve her skill as time goes on.

When the opening of the cervix is about two inches, or five centimeters, in diameter, many women will begin to feel the strain of waiting, impatient with contractions that seem to be doing no good. They may become restless, not relax as well during contractions as before, and thus begin to have some discomfort. This is a typical emotional reaction, and the husband and/or attendants should reassure the mother with explanation and help her reestablish adequate relaxation and deep, quiet breathing with each contraction until she is comfortable once more.

It is still not necessary for her to be in bed. In fact, it has been demonstrated that mild activity and an upright position are a stimulus to labor. A rocking chair *for the mother* should be in every labor room. The gentle rocking motion provides mild activity, while at the same time supporting her comfortably in an upright position; her feet can rest on a footstool or pillows. During contractions she should stop rocking, let her head drop forward, and relax totally.

If she is walking around, during contractions she can rest her upper body on her husband for support so that she is bent over, and totally relaxed without danger of falling. If she is on her hands and knees, her upper body should be supported across the side of the bed. If she prefers to lie down, she should assume the position most comfortable for her, either the reclining-chair position with her back and shoulders raised, or the left lateral position.

No woman should lie on her back during any stage of labor for more than brief moments, for the weight of her baby and uterus places pressure on the major veins and arteries found in her lower back, and blocks adequate circulation. This can reduce the oxygen the baby receives and can cause a sudden drop in the mother's blood pressure: the *hypotensive syndrome,* as it is called, has frequently been observed by attendants without an awareness that the woman's supine position was its cause.[3]

## LATE FIRST-STAGE LABOR

### POSITION

As labor progresses and the contractions come more quickly and become stronger, the woman should assume the labor position most comfortable for her, keeping her back rounded and being completely supported. She should remain fairly relaxed *between* contractions from now on, in order to deepen her level of relaxation during each one. But even if she is relaxing well and seems comfortable, she still *must not be left alone.* She will be aware of the presence or absence of her husband and/or other helpers. Nor must she be bothered with unnecessary vaginal exams or other unnecessary intrusions. The baby's heartbeat can be monitored from time to time without disturbing her unduly or making her change positions.

It is important that her bladder be kept empty, and that she use the bathroom frequently during early labor, and then again before getting into bed to relax completely. All her joints should be loose and bent slightly, and if she is on her side, her knee and upper thigh need to be firmly supported by a large, firm pillow. She must consciously "let go" all muscular tension in the upper thigh, lower abdomen, and lower back, relaxing the pelvic area so completely that the outlet seems to be falling open of its own accord.

Relaxation during the first-stage contractions has the most astonishing effect. If the patient has been sympathetically treated and

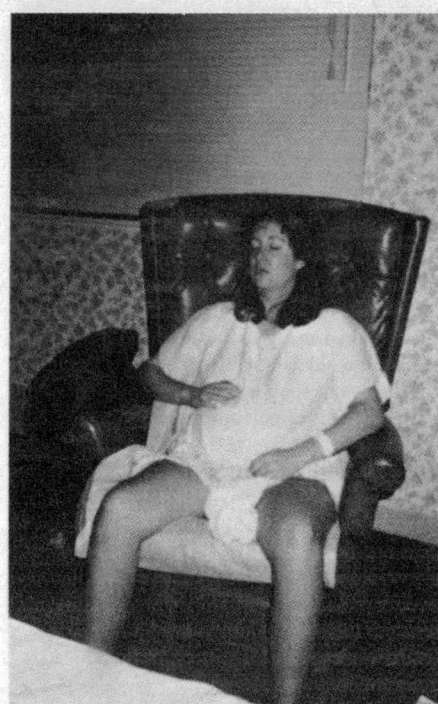

Relaxation in
upright position
during labor

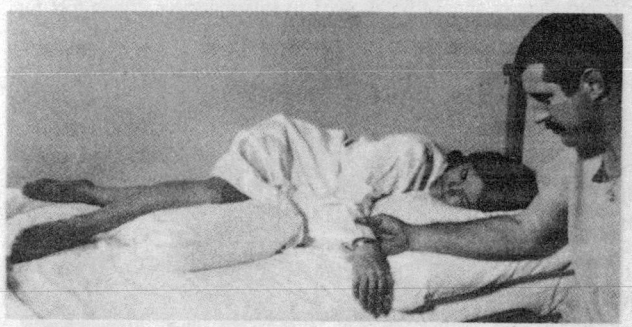

Complete muscular relaxation in left lateral position

well instructed, she should have no difficulty whatever in avoiding all pain during the first stage of normal labor. It may be that it will not be easy for her, during the last part of the first stage, to avoid discomfort, but the calmer she is the more relaxed she will become. It is difficult to relax when under the influence of strong emotional disturbance.

When a physician has a patient who reaches a degree of relaxation, he or she should remember not to be too ambitious and expect too much of her. But occasionally there will be the absolute delight of finding a woman who becomes adept at relaxing. In this case, if everything else is normal, he or she should call in medical friends, gather the students around, collect the nurses, and let them come and see a real natural labor. I have had many such cases. Some of them have appeared to be lying as if in a daydream from the beginning of their labor until the end. Their relaxation was so complete that they became almost oblivious to the fact of parturition, and, at the end of the first stage, relaxation during the contractions of the so-called pain period of labor enabled them to pass through it without discomfort. They then automatically brought into play the muscles of expulsion as the second stage began, but continued to lie in a completely relaxed state when not pushing.

The idea of pain-relievers and pain to such completely relaxed women is quite absurd. It does not enter their minds. They have no desire for it, for they do not have pain. But they understand what is said to them, listen, and carry out instructions in full cooperation.

### DISCOMFORT

No woman should be allowed to suffer greater discomfort in labor than she is willing to endure for her child's sake. In my experience the use of anesthesia presents no difficulty. If there are clinical indications, the signs and symptoms determine the most suitable method of pain relief. But even with the array of simple and effective methods of pain relief available, considerable experience is required in order to obtain the desired results. It should not be overlooked that if any reagents are used contrary to clinical indication, or at the wrong time in labor, serious trouble may ensue. The most important factor, therefore, in the use of analgesia and anesthesia in childbirth is the skill, experience, and judgment of the attending physician. Without these nothing is either safe *or effective.*

Before any method of pain relief is employed, however, the

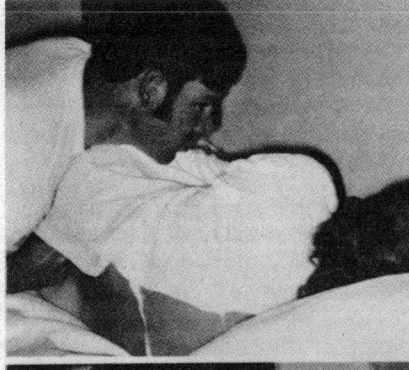

Husband applying pressure with fist for backache

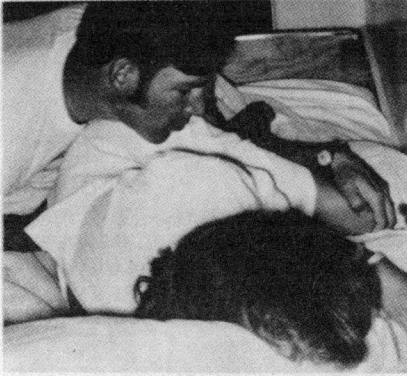

Husband massaging back and giving emotional support

physician should attempt to diagnose the *causes* of the pain. If the mother is unhappy and unable to relax, this may be the reason *for* her pain, rather than pain causing her tension and dismay. Has her peacefulness been disrupted by interventions—catheters, oxytocin, vaginal exams, IVs, monitors, and so on? Removing the causes of stress, helping her to get into a comfortable position, slowing her breathing down and relaxing her again may be all that is needed.

On the other hand, if she is doing all these things and yet complains of severe pain, this may well be an important signal that all is not well—that the baby is not in an advantageous position, that

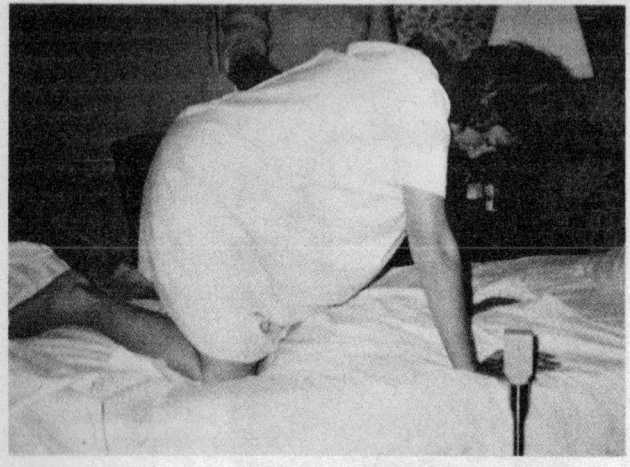

Hands and knees (pelvic rock) position for backache

its head is too large for the bony rim of the pelvis, or that there is internal bleeding or laceration. Only after attempting to determine the *cause* of her pain should action be taken and/or relief given appropriate to the problem.

## TRANSITION

Just before the cervix is fully dilated, that is to say, stretched wide enough to allow the baby to pass through into the vaginal portion of the birth canal, certain changes occur. In about 50 percent of women the ultimate stretching of this rim of muscle tissue at the outlet of the uterus gives rise to a backache over the sacrum or bottom end of the spine. The pain is caused by the stretching of the tissues but is referred to the lower back and felt as backache. This ache can be relieved by firm pressure of the hand of husband or attendant, or by slow, heavy rubbing over the lower back and sacrum.

The contractions are strong at this point, for it takes powerful contractions on the part of the uterus to pull the circular muscles completely back over the baby's head. Yet this is a most important

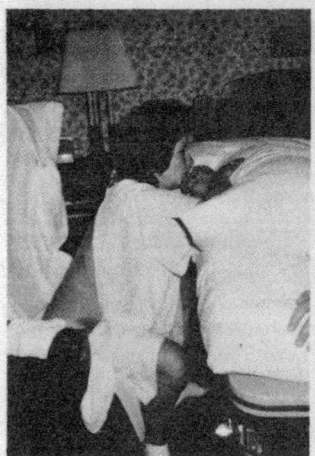 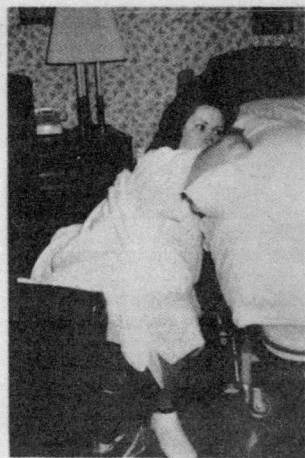

Alternate positions for pelvic rock, for backache

Husband massaging for backache

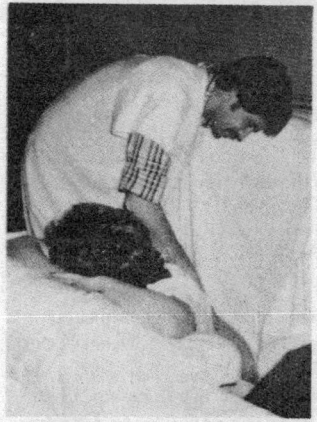

time for the mother to be able to relax with each contraction and not oppose it.

The temporary discomfort of the backache often is accompanied by a second change in the attitude of the woman toward her labor. Not infrequently it is the first time she has been aware of any physical uneasiness, and it awakens in her mind many fears lest this backache resolve into a more severe pain. Fear definitely assaults the minds of many women just before full dilatation of the cervix.

Back pain due to the baby being in the posterior occiput position is a different problem! When the baby is in the usual position, however, this backache only persists for about nine to twelve contractions. A woman should be informed of that, for a temporary discomfort is much more easily borne than one which is likely to persist.

Now for the first time vague signs of pressure, those early symptoms of the second stage, appear. Even a well-prepared woman can be confused. She needs guidance, coaching, encouragement. She needs the skill of her helpers in guiding her in deep, even breathing to relax completely with each contraction. At this point, it may be more comfortable for the patient to be propped up in the reclining-chair position, her back raised, and knees raised and resting on supports. Her head and shoulders should rest on a pillow, her neck relaxed and head turned slightly to the side. Her arms and legs should also remain completely limp during these contractions.

As this transition from the first to the second stage of labor develops, there may come an irresistible desire to bear down, even before the cervix has quite finished complete dilatation. Sometimes the mother may follow this urge, and bear down ever so gently during a contraction, and this will help draw the rim of the cervix up over the baby's head so that it is in position for the second stage of labor. This bearing down is to be ONLY in response to a truly relaxed patient's urges, and ONLY to the degree signaled by her body.

## EARLY SECOND-STAGE LABOR

Once the second or expulsion stage of labor begins, a woman not only gives the appearance of, but often expresses, great relief. Now she can take a more active part. Her backache disappears, things are making progress, and soon, in an hour or two, her baby will be born if she works with a will. *It is from this second stage that giving birth has earned its name: Labor.*

When the second stage is established, the routine of labor changes. The patient should NOT be allowed to push violently, but merely to hold her breath and exert a little pressure with each contraction, leaning forward and pressing down on the top of the uterus. It is a great mistake to wear a woman out with violent muscular effort in the beginning of the second stage of labor. The uterus will do its work perfectly well with a minimum of assistance.

Pushing with second-stage contractions requires physical effort; therefore it is obvious that relaxation during contractions must be discontinued. But as soon as a contraction has ended, the mother should lean back comfortably against a raised back support, close her eyes, take one or two deep in-and-out breaths, and completely relax *between* contractions. These contractions may come every five or six minutes at first, or every two or three minutes.

After ten or twelve contractions it will be observed that the woman becomes very drowsy between them. This state of inattention to surroundings is nature's way of keeping the mother relaxed. It is not, however, for the purpose of taking pain away, because very few

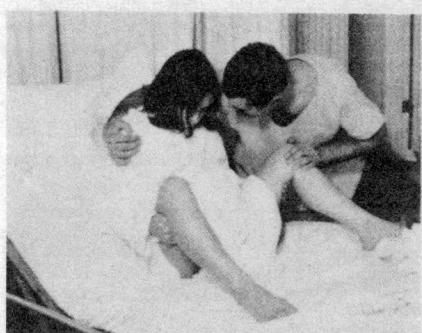

Bearing down in early second stage, knees drawn up and widely apart, back rounded, head bent forward

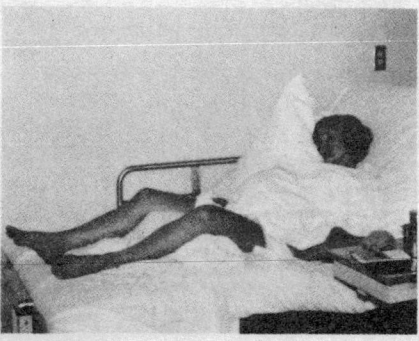

Complete muscular relaxation in reclining-chair position, between bearing-down efforts

women have any physical discomfort at this phase of the second stage. It is the means by which a woman's mind and body are completely rested, creating a condition in which the body can *recuperate with great rapidity between its violent efforts.* She is thereby prepared for each succeeding contraction without becoming exhausted. It is essential therefore that *absolute quiet* be maintained in the labor ward. Inconsequent conversation between attendants, clumsy movements, heavy footsteps, and banging doors are unforgivable sins in the presence of a woman advanced in labor.

Subdued lighting is important as an aid to her relaxation. Many women sleep between contractions, while others remain quietly unresponsive to their surroundings. Sometimes it is difficult to make them understand what is said without speaking loudly into their ears. Since they will often respond more automatically to a command given by the husband, the doctor can give the instructions and the husband relay them to his wife.

There is usually no need for the woman to be removed to a separate room for a normal birth. This is an American custom. In most of the world it is accepted practice for the mother to labor, give birth, and recover in the same bed, without being removed from her room.

### POSITION

As soon as the second stage is under way and the mother is helping to push her baby through the birth canal, she should be placed in a semisitting position with her knees wide apart. Adopting this modified squatting posture gives the greatest freedom of muscular action to her, and also allows for the maximum size of the pelvic outlet to be obtained.

In order to achieve this position she should be propped up on a backrest to an angle of about 45 degrees, the angle varying according to the desires of the mother. During a contraction she is to lean forward over the abdomen, with her knees drawn up beside her body, near her armpits. As she grips under her knees with her hands and pulls them outward and upward, her feet are to be supported either on the stirrups or by her attendants.

The mother may prefer to be out of bed, leaning against the wall in a squatting position, on her hands and knees, or in a kneeling or standing-squat position with her upper body supported by her husband. Squatting helps to widen the pelvis by as much as 15 degrees, as well as providing the advantage of gravity.⁴ The pelvic rock, kneeling, or standing-squat positions are especially helpful when the baby is in the posterior or breech position. In any case, the attendants should make every attempt to cooperate with the mother in the position she finds most helpful and comfortable. The physician or midwife can be humble enough to kneel and spread the sterile sheets and so forth on the floor beneath his or her patient for the birth if necessary.

## WELL-ESTABLISHED SECOND-STAGE LABOR

### BREATHING

Once the pushing reflex is well established, the woman leans forward and bears down in an expulsive effort at the height of each contraction. She should take a breath or two as the contraction starts, and then bear down as it increases, keeping her jaw relaxed and lips slightly apart, and exhaling slowly and calmly as she bears down. She may take additional breaths as needed. There is no need for violent effort, and she should not hold her breath for long periods as this reduces her oxygen intake and causes a high quantity of carbon dioxide to accumulate in her blood, giving her skin a dark red-blue color. If this occurs, remind her to take another breath, and to keep breathing out through her mouth. Having the mouth open helps the perineum open up below. She can think of her body as gently "breathing out" the baby below, as she breathes out through her lips. It is not hard pushing but *effective* pushing that moves the baby along. It is not necessary to rush this stage.

After each expulsive contraction she should lean back, take two or three deep breaths, and then completely relax and wait restfully for the next contraction in a state of peace.

Whether pushing or relaxing, the mother must be *fully supported* at all times, regardless of the position she has chosen. Some women have become exhausted raising themselves up, lifting their legs to hold them during expulsion, and then trying to push. This is not the time to make the mother do sit-ups and leg-raises! Her energies are to be totally conserved for the pushing alone.

There is no need to pull on the legs or push with the feet, as this creates muscular tension which can spread to the perineum. The mother should feel loose from the waist down, the legs relaxed and

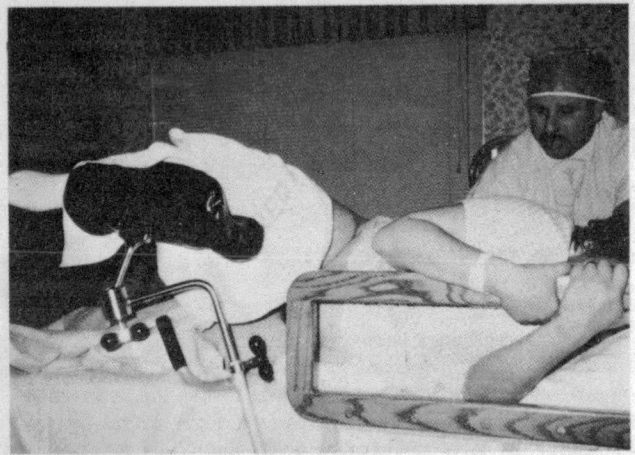

Side-lying position for backache, rotating posteriors, or birthing on the side (birthing room bed)

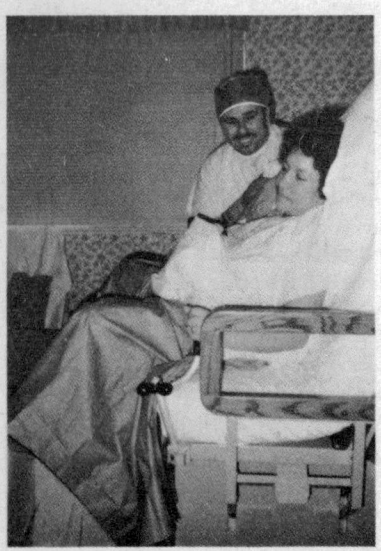

Upright position for birth (birthing room bed)

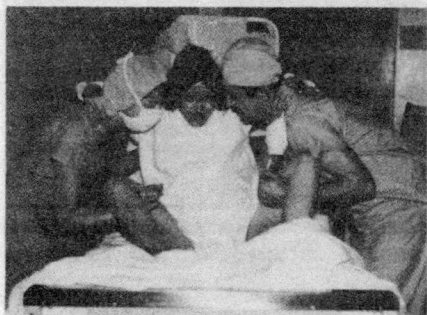

Bearing down correctly, with husband and nurse assisting

spread apart, her knees resting on pillows or supported by attendants. It is helpful for her to have something to grasp with her hands when bearing down, perhaps the hands or forearms of her attendants.

## RELAXATION

One could not require, nor would it be possible to obtain, physical relaxation during expulsive contractions of the second stage. The idea of nature here is that, the door being widely opened and the birth canal ready for the baby to pass through, the mother can assist the muscles of the uterus by pushing down to the degree of the urge. This requires real physical exertion, and since after each second-stage contraction the woman will be plainly out of breath, deep in-and-out breaths must be taken to quickly replace the oxygen used. Then, *between* the contractions complete relaxation is necessary, for relaxation is the most effective manner of quickly reconstituting muscle power.

It is usual for the membranes, the bag of waters in which the baby is contained, to have ruptured before this time. *A woman should always be reminded of the imminence of this event,* because many are alarmed by the sudden and unexpected flow of a large amount of water.

There is very little, if any, discomfort in the average, properly conducted second stage of labor, when the pelvis is adequate, the size and position of the baby are normal, and the mother is free of fear. Other pain may indicate a baby too large for the mother or an abnormal fetal position.

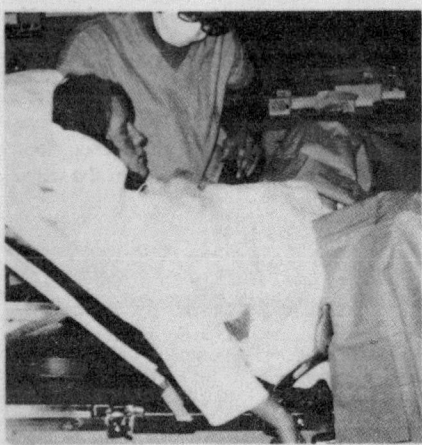

Laboring with twins, totally relaxed between second-stage contractions

During the first stage many women become bored, and a little tired of the feeling that nothing can be done. Thus a tremendous sense of relief very often fills a woman's mind as she realizes that not only can she help, but the greater effort she applies, within reason, the greater sense of comfort she will get. There is no pain with a good honest second-stage expulsive effort until the first awareness of dilatation of the perineum is felt. I am not, of course, speaking of abnormal cases, such as those in which large masses of piles come down as the head stretches the anterior wall of the rectum, but of the normal, unimpeded case in which no pathological condition is present at all.

When the head gets down onto the muscles that form the floor of the pelvis, a woman often finds it difficult to relax the outlet, because she feels a sense of the passageway opening up, a new sensation to every first-time mother. If she is alarmed by this sensation and endeavors to resist as the head arrives within an inch of the outlet, contracting her pelvic floor and squeezing the vulva and rectum tightly, she runs a very good chance of having not only acute pain but also, by increasing resistant tension, a torn perineum.

At this time a definite wave of fear comes over most women, caused by this feeling of opening up below, and an uncontrollable desire to *escape*. It is important not to yield too quickly to the assumption that the woman is in pain, for this threat to her self-control is not difficult to overcome. She must be strongly reassured that she will not "burst," that the opening will not hurt as it stretches further; she must be told how to overcome the discomfort. At the next contraction she is *to concentrate and push as firmly as she can*. As soon as she exerts this *maximum* pressure, the pelvic floor becomes distended and the head rapidly passes down to the vulva without further discomfort.

## CROWNING

When the head is visible and no longer slips back between contractions, what is called *crowning* has occurred. As the vulva dilates to about two inches in diameter the outlet can be felt stretching, a sensation that has been described as one of burning or bursting.

It is important that a woman *relax completely* at this time, letting her jaw fall slack and *breathing with her mouth open*. The muscles of the perineum relax as her face and mouth relax. She should be told that the sensation of bursting is a myth. The head will not tear the perineum if she is *completely relaxed*, all her muscles slack and her facial muscles relaxed, and if she breathes softly in and out through her *open mouth*. It is astonishing how large a baby will then pass through what appears to be a small vulva without any tear to the perineum at all. If, between the final second-stage contractions, after the head is adequately crowned, the attendant can persuade a woman to remain relaxed in this way, the complete absence of difficulty with which the head can be produced is surprising. I am sure that a large number of torn perineums are due to the effort of the woman to resist the oncoming head by violently contracting the muscles at the outlet. If her husband sees her close her mouth, or set it in a grim line, he should immediately remind her to relax her face and breathe through her open mouth.

As soon as the head has crowned, *all efforts to bear down should be stopped*. During contractions the uterus itself will slowly urge the child forward while the woman fully relaxes, opens her mouth, and breathes in and out quickly, to keep from pushing. In this way the vulva is gradually distended without discomfort. It must be distended gradually without any violence, for tears of the skin and even of the muscles are frequently produced unnecessarily because a woman is erroneously encouraged to bear down at this time.

## *BIRTH*

As the head is born, it must be supported by the attendant and turned up over the pubis of the mother. Once the baby's head is born, there is often a pause. It may cry before the shoulders arrive. With the next contraction, which again must be completely controlled by the attendant to keep the baby from moving too quickly, the baby's body emerges. The attendant may ask the mother to refrain from pushing during contractions, or may have the mother bear down very gently if the uterus requires a little assistance.

When a baby arrives under these conditions, the woman, being conscious and not filled with anesthetic, often realizes that her baby has been born only after she hears it cry. A child passes through a relaxed vulva with almost complete absence of sensation to the mother. There is no doubt that with relaxation of the vulva there is also a temporary natural anesthesia of its sensory nerves.

The case of a young woman whom I attended is an example of this. As her second stage of labor began, I instructed her in how to bear down, and asked her gently to increase her efforts. Then I sent for the medical students to come observe. They seemed unable to believe that she had passed so smilingly and so comfortably through the first stage. After a few more honest contractions, the rectum

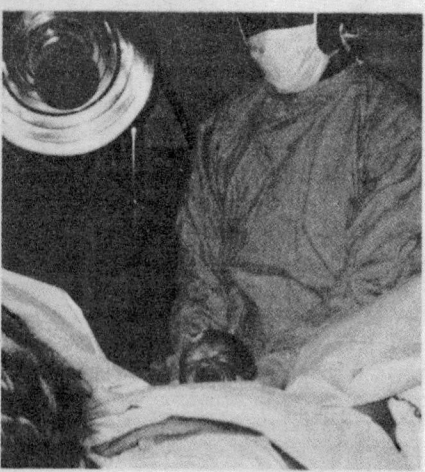

Baby's head is born, supported upward toward the mother

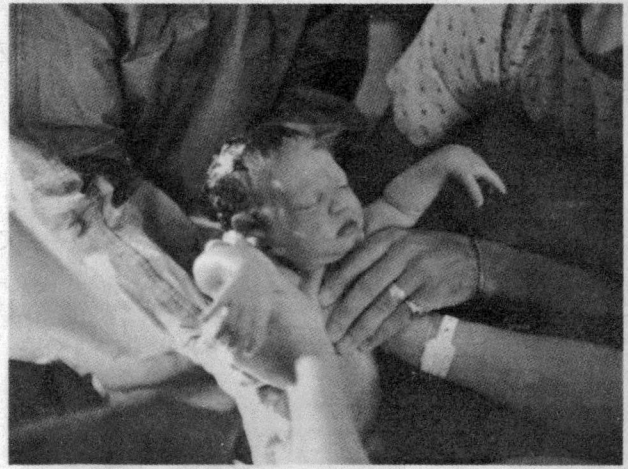

Mother and father assisting birth of baby

bulged. Soon the head appeared, and she looked at me inquiringly and said, "Can I really stretch enough? It feels as if something must give way." I pointed out to her that this was the invariable sensation of a conscious woman, but that it was only a temporary sensation, for as the head was born it turned away from the point where she was feeling the pressure. She accepted my assurance confidently, and in three or four more contractions a large baby's head was born easily and painlessly into my hands. I told her that her baby's head had arrived and that it was a lovely child. She was unwilling to believe that I was not encouraging her by making her think the head had come when it had not, so I pointed out to her that she could feel the child's head against her thigh and also see it if she looked. She was incredulous as she looked down and saw her child.

I asked her to bear down gently so that the rest of the child could be born. She said, "Tell me at once if it is a boy. We are longing for a boy." And so I was able to lift up to her a crying, beautiful baby boy of eight pounds one ounce, as we soon discovered upon weighing him. Her joy was indeed a picture to behold. There was no question of pain; she had been instructed how to use the inhalant but had refused, assuring us that there was nothing in this experience but the most unqualified delight. At first she was too excited to speak as she

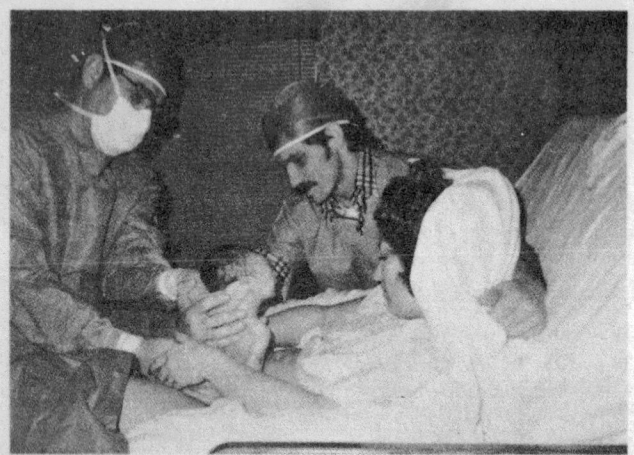

Parents assisting the birth, drawing baby up over mother's bare abdomen

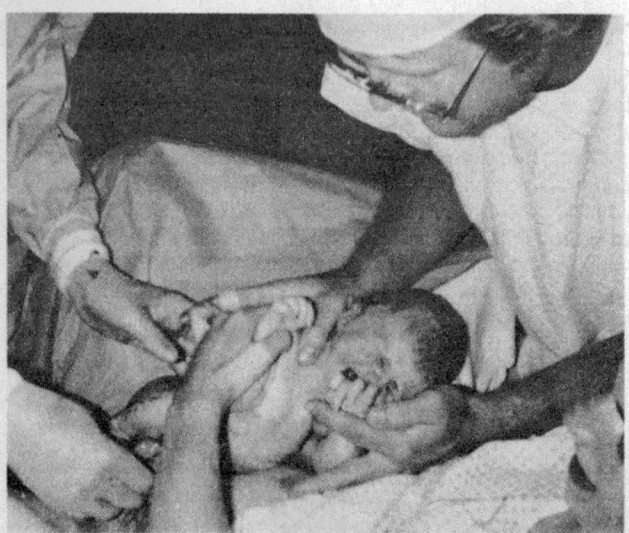

Immediate newborn skin-to-skin bonding with parents' hands

took the child in her hands, but then she said, "I must look carefully —it is difficult to believe I have a boy. It is wonderful!" And as she laughed and fondled her child, tears of joy rolled down her cheeks.

## THIRD-STAGE LABOR

In natural childbirth, once the baby is born, there is no need for relaxation. Here we get the beautiful *tension* of satisfaction. The sympathetic nervous system sweeps in with all its joys and its pleasing emotions, and so there is no desire for relaxation. The weariness of muscular effort is swept from the mother's memory by the sound and sight of her newborn child, and this stimulates the uterus into the action of the third stage.

Often the mother assists in the birth by lifting out her child as it is being born and taking it right to her breast. Her husband may also assist by placing his hand under the baby, so that it is receiving touch from both parents even while being born. A warm blanket is thrown over mother and baby. All babies should immediately be put to breast, for the human baby is genetically and instinctually programmed to do so.

There is no hurry in cutting the cord. Sometimes it may be four or five minutes before pulsation fades. At this time the father may cut the cord if he desires to be the one to do so. He should be encouraged to touch and caress his baby with his hands under the blanket in direct skin-to-skin contact.

The contact of the baby at the mother's breasts stimulates, by direct reflex, strong contractions and retractions of the uterus, thus hastening separation of the placenta and the closing of the blood vessels in the part of the uterus to which it was attached. This may be confirmed if one's hand is placed lightly on the abdomen as the baby is put to the mother's breast. Thus one important benefit of the physical contact of the newborn with its mother is this rapid separation of the afterbirth, and the absence of any excessive hemorrhage. Those of us who are aware of the results of the mismanagement of the third stage of labor can adequately assess the importance of this phenomenon.

If there has been a small nick of skin which the obstetrician considers will heal better with one or two stitches, these can be inserted while the perineum is still numb, with a minimum of discomfort to the woman and without any anesthetic. The woman is asked to relax while they are being inserted. A semicircular needle

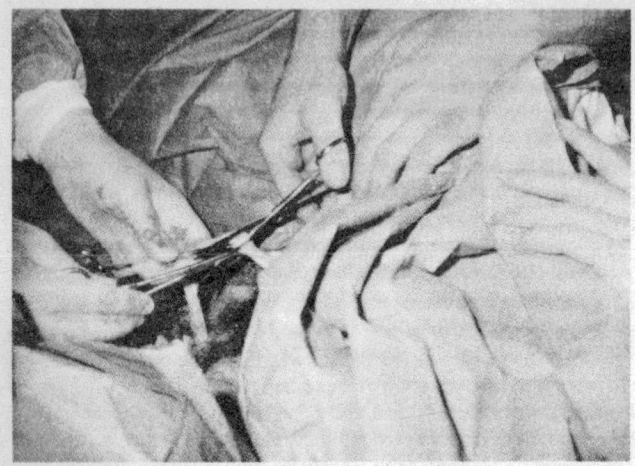

Father cuts the cord

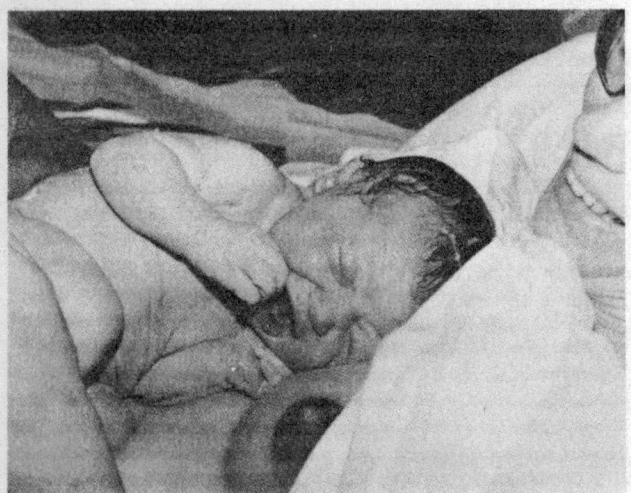

Baby skin-to-skin at mother's breast

of an inch or an inch and a quarter in its greatest diameter can be used, passing the point quickly at right angles to the surface both in and out.

This must be done at once, however, because the natural anesthesia of the vulva disappears in a very few minutes. If it is delayed for a quarter of an hour or more, then some local anesthetic, such as 1 percent novocaine, should be injected into the area through which the ligature is passed. This relative natural anesthesia of the perineum persisting in the early part of the third stage of labor is worthy of note, for it permits immediate suture, if needed. It is probably true also that lacerated surfaces brought into apposition before coagulation has occurred heal more quickly and more firmly than those which remain open before they are repaired. If an episiotomy is performed and a more extensive repair is required, the routine procedure of the attendant physician or midwife will be adopted.

It should not be overlooked that many women believe the delivery of the afterbirth to be an event of considerable severity and discomfort. Therefore the care of a woman's mind during this eight to twelve minutes or so continues to be important.

She need not relax, but may be asked to bear down gently with these painless, miniature second-stage–type contractions. Not infrequently a mother will expel the afterbirth without any assistance from the physician, and with a minimum of blood loss. This is possible because of the absence of either exhaustion or shock in a natural birth.

The placenta is a spongy, soft organ that varies in size with the size and weight of the child. Usually oval or circular in shape, it measures from six inches to nine inches wide and about three fourths of an inch deep at the center, thinning off at the edges. The average weight is about one pound. It shapes itself very easily to the contour of the birth canal and is passed without difficulty.

Years ago it was unheard of that a woman should wish to see the afterbirth. Today nearly every mother who watches her baby born asks to see the placenta. (A few women have no desire to look at it.) This I do if she requests it, pointing out the bag in which the infant, now lying peacefully in her arms or by her side, developed and became a perfect little human being. I show her the cord and its attachments, and the manner in which substances are filtered from the maternal blood to build the body, mind, and nature of her child.

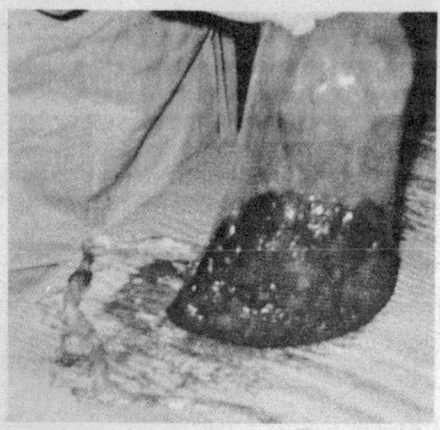

The placenta in the membranes

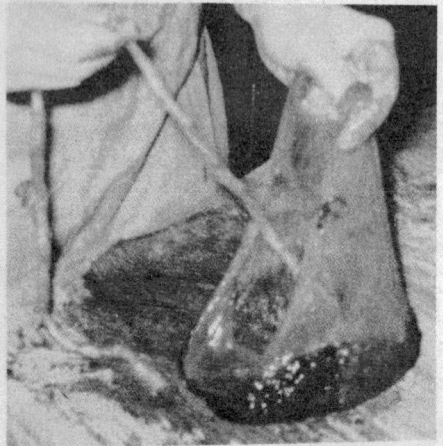

The membranes in which the baby lay, and the cord attached to the placenta

The amazing powers of selecting and rejecting substances that the placenta has for the fetus at its different stages of growth is remarkable. Its capacity for selecting the correct food in balanced quantities and refusing to admit much, though not all, that might be harmful,

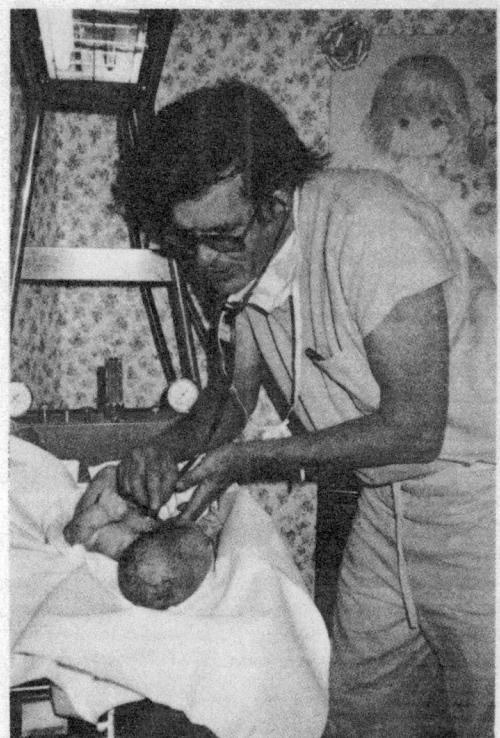

Physician (Harlan Ellis) checking newborn

makes the intelligent mind appreciate the incalculable genius of creation in all its phases and designs.

"Madam," I tell my patient, "when man can make one of these, he will have reached the footstool of the Creator. As I hold this discarded mass in my hand, I am humbled by the limitations of science." Such references create respect and help us visualize childbirth in its correct perspective. By speaking of the placenta in these terms, the importance of judicious diet and the influence of harmful chemicals that may pass into the baby's blood can be more fully appreciated.

Walking to room with husband after giving birth to twins, orange juice in hand

After the placenta is expelled, the nurse then swabs the vulva and perineum carefully with an anesthetic and a sterile napkin is adjusted to receive what is known as the *lochia*. So labor ends, and the woman, accompanied by her husband, is returned to her bed, where she is given a cup of tea, orange juice, or other nourishment and made comfortable to rest from her exertions. The newborn baby should remain with the parents, skin-to-skin.

## CHAPTER 7

# The Human Potential of the Newborn

**A** newborn baby remains part of its mother just as much after birth as it was while *in utero.* Indeed, the added association of personality and behavior brings them even closer together. When a baby is born, it is equipped by nature with the means of survival in relation to its mother.

In the absence of experience, it does not interpret incidents in the adventure of living with adult understanding. Its physical demands are for food, warmth, rest, and the security of human contact. Its awareness of things and people is acute, as are its senses of being touched, hearing, seeing, tasting, and smelling. From the moment of birth it seeks security in the widest provision of the essentials for survival and protection from outside injurious influences. *For that security a newborn baby turns to its mother.*

## BONDING WITH THE NEWBORN

Bonding may already be taking place before birthing is completed, as the mother reaches down to help lift out her own baby. Many times the baby's eyes are wide open, and eye-to-eye contact between mother and child is made as he or she is being born.

Ideally, the father and the newborn also bond immediately. At times he can even place his hand behind the baby and help bring it

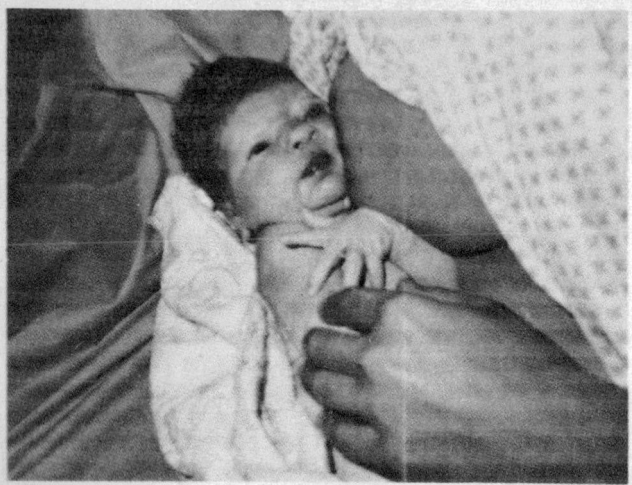

Stimulation of newborn through mother's hands and eye contact

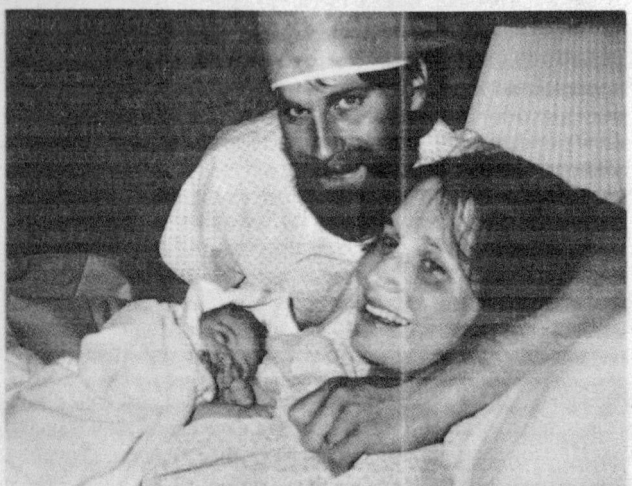

Parents bonding with newborn (baby naked against mother's skin under blanket)

on up to the mother. The baby is immediately placed skin-to-skin on the mother's abdomen and drawn up to her breast. After the cord has stopped pulsating, the father, as a symbolic act, cuts the cord. He then continues bonding by keeping his hand on the baby under the blankets which have been placed over both mother and baby. The heat from the mother's body under the blankets keeps the baby warm and at the right temperature.

The Apgar ratings taken at sixty seconds and again at five minutes after birth can be accomplished without removing the baby

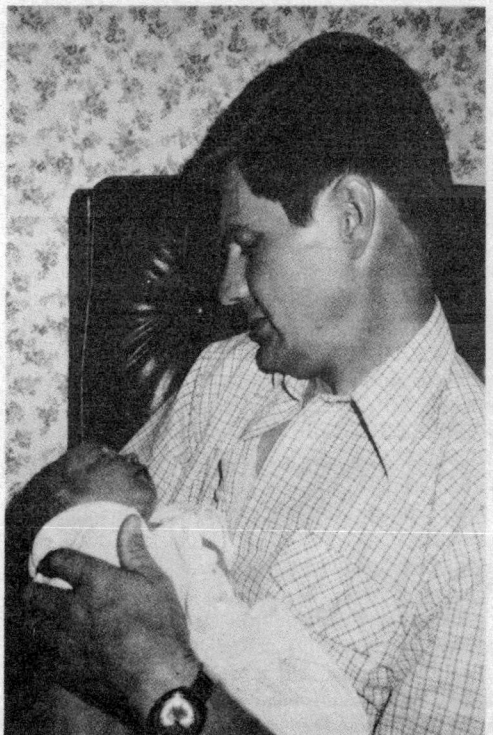

Newborn making eye contact with father (baby should be skin-to-skin with father under the blanket, not wrapped separately)

from the mother, as can any other essential care. The only separation that need occur should be after a delay of twenty to thirty minutes, when the baby is removed a few feet to be weighed and so on under the watchful eye of the parents, and cleansed of any blood or meconium with lukewarm water. All vernix caseosa is to remain on the baby, which is to be returned skin-to-skin to the mother as quickly as possible. Administration of silver nitrate or alternatives in the baby's eyes is delayed for a period of hours so as not to interfere with the eye-to-eye contact (visual bonding).

### DEFINITION OF BONDING

Klaus and Kennell in their classic book on bonding discuss a special sensitive period of time immediately following birth during which bonding takes place.[1] There appears to be an interaction between the newborn and the parents that is profound and tends to be life-long. In subhuman animals, this is usually referred to as *imprinting*. It appears that the most sensitive bonding period would be the first two hours of life (which might be called *primary bonding*). This sensitive period then is extended into the first twenty-four hours (which might be called *secondary bonding*). In fact, the sensitive period seems to continue in humans for the next nine months, to a time of a more natural separation of parent and child (which might be called *tertiary bonding*). Bonding is difficult to explain completely in terms of what happens physically, physiologically, and psychologically, but the following are some of its special characteristics.

1. It occurs between the newborn child and the immediate environment into which he or she is born, usually and more naturally between mother and newborn.

2. It takes place through the five senses of hearing, touching, sight, taste, and smell.

3. In the human baby, bonding appears to be most significant in the first few minutes immediately following birth.

4. Bonding is occurring throughout, not only during the first twenty-four hours, but for a period of nine months.

5. The effects of bonding may last a lifetime.

Primary bonding is the result of that special relationship that develops between the newborn and the parents in the period immediately following birth. It is the way in which all newborns are genetically and instinctively programmed. This bonding occurs through skin-to-skin contact, talking to the baby, stroking the baby with the hands, developing eye-to-eye contact, breastfeeding, taste, and smell. Many babies start nursing even before the cord is cut.

In the animal world, the term "imprinting" has been used to describe this process. The more one goes against the instinctual and genetic patterning of any species, the more abnormal is the behavior evidenced in the adult animal. Why then should we be surprised to have a few problems in our young adults, when there are large numbers whose births and bonding experiences violated their genetic and instinctive programming?

In our hospitals, do we not tend to do just the opposite of what Margaret Ribble advises,[2] by separating the mother and the newborn child and thereby subtracting just a little bit of the potential of a child? We are not talking about extreme separation, in which children are separated from their mothers for months at a time. We are talking about what frequently goes on at the hospitals in our Western culture. The pattern is set in the hospital and continues afterward at home, where the infant lies isolated in crib or playpen while its mother works around the house. As Harlow at Wisconsin has pointed out in his studies with primates, it may not be the milk that is so important. But when he separates a newborn monkey from its mother for any significant period of time, he finds this does affect the ability of the baby monkey to develop in a normal psychological way.[3]

And what about the effects of imprinting that Hess writes of in relation to human babies?[4] Have we not learned much from Konrad Lorenz about imprinting, the significance of early skin-to-skin contact, and the importance of continued skin-to-skin contact?[5] James Clark Moloney writes about healthy primitive cultures in which the care of the newborn baby includes a continuous maternal newborn relationship.[6] And it is a rare breeder of animals who would in any way encourage early separation of a newborn from the mother! Dog breeders who are interested in the temperament of the grown dog are emphatic about not separating the newborn from the mother until the seventh week. More information comes from studies by Clarence Pfaffenberger,[7] and from Pfaffenberger, John Paul Scott, and John I. Fuller in their book, *Genetics and Social Behavior of the Dog.*[8] Margaret Mead also writes much about the so-called healthy primitive cultures versus unhealthy primitive cultures and the differences in their early child-rearing practices.[9] This type of data should be presented, or at least discussed, when talking over the emotional potential of the newborn with prospective parents.

From what is said in *Childbearing: Its Social and Psychological Effects,* edited by Stephen A. Richardson and Alan F. Guttmacher, it is apparent that cultural, social, and psychological factors have significant influences on the course of the pregnancy, on the birth, and on the outcome.[10] The outcome, of course, represents the quality of the child. Dr. Norman Morris, professor of obstetrics from the University of London, stated at a New York Maternity Center Association symposium that if we could use pregnancy as a time for couples to learn what is known about the family and newborn growth, the repercussions on our society would be remarkable.[11]

Much of the future of the newborn depends on the parents' attitude and relationship toward it, *starting at birth,*[12] with skin-to-skin contact and breastfeeding. These are not minor matters but essential elements for the growth and development of the newborn. Work by such noted men in behavioral animal science as Konrad Lorenz of Austria or Harry Harlow at the University of Wisconsin are too often ignored. It seems we have learned much about imprinting in monkeys, dogs, birds, and even fish, but what have we learned about the imprinting effect in the human newborn? What animal breeder would ever think of causing any type of separation of the newborn animal from the mother following birth? Only among humans is this done. Could it not be that some of our social ills actually take root because of a nonimprinting environment in humans during the first several months of a newborn's life?[13] We live in a society which seeks answers to the causes of tension, anxiety, and depression, as well as the inability of parents and children to communicate with each other. It may be that we should not ignore too quickly studies of so-called healthy primitive cultures that seem to be able to raise children with lower levels of aggression, anxiety, hate, and competitiveness.[14] Mother-child closeness appears to be a constant finding in so-called healthy primitive cultures,[15] and the absence of this closeness is a frequent finding in retrograde studies by psychiatrists of deeply disturbed children.[16] It is also suggested that the worse the birth and the bonding experiences, the more likely it is that the child will be subject to child abuse.

The Rhesus monkeys separated from their mothers at birth show degrees of emotional disturbance later in life that are directly related to the degrees of early separation.[17] One farmer refused to sell his three-day-old calf because the animal had not been fed during the first four hours; for this reason he did not expect it to live, although it appeared healthy enough. One might surmise whether this was due to the lack of imprinting to the mother, or having missed the colostrum (the substance preceding milk following birth) with its antibodies. Is it possible that there is a connection between this same lack and the incidence of sudden infant death syndrome? Reports indicate little difference between breastfeeding and sudden infant death syndrome. But breastfeeding that *starts* at birth may be different from the usual breastfeeding as it is done in our society.

## BONDING AT VAGINAL BIRTH IN THE HOSPITAL

There needs to be an adequate hospital philosophy concerning the need for bonding at birth, from the administrator on down. The obstetric supervisor must consider this important, and the nurses must understand its importance rather than be impatient to handle and care for the newborn themselves. The doctor must make bonding a high priority for each infant he or she assists at birth. With this kind of cooperation, bonding can at times occur more completely in the hospital than at home births, if the couples birthing at home do not understand its importance. Sibling bonding is frequently more easily accomplished at home, however, although it is possible in a hospital setting if all concerned realize its importance and cooperate in making it possible.

## BONDING AT CESAREAN BIRTH

It is essential that cesarean-section patients learn that they can totally breastfeed, and that they can bond with their infants. When regional block anesthesia is used for the surgery, the baby is given to the mother so she can touch it, talk to it, and make eye contact. The baby is then given to the father for continued bonding while the mother is cared for.

The father's shirt should be opened and the naked baby placed in direct skin-to-skin contact with him, with a blanket thrown loosely over them. In a rocking chair the baby remains in the father's arms until it is time to take the mother to her room, and then he accompanies the baby to the nursery.

## PREMATURE BABY BONDING

Bonding is essential for the premature baby as well. The parents should have access to the intensive-care nursery at any time, to talk to and touch their child, and if possible, to hold him or her from time

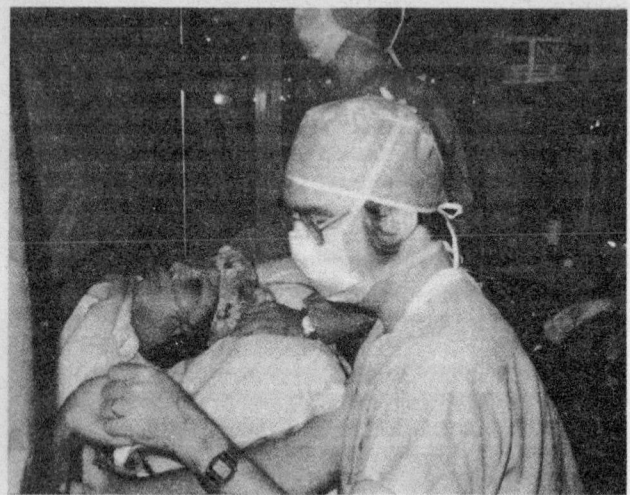

Husband supporting wife at cesarean birth

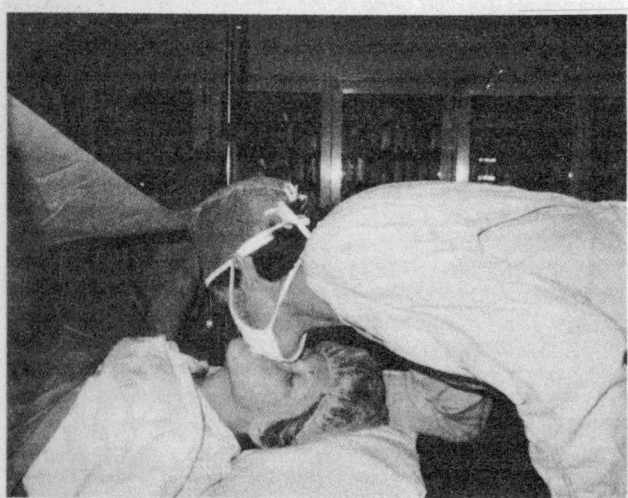

Husband comforting wife at cesarean birth

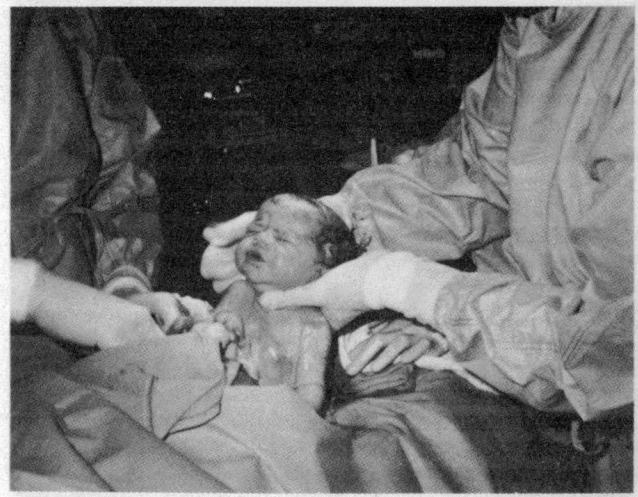

Physician lifting baby from mother's abdomen

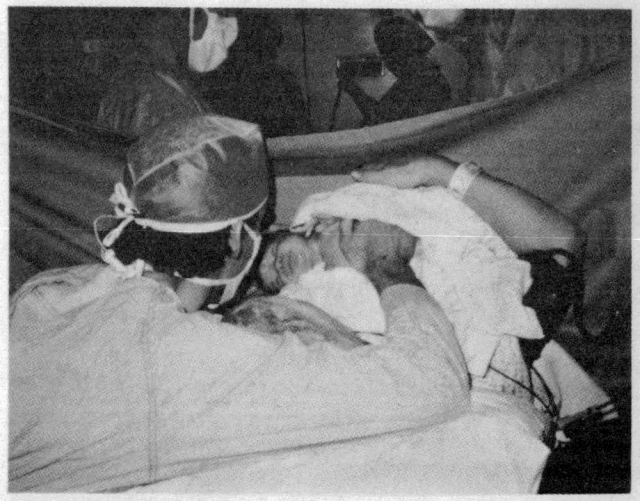

Immediate cesarean newborn contact with parents skin-to-skin

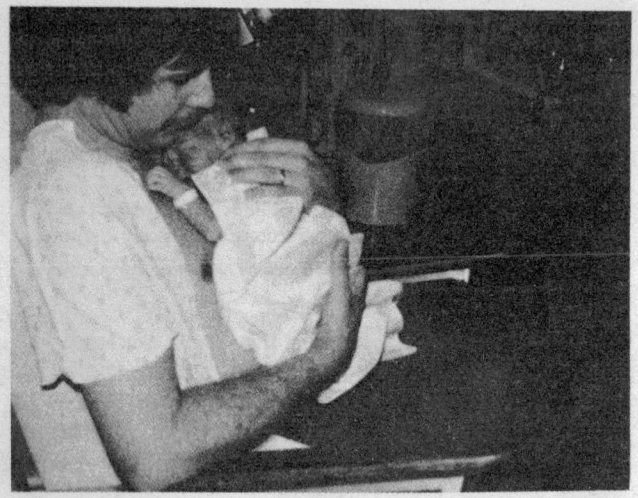

Cesarean father bonds skin-to-skin with baby while mother is cared for

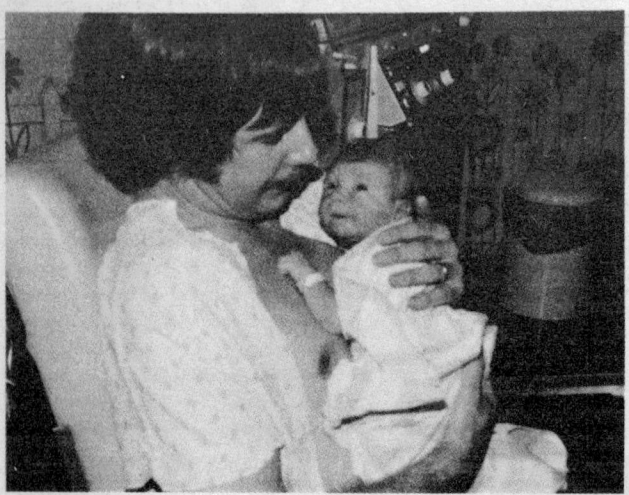

Cesarean newborn making eye contact with father

to time. This intimate contact should continue as frequently as possible until the baby is stable enough to go home. The mother can pump her breasts to supply milk, and be allowed into the nursery to breast-feed as soon as the baby is able to nurse.

## SIBLING BONDING

As mentioned earlier, classes for the siblings of the baby can be held prior to the birth. The siblings can accompany the mother on a prenatal visit, visit the hospital and the birthing room, and so on. Siblings can talk to the fetus before birth, and start relating and bonding long before the little brother or sister arrives.

If siblings are not to be present at the actual birth, they should be in the immediate vicinity so that they can bond as soon as possible, preferably within the first ten minutes, but at least within the first two hours after birth, touching, talking to, and making eye contact with their new brother or sister.

Big sister bonding with newborn

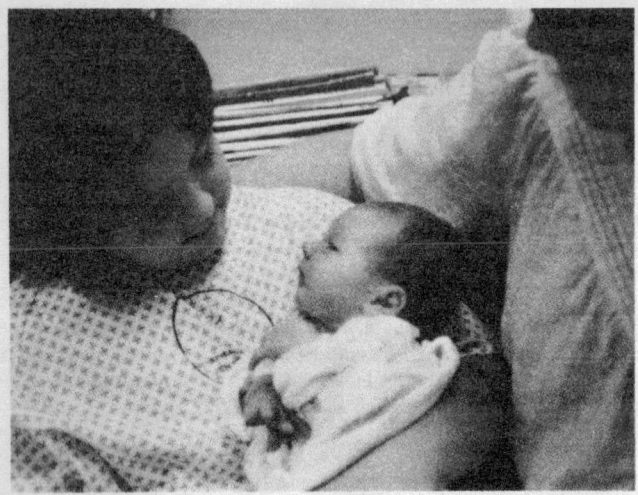

Newborn making eye contact with big sister

Preschooler bonding with newborn

## THE AMAZING NEWBORN

For too long it has been thought that the newborn was incapable of feeling pain, of seeing, of distinguishing sounds, or of remembering anything that occurred during the birth or the early days and weeks of life. The newborn was held up by its feet, perhaps slapped, then weighed, measured, tagged, wrapped in blankets, and carried off to an isolated bassinet in a central nursery.

More recent scientific studies have demonstrated that the newborn is as capable a young organism as any other in the animal kingdom. One expert in neonatalogy has said that "Newborns can learn better on the first day of life than they ever will be able to again."[18] They can turn in the direction of a sound: newborns only seconds old may even turn their eyes as well their heads in that direction, as if expecting to see something as well as hear it.

Babies not only move their heads and eyes to observe, but if held correctly along a table top will use their feet and legs to move in a stepping motion. (This ability appears to fade after the first few days, then reoccurs some weeks later.) Newborns can reach out and hit or grasp things.

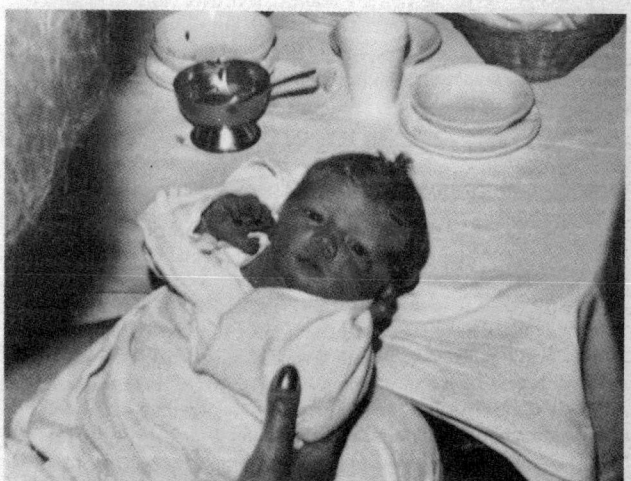

Newborn uses all five senses, able to see and make eye contact, hear and turn head in direction of voice or sound (recognizes voices heard *in utero*), feel, taste, and smell

Babies less than a week old have been shown in research studies to have visual preferences for certain colors and shapes. They can imitate other people's facial expressions. For example, if a mother sticks out her tongue, the baby may do likewise. If she flutters her eyelashes, it will blink back. If she opens and closes her mouth, the baby will do the same in sychronization.

A newborn already knows the voices of its mother and father. When placed on her abdomen immediately after birth, the baby attempts to make swimming motions up toward the sound of the mother's voice and turn its head in that direction. The newborn not only makes eye contact with the parents, but learns to recognize their features, and within a few days may avert its face from that of a stranger.

A baby is genetically and instinctively designed to be in complete physical contact with its mother from conception through nine months of age. The old idea of removing the newborn and wrapping it in a blanket to keep it warm may be just the opposite of its best interests. Mother's skin is a much better thermostat and *at the right temperature*. A blanket prevents this skin-to-skin thermostat, and also prevents the security that comes from skin-to-skin contact. Complete contact for the first twenty-four hours, with the mother bare to the waist, is best. *There is no security to match the feeling of being close to the parent's body,* carried next to it in the daytime, snuggled close to mother and father at night.

Ashley Montagu has long stressed the importance of touching, maintaining that babies who receive inadequate touching fail to thrive physically, mentally, and emotionally.[19] Janov says:

> From the time of birth until the first year, the infant needs to be in frequent physical contact with its parents. The closer to birth, the more continuous the contact needed; and the greater the trauma when it is missing. If the baby is left without physical contact with the mother for the first minutes or hours of life, there is a heavy penalty to pay in terms of stored pain and lifelong tension. . . . The implication of what I'm saying is that very soon in life the baby should be sleeping with its parents—and not in a separate crib. After several months of life, if the baby is carried in a papoose carrier when the parent goes out for a walk or to shop, those secure feelings are continued.[20]

These factors are so important to the full development of the physical, mental, and emotional potential of the newborn that they need to be stressed during pregnancy and even before. Appropriate information can be found in Montagu's *Prenatal Influences*[21] and *Human Heredity,* and in *A Matter of Life* by Dr. W. Coda Martin.[22] Klaus and Kennell's *Parent-Infant Bonding* is another valuable resource. Maria Montessori writes that most of a child's ability to learn, and his or her pleasure in learning, is determined in the first three years of life.[23]

## BABY'S PERFECT FOOD

Mother's milk has certain qualities that cannot be exactly duplicated. It has been created specifically for the human baby's own digestive system, and develops within the child an immunity against certain diseases, infections, and tooth decay. In families that suffer from such allergic diseases as asthma, eczema, or hives, infants who are entirely breastfed for the minimum of nine months, and continue to be breastfed well into the toddler period after other foods are introduced, are less prone to develop these problems.

The baby should be put to breast immediately after birth, and frequently thereafter, for the valuable, thick colostrum which precedes milk in the breasts for the first couple of days. We know that this contains substances that produce within the infant immunities to certain bacteria which might cause diseases. It comprises a certain amount of milk globules and cells containing fat, called *colostrum corpuscles,* although the actual value of these to the baby is not yet fully understood. Colostrum seems to have a beneficial effect upon the baby's bowels, helping to expel the meconium that is contained in the intestines of the newborn. It may be of help in breaking down the mucus in the throat when the baby nurses immediately after birth, by stimulating the swallowing reflex or causing the infant to cough before it can swallow. Colostrum may also provide enzymes for protein metabolism.

Colostrum is also of great use to the breast and nipple of the mother, for the suckling of the baby helps to stimulate the activity of the glands by which the milk is secreted. By the third day or less after the baby has been put to the breast, these milk glands become enlarged, filling the ducts leading from the breast to the nipple, of which there are about twenty. Since the baby has drawn away the thick colostrum from these ducts, the milk flow is much more quickly and easily established without engorgement, for *where the infant feeds there will be food.*

Nature provides the newborn infant with a considerable amount of fat. During the day or two before the milk is secreted in the breast, this fat in its own system is absorbed as its own natural nutrition. It is largely this provision of food within the newborn itself that accounts for the loss of weight until the mother's milk supply is established. The baby has enough nourishment in its own body to live comfortably on the colostrum until the mother's milk supply has been adequately stimulated.

Breast milk is important for the infant's well-being throughout the first nine months of life. One of the valuable amino acids found in high concentrations in breast milk is *cystine,* which is important for brain development. Studies of sudden infant death syndrome have indicated that one cause may be poor development of neural transmitters in the brain tissue. If the baby received a full quota of cystine in the mother's milk right from birth (no other water, formula, or supplements), might there not be better development of these neural transmitters, and less risk of sudden infant death?

A baby does not wish to nurse continuously. At first, when hungry, it will swallow as rapidly as possible, but it must rest. Although it does not relinquish hold on the nipple, it will stop taking milk for a short time. If it appears to be drifting into sleep, a gentle touch on the upper lip with the mother's finger will restimulate the sucking reflex.

While it is not strictly accurate to say that the infant sucks the milk from the breast, we will use this term for the sake of simplicity. In reality, it presses the milk out by closing the mouth on the nipple with a squeezing action. The only real sucking is the action of the baby's tongue in lifting the nipple up to its palate.

A newborn baby requires feeding again as soon as its last meal has been digested. One will take a large amount, and four or five hours pass before it feels it wants more and cries to gain the mother's attention to his hunger. Others may take smaller amounts, or have a more rapid digestion, and will cry after three hours or even less. The demand in a baby's voice is recognizable from all other cries, and a mother quickly learns the difference between the cry of hunger, the cry of colic, the grumble of an uncomfortable diaper, or the irregular bursts of a cry due to pain. Mothers learn to recognize swiftly the normal conversational cries of their children by close association from the time of birth.

Demand feeding has many advantages. It is obviously wrong to force a baby to take food into a stomach that is not demanding it, and, although many will do so, they are more predisposed to colic or spitting up than those who only accept a meal for which their stomach is ready.

Much crying in a frustrated baby is undoubtedly a greater evil than has been recognized in the past. Violent crying deprives a child's brain of the full quota of oxygen that he or she would have in a restful state. Many babies cry very violently when they are annoyed by not having what their body obviously demands, and these fits of irritation may do harm, not only to the child's personality, but also to his or her physical and mental development.

No hot blanket, guardian nurse, or weaning bottle can replace the physiological character formation of the breastfed baby. There is no substitute for mother love. The relationship between those who love and those who are loved is not a sentimental association but a reality.

Man cannot feed the baby within the uterus. What justifies his presumption that he is able to improve upon the physiological provision because the child has recently left the uterus? We can fortify and reinforce with certain substances the adequacy of both the placental and the breast nutrition, but the basic natural nourishment supplies something no concoction can contain. And although skilled physicians can write prescriptions for mixtures upon which children may thrive, they cannot include the personality factor of successful mothering.

The child who develops on natural food becomes familiar with the comfort of being cuddled in soft warmth while it feeds, in the strong, possessive, and protective arms of its mother. In this way the earliest foundation of the mental stability of the child is laid, discernible in the ease with which it adapts itself to the new environment of extrauterine life. The absence both of frustration and of fear of insecurity can be seen in the placid, cooing child who lies awake in his crib and gurgles at the discovery that his fingers belong to him and he can make them do things.

Many psychiatrists have stated from time to time, not only that man relives the moment of his birth, but also that his mental development will arise upon his earliest associations with life. If this is true, the happiness radiated by the feeding mother to her child must envelop the infant in the aura of blissful associations with its earliest beginnings.

The ability of a mother to feed her baby at the breast is commensurate with her ability to give birth to her child by natural childbirth.

The mothers who witness the arrival of their babies and experience the sensations of relief, joy, achievement, and pride that are the natural accompaniment to the birth of a child invariably desire to feed their babies, and almost always are able to do so efficiently. We cannot disassociate breastfeeding from the manner of birth. This is a reason to pay special attention to the manner of bonding when the birth is by cesarean.

The profound importance to the baby of the first forty-eight hours of its neonatal life does not receive the emphasis many of us would wish it to have. For my own part I extend that thought to the development of the mother in the first forty-eight hours of motherhood.

We find that, where women are subjected to interference either with regional or general anesthesia, the wish to feed their babies is less frequent. This could be put in another way: the nearer the birth

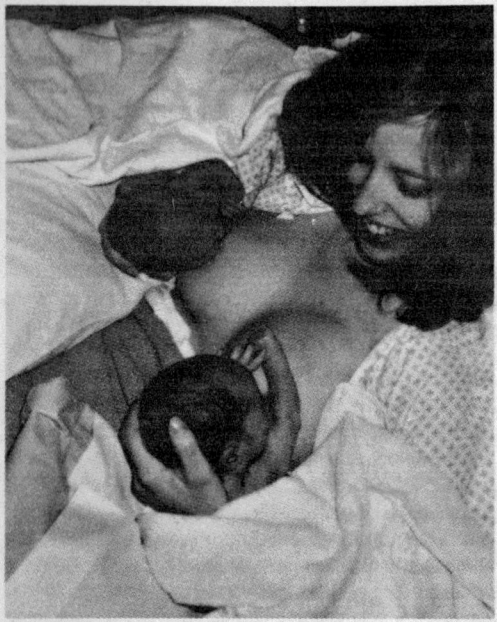

Breastfeeding twins after cesarean birth

of a child is to the normal physiological function, so much the more likely it is that the continuity of the natural sequence of events of human reproduction will be maintained. When a mother takes her baby to her breast immediately after she has witnessed its arrival, its contact stimulates, by direct reflex, strong contractions and retractions of her uterus. This activity hastens separation of the placenta and the closing of the blood vessels in the part of the uterus to which it was attached.

The reflex action of the uterus and other structures within the pelvis continues after the placenta has been extruded, for each time the baby goes to the breast it stimulates retraction or shortening of the muscle fibers and diminution in size of the vast blood vessels that have been formed around and within the uterus during pregnancy. This process, known as *involution,* or restitution of the uterus to its nonpregnant state, is most satisfactorily completed under the urge of breastfeeding. In the first week or ten days after giving birth, the activity of the breastfeeding baby may establish within the maternal pelvis a healthy condition that will be a blessing to the mother for all time.

If, as we are led to believe, lactation and the flow of milk are associated with an outpouring of secretion from the pituitary gland, the stimulating influence of that secretion upon the pelvic organs is evident in a breastfeeding mother.

The feeding of the child induces certain conditions in the mind of the mother. There is a complacent, peaceful sense of achievement associated with the knowledge that she is giving herself to her beloved possession. Her pleasant physical sensations when the baby feeds not only give rise to uterine contractions, but to a reaction closely akin to eroticism, which in many women stimulates contractions of the muscles of the pelvic floor and activates the glands of the vagina and vulva. I have heard it said that this intrusion of sexual feelings upon the purity of peaceful motherliness has so revolted some women that the conflict has inhibited the milk supply. In my considerable experience I have never met this psychopathic phenomenon. If a woman has accepted, for a variety of reasons, sexual gratification without love, I can understand the basis of conflict when, maybe at long last, she has learned the power of spiritual love for her baby. Love and sex can be two strongly opposing emotions.

It has been observed that a woman who has breastfed her baby may require a smaller contraceptive diaphragm than was used eighteen months before pregnancy. I have no recorded case of this in a mother whose baby was weaned to the bottle from birth. The significance of this is clear to married people.

## THE HOME

When successfully breastfeeding his child, a wife is supremely attractive to an affectionate husband. Sometimes when we are writing upon obstetric subjects we forget to call attention to the profound love for the baby that possesses many fathers. We do not remember how deeply they feel the emotional changes of their wives, nor the exaltation and personal satisfaction they enjoy when all goes well. The lack of a father relationship early in life can leave a painful gap in a child's feelings.[24] And husbands fail to realize what indignity their homes suffer from the alienation of mother and baby, if the infant is given at an early age to the care of a nursemaid, to be seen only for a few hurried moments in the evening before its parents change for dinner.

Of course there are those miserable creatures of society whose babies are due to arrive invariably at just the wrong time—who want a baby very much, but it *is* an awful trial and they are not at all sure what their husbands think about it. They would like to nurse the baby, but they have so many social engagements booked—things they do not want to do but must—that they are afraid they will not be able to . . . and so on, ad infinitum. Marriage itself, as it is understood in modern civilization, introduces complications into the mind of the young mother that never could have existed in the natural state of *genus homo,* when the instinctive desire of the male was reproduction, the reciprocal instinct of the female was parental, when the fullness of their mutual harmony was inspired by nature to the continuation of the species. Social engagements, economic considerations, and procreation out of a sense of duty were limitations unthought of.

The care of the breasts is of far-reaching importance to a woman both as a mother and a wife. If she loses her figure and adopts an unbecoming posture, it may affect her personality. Some women become self-conscious, develop a sense of inferiority among others, and an apologetic retiring manner, sometimes akin to shame, before their husbands. They blame lactation and even the infants whom they have breastfed, although these troubles arise after weaning to the bottle from birth more frequently than from breastfeeding. It is too frequently overlooked by those who attend childbearing women that the breasts are reproductive organs. They have a sexual as well as a personality value, which subjects them to the buffetings of a variety of psychological assaults. For that matter, I know of no literature, except that which today is considered Victorian and grossly sentimental, that places childbirth itself in its true position and understands that labor is of love.

Perhaps it will be forgiven if I issue a warning of the nature of things. Every act that leads, in a normal sequence of events, to the association of painful childbirth will become inhibited by the primitive instinct of escape. The chill of fear creeps into the warmth of love: the kiss becomes a mere peck and an established routine; the passion that was possessive and overpowering no longer binds life partners in the masonry of marriage. Coitus becomes an unjustifiable risk; its pleasures fade and disappear before the ever-present fear of impregnation. And so the seeds of domestic strain and misery are often sown by painful childbirth.

These feelings are often intensified during the first weeks a baby born so painfully spends at home, especially if the baby is not breastfed, for breastfeeding does not extend its benefits only to the mother and child. Many fathers are distraught with the troubles of their wives and the cries of a restless baby who does not thrive. It is by no means infrequently the cause of one-child families, the father and mother agreeing that, quite apart from the trials that the labor brought to them both, they could never go through six or eight weeks of nerve-racking experience, physical weariness, and sleepless anguish that fell to their lot when the baby struggled to attain a standard of health and behavior in which the parents had lost all confidence.

Fortunately, the converse also applies. Some of those women who have experienced the happiness of their child's arrival say that they have never known the fullness of love until possessed by the irresistible desire to have more children. Again and again they recall and dream of that transcendental joy that shines like a persistent orb of light, illuminating the wonders of their new life of motherhood. Every act of love is enhanced; the physical and mental desire for the fullness of their husbands' affection perfects the mutual delight of their companionship. Restraint is flung to the four winds of heaven. As one they join together in the search for new and yet more delightful experience. Their coitus is a spiritual union blessed with profoundly pleasurable physical reaction.

The birth of a child is not a woman's monopoly. It is the major incident in the lives of three people—father, mother, and child.

Indeed, many husbands suffer more in childbirth than the women who bear their babies. To overlook or prevent the mutual companionship and assistance of husband and wife during pregnancy and labor is to show a grievous lack of human understanding.

The love of a woman for her child and the love of a woman for her husband have different foundations and manifestations. When a baby is born, the first questions of a young mother concern the welfare of her baby. The first questions of a young father concern the welfare of his wife. This persists until the child is able to care and fend for itself. Experience has shown in the past, on many occasions, that in time of danger a woman will save her child before her husband, whereas a man similarly placed normally saves his wife first. This does not mean that the wife has no love for the man, or that the man has less love for the child, but demonstrates the instinctive valuation of love between the three of them. This is well recognized in the traditions of the sea, where the shipwreck order is "Women and children first."

A woman should bear in mind that a little more tenderness to her husband after the child has arrived will strengthen the bond of affection between them. But this will not have the same effect if during the pregnancy the birth of their child has been the interest only of the mother and not of the father. Therefore the woman must interest her husband in pregnancy, must point out that it is his child as well as hers.

Most men want families and will love their babies in a man's way from the earliest age if they are encouraged or even allowed to learn. Paternal love is different from maternal love, but it is an equally deep emotion. Women must not pride themselves on being the only incomprehensible component of the human race; husbands are just as difficult to understand at times as wives. A man may consciously or unconsciously be confronted by dangerous reactions to his wife's pregnancy. He may fear for her safety or her health and beauty afterward. He may resent the child's arriving, being jealous of the love his wife will give it. He may desire her for himself alone and foresee a rift in the early companionship that they have enjoyed together. He may be disturbed by the immediate cost and future expense. It is thus we can say that the birth of a child may bind or break a marriage, and the possibility of these things happening consequently calls for special attention on the part of the wife. She must take care of her husband, for above all things she desires to keep him for herself, and she knows that she and her child depend upon him.

Women, therefore, must share fully with their husbands the child that is born to them. The love of husband and wife, which gives them children, needs more care than the children that this love brings. It is a delicate and beautiful thing, fragile and sensitive. It must be nurtured, watched, protected, if it is to survive. It fades quickly if left without attention and must be looked after carefully as it strives to mature with the years. The husband must become interested in the affairs of the wife, which primarily concern the children and the care of the home. The wife must become interested, though not necessarily active, in the affairs that concern her husband, primarily the maintenance of the family and home.

From the foundation of a happy childbearing experience, shared by the mother and father, children can grow secure in the knowledge that they are loved and wanted. As boys and girls grow older, they will be prepared to learn and understand about parenthood. No prudery or lying pose of innocence will tarnish the personality of such educated, understanding young people. Thus it is that successful home and family life must become the ultimate objective of modern obstetric teaching.

Let us suppose, therefore, that from infancy to puberty the sexual education of the child is carried out by the parents in the home. If parents wait longer than the immediate prepuberty years, or if the instruction is given over to others outside the family, then the child may be deprived of that security which is so essential to all the changing phases of development. In some ways this is comparable to the mother who is emotionally absent, and the father literally absent, from the birth of their child.

A similar series of events demands the closest maternal care and love during the premenstrual phase of a girl's life. I teach that mothers can make better mothers than those who are not mothers can ever make. I do not decry the work of those unselfish people who sublimate their own maternal love in an effort to fashion the lives of the young. But it is like breast milk as opposed to milk from a bottle —one is ever present, already prepared for immediate use when so desired, while the other is the acquisition of an unnatural regimen, satisfying the stomach but never penetrating the deep and spiritual self within the consciousness of the child.

Human nature has not changed since the days of the Psalmist. The man who has a "full quiver" of children and an adequate income is the peace-loving worker whose presence in the community is an influence toward moderation and reason. But should his home be in jeopardy or his family in danger, he knows no fear, but flings himself in to the fray with the violence of desperation. Is it for his own comfort or for his childless wife he fights to the death? Is it in the cause of justice among nations or is it for children who crowd his small home and climb upon his knee? From whence is the power in a man's arm? Let fathers of families answer, and husbands with good wives who mother their growing sons and daughters. The phylogenetic development of man has equipped him physiologically and mentally to fight for the protection of his children and their mother. Perhaps that is why peace-loving men who are forced into battle by an aggressive enemy fight with such fury that the professional soldier is amazed.

From my contact with men and women of all classes, I have been led to believe that it is for homes and families our people will cry out. The demand will be for parenthood, and for income from their work adequate to provide for children in health and happiness. Unfortunately, the prestige of a satellite in orbit around the earth is too often infinitely greater than the prestige of a revolutionary approach to the breeding of better human stock, or the founding of homes and family units of happy and contented people. The uninhibited development of a simple philosophy and sound physiques, which enable men and women to adjust themselves to an ever-changing world, is allowed to occur where it may, if it will. Rockets and satellites, spaceships and hydrogen bombs, absorb thousands of millions of the wealth of nations, while the development of the human race to a higher standard of mental and physical efficiency is granted a disgraceful pittance. We do not demand greater numbers—the objective must be the *quality* of the child. As the quality of the mother, so the nature of the offspring will vary; the mother herself has been molded by the manner of her birth and the environment in which she was influenced by her parents as a small child. The bondage or the freedom of her puberty guides her to accept or to distrust the father of her own children, and so the cycle starts again in the birth of a baby.

# PART II

# The Philosophy of Natural Childbirth

The philosophy of natural childbirth is as relevant today, in this last portion of the twentieth century, as when Grantly Dick-Read first enunciated it in 1919. For its truths evolved from his observations of and listening to women who labored and gave birth gladly, without interference and without suffering. *Women* taught him the truth, and the truth stands.

The question was first raised in his mind by a young woman whom he attended in 1918. She astonished him by refusing the anesthesia he offered. After her child was born, she said, "It didn't hurt. It wasn't meant to, was it, doctor?" He came to the conclusion, No, it was not meant to hurt; and then had to find answers to the inevitable second question, Why, then, does it hurt?

The following portions summarize his answers, selected from the best of his writings from 1933 until his death in 1959. Terminology may change; medical research may reveal more and more details about the intricate workings of the human body than he knew. Many of the obstetric practices he objected to have been changed, for his teachings revolutionized obstetrics around the world.

Yet new obstetric practices are continually being introduced which still violate the principle of childbirth as a natural process. Every person involved in any way with the birth of a child should be required to read what he had to say, and challenged to justify their procedures by providing better answers than his.

## CHAPTER 8

# Childbirth as a Natural Process

We cannot think of motherhood only in terms of its satisfactory completion. We must look back into the life of a young woman and consider the thoughts and experiences that eventually lead her to become a mother. We need not delve into that experimental playground of psychologists popularly known as the "sex life." We have only to recall the normal sequence of events every healthy-minded girl and young woman of our time goes through. At an early age she learns all the happiness of love; it is an emotional development that radiates from a young girl. It will often be found that in her untrained and undifferentiated affection life holds some joys too deep and too unfathomable for her to understand. This irresistible urge to love is so mysterious that my daughter, when fifteen years of age, wrote to me from school:

> I wish you could explain to me why I feel as I do this term; it has never been like it before. I am so deliriously happy. There is no reason that I know of, but I am fond of everybody. I seem to see the good in them, and want to *think* lovely things, as if I were possessed of a heavenly spirit making me so much better than my real self.

And so, with most every young girl in varying degrees, this love of life begins to develop at an early age, until in due course she may find herself in love, and here her emotional life becomes concentrated, with all its thrills, its joys, and its anxieties, upon one semidivine individual. It is the spiritual refinement of her own ideal, and in the normal course of events she becomes engaged, unwilling to believe that there are others who are equally fortunate, and blissfully ignorant of the fact that she and her suitor are instruments in the design of nature. Eventually she marries, and if all goes well she conceives and prepares to bear her child.

The average woman associates much that is beautiful in her life with this series of events. It is the implementation of the power of life by the universal forces that govern all things to the end that the human race shall survive. From earliest girlhood, each forward step in this progression is made because of a desire to bring her joy or a fuller realization of her dreams. The law of life does not beat a woman on either by fear or physical necessity, but attracts her development by the presentation of increasingly beautiful experiences, which she is not slow to grasp. Love may be beset by anxieties and doubts, but of itself it stimulates all the noblest and greatest qualities by which human nature is characterized at its best. It is the greatest power in the world, and without it the races of mankind would be finished in a few generations.

When the time comes for giving birth, each woman must be treated according to her understanding. Childbirth is divided into three definite stages by signs and symptoms. The first stage is not just the opening of the outlet of the uterus; it presents certain features of the process of labor, all of which can be shown to be purposeful. Where education has been satisfactory and the beginning of labor can be seen as a joyful prelude to her child's arrival, a woman is conscious of each uterine contraction as a promise of her child's arrival. Elation, rejoicing, and a strong sense of contentment and relief are the natural emotional reactions to the onset of labor.

I use the term "elation" in its strict meaning. It is not a simple happiness, but an exaltation of the mind resulting from the feeling of success and pride in the confident approach of the reward of pregnancy. Many women become conscious of their own importance at this time, and the strong instinct of self-assertion may be observed. Such women will telephone their friends, and many will advertise widely to the world the fact that at last the great moment has come. This is a time when doctors are not often with their patients, but a doctor may detect this elation when a woman who does not fear labor calls on the telephone when she thinks she has begun labor. She will say, with a cheerful spirit, "I think I have started. Isn't that great?" or, "Things are happening—I am so thankful." This emotional state was described to me by a vivacious, intelligent young woman in simple yet dramatic words.

"I have never known such a sense of joy," she said. "I walked out into the garden; I felt an irresistible desire to parade myself. I made a point of going to speak to the gardener. I told the chauffeur to be ready to go out in the car at any moment. I have no idea why, but it seemed as near as I could reasonably go to telling him that my baby was coming. I walked down the drive and up and down the road for five or ten minutes, feeling in the back of my mind a hope that I should meet some of my friends. My time had come, my baby was on its way—after all it was true. I believe now that I actually exaggerated my shape."

This is only one example of many instances that have been told to me. Although few women will volunteer, without questioning or an inquiry being made, to describe the profoundly stimulating emotions that accompany the onset of labor when complete confidence in its outcome dispels all fear, most women do not hesitate to say they are glad when their baby is coming at last.

To all doctors, midwives, and husbands and/or other birth attendants, I say: Do nothing to destroy the cheerful courage and confidence of the woman who has begun labor with her mind in that state; bury your own anxiety and fear and share with her the spirit of victory about to be achieved. You will thereby assist in paving the way for her progress to uncomplicated motherhood and ward off the greatest enemy to her neuromuscular perfection. There are few greater obstetric crimes than to become a serious busy body who demands compliance with illogical and baseless conservative principles, requesting silence, speaking in whispers, parading a mass of so-called essentials ready to deal with all emergencies. The kindly sympathy and word of warning advice are disturbing to a happy woman who sees only the impending joy of her child's arrival, and believes it will come quickly and easily. Elation is an emotional state, but it has profound physical manifestations; it is not only a part of the reward of childbirth, it is a phenomenon of which nature, to facilitate the safe reproduction of her species, takes most subtle advantage.

The first stage of labor demands peaceful relaxation, quiet assurance, and the ignoring mentally of what is going on in the womb, or uterus. Any effort actively to assist first-stage contractions will defeat its own ends. The secret of rapid opening of the outlet (the cervix) of the uterus is to allow the skeletal muscles to become limp and thus let the uterus work by itself. The more relaxed and unresisting both the abdominal muscles and the muscles of the pelvic floor below the uterus are, so much more easily can each uterine contraction pull the cervix over the baby's head and press the head gently down into the birth canal. If the woman's muscles outside the uterus are tensed and rigid—as they will be if, for example, she grabs something tightly with her hands, resisting the contraction—this will tighten the circular muscles of the cervix. This creates in the uterus the need to work harder to push the baby out, and causes pain.

Relaxation must be recognized as a necessary phenomenon of natural labor, and it should be accompanied by resting the mind from any active interest in the uterine function. How often have I said, "You can do nothing to help yet—allow your uterus to get on with its work undisturbed by your inquisitive interest. If you interfere it will resent it, and hurt you." Almost invariably that advice, when acted upon, results in the relief of pain and discomfort caused unwittingly by efforts to assist.

But even if efficient relaxation is practiced, there is always the possibility of a few relatively painful contractions at the end of the first stage—the final dilation of the cervical canal. On many occasions I have formed the opinion that the only true pains of normal labor, if present at all, are the last few contractions that completely dilate the cervix. When this discomfort is recognized and its significance appreciated, a woman may confidently be asked to put up with about six or eight such contractions. The reaction to such a request is almost invariably an easy compliance. "If it is only six or eight, I don't mind, but I thought it might be going on and getting worse all the time now." And so it proves true; this short phase passes into the more definite but completely different second stage. The discomfort of the end of the first stage lifts, either gradually or suddenly, depending upon the mode of onset of the bearing-down reflex.

I have in mind a nurse who attended cases with me until she herself was seven months pregnant. About two weeks after her baby boy was born, I had an opportunity to ask her in detail what she thought about the whole process. We discussed at length everything that had happened during her pregnancy and labor. She had closely followed my teaching, which she had seen practiced in the maternity home, and her final judgment was that she could not understand why some women made such a fuss about having a baby. At one point only—and then for a very few contractions—was she in discomfort, but other than that the whole thing, as she put it, was an exciting and marvelous experience.

As the second stage becomes fully established, acquired social habits and manners are thrown off. The woman becomes aware of the conscious effort demanded of her to help, so far as possible, in the expulsion of her child. She is engrossed in her task, concentrating upon the all-important occupation of the moment. When the muscular effort ceases, her mind and body relax and she passes into a restful, sleepy state, sometimes into a deep, snoring slumber. This condition of complete release from any thoughts or associations either causes or passes into a state of inattentiveness and partial anesthesia; the perception is dulled and the interpretation of stimuli through the normal channels is clouded. She rests peacefully, arousing only to work with each contraction.

I cannot lay too much stress upon the necessity for recognizing this inattentiveness and the changes in perception, interpretation, and reaction that accompany it. If conscious control is relaxed, the mind remains undisturbed and confident. A quiet peace stays, a fact best demonstrated by the relative absence of discomfort when a woman retains both confidence and courage. "Hard work, yes—the hardest work I have ever known," was the comment of a fearless woman. The physical reactions to the emotional state in the second stage must be more clearly understood if interference is to be avoided in normal labor.

Take, for another example, the grunting moans during a second-stage contraction. In a natural, uncomplicated labor they vary, not only according to the strength of the woman's muscular activity, but according to her emotional state, and they have no association with physical pain. The large majority of undrugged and fully informed women have very little if any discomfort with second-stage contractions, but a deal of hard work. Their grunts and moans are like those of a man who pulls successfully upon a rope, his physical strain at the utmost. His determination adds to the violence of his effort; when he relaxes, it is with a groan of satisfaction and relief that he may rest in preparation for the next pull, and having rested he is ready for a renewal of his exertion. So he struggles in the sure confidence of victory until at last his objective is attained, and according to his valuation of the prize, so is the joy with which he hails success. His contortions have not been accompanied by physical agony, though his facial expression may well have represented it. His groans have been physiological, for our bodies abhor a sudden change of tension and most of all a sudden drop of intra-abdominal pressure. The diaphragm must be gradually released and the muscles of the chest slowly relaxed from the strain of their rigidity. There is nothing to cause purely physical pain, but the partial closure of the larynx, which produces the grunt, groan, or long-drawn-out moan, is a part of the design for safety after effort.

There is yet one more observation upon the natural anesthesia and analgesia of the second stage. The stretching of the *vulva* (external genitals) just before the baby is born is felt as a burning sensation. But this is temporary, and the actual passage of the baby through the vulva is often accomplished with so little sensation that the woman is with difficulty persuaded her baby has arrived; until she sees or hears it she is unwilling to believe it is born. In a natural labor the *perineum,* the area between the vulva and the anus, is practically insensitive.

It is my custom to lift up the crying child, even before the cord is cut, so that the mother may see "with her own eyes" the reality of her dreams. I have been told that no woman should see her baby until it has been bathed and dressed; my patients, however, are the first to grasp the small fingers and touch gingerly the soft skin of the infant's cheek. They are the first to marvel at the miracle of their own performance; to them indeed is due the inspiring reward of full and conscious realization. That there is anything unsightly in the appearance of a newborn babe is nonsense; that a mother might be shocked at her own baby is fantastic. Its first cry remains an indelible memory on the mind of a mother; this is the song that carried her upon its wings to an ecstasy mere man seems quite unable to comprehend. But like all other natural emotional states, it is part of a great design; its magnitude is significant of its important purpose. No mother and no child should be denied that great mystical association. It is not only advantageous for the immediate present, to perfect the restoration of the muscles and tissues involved in the birth to their nonpregnant state, as we shall see in a moment, but it lays a foundation of unity of both body and spirit upon which the whole edifice of mother love will stand.

Many times I have called attention to the wonderful picture of happiness that we see at a natural birth. Women of all ages and types have testified to this "greatest happiness in their lives." It is a mo-

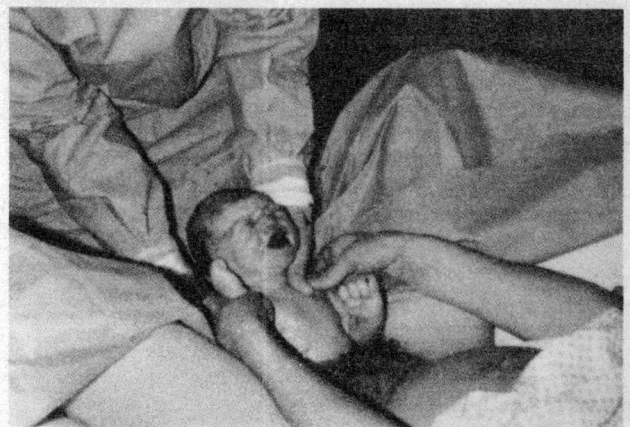

Baby emerges toward mother

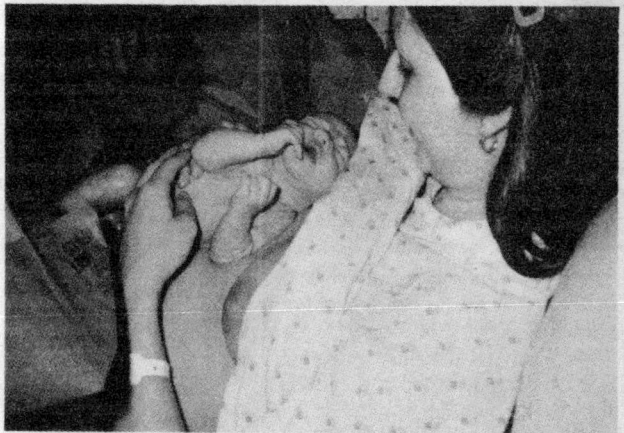

Immediate newborn maternal closeness

ment when, in the full consciousness of their achievement, they experience the most intense emotional joy. "I have never felt anything so marvelous—it cannot be compared to ordinary pleasure." If this is intended, and is one of the series of physical and emotional states in the natural law of parturition, what reason can we assign to it? Why should the serious hard work of the second stage, with its dulled senses, lowered receptivity to certain stimuli, and sleepy relaxation between the contractions, suddenly disappear? It is not just an accident that the brilliant sunlight of motherhood breaks through and dispels for all time the clouds of her labor. No change in human emotions is more dramatic. The quick temper that flashes from calm to rage, with all its disturbing variations of sound and appearance, is dull and crude when compared with this amazing transformation. I have sometimes been constrained to desert my established custom of observing with impersonal interest the phenomena of childbirth. Such an aura of beauty has filled the whole atmosphere of the room, and such superhuman loveliness has swept over the features of the woman whose baby is crying in her hands, that I wonder if I am right in my stolid abstinence from spiritual participation. "Strange talk," my reader may remark, "from a one hundred and ninety pound athlete!" But with all sincerity I repeat that I myself have experienced a sense of happiness much more akin to reverence and awe than to the simple satisfaction of just another natural birth.

This phenomenon is so definite and so inevitable, if preceded by the uncomplicated events of a relaxed and relatively painless labor, that it is not unreasonable to ascribe to it some result. All emotional states have a definite purpose, and the more closely we examine the physiological changes consequent upon emotional activity, the more apparent does the functional advantage of such states become. The overwhelming delight activates the sympathetic nervous system, and all the forces of that great protective mechanism are brought into play. The inhibitory fibers no longer lie relaxed and passive in the birth canal; the circular bands bind firmly the muscles of expulsion, and the uterus, as if in answer to the cry of the newborn child, becomes hard and remains contracted. Let every obstetrician feel once the brisk contraction of the uterus when the mother hears her child; it is the natural stimulus to close the great blood sinuses, rendering the placental site anemic and so hastening the separation of the useless afterbirth. "No bleeding at all" is frequently recorded, except the ounce or two of placental blood that comes away at the end of the third stage. Thus the physical reaction to this natural emotional state protects the mother from delayed expulsion of the afterbirth, excessive loss of blood, and postpartum shock.

But this is not all. When exhilaration and intense joy are experienced, physical changes occur that are readily diagnosable at sight and strangely infectious. The ecstasy of love that floods the whole personality when the earliest call of a new life awakens a woman to the realization of motherhood is a transport akin to mysticism. It is the spiritual perfection of physical achievement. Many women have written to me of this highest plane of human happiness: "Something of which no woman should be deprived," "A moment no words can describe," and so on. What does it mean? I do not know what inference should be drawn from such spontaneous and superlative expressions. The thoughts and words of women who watch their babies being born are so constant that in spite of the different terms in which they are couched they must be included in the purposeful phenomena of labor. Excitement, emotionalism, or sentimentality may be offered as an explanation, but it does not account for the uniformity of these manifestations in that most variable and unpredictable field, the mind of woman. Young mothers with no pretensions to piety have unhesitatingly told me that at the birth of their child they felt nearness to God, or the presence of a superhuman being—"a heavenly feeling that they have never known before"—and that it was difficult for them to believe in the reality of the present. They spoke with awe and respect for the unpremeditated wonder of their experience.

And so, when a child is born unhampered by the limitations we moderns put upon the natural laws, I am humbled before the miracle of birth and all the host of wonders that awaken its mechanism. It lives, we do not know why; indeed, we do not know the source of life itself. But here, from the indestructible forces of the universe, arrives a new human form. It is unlike any other we have ever seen, different in a thousand ways from its most similar brother. It has, however, the great common denominator of all humanity, life, that inestimable gift which from the first moment is our responsibility—life, which arrives, is marred or magnified, and passes on. Is it surprising that, at a moment of such stupendous significance, the woman who has been chosen to be the perfected instrument in the natural law of survival should be rewarded by a sense of exaltation? A new life, which of its very potential power is greater than death, should logically be heralded with pride and joy. In every newborn child there is new hope—to every mother the people should give thanks.

## CHAPTER 9

# The Influence of Memory

Is it unreasonable that we should pause to consider the mental picture of labor within the mind of a woman? Is it not essential that we should create by education and instruction the true and natural happiness of motherhood within the vision of her mind? The mental picture of her anticipated experience should be the image of all that is beautiful in the fulfillment of her love. For the body is only a vehicle in which and from which a child is miraculously made and produced. It is the *mind* of woman that knows passion and desires the fulfillment of her biological purpose. It is the mind—its receptivity and its ability to integrate the fund of new thoughts and feeling that are the physiological visitations of love and pregnancy—that molds and fashions the child. It is the mind that bears the spiritual imprint of the newborn child and around it writes indelibly the mysterious circumscription of love.

Francis Galton wrote much on the importance of the mind that has been overlooked in the modern teaching of medicine.[1] His investigations emphasize the vividness with which images, based upon thought and association, can be reproduced in the mind. Sights, sounds, and associations, real and imaginary, imprint themselves upon the human mind to mold and influence its reactions.

As Pavlov points out in his important work on conditioned reflexes, the things that give the greatest pleasure will become conditioned causes of acute fear and hatred if continually offered with a terrifying accompaniment.[2] Both objective and subjective associations can condition stimuli that provoke fear reactions to labor. I know single women who, their natural longing for a child obliterated from their minds, shudder when childbirth is mentioned. Associations of pain and mental pictures of agony and death have become conditioned stimuli for such fear and abhorrence that these women seek permanent refuge in virginity and spinsterhood. There are some women who have had one baby who have been known to refuse all marital relations forever after for fear they should have to experience labor again. Even love for the child cannot override the fear and pain that its arrival occasioned. What devastation to homes, husbands, and children one ill-conducted labor can bring!

Owing to the nature of Pavlov's experiments, the concept of the conditioned reflex is often associated only with salivating dogs, meat, and bells. But earlier writings, such as Galton's in 1883, made it apparent that the recurrent stimulus frequently arises *within* the mind. The memory, or even the visualization, of an incident may surround a natural and physiological function with an aura of pain or pleasure so vivid that normal reflexes are disturbed. Just as a colored light will produce defense reactions of pain in a dog who was hurt when the light appeared, so will the words "baby," "childbirth," "labor," or even "motherhood" produce emotional states and their physical manifestations in women who suffered in parturition, and every act that leads, in a normal sequence of events, to the association of painful childbirth will give impetus to the primitive instinct to escape.

Fear of childbirth, then, becomes the great disturber of the neuromuscular harmony of labor. I do not wish it to be inferred that childbirth should be looked upon as a mental process. But obviously the mechanical efficiency of this function not only depends upon the structures and forces of the body but upon emotional stimuli, and upon the integrity of the influences to which the emotions are subjected.

## NEGATIVE INFLUENCES

Many young women from the age of puberty and even before have inquiring minds, particularly in relation to childbirth. Few hear much that is encouraging from those of their own age, but since the temptation to seek information is not curbed, again and again, drawn as if by sirens, they satiate their greed for knowledge by listening to voices that capture the imagination but utterly distort or destroy the truth.

The facts of childbirth may be withheld by the mother, the logical source, for the mother may have had such unpleasant experiences herself that she has no wish to communicate them to the daughter, who she believes will also suffer in childbirth. If, in a moment of confidence, she gives any information to her daughter, it is more likely to be fear producing than a stimulus to pleasant anticipation. Thus the influence of too many mothers upon their daughters, either through the subtlety of their information or through the mystery of their silence, is a serious factor in producing a feeling of fear in regard to childbirth.

We must remember, also, the influence of the friends of a woman about to have a baby. Wherever women are gathered together and the subject of childbirth arises, someone may remark that childbirth is a kind of martyrdom, the suffering during which, though probably best forgotten, is satisfactorily recalled with obvious pride. Here it must not be overlooked that those who have suffered are justified in believing in suffering. There is no blame to be laid upon those who are honest in their opinions; neither was it their fault if they suffered. This does not, however, mitigate in any way the crime of their propaganda, for to produce alarm can never assist in the accomplishment of a task, however unimportant.

The influence of husbands is another potential source of anxiety concerning childbirth, if the husband has formed his opinions upon hearsay. His ignorance leads to an understandable anxiety over the welfare of his wife. Unfortunately, he communicates his anxiety to her.

Apart from the more intimate sources of information about childbirth, women cannot escape the influence of the general trend of public and popular opinion. Constantly in contact with the modern foundations of both education and amusement, they read books, study papers, listen to radio and television broadcasts, and see motion pictures. In far too many of these the same atmosphere is found: childbirth is an ordeal, essentially painful and dangerous to the life of the mother.

If the dramatist finds it necessary to increase the interest of the story by describing the events that occurred when one of the chief characters gave birth to a child, the incident is often fraught with poignancy and tension, drama, suffering, and possibly death. As a student of human nature, the dramatist well knows that nothing is more likely to gain the attention of the reader. Do we often read of a normal character experiencing any happiness in childbirth, or see such a presentation on the screen? Similarly, the tense anxiety of the husband gives the author or producer a wonderful opportunity for drama. Fortunately, this is sometimes so exaggerated as to become laughable.

The daily papers are also printed in order to attract readers. The story of a straightforward birth is not news, unless it occurs in a taxicab or a telephone booth, but the story of a mother's death when a child is born is almost worthy of headlines.

## CULTURE VS. NATURAL LAW

I have chosen the term "indigenous" below in reference to woman in her original condition, as opposed to "cultured" or "civilized." It is obvious that such a term requires explanation. I am using it to convey the idea of first or original, primary; that is, women whose tribal lives and traditional limitations of experience have not been affected by medieval and/or twentieth-century culture, compared to the "cultured" woman of today. There is very little evidence that modern woman is in any way less fitted to produce children painlessly than the woman without the influence of Western culture and civilization.

Woman, indigenous or cultured, has before her no evidence suggesting that nature ever intended pregnancy to be an illness. The indigenous woman continues her work—in the harvest field, on trek, in the rubber plantation, or wherever she may be employed. The child develops while she herself lives a full and natural existence. Muscularly strong, physiologically efficient, her mechanism carries out its normal functions without discomfort, difficulty, or shame. The child then is born easily, small and firm fleshed. Among cultured women we see this too—the athletic young woman who continues her active life, who plays golf to the seventh month, who walks three or four miles a day to the full term of her pregnancy, who eats sensible food in a sensible way, who is not diverted from her normal routine by those who try to advertise special care, rest, diets, and enormous quantities of milk.

Such exaggerated concern is an offense against nature; it is a presumption that natural methods require unnatural fortification, and to those of us who believe in nature it is little short of inducing a pathological state into a very perfect physiological function.

Whichever of the many definitions of culture is adopted, one thing is certain, that culture is dependent primarily upon the activity of the mind. The greater the education, the more "cultured" the type. But, unquestionably, we have very largely lost many of the higher sensibilities that in the original state were essential to our personal survival. One has only to spend a few weeks with those who depend upon their wits for the supply of their food from natural surroundings to appreciate how soon we should die out if once again we were bereft of cultural attributes and were called upon to return to the original state!

From this the question naturally follows: To what extent can the influences of culture have affected those functions that remain with us as natural physical functions, childbirth in particular? The mind has developed, and the enormous fund of stimulus that passes from the consciousness to the autonomic nervous system has to meet new conditions. The lives of the cultured have gradually changed as Western civilization has developed. With repression, emotions of varying intensity have found new means of expression. The physician of today looks to the emotions and sentiments of his patients when endeavoring to find the original cause for many of their physical complaints, practicing "psychosomatic medicine."

Herein lies the fact of pain in childbirth. Modern woman is physically competent; modern childbirth is physically unaltered from earlier times, but our culture has brought to bear upon this function neuromuscular activities caused by intensifying certain emotions that inhibit the progress of the birth and thus create pain.

Yet there is no reason why culture should be allowed to destroy all that is beautiful in the primitive. True culture should enhance original beauty and purify where contamination has crept in. If childbirth among indigenous people unaffected by Western culture still persists today as a relatively painless procedure, it is indeed a slur upon our utilization of culture that the most dramatic, the most beautiful, and the most essential of natural functions should be made unpleasant for so many.

A woman may be conscious of uterine contractions for hours, but have no discomfort until she is told she is in labor. This verbal stimulus to her mental expectation alerts her attention and anxiety. Although she may appear to be quite calm, a woman in labor has an inborn alertness to danger, and evidence of anxiety, however courageously suppressed, will forewarn her attendants of the special care she may need. In anxiety, the heart beats strongly and often rapidly, breathing is quicker and sometimes irregular, and is interspersed with a series of deep, sighing respirations. The nostrils may be widely dilated to facilitate the intake of air, and not infrequently the mouth is slightly open for the same reason.

If women are to be taught to anticipate childbirth with relaxed confidence, it is necessary to eliminate the tension that gives rise to pain by removing the causes for fear. Those who seek to follow as closely as possible the natural law of childbirth should do everything possible to allay a young woman's anxieties and give her confidence by simple and truthful reiteration of the facts of natural childbirth.

## HISTORICAL AND RELIGIOUS INFLUENCES

If we survey the history of childbirth in European civilization, we discover that suffering is often presumed, the minds of both men and women being conditioned to the idea of suffering as essential to childbirth. Since it is expected, it is thus caused and aggravated. For generations the necessity of pain has been accepted as a fact, even though the motivation for earlier stories and dramas may have been to concentrate on the negative in order to attract an audience, just as in our day.

### ANCIENT PRACTICES AND PAGAN RELIGIONS

At the time of Hippocrates, four or five hundred years before Christ, we read of a different outlook. Even prior to his day, three thousand years before Christ, the priests among the Egyptians were called to assist women in labor. In many societies witchcraft was resorted to, often very successfully due to the power of suggestion, and old writings suggest that herbs and potions were used to help a woman give birth easily. In fact, it may be said with some accuracy that among the most primitive people of whom any record exists, help was given to women in labor according to the customs of the time.

Hippocrates lived from 460 to 355 B.C. His aphorisms should be read by every medical man. It was he who realized that "our natures are the physicians of our diseases"; it was he who recognized in the routine care of human ailments that prevention was more important than cure. He emphasized that the daily discipline of a healthy person was to include diet, exercise, and fresh air. All the simple things of life to correct an illness were to be used before medicines, and last of all came surgery. It may seem strange to some of us that these things were written so long ago!

Today in the United States, England, and many other countries, everyone who qualifies to be a doctor has to take the Hippocratic Oath, an oath of allegiance to our science. This oath is a magnificent concept, to which one who is accorded the privilege of attending patients should adhere, for it stands as fresh and noble as ever. It says in part:

> I will prescribe regimen for the good of my patients according to my ability and my judgment and never do harm to anyone. To please no one will I prescribe a deadly drug, nor give advice which may cause his death. . . . If I keep this oath faithfully, may I enjoy my life and practice my art, respected by all men and in all times; but if I swerve from it or violate it, may the reverse be my lot.

Unfortunately, even today in my professional career, I have often seen only lip service paid to this oath and its tenets ignored. Yet it is upon the Hippocratic teaching that all modern medicine is based. If the principles of Hippocrates were reenacted today in all their simplicity and wisdom, they would undoubtedly alter the whole tone and tenor of our lives. Hippocrates made stern demands upon his pupils, but he always practiced what he preached.

There is no authority but *fact,* Hippocrates taught, and deductions are to be made only from facts. Since observation, common sense, and clear reasoning are not compatible with the speculative practice of medicine, a physician should be persuaded by no influence that cannot be justified by accurate observation. True science begets knowledge, but opinion, ignorance.

Hippocrates' teaching was largely based upon the laws of nature as they were understood in his time, that is, exploring the secrets of life, its origin, its maintenance, and its reproduction. He endeavored to organize and instruct midwives. He found no place for fear in childbirth except in the presence of abnormality, which may or may not have been caused by a faulty regimen in the life of the individual. Such confidence was placed in the ability of the natural law to carry out the work of reproduction that one statement was frequently impressed upon the students and doctors of that time: "We must refrain from meddlesome interference!" A statement particularly applicable to the care of women in childbirth. Indeed, it is important for us to realize that there is nothing *new* in the concept of natural childbirth. It is but a revitalizing and uncovering of that which conforms to the laws of nature.

Aristotle (384–322 B.C.) went further, and in some of his writings we find accurate and very desirable observations upon childbirth. He was probably the first man who ever urged *care of the mind* for a woman having a baby. A great naturalist, he was the first investigator of the development of the chick within the egg.

Followed by Aristotle and other great scientists, the Hippocratic and Grecian school of medicine held sway until after Soranus of Ephesus, who, living at the end of the first and the beginning of the second century after Christ, continued the emphasis upon the high level and humane principles of Grecian obstetrics. Writing a famous treatise on obstetrics in about A.D. 79, Soranus was quite possibly the greatest of all the ancient obstetric clinicians, and must be regarded as their leading authority upon childbirth and pediatrics. He denied the truth of certain superstitions about childbirth, and he stressed consideration of the *feelings of the woman* herself. He makes no mention of fear, and did not expect it to occur unless some abnormality disrupted the healthy function. His writings, as true today as nineteen hundred years ago, were collected by monks and, buried in the cellars of great monasteries, were soon forgotten, not to be rediscovered for many centuries.

Pain in childbirth has been recognized as far back as we can go in the history of man, but only in the presence of something contrary to the natural or physiological law, which then gives rise to fear. Fear is an emotion that, emerging from the primitive instinct of survival, is the natural protective agent prompting the individual to escape from danger.

There seems to be little doubt but that the unnatural, pathological, and destructive condition of fear in childbirth is found more intensely and frequently in the European civilization than in any other. Those of us who have traveled among groups who have not yet come into contact with European civilization have found that the presence of fear of childbirth affects only a small percentage of the population, confirming what we have read in the ancient writings, and those who do suffer from fear almost invariably have a reasonable cause.

The general tendency is to pass quickly from the discussion of fear to that of pain. But the origins of fear are important, because the association between fear and pain is very close. Thus it is necessary to draw attention to the influences of superstitions and religious customs, and all those things which pertain to ethical conduct and beliefs among various peoples. Fear produced by religious beliefs becomes an offense to the mental or physical integrity of childbirth. Unnecessary fear is a pathological condition.

Pagan religions demand an absolute belief in an outside controlling influence over the events of one's life. That control is exercised, directly or indirectly, by one's ancestors. All goes well with the individual, so long as he obeys the rules and does not offend his or her ancestors. It is the woman who carries, hidden in her mind, the knowledge of her disobedience of this law who becomes depressed and filled with fear during labor. She is anxious not only for her own life but also for the life and fitness of the child. Pain and suffering in childbirth then becomes the corollary to "the wages of sin is death," an idea common to all ethical teachings and religions. Thus if a dead or abnormal child is born, it is considered the reward of sin and disobedience of the law.

We found that some tribes in Africa go to extraordinary lengths to appease the wrath of their forefathers or their gods. When trouble arises in labor, as it surely does in the presence of this sin-born fear, free confession overcomes the trouble of a delayed or prolonged labor. This form of pain relief in difficult labor is well recognized among many tribes. In the Congo we obtained first-hand evidence of the curative influence of confession as a means of palliating the angry ancestors or gods during labor; in the absence of abnormality, the baby was usually born soon after confession. Thus the ethical beliefs of an individual, and the consciousness of sin or disobedience in respect to these beliefs, do influence the course of labor, through the emotions.

#### THE MIDDLE AGES

It was about three hundred years after Christ that a big change in attitudes came about in Western civilization, due to a distortion of earlier Judeo-Christian teachings. It is generally accepted that the institutionalized Christian Church during this period, more than any other influence in the last two thousand years, retarded the progress of medicine and medical science. One of the principles of Christ's teachings is that we should visit the fatherless and the widows in their affliction, and heal the sick. But the priests of this middle period —interpreting any efforts on the part of man to heal the sick as being presumptuous, placing oneself on an equal with, or even preeminent over, the God of Christians—went back to pagan practices, where prayer and fastings were the total remedies. If medicines or potions were used at all, they came from the monasteries through the Church, and it was the special prerogative of the priests to prescribe and distribute them. To study and believe in the laws of nature became an offense against the authority of the Church, and all books on medicine that had been written, including those of Soranus, were seized and buried beneath the monasteries. When the Roman Empire fell, all medicine reverted to the lore of superstitions, legends, salves, poultices, and talismen. The sick were no longer healed; they either lived or died.

With this as background, it is no wonder that the rites of paganism were relatively simple, pleasing, and acceptable when compared to some of the horrors to which women in medieval times were subjected, owing to the ignorance of those who were entitled to look after them in childbirth. During the thousand years up to 1520, the responsibility for childbirth was entirely usurped by the Church. No man was allowed to attend a woman in labor unless he was a shepherd or a man who looked after animals in sickness. Childbirth was considered the result of carnal sin, to be expiated by suffering in giving birth. Should the woman have trouble during labor, the Church, according to its ethics, demanded a live baby, whatever might happen to the woman in question. In fact, if a woman was dying it was not unusual for the baby to be taken from her through the wall of the abdomen, for which purpose men accustomed to castrating animals, usually hog-gelders, were employed.

## THE SIXTEENTH AND SEVENTEENTH CENTURIES

It was not until 1513 that a German, Eucharius Roesslin, discovered the hidden writings of Soranus and others. He wrote the first obstetric book in nearly fifteen hundred years, gleaning his manuscript from the works of those ancient, astute physicians, profound philosophers, and most accurate clinical observers the world has ever known.

The book of Eucharius Roesslin stood as a monument upon the high road of the development of care in childbirth. Nine years after its publication a doctor in Hamburg, thinking that too little was known about childbirth except through books, decided to observe the birth of a baby. Since no man was allowed to attend a woman in childbirth and the law was extremely rigid, he dressed as a midwife and joined the midwives at a birth. His observations were invaluable.

Success in midwifery had begun to be established once more, but then he was deceived by a personal acquaintance and reported to the authorities. For that crime, that heresy, Dr. Weiss of Hamburg was burned at the stake. Only four hundred years ago!

It was not until 1580 that shepherds and herdsmen were prevented by law from attending women in labor, though physicians were still not permitted to assist midwives. Two hundred and fifty years ago physicians took over the work in certain cases, and later surgeons applied their skill, but even then little consideration was shown for the woman's feelings.

In the so-called ages of religious faith, the sixteenth and seventeenth centuries in England, if there was any difficulty in labor it was the custom to baptize the child before it was born so that its soul might be saved, the holy water being introduced onto the unborn child by use of a special instrument. The fact that the mother died still called for no remark.

The most important of all historical writings, and the most likely to be read, is the Bible. It is still the world's best-selling book. Many women read and study their Bibles—and many have been influenced to believe that childbirth is a grievous and painful experience because of passages in the King James Version like Genesis 3:16, which quotes the Lord as having said to Eve: "I will greatly multiply thy sorrow and thy conception; in sorrow thou shalt bring forth children." This passage has been known as the "curse of Eve," with its assumption that misery, pain, and sorrow automatically accompany every birth. Thus many still are of the opinion today that the teaching of natural childbirth is contrary to the Bible.

Nothing could be further from the truth! For those who believe the translators and others who compiled the various editions of the Bible were under divine guidance no argument will be of any avail, but if the Bible had divine inspiration, it is likely that the writers of the original manuscripts were inspired, and not the translators of the various editions in different languages.

Biblical scholars have carefully reexamined the Hebrew and Greek manuscripts from which much of the Bible was translated, and have concluded that the words referring to childbirth do not signify pain, but refer to "labor," or to "a woman in childbirth."[3] Being interested in this subject myself for many years, I have acquired in my library a considerable collection of ancient Bibles, and find that some of the translations differ from those of the great King

James Version, which was started in 1604 and completed in 1611, in the reign of James I.

Take, for example, Isaiah 21:3. I turned this up in my copy of the Geneva Bible, first published in 1560, and find that the words "pain" and "pangs" were not used, but "sorrow" was repeated three times. In my copy of the Bishop's Bible, however, first published in 1568, the words "pain" and "pangs" appear, and since the King James Version was largely a revision of the Bishop's Bible and not the Geneva Bible, the same terms have been repeated by the translators.

This matter was referred to Hebrew scholars, one of whom, the Reverend B. D. Glass, spent much time investigating this subject and wrote to me as follows:

> One thing, however, that puzzled me was why the Bible referred to childbirth as such a painful and dangerous ordeal. That is how I was taught, and later on taught my pupils. After studying your book, *Revelation of Childbirth,* [4] I felt I had to search the Bible more thoroughly to find the deeper meaning concerning expressions about childbirth.
>
> I was very pleased when I read the first sentence of Genesis 3:16, where the Hebrew word *"etzev"* which is usually translated as sorrow and pain, has obviously been misconstrued. The words of pain in Hebrew are *"ke-iv"* (pain) *"tzaar"* (sorrow) *"yesurim"* (anguish).
>
> At no time would any Hebrew scholar use the word *"etzev"* as an expression of pain. The meanings of *"etzev"* are manyfold, i.e., labour (vide Gen. 5:29, referring to Noah: "The same shall comfort us concerning our labour and toil of our hands").
>
> In Proverbs 14:13, *"etzev"* is used as expressing labour, e.g., "that in all labour there is profit."
>
> *"Etzev"* can also mean "concerned" or "anxious" as is mentioned in Genesis 6:6, where the word "grieved" is not used in its proper sense—"displeased," or "concerned" would have been more in keeping.
>
> In chapter 45 para. 5 although *"etzev"* is again translated as "grieved," it is used in a wrong sense, "displeased" would have suited the expression better.
>
> Again in King I 1:6, the correct translation of *"etzev"* is given, namely, "displeased"—"and his father had not displeased him," etc.

"*Etzev*" has yet another meaning—that "of being perturbed," as it is expressed in Samuel I 20:3, "Lest he be perturbed."

I find that throughout the Bible the word "*etzev*" is used approximately sixteen times, and not once does it convey the meaning of pain as we are made to believe. "*Etzev*" can assume different shades of meaning, regarding the sense in which it is used.

I think that is why the translators of the Bible in the olden times, believing in the ordeal of pain and anguish in connection with childbirth, translated the word "*etzev*" to imply such. None of the prophets ever used this word in their expressions regarding childbirth. They used the words "*tzirim*" (hinges) and "*vchavalim*" (threads) which mean hinges and threads, or nerves. Not being a medical man it is hard for me to explain these terms. I can, however, explain "*vchavalim,*" which means the contractions or stretching of the muscles and fibres.

In all your quotations from the Bible, the above two words were expressed and they do not really signify pain. It is only because "*yeloda,*" which means "a woman in childbirth" is always used in conjunction with these same two words in question that the translators added on their own behalf these words as meaning "pain and travail."

If we put ourselves in the place of those brilliant classical scholars of the time of James I, from A.D. 1604 to 1611, the years occupied by them in completing this translation, we can see why their negative thoughts on childbirth were expressed in their translations. They used the word "pain" because they had no reason to believe any other term was applicable. During this era, obstetrics was at a low ebb. Anesthetics and antiseptics were not discovered until two hundred fifty years later. The first English book on midwifery had been published only fifty years earlier, and although several manuscripts appeared, mainly for private circulation, they demonstrated little advance upon the works of Soranus, who flourished in second century A.D. Women died in large numbers in maternity hospitals, and the appalling conditions of the Hôtel de Dieu in Paris due to epidemics of childbed fever were found to some extent in English institutions as well. Surely it was reasonable that the translators used the word "pain" in keeping with the accepted belief and experience of their time. It was not until the nineteenth century that the foundations of our present knowledge of antiseptics were laid, and there were no antibiotics for infections until the mid-twentieth century. We tend to overlook the fact that until 1847 anesthetics or pain-relievers were not even known, so that when a labor was abnormal the suffering was appalling.

An investigation by Herr Ernst Burkhardt, who translated *Childbirth Without Fear* into German, states that the German word *"Wehen"* (pain) was not found in German writings before the Middle Ages:

> I enclose an article of mine, published recently by *Die Neue Zeitung.* Professor Joseph De Lee (in the preface of his *Principles and Practice of Obstetrics,* 1947 edition) says that since unthinkable times all races understood contractions in labour as a painful experience and accordingly spoke either of pains, dolores, dolori, douleurs or (in German) *Wehen.* There is no evidence for this assertion. On the contrary, it seems to be sure that these termini developed only with civilization. Our German word *"Wehen"* cannot be traced beyond the Middle Ages. Our frequently used pain-suggesting word, *"Wehmutter"* ["midwife," literally, "mother of woe"], I found, had a definite artificial origin. Dr. Martin Luther invented it when translating the Bible. It does not exist before the year 1540.

Dr. Rudolf Hellman of Hamburg, in his paper "Schmerz oder Erlebnis der Entbindung" (January 1959), gives additional consideration from the German Bible translations:

> Dick-Read maintains that the underlying Hebrew word *"Etzev"* should not be translated as "pain" but as "toil, trouble, distress and labour." It is all a question of a predominant psychic understanding. H. Adler and other investigators I have questioned have moreover come to the conclusion that there is here no command of the Lord. Several years ago Dick-Read showed that a confinement, as a natural event, need not be, and should not be, associated with violent pains. He is convinced that it could not have been the will and intention of the Creator.
>
> In the Bible we also find references to easy deliveries, just as today they are happening in "natural births." In the Second Book of Moses (Exodus) 1:15, the King of Egypt commanded the Hebrew midwives Siphra and Pua to kill the sons immediately on the stools (here no doubt the reference is to the birth-stools which were in use in Luther's time). The midwives referred, however, to the easy deliveries of the Hebrew women with the words: "They have been born before the arrival of the midwife." This expression is recognized as sound. Luther, who liked to associate the birth with

pain, probably invented the painful-sounding "Mother of Woe," a translation which was only discarded after 1540.

Graf Wittgenstein, in his book *Man Before Delivery*, translated after Gunkel: "Much will I prepare your toils and groans; in labor wilt thou bear children . . ." Archaic, inaccurate explanations and translations were learned, in good faith, by clerics and teachers, and by children and grown-ups true to the words of books and letters.

Wittgenstein also mentions in this excellent contribution that the Greeks called pain the "barking watchdog of health," and that pain occupies an important place in the extensive system of warning and protection of the organs: ". . . it seems to us rather senseless that it should be the alarm signal of delivery as at the same time it hinders the mother in her activities."

It is forgivable that the translators of nearly four hundred years ago should interpret as they did, but I find it difficult to understand how these obviously controversial translations can continue to be accepted by many modern scholars of the classics, who copy and even intensify the mistakes, although they have many more manuscripts and advantages from which to deduce the significance of the words.

But that is not all, for a woman's fears are supported by the Prayer Book, in which there had been no substantial alteration, until recently, since A.D. 1662. There was a special service known as "The Churching of Women" which was supposed to be a thanksgiving after childbirth, which ends: "Oh, Almighty God, we give Thee humble thanks for that Thou hast vouchsafed to deliver this woman, Thy servant, from the great pain and peril of childbirth."

Could we still expect women to believe childbirth was to be painless, that it could be a moment of transcendental joy? When I was discussing this service with a girl of twenty-three, she said: "But you would not expect the most wonderful gift of God to come unpleasantly." Is the pride of possession and accomplishment that fills the heart of every young mother when she first sees her baby unworthy to be recalled? Is a lame apology for gratitude adequate thanks to the Almighty for the gift of a child? Yet the Church has asked her to say: "Thank you very much for having allowed ME to come through all that frightfulness unscathed; it is so nice to be alive in spite of having performed the greatest of all natural functions for which You especially built me, although You did make it dangerous and painful for me."

What a travesty of the truth! It is not for the escape from pain and danger that women thank God. In my experience mothers are not made like that. They give thanks for their child.

The Church must once again teach the beauty of childbirth and encourage confidence in normal, natural function, which is in harmony with the basic teachings of the Bible. We must not forget the significance of Christmas or the manger in the stable of a wayside inn. Millions of Catholics honor the Madonna and Child, and Protestants also recognize the spiritual implications of childbirth.

In the meantime, let us assume as historical necessity the teachings of the past that emphasized the negative aspects of childbearing, keeping in mind that there can be no more horrible stigma upon civilization than the history of childbirth.

## THE LAST HUNDRED YEARS

In 1847 a brighter picture began to emerge for women in childbirth, with James Young Simpson's discovery of chloroform, creating the beginning of the era of pain relief. Simpson was harshly criticized by the Church for giving women anesthesia in abnormal labor. A dignitary of the Church wrote in condemnation of his work: "Chloroform is the decoy of Satan, apparently offering itself to bless women but in the end it will harden society and rob God of the deep cries which arise in time of trouble."

That in my father's time! But anesthesia had come to stay—and to such an extent that it was used in all labors, abnormal or not. Why *always* anesthesia, when in the natural state it is unnecessary? It has always been easier to utilize the pain-relieving discoveries of science than to investigate the complicated causes of pain. Since 1850 a hundred ways and means have been discovered to rid our women of the pain that has invariably attacked them, even when they most deserved the natural joy of their supreme accomplishment. Nevertheless, anesthesia has been of the greatest service to women, and an important step forward in the development of humane care during childbirth.

In 1854 Florence Nightingale became the first person to make it widely known that cleanliness and fresh air were fundamental necessities of nursing. It was largely because of her work during the Crimean War that the standards of both the training and practice of nursing were raised. The gin-drinking, reprobate doctors who were found in great numbers at births both in hospitals and at home began to disappear. With their exodus, childbed fever occurred less frequently in maternity cases, but even so, women were still dying in hospitals at the rate of 12 to 15 percent of all normal labors. This means that one in every eight perfectly healthy women admitted died through childbed fever!

About this same time, Ignaz Philip Semmelweis, a nervous young man who was a physician at the Maternity Hospital in Vienna, came to the conclusion that the cause might be due to something arising within the hospital. He therefore made his students wash their hands in a solution of chloride of lime before attending women in childbirth. In one year, 1858, the death rate in his wards tumbled to 3 percent and soon afterward to 1 percent. This was the first great step toward preventing the attendant from taking death to the patient; for Semmelweis had discovered what the ancients had always preached, that to interfere with the law of nature was to invite the hand of death. For his success in saving lives Semmelweis was asked, for some made-up reason, to leave the staff of the hospital. He was told he had no right to require this washing, and was sent away. He returned to his home and died, a broken man.

Until 1866 there was no knowledge of asepsis. Hospitals were originally organized by priests whose humane intention was to move people from the hovels in which they lived to be cared for by doctors in hospitals. In the homes a certain number died; those who went to the hospital for safety and good treatment died in much greater numbers. It is difficult to visualize the state of affairs that prevailed when limbs were amputated, abdomens opened, and cesarean sections performed without any anesthesia and with an almost sure supervention of sepsis, giving rise to a high percentage of mortality in the simplest operations.

Probably all of us, if we are wise, pause to think sometimes how much harm we do in our efforts to do good, and how much trouble we cause when conscientiously endeavoring to prevent it!

In 1866, long after my parents were born, Joseph Lister first practiced aseptic surgery, and he continued to use antiseptics in spite of the opposition and ridicule of his colleagues. Then Pasteur discovered fermentation and inoculation and Koch discovered bacteria, the two men becoming co-founders of the science of bacteriology. This is all recent change and innovation!

The care of women in childbirth benefited by the advance of these other branches of medical science, but in obstetrics itself little happened. At the beginning of the twentieth century the death rate from childbirth was lower, and severe pain was relieved, but still childbirth was an ordeal for a woman to face. Much pain still remained, pain that was unexplained and could only be obliterated by unconsciousness, which carried its own dangers. Was unconsciousness safe for mother and baby? It is incredible how pain was and still is accepted by many doctors and scholars as an inevitable accompaniment of childbirth.

I cannot understand anyone who says women in childbirth should not be afraid, for who among us would not have some qualms about entering into an experience that we desired above all else, but that we believed must occasion severe pain, danger, possible mutilation, and even death to either ourself or our child? We know of only a few who have no fears: there are a number of women who faithfully believe in the rightness of their God and the sanctity of their bodies, and in my opinion there are also women who have an inborn belief in the laws of nature, not by formulating them to themselves, but because they are natural in their outlook and experience.

The extent and magnificence of the medical discoveries made during the last hundred and fifty years is beyond both praise and gratitude. Gradually truth has been discovered, and the safety of women in childbirth has been made an object of investigation, with results that would have been unbelievable when the mothers and grandmothers of many of us were born. But now that many of the troubles and dangers have been overcome, we must move on—not only to save more lives, but actually to bring happiness to replace the agony of fear. For although the consciousness or sensations of a woman's discomfort can now be dispelled, it is only at a price, for with it goes the awareness of birth and the joyful sensations and emotions that should accompany it. Now we must bring a fuller life, truer to natural law, to the women who are called upon to reproduce our species.

It is not only that we want to bring about an easy labor, without risk of injury to the mother or the child; we must go further. We must understand that childbirth is fundamentally a spiritual as well as a physical achievement and throughout this book it must be understood that the birth of a child is the ultimate perfection of human love, the culmination of the love between a man and a woman. In the Christian ethic we teach that God is love. The blessing of sexual necessity and pleasure is but an essential part of the love God has given to man and woman. It may be that in time scientists will be able to give such complete proof of the rightness of materialism that religion will become a weapon in the hands of the psychiatrists and the Church will be replaced by the clinic. But my close association with the birth of a child has led me to believe there is a limitation to science and that the extending boundaries of human knowledge have only reached the foothills of the towering mountains of Omniscience. This philosophy of childbirth is written, therefore, in terms of a belief in God.

For my own part, I stand in awe and utter humility before a woman with her newborn babe. There is so much to see and learn in their presence, so much that I am unable to understand or to explain, so much that makes me aware of the limitations of my own ability. It may be that among my colleagues there are those who feel the same. Obstetrics must be approached as a science demanding the most profound respect.

One woman who had feared, because of all the accepted causes, the arrival of her child, gained confidence and understanding before her baby was due; she had a natural and happy birth. Toward the end of the labor that produced her second, and much larger, child, she worked with tireless energy. "How many more?" she asked me excitedly, as she rested between the contractions.

"It will soon be here," I replied. "Why do you ask so anxiously? I hope you are not too weary."

"No, no, not that—but this brings back to me so clearly John's arrival. I can hear his cry and see his fat pink body in my hands. I'm longing for that heavenly feeling again—I simply can't describe it to you. It won't be long now, will it?"

Could we wish to blot out the memory of her first experience? In the natural state the emotional experience of childbirth raises a woman to such delight and thankfulness that her mind turns to spiritual and metaphysical associations to express her gratitude and joy. Materialism and atheism are not included in the makeup of motherhood; neither can a robot lead a blind man across the road.

## CHAPTER 10

# The Neuromuscular Harmony of Labor and Birth[1]

There is a tendency these days, when publication in the press familiarizes the man in the street with the most dramatic exploits in the laboratory, to accept each new discovery as "the last word." So wonderful do the revelations of science appear that the idea of introducing simplicity as a means of unearthing the even greater revelations of nature is not well received. But it is essential to good obstetrics to begin with a clear understanding of the knowledge we have of the structure and mechanics of the uterus and birth canal when it is time to expel the fetus.

## STRUCTURE OF THE UTERUS AND BIRTH CANAL

### THE UTERUS

There are three definite muscular layers. Externally, longitudinal fibers sweep up from the lower uterine segment posteriorly over the *fundus uteri,* and down to the lower uterine segment anteriorly. These fibers have become enormously enlarged with the growth of the fetus, and many new fibers, or muscle cells as they are sometimes called, have made their appearance. They may be increased to fully ten times their length and five times their breadth during pregnancy. The middle layer has fibers interlaced in all directions, among which are the large and relatively dilated uterine blood vessels; the contraction of these fibers obliterates the passageway of the blood vessels. The inner layer is formed by the circular fibers that surround the body of the uterus.

Longitudinally, the uterus may be divided into the upper uterine segment, which comprises the greater part of the organ—its muscle wall is thick and powerful—and the lower uterine segment, which is a thin part of the uterine body, comprising approximately three inches of uterine wall above the internal os. These two merge into each other imperceptibly, but the musculature of the lower uterine segment is weak compared to that of the upper.

It must be recognized that these divisions of the uterus are not defined by any anatomical limits. Uteri vary, and there is no fixed law where the upper and the lower uterine segment shall join.

In the same way it must be fully recognized that although the presence of (1) outer longitudinal, (2) the middle mixed, and (3) the inner circular muscle fibers is described as if they were anatomically separable and structurally apart from each other, this is not really so. The most careful dissectors have found it difficult to demonstrate clearly the muscle layers of the uterus in any given case; but the general structure and the whole organ do show that there is some such division, and although fibers in all directions may be intermixed, there is little question that they each play their part with an individuality essential to the perfection of the process.

### THE CERVIX UTERI

The cervix uteri, like the body of the uterus, develops rapidly during pregnancy, although to a relatively small extent. Increased vascularity alters its hard, almost cartilaginous consistency to a loose and spongy elasticity. Some physiologists have observed a lengthening of the circular muscle fibers in the cervix, but its most definite property during pregnancy is elasticity. It does not have a sufficient supply of longitudinal muscle fibers to give it any power of expulsive contraction, and the internal os begins to dilate at the earliest stage of parturition. Some authorities consider that the internal os disappears and the upper part of the cervix uteri merges into the lower segment some weeks before the termination of pregnancy. The cervix uteri is attached around its whole surface to the vagina, higher posteriorly than anteriorly, so that its protrusion into the vagina makes it appear that the posterior wall is longer than the anterior. This explains the disappearance of the posterior lip before the anterior lip when the cervix is fully dilated. As the longitudinal muscles of the body of the uterus draw up the lower uterine segment, the cervix uteri is not so much stretched by the wedgelike mechanism of the descending structures but absorbed and pulled up by its continuity with the lower uterine segment, until the power of retraction of the uterine muscle fibers has flattened the cervix in continuity with the lower uterine segment and the upper limits of the cervical vaginal attachments. The whole birth canal thus becomes uniformly smooth, without any constricting bands of protruding or thickened tissue, and the fetus will rotate within a well-lubricated and homogeneous surface in its passage down to the vulval orifice.

*The influences that may adversely affect this apparently simple mechanical procedure are largely dependent upon the ease with which the cervix uteri is pulled over the advancing presenting part, and the elasticity with which it merges into the wall of the birth canal.*

## THE VAGINAL CANAL

The vaginal canal also has circular and longitudinal muscle fibers. They are weak and relatively ineffective during labor, and, unless some gross abnormality in either the fetal or maternal structure occasions undue pressure upon its walls, the dilation of the vagina seldom gives rise to any complication. Its mucus lining pours out a copious secretion of lubricant.

## THE VULVA

The vulva, like other parts of the birth canal that have to dilate in order to allow free passage of the fetus, is endued with enormous elasticity. Unless some influence mars the natural process of labor, the vulva and—most important—the skin of the perineum itself will stretch without damage. The muscles of the pelvic floor will normally relax, as will the sphincter muscles of the vagina. The anterior triangle is relaxed and pulled upward by the attachment of its apex to the anterior surface of the cervix uteri. The posterior triangle goes downward, its apex being attached to the perineum. Thus, as every student is quick to appreciate, the descending fetus passes through a pair of swinging doors—one that has opened inward and upward, and the other downward and outward.

When the integrity of this mechanism is maintained and the forces applied without aggravating stimuli, such operations as episiotomy or artificial stretching of the vulval orifice should never be necessary. In the absence of unnatural resistance to the normal forces of parturition, there should be no laceration or injury to any muscle of the pelvic floor or at the outlet. And unless subjected to sudden force or quick distension from below before the tissues are physiologically prepared, the perineum should rarely suffer injury.

These remarks upon the structure of the uterus and the birth canal must be very clearly in the mind in order to appreciate how easily complications of labor may arise from direct or reflex activities consequent upon abnormal influences invading a normal labor. Injury arises in the majority of cases from the imposition of resistance, either from the birth canal itself, opposing forces from the uterus above, or within a normal birth canal that is called upon to accommodate itself to applied forces from below.

## AUTOMATIC CONTRACTION OF THE UTERUS

Having briefly outlined the anatomy of the uterus, and illustrated how its structure relates to its peculiar function, we must endeavor to make clear the peculiarities of the nervous mechanism of the uterus during parturition.

In an experiment in 1902, when the uterus of a rabbit was separated from all its extrinsic nerves, the young arrived by spontaneous birth. As early as 1904 it was confirmed that the uterine muscle has the power of rhythmic contraction irrespective of nerve supply, for contractions are not dependent for their origin upon impulses from the central nervous system. Experimental work in that same year demonstrated the capability of the uterus cf a woman to contract even when separated from the body, and also proved that impulses from the central nervous system are not essential to contraction. Although there are variations in the activity of the virgin uterus, these observations apply without exception to the pregnant uterus.

Although it can be clearly demonstrated that the various nerves supplied to the uterus appear to have branches that are inhibitory as well as branches that are motor, one faculty of uterine muscle that is extremely important in the unraveling of the mysteries of difficult labor is *the ability of the circular muscle fibers to contract independently of the longitudinal.* The importance of this power of individual contraction will easily be understood when we come to discuss the activity of the cervix uteri under impulses peculiar to fear or stress.

As well as having the power of automatic contraction of itself, irrespective of nerve supply, there are also nerves to the uterus that govern and control its contractions either to assist or impede that automatic action. There is also evidence of some form of inhibitory center for uterine contraction that exists in the medulla oblongata. Thus the "pains" of labor can often be inhibited by the emotions and other contemporary actions of the central nervous system.

Many cases have been observed and reported of automatic birth, where the lower half of the spinal cord has not functioned and the lower half of the body, therefore, has been completely paralyzed. The painless character of labor in patients suffering from *tabes dorsalis* (spinal cord disease) has been noted and the powerful character of the muscular contractions of the uterus in these circumstances observed.[2]

Physiologists have also recorded that the muscular contractions of the uterus appear to be *definitely stronger when separated from their nerve supply than in the natural state,* so that the normal nerve supply to the uterus conveys an inhibitory influence.

Several cases of normal parturition have been recorded in women who were suffering from paraplegia caused by lesions in the spinal cord in the mid-dorsal region.[3] In these women no impulses from nerve centers were received above that point, but they all had normal labors without sensation. It is therefore suggested that if there is a special center for the impulses necessary to parturition it is situated below the mid-dorsal region of the spine. Efferent nerve fibers from the lumbar region of the spinal cord make their way to the uterus via the inferior mesenteric ganglia and aortic plexus.

We can therefore see three apparently definite and separate controlling influences in uterine contraction during parturition, and this is clearly set out by Marshall in his general conclusions regarding the mechanism of parturition:

1. The act of parturition is partly automatic and partly reflex, these actions corresponding in the main to the first and second stages of labor respectively, the spinal reflexes usually commencing immediately the membranes have ruptured.

2. Direct communication with the brain is not essential for the proper coordination of uterine action, but the brain appears to exercise a controlling influence of some kind. Thus emotions often become a hindrance to the progress of parturition. It would seem possible that this inhibition of uterine contractions is brought about by an inhibition center in the brain.

3. Direct communication between the uterus and the lumbar

region of the cord is generally essential for the occurrence of those rhythmical contractions which take place in the progress of normal labor. There is experimental evidence upon animals, however, that the uterus is sometimes able automatically to expel its contents at least as far as the relaxed portion of the genital cord, even when entirely deprived of all spinal influences.[4]

More recently we have similar conclusions based upon different methods of examination. Albert Kuntz in *The Autonomic Nervous System* states:

> In view of the experimental data available at present it may be assumed that the uterine musculature, *like other smooth muscle,* possesses the inherent capacity to undergo rhythmic contractions, but under conditions of normal innervation the activity of this musculature is subject to both motor and inhibitory nervous influences, which may be of reflex or central nervous origin.[5]

These important conclusions have a very definite bearing upon the mechanism of labor, and in particular we must note the influences that give rise to the inhibition of muscular activity, and the means by which that inhibition of rhythmic contraction is brought about.

The conclusions of Beckwith Whitehouse and Henry Featherstone, in the *British Medical Journal,* are of profound importance, and a full realization of their value to clinicians will be the means of preventing much pain and distress in labor. They are as follows:

1. The nervous mechanism controlling the uterus is constituted by three systems: (a) Local; (b) Sympathetic; (c) Lumbosacral Autonomic.

2. The "local" system is capable of producing rhythmical uterine contractions, and is independent of the sympathetic and autonomic systems in common with other voluntary muscle.

3. The sympathetic stimuli are motor to the circular muscle fibers and inhibitory to the longitudinal bundles.

4. The lumbar cord stimuli are motor to the longitudinal fibers and inhibitory to the circular fibers.

5. Both autonomic and sympathetic stimuli are controlled by higher centers in the medulla and possibly the cortex, but are capable of acting independently of the same.

6. Reflexes, both (a) autonomic and (b) sympathetic, are probably important factors in normal uterine contraction. (Reference may be made to mammary [breast] and perineal stimulation.)

7. Uterine contractions, to be effective, depend equally upon

the integrity and correctly adjusted balance of autonomic and sympathetic impulses. Disturbances in either, whether in the direction of augmentation or diminution, will interfere with the normal course of parturition.[6]

## EFFECTS OF SYMPATHETIC STIMULI

### NERVE SUPPLY OF UTERUS, VAGINA, AND VULVA

The nerve supply of the uterus is derived from the tenth, eleventh, and twelfth thoracic nerves, through the hypogastric plexus to the uterovaginal plexuses, which receive supply also from the first lumbar and the second, third, and fourth sacral nerves. In this way it is seen that the sympathetic and the lumbosacral autonomic systems merge in the formation of the great uterovaginal plexuses, and send their fibers freely into all parts of the uterus. Some physiologists add that fibers from the lower lumbar roots also send branches to these plexuses. The uterovaginal plexuses, as their name implies, supply also the muscle wall and mucous membrane of the vagina.

The labia are supplied anteriorly by the first lumbar cerebrospinal nerve through branches of the ilioinguinal, and posteriorly from the second and third sacral nerves through the inferior pudendal and the perineal cutaneous branches of the small sciatic nerve. The vaginal plexuses supply them with the lumbosacral autonomic fibers.

There is nothing to add concerning the inherent ability of the uterus to contract irrespective of nerve supply. The next step is to state briefly the effects upon the uterus of stimulating the various nerve supplies.

The sympathetic stimuli appear to be definitely inhibitory to the longitudinal fibers of the uterus and motor to the circular fibers, and, acting in antagonism to these stimuli, the influence of the lumbar cord is motor to the longitudinal fibers and inhibitory to the circular fibers.[7]

Although both parasympathetic and sympathetic stimuli are dependent for their activity to a certain extent upon the medulla and possibly upon the cortex, it has been clearly demonstrated that they can act quite independently of central influence. It is also probable that the sympathetic stimuli are controlled directly or indirectly to some extent by the posterior part of the optic thalamus.

The point of greatest importance to the clinician in these observations is the functional activity of the sympathetic nervous system, for the contraction of the circular muscle fibers during the first stage of labor is obviously inhibitory to the whole function. Under certain circumstances the sympathetic division of the autonomic system completely overrules both the cranial and the lumbosacral autonomic, so that in the presence of strong sympathetic stimuli the influence of the lumbosacral autonomic is relatively negligible.[8]

If we turn back to review the structure of the uterus, we find that the proportion of circular fibers in the cervix uteri is much higher than anywhere else in the organ, and conversely the strength of the longitudinal fibers is much less. Although the lumbosacral autonomic system is motor to the longitudinal fibers, the uterus does not depend upon it for its power of contraction. Should these stimuli be entirely nullified, the uterus will continue to contract of its own automaticity, even though the sympathetic nervous system is acting directly contrary to the normal mechanism.

We may summarize the effects of the various nerve supplies under four headings:

1. The local innervation, which is responsible for expulsive contractions.

2. The parasympathetic nerve supply, which stimulates the muscles of expulsion.

3. The sympathetic nerves, which inhibit expulsion.

4. The sympathetic nerves, which cause the muscle fibers around the large vessels of the middle layer to contract.

#### FACTORS RELEVANT TO NERVE SUPPLY

Now, it is clear that *one of the primary and essential factors of a relatively easy labor lies in the elimination of this sympathetic stimulus.* The sacral autonomic supply is a comparatively small and localized area of distribution from definite and separate upper-ganglionic fibers. On the other hand, the sympathetic division of the autonomic system is of widespread distribution and allows the reception of stimuli by one means or another through a variety of causes from practically the whole body. A metaphor facilitates the understanding of this: "The sympathetic is like the soft and loud pedals, modulating all the notes together, but the cranial and sacral autonomic are like the separate keys."[9] *The contracting cervix resisting dilation and increasing uterine tension is but a single symptom of the general intensification of sympathetic activity.* That it may of itself become a secondary or contributing cause of further sympathetic stimulation is highly probable, for the fact that it inhibits a normal function invites psychical as well as physical reinforcements to the already adverse influences proceeding from the higher centers through the sympathetic back to the uterus.

From the point of view of the clinician, it has long been difficult to understand why a cervix that, between contractions, appears to be patulous, soft, and elastic, resists dilatation, even though the mechanism of labor is otherwise perfect. No obstetrician has failed to notice how frequently the nervous patient is the slow dilator; so much so that the slow labor has been attributed to the resistance occasioned by the fetal head to the birth canal, or by the relative weakness of the uterine contractions, and to the slowness of the labor has been assigned the mental and physical anguish of the patient.

*Surely cause and effect have been transposed!* The mental anguish of the patient has added general sympathetic intensification, for the physical signs of her emotion are in reality the physical signs of an intensification of sympathetic stimuli. As surely as she vomits, has a rapid pulse, large pupils, and a cold, pallid, perspiring face, so surely *in harmony with these manifestations is the presence of the resistant contraction of the circular fibers of her uterus—in particular those of the cervix uteri,* which series of events calls for a further excitation through the whole vicious circle. When the longitudinal fibers press down the fetal head, it causes intense discomfort which increases as retraction as well as contraction takes place. Probably the discomfort itself adds force to the sphincterlike constriction of the cervix.

### PAIN

The phenomenon of pain has been evolved with a definite purpose. It is so general among all the higher forms of animal life that it is probably beneficial and not of itself harmful. It is an important device employed by nature to protect the individual from injury or the results of injury. The reaction to irritation is movement, which is demonstrated by the amoeba, the simplest unicellular form of animal life: if we place minute granules of methylene blue in contact with its surface, the response is movement in order to escape from or rid itself of the irritating particle. As we ascend the scale to the higher mammals, awareness to stimulation increases. Whether reaction is associated with volition is open to discussion, and we must presume that in the absence of consciousness, defense movements are purely tissue reflexes. We can learn very little about pain from experiments upon animals. Our knowledge must accrue from observation upon conscious human beings; they alone are able to describe their feelings. If we remove the consciousness, by any means, there is no pain appreciation and therefore vital resistance to pain is absent.

Over the surface of the body and upon various internal organs and structures, there are minute nerve endings that we know as pain-receivers, or nociceptors. In the pristine eras of human development we were exposed to attack by tooth and claw; therefore the greatest profusion of nociceptors are found over the vulnerable areas of the body where injury would have most serious consequences. The sides of the neck, under the arms, the abdomen, and the chest are all extremely sensitive places, for, if engaged in combat, it would be here that tooth and claw would inflict damage and cause the physical shock that places a fighter at the mercy of his foe. If we watch kittens, puppies, or young bears at play, we can see where nociceptors are liberally distributed. There are definite areas which each endeavors to claw or bite—they roll, feint, and jump to shield these places. They are playing, but unwittingly practicing the more serious art of attack and defense.

But we need not discuss the pain-receivers of the body surface, for we are interested in those within the abdominal cavity. The uterus is poorly supplied with nerves that register pain *(nociceptors),* for it conforms much more to the distribution and behavior of nerves that supply the internal organs of the abdomen. The intestines and the internal organs, in particular the uterus, are not affected by external cold or heat and the abdominal wall has to be severely injured or ripped open before they can be damaged, but they are well supplied with pain receptors that record *excessive tension* or *laceration of the tissues.* No other nociceptors have been demonstrated within the abdomen—the intestines and the uterus can be burned, cauterized, handled, and moved without any sensation of discomfort to the patient, but if either of these structures is stretched or torn, considerable pain and shock result.

All nociceptors are specific, that is to say, they react to only one form of pain stimulation. It follows thus that the only pain stimulus that the uterus can record is excessive tension or actual tearing of tissues. I have been persuaded from experiment and experience that specificity is a constant phenomenon in both conditioned reflexes and sensory receptors.[10,11] The pain of labor, whether referred or otherwise, must result from one, or both, of these specific stimuli. So we must ask ourselves: Does nature intend that childbirth should be accompanied by laceration and injurious tension? If it does, why has not this important structure adapted itself to its function, according to the law of Professor Julius Wolfe, which was, in short: "Structure is adapted to function"? If nature does not intend this laceration and injury, then those pain-receivers are there to respond only to stimuli other than normal. We must inquire: Against what is the uterus protecting itself by giving pain sensations in carrying out a perfectly natural function? The physiological perfection of the human body knows no greater paradox than pain in normal parturition.

The biological purpose of pain interpretation is protective, and it results in muscular activity to the end that the individual may either defend himself or escape from impending danger. For instance, if a finger is accidentally put on a hot stove, almost before there is any conscious mental interpretation of what has happened it has been removed; the muscular activity of protection has been immediately employed by lifting the finger from the injurious stimulus. Pain also instructs us, lest its horrors be repeated through our carelessness. The creation of such association and experience is exemplified by the unfortunate boy of earlier days who withdrew his hand as the master's cane descended.

There are, however, pains from which we cannot escape so easily, arising from the internal organs and known as visceral pains. The uterus and the pelvic organs are visceral, and therefore in this discussion we are primarily concerned with visceral pain. It must be borne in mind, also, that we are not concerned with disease but with healthy women carrying out a normal and natural function.

*There is no physiological function in the body that gives rise to pain in the normal course of health.* When the natural urges to perform are uncomfortable, it usually indicates that the physiological balance is being strained.

All over the body there are groups of muscles whose actions are opposed to each other. A simple example is the action of the biceps and the triceps. If we wish to bend the arm at the elbow, the biceps contract and the triceps, which normally oppose it, relax. If, on the other hand, we wish to straighten our arm, the triceps contract and the biceps at the same time relax. If both these muscles function at the same time, the arm goes into a state of rigidity. If the contractions are strong enough the whole arm quivers, and in a very short time there is considerable pain in the limb.

This arrangement also holds good for all organs of the body that fill and empty. In normal physiological action one muscle group by contraction prevents emptying of the organ, but is completely relaxed and loose when the opposing muscle groups contract to empty the organ. This convenient harmony of muscle action is seen, for example, in the bowel and urinary bladder. When the bowel is emptied, the muscles that are brought into play in order to expel its contents are not opposed by the ring of muscles, or the sphincter, at the outlet, which normally holds the bowel tightly closed. When an expulsive effort is made, the outlet is relaxed. The same also applies to the urinary apparatus. Both these mechanisms may give rise to acute pain if spasmodic contraction at the outlet occurs and resists the efforts of the expulsive muscles. The condition called fissure of the anus, which is extremely painful, may cause a spasm of the sphincter muscle so that it will not relax. The two opposing muscles, acting at the same time, combine to produce acute pain from abnormal pressure. The same is true in the spasmodic tension of a baby's anus when it becomes constipated. The reflex relaxation of the sphincter ani is overcome by the unconscious influence of the sympathetic, stimulated by the anticipation of increasing pain when the tension of a hard motion causes discomfort with each expulsive effort. We see it again in the retention of urine in cases of acute urethritis, for pain inhibits the reflex relaxation of the sphincter. How often emotional excitement is the underlying cause of painful coitus, particularly when laceration of a rigid hymen conserves memory not only of surprise but of physical pain. Similarly, the spasm of vaginismus has unquestionably a strong relationship to the sympathetic stimuli emanating from the pathological emotional reactions of a psychoneurotic.

The same harmony of muscle action is seen in the uterus during childbirth. The longitudinal muscle fibers, whose action is expulsive, contract. In normal conditions the circular muscle fibers are relaxed and flaccid, allowing dilation of the outlet to the womb and free passage of the child.

From the general principles of the construction of the uterus, we deduce that labor without the pain of tension or injury depends upon:

1. Expulsive muscle activity *without resistance* from constricting muscles.

2. Expulsive nerve impulses being active and constrictor nerve impulses inactive.

3. Elasticity of structures around arteries and veins between expulsive contractions so that a full supply of fresh blood may be maintained and the waste product of muscle action freely removed.

## INFLUENCES OF EMOTION UPON LABOR

In order to appreciate the influences of the emotions upon any function, it should be clearly understood that emotion is probably the cause of physiological activity, and not physiological activity the cause of emotion. The perfection of the human body as a working machine is beyond criticism. If its imperfections are to be considered, then first let the applied misuses to which it is subjected be given their full significance.

The emotions do not arise from physical stimulus; but from emotional stimulus physical changes occur that, given normal and natural circumstances, are to the end that the body itself shall be more efficient to meet the physical or mental responsibility that time and circumstance may place upon it.

It is impossible to give even an outline, in such a work as this, of the discoveries that have been made pointing to the increased efficiency of the body to meet emergencies under the influence of emotional stress. The secretion of the adrenal glands is said by some physiologists to play a large part in the quality of our emotional reactions. Under certain circumstances blood corpuscles are poured out into the circulatory system to meet an emergency; under others, the blood sugar is suddenly increased, thereby augmenting the fuel value within the circulatory system. Certain mental and emotional states have been shown to call for such reaction as will increase the coagulation power of the blood. The reserves of the body, in hiding and apparently nonexistent, are suddenly called into the fray like strong reinforcements that have been lying in readiness until such time as emergency shall demand their help.

Let us consider what occurs in natural labor. Some biochemical or mechanical change—concerning which many theories are at present not yet proved—sets up rhythmical expulsive contractions of the uterus, and the lumbosacral autonomic system, under normal circumstances, proceeds to carry out its primary function, which is the emptying of viscera. It stimulates the longitudinal fibers of the uterus to contract, or it may be more accurate to say that the local and inherent stimuli derived from the uterus itself to produce rhythmical contractions is augmented by the lumbosacral autonomic system. The lumbosacral autonomic system antagonizes the sympathetic stimuli which are motor to the circular muscle fibers and inhibitory to the longitudinal bundles, with the obvious consequence that the contracting neck of the uterus and the cervix uteri, which are chiefly composed of circular muscle fibers, adopt a state of complete relaxation. This relaxation enables the cervix quickly to be taken up; it enables the uterine muscle cells by the faculty of retraction to draw up the cervix around the well-lubricated presenting part.

It is open to very serious consideration whether or not the teaching of dilatation of the cervix has, in the past, been entirely accurate. Few obstetricians can be satisfied that the presenting part forces open the cervix uteri. Unquestionably, a well-formed bag of waters or a pronounced caput succedaneum are of great assistance to the retracting longitudinal muscle fibers in their efforts to pull the cervix upward over a presenting part. How many who have been called upon to do a podalic version have found that the cervix will admit the whole hand with practically no resistance, when it has been subjected to none of the so-called dilating structures from above. I suggest that the greatest factor in the dilatation of the cervix is the inhibitory effect of the lumbosacral autonomic system upon its circular muscle fibers, and the absence of any overpowering stimulus that would retain its muscle fibers in a state of contraction.

Normally, therefore, the integrity of the process of parturition depends upon the antagonistic action of those nerves which supply the longitudinal fibers on the one hand, and the circular fibers on the other. *This applies throughout the birth canal, even to the perineum itself, for the muscles of the pelvic floor and the sphincter muscles of the vagina, and the elasticity of the perineum, are each in their turn dependent for complete relaxation upon the harmony with which the integral parts of the machinery carry out their work.*

Look upon labor, therefore, in its simple form, as being carried out primarily by the lumbosacral autonomic stimuli, in conjunction with the automatic rhythmical stimuli from the uterus, antagonizing to a very large extent any interference from the sympathetic nervous system. Although it may be that there are higher centers in the medulla and in the cortex, which can, under certain circumstances, influence the course of parturition, there are sufficient cases on record to demonstrate that no activity is required on the part of these higher centers, and if they have any control over the lumbosacral autonomic or the sympathetic nerve distribution, it plays no part that is essential to uncomplicated labor. The same applies to a cortico-thalamic interaction, and whatever part the optic thalamus may play when deprived by anesthesia of its subservience to cortical influence, it does not appear to affect the main principle of nerve control of parturition.

If in outline this describes the muscular activity dependent upon the nerve supply throughout the birth canal, it also enables us to see that birth itself should occasion no pressure sufficiently great to give rise to objective peripheral pain. Where there is no gross abnormality of structure in the female pelvis, the elasticity of the fetal part is such that, during the processes described above, pressure is not increased to an extent that can cause injury to the surrounding tissues.

These principles of interaction of the longitudinal and circular muscle fibers are applicable right through the pelvic canal. The pelvic floor is extremely elastic; the levator ani offers no resistance where there is no spasm. The sphincters of the vagina are not only extremely elastic, but when in a state of relaxation offer no resistance whatever to the descending fetus. The skin of the perineum, if it is not subjected to any unnatural force, will dilate without rupture in a very large number of cases—in fact it may be said that any tear in the perineum in normal labor is an injury for which the obstetrician is probably more responsible than the woman herself. Thus we see that where there is complete harmony in the action and interaction of the muscles of the birth canal, and where that harmony depends upon normal stimuli to the nerves concerned in parturition, there is no anatomical feature that creates difficulty, undue strain, or pressure too great for the surrounding tissues.

When the baby is born in the natural state, the mother is not only conscious, but she hears, as a reward for the hard work that has been hers for the previous few hours, the cry of her child. The powerful emotion known as mother love sweeps throughout her whole body; she receives stimuli from sight, from hearing; the joy of accomplishment adds to the intensification of her sympathetic activity. The first cry of a baby after a normal labor, if clearly heard by a fully conscious mother, has, in my experience, an action upon the uterine musculature as immediate and as powerful as pituitrin extract. Not infrequently have I called the attention of nurses and attendants who have been assisting me in maternity work to this phenomenon. I have rarely seen a postpartum hemorrhage when a fully conscious mother has heard the first cry of her child; I can remember no case of healthy retained placenta under those circumstances. But more frequently I have noticed that the placenta has been expelled from the uterus into the vaginal end of the birth canal painlessly and without any hemorrhage, before the twenty minutes have passed that I adopt as my arbitrary minimum for the time of the third stage of labor.

Such cases as these demonstrate that loss of maternal blood is pathological; that a certain amount of placental hemorrhage should occur is probably not only natural, but physiologically necessary, for, as the placenta separates from the surface of the uterus, there must be a certain amount of blood retained within its meshes distal to the point of closure, and separation of those vessels which interchange supplies upon the placental site of the uterus.

The importance of this emotion to the success of parturition cannot be exaggerated. I am persuaded quite definitely in the fundamental truth of this observation that the conscious knowledge of accomplishment of which the mother becomes aware at the end of the second stage gives rise to those emotions which nature intended as agents to the perfection of the third stage of labor.

Now let us consider what occurs throughout this process when fear creeps into the mind of the woman—when that part of her autonomic nervous system which is stimulated most strongly by this emotion takes precedence, and wields its influence to antagonize the natural stimuli of the lumbosacral distribution.

### THE MECHANISM OF FEAR OR EMOTIONAL STRESS

Fear is alertness to the presence of danger. In other words, the reception of impulses making us aware of the actual or possible presence of phenomena is associated in our minds with pain or injury.[12] Fear or stress gives rise to action; it produces motor responses. In order to do this, the sympathetic nervous system is activated by impulses that are inhibitory to all visceral action, for, to utilize all possible physical strength for the purpose of defense, those parts of the body that are of no service in defensive action are deprived of motor activity. At the same time the adrenalin excretion is increased. In short, the influence of fear or stress, being conveyed through the sympathetic nervous system, inhibits the pelvic autonomic. As a result, *the neuromuscular harmony of labor in the presence of fear or stress is disturbed in a manner exactly similar to that produced by pain.*

In all cases where there is injury or pain, action is demanded by the body's protective motor responses; and where there is fear, fight or flight is its only outlet. Yet in labor, neither fight nor flight is possible. Injury without action rapidly exhausts nervous energy, but an acute emotional state that must be suffered without escape has been shown to exhaust the cytoplasm of the Purkinje cells of the cerebellum even more rapidly. Thus acute or persistent pain, whether caused by injury, fear, or stress, actually destroys certain elements of the nerve cells of the brain that are concerned with the integration and interpretation of pain stimuli. Therefore, one of the first duties of a good doctor is to see that his or her patient does not suffer any unnecessary pain.

The effect of pain on the human body has been observed in all the variations of its manifestation by every physician, but in particular we must consider its effect upon women in labor. We must know to what extent the nerves supplying the muscles that take part in this act can be affected by emotional stress. The experimental evidence for this can be found in the works of investigators in regard to the other internal organs of the body.[13]

The essential protective emotion, fear, brings about the strongest and most efficiently reinforced of all motor responses. Its influence is diffused throughout the entire receptor mechanism and the urgency of the inborn sense of self-protection amplifies or distorts the interpretation of both facts or fantasies of the emotions. The exaggerated messages prompt the cortex to precipitate a state of emergency in preparation for offense or defense. In this way, somatic or physical changes may occur as a direct result of psychological states. Sir Henry Head, one of the great pioneer neurologists, said: "The mental state of the patient has a notoriously profound influence over the pains originating in the pelvic viscera."[14] In other words, the interpretation of sensations arising from the uterus may be influenced in most astonishing ways by the mental condition of the woman concerned.

Outer impulses arrive within our consciousness through the special senses; we may see danger, or hear sounds we associate with danger. But we are also capable of imagination. In civilized life the majority of those who suffer from fear or anxiety states are not threatened by reality of danger but by the elaboration of possibilities that, being exaggerated by mental processes, produce a condition of tense alertness to the presence of danger, when in reality no danger exists. That, unfortunately, does not prevent the physical manifestations of this emotional state.

When labor begins, there is a danger that anxiety may sweep aside any sense of elation the woman may have experienced initially. But anxiety activates the sympathetic nervous system, which overrides, by its powerful influences, all other nerve stimuli throughout the body. It activates the machinery for either fight or flight; it creates a state of tension throughout the individual that provides for an increase of muscular power. Yet the sympathetic nerve supply to the uterus unfortunately supplies the circular fibers that inhibit the opening of the uterine outlet and resist the expulsive efforts of the longitudinal fibers of the uterus. As soon, therefore, as this protective apparatus is brought into play in order to overcome or fly from the painful recording of uterine sensations, so much more is the cause of pain introduced.

Since anxiety causes resistance by interfering with the normal harmony of muscle action, two powerful muscles are set against each other. This quickly increases enormously the tension of the uterine muscle. Tension above a normal amount is registered by special nerves and interpreted as pain in the higher brain centers, which creates a very serious complication of labor concerning the blood supply to the uterus through the placenta to the baby. This is sometimes overlooked.

Through this fear system or sympathetic system, the body reacts primarily not in a separate focus but *all over at the same time,* in order to protect itself against danger. The first principle of protection is to see that all possible fuel is conveyed to those muscles that will be used either in order to fly or to fight. At the same time, all the organs of the body that do not need the maximum blood supply are deprived of their blood to a large extent simply by contraction of the arteries supplying the organs that are useless in the act of defense. One of the organs useless in defense is the uterus. Under the influence of fear the blood vessels and the muscles supplied by the sympathetic or stress nervous system actually limit the amount of blood going to and coming from the uterus. For a short time this can be done without disturbing the well-being of the infant, for it requires a very much lower oxygen pressure in the blood with which it is supplied than the adult musculature. But if this persists for any length of time without remission, it is quite likely that anxiety itself is enough to deprive the baby within the womb of oxygen, and therefore to cause injury to some of its intricate organs, particularly the brain, and sometimes even cause intrauterine death.

Fear or emotional stress strongly stimulates the circular muscle fibers of the birth canal. As these circular fibers contract, their tone is increased while their elasticity is impaired, and the relaxation of the fibers is incomplete. The automatic action of the longitudinal muscle fibers of the uterus and pelvic canal not only presses down the presenting part, but the lower uterine segment adds tension in its endeavor to pull up the cervix and slide it gently over the fetal head.

So we find that *where unpleasant emotions rule, the first unnatural factor becomes physically manifested in the mechanism of labor itself by a definitely resistant cervix*—resistant not only to the downcoming presenting part, but to the efforts of the longitudinal muscle fibers to draw it up by their faculty of retraction. For it must be remembered that there is also a local nerve supply for the uterus, which enables the longitudinal fibers to continue to contract even though the autonomic supply has been cut out by sympathetic overstimulation.* So the uterus goes on contracting just the same, in spite of the sympathetic nervous system being activated. We have then a condition of the expulsive fibers pushing against the circular fibers: two opposing groups of muscles working one against the other. The normal and natural result of this is that there is excessive tension, and soon a painless natural function is made into an extremely painful and therefore abnormal condition.

Tension is thus introduced from above, tension from within, and from the fact that the presenting part is pushed down into the pelvis, the lower part of the cervical canal, long after the cervix should be completely drawn up and contiguous with the lower uterine segment. Instead, it is pressed low down into the pelvic cavity, maybe to the coccyx posteriorly, or even to the upper surface of the pubic bone anteriorly before full dilatation is achieved.

---

* In a paper by E. H. Shabanah, A. Toth, and George B. Maughan—"The Role of the Autonomic Nervous System . . .", *American Journal of Obstetrics and Gynecology,* 89, no. 7 (August 1, 1964): 841–880—reporting from McGill University, the following statements (reprinted by permission) are made as the result of some impressive experiments:

"Impressions creating anxiety and fear or, on the other hand, excitement or painful sensation, awakening the primitive defense reaction, produce a form of stress which brings about sympathetic hyperactivity. Spontaneous pain sensation due to a pelvic lesion or pain triggered from the parametria as in dyspareunia may precipitate a vicious circle. Sensory impulses travel through the two reflex arcs, the spinal and the cortical, referred to above. Since both the sympathetic and the parasympathetic contain sensory fibers, both systems are stimulated equally and, therefore, remain in balance as long as pain is not registered at the cortical level. When it is, as is normally the case, *sympathetic hyperactivity* [italics ed.] is thus created, affecting the uterus partly through its nervous connections and partly through the adrenal glands. This results in an elevation of the tissue and blood catecholamines, which in turn impair myometrial activity and induce vasospasm" (pp. 855–856).

"The preceding experimental findings in addition to other experimental and clinical observations raise the possibility that most if not all the previously mentioned, unexplained obstetrical and gynecological clinical conditions may well be etiologically related to abnormal neurohumoral causative factors reflected in a final picture of *autonomic imbalance—sympathetic hyperactivity*" (p. 856).

This is the painful first stage. It is pathological because it is opposed to normal physiological activity. Fear or apprehension mean real physical pain, not only subjective but objective, organic pain, intrinsic and extrinsic in the periphery that is active during labor. With what torment the cervix becomes fully dilated—the fact of pain is established in the mind of the woman—the dilatation of the outlet begins, and a similar series of events follows. The pelvic floor has been damaged, the levator ani injured because its anterior attachment has not been drawn up before pressure is occasioned by the presenting part. The vaginal sphincter can be seen, by anyone who has ever observed it, as two strong muscle bundles, tense and inelastic. This hypersensitiveness and tension is carried backward to the sphincters of the anus, and it may be noticed that when fear is present, the pains of the second stage are frequently heralded by spasmodic contractions of the sphincters of the anus and vagina. Instead of relaxation and elasticity, tension is encountered, pain is experienced, protective spasm again augments the tension, and so again the forces join in battle on unequal ground, for sooner or later the great muscles of expulsion will either break down the resisting tissues or injure the fetus in their efforts.

In order to combat this situation, fear and stress of all kinds must be prevented. Physical relaxation is essential, and the learning of relaxed breathing patterns during pregnancy in order to employ them in labor. Education, correct relaxation, and breathing will prevent, so far as is possible, the harmful effects of fear or emotional stress, which are pain, tension, and the deprivation of oxygen in the tissues of a healthy woman.

#### THE MECHANICS OF DILATATION

If we examine the action and reaction of the forces about the fetal head during the first stage of labor from the point of view of pure mechanics, the importance of cervical tension in relation to the expulsive and dilating force of the uterine musculature may be clearly demonstrated.

In consideration of the normal case, resistance occasioned by molding of the bones of the fetal head upon the bones of the pelvis during the first stage cannot be taken into account. It is, in fact, extremely unlikely that the bony structure of the pelvis during the first stage of normal labor exerts any force upon the fetal head that is relatively important in the dilatation of the pelvic canal. Cases of abnormalities of bony structure of pelvis or fetus do not come under this heading.

Let the fetal head be likened to a ball passing through an expanding ring, the cervix uteri. More accurately, the cervix may be described as a series of expanding rings. If the tension of the cervix uteri is increased, then the expulsive force must be proportionately increased. Retraction and automatic expulsive contractions continue, irrespective of the inhibition of the pelvic autonomic stimuli, until gradually they overcome the resistance either by dilatation or by rupture of the ring muscle. Rupture occurs in the majority of cases when the tension remains abnormally great.

It is obvious also that parturition under these circumstances necessitates a muscular strain upon the mechanism out of all proportion to that which nature intended. It is not difficult to appreciate why modern woman may suffer from lacerations, displacements, bruisings, and internal injuries. It is also clear that such tension cannot exist without pain.

It is my belief that subinvolution of the uterus is not infrequently due to an excessive strain placed upon the fibers of expulsion in their efforts to overcome the inelastic and tense circular fibers of the cervix uteri. This is augmented by the tension that is placed upon the thin and relatively meager musculature of the lower uterine segment. When the cervix is torn by the oncoming fetal head, large vessels are frequently ruptured, for the blood supply of the cervix at that time is enormously increased. Many serious postpartum hemorrhages have occurred from the split lateral walls of the cervix uteri.

Cases have been noted in which the fetal head has started to come down in the occipito posterior position, when the pelvis presents no abnormalities, and when no reasonable cause has appeared for so serious a complication.

It can be shown that rotation into the posterior position is much more easily accomplished when the cervix uteri has resisted full dilatation and has been pushed down only partially dilated before the fetal head. By presenting a thickened, almost obstructive band upon the wall of the birth canal, it deflects the occiput from the simple course, and by its presence influences the occiput to swing through the greater segment to the posterior position.

The ease with which these cases of persistent occipito posterior presentation, without any skeletal abnormality, can be rectified after full dilatation of the cervix, must be considered from this point of view, that in the absence of full dilatation the cervix uteri played some part in the presentation of the fetal head. A state of complete relaxation is necessary before rotation can be performed, but how frequently with the attainment of the occipito anterior position the child will almost fall through the pelvic canal.

At the outlet, *tension* is the greatest of all predisposing causes of rupture of the perineum. The fourchette may go, but too frequently the sphincter of the vagina is either partially or totally torn at the posterior end. An effort may be made by the insertion of a few stitches to obviate this trouble, but rarely does a torn sphincter regain its full power of contractility.

To the casual observer these points may be of small importance, but above all things an obstetrician must be a humanitarian. To produce a child and injure the mother is the same thing as producing the mother and ruining the wife, and many physicians will readily acquiesce to the suggestion that this is synonymous with domestic strain, if not ultimately with personal estrangement.

It is almost superfluous to add what must be obvious to the least critical, that these observations are not intended to explain the origin of all complications of labor, but rather that in intensified emotions, we have a factor that not only makes labor painful when it should be painless but introduces difficulties and complications that need never arise.

One of the most astounding results of the application of the principles outlined above is the almost entire elimination of such complications to labor as have been mentioned. Given anatomical efficiency, physiological integrity can then be acquired by the elimination of negative emotions, substituting the peacefulness of a relaxed, confident woman.

. . .

*This chapter on the neuromuscular harmony of childbirth was compiled from material written by Grantly Dick-Read in 1933. The chapter was then submitted for comment to Dr. Berry Campbell, Ph.D., Professor of Physiology and Acting Chairman at the California College of Medicine, University of California, Irvine. The following reply was received:*

I have read the chapter of Grantly Dick-Read's book on natural childbirth with great interest and I have enjoyed the search through the literature to which it led me.

The chapter in question is remarkable. Before the discovery of the important role of estrogen and progesterone in the conditioning of the uterus to nervous regulation and even before the understanding was had of the role of acetylcholine, norepinephrine and epinephrine, not to mention oxytocin and the prostaglandins, a consideration of the clinical role of the balanced autonomic innervation of the uterus is given which still has great logical force.

Compared with other medical fields, the amount of scientific publication in obstetrics is remarkably sparse. However, there is a scattered literature on the subject in the last decade in which the same matter is reviewed in the framework of modern neuro-endocrinology. The modern work is best exemplified by [E. H.] Shabanah, *et al.*

The chapter from Grantly Dick-Read's book is most impressive when one realizes that the succeeding fifty years, though bringing much new and unexpected factual knowledge into the picture, have borne out his essential thesis completely. The reason for this, it seems to me, is that the base of his viewpoint is an astute and valid clinical observation. The physiological data are presented to show that they are compatible, but I doubt if it was from the physiological data that he drew his conclusions. It is most impressive that Dr. Read has been borne out so well by recent scientific advances.

## CHAPTER 11

# The Relief of Pain in Labor

When we speak of normal, natural, or uncomplicated labor, we infer that the child is the right size and in the correct position to pass through the pelvic canal without undue strain or injury to the surrounding parts. In the majority of labors, everything appears to be perfect; the muscles contract well, the child is the correct size and in a good position, yet in spite of this there is pain. Why is this, when there is no other physiological function in the body that gives rise to pain in the normal course of health?

A close clinical study of natural childbirth has taught us much about the cause and origin of nervous impulses that are not physiological. *Fear* is a natural protective emotion without which few of us would survive. When through association or indoctrination there is fear of childbirth, resistant actions and reactions are brought to the mechanism of the organs of reproduction. This discord disturbs the harmony or polarity of muscle action, causing *tension,* which in turn gives rise to nervous impulses interpreted in the brain as *pain.* This is in keeping with the natural law of protection of the individual from abnormal or harmful activities in or about the body. Therefore, fear, tension, and pain are the three evils that are not normal to the natural design, but that have been introduced in the course of civilization by the ignorance of those who have been concerned with attendance at childbirth.

The fear of pain actually produces true pain through the medium of pathological tension. This is known as the "fear-tension-pain syndrome," and once it is established, a vicious circle demonstrating a crescendo of events will be observed, for with true pain fear is justified, and with mounting fear resistance is strengthened. Thus the most important contributory cause of pain in otherwise normal labor is fear.

But fear also affects the circulation of the blood to and from the uterus, for persisting tension of the uterine musculature prevents complete relaxation between contractions. The great blood sinuses of the uterus, deprived of full expansion, and the venous blood replete with metabolites or waste products of muscular action, are unable to discard their contents as freely as they should. Further, stimulation of the sympathetic nervous system results in constriction of the arterial blood vessels bringing fresh fuel to the contracting muscles. As a medical student at Cambridge I watched Professors Langley and Anderson[1] stimulate the sympathetic nerves to the uterus. In a short time the organ became pallid, firm, and bloodless, but when the stimulation was removed it rapidly filled with blood and once again became an elastic, deep-pink organ. I have also seen, on more than one occasion, what is known as a white, or *ischemic,* uterus. Because of urgent fetal distress, a cesarean section has had to be performed, labor having been inhibited by strong but ineffective contractions. The women in these cases had no anatomical obstruction or *abruptio placenta* (premature separation of the placenta from the wall of the uterus), but uncontrollable fear had caused, through the resistance of the circular muscles, such tension within and ischemia of the uterine muscles that the baby, through excessive intrauterine pressure and restricted oxygen supply, was unable to survive a protracted labor and vaginal delivery. The white uterus persisted in spite of surgical anesthesia, which demonstrates the depth of fear that may remain within the psyche of the individual.

Sir Thomas Lewis described the results of experiments dealing with the effect of partially restricted circulation upon muscle pain.[2] He suggested that an impairment of circulation is a cause of pain because the blood flow is too slight to dispose of metabolites. These substances, which may be crystalline in form, when in high concentration irritate by laceration the inner walls of the blood sinuses and smaller vessels within the muscle fibers, so that restricted circulation or relative ischemia could easily give rise to severe pain in muscle tissue. Not infrequently I have observed in the prolonged labor of frightened women a tenderness of the uterus; even gentle palpation of the womb through the abdominal wall gives rise to acute pain. A labor without disproportion or malpresentation of the baby is long because it is painful, not painful because it is long.

It is an indisputable statement that a very large majority of women today—however brave, however anxious to have a child, with whatever honesty they may say, "I am not worrying in the slightest"—have a background of fear. Unless their anxiety is alleviated, the fear-tension-pain cycle is set in motion because of the stimulation of the sympathetic nervous system. The circular or inhibitory muscle fibers of the uterus are among those activated by this system, rendering the lower uterine segment and the outlet resistant to dilation. This rapidly produces tension greater than normal within the walls and cavity of the uterus. This excessive tension is recorded by the nerve endings specific for that form of stimulation and is correctly interpreted as pain.

One of my patients was a tall, athletic girl of twenty-two, being in every way what could reasonably be described as a fine type of British youth. But when her labor began I found a pale, anxious girl, whose natural sense of courage was being severely tested. Her mother resented what she described as my cheerful confidence—she took me aside and explained to me that she did not consider it a time for smiles. Since she refused to leave her daughter, I decided to go out of the house, instructing the nurse in charge to call me later. I heard nothing for five hours, so I telephoned and received word that progress seemed to be very slow. After nine hours, having heard nothing, I went back to the house.

There were no obvious signs of the end of the first stage, but the patient showed all the symptoms of fear. The distracted mother rushed out of the room with me—an opportunity for which I was grateful!—demanding to know how I could allow such agony. I pointed out to her that so long as she was in the room I could do nothing. Fortunately my advice prevailed, and she stayed away.

I made an examination, and found a loose, flaccid cervix, which I could dilate sufficiently with my fingers to feel the ears and nose of the oncoming head, indicating an *occipito-posterior* (face-up) presentation. As I examined—and it is not without interest that my examination occasioned no discomfort—a contraction occurred. The picture of agony was typical in all respects at the very earliest signs of a contraction. The nurse was clutched around the waist, the corner of the pillow seized in an agonized apprehension of pain. *The cervix tightened to a size no bigger than a quarter.* There was, of course, no advance.

I sent for an anesthetist. With the greatest of ease an *occipito-anterior* (face-down) presentation of the head within the pelvis was obtained. Under anesthetic the cervix admitted my whole hand with practically no tension. I did not apply forceps. The anesthetic was lifted, and within three quarters of an hour a baby of seven pounds was born to a conscious and relatively calm mother.

I made full use of the third stage; the mother heard her child's first cry, and from that time all went well. Three years later I heard from abroad that her second baby had arrived. In three and a half hours she had produced a fine son weighing seven pounds three ounces. There had been no trouble. She had apparently suffered no pain, and no anesthetic had been given.

A more common cause for anxiety today is the stress of *time.* The water has broken, and the mother knows, "If you don't go into spontaneous labor within twenty-four hours, we'll have to induce labor." Or, "If your labor doesn't speed up, we'll need to augment it" (with pitocin, etc.). Or, "It looks like we'll need to do a cesarean if your cervix doesn't make better progress soon." All these "by-the-clock" rules cause emotional stress, inhibit the neuromuscular harmony, and lead to pain. Even "timing contractions" can be a cause of stress: how long a contraction, how long between, how strong, and so on. Usually it would be better just to throw the watch away! Birth is not a mechanistic event, which can measured by minutes and hours. What the mother needs is *peace,* so that she may relax with perfect confidence not only in her own body, but also in her surroundings, and her labor proceed without worry.

Of course the prenatal instruction is also extremely important. Nothing can be of greater importance, from the point of view of the mother, the infant, the family unit, and ultimately the social structure of the nation, than to persevere in the preparation of the woman's mind during the early weeks of pregnancy. By teaching the facts, thus implanting confidence, and by giving instruction in muscular relaxation, a state of anxiety may be replaced by a sense of well-being throughout the receptive months of pregnancy.

Prenatal preparation of the mind has been observed to have a close association with the pregnant woman's physical condition. A fear-conditioned mind often calls up physical complaints, backache or headache, dyspepsia or constipation, listlessness and muscular apathy, depression or weariness of mind and body. But many of these complaints, along with many persistent anxieties, will be removed by a psychological shift from the expectant mother's introvert self to her unborn child, particularly after she feels it moving within her. Her psychological constitution will become re-formed, and a more care-free state of mind will take the place of the anxiety tension to which she has been subjected for perhaps many years prior to childbirth.

*Depression and disappointment* are potent pain-intensifiers. In labor, when the long first stage seems unending, when there is no reason to believe the contractions are "any good," women are liable to become depressed and acutely disappointed. The sameness of the cycle of events, the uselessness of self-control, wear down their forti-tude. There is no relief but in tears, no comfort in protracted hope. The misery of labor when depression and disappointment overcome the patient's spirit of courage is a picture of which all obstetricians should be ashamed.

*Loss of control* allows all stimuli to run riot. The slightest dis-comfort will become an unbearable agony, and all the wiles and violence of animal nature are utilized in the effort to be freed from torment. Care must be taken during pregnancy. All influences likely to intensify the pain-producing stimuli must be removed as far as possible. And let us remember the value of sleep, that most salutary means of increasing central control.

*The centralization of thoughts upon new sensations,* upon their causes and results, intensifies the reactions to stimuli that normally would never reach consciousness. Do you want to know how to make a uterine contraction *hurt* during labor? Inquire of the woman before it starts where the last one hurt her. Agree that it was a bad pain. Put your hand on the uterus and feel it beginning to contract, then say briskly, "Now it's going to hurt. Try to tell me when the pain is at its height. Grip my hand; set your teeth; concentrate on your pain; close your eyes and suffer!!" Then you will see a woman having pain! Some researchers have attempted to measure the intensity of pain during contractions by just such a foolish procedure, unwit-tingly causing the pain they are attempting to measure.

This brings us within sight of the influence of suggestion. As education in childbirth is largely concerned with protecting women against the evils of false suggestion, so helpful suggestion is used during the conducting of natural labor as a means of infiltrating the subconscious with truth. If those who attend women in labor view helpful suggestion with disfavor, must they continue to inflict strong and harmful suggestion upon women who would be willing to accept the truth?

For suggestion works either way, whether it is intended or not. The physician who scorns the use of mental reinforcement has overlooked the fact that by actions, thoughts, and sympathies he or she has unwittingly applied the most powerful negative suggestion. During pregnancy the doctor has searched for abnormalities, has suggested the possibility of illness and danger. By the promise of drugs and anesthetics he (or she) has introduced his own belief in their necessity, and therefore has suggested that the patient will have pain to bear. By his or her manner the obstetrician has conveyed the idea that he or she is guardian against the assaults of mysterious and harmful eventualities. Further, the drama of labor is awe-inspiring to the average woman who has not been educated in what her own experience in giving birth will be.

When she enters the hospital, unprepared, the whole atmosphere may become a potent agent of harmful suggestion. The rubber gloves, expectant searchings down below, and quiet steps awaken in a woman's mind a host of fears and doubts. She may presume, and not unjustly, that the climax of all this must fulfill her worst and most vivid imaginings. When she is taken into the delivery room, its polished furnishings, the instruments laid out in scintillating readiness before her eyes, the mask, the gown, all suggest that this is no simple affair. Her conscious mind remains alert, and her body misinterprets its sensations. Ultimately, these false suggestions are blotted out by anesthetics and drugs.

But if anesthetics are required to circumvent the prevalent influences of false and harmful suggestion, why, in order to avoid anesthesia, is the use of true and helpful suggestion so often tabooed? The truth of natural labor is that there is no discomfort greater than healthy women are willing to bear. That is why women in labor are so susceptible to suggestion, if their prenatal education has prepared them for what to expect as a natural function.

We must also emphasize the *necessity for teamwork*. We cannot expect women who have been trained to carry out the procedures to be successful if, upon arrival at the hospital, a number is assigned to them and instead of a friendly greeting they are commanded to do as they are told with the "You-have-not-come-here-to-tell-*us*-what-to-do!" attitude. I do not wish to exaggerate this type of reception extended to both husbands and wives, but it does sometimes still happen.

As for the organization of trained teams, all those who educate or care for a pregnant woman should combine to follow the natural childbirth principles from early pregnancy through the weeks after the baby is born. The doctor, too, must carry through on this humane approach and should not be willing to interfere in a normal labor, or to do those things of which Aristotle so sternly warned us over two thousand years ago. If we interfere with nature there is a price to pay.

Of course, whether or not one is successful in protecting the woman from her fears or from other forms of pain, she must not be allowed to suffer. The scars of physical pain do more to ruin a woman's life, her marriage, and her motherhood than is generally recognized. It is necessary for a woman to have a scar from a cesarean section, too often an emergency operation; but I would rather see the scar tissue of safe healing than the evidence of brain tissue incurably damaged by the shock of pain and terror.

Teamwork is essential, and there will be no good results without it. Today wives demand to be taught about childbirth and husbands are taking a great interest as well. All personnel involved in care of the pregnant woman also need to know what is to be expected of them. Today many hospital staffs are organizing classes for those whose children are to be born under their care; this serves not only to impart information, but to establish a rapport between the expectant couples and those who will be serving them later, when they return for the birth.

It has become the custom in some childbirth classes to describe the various methods of inducing anesthesia or analgesia; different apparatuses are demonstrated and the women taught how they will be used. I have found that this introduces a serious fear that the rest of the instruction will be of no avail in labor. If the women are taught how these are to be utilized in labor and delivery, they expect that they *will* be required to relieve pain, and that the implication is that they will suffer.

But no difficulty arises if analgesia or anesthesia needs to be introduced when a woman is in labor. A few words of advice and instruction at that time if she needs pain relief, and she quickly understands. Since over 95 percent of women who have been adequately prepared for a natural labor neither need nor desire such relief, there is no need to discuss the various means of pain relief. The risk of introducing fear during pregnancy to conflict with faith is unjustifiable.

I have never taught a woman during pregnancy how to use an inhaler for a whiff of anesthetic. I have never instructed a patient in the use of a hypodermic syringe and needle in case she requires an injection, *nor have I ever tied down a pair of hands or legs!*

These deflections from "orthodox" prenatal and obstetric procedures have not prevented me, however, *from eliminating all possible discomforts from normal labor.* Analgesia should always be available, for pain is the enemy of childbirth, *not* its natural accompaniment. It is, therefore, the first principle of an obstetrician to avoid or to overcome by the quickest and safest method any discomfort a woman in labor feels is more intense than she wishes to bear. The means of *preventing* pain from occurring in childbirth is the cornerstone of prenatal education; not teaching the necessity for pain and the methods by which it may be relieved. It is the quality of the instruction that makes these alarming demonstrations of pain-relieving apparatuses unnecessary.

## ANESTHETICS AND ANALGESICS

In childbirth there are two types of pain, each of which requires a different method of treatment. The first, which is unavoidable, accidental, and relatively rare, arises from abnormalities in the mechanism of birth, which require interference to rectify. This is true primary pain. The second, which is avoidable and relatively common, arises from the emotion of fear, which causes tension, which in turn causes pain—the fear-tension-pain syndrome already mentioned, which is responsible for nearly all the discomforts of normal labor. It is a vicious circle, for the increase of any one of these magnifies all three.

No woman should be allowed to suffer pain in labor, and every method discovered by science should be used to prevent it. If there is true pain, anesthetics and analgesics should be exhibited at once, but the absence of severe discomfort contraindicates its use. *It is as great a crime to leave a woman alone in her agony and deny her relief from her suffering as it is to insist upon dulling the consciousness of a natural mother who desires above all things to be aware of the final reward of her efforts. Each of these two unforgivable errors is constantly committed.*

There should always be an anesthetic or analgesic apparatus at hand during labor. Women adequately trained for natural childbirth very rarely desire anesthesia and frequently refuse its use. Women who have not had the advantage of preparing themselves to give birth may have considerable pain, which they are causing themselves; therefore analgesia and anesthesia should be used. It must be recognized, however, that 95 percent of these deprived women could have had natural labors if they had been properly prepared.

When there is a *definite abnormality,* such as disproportion or a malpresentation or one of those rare complications that must be diagnosed and treated by an experienced obstetrician, drugs and anesthetics should be adequately applied under his or her instructions as quickly as possible. *That is one of the greatest benefits anesthesia has brought to humanity, and when a woman suffers the pain of abnormality in childbirth it should never be withheld.*

The administration of anesthetics and analgesics should have definite indication in obstetrics as it has in every other branch of medicine or surgery. Pain is the most frequent justification; it does not matter whether the pain is secondary to fear or whether it is primarily physical. Natural childbirth mothers have no fear and therefore little discomfort. Because the discomfort is minimal, few, if any, of these prepared women demand relief.

When deep anesthesia is required, a skilled and experienced anesthetist should be called in. The reagent to be used must be carefully selected after consultation between the obstetrician and the anesthetist. One method of pain relief is induced by deadening certain nerves in the pelvis with injections of anesthetic agents. When this method, in the hands of a highly skilled performer, is completely successful, it has certain physical advantages; but it has disadvantages that make unlikely its permanent or general place in normal obstetrics. It requires the constant attention of a specially trained and efficient staff, not only while it is being administered, but also after the baby is born. Apart from the possibility of physical injury there are serious risks to the mental processes of a woman who, although conscious, does not feel the sensations of childbirth. When she hears the first cry of her baby, the normal flood of mother love is restricted by the absence of the pride of personal achievement. She may have a sense of failure and resent the fact that she did not take an active part in its birth.

Analgesics do not relieve severe physical pain. They are sometimes used to relieve pain resulting from the influence of fear and tension in an otherwise normal labor. By their administration the senses are numbed and the pain-causing tension relieved. Such analgesia for short periods is the least harmful method of restoring confidence and releasing tension. If, however, too much is given or it is continued too long, risks are incurred both to the mother and the child.

One of my early colleagues stated that "the relief of pain by drugs is also a powerful means of conquering fear, and drugs are available which in my judgment provide a much simpler method. Incidentally, though the careful administration of drugs demands much sacrifice on the part of the doctor, it is probable that it is less exacting than the instruction in Read's technique, and that is a consideration to busy men and women."[3]

Does this really suggest that had I ever been unfortunate enough to be busy I would have learned that the easiest, safest, and simplest way to cure a poisoned mind is to poison the body as well? I have tried both methods, and find drugs more exacting, more uncertain, and less satisfactory. The women under my care have no doubt which they prefer.

## MISUSES OF ANESTHESIA AND ANALGESIA

I must emphasize once more the unforgivable custom of anesthetizing a woman as routine, or the giving of tranquilizers and analgesics *irrespective of her wishes and demands.* In the British Isles, the United States, and many other civilized countries this astonishing and deplorable interference is accepted as normal treatment, without any clinical indication for its exhibition.

When we read the opinions of authorities from all parts of the world on analgesia and anesthesia, as well as the experimental and clinical reports from those who are never likely to be authorities, we become lost in a tangle of words. I am reminded of one eminent obstetrician who commented: "Obstetrics presents a large and varied field for *practice* and observation for the *student* of anesthesia." Walt Disney could hardly do justice to the silly symphony of obstetric analgesia.

I could only picture a crowd of men in white coats and large hornrimmed glasses, seeking fame and fortune by searching for a weapon with which to protect all women from an enemy which in 95 percent of cases did not exist, their chosen method of protection being to risk the life of the woman and her baby by using that weapon upon them, rather than upon the enemy they erroneously presumed to be present! It did not seem to matter how a woman was robbed of her consciousness or sensations; the more awkward the means of administration, or the longer the name, so much the more likely was it that fame might be achieved. Simple inhalation of an analgesic agent was soon left behind. Drugs were injected under the skin, into the stomach, into veins, deep into muscles, into the rectum, into the spinal cord, into the sacral nerves—in fact, anywhere that they can be put into the human body. A mid-1980 felt-graphic visual presentation for childbirth education classes includes one fully jointed baby, one fetal-position baby (two-sided), one silhouette of the mother's abdomen (side view), one pelvis, one umbilical cord of yarn, and *twelve* anesthetic indicators! These felt syringes and needles were each labeled in descending order illustrating the site of injection: tranquilizer, barbiturate, narcotic, scopolamine, spinal, saddle block, epidural, caudal, pudendal, paracervical, local. One needle was left blank for some other possibility.

The length of the names of these inflictions increased as the field of operations spread. Pentothal and thioethamyl swept aside our old friend paraldehyde, which appears to be equally effective whether introduced from below or from above; but sodium-prophymethyl-carbinyl-allyl barbiturate scopolamine won in a canter. Robert A. Hingson did magnificent work upon the use of anesthetic injected either around or within the spinal cord.[4] In many abnormalities and illnesses his methods have been of life-saving service; but, unfortunately, enthusiasts have mutilated thousands of normal labors by this dangerous and unjustifiable procedure, in which nearly all babies are delivered by forceps extraction, the majority of mothers have deep episiotomies performed, and the women do not know the joy of spontaneous delivery of their child. It is a painless, sensationless birth, without emotional rectitude. There is no sense of personal achievement. An offspring is produced by a magician from a paralyzed birth canal.

The development of spinal anesthesias has led to the proliferation of cesarean sections in which the mother can be "awake" for the birth; nine months of happy anticipation of her highest natural ambition, finished off by unnatural interference! Are there any advantages in this to offset the disadvantages of spinal anesthesia? Professor Nicholson Eastman, one of the great obstetric authorities, believes spinal anesthesia is to be blamed for more maternal deaths than any other form of anesthesia.[5] How long, oh, how long will this nonsense go on? Can the scientific mind see no further than drugs and anesthetics? Why the urge to persist in this search for an elixir to cure all ills, which in the vast majority of women are preventable with the utmost safety?

I find it most reprehensible that such a gross misunderstanding of the phenomena of childbirth should be allowed to infiltrate and persist in the procedures of so great a science. It can only indicate a deplorable lack of clinical observation, or a domineering and pompous attitude toward parturient women that says: "We are producing this baby for you. What we do is not your business, and what you want does not concern us."

I have received from far and wide some remarkable reports of inhumane and unsympathetic treatment of well-informed and intelligent women during their labors.

I do not promise "painless childbirth" and never have done so. Some women have their babies with no pain, but there is a certain amount of discomfort in most first labors, either backache or stretching feelings. If a mother and her attendants understand how to overcome these unpleasant sensations, they become of so little consequence that only three or four women in one hundred wish for or need partial or total insensibility.

Let it be clearly understood that I am not criticizing the justifiable uses of analgesia and/or anesthesia. It is the *misuse* of methods, machines, techniques, and reagents to which I call attention. Any discomfort that can be overcome by the use of light obstetric analgesia or tranquilizing agents can also more helpfully be avoided or relieved by reassuring the woman, helping her into a more comfortable, advantageous position, and seeing that she becomes physically relaxed. This is not theoretical, but is the experience of thousands of obstetricians and midwives throughout the world.

Let me summarize this matter:

1. For the perfect labor anesthesia is unnecessary because there is no pain.

2. The pain of labor should be *prevented* from occurring rather than obliterated.

3. Where the woman's ability to relax is absent and pain-producing emotions occur, analgesics should be used. Carefully administered pain relief during labor is one of the greatest gifts that our profession has made to civilization.

4. The misuse of drugs and anesthetics is the cause, directly or indirectly, of a large number of the complications of labor. It is the cause, not only of maternal and infantile morbidity or mortality in many cases, but of ill health and domestic unhappiness in the lives of a great many women.

Anesthesia is only a veneer to cover up pain, trauma, and damage. It is sound and right in every way *if* used correctly in order to dispel pain. But if it is used in normal labor as a routine or to alter nature's intentions for either mother or baby, it is wrong—morally, ethically, and physically!

How much better it is for both mother and baby if the pain and damage can be kept from occurring in the first place.

*The safest and most effective way to minimize the discomforts of childbirth is to enable a woman, by preparation for, and understanding attention at, labor, to have her baby naturally.*

## CHAPTER 12

# The Four Pillars
# of Parturition

**M**any of my friends have asked me to give a detailed account of the conduct of labor embodying the fundamental principles of what has become known as "natural childbirth." It will be necessary to begin by accepting the teaching of our great masters of obstetrics so far as the ordinary routine of obstetrics is concerned. *The general principles of good obstetrics must be recognized and practiced by all who undertake attendance upon women in labor.*

The obstetrician must be fully prepared to meet or provide for all emergencies, and, since chapters on the conduct of labor are usually concerned with the imminence of the unforeseen, it would be vain repetition to delve into the abnormal. Let it be presumed, therefore, that all the sound general principles are employed for the safety and care of women so far as the purely physical process of childbirth is concerned.

Here we will examine the conduct of labor from the point of view of the woman herself, her mental condition and changing emotional state. This chapter is not intended as a panacea for all the ills of labor, and will have but little influence in rectifying genuinely abnormal conditions or occurrences. But it does shed light on troubles that may appear to be relatively unimportant but that in reality are the roots of many serious evils.

*Elation, relaxation, inattentiveness,* and *exaltation* are the four pillars of parturition upon which the conduct of labor depends, each in its proper place maintaining, supporting, and controlling the impulses, both sensory and motor, upon which the neuromuscular harmony of the function relies.

Parturition is the great event in the reproductory cycle of woman. Although in recent years prenatal care has become increasingly important and its value fully recognized, labor is the real excitement for the patient and her attendants. But the nature of labor depends basically upon the efficacy of prenatal education, care, and, if need be, treatment, and the act of parturition should be complementary to the conduct of pregnancy.

## ONSET OF LABOR (ELATION)

There is still some controversy on what indicates the establishment of true labor. The waters may leak for a number of days before labor starts—in fact, on several occasions I have observed that the water has stopped, the bag of membranes apparently closing. The "show" may appear some days before labor is established, but this sign is probably the most common of the three usual indicators of labor.

The recurrence of contractions or tightness of the uterus may be misleading, for some women who have not been prepared for labor and are still wrapped in anxiety may have contractions of the circular fibers in the lower part of the uterus for two weeks, three weeks, or even longer before the longitudinal fibers go into action and true labor starts. I have met women who believed in all seriousness that they were in labor from ten to fourteen days before the arrival of the child, but when the signs and symptoms that they had observed were discussed with them, it became clear that true labor had lasted for not more than twelve hours.

It is my opinion that the onset of parturition is best diagnosed by rhythmical contractions at shortening intervals, and a sense of generalized tightness of the abdomen without pain so long as the woman remains relaxed. The intervals will decrease from a quarter of an hour to five minutes or even less.

Women are all asked to go to the hospital as soon as it is established that labor is well under way. *Multipara* (women who have already had two or more children) recognize true labor contractions and waste no time, since they know how rapidly labor may develop under the influence of relaxation. *Primigravida* (women who are having their first child) have more time. My practice is to have them check with me on the telephone as to when to leave for the hospital.

## TO THE OBSTETRIC ATTENDANTS

The arrival at the hospital or birth center should be a cheerful event, and it is essential that those who greet patients know the value of maintaining an atmosphere of cordiality and confidence. After admittance procedures, the parturient woman is taken to a labor room and prepared for labor in accordance with instructions from her physician.

*Look upon emotional stress as the great enemy of the patient;* neither say, do, nor insinuate anything that will stimulate anxiety or fear of intervention. Think, therefore, what does she fear? She may fear pain and may believe it to be essential. Her contractions are spoken of as "pains," and what are known as "pains" must be painful. *When will our nursing and medical professions cease to use this hideous term?* They are contractions, and if contractions, each becomes an effort to an end, each effort one more push that brings her baby nearer. Each contraction may be stronger than the last—therefore more effective, therefore more excellent—but if a "pain," the stronger it is the more intense the pain, and as the next one starts, the greater the expectation of agony.

She may also fear intervention—that others will interfere with her relaxation and control of her own labor, with routine uses of intravenous solutions, internal or external monitors, too frequent vaginal exams, injections, lack of freedom to move about or to have her wishes fulfilled, and so on. Fear, or emotional stress, is the great enemy of childbirth. Even women who are well prepared and unafraid may be placed under a great deal of emotional stress by uncooperative surroundings or staff and unnecessary interventions.

*Anything that disturbs the confidence and peacefulness of the mother disrupts the neuromuscular harmony of her labor,* and blocks the normal flow of the process to a lesser or greater degree. Attendants can stimulate confidence in the woman by quiet attention to her needs and comfort, respect for her privacy and wishes, and encouragement that she is doing well. She should be helped to relax during contractions from the beginning of labor, and subjected to no emotional stress caused by rudeness or unnecessary routines. The attendants (including her husband) can provide emotional support as she desires, but without in any way threatening her privacy or rights.

## FIRST STAGE OF LABOR (RELAXATION)

As early as possible after the patient's admittance to the hospital, my visit is made. This is not a hurried rush in and "Glad you've started! Get on with it—I'll be back in time" sort of visit, but a prolonged stay, possibly for an hour or more.

Elation, rejoicing, and a strong sense of contentment and relief are the natural emotional reactions to the onset of labor, as was mentioned earlier. As her physician or midwife, be interested in her elation, encourage it, and mildly share it; she will feel that you are in harmony with her and will more readily accomplish relaxation of both mind and body as the contractions become firmer. Then as the spirit of jocularity wears off, as it will, the reality of her task will dawn upon her consciousness with a calm confidence.

It must not be overlooked that sometimes the most cheerful and apparently carefree woman may be very frightened. Beware of an excess of laughter between contractions; this is often a manifestation of tension of the mind and may well turn to tears when real effort and control become necessary in the later stages of labor. This anxiety or anticipation near the beginning of the final episode must be overcome by kindly but careful explanation of the sensations she is experiencing. During the visit a calm, reassuring, but firm kindliness is desirable.

If relaxation has been practiced and acquired as a habit, it will easily be accomplished during first-stage contractions. Complete relaxation of legs, arms, face, and therefore mind is the secret of a calm, quick labor. The points to remember are the few deep breaths to aid relaxation as the uterus comes into action, and that the eyes should be open and the face relaxed—that is, no frown or puckered brow, no screwed-up eyes, no pursed lips or grinding teeth. There is no need for these exhibitions; they do no good. They are either demands for sympathy or manifestations of anxiety, and they increase neuromuscular tension.

How many doctors have been told, "Everything seemed much easier when you arrived"? The importance of the obstetrician or midwife's presence is not sufficiently realized, and one who fills this high office should be sure that he or she does not disappoint the woman who relies so implicitly upon his or her judgment, knowledge, and skill by appearing disinterested.

With the utmost patience, persevere until your patient is well relaxed during the contractions of first-stage active labor. Such patience will be amply rewarded. Speak quietly and with understanding; be honest in your advice and gentle in manner; point out once again the significance of these first-stage contractions: "They are pulling open the outlet of the womb. Step by step it expands and muscle is collected up and shortened, so that it cannot close again until the baby has passed through. The uterus must be left alone—it can do all this without any effort to help on your part. Consider it a machine apart from yourself, and in due course the dilatation of the outlet will be complete. There is no hurry—the door will open, but you must not make the work harder for the uterus by tightening the door. If you are rigid and squeeze up your face, then the muscles of the outlet will squeeze up, too. The uterus is astoundingly strong and persistent; the result of your resistance will be pain. But the more completely limp your muscles become, so much the more elastic will be the mouth of the womb, and so much less discomfort will you experience."

Women frequently comment on how different labor becomes once relaxation is obtained. They should be encouraged to maintain this state because it is common sense that an elastic opening is not only more easily but more quickly expanded. *Until a controlled relaxation is obtained by the patient, the physician should not leave.*

A peaceful, confident atmosphere should be sustained and a close watch kept upon any untoward trend in conversation. The acute sensitiveness of women in labor must be constantly borne in mind. If you wish to try to deceive them you will fail. They miss nothing, and have a way of turning over in their minds the things they see and the words they hear. They are keen observers, not only of their own actions, but of the reactions of those about them to every fresh event or incident. This keenness of their perception must be appreciated; every expression, movement, and incident is observed, and no word or action passes unnoticed, for the occasion demands their fullest concentration. Any communication from those in attendance that can possibly be construed as disturbing their peace is harmful.

Nothing is more irritating than noise and restlessness when relaxation is sought. Nothing is more exasperating than inconsequential chatter when the mind is occupied with an all-absorbing interest. Disturbing interludes of tune humming or muffled tap-dance rhythms on the bedside, frequent comings and goings, openings and closings, shufflings and solicitations, are thoughtless actions and indicate lack of human understanding. Women in labor also abhor loud voices, terse commands, and bright lights.

The patient's physical comfort should be attended to without ostentation. She should be reminded that the bag of waters in which the baby lies may break, and that this is perfectly normal.

Care should be taken that adequate nourishment is given during the first stage of labor. It is a great mistake to leave a woman for ten or twelve hours without adequate nourishment. She is doing hard muscular work during this time and requires fortification, as we all do when we are occupied with physical exercise. Her hot or cold drink—whichever she prefers—may be given without any need for gratitude.

When the opening of the cervix is about two inches, or five centimeters, in diameter, a series of new sensations will be experienced, which will require explanation. It is not a question of physical pain that arises, but one of the emotional attack to which most women are subjected at this time. They wonder if they can possibly carry on; they feel the strain of labor, presenting an added impediment to complete relaxation.

This is *the first emotional menace of labor.* There are some women who, finding it very difficult to overcome this phase, become restless and, by their inability to relax, have a certain amount of real discomfort. A word of encouragement or explanation during this phase is of the greatest help, and should never be withheld. With the assistance of a nurse or medical attendant and husband who recognize the importance of this change, a calm and purposeful attitude toward labor can be reestablished. The contractions become stronger but the ability to relax improves.

*Natural childbirth is not just sitting by and allowing what comes to take its course!* The law of nature has a host of enemies not only in the mind and body of civilized woman but in the good intentions of those who are concerned with her well-being. An obstetrician should be a private detective who watches, guards, and unostentatiously accompanies a woman during her parturition. Should unpredictable emergency arise, he or she is able to meet it, fully equipped from the various departments of modern science with devices to overcome the misadventure, and safely deliver the woman of her baby.

At three in the morning we may be harassed by ruminations and imaginings that raise doubts in our minds and even warp our judgment. It takes a strong moral courage to be able to set out all the facts and review the situation with a calm, logical precision, particularly if the patient has detected a weakening in the support you have given her. During labor, a woman can spot a doubt in the doctor's mind as quickly as a falcon sees a rat in the stubble. However good an actor or however suave a humbug, confidence has no counterfeit. It is neither looks, words, nor works, but a special sense borne on the atmosphere of truth and inflexible honesty of purpose.

But always be on the watch. Concentrated observation need not be obtrusive, but it must be accurate and keen. You are more likely to find abnormalities by delineating the boundaries of good health than you are to find good health by concentrating upon real or phantom abnormalities. Your tranquillity must be tempered with vigilance lest any harmful thing occur. It is astonishing how often patience will overcome difficulties and solve the host of mythical problems the long, quiet, waiting hours of night will create in fertile minds.

In general outline, I have drawn attention to some of the advantages of personal interest in a woman in labor, but the evils of its absence are not usually recognized. All sensitive women are hurt by friends who appear disinterested when friendship is most salutary. When, in times of anxiety, the support we expect of those in whom we have implicit faith is withdrawn, and when our self-confidence and fortitude are severely tested by the manifestations of a mysterious assailant, we long for the comforting voice of calm. However well prepared and confident in her ability to achieve a satisfactory and natural birth a woman may be, *ultimately her success depends on each individual of the team of people* to whose influence she has been subjected during the changing phases of her reproductivity. She does not want to hear soft words and sob stuff, but explanation, instruction, and encouragement. She wants to hear that all is going well, that the baby is fine and that she is conducting her job in an admirable manner. If she is left alone and not told these things, she may assume all is not going well and become alarmed with each new, though normal, phenomenon of labor.

Hospital organization, we know, makes constant attendance by medical personnel upon all women in labor extremely difficult, but *no patient should ever be left alone!* No greater curse can fall upon a young woman whose first labor has begun than the crime of enforced loneliness. Why cannot every obstetrician realize the enormity of this medieval torture? Library

Hear from women who have experienced this truly human attention what aid it gave to them; I suspect it will make you visualize their labors as something almost unbelievable. But observe as well whether your patient wants you there or not; some women dislike intensely the presence of anyone at all, and a good many do not want the doctor until they feel they must have him or her. Tactfully find out why, if you can. It may teach you a lot about your patient that you had not previously suspected.

### THE TRANSITION

During the latter part of the first stage it is of vital importance that nothing be said or done to allow tension. It is an interesting fact that neuromuscular tension is not relieved by analgesic drugs, for its influence emanates not only from the conscious but also from the subsconscious mind. Long after consciousness is lost the anesthetized patient will exhibit a picture of unrestrained anxiety; the reaction of muscular tension to a partially narcotized mind can be attested to by every medical student who has been called upon by the anesthetist to restrain the coal heaver, longshoreman, or powerful seaman during the early stages of anesthesia.

The final dilatation of the cervix is the phase that calls for the greatest control. At this time a woman demands that her courage be sustained, for real discomfort may be present in the most natural cases. Normally, a cervix is dilated much more rapidly from three inches to full than from half an inch to one and a half inches. The last few contractions increase the tension in the already well-stretched tissues of cervix and lower uterine segment, and the normal *nociceptors,* or pain sense organs, record pain stimuli as reactions to stretching and the small lacerations of tissue that may occur, for not infrequently such contractions are followed by a definite show of blood. Occurring in the area of the *sacrum,* or lower end of the spine, in about 50 percent of the cases, this tension is felt as an acute backache, and sometimes persists between contractions.

This discomfort is accompanied by a second change in the attitude of the woman toward her labor. Not infrequently it is the first time that she has been aware of any physical uneasiness, and it awakes in her mind many fears lest the backache resolve into a more severe pain. Fear definitely assaults the minds of many women just before full dilatation of the uterus, and this is the *second emotional menace of labor.*

The backache, however, only persists for about nine to twelve contractions, a fact that a woman should be told, for a temporary discomfort is much more easily borne than one which is likely to persist. She should also be told to breathe slowly and deeply to help stay relaxed. *It is possible to relax efficiently* in spite of the fact that respiration is a little quicker and deeper. The backache can be relieved by firm rubbing, or more often by really hard pressure on the sacrum.

If, at this stage of labor, there is pain anywhere else, it is probably due to some factor not usually present in normal labor. For instance, acute pain in the twelfth dorsal or upper lumbar region is not uterine in origin, but arises in the structures that take the strain of labor but that, if healthy, should do so without discomfort. Occasionally a woman will vomit during this latter part of the first stage of labor.

On one occasion I delivered a multipara, aged forty-two, of her second child, the first one having been born elsewhere some eight years before. She had accepted all the teaching she instinctively knew to be right, had practiced her relaxation to the best of her ability, and had taken a great interest in all the information I had given her upon the mechanism of labor. So little had appeared to be going on in her labor that I was not sent for for some time. When I arrived, I found her lying on her side, quiet and quite contented except, as she explained to me, for the considerable aching in her back. It was not a pain, she said, but a dull ache; it extended through to the front, and she felt it quite definitely along the lower backbone and above the bone in front.

When this occurs, I always do the same thing: I turn the patient over onto her back with pillows under her shoulders and the head well up, and during the next contraction I bring the knees upward and outward as far as possible; this almost invariably removes the pain in the front and relieves the discomfort in the back. This is, of course, different from the sharp acute pain that the persistent occipito posterior will complain of just after full dilatation of the cervix. I explained to my patient the use of the gas apparatus, having placed it, as usual, in her hand so she could use it when necessary. She said there was no need for it, but it lay on the bed beside her so that she could use it if she wanted.

She told me that the pain in front disappeared after one or two contractions in that position, but that there was still a considerable ache in the back. She thought, possibly, that being forty-two her bones were a little stiffer than they should be; otherwise she felt quite convinced that there was no need even for the ache that she felt over the lower sacrum. She had not, up to that time, been using contractions very well, so I explained to her the best method of using them. "Wait," I told her, "until the contraction is at the top—you will understand what I mean—then draw a long breath and hold it. Do not push violently, but just lean on it." She did this and told me it was much more comfortable.

Her contractions came at about six- to seven-minute intervals; in between them she slept. She was quite comfortable. When she awakened for a contraction, she said, "Now it is coming," and we lifted up her knees and let her push her feet against our hands. She hung onto her knees once or twice, but managed to do very well without exertion, and I told her not to press violently, as the baby would come easily. Her baby was born quite perfectly about an hour later.

On another occasion, on a Christmas morning a primipara was nearing second stage. She was getting good contractions; my opinion was that they were contractions that should have fitted in with the second stage, but she told me she had no inclination whatever to help them, and by relaxing in between times she was extremely comfortable, got on with her job in the most excellent way, and did everything she was told. She seemed very happy.

An hour later I was quite sure the contractions were second-stage ones, although she had no sort of urge to push down herself. So I told her to take a deep breath when the next one got to its height, and to "lean on it"; that is, to hold her breath and let herself contract in the upper abdomen so as to bear down slightly. She understood that well, and told me it gave her a good deal of comfort; she liked the feeling, but her back was painful. Now, this pain in her back was not in the sacrum, the usual area, but was more in the region of the second and third lumbar vertebra. When I pressed on those, she said it relieved it a little but not altogether. She then turned over onto her back, drew up her knees and pushed against my hands—or, rather, my hands on one side and the nurse's on the other—held her knees and pulled on them, at the same time opening her legs as widely as she could. With the first contraction the baby's head appeared at the vulva, but after this progress became very slow. I watched several contractions carefully and could see no obvious reasons for the delay, but then I noted that she was arching her back when she pushed down. Since that is an unnatural position, I showed her how to round her back with her head forward. She said this was much more comfortable, and, indeed, seemed to work well. Suddenly, after three or four contractions in the rounded position, a loud, dull crack sounded in her back. I asked her whether she had felt it and she said she had, and from that moment she had no further pain in her back at all. She herself said to me, "That seems to have cured the pain in my back." This was interesting, because I am persuaded that a good deal of the pain in the back during labor is owing to the posture in which the patient lies and the posture adopted during contractions. This particular patient had no pain whatever from that point on in any place at all.

## SECOND STAGE OF LABOR (INATTENTIVENESS)

Sometimes a uterus calls for external help immediately after the cervix is fully dilated, but at other times the cervix may be fully dilated for some time without any reflex demand for assistance from the extrinsic muscles of expulsion, as in the cases mentioned earlier. Therefore it is advisable to introduce during the contraction a respiratory stimulus to this important reflex.

In the first stage, breathing is naturally free and easy, increasing automatically in rate and depth as dilatation progresses. After each contraction it is wise for the mother to take one or two deep breaths as the uterus relaxes, as one would naturally do after the prolonged use or strain of any muscle in the body. But in the second stage, as a contraction develops to its greatest height, a deep inspiration is made for the bearing-down effort.

Once the cervix is dilated fully, the woman should take a deep breath and hold it at the height of the contraction, even if she doesn't feel a bearing-down reflex. Not infrequently, after doing this once or twice she will begin to bear down, and will remark upon the satisfaction the effort affords her. The mother should keep her mouth relaxed and open during the contraction, breathing out slowly as she bears down, and taking another deep breath as needed. Once the reflex is started in that way it continues, and the distinctive phenomena of the second stage become increasingly apparent. With the uterine contractions somatic relaxation is impossible, but between them it is easier than at any other time during labor; in fact, as the uterus works more intensely in its effort to expel the baby, a relaxed sleep in the intervals between contractions is commonly observed.

If the woman's confidence has been maintained by a sympathetic comprehension of her reactions to psychical and physical stress, she will pass quietly into the second stage, with its lowered mental appreciation and its modified interpretation of sensory stimuli. As this *inattentiveness* occurs, she demonstrates the relative inactivity of her senses of discretion and discrimination; she becomes oblivious to her surroundings and careless of her appearance, expression, and speech. Normally—that is, in the absence of any dominating fear—she is devoid of any consciousness of herself and employs all her energies in the fulfillment of the immediate purpose.

Sit always at the *head* of your patient, for this is the center of activities. To sit, as is so frequently done, at the other end is wrong. Not only is your patient unable to see you, but she naturally concentrates her mind upon what is going on down below, feeling that you would not be there unless you expected something to happen. But in reality the doctor is frequently there long before he or she expects anything at all to happen at that end of the body that is worthy of attention. Certain attentions may have to be made below from time to time, especially if preparation has not been efficient and complete, but surely a competent nurse in attendance can deal with this just as satisfactorily as the doctor.

During the second-stage contractions, explain carefully to your patient how she can help her contracting uterus. This requires considerable experience. Do not allow her to be violent in the expulsive stage, because there is no need for such exertion. She must take a full inspiration and bear down only when and as the uterus demands. With a first baby this is important, for unnecessary tiredness or fatigue, which should not occur, may create difficulty in the final dilatation of the outlet.

A patient of mine began labor with her third child. She had come to me rather late in pregnancy, telling me that she had had considerable trouble with her children before, and found it difficult to believe in the teaching of natural childbirth although, having heard of it, she wished to try. She practiced her relaxation assiduously, and did her exercises as well as she could, but she was stiff and rather tender in the back; she did not have what one would call a good obstetric back.

During her labor I asked her whether she would like me to sit in the room next to hers or whether I should be with her, and she was very emphatic about my not leaving her. She preferred absolute quiet and peace, and I must say that the nurse assisted me in that. There was not a sound of any sort—even walking was on tiptoe—and my patient relaxed beautifully during the contractions and slept in between them. Then I noticed suddenly that there was a drooping of the eyes and a slight listlessness. She was obviously passing into the second stage, but not before proclaiming that her back was extremely sore; there was an aching pain low down in the sacral region. This was relieved by pressure and rubbing, and we went quietly and patiently on. I told her that all that was required was patience and hard work, and that if she felt any pain I would certainly do something at once to relieve it.

And so, from the beginning of the second stage, she became a typically inattentive woman. She found it rather difficult to hold her breath and to—as I describe it—"lean on it," and also at first she quite definitely tensed her pelvic floor whenever a contraction started. The nurse, who was watching the contractions from below —as I naturally could not see—told me that there was definite contraction of the whole pelvic floor, the anus being quite drawn in when the uterine push was at its height. We overcame that with a little instruction, and got on well. The pain in the back became rather more acute. The patient could not get comfortable or get into a good position. As soon as she raised her knees she got a cramp, and so I decided that, since the head was obviously coming down well and there was slight distention of the anus already, she should turn onto her back and adopt the semisitting position I frequently ask patients to adopt at that time. As she did so, the very first contraction seemed to present a different picture: the head came down until it was visible, the pain in the back was much less acute, and after about four or five contractions at long intervals—ten minutes or so—the head was born perfectly.

I do not know the cause of that state in the second stage which dulls the conscious brain, but, from watching closely all the signs and symptoms, the first thing I should like to investigate would be the oxygen metabolism. The enormous muscular exertion must produce chemical changes altering carbon dioxide, oxygen, and lactic acid balance. On these lines the nature of the second stage of labor anesthesia can be explained. It is upon suboxidation that the conscious brain fades out and the instinctive reflex activities of the subconscious are made free to act. The ideal anesthetic state during labor is the subconscious, not the unconscious. This state is frequently present as a natural process in normal labor, and demands understanding, not narcosis.

For your patient's sake, be interested in her mental and physical well-being during labor; for your own sake, observe closely her reactions to its demands. You are dealing with several different women during labor; the woman who is reacting to her social environment in the early first stage has little physical and mental resemblance to she who reacts to the uncontrollable neuromuscular energies of the late second stage. The old saying that women are always unpredictable is never more true than in labor.

The course and progress of labor must be watched and followed in all its stages, particularly at the end of the first stage, when the second emotional menace of labor makes its subtle attack upon a woman. And so it may be again in the latter half of the second stage of labor, especially if the woman, strong and healthy, is bearing her first baby. The thick perineum must gradually be thinned out by successive uterine contractions until it can allow the baby's head to pass. It is so slow—there seems to be no progress, no advance—the weary hours hang heavily upon the attendant's expectation. The woman, inattentive and contented, is not aware of time.

When the head is in the midpelvic cavity—possibly the bag of waters or the baby's head is just showing—extra effort may be called for, providing that rest and relaxation are obtained between the contractions. Waken the patient to the conscious reality of her surroundings and be alert to advise her on how to get a relaxed outlet and the best method of mechanical advantage for her efforts. But do not presume that she is unaware of what is going on. *She may appear to be asleep and behave in a dull and inattentive state, but she is not asleep and will hear and understand everything as her contraction begins again.*

As the head advances through the birth canal and reaches the muscles that form the floor of the pelvis, a sensation of internal pressure is felt. Some women have described it as resistance, and it is the third occasion during labor when a large number of women feel a definite wave of fear and exasperation. It is at this time, when the baby's head may be only one inch from the outlet of the birth canal, that many women become frustrated and disappointed with efforts that they feel are of no avail. It is so marked that it has been termed the *third emotional menace of labor.*

The desire to escape, very largely exaggerated by the absence of discretion, may easily be misunderstood by those who have not examined this phenomenon closely. When a woman desires to escape from anything that she does not wish to experience, she may use all manner of wiles to obtain her object. Many will complain of agonizing pain while their pulse remains at seventy. Many will ask for anesthesia—not for pain, they will explain, but because they have "had enough." Some will say that they are completely exhausted and cannot possibly go on: "Will you please help me?" On occasions the attendant obstetrician will be told exactly what the patient thinks of him or her!

*Great care is needed on the part of the attendant not to be misled by emotional exhibitions and not to mistake them for physical discomforts.* Severe physical discomfort at this phase of the second stage of labor is extremely rare in a normal presentation of the child, a fact that has been told me after labor by a large number of women. Several women doctors, who have had their babies and observed the processes of physiological labor closely while they have been experiencing them and communicated their sensations to me, have explained afterward that in their opinion the most terrifying part of labor was the uncontrollable desire to *escape* at this third emotional menace. One went so far as to tell me that *I had not emphasized sufficiently the importance of this incident,* and that in spite of my reassurance, she had had considerable difficulty in accepting, at the time, the advice I gave her.

Now, this threat to a woman's self-control is in no way difficult to overcome. The method is that at the next contraction she should be told to *concentrate* and *push as firmly as she can,* for as soon as she exerts the maximum pressure all discomfort ceases and confidence is restored at once. The third menace of labor is negligible if it is met with a combative determined effort, for once the pelvic floor is adequately distended the head passes down the vagina rapidly and without discomfort.

#### CROWNING

As the head comes down onto the vulva it becomes visible, and the patient should be told that the baby can be seen. This is a most encouraging moment, but she should *not* be told it will be there in five minutes. It may take half an hour for a baby to be born after the head is first seen at the outlet, particularly if it is a first baby.

The contractions now should be used fully. When the vulva is dilated to about one and a half to two inches in diameter, the woman will feel the outlet stretching. This is natural, because the opening has to stretch. Since the sensation is one of burning, the woman must be forewarned, for it may be very frightening and may become acutely uncomfortable if not properly managed. *At this point all efforts to bear down should be stopped.* The burning varies in intensity but is rarely of such significance that the patient feels it desirable to resort to the analgesic inhaler. The sensation is intensified by an alarmed woman—she resists by squeezing up her pelvic muscles. An understanding attendant will overcome the slight and transient discomfort, as described below, and with full crowning of the head the sensation ceases.

This stretching of the vulva is rightly termed the *fourth emotional menace of labor.* Many feel that they must inevitably burst or tear and, in an effort to prevent this, will actually endeavor to contract the muscles of the pelvis in resistance to the oncoming head. Watch carefully the beginning signs of a contraction. If the patient automatically tenses up her pelvic muscles, if the anus is contracted and the muscles tense about the vulva, help her to relax. The woman must be reassured that she will not burst, but that she must relax and allow her baby to come in a quiet and controlled manner, without pushing, and that the sensation will disappear as the vulva is more fully dilated. I have wondered at times whether the dilatation of the vulva in some way or other does paralyze certain sensory nerves, for as soon as the vulva is nearly fully dilated it loses the sensation of burning and becomes quite anesthetic.

The absence of tension from the muscles comprising the floor of the pelvis, the relaxation of the vaginal sphincter, and, what is more difficult to explain, the apparent increased elasticity of the skin of the vulva, facilitates the passage of the infant through the birth canal. The uterus, of itself, will slowly urge the child forward. *During contractions the woman should be told to breathe in and out rapidly.* It is a comforting dispensation of nature that the pushing reflex can be overcome voluntarily at this stage of labor, and that a woman can breathe freely without giving way to the urge to bear down.

In this way the vulva is gradually distended—and it should be distended gradually without any violence, for tears of the skin and even of the muscles are frequently produced unnecessarily because a woman is encouraged to bear down violently.

Allow full crowning of the head and *do not hurry by pressure from behind or efforts to stretch the vulva over the forehead;* it will slide over quite easily without tear or injury if left to itself. Not infrequently a woman is unconscious of the birth of the baby's head. There is no doubt about the relative anesthesia of the perineum during the late second stage and for some minutes after the child has been born.

And again, when the head is born there is no immediate hurry

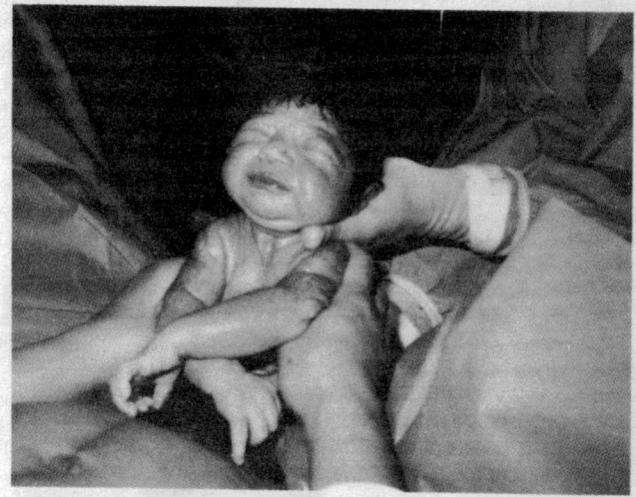

Baby emerges toward mother, mother assisting

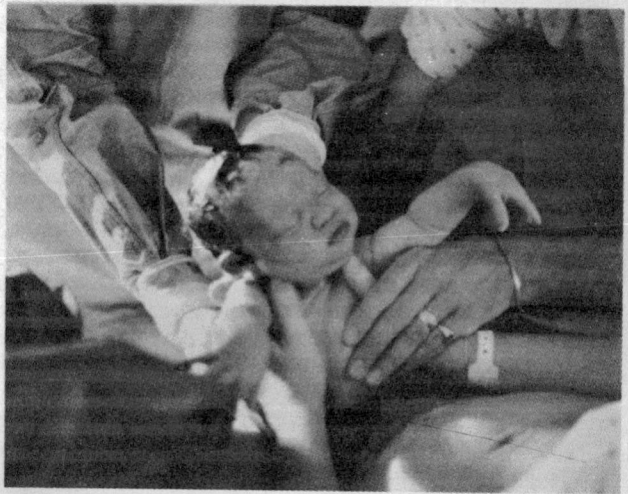

Father assists the birth also

if all has gone smoothly. It may cry before the shoulders arrive. Check the cord; a hand may be out of place; resist expulsion by violent contraction, or you may have a tear by shoulder or elbow. Support the head in the right hand and allow the child to awake its mother from her light inattentiveness. With the next contraction, the attendant may require gentle assistance from the woman and invite her to bear down. It is my custom to wait until pulsation has practically ceased before severing the cord, even if it is four or five minutes.

One of my patients provides a good example of several of these phenomena. Eight years previously, at eight months pregnancy, she had been delivered of twins by forceps. One had died, and the remaining twin was brain-damaged. She had come under my care for this birth, and was very nervous and alarmed about it all. But her labor went well, and there was not much discomfort until near the end of the first stage. Then she began to feel a certain amount of discomfort low down in the back, which was different from any previous sensation. I pointed out to her that if she would put up with one or two of those twinges in the back—which, by the way, entirely disappeared when I pressed firmly over the sacral region—they would pass off quite quickly and that it was just a phase in the labor.

Then the really interesting part of her labor began. She had a prolonged and good contraction, lost her smile, and became a serious woman starting her second stage. She flung her head back, and when I looked to see whether there was any change at all down below, she said, "Oh, take off those clothes—it is quite impossible to be a lady now!" She lost all her natural reserve and shyness and the rather unusual refinement of speech that characterized her. She had one or two more similar contractions, and I said, "Now, I want you to draw a deep breath and find out whether you have any inclination to bear down." She tried this and found that it was not only pleasant, but that it was a distinct relief to her just to give a gentle push down when a contraction was at its height.

From that moment onward I saw one of the most perfect examples of what I have so frequently described as the inattentiveness of the second stage—the phenomenon I believe to be so important and to which so little attention is paid in modern obstetrics. She became an entirely different woman. Her natural, quiet voice and controlled self disappeared, and she seemed to alter in every way. She paid no attention whatever to the dishevelment of her hair, the position of her clothes, the position of herself. Her eyes were half closed; between the contractions she passed into a quiet, sleepy condition, not answering when spoken to, and when a contraction started she suddenly brightened up and, saying, "Here's another one," grasped her knees, pulled her legs into the correct position, and helped for all she was worth. After a time she gave vent to an exaggerated groan, because it was nature's demand that she not relax the tension too quickly. I also pointed out that there was no need for her to suffer pain at all—I had already explained to her how to use the gas apparatus that was in her hand or on the pillow beside her—and she quite violently said, "It isn't a question of pain—it is this frightful bursting feeling. I feel I am going to burst down below." I assured her that she was not going to burst down below, and her reply was, "You don't know." She generally became an aggressive, different woman altogether, but still assured me that it was not a question of pain. As each contraction faded away she became listless, semiconscious, and sleepy.

The head came down nicely; the crown began to show; the membranes had ruptured previously. The second stage was only twenty-five minutes from beginning to end. When the head began to crown, I said, "Are you quite sure you are having no pain?"

She looked wildly at me again, grasped my arm, and said, "Pain? What do you call pain? The whole damn thing is painful—you ought to know it by now."

I said, "Why have you not taken your gas, then? It's there, and I asked you to let me know if you felt anything that hurt you, and you haven't taken it. Now, will you please take your gas, because it is not necessary for you to have pain. In fact, I object to your having pain."

And then, in quite a feckless way, she said, "Oh, it isn't really pain. Let's get the thing over—I'm sick of it. Can't you do something?"

I said, "No, certainly not—there is nothing to do. If you will do as you are asked now quietly, sensibly, and in a controlled manner we shall have this baby in a very few more contractions."

And she said, "All right, get on with it."

I said, "Won't you have some of that gas?"

"No, I don't want the gas."

The head came down and crowned, and there was a lot of scar tissue all around her vulva, and she said, "I think it is going to tear—it feels as if it is going to tear."

I said, "Does it hurt you?" and she replied, "No, it doesn't hurt me, but it feels awfully tight."

I said, "Very well—I think you had better have a few whiffs of gas."

So she put the mask over her face, and took a few whiffs of gas, and then said, "It doesn't hurt—what do I want that for?" And so on.

That was her sort of behavior the whole way through. She was certainly not a woman who was conscious of what she was doing entirely, and certainly not the Mrs. X I had known for five or six years as a rather mild, gentle, and refined person in her manner. Here was the changed woman whose consciousness had been driven below the normal level, whose powers of discretion and discrimination were dulled and whose sensory receptors were inhibited.

The baby was born naturally, and there was only a small tear —a little slit of less than half an inch long in the scar tissue that was kept together with one small stitch, the immediate insertion of which appeared to cause Mrs. X no discomfort.

When the baby arrived, it was quite an astonishing picture. Mrs. X came out of that inattentive state, and I said, "Here is your little girl."

She looked at me. "That isn't true."

I said, "It's quite true."

Her eyes were half closed, and she continued to look at me in a suspicious way. The baby cried lustily, and I held it up.

She asked, "Are you sure it is normal?"

I told her, "There is nothing the matter with this baby."

But she said, sighing, "Ah, you don't know."

After possibly three or four very trying minutes, she took the child and held it in her hands. Then she seemed to cast her doubts and fears away; it was really a very dramatic picture as she suddenly cried, "Then I'll believe you!" In a flash her restraint disappeared and she was wreathed in the smile of incomprehensible happiness.

## THIRD STAGE OF LABOR (EXALTATION)

Whether the first cry of a baby indicates its pleasure or displeasure upon arrival we are unable to say, but physiologically it is essential to the life of the child and extremely beneficial to the well-being of its mother. At the sight of her child the mother becomes an entirely different person. The inattentiveness has gone. Her happiness and the expression of delight are so dramatic that the birth of the child, which is the change from the second to the third stage of labor, has been called a state of exaltation.

There is a purpose in every natural phenomenon that occurs during labor. *This joy is not only the first flood of maternal love,* but, as has already been mentioned, in the more banal sense of physiological reaction it causes a violent contraction of the uterus, prevents any excessive loss of blood from the site of detachment of the placenta, and hastens the expulsion of the afterbirth. As a mother fondles and toys with the fingers of her child, the great muscular organ is a hard solid ball of safety within her abdomen. I say "of safety," because from the obstetrician's or midwife's point of view, should he or she have an anxious moment, it is when the uterus during the third stage of labor is flaccid and will not contract upon the afterbirth.

The child is placed in the mother's arms. After perhaps ten minutes, she will feel again gentle contractions of the uterus, or indeed the uterus may contract firmly without her being conscious of it. The attendant will know when the placenta has passed from the uterus into the vagina, and, about twenty minutes after the child is born, the woman may feel a definite desire to bear down and extrude the afterbirth. This is not done by the attendant, as it used to be years ago, for there is no necessity to help the uterus.

It should not be overlooked that many women believe the delivery of the afterbirth to be an event of considerable severity and discomfort. Therefore the care of a woman's mind during this twenty minutes or so is important. After a natural birth the attendant may be carried away by the atmosphere of happiness radiated by the mother, but *the emotional changes of the third stage are quite definite, conforming to a miniature labor.* The reaction to the first exhilaration may occur with the reestablishment of rhythmical uterine contractions. These are accompanied by slight drowsiness, which is disturbed by an irritated attitude toward the unexpected anticlimax of the recurrent uterine activity. The reestablishment of the expulsive reflex is received with satisfaction and success of the ultimate effort, a long persistent bearing down as the spongy mass is extruded. This is greeted with a sigh of relief and a feeling of final achievement. The delivery of the placenta is the end of labor.

If labor is conducted in this way you will be preventing many of those complications of labor which experience has led you most to fear: you will be surprised how seldom an occipito-posterior presentation delays labor; you will notice how rarely the placenta is slow to separate. A torn perineum will become to you a personal disgrace and not an unavoidable occurrence. And this kind of labor is more than parturition. Not only does the body of the mother suffer no damage, but her organs return to normal. Her muscles, uninjured, become reinstated; her nervous system suffers no trauma. We do not find the puerperal neurasthenia; we do not find the sleepless, wasting babies. The mother becomes again the wife, physically and mentally equipped to retain the affection and admiration of her husband. May the importance of this never be overlooked by the obstetrician who allows a torn perineum to go unmended, a pendulous abdomen to go untreated, and breasts to become straplike and unattractive. We are not so civilized that there is yet anything to take the place of sexual attraction in the maintenance of happiness in the homes of the people.

There is no more beautiful event in the life of a human being than the natural birth of a child. Subtract from modern childbirth the inflictions of ignorance, and it becomes a joy to the mother; protect a healthy woman from the influences of cultural contaminations, and parturition may be witnessed as a physiological masterpiece. Look with quiet, comprehending eyes at the miracle of nativity; each reflex is a reasoned part without which the intricate machinery would break down. No sound or movement of the newborn babe is without significance to its survival; already it is predisposed to a familiar pattern, but we see it suddenly possessed of individuality. It has not the ability to speak our tongue; its cries are not the tears of sadness but commands and demands for essential services. It looks at us and sucks its fingers; it sneezes and expands its lungs in physiological songs; it kicks and waves its arms; it urinates and grunts to expel meconium; within a few hours it learns the reward of importunity.

No science knows the origin or the nature of those forces which united in harmony to vitalize and perfect this new life, cast off from the uterus of a woman whose facultative genius has developed, nurtured, and ripened the physiological facsimile of herself. The cultural acquisitions of the human race are not yet comparable to the works of God.

## CHAPTER 13

# Natural Childbirth in Emergency

There are times when we all have to face unexpected emergency, and our reaction to it is often more important than the sudden unexpected occurrence or situation with which we are confronted.

Women all over the world are, and may continue to be, caught in the emergency of unexpected labor—if only because they are alone at home or in the country or, as I have seen several times, in a public place or vehicle. Labor is not a frightening incident in the life of a woman if she has learned what goes on and how her body produces the child when it is ready to leave its mother's womb.

What can a woman do when and if in circumstances of unexpected emergency her labor begins, with no competent person to help her, and perhaps only herself to help her child safely into the world? Her first need in such circumstances is to be prepared in advance by knowledge and understanding of how to give birth to her child.

When the baby is ready to be born it lies comfortably in the uterus or womb with its *head downward,* for it is usual and best for babies to dive, not step, into the world. The baby announces its coming arrival in three ways: by a *show* of mucus or blood from the outlet of the birth canal, by a *leaking* of water from the uterus, or by *rhythmical contractions,* which increase in frequency and in strength.

The first two of these warnings, in the absence of the strong contractions of the uterus, usually give plenty of time to prepare for the baby's arrival. But under the stress of accident or the threat of death-dealing danger, as in time of war, the intense defensive reaction to paralyzing fear is almost complete relaxation and inactivity of the muscles that control the passage of the baby from the womb. Under these circumstances labor is often what we term "precipitate," and the baby arrives with very little discomfort or difficulty to the mother. Terror-caused paralysis of the muscles of the pelvic floor, allowing spontaneous evacuation of the bowel and urinary bladder, is well known, and at the end of pregnancy the same reaction to terror may occur with the uterus. This unusual state is the reverse of the fear-tension-pain syndrome.

When the intensity of fear diminishes and brings conscious realization of being in labor, women resist the effort of expulsion and thereby create a state of tension by opposing the muscles that are contracting to push the baby out. This is the reaction of emotional stress. *There is a very real difference between the emergency of precipitate labor due to external stress,* with the primitive defense reaction to violent and imminent destruction, *and the labor of a woman in fear of labor itself.* The defensive reaction in cases of external fright is one of emotional and physical paralysis, but in the fear of labor alone it is one of emotional and physical resistance to the work of the uterus. I have seen in trenches, on shell-swept plains, and in the rubble of bombed cities women in such emotional terror that they have lost all voluntary muscle control so that their babies came quickly, and have compared them with women in perfectly safe surroundings, frightened by the process of labor itself. These latter women suffer even though under the care of well-meaning attendants, whose tender ministrations and sympathetic manner reveal that they expect their patient to be in pain, and thus add to her tension and discomfort.

The most important thing to remember, then, is that it is *fear* of pain that produces all the severe and unbearable suffering of labor. In an emergency, a *calm* woman who remains in control of her actions will have little discomfort as she awaits the progression of the natural events about which she has learned.

During labor a woman should pass urine from time to time, in order to keep her urinary bladder empty. This should be done in a squatting position at any reasonable place, according to the dilemma in which she may find herself.

Then, wherever she is, in a wayside ditch or a ruin-covered cellar, in a stranger's house, a caravan, or tent, she should find a place *to sit down and lean her back against*—a wall, a bank, or any available support. She should pull up her knees and rest her buttocks on a folded coat, a bunch of leaves, or anything that will lift her slightly off the ground. She should *not lie down on her side or her back, but sit* as nearly as possible in a squatting position, taking the weight of her body upon her buttocks. If left alone in labor, she may escape one of the greatest causes of trouble, which is interference by those around who, being kind but misinformed, feel they must *do* something for her. The safest medical attendant in such an emergency is nature, by whom woman has been marvelously equipped for this purpose. The baby is not to be interfered with by its mother's mind or a volunteer assistant's hand. Just courage and patience are required, and faith in God, if she is a believer, to produce a healthy baby and be a happy mother.

As the woman sits and waits patiently for the baby, she will soon feel a desire to push down. At first the effort to push must be very gentle. She should only take a deep breath and hold it, without pushing. There may be some backache, but it will soon pass. If there is no one there to rub her back she must relax and try to put it out of her mind, for the backache will soon disappear. When the desire to bear down becomes too strong to resist, she may begin to push firmly, but not too hard, and without expecting immediate results. If it is her first baby, it may take one and a half to two hours of expulsive effort before the baby appears. Sometimes two or three deep breaths, in and out, may be taken during one contraction, if it is too long for one breath alone.

As the contraction fades she will relax sleepily, first taking two deep in and out breaths, then quietly resting until the next effort begins. Her drowsiness may be so deep that her mind is concentrated only on the one task of producing her child. I have seen women during air raids who, although by nature nervous people, were not disturbed by the noise or the flashes of bombs that rocked the walls about us. On one occasion, being disconcerted myself by the volume and proximity of missiles, I was slow to notice the onset of my twenty-two-year-old patient's next contraction. She said testily, "Another push, doctor. Come on, don't worry about the noise!"

Just before the head can be seen, some women have a strong desire to "escape" the impending birth. When this occurs, the woman should remember to ignore the feeling and *push firmly* for the next two or at the most three contractions. Such concentrated expulsive efforts to help the contraction will quickly overcome the temporary discomfort and desire to escape. Shortly after that the hair on the baby's head will show at the outlet. If there is a looking glass handy, so the mother can see her baby, it will help her take an active interest in helping it to arrive. She will then concentrate upon the baby and its arrival and forget thoughts of her own well-being. The second or expulsive stage of labor need not be painful if the mother is in the correct squatting position, keeping her outlet relaxed and pushing properly with the contractions, though it may be hard work for the birth of a first baby. This stage is to be a conscious, controlled, and painless repetition of pushing to urge the baby forward as it moves through the natural twists and turns, flexions and extensions of the head that prevent damage to both mother and baby.

As the head starts to distend the vulva, a feeling of burning of the labia or lips of the outlet may alarm her. She must realize that it will quickly disappear *if* she does not squeeze up against it. The outlet must be relaxed and allowed to bulge as it will. But she *must not bear down* any more. Instead, she should breathe short breaths in and out, letting the abdominal muscles stay relaxed, allowing the uterus itself to urge the child slowly forward in a relatively painless birth of the head.

At this time she will have lost her drowsiness, and will be able to adjust her position, leaning back at an angle of 45 degrees—about halfway between flat and upright. With contractions she should pull her knees up and, with her hands, hold them wide open and at right angles to her body, with her feet resting on whatever support is handy.

As the baby emerges into the world face-downward, the woman should lean over and put one hand on the area between the anus and the vaginal opening, so that the child's head may pass gently into her waiting hand. The child's head rotates to one side before the shoulders are born. The mother can support her baby's head as the shoulders are born. The baby keeps rotating during the birth of the body until it is facing the mother. As the baby is born, the mother is to direct it *upward* toward her abdomen. Under no circumstances should she pull the baby out straight before her! She must remember to *help the baby upward and over the bone of the front of the pelvis,* using her second hand to support the baby's body as it emerges. Lifting the baby upward helps prevent tearing of the outlet.

If she is alone or with inexperienced people, she must not become excited or hurried. Slowness, quietness, and gentleness are the qualities of a good delivery. The crying baby is then to be laid on her abdomen, the head still supported in her hand. Then she may lift the child (without any pull on the cord) to her breast, raising it gently with one hand under the head and the other under the hips. Cradling the baby so that it lies level along her arm, she should allow it to grasp the nipple. If the infant will not take it as most do, she should gently rub its mouth and nose against the nipple, to stimulate her uterus.

Soon contractions will begin again, and the second stage of labor is then repeated, in a diminutive form, for the birth of the placenta, the third stage. If the afterbirth does not come of its own accord, the mother can keep the baby supported on one arm and place her hand on her abdomen above the uterus, which will be felt as a coconut-sized lump reaching just above the navel. If she presses gently on the abdomen with the palm of her hand, and then gives one or two sharp coughs, the afterbirth may come out easily.

*In emergency labor the cord should not be cut until after the afterbirth comes away.* Until then the baby is kept warm in its mother's clothing against her skin, preferably held to the breast. When the afterbirth has been expelled, it is to be wrapped up with the baby, the cord uncut, until experienced medical help is available.

Whatever clothing is available may be used for the baby and for the mother. As little as possible should be put over the birth-canal outlet, which must not be touched with unwashed hands if this can be avoided, although emergency labor seldom results in infection.

Most women, after the labor is completed, are able to walk with their babies to a place where clothing and cleanliness may be obtained, and perhaps medical aid and advice.

The *dignity and control of childbirth* can be maintained even in circumstances incredibly different from our accepted standards. I have attended women in many strange places and circumstances and know that this is true. A woman must remember that faith is not only an ethical and emotional acquisition. It is also a state of mind, which creates within the body physical harmony in the activities of living that maintain the highest standard of health and resistance to disease.

# PART III

# The Autobiography of Grantly Dick-Read, Pioneer of Natural Childbirth

These chapters have been compiled from the many personal experiences about which Grantly Dick-Read wrote, scattered through his books and letters. They give us an understanding of the man as a person that few of his contemporaries had.

During his life he was an enigma to many people. He was a far-seeing man who looked beyond the immediate. He observed details in the natural world around him that escaped the attention of others. He looked back through the centuries in search of wisdom and forward into the future of the human race.

As the years passed, his goal in life focused increasingly on one essential purpose: to make this world a better place in which to live, through happier mothers and homes. As he grew older he became increasingly outspoken in his views, in contrast to the timidity of his earlier years. The fact that he was right did not increase his popularity among his colleagues!

Yet it was not arrogance that drove him on, but an inner anguish over so much needless suffering that he had found clues for overcoming. It was the anguish similar to that of another prophet, who cried, "There is a fire burning my bones, and I cannot keep silent!"

## CHAPTER 14

# Early Impressions

In my library there are thirty-seven volumes, each leather bound and stamped in gold: *Mother's Letters, from 1915 to 1941.* These manuscripts of indescribable beauty are not to an only son, for I was born in 1890 as the sixth of seven children. In these letters, school-days and Cambridge, the London Hospital and World War I are all recalled and reviewed in terms of sympathy and understanding, admonition and advice. Betrothal, marriage, and parenthood are discussed with me in words of which Madame de Sévigné might well have been proud. Year after year this fount of mother love poured its influence into my life and still, at eighty-eight, this grand old lady filled me with pride when I read her views on things of today, written in the light of long years of quiet observation and deduction.

There is no logical reason to presume that the influence of one mother is exceptional. It is my belief that I quote an example only from many thousands, and there would be many more with each generation if this great source of power were fostered and nourished by the obstetric physicians. The science of obstetrics must be recognized as an invaluable adjunct to the health and happiness of human-ity. From earliest childhood, since as far back as my memory reaches, I have devoted nearly all my interest, and most of my energies, to this cause.

When I was a small boy, I delighted in hearing my sister play

"The March of the Gladiators." Many evenings before my bedtime she would sit at the piano and play it to me, until "old Ellen" came to take me up to bed. One night I sat by her, listening and supremely happy, when three revolver shots rang out from the woods at the bottom of the drive. Then I heard that "old Ellen" had been shot dead by the soldier she had been going to marry.

For the rest of my life, one phrase in that tune, if ever I am forced to hear it, brings back to me the chill of horror, the agony of fear, and the inconsolable anguish that I suffered that night. "The March of the Gladiators," by association, ceased to bring me pleasure, but was a conditioned stimulus for violent emotional disturbance—so much so that, ten years later, when I was in medical school at Cambridge and it floated across the campus to my room during lunch, I suddenly felt sick and had to leave the table, only realizing afterwards that it was a reaction to an almost forgotten emotional state. This experience later helped me to appreciate the negative emotional reactions of a woman to any mention of childbirth, if she had unhappy memories concerning it.

As a child I was very happy and fortunate to spend at least six months of the year at our Norfolk home, which was a farm, where I became acquainted with nature and enjoyed it far more, I regret to say, than I enjoyed the society of my older brothers and sisters. I got to know my animals, the cows, the pigs, and the horses. I sat with my bitches when they had their puppies, and caressed Topsy when she had her kittens, those natural things children do under the happy circumstances of such an upbringing. I spent much of my time on my own because I believed so unquestioningly in the miracles of nature—they were all mysteries to me of absorbing interest. I sought the loneliness of silent places where only naturalists really find companionship.

On one occasion during my obstetric practice in later years, a nursing student remarked to me: "We have only had normal cases lately, but Dr. X is coming in later on this afternoon to put on forceps. The woman has been in labor two and a half days—we think she is an occipito posterior. It should be quite interesting."

"Ah, splendid," I replied to this lady, who though a student was a potential mother of tomorrow, "very interesting. I expect the woman is getting interested by now!"

Of course it is exciting to see the abnormal, and necessary for training, but must the normal and natural be considered dull? It is only in these cases that any beauty can be found in obstetrics. The simple, straightforward performances are the perfect initiation into motherhood; surely here is the field for observation. Each constituent of the ordinary is so extraordinary when understood. It is so in nature, in every sphere, one of its great fascinations. It is more thrilling to watch an avalanche crash in a cloud of snow to the bottom of a ravine, to hear the roar of its thunderous progress and witness the devastation in its path, than to lie on the edge of a Norfolk marsh. Yes, more thrilling—until you have looked quietly and closely into the reeds.

Here as a boy, prone on the grass, I observed the peaceful beauty of nature as its constituents gradually appeared. Silver fish lit up the shallow water, great swallowtail butterflies flitted decoratively from ragged robin to wild flower; small cotton tufts revealed the newly hatched cocoon; each wee spider was a thrill as it set out on its great adventure. I heard the moorhen call and hurry her fluffy offspring past my observation post as a bittern* boomed in the distance.

At every turn of the eye the simplest form of nature is found to be full of excitement and fresh beauty to the quiet, respectful observer. As we look more closely, the treasure-house opens fresh doors of wonder until we become absorbed in the perfection of simplicity and the magnificence of the ordinary. I have continued to do this so often during my life that the intrusion in these marshes during the past several years of foreign bodies in smelly motorboats is equivalent to disease attacking the peacefulness of natural beauty. The thought of these disturbers brings resentment; they are not interesting. They upset the natural order, and are unheedful of the beauty around them.

In all observation of a natural state, the more concentrated and penetrating it becomes, so much the more is found to observe, to understand, and over which to marvel. Many people think the Norfolk marshes dull. They abhor the silence, so they bring radios and tape recorders and regale the voices of nature with ragtime. These are the same people who love to be on the Jungfraujoch with me and count the roars of avalanches and say, "Stupendous!" while I say, "Dead ends falling off dead beginnings." These are the type of people who also find normal labor dull, but who are thrilled with a forceps operation, a postpartum hemorrhage, or a face presentation. If only they would look closely into uncomplicated labor, observing every

---

* A medium-sized heron notable for the booming sounds it utters.

change in the mind and body of their patient, how much they would find of absorbing interest, and how all-important the harmony of nature would become!

One day in 1907 I made my first observation upon the pains of childbirth. There were a number of cottages on the Norfolk farm, and I had discovered that when a woman in one of the cottages had her baby, it was an anxious day of woe and sadness. The maids climbed up at our windows to see when the doctor galloped past our house on his horse. My mother went quietly down the drive to the cottage with a basket on her arm in which was a chicken or jelly or something she was taking to Maria, Mary Anne, Robina, or one of the others.

I questioned my mother about this, and she told me that it was a dreadful thing to have a baby. This didn't make sense to me, for as number six of seven children born in eight and a half years, I thought my mother looked awfully well to have gone through seven really dreadful experiences in such a short time! But, owing to the peculiar nature of my extremely pious and religious upbringing and my observations on the marshes, I turned to her and said something that was probably the stepping-stone that changed the course of my whole life. "That's not true, Mother! It must be man who is making the mistake, not the God of nature in Whom you have taught me to believe!"

After an awkward moment she said to me, not unkindly, "I think you must realize that these are things you should not discuss. You are much too young to understand. But in time, perhaps, you will realize what a serious thing it is for a woman to have a baby."

For years her answer troubled me, and prompted me to keep my thinking on the subject to myself, but inwardly the direction of my thought had been determined. I had learned by this time that the Creator uses neither the words nor the methods of human beings to obtain results more magnificent than our greatest scientists can ever aspire to. It is an essential law of nature that all species should be reproduced in the safest and easiest manner possible. Two of nature's greatest laws are the law of reproduction and that of the maintenance of the species. If either fails, we all fail.

Sir Thomas Browne's statue stands in the marketplace of my own home town. It was there he lived and wrote the famous *Religio Medici* in the seventeenth century. From the time I was a boy one of his most famous statements has remained in my mind: "Nature does nothing in vain." I have learned nothing new from the work and writings of man. Man's discoveries, innovations, creations, and cleverness are only nature opening a little wider the window through which all knowledge will, in time, be found. Nature separates the apple from the tree. We must learn to work in harmony with the law of nature if life on earth is to survive.

In the following year, 1908, I started my medical career with these impressions already forming in my mind. But my sense of discovery and adventure soon brought me face to face with inflexibility. My chiefs were more rigid and less approachable than any senior staff is today. Their noses were so long, it seemed to me, that when one looked down his at the junior who was inquiring, he became an indistinct object that could not be clearly focused. His questions were an even more distant blur upon the horizon of the great man's dignity. The answer I received in the classroom was, "My dear boy, we are trying to teach you, and before asking questions you don't understand, I suggest . . . etc., etc."

Fortunately, because of my love for sports, I soon learned to appreciate the reality of blunted noses against my boxing gloves. Some of the owners of these previously haughty noses became my lifelong friends. Strangely enough, it was here by the ringside, on the playing field, on the football field, the tennis court, or golf links that my chiefs, off duty, approached their juniors without restraint. Here I learned that they were men of great accomplishment and human understanding. They were people who could laugh at themselves more readily than at their colleagues, and whose hands were always outstretched to receive the grasp of a man who needed guidance and help. A little later on I began to realize that long noses were only lifted as a means of self-protection, protruded when difficult situations or even more difficult questions threatened the proprieties of orthodoxy.

It was my good fortune during the years of my training to have been under the able teaching of Professors Shipley and Gardiner,[1] John Baxter Langley, and Thomas McCall Anderson at Cambridge. I reveled in the study of zoology, biology, and physiology because of my hobby of natural history. The notions and ideas upon the birth of the young of any phyllum, class, or order that I saw or studied filled me with wonder and curiosity. It was not inherent discernment that drew me to this research, but a resentment that the law of nature should be held responsible for such injustice to women.

I was also privileged in having such men as Rivers[2] and M. D. W. Jeffereys as my professors for my courses in anthropology. In the years 1908 and 1909 I often sat with one or two of my friends on the floor of Professor Rivers's rooms at Cambridge, drinking tea and eating cookies with him, while listening to much that was fascinating, interesting, and almost terrifying to us undergraduates, as he related the experiences he had had in his life of pioneering work in social anthropology. And Professor Jeffereys had spent thirty years of his life as a government official in East Africa before retiring to a university appointment as senior lecturer in anthropology. From these men and others I learned that we must not draw deductions from small premises!

In 1910, while still at Cambridge, I spent considerable time in collecting varieties of color associations and the visual patterns of numerals. This was especially interesting to me as I have, among other peculiarities, a certain form of color blindness. Later I persuaded some of my musical friends to record the forms and colors connected with sound. We found that, with practice, definite types of color patterns were consistently associated with the characteristic works of different musicians. Here, in musical works, we discovered that the mind of the creative genius not only conveyed clear and unmistakable pictures to us by sensuous auditory paths, but imprinted them on our memories as well. When these pictures were reproduced in mental imagery behind closed eyes, they aroused again in our minds the musical patterns, airs, and harmonies that they represented. Dvořák has painted the simple pathos of the Negro slave; Tchaikovsky has unveiled the panorama of tragedy and woe; Handel has opened our eyes to a great celestial choir massed upon white clouds beneath the azure dome of heaven, flinging its song of praise across the amphitheater of illimitable space. Thus I found that sights, sounds, and associations, real and imaginary, imprinted themselves upon the human mind, molding and influencing its present reactions to past experiences.

These observations later raised in my mind the question concerning what mental picture might be within the mind of a woman in labor, and how this might influence her actions at that time. But I still kept such thoughts and impressions to myself, unable to find anyone with whom I felt free to share. Once I mentioned my loneliness in a letter home, and my mother replied: "I know that you are lonely; it is possible that you will be for many years. But we are close together in spirit and you are never alone, for God is with us both."

During my four years as a medical student at Cambridge, on only one occasion did I gather courage to ask specifically about pain in childbirth. I was watching one of the experiments by Professor Langley, in his study of the sympathetic nervous system. In this instance the nerves to a cat's uterus were being stimulated with nicotine, and I asked, "Is it possible that these sympathetic nerves have some bearing upon pain in the uterus during childbirth in a human being?" Professor Langley looked up sharply, and then, after a moment's pause, said, very quietly and very slowly, "Yes—yes, that is indeed possible." That is all that was ever said on the subject.

In 1912 my internship began at the London Hospital. It is situated in the heart of the East End slums in an area called Whitechapel, where fifteen hundred to two thousand patients passed through the outpatient department every day. It was an exciting and a busy time for me. On the surgical side I felt that I was dealing with real science, and on the physician's side with humanity, which interested me even more. But nothing so far turned my interest so close to excitement as gynecology and obstetrics. When I first arrived I had not yet seen for myself what childbirth was really like, but felt that at last I was on the threshold of discoveries that would help answer the troubling questions in my heart and mind concerning it.

Among the women I attended at Whitechapel there was one in 1913 whose casual remark had a far-reaching influence on me. The whole picture made an indelible impression upon my mind, although at the time I had no idea that it was the seed that would eventually alter the course of my life.

I had plowed through mud and rain on my bicycle between two and three in the morning down Whitechapel Road, turning right and left, and innumerable rights and lefts, before I came to a low hovel by the railway arches. Having groped and stumbled my way up a dark staircase, I opened the door of a room about ten feet square. There was a pool of water lying on the floor. The window was broken; rain was pouring in; the bed had no proper covering and was kept up at one end by a sugar box. My patient lay covered only with sacks and an old black skirt. The room was lit by one candle stuck in the top of a beer bottle on the mantel shelf. A neighbor had brought in a jug of water and a basin; I had to provide my own soap and towel. In spite of this setting—which even at that time, near the turn of the century, was a disgrace to any civilized country—I soon became conscious of a quiet kindliness in the atmosphere.

In due course the baby was born. There was no fuss or noise. Everything seemed to have been carried out according to an ordered plan. There was only one slight dissension; I tried to persuade my patient to let me put the mask over her face and give her some chloroform when the head appeared and the dilation of the outlet was obvious. She, however, resented the suggestion, and firmly but kindly refused to take this help. It was the first time in my short experience that I had ever been refused when offering chloroform. As I looked at her, I saw an expression on her face that showed she hoped she hadn't hurt my feelings by refusing the offer.

As I was about to leave some time later, I asked her why it was she would not use the mask. She did not answer at once, but looked from the old woman who had been assisting to the window through which was bursting the first light of dawn. Then, shyly, she turned to me and said, "It didn't hurt. It wasn't meant to, was it, doctor?"

For weeks and months afterward, as I sat with women in labor, women who appeared to be in the terror and agony of childbirth, that sentence came drumming back into my ears: "It wasn't meant to, was it, doctor?"

That young woman doesn't know what a tremendous fund of comfort and happiness her casual but purely honest cockney remark has made to the women of the world. So it is from the seeds dropped unknowingly and in unexpected places that the greatest trees may grow.

Not long after successfully completing my final medical examinations at the London Hospital, I was called into military service, as World War I was raging. Dejected, I wrote home that "I had hoped my life would be in the reproduction of the human race. I don't want to be called on now to attend to those who are mutilated, and watch them die!" But England was at war, and, like countless other young men, I had no choice but to serve my country. I was attached as a doctor to an ambulance unit, and soon sent overseas to Gallipoli.

I do not lightly recall my most hideous hour; it was in August 1915, shortly after we had landed at Suvla Bay. My watch upon the beach began at 2:00 A.M. On the edge of the mud of Salt Lake, crystal-coated and faintly glistening in the brilliant starlight of a moonless sky, was my first-aid station. Some three hundred badly wounded men were lying shivering in the cold night air; the fierce heat of the day had fled with the fading light, and in a few hours men's breath was frozen on their beards. To those who were in pain I gave the maximum dose of morphia; rifles and bayonets used as splints required adjusting; tourniquets had to be released and reapplied. Water was scarce, but some could ill afford to be left without their share of our meager supply. The monotony of this round was depressing, for there were no ships' boats to take the wounded off the beach. From time to time, Death seemed to reach down from the empty spaces and seize this man or that, and, on each round I made, a carcass lay where but a short time past I had heard courageous words of patience and gratitude.

I sat to rest upon a mound of sand from which I could hear any call from my stricken flock, and wondered if the living knew that their silent neighbors had passed on. It became so still that only the breathing of the sleepers could be heard, and suddenly I became aware of utter loneliness. I thought afterward that some instinctive warning brought that strange desire to fly. In fact, such an impulse was unthinkable, but in theory at least I was reacting to an undefined fear. I had not many moments to wait for the explanation: from only a mile across the bare lake, on Chocolate Hill, a rifle was fired, rending the stillness so unexpectedly that I started and became alert. It was followed by a sound of war that still rings in my memory, more terrifying than the bombs of World War II that are bursting nearby as I pen these lines, falling close enough to rock the lamp on my table.

It was the sound of a bayonet charge: the lights leaped from beyond the hill; the shrill yells of madness and bloodlust mingled with the wild whoops and screams of victor and vanquished. A few revolver shots, and soon the lights died down. The stillness was a thousand times more intense after that mad quarter of an hour. I knew our line was feebly held by tired and battle-strained troops. I peered into the distant blackness, wondering who had won. Had the Turks broken through, and should I see the gleam of steel and the fire of mad eyes looming up from the darkness?

I would have given anything within my power to have had a trusted companion with me, even if only to ask him who he thought had won. But I was alone, and that sickening doubt wore down my vitality. I stumbled, tired and frozen, around my patients; my hand shook as I held the water bottle to their lips; my eyes turned unwillingly, but half expectantly, to the black mile that stretched to Chocolate Hill. My mind ran riot, and I suffered agonies of apprehension and fear. Not long after, dawn broke in gray and purple lines across the hills. The doctor who was to relieve me came with the first rays of the sun, and he asked me about the night. I gave him my report, and he looked at me and said: "You look worn out. What's wrong?" He was an old Cambridge friend of mine, and my answer was: "I have never known before how frightful loneliness can be."

The landing on August 6, several days earlier, with its hail of fire over our heads, had been the reality of slaughter; but it was not so fearsome as that lonely night on which I died a hundred deaths. Later on I was in many battles—on the Somme, at Ypres, Arras, Amiens, and Cambrai; Bourlon Wood, Farbus, Flecquière Wood, Fampoux, and a dozen others where there was ample reason to be afraid—but I never suffered so acutely in any of these as when I learned that night what loneliness can mean.

Perhaps that is the reason why I shudder when I pass the door of those wards where women lie alone, enduring the first stage of labor with no understanding of what is taking place, fearfully imagining what greater agonies may await them.

One day while still at Gallipoli, a shell burst over me and I was seriously injured. Some time later I regained consciousness enough to discover that I was on a hospital ship, a converted cattle boat, bound for Malta. There I was taken, along with the other wounded survivors, to the Blue Sisters Convent for medical care. As I sit with women in labor, I not infrequently remember those dark days in 1915 when I arrived there, blind in one eye and with clouded vision in the other, almost completely paralyzed below the waist, weakened by dystentery, my pulse at thirty, and with a raging fever. The surgeon would have removed my injured eye if he had not been so pressed with caring for those he thought more likely to survive. As the weeks slowly passed I longed to live, yet at the same time wished that I could escape from life.

I recall the horror of those sympathetic visitors who brought me flowers I could not see; told me to cheer up, I should soon be home. "Remember how lucky you are to be alive," was their parting comfort. It made my whole body burn with agonizing tension; my head throbbed and uncontrollable twitchings came into my legs; my spine felt as if it were torn in two at its fractured vertebra. I perspired, and had I been able would have yelled in a wild mixture of pain and fury.

One of the sisters came in after they had gone and saw me alone in my trouble. I had been given a room to myself. She was a tall, stern-looking woman of some fifty years whose features I could not clearly define. She took my hand in hers and stood silently beside me. After a time she knelt beside my bed, and in broken English said: "I will stay with you. We will be peaceful, you in your way and I in mine."

Can I ever forget the miracle of that understanding? My back relaxed and ceased to torture me; the uncontrollable spasms left my legs; my clouded eye seemed to clear, and before I sank into my first long sleep for weeks I saw her head bowed and her eyes closed as she sought in her own way the peace that swept over me.

We may all have our own way of bringing peace to women in labor, but it is in the end a balm of restfulness to a tired mind—a mind that has no energy to withstand the irritations that intensify its discomforts.

I finally recovered enough to be sent home to England for further rehabilitation, fifty-six pounds lighter than my usual hundred and ninety pounds. Determined not to remain a lifelong cripple, I cooperated fully with the hospital program of heat and massage to restore feeling to my legs. Grimly I exercised my useless legs day after day and week after week, until gradually coordination began to return.

Because of the great shortage of doctors on the battle front, I was sent back to active duty in foreign lands soon after regaining the use of my limbs. This time I was attached to a cavalry unit. One of the things that occupied my mind during quieter hours was the weighing of the reactions of the men around me to danger. I described my reactions in long letters home:

> I am not pretending to like shells nor to pose as a fearless fire-eater. I know well enough how I loathe it all. The excitement for me is the fight between body and mind. Instinctively I should run away, fly to cover although the shell is nowhere near. But of course one doesn't. I have that instinct more or less under control. Then comes the fight to stand still, to continue dressing a wounded man; not to start or jump but to continue talking, eating, writing.
>
> People will confound and muddle the terms "fearless," "brave," "heroic," "gallant." The fearless man cannot be brave, he has no physical fear (and there are such). He has no battle of the mind versus body. He can be heroic or gallant—but never brave. The only brave man, to my mind, is the one who is afraid. That sounds like a paradox. But the man who cannot breathe because of fright, who is pallid, whose legs shake and whose voice quivers, who feels death at his very throat, at whom each shell is personally aimed, but who yet forces his legs up the embankment, who sees

men fall back dead and wounded, who forces words of encouragement through his teeth and leads the first wave over; that is the man.

He is the man who has all the glory for me. He is the best fighter, fighting as no other man can, because suddenly the bonds of fear become loosened and the whole tense physical strain relaxes into an overwhelming reaction.

It is no honor to be fearless; it is a gift. To be brave is more than glorious. If I won honors or died, I could wish for nothing less than for it to be said of me, "He went fearlessly into his duty." That is no praise! It is but making light of an arduous duty. Let it be said of me: "He was afraid, but went because it was his duty." Then honor is earned.

I am afraid. I have not won so far because I have not yet had a severe test compared to many. I am not brave, and that does not apply only to war. There are many things at home around which the same conflict rages. What I want you to do for me is to send me the thoughts to win on. And if I am not here to write, you will know that I have won. . . .

But I learned more on the battlefield than just from observations of myself and the men around me. It was during this time that I witnessed several women having their babies in the most natural and apparently painless manner. But I also saw those who suffered pain and to whom the birth of their child was an experience horrible to remember, and weighed in my mind what it was that made such a difference. I learned more that was to be of service to me in obstetrics than I would ever have learned had I remained safely in England.

On one occasion a young woman approached the trench and asked for a doctor. The soldiers brought her to me, as she was obviously very pregnant. I had sacks hung up at the end of the dugout and placed her on a stretcher there, while the orderlies on the other side of the improvised screen continued dressing the wounded men who were being brought in. I examined her and found her well advanced in labor. She seemed to be having no discomfort at all. Soon the baby appeared and all was well. She seemed oblivious to the noise of war all around us, sat up on the stretcher, laughed, and took the child in her hands at once.

Four British soldiers came to carry her gently away on the stretcher, rather than the usual two. I could not forget the look of joy on her face as she was carried off with her new baby. She probably would have walked away had the soldiers permitted her to do so. If this is childbirth, I thought, how can childbirth be compared, as it is, with the pains and agonies and hopelessness I see among the wounded men who are brought down to this very same place where this child was born?

One day I had been off the base playing polo, and on my way back to camp came across a Flemish woman leaning against a bank in the field where she appeared to have been working. I tethered my horse and walked over to her to see if anything was wrong, telling her both in French and in English that I was a doctor. She spoke only Flemish, but indicated with gestures that she was bearing a child. She did not in any way appear to resent my intrusion. With the recurrence of the contractions, which appeared to me to be out of all proportion in their strength to those of the average European woman, her face became set, not with pain or fear, but with an almost stern sense of expectancy. I sat down and smoked a pipe and waited, knowing enough of this people's customs to realize that no interference would be welcome.

Within a short time a child arrived. It is possible that during the last ten minutes her expectation almost became apprehension. The child appeared when she was in a half-sitting position. She smiled almost immediately. I felt then that my presence was unnoticed. For some minutes the child lay on the ground and cried, and then she took it in her hands. After a time its yells were all that could be demanded of a newly born baby, and I observed that the cord was already like a thin white string. She took this in her fingers, about six inches from the umbilicus, and neatly severed it—whether by tearing or with her long nail I could not see. She wrapped her baby in the cloth that was around her own shoulders and then looked at me and laughed. It may possibly have been five minutes later when contractions recurred, and with minimum effort the afterbirth arrived, certainly with minimum hemorrhage, for there was none that I could see.

I left her then, hastening into the village on horseback to see if any of her people would come to help her home. They appeared unconcerned and shrugged their shoulders, so I galloped back to where I had left her. I met her walking back to the village, carrying her baby.

The spirit of joy, the spirit of happiness and pride at the arrival and sound of the child, appealed to me. I had never seen a cord so rapidly anemic. The separation of the placenta and its expulsion all appeared to be carried out under the influence of the joy that the mother was experiencing. For the first time it entered my mind that this joy was not for nothing, and that this perfect physiological process could not be an accidental occurrence. My visions of postpartum hemorrhage, blue babies that would not breathe, uteri that would not contract, and placentas that would not separate, all seemed entirely foreign to this exhibition of labor, conducted more efficiently than I had ever visualized in my most ambitious moments. Elation, wonder, tenderness, and the pride of creation appeared to combine in a great storm of pleasing emotions, and under their influence the birth of a child had been perfected.

During the war I was transferred from my unit to the Indian Cavalry Corps, as deputy assistant director of Medical Services. One of the black-bearded Indian officers noticed one day how tired and jumpy I was after having cared for the wounded under fire and losing several men. He approached me and politely asked if he might demonstrate how he and so many of his people overcame tiredness. He explained in great detail how to achieve complete muscular relaxation. Afterwards, on many occasions I recovered from the stress of my duties by relaxing completely on the little broken-down sofa in my quarters, breathing deeply and quietly as he had taught me.

As the end of the war approached I gave many thoughts to my future, and wrote home how I felt about it:

> I am not suited to be a general practitioner. My object is not to become popular. It would be madness for such a man to settle down in suburbia. It is far better for him that he should aim at a position where the work matters more than the pay he receives, where the service to which he is called is not constantly and obviously in view, where he is not overloaded with the various social and domestic impediments which have spoiled the work of more than half of our good men in the provinces.
>
> . . . Some months ago I was thinking about things, just sitting quietly with my feet on the table, trying and managing to pick holes in myself. Then I turned and picked up a *New Testament* and read, for no reason at all, *James*. I just seemed to drop on to it and came upon some rather startling phrases when you remember the trend of my thinking. I know that service and not self-aggrandisement is the only life one is justified in living. I *know* it. That is the great subconscious influence governing and guiding the whole trend of my thought, and then I read it as if I had been arguing with James himself: "To him that knoweth to do good and doeth it not, to him it is a sin." That is plain enough, is it not?

Again I was injured near the front—playing football! Some of the men and I were enjoying a bit of recreation on a stretch of open land just beyond reach of the German shells. I was returned to England with a broken leg, shattered by a swift kick in the shin from one of the men who had been aiming at the ball. But I recovered before the Armistice was signed in France. I was reassigned as a brain surgeon in a hospital at Le Havre, meticulously taking shrapnel out of wounded heads.

When eventually the war ended in 1918 I returned to the London Hospital as the senior resident obstetrician, overjoyed to be back in obstetrics. I got out all my old papers and research notes on childbirth and began going over my developing theories again. Here in the hospital I found the same contrast occurring that I had seen on the continent of Europe. Most women seemed to suffer greatly, but here and there I met the calm woman who neither wished for anesthetic nor appeared to have any unbearable discomfort.

It was very difficult to explain why one should suffer and another be free, apparently, from pain. There did not seem to be much difference in the actual labors; they both had to work equally hard; the time factor was not markedly different one from the other. Perhaps those who had suffered had slightly longer labors on an average than those who had less discomfort. In those days we did not know the mechanism of pain as well as we do today, and a good deal was overlooked that certainly would not have passed unnoticed in the light of our present teaching. It slowly dawned on me, however, that it was the peacefulness of the relatively painless labor that distinguished it most clearly from the others. There was a calm, it seemed almost faith, in the normal and natural outcome of childbirth.

So gradually my mind was influenced by these observations to investigate the part played by the emotions in the natural function of reproduction. Was the nature of the labor responsible for the emotional state of the woman, or was the emotional state of the woman to a large extent responsible for the nature of her labor? Which was primary and which secondary? Could it be that fear of impending pain actually set in motion those factors that caused pain?

Fear is not necessarily abnormal; it is a natural protective state. In the presence of danger, fear engendered by knowledge is the stimulus that prompts escape according to that which threatens. For example, we slow down, if we are wise, when passing through dangerous crossroads. There is, however, an exaggerated state of caution. As students at the university we heard many stories about the "height of precaution," like the decrepit old gentleman who always wore the armor of a first-class wicket-keeper when he went out to play croquet.

In childbirth, fear and the anticipation of pain give rise to natural protective tensions in the body. Unfortunately, the natural muscular tension produced by fear also influences the muscles that close the womb and thus delay the progress of the labor and create pain. What I was witnessing in the labor wards of the hospital convinced me of the truth that this aspect of childbirth held. The Whitechapel question still came back to me: "It doesn't hurt. It wasn't meant to, was it, doctor?"

Now at last I knew that I had found an answer, and that answer was "No. It was not meant to hurt."

## CHAPTER 15

# Prophet Without Honor

It was my good fortune to serve as house physician under Sir Henry Head[1] for a time after my return to the London Hospital. He is one of the great pioneer neurologists whose writings have helped form the framework for the later rise of the branch of science known as psychosomatic medicine. He demonstrated that somatic or physical changes may occur as the direct result of psychological states. I had the privilege of many conversations with him. These were always a source of great pleasure, because of his enthusiasm not only for his specialty but for the art of living. This stimulated most interesting discussions filled with observations upon his wide experience of human relationships.

Knowing my interest in gynecology and obstetrics, he turned my attention on a number of occasions to the mind of woman and its activities under different circumstances. The obstetric orthodoxy of the day required the mother to be drugged into unconsciousness during labor and birth to spare her from "suffering." Nothing is more to be abhorred. The forceps deliveries of normal babies—blue and flabby babies who will not cry, babies drugged and anesthetized —were common pictures in current practice.

As senior resident obstetrician I began probing deeply into my patients' backgrounds, hoping for more clues, observing their state of mind. I sat for long hours at their bedsides in labor, seeking to ascertain the strength of the relationship of fear and tension to pain. In every spare moment I searched through every textbook that might provide a clue. I could not relax until I was satisfied that I had found an answer.

And then, in 1919, when I was nearly thirty years old, I gathered together my conclusions from my copious notes into a manuscript painstakingly written out in longhand, hoping eventually to have it published. I had had no one with whom I could share my views freely, but finally I gained courage to present it to my three obstetric professors for their evaluation. They were kind men, and accepted the manuscript graciously.

For some time there was no response. But finally I was called in to meet with them and given their decision. "Look here, old chap," the spokesman of the three said quietly. "The truth is we think you really ought to learn something about obstetrics before you start writing on the subject."

Deep in my heart I had known that this would be their reaction. Although my thesis still contained a great deal of orthodoxy that I had not yet discovered could be discarded, it still represented a major change from current obstetric thinking. "All right. I'll learn," I told them. Returning to my room I buried the manuscript and notes deep into my trunk and went for a long walk alone through the gray, dismal back streets of the East End slums. I never brought up the subject again while at the London Hospital.

When the time came for permanent appointments to the hospital staff to be made, I was passed over, much to the astonishment of my fellow classmates. This meant I had to leave my loved work in obstetrics and go into general practice after all.

Soon after entering general practice, in partnership with an elderly physician in a small town away from London, I married, and in due time our first child arrived. I was not permitted to be present, and was found, when informed of the child's birth, reading the daily paper, apparently calmly—except that the paper was upside down! This, I regret to say, was true, for every obstetric abnormality I had ever seen was, to my knowledge, occurring upstairs.

A few years later, in May 1926, I entered into a clinic practice with three other doctors so that I could devote my time completely to obstetrics. The idea of specialists working together from a single clinic was such a new concept in medical circles that what we had done was not well received. A wave of resentment among the doctors who heard of our action set in, and one of them reported us to the ethical committee of the local division of the British Medical Association. They investigated us, but eventually ruled in our favor.

Now at last I could concentrate fully on my specialty, continuing to apply my theories to my patients, perfecting my methods both from their comments and from my own observations. On one occasion I had spent three hours with a girl of nineteen, and just at the beginning of the second stage of labor she assured me that everything was fine. She had learned how to conduct herself and her labor, and everything was going extremely well when her mother tiptoed into the room. Wearing an agonized expression on her face, she went to the other side of the bed and took her daughter's hand. She stood there during the next contraction, and then, with tears rolling down her cheeks, whispered, "Darling, if only I could bear some of your agony for you!" Fortunately, by that time my patient had transferred her confidence to me, because she smiled at her mother and said, "Yes, it must be painful for you to watch. Now please go." I added in a stage whisper, "Yes, please go."

I shall never forget the harassed, agonized expression on the face of another nineteen-year-old girl whose doctor had sent for me. The labor had been slow, and the mother-in-law—a perfect example of one of the major pests of parturition—rushed dramatically into the driveway and flung open the door of my car before the chauffeur could leap from his seat. She tugged my arm and cried, "Come, oh come quickly. They are killing my daughter. Save her! Save her!" I ceased to be popular when I looked down upon her and asked with a smile, "From whom?"

The scene upstairs was one of tribulation and turmoil. The girl, uncovered from the waist downward, was biting a towel that had been stuffed into her mouth. When I entered the room the towel was taken from her mouth, and she flung a tired arm across the bed to me and said, "For God's sake give me peace!"

There was nothing abnormal in her labor except its conduct. Each contraction had been a signal for loud shouts of "Push, shove, pull, hang on!" Pressure on the abdomen alternated with the raising of the left buttock to see if the child was appearing. Nurse, doctor, and even mother-in-law gazed at the inoffensive outlet in an agony of anticipation. But the cervix was not fully dilated. It was suggested that they were all very tired; I advised a large brew of tea—downstairs, away—and a cup of tea for the patient and myself upstairs, weak and warm. In one hour a normal second stage had produced a healthy baby. A few whiffs of gas just at crowning time, for she was still very alarmed, and peace reigned. The pitiable request of that girl, tortured by the turmoil of her parturition, "For God's sake give me peace!" embedded itself in my mind and left an indelible impression of the power of calmness and confidence.

It had become obvious to me long before this that the first place to strike in eliminating pain was at the cause of tension. An aphorism was already imprinted on my mind: "Tense woman—tense cervix." All obstetricians know the effect of a tense cervix: pain, resistance at the outlet, and the innumerable complications of a prolonged labor, with probably an operative finale. I believed the cause of tension to be fear. Restoring a measure of confidence to this badly frightened young woman had released tension enough to produce the baby without difficulty within a short period of time.

However, the fear of childbirth originated from so many sources and from such high places that the whole scheme of society would have to be altered if the attack were made at the source! It was equally obvious to me that those who had suffered were very unlikely to refrain from saying so, and even less likely to preach that their suffering was unnecessary. It was also rather difficult to go around saying that the Bible and the Prayer Book did not really mean what they said on the subject! The Prayer Book had not been altered since 1662, and contained the special service known as "The Churching of Women." The following is from the Prayer Book of my grandmother, to whom this service was read many times:

> Forasmuch as it hath pleased Almighty God of his Goodness to give you safe deliverance, and hath preserved you in the great danger of childbirth; you shall therefore give hearty thanks unto God and say . . . "The snares of death compassed me round about and the pains of hell gat hold upon me. I found trouble and heaviness, and I called upon the name of the Lord . . . I was in misery and he helped me. . . . Thou has delivered my soul from death."
>
> Oh, Almighty God, we give Thee humble thanks for that Thou hast vouchsafed to deliver this woman, Thy servant, from the great pain and peril of childbirth.

And finally, I came to the conclusion that it would not be much fun to shake a theory in the face of my contemporaries in the attempt to persuade them that all our greatest obstetricians were wrong, and on no account should anyone believe what they were saying! It appeared to me to be rather like a flyweight squaring up in the corner to not one, but a dozen professional heavyweights.

It will be seen that the correct line of procedure was not obvious. On the other hand, I must own to a profound affection for my theory, and that, combined with a modicum of quiet pigheadedness that always stimulates a Norfolk man to discount odds, prompted me to get on with it without further "quavery mavery." Thus I began making an effort to educate women in the facts of childbirth during their pregnancy, in addition to striving to calm their fears during the labor itself. I soon received encouragement, for many women instinctively felt the truth and disbelieved in the necessity for suffering.

At first this did not appear to be enough, for too often, as soon as labor began, the exaggerated receptivity of the mind to all forms of stimulus, both physical and psychical, swept aside their good intentions. Some method had to be found to overcome this main weapon of the enemy, which was muscular tension.

So the practice of physical relaxation that I had learned from the Indian officer during the war was introduced. I had my patients learn to relax well, applying it during the last four or five months of pregnancy for health reasons. Again in labor they were to relax all muscle tension. It was found that when the muscles were flaccid, the mind remained at rest. More gratifying than anything was that the interpretations of the sensations experienced during labor were not invariably that of pain.

Relying almost entirely on this simple, Oriental method of muscular relaxation, in a short time I was more astonished than my patients. In the absence of turmoil, anguish, and misunderstanding, many of the phenomena of labor appeared in their true light. After not more than two years the results of the application of these procedures had not only established my own belief but—what was more important—the large majority of the women whose labors had been conducted in accordance with them had an entirely new attitude toward childbirth.

It was during this period that I began including the husbands in prenatal education, encouraging them to learn and to be with their wives during labor and birth. Our clinic practice was prospering, and my file of case histories growing. Each time I returned from attending a birth I carefully recorded all details of the case, the woman's attitude, and my own handling of the labor and birth, including my mistakes.

By 1929 evidences and experiences in homes and hospitals satisfied me and a large number of patients that the effort to learn and follow the untarnished physiological pattern of normal childbirth was acceptable to nine out of ten women who knew there was such a procedure. I began preparing a book on childbirth, working from my 1919 manuscript and compiling material from the massive library of case histories that I had been building. I did most of my writing at night. Now for the first time since my mother's rebuff to my boyish question during my teen years, I ventured to bring up the subject to her again by letter:

My work has led me to a line of thought which I believe will become of tremendous importance to all women one day. It is to the end that motherhood in the normal case is not a painful and terrifying proceeding but one which is without pain and beautiful beyond all other experiences.

Since the work has developed, a large number of women have testified to the truth of the teaching. Without any anesthetic and with no pain or discomfort they have learned the joy of natural motherhood. To have had children has been their greatest happiness and the act of childbirth has been the most wonderful experience of their lives.

Now you will agree that is a work which may justifiably enthuse any man. It is a service which it is more than a privilege to render. If motherhood can become a painless joy, how great a change in the whole nation. That is my ambition . . .

But behind my enthusiasm is the drag—opposition to my greatest usefulness. Again my old enemy, professional jealousy, is working slowly to take away from me what might make me so worthwhile to others. But this time I say: "NO! It is too big to give up." It is my only justification for being alive at all.

And so I go on firmly, quietly, certainly. Perhaps in the end the Prayer Book will be altered . . . and there will just be a simple thanksgiving that a woman has, by God's grace, been admitted to the joy and wonder of motherhood and all the marvels of childbirth —God's greatest miracle.

You will keep this confidential to just us, won't you? It has been so nice to write this; so grand to have you still there, so many years after my leaving home, to pour out my whims and my grouses, my ideals and ambitions, knowing that you will understand and sympathize.

By 1930 my manuscript was completed, and I chose as a title the words *Natural Childbirth*. Before submitting it to a publisher I first showed it to one of my personal friends, Dr. John Fairbairn, who was at that time one of Britain's finest obstetricians. He returned it to me later, thanked me for letting him see it, but then added, "Look here, my boy" (He still called me "my boy," even though I was over forty!), "you aren't really going to publish this, are you?" I told him that I hoped to.

He said soberly, "It will ruin your practice, you know. Ruin it!" I asked him why, and he replied, *"Because it's true,* my boy. It's true. But it's a truth which will not be accepted by our profession. If you can stand having that sort of trouble, go on; but if not, then my advice is that you should give it up." He patted my arm, and left.

In the months that followed I submitted the manuscript to one publisher after another, all of whom rejected it, some without comment, some with formal "regrets." Finally, two years later, William Heinemann (Medical Books) Ltd. accepted it for publication with certain reservations, upon the recommendation of Dr. Johnston Abraham, a well-known London surgeon who was one of their directors. A letter from them in October 1932 stated:

> We have now received the report from our reader on your manuscript and while he considers it an extremely interesting work, full of valuable ideas, he does not think, owing to the fact that you have no definite obstetrical appointment and are comparatively unknown, that it would have any commercial value for a large sale.
>
> If you like, we will be pleased to publish it at your expense with the proviso that as soon as we have sold a sufficient number of copies to cover our cost, the money will be returned to you and a royalty paid on subsequent sales. We shall only print 1,000 copies to start with and probably 500 will have to be sold before the cost is covered. If this idea appeals to you, will you be good enough to let me know and we will send you an estimate for same.

It was nine months before the book was ready for publication, but in 1933 *Natural Childbirth* was published, and not only did the subject become controversial but the author "a controversial figure"! At first the book was received with gentle kindliness, more like sympathy, by my colleagues in obstetrics. The first reviews were surprisingly favorable. When my friends heard what I had found off the beaten track, they listened politely—much too politely for my comfort.

After the initial fairly favorable response, the reaction set in. My clinic partners dissolved our relationship, bringing against me charges of unprofessional conduct. For a year my professional life hung in the balance. I could not legally practice until the charges were resolved. Ten months later the court cleared me of every charge for lack of evidence, and I was free to open a practice on my own.

But it was difficult to find patients. At first I did not understand why, until someone informed me that I had been anonymously reported to the General Medical Council for advocating cruelty to women! Husbands called me on the phone to cancel appointments for their wives. Pregnant women hurried past my door like scalded cats. But in spite of it all I was satisfied to be nobody with something special, rather than somebody with nothing.

On the advice of friends, I applied for a chair of obstetrics that was vacant at one of the universities. My application was rejected. During this difficult period my health became affected. The old war injuries in my back and legs caused increasing pain and paralysis. I was able to get around with difficulty by using walking canes, but could only manipulate stairs to reach my patients by dragging up on hands and knees.

But encouragements as well as discouragements began coming. Eventually my practice began to grow again, prospering far more than it had in group practice. I maintained a second office on Harley Street in London during part of each week.

I began receiving an increasing number of invitations to lecture on obstetrics. In 1933, before the Ninth British Congress of Obstetrics and Gynecology I read a paper that I called "Prophylaxis of Fear," using that name to explain how to prevent the pain of uncomplicated childbirth. I was invited to address religious gatherings as well as medical groups, in which talks I laid stress upon the family and the importance of the husband's role. Among the addresses I made were to two conferences of Catholic priests in 1936, one in March on "Psychological Aspects of Maternal Welfare," and one in July on "Maternal Happiness," explaining the importance of the husband for a woman's good childbirth experience.

I was invited to contribute a chapter in Professor Francis James Browne's textbook, *Antenatal and Postnatal Care,* which was published in 1935.[2] Apart from my own book, this was the first time that either the practice of relaxation during childbirth, or the thesis relating to the cause of pain, "The Fear-Tension-Pain Syndrome," had ever been published and widely circulated in the medical world.

From America a letter of encouragement came from Joseph De Lee, Emeritus Professor of Obstetrics at the University of Chicago, dated June 29, 1936:

I thank you for the book [*Natural Childbirth*] which you have kindly autographed.

I had already been reading the book, having obtained one of the first copies that came from the press. I agree with you to a very great extent on the thesis which you have therein set forth.

It may interest you to know that I loaned your book to Dr. Paul de Kruif, who made rather extensive references in some articles that he wrote for the *Ladies' Home Journal.*

I will incorporate some of these ideas in the next edition of my book on obstetrics,[3] which will probably be finished some time in 1938.

With best regards . . .

These encouragements made me eager to complete a more comprehensive book on the subject. Dr. Johnston Abraham assured me that Heinemann would publish it, and Dr. Browne kindly offered to read the proofs.

When De Lee's book came out in 1938, he wrote: "It will take several thousand generations before we can train women back to the state which Grantly Dick-Read speaks of as 'Natural Childbirth.' " Because of his comment, it seemed best to prepare my new book as a teaching book addressed to women, and once again I spent long nights poring over my notes, and writing. I am sure that, had this great obstetrician lived, he would have modified his opinion concerning the ability of women to learn, for he set up an experiment using a hundred of his former students to examine the procedures. At the end of the experiment he announced the principles as sound and wrote asking if I could hurry along the completion of the new book. A few weeks later he died without having seen it.

My growing practice and lecture opportunities made progress on the book slow, but I learned from these as well. I was lecturing one time in a large county center. There were a number of medical personnel present, as well as two or three hundred practicing midwives who listened appreciatively to my observations. The matron, whose brilliant career at a London maternity hospital justified her appointment to a large county maternity organization, rose to speak. She spoke with simplicity and a charm of manner that accentuated the sincerity of her revelation:

"I feel it is the moment to disclose a secret. For a long time after I became matron I failed to understand why so many women asked to be looked after by the nurses and not by the medical men who attend the hospital. I was constantly embarrassed by the situations which arose, and finally decided to inquire why the request was so frequently and so urgently made. The reply I had was astonishing: 'Because the doctors all make us have chloroform whether we want it or not, and the nurses don't.' "

The matron in another maternity home told me, "The more I see of this natural childbirth, the more I am persuaded that education is what really matters." I asked her frankly if there was any obvious difference in the conduct of labor in my cases from those of other obstetricians who also practiced there. She said, "Yes, in your technique, but the outstanding difference is in the women. They seem to know their job before they start. They understand why relaxation helps and why it prevents pain in labor. . . ."

Two brilliant and progressive headmistresses of large girls' schools in England became persuaded that the teaching of elementary biology and anatomy should be extended, in the higher classes at school, to human structure and reproductive function. It was believed that confidence in discussion would make it easier for girls to have a balanced acceptance of womanhood upon leaving school. But before introducing the subject they felt it necessary to obtain the opinions of the parents of the three hundred girls in one of the schools, as a guide to what the reaction would be in all the others. The response was prompt and dogmatic. If, under the guise of biology and physiology, the parents said, their daughters were to be introduced to the subject of sex and reproduction while still in school, they would be removed immediately!

The tremendous need for such training was brought home very closely to me when one of my own daughters, at the age of seventeen, made these remarks in her weekly letter home: "Jenny's mother is going to have another baby; she is terribly upset about it and awfully worried because her mother told her it was absolute hell. Isn't it too frightful for her?"

It was near the end of the term, so I did not reply in any controversial manner, but neither did I waste any time at the beginning of the holidays in introducing my daughter to the opinions of those who not only entirely disagree with Jenny's mother, but who would have liked to tell her of the infinite harm this effort to gain the sympathy of her daughter had done. To my own child this was an example of the hearsay with which sooner or later all girls become familiar, even in those schools where it is not a frequent subject of conversation among the girls themselves.

One problem that frequently confronted my patients was the

unhappiness of the other women in labor. One of my patients was very comfortable and progressing well toward second stage when the loud cries and moans of a woman in labor from a neighboring ward floated through to the peaceful room in which we were situated. My patient hastily grasped my hand, looked appealingly at me, and said, "How unnecessary it is that she should suffer. Can't you go and help?" I said that I was indeed grieved, but it was no business of mine to interfere uninvited with other cases. I assured her that the chances were the cries were not of suffering, but of fear, and under the influence of narcotic drugs. About an hour later, from the ward on the other side, groans obvious to me to be those of a woman in real pain came loudly across the passage. In a few minutes we heard clearly the crescendo of her screams for help. This was extremely disturbing to my patient, who said, "Surely that is not another?"

I explained to her that a perfectly competent doctor was attending her, because I had gone out to see whether she was asking for help that could be given by me. This went on for an unhappy quarter of an hour and I was afraid it would disrupt the harmony of my own patient's labor. But she proceeded quietly, saying, "I am not having any pain, why should they?" Some time later her baby was born perfectly.

Two women medical students were present at her labor. They had asked to see how natural childbirth was conducted. I was as much interested in the expressions upon their faces as I was in the normal, peaceful birth that I was conducting. Their mouths opened, and, in silence, their eyes opened wider and wider. They looked at the woman as though she were mad or demented; they failed to understand that she was speaking the truth. They had, each of them, seen and conducted many labors, but did not realize the importance of certain simple phenomena of labor that can only appear under these conditions. As I came away after the birth, one of them commented, "It's perfectly simple to have a baby like that. If that is what obstetrics means, there is nothing in it." I replied, "Exactly. Obstetricians are essential to deal with the abnormal—they should not complicate the normal."

When I stopped by to see my patient later, she asked about the two other women whose babies had been born that same night. I told her in plain words that all was well with them, but did not tell her that one of the women had been deeply anesthetized for an hour and a half, her child extracted by forceps, and a large tear of her perineum repaired. The other one had had her perineum repaired later in the night. I kept for myself all thoughts, and merely left her with the knowledge that they were two mothers with two babies.

All this did not endear me to some of my colleagues! There were those who encouraged and helped, but there were others who not only disagreed, but continued to make a number of untrue accusations. The most frequent and most damaging of these continued to be that I did not allow anesthesia or anything else to relieve pain. This accusation was brought to my notice by a doctor whose wife wanted me to attend her. He had read a book in the medical library that stated that I would not give anesthesia. I knew at once the book to which he referred. It was popular with medical students because it was short and easy to read. The author never corrected the statement, although he knew full well that it was a deliberate falsehood. My teaching on this has always been clear: (1) no woman should be allowed to suffer; (2) analgesia must always be available for the woman to use if she needs it; (3) analgesia is to be administered according to the clinical indication and the judgment of the attending physician.

One lady wrote and told me my name should be struck off the medical register; such inhumanity was unbelievable in our enlightened age. Society whispered that I sat and watched women writhe in agony. A doctor who had intended to invite me to attend his wife wrote and explained that he did not think I was quite good enough as an obstetrician.

Another startling accusation was that there was some kind of mystic quality I possessed that made the good results possible, but of course other physicians were not so endowed and could thus be excused from even trying to achieve the same results. Others dismissed the results as a kind of personal hypnotism. Frankly, when I saw myself in the mirror mornings, I hesitated, for one brief moment, before even considering this distinction!

I had considered hypnotism in my early research, along with anesthesia and every other means of relieving suffering, but had dismissed the thought of learning to use it. Why hypnotize when education and understanding give better results? Hypnotism only hides the phenomena of normal labor behind the ephemeral curtain of disassociated consciousness.

It is true that I possessed one personal quality that helped make the good results possible. But it is a quality I share with tens of thousands of other doctors the world over. It is said by psychologists that in the subconscious mind of woman there are but two types of men: those who injure and abstract from her and those who protect and give to her. The first of these is the materialization of cruelty, and the second the personification of kindness.

There is no more definite division of men than that which is found among the attendants upon women in labor. For, without any question, some by their presence alone stimulate the normal neuro-muscular activities of parturition, and others, in spite of the utmost sympathy, appear to cause delay and suffering. In short, there are "motor men" and "inhibitory men" in obstetrics.

An example of the sympathetic yet inhibitory physician is a medical man I once overheard try to encourage his patient. "Ha, ha. Cheer up, old girl. You've got to go through hell, but I'll go anywhere with you, so keep smiling. Ha, ha!" Then there are others who inhibit because they are prompted by the impulses necessary for the perfection of the work *they* have to do during parturition.

Fortunately there are many others who are truly activated by motives of kindness and human understanding, willing to assist the woman in her work of giving birth and to let her be the "star" of the show. These I characterize as "motor men." One of the many accusations made against me was that I was a "motor man," but this I did not mind.

One thing I would never do was to induce labor unnecessarily or hurry things along for my own convenience. We still hear of normal cases having the membranes ruptured early or the labor induced in some other way, so the physician can get the case over in time to do this or that. We still hear of anesthesia and forceps being employed to assist in the maintenance of a social program, and even for the purely selfish motive that it is the quickest method. Obstetricians are sometimes busy men, but there is no reason why busy men should not be good obstetricians! I have frequently been told, "But my dear so-and-so, I simply do not have time to do all this. There are other things to attend to, and other things to be done."

For three years in succession my summer holiday was planned for three weeks, giving ten days clear at each end from any booked dates for births. Each year from ten to fifteen days of that three weeks had to be sacrificed to infants who insisted upon remaining *in utero*. It is not surprising that my family had a poor opinion of obstetrics as a hobby! To invite friends to dine was to precipitate a labor during dinner, and to fulfill a long-standing promise of a family evening at the theater was practically impossible. The special days of the school term when the children looked forward to a visit from their "baby doctor" father were frequently days of disappointment.

Late in the summer of 1939 I had finally been able to take my family for a short two-week holiday at the beach. On the last Sunday, we were all in church when the pastor made the announcement that war had been declared on Germany just a few minutes before. We hurried back to our home, which was only twenty-five miles from London, only to find it filled with evacuees. Our first air-raid warning came quite soon after, and, in the absence of any proper shelters, the women and children hurried to the cellars in which we have the boilers and furnaces. I stayed upstairs to make tea for the "party," feeling that bomb splinters upstairs were preferable, should they arrive, to a nightgown party in the cellars with females and boys.

My practice on Harley Street in London was gone. My big car had to be put away for lack of fuel, though two small cars were still available for my local practice. During the Christmas holidays that year war and peace were strangely mingled. I sat in my study after an air-raid warning was over one day. Suddenly the irregular zoom of an airplane, quite low and coming toward the house, attracted my attention. I listened and, as I did so, there was a loud, shrieking rush of a heavy bomb seemingly howling past my window.

Within a few yards of the house I found myself at the raised edge of a crater sixty to seventy feet wide and about twenty feet deep. The cottages near were blasted to a ruined, dusty mass of rubble. All of us, including a nurse who was staying with us, worked like Trojans to find some traces of life. By pushing my arm in the rubble I came upon a small hand. It had a pulse, firmly and surely beating.

Hurriedly working my way up the arm I gave directions to the others to clear away the debris from the face to which the hand belonged. Soon the mouth was free, and then the head and shoulders. A little more clearing and I pulled the child out by the shoulders. He was a boy of about twelve, who soon recovered consciousness and was taken away by the nurse.

I delved again and found another hand and arm—but this time, no pulse. The body was quickly pulled out of the wreckage. Together we worked rapidly until all were accounted for, some dead, some surviving.

That evening my daughters gave a previously planned party for about twenty couples. The evening went well. We had no near bombs that night, and at 3:00 A.M. the last guest went out into the darkness, cheerful, war free, and contented. So life and death lived side by side.

Inwardly I had decided to burn my new manuscript. I was fifty years old, and although my teachings had become known throughout Europe and in America, they were still unacceptable to the majority of medical men in my own country. Besides, no one knew when this dreadful war would end. I gathered up the chapters that were finished, and the notes, and stuck them into a far corner of the library.

Babies keep coming in wartime, too. A doctor's wife had come to the maternity home in labor. As her baby was born, the labor ward was shaken by the concussion of guns and shells; the first cry of the baby was in concert with hordes of German airplanes going over the maternity wards. I looked at the maternity supervisor and we wondered what might happen next. The blitz was at its height, but the mother, who had been very nervous of these things, took her small child in her hands and played with it with all the utter carelessness of joy that only this occasion witnesses. It was an extremely pretty picture.

But as I stood and watched these two, still the German hordes went over our heads; the roar and thrum of their engines, the crash of guns, the bursting of shells, and from time to time the bursting of their bombs seemed to make the picture of peacefulness in that labor ward unreal, ephemeral, or a figment of the imagination. It was the permanent record of humanity at its best, and overhead were the emblems of humanity in its most primitive barbarity.

I think perhaps I shall never forget this series of events. In the immediate presence of childbirth there was no thought of fear within any mind in that labor ward. Our work was the privilege of those who assist in laying the foundations of a fuller life, and our thoughts were far beyond the activities of those who seek to destroy. When I went out, having put on my tin hat and placed my gas mask beside me in the car, and drove the three miles home through the blitz that was harassing the countryside, I was possessed of a sense of elation that here indeed is the true calling of an obstetrician.

CHAPTER 16

# Man Without a Country

There were bombs and many deaths in those days. It may have been despondency or frustrating incredulity that men, so gloriously born, could be such fools that made me lose all faith in purposeful writing. But my wife Jessica rescued my original manuscript from being consigned to the flames. She found it, unfinished, discarded in the corner of my library. She placed it before me on my table, asked me some rather pointed questions about myself, and finished by saying, "Don't you realize? That is what women have been wanting for centuries!" So, thanks to her encouragement, the book was finished.

In 1942 William Heinemann published *The Revelation of Childbirth*. It was a more complete book upon the principles and practice of natural childbirth than the one I had published nearly ten years before, its thesis tested and perfected during the decade between. It was followed in 1943 by the publication of *Motherhood in the Post-War-World*.

The early reviews of *The Revelation of Childbirth* were not discouraging. The British medical journal, *The Lancet*, spoke of it as "this rather 'Through the Looking-Glass plan,'" but ended by saying, "The book is simple, kindly and often brilliant."

The reviewer in the *British Medical Journal* said:

This book accuses the medical profession in general and the consulting obstetrician in particular of gross mismanagement of all cases of normal pregnancy and labor. . . . In spite of all this, no one can doubt Dr. Read's sincerity and the book contains a message to all who work in the field of midwifery—namely, that the physical condition is considered at the expense of the psychological and that neglect of the latter frequently converts what would have been a normal physiological function into a pathological process.

The *Journal of the American Medical Association* advocated that "this small volume should be read by every obstetrician and every student in the physiology of reproduction."

But some of my colleagues, for whose academic attainments I have great respect, argued: "You assume too much. This is not proved—this is not strictly scientific. We disagree with your neurology and your psychiatry is misleading, therefore you must be wrong."

My reply has been, with all humility, "Yes, of course," and I have returned to the labor ward to be greeted by happy women with their newborn babies in their arms: "How right you are, doctor, it is so much easier that way." Frankly, if there is a whole series of academic flaws in my argument, I cannot be too seriously concerned, for its practical application shows clearly that "it works" with considerable success. My thesis was evolved from observations made by the bedside, not in the laboratory.

Reviews continued to pour in from all over the world, nearly all of them favorable. Natural childbirth became the topic of many lively discussions from Canada to Australia. Requests for translation rights began to come in from several foreign countries and were granted. A request came from Harper's in New York to publish the book in the United States, and it was thus that in 1944 *The Revelation of Childbirth* was published in the States, under the title *Childbirth Without Fear.* *

---

* *Childbirth Without Fear* was published by the staple trade department of Harper & Bros., which was under the direction of George W. Jones for about twenty-six years. The book sold slowly at first, but by the early 1950s had reached a sale of 100,000 copies.

When the sales of a book reached this figure, it was the custom at Harper's to have a copy hand bound in leather for the proud author. Grantly Dick-Read was in South Africa at the time, and he and Mr. Jones had not yet met. Mr. Jones had the book leather-bound as was the custom, and shipped to South Africa, "expecting

At first the book followed a course in the United States similar to the original publication of *Natural Childbirth* in England eleven years previously. It brought new thoughts from an unknown pen and introduced theories upon the pain of labor that appeared at first sight to challenge the validity of much that was considered basic orthodoxy. It did not die, however, but survived in spite of small support from the obstetric field. It was neither obstetric nor academic perspicacity that gave it security, but women, from whom letters began arriving in increasing numbers, thanking me for making possible the beautiful births of their babies, and often relating by contrast previous unpleasant childbirth experiences. Many thousands of similar letters have swelled my files as the years passed.

As the war came to an end, invitations to lecture in other countries increased. Among the invitations was one from the United States that arrived at Christmas time, 1946. The president and board of directors of the Maternity Center Association issued a large number of tickets for a meeting at the Academy of Medicine in New York: "Dr. Grantly Dick-Read of London, England . . . comes to this country to discuss for the first time on this side of the Atlantic his concepts of natural childbirth. . . ."

Over twenty-five hundred medical personnel were present, an opportunity greater than I had ever had in my own country. The kind reception and interest in the United States overwhelmed me, although not all agreed with my beliefs.

While still in New York I was invited to attend a meeting of the senior obstetric specialists in the city. They gathered once every two weeks to discuss problem cases or current difficulties. I had gone as a spectator, but after the first case had been reviewed the moderator turned to the hundred and twenty or more medical men and women and said, "And now, since we have him here, we'll use him, and he can spend the rest of this session telling us all about his teaching and explaining to us how it works." I need hardly say that before such

---

the letter of burbling gratitude authors usually send on such occasions. He was deflated but also amused by Dick's reply, 'Thank you for the handsomely bound book. However, I wish to point out that there are 3½ million babies born every year in the U.S., and I think you have merely scratched the surface.' " When the doctor returned to England he and Mr. Jones became firm friends, and remained so until Dr. Dick-Read's death in 1959.

By the mid-1960s the book had reached a sale of 275,000 hard-bound copies in the United States, and a million copies throughout the world. It has been translated into many other languages. —Ed.

an illustrious audience, to be thrown unprepared into an hour and a half's lecture and discussion might well have been an ordeal. But again, there was the same spirit of friendliness in our differences of opinion, and we had many reasons for good laughter.

Toward the end of the afternoon a brilliant psychiatrist and scholar, who stood well over six feet, suddenly strode to the foot of the platform and addressed the moderator in a furious voice: "What sort of nonsense is this? Are we supposed to believe his ideas?" He turned on me. "Tell me, sir, could I pass a coconut through my anus without pain?" There was a pause while we all collected our wits. He pressed his question: "Well, doctor, what have you to say to that?"

Fortunately, the gods visited me hurriedly and fairly. I apologized politely that I was unable to give him a definite reply. "Because," I added, "I am not familiar with the orifice!" His anger turned to friendliness, and the perspiration dried off his forehead in the good humor that followed.

I found that some senior gynecologists who teach abnormal obstetrics disagreed with prenatal instruction of women. "It is better for us if they don't know anything about childbirth, and anyway, it is our job, not theirs," I heard more than one say. That is the war I have referred to of *man against woman.* There existed a demand that women be kept in ignorance of the truth of childbirth, so that they would be unquestionably submissive to the recommendations and demands of the orthodox obstetric profession. The women did not know that this submission might expose them to routine interference and physical injury, without any clinical indication that could justify such assaults upon their bodies.

I was proudly told by a gynecologist, before a gathering of colleagues at another meeting, that 75 percent of his women were delivered with instruments. The labors of 85 to 90 percent of his patients were surgically or medically induced to have their babies at a time convenient to all concerned. He said also that no woman was allowed to be either sensitive to the sensations of labor or conscious when her baby was born. "No human being," he exclaimed vehemently, "should be allowed to suffer this appalling agony." All women having their first babies were operated upon by having the outlet of the birth canal cut open to make it wider, and he did not advise women to breastfeed their babies. It was an unnecessary call upon their time and it made them tired; social and domestic routine was disturbed and formula feeding gave better results.

He refused to listen to argument or discussion. "I have used my methods for twenty-five years," he said, "and I see no reason to alter my ideas."

I asked him if he was interested in cerebral palsy. He was not —it was the pediatrician's business. Had he read the results of the recent wide-scale investigation and the report that medical authorities believe that over 70 percent of these disabled children had been crippled by interference at birth? He replied that there was undoubtedly a lot of bad obstetrics, but what could be done about it? I pointed out that there were thirty thousand new cases in the United States every year, making a total of one and a quarter million—did he not think that the natural or physiological method might be worth a trial in this fight against the tragedy of so many maimed babies?

He replied that with all respect he must tell me that there was no such thing as natural childbirth. It had ceased to be a physiological function; culture had seen to that, and civilization must be blamed for the diseases it brings with it.

Did he know that 10 percent of all the children of low-grade mental development were in their sad plight because of meddlesome obstetrics? He found the evidence difficult to accept and preferred to leave the cerebral trauma children, epileptics, and the results of birth-oxygen starvation to the experts. He was an obstetrician.

Had not the obstetrician a great responsibility to the nation as well as to the parents and homes? "Yes, certainly, most important," he said. And so the conversation finished.

Only twelve weeks after returning from the United States I gave a course of lectures at the Clinique Tarnier in Paris, in May 1947, at the invitation of the late Professors Brindeau and Lanteujoul. I mention this to demonstrate that the general acceptance of this work resulted in a large number of invitations and requests to lecture. I lectured in French. It was at these lectures that the late Dr. Ferdinand Lamaze of Paris first became aware of natural childbirth or, as it was later termed by him, "painless childbirth."

During the years since 1933, the year my first book appeared, I had lectured upon this obstetric teaching in seventy-one different universities and maternity organizations in the British Isles and at forty-two universities and maternity organizations in different countries on three continents.

On a visit to a certain country in Europe I was shown, rather proudly, a first-stage ward where there were nine patients. When I went in with the professor who was conducting me around, I realized that there was no nurse present. We walked among the patients and

I noticed that three of the nine were already in second stage. They all thought their neighbors were suffering the most intense agony, and when kindly spoken to they nearly all expressed sympathy with others. Only one demanded sympathy for herself because of her own personal discomfort. This distressing scene impressed me with the fact that prenatal care was at fault more than labor. Had these women understood labor, learned and practiced what to do, and been helped by trained attendants, it would have been so different.

Reports were becoming public by this time of several controlled series of births carried out under the natural childbirth procedures, from as far distant countries as the United States in 1946, by Blackwell Sawyer of New Jersey, and Durban, South Africa, in 1947, by the Department of Anesthesia, Addington Hospital.

In 1947 I published *The Birth of a Child* and began compiling material for *Introduction to Motherhood.* At this time the National Health Service was about to be introduced in Britain, so I went to inquire of Sir William Gilliatt, president of the Royal College of Obstetricians and Gynecologists, whether there might not be opportunity to be accepted as a member under the new arrangements. I asked for an assignment to carry out controlled studies in Britain itself, such as those being conducted in other places. He was very charming in manner but offered no hope, and hinted broadly that I should consider leaving the country! On my return home, I wrote him a long letter:

> . . . In the absence of any official investigation or indeed recognition of this doctrine by your College, I must ask you to accept my statements as accurate, full of evidence which surrounds me here in my library as I write to you. From all over the world there is a vast fund of evidence that this approach to childbirth has brought safety and happiness to thousands of women. . . .
>
> A frequent request from doctors, matrons and sisters of maternity establishments is: "Where can I come and study these methods?" Doctors in China, America (many), South Africa, Australia, Sweden, Holland and France have all expressed the desire to visit a hospital in England to learn and witness this work. . . . Books upon this subject are bought and read by thousands in the British Isles and America. They are translated or extracted in ten languages at least, probably more by now. Few editions of medical, obstetric or nursing journals are published without some favorable reference to the benefits of the "new approach to childbirth." . . .
>
> To me this work is no longer an obstetric practice only, but

a mission—no longer a pursuit, but a calling. I am not holy or pious, but I sincerely believe that time has shown clearly that the only justification for my personal existence, now that my family is grown up, is to give up everything to spread this gospel of safe and happy childbirth. I mean everything—my practice and, if need be, my home. I cannot sacrifice wealth as I have not attained it beyond providing for my wife and the future of my children. I want to teach and demonstrate and have a platform where all who wish may listen and learn and, in due course, perfect the technique of which I have evolved the elementary principles. . . .

I must set my course for the future. I hope to have ten years or more of life given to me in active work. I want to use it to good purpose. Can you therefore tell me, in order to assist me in deciding on my disposal: Is there a place for me in this country where practical teaching and demonstration may be given to those who accept these tenets? Do you still consider that my best course is to leave the country and try somewhere else? . . . I know this thing has got to come—and in the near future. The demand for it is growing like a rolling snowball across the face of the earth. Do you wish it to come from within or without?

By November 26 word came that my request was being considered, and on January 25, 1948, I received word that an eighteen-bed unit at Isleworth was to be placed under my clinical care. It had two labor wards and facilities for a prenatal department. The hospital would provide two obstetric nurses, and one or two of the medical residents who would be trained to carry out my teachings.

It seemed too good to be true! And it was. I discovered that the unit was separate from the main hospital, and had been damaged in the war. The eighteen beds were rickety and old. One of the only two toilets in the unit was out of order. In the room where the babies would be changed and bathed, the washbasin was broken and the baby tub of cracked enamel was covered with a plain wooden board, on which were piled the dressings that were to go into the sterilizer. Shelves in the walls around were stuffed with an assortment of cups and saucers, bedpans, and spare rolls of toilet paper. Paint and plaster were peeling off the walls, and some of the windows were broken and boarded over. The labor wards were tiny, with bare wooden floors. In one of them the only ventilation was through a small window fan, set in a window that would not open. Instruments would have to be boiled in an enamel basin on the kitchen stove.

I inquired if the place could be repaired and brought up to date.

The answer was no. I invited the maternity supervisor of a large hospital to take a look at the place the Royal College had offered, in which doctors from all over the country and world would come to witness demonstrations of my teaching. Her reaction was the same as mine. It was impossible.

I was nearly sixty years old. My health was breaking under the strain of opposition. The old World War I injuries were again causing searing headaches and problems with my back and legs. My world seemed shattered around me. Where could I go? What should I do?

Then I remembered what my mother had written me many years before: "Put your hand in the Hand of God. I have done so in all my troubles and have never failed to find comfort and help." I followed her advice, got down on my knees, and prayed.

### Editors' Addendum

A new possibility presented itself to Dr. Dick-Read when a group of South Africans proposed building a magnificent hospital for women just outside Johannesburg, and invited him to take full charge of the obstetric section as soon as it opened. On March 27, 1948, he made a preliminary visit to South Africa, prior to another lecture tour of several countries, with the promise to return to the position in the fall.

But it was not to be. His teaching had caught the attention of the press, and this nearly caused the end of his practicing career. On June 28, 1948, the following article appeared in the London *Daily Mirror:*

> I understand that Princess Elizabeth is preparing, by careful study of the nature of childbirth and by doing muscular exercises, to have her baby without an anesthetic. The Princess has told friends her belief that pain in childbirth can be greatly reduced if a woman has a calm understanding of exactly what is happening when her baby is born. . . .
>
> In all these matters she will, of course, be advised by her obstetrician, Sir William Gilliatt. But I am told that Sir William is not a great believer in natural childbirth. And the Princess will be giving a lead and encouragement to millions of women who fear confinement because they believe it must necessarily be accompanied by dreadful pain.
>
> This "natural childbirth" system was first advocated in modern times by Dr. Grantly Dick Read.* Though it is accepted by many doctors all over the world, an early book on it nearly put him out of practice. . . .

---

\* The English do not hyphenate compound names. Because Americans did not realize that "Dick" was part of the surname, American editors began using the hyphen in American editions.

> Princess Elizabeth has read Dr. Read's book. When it first came out it was almost impossible to sell it. Now it has been translated into five languages, is a best seller in America and is selling at the rate of thousands of copies a month.
>
> Dr. Dick Read is a tall, jovial man with a Cambridge degree, a Harley Street practice and a private clinic in Surrey. . . .

Once that story appeared, the rumor of Princess Elizabeth's proposed natural delivery swept the world. The French newspapers came out with bold headlines such as this: ENGLAND IS DIVIDED INTO TWO CAMPS —FOR OR AGAINST PAIN. In Australia the *Melbourne Sun* reported:

> Princess Elizabeth, who is known for her enquiring mind and logical approach to life, has taken an intelligent interest in motherhood. . . . Although it is reported that she is doing regular muscle exercises hoping that she will be able to have her baby without anesthetics, bushy-eyed, sixty-year-old Sir William (Gilliatt) says that he thinks it most unlikely. . . . But the Princess has read *Revelation of Childbirth* by Dr. Dick Read, first advocator of "natural" childbirth. This book sells over a thousand copies a month in England, has been translated into five languages and is a best seller in America.

Some news reports even rumored that Dr. Dick-Read was replacing Sir William Gilliatt as the Princess's obstetrician! Yet at the time the articles appeared he didn't even know she was expecting, or that she had ever heard of his books. The news preceded him to South Africa, where the Natal *Daily News* said:

> South African women, accustomed to having things done for them, will not take too kindly to the advice of Dr. Dick Read, whose theory of painless childbirth has created tremendous interest in the United States. But perhaps the fact that Princess Elizabeth is having her baby the "Dick Read way" may give a fillip to a revolutionary concept of childbirth which, paradoxically, is as old as woman herself.

Other headlines in South Africa appeared, such as the one in the Johannesburg *Sunday Times* on October 31, 1948:

JOHANNESBURG TO BE NEW WORLD CENTRE
OF PAINLESS CHILDBIRTH

> Johannesburg is to become the world centre of "painless childbirth." Dr. Grantly Dick Read, the famous British obstetrician who has taken terror out of childbirth for women all over the world, plans to move his entire organization from London to Hurlingham, a suburb of Johannesburg. A South African architect has visited Dr. Read in London and discussed with him his plans for the proposed hospital. . . . The building of the hospital in South Africa will mean that students of the new system of obstetrics will have to come to So. Africa for training.

Dr. Read visited Johannesburg in April of this year and demonstrated to doctors and women that normal childbirth can be free from pain. . . .

Thus it was that news items, many of them inaccurate in a number of details, caused him far more harm than anyone could have deliberately planned. The day he left England, December 19, 1948, millions of Britons read the untrue headlines of the *Sunday Pictorial:* DOCTOR QUITS IN DISGUST.

The news flashed around the world, in varied and distorted ways, and thus, predictably, on March 26, 1949, the London *Evening News* carried another item:

HARLEY STREET MAN BANNED IN SOUTH AFRICA

British obstetrician, Dr. Grantly Dick Read, who took fear out of childbirth for women all over the world has been refused registration by the South African Medical and Dental Council.

The council took its decision in committee and later confirmed it in open session. Officials of the Council refused to comment on the decision. . . .

The charges against him by the council were that he had solicited "advertisement" from the lay press, and thus was not a "person of good character," and was unsuitable for registration as a practicing physician in South Africa. Dr. Dick-Read hired a lawyer to prepare an appeal. While the legal argument raged he was without income and forbidden to practice, though scores of women wrote or besieged him by telephone begging him to attend their confinements. Scouts were even sent to spy on his home, in case he might be accepting patients secretly.

Finally the Medical Council held a special session to hear the appeal, given by A. J. Israel, one of South Africa's most brilliant lawyers:

According to the evidence before you, Dr. Read is a man whose work is well known. . . . Whether his methods and teachings are correct or not, it is not for me or you to say. This application is not concerned with that aspect. It therefore seems that an unnecessary attempt is being made to prejudice him when one sees that members of this Council wish to indicate that here is a man who is nobody and has done nothing. The type of question put by a member at the meeting of the Executive Committee indicates this. It is wrong to have put that type of question, to belittle a man and his work. It has nothing to do with an application for simple registration. . . .

We have put in letters and evidence from famous obstetricians and gynecologists and other medical practitioners who have written and read papers on his work. . . . I handed in today letters from the Lord Chancellor of England and from Dr. Thoms, head of the obstetrical department of Yale University; letters from the School of Medicine at Boston; letters from Canada and other places where Dr. Read's work and lectures are known and appreciated and he is treated with consideration because obviously his work is recognized as of some value to the profession.

But here, without any necessity, it is suggested that his lectures and work are, in effect, so bad that an application for him to practice is treated with contempt.

. . . Mr. Chairman, I think I am putting the case fairly when I say that, at the Executive Committee, Dr. Read laid himself open to examination and not only to examination but severe cross-examination of himself, where there was no right or even necessity to hold an enquiry. But nevertheless, he answered every question put to him candidly and he must have dispelled any impression that he is not a "person of good character."

Following the appeal, the nineteen members of the council took a vote. One abstained, and eighteen voted against permitting Dr. Dick-Read to be registered!

Only one recourse was left—an appeal to the Supreme Court of South Africa for a judgment. Three separate hearings were held, and on June 23, 1949, the Supreme Court ruled that he was to be issued a certificate of registration without further delay.

In the meantime, the plans to build the new hospital had long since been abandoned. But once he was entitled to practice in South Africa, a small but beautifully equipped maternity hospital, the Marymount, run by nuns of a Dominican order, invited him to come, promising to cooperate fully with his teaching. He had not been there many weeks before he said to them, "In another eighteen months it will not be a question of keeping the beds full, but of building to provide double the number, so that we can cope with all the demands for our services." His prediction was correct.

## CHAPTER 17

# African Journey

My wife Jessica immediately organized a series of prenatal classes for expectant mothers. The classes were held once every two weeks for women who could attend. Usually ten was the maximum number taken in any one class, which started about the eighteenth week of pregnancy. It was fascinating to watch the difference between these organized classes conducted by my wife and my early efforts at trying to teach women myself. The clumsiness and misunderstanding of men—I don't mean to derogate my sex—but the advantage of women being taught by women is that they understand the mysteries of a woman's mind, as man cannot.

The women were taught many things at these classes, including all the principles of postnatal care from the day the baby was born. It was soon found that these classes became gatherings of friendly women, even though they were very mixed in terms of social position or deprivation. They had a common interest and a common desire to learn the truth and apply it.

I slipped into the prenatal classes one day while the women were relaxing, to see if I could discover to what extent the relaxed women showed any sign of residual tension. The room was darkened and quiet; I entered without any unnecessary noise, the instructress greeted me, and although speaking quietly she used her normal voice. I walked around the women, some of whom were in the left lateral and some in the right lateral position. They had been relaxing for about ten to fifteen minutes. I sat in a chair and watched them individually, and although several had obvious evidence of incomplete relaxation, which was not unreasonable since they had only attended four classes, I was astonished at the sleepiness of all these women, who were not actually asleep. As I sat there in the peace of the room it came to my mind how easily anyone who was not initiated might have presumed that these women were being subjected to some form of hypnosis. When given instruction they reacted slowly but accurately, and it reminded me of the dictum of Edmund Jacobson, referring to relaxation: "No university subject and no patient ever considered it a suggested, hypnoidal or trance state, or anything but a perfectly natural condition. It is only the person who has merely read a description who might question this point." I talked for a short time with the instructress and left the room. I learned afterward that only two of the class had known of my visit.

What was the result of this preparation of women? The result has been that all over the world today the tenets that emerged from that relatively small school are the basic foundation for the organization of prenatal care of women in universities, teaching colleges, and maternity homes. They are not yet as common as I would wish, but that time will come.

The actual time I practiced in Johannesburg was just under four years. In that cosmopolitan community all sorts and conditions of people came under my care. I saw about six hundred babies into the world, of almost every European nationality under the sun. For simple enjoyment it was too many, but for the privilege of attending different types it was unique—English, American, Belgian, Czechoslovakian, French, Latvian, Norwegian, Italian, Spanish, Greek, Yugoslavian, German, Armenian, and Jewish women who had lived in or been born in Russia, Poland, Bulgaria, and Austria. I mention this at length because the physical and psychological characteristics of these people differed considerably. The mental background of the refugees, those who had been in concentration camps, differed from any I had previously met. Some had witnessed the indescribable horrors of slaughter and torture, and others had seen friends and parents walk away from them forever, to be deported to a distant country or to death in the gas chamber.

There were also the women of old Boer stock, physically fit and strong, mentally imperturbable, without fear or frustration. These were women of families of the gold rush whose grandparents had farmed the grasslands, and whose cattle had grazed upon pastures with millions and millions of dollars' worth of gold beneath their feet. These people demanded my books and translated them into Afrikaans.

Here indeed was a heaven-sent opportunity to observe the influence of the new approach to childbirth; call it natural, educated, or physiological, what you will, the result was the same. Physically, in the mass, all women are the same—good, bad, and indifferent anatomical structure. Disproportions between fetus and the maternal pelvis occurred much as they do in England and probably all over the world. But psychologically the picture was different and, in my opinion, more difficult: I attended women with neuroses, psychoneuroses, hysteria, and anxiety states, with real terrors of death and conflicts at diverse psychic levels and intensities. Some had emotional struggles and the mental suffering of ambivalence—for and against children, husbands, marriage, motherhood, homes, social life, and sexual desires. All these came to learn to the best of their ability, at the magnificent prenatal school organized and superintended by my wife.

Of all these, except for those few who required, through disease or disproportion, some operative interference, 96 to 97 percent, of their own free will, refused the analgesia within their reach, preferring to be fully conscious and watch the birth of their babies.

It was possible during these years to make a sixteen-millimeter sound and color film of three natural births, as well as a sound recording. It was not possible to pick and choose "ideal" cases, but when the cameraman was hired, the film was made of the next women who came in to have their babies.

But I still had one lifelong dream unfulfilled, that of investigating the childbirth customs of the people who lived closest to nature and furthest from both the advantages and disadvantages of modern science. For weeks and months my wife and I talked about such a project. There were still villages where tribes of Africans were living, in the jungles and on the mountains, in the swamps and on the sand-swept plains, where white men seldom went and never stayed. We decided to go and see for ourselves what the customs of these people were.

For over forty years I had held the beliefs of my medical colleagues as suspect, feeling that they were misinterpreting the laws of nature. I felt that they had used modern scientific methods, not only to hide the pain of childbirth, but also to hide their own failure to understand its cause. I had satisfied myself that the physiological and anatomical apparatus the Creator had evolved for childbearing women was a magnificent manifestation of Divine genius. No further observations were necessary to uphold the belief in my contentions. But the years were telling on me. Night work took toll of my vitality, and tiredness such as I had never known brought home to me the fact that many of my contemporaries had already reached retiring age from hospitals and medical schools.

So the plans were made, and we sold home and practice, had a mobile home built on a bus chassis, and set off into the unknown, hoping to visit not just a few tribes but a hundred, two hundred if possible, to learn of normal childbirth in its natural environment. We wanted to prove or disprove the reports we had heard of the horrors of childbirth among the unwesternized people, the sufferings of women, and the enormously high rate of neonatal deaths. In our hearts we would not believe these stories without a closer examination of the facts.

During our journey through Africa we found doctors, priests, and others keenly interested in helping this project with personal experiences of their life among the African tribes. They brought Africans in to add their information on tribal lore and custom, and interpreted for me. It was generally agreed that childbirth had earned a bad name because of the relatively few complicated cases that were seen by medical people, who never saw the normal. And, further, I discovered that difficult labor cases were only brought in after a long wait in the villages, so that women who could have been successfully treated without any danger were much worse when finally brought in than those with similar complications among Europeans. This was due either to the distances involved, or to the ignorance and delay caused by the witch doctors.

One of my first visits was to the Moffatt Mission, where Dr. Manson from Scotland was in charge. He was certainly typical of the best of the doctor missionaries we came across. It was a strange coincidence to find that I was no stranger to him, although I must say I did not remember him myself. He had been present at my lectures in Scotland during the days when I lectured at the university there, bringing to the attention of the students the physiological approach to childbirth. He told me a lot about childbirth among these people. He was a keen obstetrician, and made me realize how much we had to learn.

From there we went a short distance north and called on a

Canadian doctor at the Seventh-Day Adventist Mission Hospital, Dr. Jack Hay. When I told him my name he said, "This is nothing short of a miracle! My wife has had three babies, and studied your books very carefully with each one. She had not the slightest trouble or difficulty. In fact, she was so enthusiastic about the method that she started prenatal classes for the African women." After a year she found the numbers to have increased so much that seven hundred women attended in that one year. And it was the old women who usually insisted on the girls coming to learn.

I learned that the law of the jungle has two main branches. The Africans told me of the manner of the *maintenance* of individuals and their tribes, their systems and organizations, religions, food and drink, victories and defeats, drought, flood, fire, and disease. But they always expressed surprise that a white man should want to know the other branch of jungle law: the *reproduction* of the people, the marriage customs, and the girlhood of the women who bore children to reinforce the manpower of the tribe.

For this information I had to speak to the women, old and past the years of shyness and reticence, those who were chosen to guide and care for mothers when their babies were born. "Why do you want to know?" they asked me, and I said, "Do you not want to hear the ways of white women?" It was an exchange of confidences freely given, and I believe most of these ancient midwives with whom I talked were honest in their replies, for so many answers to my questions were the same, although from different tribes who lived thousands of miles apart, and spoke totally different languages.

But even if they did not tell the truth it was only to be kind. Dear old Bwalya Kalunda, whose interpreter was a lady of a Protestant mission, replied to me in her own language, although she spoke reasonably good English. "Bwalya Kalunda," I said, "how many children have you had?" Miss X translated that she had had twelve.

"Was it easy to have babies?" The question was put to her very sternly as if to say, "You know the answer to this one." In English the old lady replied in a monotone, "For my sin I suffer the torture of damn."

But, choosing her moment, she gave me a naughty wink. I understood and said, "Bwalya Kalunda, you like having babies?" She smiled, and through Miss X she said, "I love it, and did not want to stop!" Miss X told me Bwalya Kalunda was an ardent Christian. My obvious rejoinder was, "A grand old lady, and very loyal!"

She was one of so many with whom we talked. The young

women were difficult to talk to, for most of them are coy and proud of their feminine assets, a fairly general trait throughout the world. They are taught it is a woman's business to be attractive to a male and on her best behavior before strangers.

But when we talked to the old dames, those who had been "through the mill," had seen life and looked after others, I found them not only charming and polite, but quiet, kindly women and surprisingly knowledgeable. They spoke of the one great experience, motherhood, not only of having their own children and all it meant to them, but of the young women they looked after. They told me, freely, so much that I came to the conclusion that white people have a lot to learn from black people, who should receive our greatest respect.

Until people have been to Africa, they are inclined to think of jungle women as subhuman types. This is entirely wrong! Within the edicts of their own laws and customs they are dignified, and many of them are beautiful people. They are essentially feminine, and there seemed to us to be very little difference between "woman" whether she is European, Asiatic, or African. The African women desire to be attractive, and spend a large part of their time beautifying themselves, particularly their hair. This is done in many different styles among the various tribes.

Black African women are people of amazing character. First and foremost we were impressed by their beauty, and when I say beauty I mean it. It isn't necessarily that they have the same outline of features you would expect to see in a London street or in New York, but they carry with them a personality that is astonishing. As we passed them sitting in groups at the edge of the forests, we stopped and laughed with them often, making signs and getting in touch with them in the different ways we had learned, because none of them spoke any language we understood. We got along well in the towns with our French and English, but in the jungle had to go back to the old primitive method of enjoying each other's company by signs, hands, eyes, and smiles. And there is nothing that gets one further with the African woman than a smile.

Among the majority of the tribes we visited the women in the villages were looked after by the older women in the families, not necessarily relatives but old people especially chosen for this purpose. Very few African women attended a hospital for birth unless there was some definite complication and delay during labor. The more urbanized Africans who lived in the town brought their wives into the hospital, and we were told that they had more discomfort and made more noise than the village women at home.

While customs differed, the following procedures were the most common: The babies are born with the mother squatting on the floor, leaning against the side of the hut. Usually there is someone behind to support them during the later stages of labor, when the midwife takes up her position in front. The village labor is conducted in silence. There appears to be very little discomfort though sometimes considerable hard work on the part of the mother.

The woman who is attended in the village is never left alone. Most of them are well instructed in the course of labor by old women in whom they have complete confidence. And while their errors are tragedies, for they do not have the knowledge or ability to treat the 4 or 5 percent of irregularities that occur, their customs do not allow the acts and interferences that account for over 60 percent of maternal morbidity in the Western countries. There will always be abnormalities in all forms of reproduction throughout the realms of nature, but the complications of pathological childbirth are few compared with the man-made troubles that emerge in civilized countries, when there is failure to understand the simple physiological mechanism and its demands. A mission doctor reported that 18 percent of his patients had abnormal labors *after* admission to the hospital. This I am willing to believe, but I found no evidence to support such a high percentage of abnormal labors in the villages.

A British provincial commissioner told me of one experience he had had when he was carrying an African man and wife on his boat. The wife began labor during the journey, so he stopped. She went into the bush and the husband waited nearby. In a relatively short time the woman emerged with her baby and the journey resumed.

We learned the profound respect that every tribe and village has for the afterbirth, and the manner of its extrusion from the birth canal. They do not interfere with nature's work, and allow no child to be separated from this wonderful structure, which gave it soul and body while it grew within the mother's womb, until it has been born and lies beside the child. Then, and only then, may the cord be cut and the offspring given to its mother to embrace. In many tribes, no one is allowed to touch the placenta, or afterbirth. It is taken away by the woman in attendance and buried. There are many superstitions concerning it, and its burial constitutes an important rite in the birth of a child.

The major cause of difficulty among the nationals, apart from anatomical disproportion or malpresentation, is that often the aged midwives insist on the mother pushing down hard from the beginning and using all her strength. This has resulted in many unnecessary troubles. Prolapse of the uterus occurs, and sometimes the pressure, before the cervix is properly opened, produces swelling and edema of the outlet, which actually impedes the progress of the oncoming child. I saw a number of fistulas from the vagina into either or both bladder and rectum, rupture of the uterus, and severe exhaustion and shock. When labor is prolonged, the woman might be accused of adultery, adding mental suffering to her physical difficulty. These were the chief complications of labor, and although compared with the normal cases they were only a small number, even these troubles could have been prevented, for the African can also learn from us.

The Africans are intelligent people, but it must be remembered they have a different culture from ours. Their way of life is that which one could expect from those who live nearest to nature, the nature from which they come and upon which they survive. In this journey of ours we found that the simple biological law of all life has stood immutable since the creation of the first living soul, and in a word it is—survival!

As we traveled through strange places among people whose manners and customs were new to us, we were conscious of the power of this fundamental principle. We found it everywhere; human beings, animals, insects, the trees of the great forests and the creatures of the rivers and lakes survive in a ruthless war one against the other, but man in many ways has a higher intelligence than other living creatures, and from the earliest records of his existence we have reason to believe that he has been aware of an all-powerful influence that rules over his destiny.

At one place we had come upon a deserted, hidden temple. It was an awe-inspiring spectacle for me, for when one has lived for over sixty years one seeks some association with our own experience, and recalls analogies from memories past. What can any sensible human being say when he sees, thrown on the canvas of today, the genius of a people long lost in an oblivion that has destroyed their entity, and the brilliance of whose work is secreted beneath a shroud of rampant vegetation? All archeologists must feel the futility of our existence in terms of man's estimate of success.

It must be accepted that greatness up to a certain standard is attained by acquisition, discovery, and organizing ability, but we very rarely hear anyone say "thank you" to the powers that placed the substance there and gave man the faculties to utilize it for the development of the human race.

I can only say there are some things the black man knows that would be of tremendous benefit to us, though other things are best left where they are, gradually dying out in the hidden places of the jungle. The African is a proud, spiritually minded but essentially practical man. He has for generations been brought up to use his physical prowess as well as his wits for the survival and the maintenance of his people.

In an international medical magazine recently I read: ". . . When modern science has said its last word, and the patient is still no better, we are not justified in saying that the case is necessarily hopeless. There are still spiritual values to be considered, and spiritual resources of prayer. . . ." We are swinging around once more to the practices of the African over the centuries, in his awareness of spiritual forces in the universe.

In the scorching brilliance of a cloudless sky and in the damp of forest darkness, when wild turmoil bent and frayed the treetops of the valley, and again in the stillness and peace of tropic night, we heard the echo of a Voice in harmony with every discord of the jungle world: "I am Alpha and Omega, the beginning and the ending, the first and the last."

Why is it that the enslavement of the body appeals more to our sympathies than the more destructive slavery of the spirit, which is the ruling force of survival in the modern civilized or cultured world? Soon this glorious array of bounties, which until recently was known as "Darkest Africa," will have been dissolved by the torrent of the white man's infiltration. I give it ten years—until the early 1960s—and then all will be commerce. The destructive hand of Western influence will take so much that is good and replace it with the crumbs that fall from the rich man's table.

Don't look too far ahead. It will give no pleasure and no reward. Go now, not to kill beasts or to find minerals, not to grow cotton, coffee, or bananas, but to open, while there is yet time, the windows of your own souls. Let in the light that floods the forest of the valleys and the hills, the light that is the law of the jungle, the law of nature, and the law of God.

And try to understand.

## CHAPTER 18

# Some Misunderstandings

During my years in South Africa, experiments in natural childbirth procedures continued to be carried out in all parts of the globe and the results made public. Among the most notable of these was that conducted by Professors Thoms and Goodrich[1] at the Yale University School of Medicine in 1948, and in 1951 by Lawrence D. Roth of Rochester, New York. Since then each year there have been one or more records and publications of controlled experiments in the use of these principles.

Shortly after arriving in South Africa, I completed writing *Introduction to Motherhood*. My books already published or in progress in several foreign languages were: *Mutter Verden ohne Vrees,* in Dutch; *Die naturlige Fødsels,* in Danish; *Mutter Werden ohne Schmerz,* in German; *Att Foda utan Fruktan,* in Swedish; *Rivelazioni sul Parto,* in Italian; and editions were also appearing in French, Spanish, Portuguese, Japanese, and Norwegian. It can safely be said that this teaching was known all over the Western world before my years in Africa began.

Painless deliveries have been of interest to Russian physicians for many years. In 1936 I read of the methods of painless childbirth in Russian papers; at that time it was spinal analgesia. In 1946 a Leningrad doctor reported on the use of vitamin $B_1$. In 1945 Dr. Velvovsky of the Ukraine, who had been studying methods of painless childbirth, first using hypnosis and then trying a variety of other methods, reached for the Pavlovian physiology to assist him in obtaining his design. In 1948 the Russians carefully investigated the benefits of the natural childbirth approach, which was then known all over the world. These natural childbirth experiments found favor among them. They were quick to appreciate its benefits for the health of their nation, but omitted any reference to factors not purely mechanistic.

At the Fourth International Congress of Catholic Doctors on September 29, 1949, the Pope gave an address, outlining the principles and practice of childbirth without fear. He compared it to the procedure in certain hospitals where the mother was plunged into deep hypnosis, stating that this procedure resulted in emotional indifference to the child, and was thus not recommended, but that natural childbirth did not entail this danger. He went on to relate the recent Soviet researches in obstetrics along these same lines, but implied criticism of the Russians for their neglect of the spiritual aspects. He said:

> The Englishman Grantly Dick Read has perfected a theory and technique which are analogous in a certain number of points; in his philosophical and metaphysical postulates, however, he differs substantially because his are not based, like theirs, on a materialistic concept.
>
> The laws, the theory and the technique of natural childbirth, without pain, are undoubtedly valid, but they have been elaborated by scholars who, to a great extent, profess an ideology belonging to a materialistic culture.

By late 1949 and 1950 the Russian experiments in natural childbirth were successful enough for them to call a conference on this subject at Leningrad in 1951. It was sponsored by the Clinical Department of the U.S.S.R. Academy of Medical Science and the Scientific Council of the U.S.S.R. Ministry of Public Health. Here Velvovsky, Platonov, and Nicolayev[2] read papers on the results of a *new* method of obstetric pain relief now being practiced in a number of institutions in Moscow, Kharkov, and Leningrad. It is difficult to know why this approach was called new, since it had been in English textbooks and used in many countries for twenty years! It can be said that this work was known practically all over the civilized world by 1951.

In September of that same year (1951), Dr. Pierre Vellay of

France wrote me a very kind letter, saying that both he and Dr. Lamaze had considered it a privilege to read the last edition of my book, *Childbirth Without Fear*. I remembered Dr. Lamaze from my lectures at the Clinique Tarnier in Paris in 1947. Dr. Lamaze was now the resident accoucheur of the Ironworkers Policlinic in Paris, and Vellay had been his assistant for the previous three years. Dr. Vellay stated that he appreciated the help my book might bring to pregnant women, and requested the right to translate it into French.

I replied, thanking him very much for his letter but informing him that the work was already translated into French, and that my publishers had informed me that it would appear on the market shortly. However, in spite of all our efforts to get it through, it was not until eighteen months later that the book finally appeared on the French market. This was always a mystery to us, but eventually my book *L'Accouchement sans Douleur* was published.

Early in 1952, while still in South Africa, I received information from Switzerland and other countries that Russian gynecologists had described a new approach to childbirth called "psychoprophylaxis," based on the work of a Russian named Ivan Pavlov. Those who sent the information stated that there was a striking similarity of what they were claiming to have discovered to what I had been writing, lecturing, and teaching for so long in so many parts of the world, even to the use of the term "psychoprophylaxis" in relation to childbirth, which I first used in 1933. So I visited the Consulate of the U.S.S.R. in Pretoria, South Africa, to discuss the matter.

The consul invited me to send copies of my book, in English and translated into German, to Dr. Lurye of Kiev. These were dispatched by diplomatic bag along with a friendly letter asking to exchange observations:

Dear Professor Lurye:

Medical friends who have written to me from Switzerland and England inform me that you are using a method of natural childbirth based, from some of its aspects, upon the work of the great Russian physiologist, Ivan Pavlov.

I feel therefore that you will be interested to read a book that I published in 1942, *Childbirth Without Fear*, which has sold just under a quarter of a million copies. It has been translated into eight different languages and has been enthusiastically received wherever it has been adopted. And my investigations upon this subject were carried out for twenty years before my first book, *Natural Childbirth,* was published in 1933.

I enclose an English copy and a German translation together with a small practical manual, *Introduction to Motherhood,* that has been published in four countries. I have no doubt that most of your colleagues will be familiar with one or both of these languages.

It seems that there is still in this world one common denominator for all humanity—motherhood. Motherhood has occupied my attention for the last forty years of my professional life and this alone allows me the presumption of writing to you and sending you a work that may prove interesting to those about you.

I shall deem it a great honor if you will read these books and send me some literature published in Russia on modern obstetrics. Please accept as from one colleague in this great work to another my cordial greetings.

Yours sincerely.

I received neither thanks for the books nor acknowledgement of the letter, although it is certain that they arrived safely in Kiev, since they were dispatched through official diplomatic channels. When I inquired at the Russian Consulate they expressed surprise, but offered no explanation.

There is no doubt that those who heard the Russian exposition of their "new" work were struck first and foremost by the resemblance of the speeches at the 1951 Conference in Leningrad to previous published papers of my own, even to the measures adopted for the preparation of women for childbirth, which in the earlier stages of my work had no relation whatever to Pavlovian conditioning. In fact, Pavlov's book on conditioning did not appear until nearly fifteen years (1928) after my own work had begun, at which time I incorporated his explanation of conditioned reflexes, with due credit, as descriptive of what takes place through mental imagery.

Two years later, in 1953, I read a Russian claim that my work had been inspired by Ivan Pavlov but had not been a success! The only successful system of natural childbirth, it was asserted had been evolved by Soviet scientists from the teachings of Ivan Pavlov.

In 1953 Dr. Lamaze, who had been in Russia for six months to study their methods, started widespread publicity from the Metallurgic Hospital in Paris, claiming that the work he was doing was Pavlovian psychoprophylactic method. Visitors to his hospital again recognized the similarity in almost every way to the teaching that had been carried on in America and Britain for many years.

The truth is that the psychoprophylaxis of fear and pain in childbirth had already been discovered, published, taught, and used for nearly twenty years before the Soviet doctors realized its value and began to examine its principles. The fear-tension-pain syndrome has been the foundation of psychoprophylaxis and has proved its value in countries all over the world. Many have made small changes to suit their people and their climate, but only one country has claimed it as their own.

It is no concern of mine whether this general principle is applied with a hundred different variations, neither can I be concerned with the academic arguments of neurologists or neurophysiologists upon the functions of the brain. There is no end to their opinions. It has been my privilege to work with some of the greatest neurophysiologists of the last fifty years, but I have only come to the conclusion that they are uncertain of all the applied doctrines concerning the reception, integration, and interpretation of the afferent stimuli to the brain and the efferent messages from the brain to the periphery of the body. I speak of *human beings,* not machines made from *cerebrocentric reflex arcs.*

So long as the fear-tension-pain syndrome is broken down by safe and simple teaching and training, our purpose is served. It is a fact that a series of events takes place that, if disturbed at any level, results in the abnormality of severe pain. I look upon the claim, therefore, of the Communists to be one of ideological rather than medical importance. My sphere is to reduce the pains of labor, to take fear from childbirth, and to bring untarnished love into the homes of the people. My concern is for the betterment of childbirth, parenthood, and marriage, for happy families within the framework of our society, regardless of individual race, religion, or political creed.

This was made clear in my original publication in 1933 and has not changed since. Hundreds of thousands of women of all nationalities have breathed gratitude for the comfort and happiness this teaching brought to them. In 1951 the Russian physicians accepted the advantages of this principle, after two or three years of testing it in practice, and in 1953 it was propagated by Frenchmen, to whom I give all honor for their determination. In the *Revue de la Nouvelle Médécine* A. Bourrel writes of the "new" preparation of women, all the details of which had been used for years by others. Lamaze, Vellay, and Hersilie write on a technique of childbirth without pain that was an imitation so similar to that already published that in its initial stages visitors who observed it in practice saw nothing new. Angelergues, in seventeen hundred words, states that I don't know anything about childbirth, that I don't understand Pavlov's work, in fact that this man Read knows nothing about anything! He forgot to add, "That is why his work has revolutionized childbirth throughout the world, and also why the Communists have rescued him from the risk of his own ignorance."

But there is a serious aspect of this work as it is used in Russia. There are still great scientists who value, before all things, *truth.* This requires a freedom not always available. I am told that in the Soviet states a scientist must say and do what he is ordered to do by officials in high places. I also understand that there is another sort of scientific worker in the U.S.S.R., he who, in full knowledge of the truth, adheres to the universal principle of academic honesty and who, for his love of science, desires neither to deceive himself nor his colleagues. The true scientist will always exist, and he must be recognized as different from the one whose work is primarily designed to support, by all available means, the ideology of Communism. If this is compatible with truth, I have no quarrel. But if ideology is upheld at the expense of truth, work loses at once its scientific value and the workers are degraded.

The claims of original production and possession of innovations are effective means of establishing the greatness of an ideology and its leaders only where ignorance and fear prevent contradiction. For instance, we believe that Signor Marconi was an Italian and that Shakespeare was an Englishman and that Columbus discovered America. When, however, we learn that the discoverers were Russians, we cease to be surprised that Pavlov, without realizing it, disclosed that psychoprophylaxis in childbirth is a means of relieving the pains of labor. Such nonsense is not taken seriously by educated people, and neither is it worthy of our attention. I have followed the writings of Pavlov for fifty years and, so far as it has been of value to physiology, I have admired it. But this hysterical effort to found a philosophy on his physiology is pathetic, particularly when much of his physiological concept is out of date.

But there is one basic principle of natural childbirth that Communism does not imitate, and in this way the Russians differ entirely from my teaching. They treat childbirth and motherhood as a *materialistic* and *mechanistic* performance with no spiritual association. The miracle of reproduction is distorted to become a means of demonstrating the absence of God and the omnipotence of the Communist leaders. Their teaching stops abruptly at that point where the spiritual associations of parenthood play such an important part. The benefits of their teaching on childbirth will be limited by the atheism and materialism of their ideology.

My teaching is exactly the opposite. I believe in the law of nature and a God-force. I do not accept man's limited understanding as all powerful; in fact, I am very conscious of the small fraction of total knowledge that is within the comprehension of man. To me, childbirth is a sacred event and brings humanity nearest to the spiritual and metaphysical world around it. It is a moment of emergence of new life with unknown potentialities.

When I see a baby born to a happy, healthy mother and witness the superhuman radiance that carries her to a new world of mystery and possession, I say to myself, "What sort of an idiot thinks he can make anything of this life without the hand of God to guide him?"

So, finally, there is no clinical difference between my teaching of natural childbirth and that claimed by the Russians in the early 1950s because there was no "new" Russian method, but only a Communist adaptation of a twenty-year-old teaching, distorted for atheistic, ideological purposes. That is where we differ. They teach antispiritual parenthood and the doctrine of mechanistic materialism. I teach the sacredness of childbirth as a spiritual event, the spiritual power of a mother's love, and faith in the truth of the law of nature, which to me is one of the great laws of God.

Ninety percent of all civilized countries profess to some form of religious persuasion. Religious teaching calls for obedience to its codes, homage to the Creator, and loyalty to its spiritual and material purposes in the mother-child relationship. This factor knits in a common bond all the people of the world. I am not persuaded that the Communist ideology can destroy in so short a time the inborn devotion of a vast people to generations of religious faith. I believe that in time these naturally devout peoples who constitute the worker masses of the U.S.S.R. will turn once more to the fervent faith of their forefathers.

Professor A. P. Nicolayev ends his lecture with the words of a Soviet woman after her labor: "I have no fear, I am happy, thanks to Soviet knowledge, thanks to Soviet doctors, thanks to the great friend of knowledge, our own comrade, Stalin."

I end my lecture: "Childbirth is a sacred subject, and I cannot be concerned with any who use it as merchandise to exploit it for personal gain, whether it be for money, social prestige, or political propaganda. I am neither the arbiter of your opinions nor partisan to your persuasions. I endeavor to raise before you the high level of loving homes and families through happy childbearing, for in the end it is the homes of the people that become the standard of a civilization."

## CHAPTER 19

# United States Tour

When I returned to London from Africa, I no longer practiced medicine. I had passed the age when appointments on hospital staffs could be obtained, even had they been available. Under the present organization of the medical health services in the British Isles, an age is fixed for retirement of physicians in order to make room for younger men.

During my years of practice and research in Africa it was not possible to accept lecture tours elsewhere, but on my return I began writing and lecturing again, in response to invitations throughout Europe. In the three years after my return from Africa I received a large number of invitations to speak in the United States again. So, at the beginning of October 1957, after completing a lecture tour in Germany, we made our way to the United States once more.

I had been invited by the Academy of Psychosomatic Medicine to speak at their Fourth Annual Meeting in Chicago, October 17 to 19. This was a great occasion, for we learned in a short time what was taking place in the United States in regard to understanding the mind of women in childbirth, much of which had not been published in English medical journals.

Our host at the congress, Dr. William Kroger, who was secretary of this occasion, met us as we arrived. We soon had a taste of the hospitality that was to be heaped upon us for the next three and a half months. During those months I was entertained by seventy different groups in the large cities and towns of the United States, as well as in several cities in Canada.

It was nearly eleven years since I had been in the United States. Everywhere we discovered some organization flourishing for the education of women in natural childbirth. The interest extended to great universities as well. Preparation for childbirth has come to stay, and although it had still not been accepted by all the large hospitals, the demand of women for knowledge, and for more personal, humane care, is not to be denied. I had found the same rapidly improving conditions in Germany, Italy, France, the Scandinavian countries, Spain, Portugal, and the great countries of South America.

While here I was fortunate in having some extremely interesting conversations with the doctors of large hospitals. I remember one staff especially, where there were environmental differences in practice, but whose fundamental approach to childbirth was as near to the natural law as was possible under their present circumstances. I was taken into ward after ward and introduced to the women whose babies had recently arrived. I was greeted like an old friend and told without inhibition the details of their labors. My wife and I agreed it was a wonderful thing to happen to complete strangers.

One of our warmest memories is of our arrival in Seattle. It was, to say the least, unusual! Our seats were near the end of the train, so we were the last to follow the luggage cart down toward the station. These platforms are very long. After we had walked about a hundred yards toward the station we thought there must be some kind of school picnic, for a very large number of small children were waiting with some adults at the end of the platform. To our surprise, one of the ladies in charge walked toward us and stretched out her hand in greeting. She was the mother of four of the children. The other women were mothers of the other children.

Two very small girls carried a banner that said: "Welcome to Seattle," with my name printed underneath. As we approached, they set up a cheerleaders' shout: "We are Dick-Read babies!" I found it very difficult to know quite what expression to wear, but the spontaneous one was an amused smile, which crept over my face. Then, very solemnly, two other charming little girls walked forward to my wife and presented her with a beautiful bouquet. Then we all gathered around and had a good look at each other, with a lot of laughter. I told them it was the nicest thing I had ever seen.

On another part of our journey, while in Dallas, Texas, my eyes could hardly take in all that I saw in the great Neiman Marcus store. Although appreciating the elegance and art that was so obviously and beautifully displayed, I found myself wondering how long I could live in comfort, without working, for the amount it would cost me to buy my wife just those things I felt sure she would enjoy wearing.

The morning went all too quickly. As we left, our taxi driver threw away three inches of a Havana cigar, which smelled excellent to me. Then he opened the box on the seat beside him and produced another one, a good six inches long, which he lit as though it were his duty rather than his pleasure. Again I began, in a very English way, to wonder how much it would cost me at home to buy a box of fifty of those cigars. Although I had given up smoking some time ago, I used to be a cigar smoker, and Havana cigars are really good. For a moment I dreamed and, in the clouds, so tender to my nostrils, worlds long forgotten formed. I sighed and my wife said, "Isn't it beautiful?" "Indeed it is," I replied. She was referring to an expensive coat, and I to an aroma!

We were in Las Vegas only a short time, fortunately, just long enough to see a little of its gaudy illuminations and mechanical decorations, and people standing for hours pulling handles. It seemed to be a place where nakedness was in great demand—postcards, boxes of chocolates, flags, toys, books, and even chocolate bars all seemed to come as close as possible to presenting a naked man or woman. I suppose it is reasonable that a doctor in his late sixties should look upon this approach to life as rather unnecessary and not a little boring, and we were not sorry to get back on the plane.

Another experience that left an unpleasant memory occurred as our hostess drove us through a beautiful mountain range. Although the trees on its slopes had no leaves on them, we could envision them covered with foliage all the way down to the river below. But there we saw vast booms of logs, like enormous water lilies on phantom lakes, gradually moving downstream, on their way to finish life in a pulp factory.

Since I was a small boy, I have never been pleased to see trees cut down, which may be associated with the respect I have always had for anything that lives. To see a tree falling to the ax seemed like murder to me, and I wondered how the pain it must have suffered was interpreted. I was told there was still enough wood to go on cutting more than man could need for a hundred years, by which time the new wood itself would have grown up to continue the supply, yet I could not help being reminded of an occasion when my wife and I were in East Africa. We had been down the Crocodile River, more sight-seeing than anything else, when we came upon two large trucks pulled up by the roadside. In a variety of uniforms and weird outfits, about a dozen or more young men were strolling along carrying rifles. We looked at the trucks and saw they were piled high with impala deer, beautiful little creatures that had apparently been herded up, driven together, then shot and carted off in that way. Little white tails, or beautiful antlers, hung over the end of the trucks. Somehow it was a shock to me that men could go out and kill hundreds on one safari and then take them back to be skinned, their flesh dried and sold. It isn't for one moment that I would suggest this wasn't reasonable, because life very largely lives upon life, and yet we need to be more careful not to entirely destroy our associations with all that is beautiful.

During one of my lectures I was asked to tell about my experiences while on safari in the Central Congo, Northern Uganda, and other places where the white man has not yet exerted any influence upon the childbirth customs of the tribes. I gave a short outline of the information we had gleaned and, so far as possible, the factors common to the two hundred-odd tribes and subtribes we had visited. I tried to put these observations in terms of physiology, and the manner in which the birth function was carried out both emotionally and physically in terms of the religious and social rites of the various peoples. In terms of pagan religions, the laws of the gods saw childbirth as the greatest gift of woman, and her happiest accomplishment.

I drew attention to the fact that I was not discussing the abnormalities that arose in 2, 3, or 4 percent of the women—who died unless they were rushed to some European hospital maybe a hundred, two hundred, or three hundred miles through the jungle—but was giving my observations upon normal and uncomplicated labor, which represented well over 90 percent of all births. This we had seen when we were given the privilege of studying the analogy of the white races and the black in the minds and hearts of women. In Africa we often witnessed the natural law of reproduction with its love and its magnificence.

I was surprised when a man who was not even on the staff of the hospital where I was speaking stood up, looking very angry, for this was unusual in my discussions in America. He firmly exclaimed to me that I had no right whatever to compare them—that is, the people of his area—with these "goddamned savages," for, he said, "We are not animals!"

That was, of course, a challenging remark, for whatever else the human being may be, he does remain an animal, par excellence, and his primarily biological reactions, whatever his color, are those of reproduction and maintenance. For my own part, I can discover no satisfactory evidence of alteration of forces or function in the reproductive equipment of *genus homo,* whether red, brown, black, white, yellow, or American.

The doctor's remark surprised me because, speaking generally, I had not heard these views expressed in public since I had been in the United States of America. This was obviously a sore point, upon which I had inadvertently trodden for the first time, but I did not feel either the person or his dogmatic assertions demanded a serious reception upon this occasion.

I replied, "You have me at a disadvantage, sir, for I would not dream of comparing my hosts and the people of this state with either 'goddamned savages' or human beings who are *not* animals, because I do not know of such specimens. I have never, in all my travels, come across any goddamned savages. In fact, I doubt if they exist, even in the most pagan tribes. I know only too well the white-damned blacks. Perhaps you refer to them? If so, I agree with you. Our lot in life is not comparable to theirs any more than mine is comparable to yours, if you are not animal."

One of the greatest joys during our long tour of America was the opportunity, on occasions like this, to gather as medical people and colleagues for discussion over a drink or at lunch, or after touring a hospital. There was no asperity in our discussions, or an absence of humor. We were earnest and thoughtful; we agreed and differed. I would not have missed one moment of that three and a half months that enabled us to exchange opinions and expose our respective ideas to analysis and dissection.

Any English doctor making a tour of the American hospitals will be struck by the luxury and magnificence of these modern buildings. I became more and more impressed with the meticulous care that had been taken to provide every possible accessory to comfort and convenience in the newer structures. The organization and equipment for the feeding of patients and staff would have left nothing to be desired in a most expensive first-class hotel. I found it difficult to decide whether I was ashamed of the English hospitals or whether I felt sympathy for the people of England that they did not have enough money to supply them with buildings adequately equipped and comfortable.

On the other hand, I often felt that the English women were much better off, particularly in regard to obstetrics. In one magnificent new hospital I was brought into a ward of twenty beds in the obstetric unit called the recovery room. It was here that women who had had their babies were put until they recovered consciousness or had settled down safely from the unnatural interferences to which the majority had been subjected at the deliveries of their normal, healthy babies. There was a special nursing staff for this recovery room, and it was not unnatural that I wondered what they were recovering from, and why there should be such a large place organized for that particular purpose. Did American women, having borne a baby, have to go through a stage of recovery requiring so much specialized attention? It was certainly not so in other countries, except in rare and complicated cases.

I noticed that over each of the beds there was a tap that supplied oxygen, this gas being available through tubes and pipes just as gas for a stove might be, or the electrical wiring for a building. I was directed to notice its proximity to the blood bank; every new mother was as near as possible to grouped blood, stored ready for transfusion should it be required. I was interested to hear that quite a number of patients did have blood transfusions, the number varying considerably in different hospitals, depending on the obstetric routine and the clinical opinion of the attendants.

We went on to a special ward for newborn babies, where they were immediately put into an oxygen tent for one hour, whether they were healthy or not, whether they were born with interference or without. Their first duty of life, impressed on them by the hospital authorities, was that they should spend their first hour of extrauterine existence in an oxygen tent. They were not allowed the security of mother's arms or the warmth of her body, but were placed all alone in an unnatural gas, water, and air mixture (40 percent oxygen, 75–80° Fahrenheit, approximately 70 percent humidity), as a psychological boost into a new life! I wondered why one hour in an oxygen tent, with a higher percentage of oxygen in the breathed air than they had been accustomed to in the placental blood, was more advantageous than lying in the arms of a healthy mother, experiencing from the moment of birth the security and warmth that are the natural heritages of a newborn child.

I passed on to a laboratory near to the babies' nurseries whose function, at first, I did not understand. Then I was told it was the milk bank, where the pediatricians came to write the formulas for the milk of each baby, because it was unusual for a woman to feed her baby from the breast. The organization of the milk bank was made quite clear to me—it was magnificently done, and had women not been born with breasts at all, I can't imagine anything that would have been more efficient.

I learned that when a woman was admitted to the hospital, she was put into a labor room and prepared for the birth by being washed and given an enema and a shave, and was then immediately given a "shot." I asked what the "shot" was and was told it was an injection given as routine when women came into the hospital. They were usually rather anxious, and this helped to calm them down before labor progressed too far. A nurse was in attendance and, from time to time, made the rounds of the labor rooms to see how the women were getting on. The nurses were advised not to answer any questions a woman asked, but simply to tell her to be patient. She was given medicine, usually atropine by injection and 100 to 150 milligrams of Demerol, when the stresses increased, usually at about three-fifths dilatation of the cervix. Some of the staff preferred to give Demerol and hyacine, sometimes combined with a dose of nembutol. It was impressed upon me that no patient who did not wish for medication was forced to have it. It was pointed out, however, that it was highly unlikely that a woman would refuse, even though she was not having much physical pain.

The difficulty is that if she is given 100 to 150 milligrams of Demerol she will react, like so many women, in a manner that *lowers her discretion and intensifies,* to a large extent, *a negative emotional attitude* toward her labor activities. If she is given hyacine, there is no doubt her discretional sense will be partly or entirely destroyed.

As we passed the labor ward, I heard two women cry out. How well I knew that horrifying noise. One woman was particularly uncontrolled; she was terrified, and only in pain because she was trying to overcome her discomfort by resisting it. The thought went through my mind, Can't she be told how to stop making it painful for herself? Hasn't she been told how to breathe? Similar thoughts always pass through my mind when I hear a woman distressed in early labor. But I knew these women were only semiconscious; a routine sedative had already been given, and they could not help themselves.

We moved on into the most immaculate changing room, where I was told the patients' attendants put on sterile garments before they delivered a woman. Nearby was a room where obstetricians rested while waiting for a child to be born. This was fitted with cupboards and closets for clothes, with a beautifully tiled and decorated washroom and shower.

I was then shown into an anteroom that contained a vast supply of instruments in glass cases, visible to all who might pass by, including the patients. There were hoards of drugs in capsules, vials, and bottles, in test tubes and mysterious boxes, all ready for immediate exhibition should occasion be deemed to have arisen. There were syringes and needles for all manner of analgesic and anesthetic injections; some were given to desensitize the whole woman and others for different areas and parts of the woman. Some robbed her of consciousness and others of discretion. It seemed there was no possibility of an emergency arising that could not be dealt with immediately, but there was *no provision for the absence of emergency or abnormality.* I was told it did not happen!

I felt that I was in the general atmosphere of a great nation, *so efficiently equipped for war under the pious persuasion of self-preservation and peace that war became almost inevitable.* In fact, the thinking seemed to be that it would be a shame to have had so much money spent without putting the equipment to use, even though this meant misusing it. Those of us who have seen three wars no longer think of that. We find the mind of man today has so reached a comprehension of the physical world that it gives him power to destroy the human race. Man tends to shrink from the belief that there is a force greater than he. There is a trend in American obstetrics toward an element of servitude to mechanization and the materialization of childbirth and motherhood. But man, however brilliant, has no right to assume command of the ship of human destiny before he even knows its purpose.

I believe there is an Omnipotence that makes our presence here purposeful. I cannot understand it, but I have only to look at the ordered brilliance of natural phenomena to seek some explanation of these mysteries in creative genius which are still beyond the comprehension of man. I am never without a sense of awe, no matter how many hundreds, thousands of babies now, I have seen into the world. I experience a sense of awe at the magnificence of the physical and emotional perfection of a woman when she takes her child into her arms and knows at last she has received the gift of God for which she has so earnestly prepared. Surely prevention is better than cure?

Women have written me of their experiences of being tied down to the table, their limbs fixed, their faces buried in a mask against their wishes, their bodies cut although there was plenty of room for the child to pass, and their infants pulled into the world by instruments in the manner that Soranus of Ephesus said should never be, for force should never be used to empty the womb.

Here in this place I was seeing it for myself. I looked at everything. By this time we had reached the delivery area. The delivery table was an astonishing mechanical contrivance upon which I understood women were pilloried so that, without resistance, all sensations, pleasant and unpleasant, could be taken from them. Consciousness was retained in some cases, but the sensations of birth were thought to be extremely painful and thus deleted.

I found on this stainless-steel and chromium-plated table a variety of pedals and handles that swung, tilted, raised, lifted, and dropped all parts and parcels of the contraption. There were rests in which a woman's legs were fixed so that she could neither move nor use them. Her body lay flat, with her head on the same level as her buttocks, reducing, almost minimizing, the mechanical advantages of the distribution and attachment of the muscles of expulsion. At the sides of the table, just about level with her hipbones, were strong metal fixtures through which saddle-leather straps and buckles passed. I asked if these were still used, having remembered that some obstetricians had discarded them, but learned that strapping down of the hands was routine practice. Every woman's hands were restrained so that she was unable to move her arms while her child was being expelled through the birth canal, or while the surgeon was removing it with instruments from the pelvic outlet, which had been operated on and had to be repaired with stitches. At the upper end of the table there were similar sockets through which straps could pass to fix not only the shoulders but, if necessary, the head of the patient, who might possibly, in her dazed condition, resist complete unconsciousness because she wished to be awake enough to see and greet her baby.

I asked my host whether a woman was conscious of the indignity of giving birth in this way, when she finds herself immobile upon the machine called a bed, fully aware of her position, her immobilization, and her exposure. My friend replied that he thought women were completely satisfied with the situation, and also commented that it made the job much easier for him. He could desensitize the whole woman or any part of her. Her position on the delivery table had nothing to do with it, so long as she escaped the agonies.

I don't wish to make my comments in any sense a satire. Rather, it is with astonishment that I wonder how such things can still be found as representing the most modern of all advances in childbearing. This vast expenditure, plan, and provision was, to me, a major condemnation of the creative genius. I had a picture of mere man, swathed in green and white masks, caps, gowns, and maybe boots, telling the Almighty it was just too bad He did not know His job. It was a good thing man was there to do it for Him. I had seen all this before, and it hurt.

I was given a gown and mask to put on and taken to observe a delivery. A young and beautiful girl was lying flat on the delivery table, her head resting on a small rubber pillow. Her legs were strapped into deeply guttered supports, and widely opened; her wrists were strapped in padded cuffs, which were attached to the table. She was still and quiet, with her eyes shut, until a contraction came. Then she opened her eyes and looked at the nurse standing beside her. It was an impersonal look received with an impersonal look. I show ... e preferred a faint smile or a gentle pat on the girl's arm.

T. ttending doctor sat on the stool between his "victim's" feet, which were on the level of his head. He looked over his shoulder and nodded to a nurse, who wheeled forward a table on which was an array of surgical and obstetric instruments covered by a sterile towel. He looked up at his professor, who was beside him, silently observing.

"She is quite normal, sir, and a pretty quick labor. She is fully dilated now, so I will get the baby. It is not big."

As he said that, he made a deep cut with a pair of scissors, about an inch and a half downward and outward, as if cutting into the center of the clock face down to seven o'clock on the dial. I turned to follow my host, who led the way out of the delivery room. Perhaps by some strange transference, he felt my feelings and guessed my thoughts correctly.

The day after this exhibition of kindness by incarceration, I happened to see, in a daily paper, a picture presented, along with a number of letters of remonstrance, that was intended to call attention to the dastardly cruelty of the Russians, the most unjustifiable desecration of life, human or otherwise, flaunted under the name of science. It was a picture of the passenger the Russians had the day before sent into space aboard a rocket—a small dog, depicted with a most benign, self-sacrificing expression on its face as it lay there, its hind legs tied down and its forepaws fixed in straps; it was manacled and shackled but supplied with artificial food and adequate oxygen. This, the fear-inducing illustration of ultimate cruelty, was thrust under my nose by a very good obstetrician and personal friend of mine, with the sort of look on his face that said, "Now, how about that?"

I am, above all things, an animal lover, and sometimes would rather see chastisement administered to a naughty teenager than to a helpless animal, but instead of rising up in my wrath I found it very difficult to suppress the most unwelcome grin that threatened to show itself on my face. For when I heard the words "ultimate cruelty," I thought immediately of the woman I had seen the day before, her legs immobilized by straps, her hands strapped down, a band across her forehead so that she could not move her head and so that she could be given an anesthetic without being allowed to turn away. I saw by her side and all around her oxygen apparatus and food for reinforcement of nutrition, should her metabolism require support. She was helpless, placed there in order to accept the tenets of science in the name of humanity. She had become an experimental piece in the hands of a scientist, and at any moment might be shot in part or in toto into the outer space of unconsciousness.

I could not help seeing a perfectly straightforward simile. I realized the indignity, indeed the cruelty that women should be robbed of the greatest natural achievement, the reward of happiness that has been provided by the physiological law. This experience, if properly prepared and conducted by an understanding attendant, could influence not only her own life but that of her husband and newborn baby, and therefore, in time, the social circle in which we live.

We need to ask again, what is the underlying purpose? What is the biological objective of the reproductive faculty? What are we breeding for at all!? Those of us who look after women bearing children must realize that every newborn child may be a potential leader of mankind. Our responsibility goes even further, for we need to be making good mothers while we make babies, in order to make a society worthy of a progressive culture. Are we going to allow our cultural desires to take us down to a level below that of our fathers and forefathers? It is our job to cultivate the stock of tomorrow.

Is the United States willing to accept the long-term results of the substitution of materialism for the metaphysical, the eternal or everlasting? The people of New York reacted strongly when the Russians put their first satellite in orbit. There was a feeling that they had suffered loss of "face," but what went through my mind was, Does this great people realize the astuteness of the Russians in adopting the use of procedures of natural childbirth?

In many of the hospitals I visited, I was confused and baffled by the passion for interference with a healthy natural function. Again and again I heard of: episiotomies, 100 percent; forceps, 50 to 75 percent; induction by appointment, up to 70 percent in some places. The high rate of forceps deliveries came as a shock to me. In most countries the forceps rate is between 5 and 8 percent. When, therefore, I was told that forceps were used in up to 75 percent of deliveries in some hospitals, I at once sought justification for this high figure. Such a percentage in a hospital in England or any of the European countries I have visited would call for an inquiry. I soon learned that a school of thought that had considerable following in the United States believed that the only safe method of delivery was by forceps operation. This necessitated some form of general or local anesthetic and, of course, an episiotomy. Childbirth became a surgical performance.

I looked up statistics published by several hospitals, and found that one of the most famous ones had published tables representing the percentage of forceps deliveries of all cases in the hospital for the years stated:

| Year | Clinic | Private |
|------|--------|---------|
| 1954 | 17.5% | 50.9% |
| 1955 | 21.4% | 46.0% |
| 1956 | 18.7% | 42.4% |

Two questions arose in my mind. Why was the forceps rate of the white, brown, and black clinic population so much lower than for white private patients whose fees were higher? Anatomically and obstetrically, private patients do not present variations that require more help or more interference, unless their "higher intelligence" made it more difficult for them to accept the natural law. The attendant factor seemed to be an influence in this case—what was it? I made some inquiries, but received no satisfactory reply.

The operation of episiotomy is another example of routine interference, without clinical indication, without consideration of its causes or prevention. In many of the hospitals I visited I find that episiotomy is considered to be a necessary routine operation and, what has astonished me even more, that students are taught it is dangerous to deliver a child without cutting the outlet of the birth canal.

Like many other phenomena of childbirth, the cause of the tight outlet has never been carefully investigated. We are told the birth canal is tight, small, or that the head is large, in the wrong position, and so on, but when I asked, "*Why* is this?" the answer has usually been, "Well, because it is." That is all that can be said about the causation of something that is obviously abnormal or pathological.

There are recognized conditions that demand this operation. In England we generally consider there are eight indications, which I need not go into now. They are quite definite, easily diagnosable, and, for one who is not sufficiently experienced to rely entirely upon his or her own judgment, make a very suitable list of the indications upon which to base practical application. But when it comes to results, I must say it is quite extraordinary.

In a large modern textbook I have read that episiotomy is a highly prophylactic operation because it prevents prolapse of the womb, incontinence of urine, undoubtedly prevents stillbirth of the child in some cases, and most certainly prevents the aftereffects of infantile cerebral hemorrhage.

I suggest that the operation of episiotomy could not possibly prevent all these complications and sequelae of labor! The damage causing these conditions is sustained *before* the head of the baby reaches the perineum. In 90 percent of healthy women attended by competent obstetricians the mutilation of episiotomy is unnecessary.

At this point in one of my lectures one of the senior members of the hospital staff rose quietly and said, "But have you forgotten so much that must be taken into account? Episiotomy shortens labor, which is good for the baby and the mother. It prevents tears and is a clean incision which is much easier to repair than a tear that may be jagged and rough-edged. We find, too, that it relieves the pressure on the baby's head, and it obviously cannot be good for a child to be pressed down on to that rigid perineum, drawn up and pressed down again, like a battering ram." At this, there were several nods of approval.

I asked him whether he had any idea how often he had seen a truly elastic perineum which stretched easily and large enough to allow the biggest of babies to pass without any trouble or tearing. He said he didn't remember having seen one like that because he never allowed them to get to that stage. I thought this was a very good reply, and I went on:

"May I assure you that episiotomy may shorten labor by five to ten minutes if it is performed at the right moment. But it is not good for the mother, and I am not persuaded it is good for the baby in the absence of obvious tensions. I am surprised you believe tears to be unavoidable because they are not, even in a primipara. Care must be taken and patient delivery understood and performed. The battering ram analogy amuses me. Sometimes it is 'ewe.' "

Then a delightfully suave little man almost leaped to his feet. He said, "But surely, sir, we ought to know. We deliver enough, and there is no doubt about it—in this part of the United States the heads of babies are much bigger than they used to be, and there is no reason to believe that women have grown proportionately larger at the outlet."

I could not resist it, and said, "So you really feel, doctor, that in this particular state some social factor has placed your women in a position of disadvantage in relation to the production of your children and your children's children? How do you account for that? Do you accept the law of Julius Wolfe, 'Structure is adapted to function'?"

Then he suggested, "Well, as the brain becomes more developed, I think it is possible that the head gets bigger!"

There was a good, cheerful laugh all around the room at this ambitious concept of development, and I added, "I am not sure I could possibly provide evidence to show that you are wrong, but I have no evidence to persuade me that the youth of this great country become swollen-headed before they are born!" Fortunately this little pleasantry was kindly taken.

Whereupon my friend the professor explained, "Episiotomy is not actually performed one hundred percent of the time, but only about ninety-seven percent of the time here. About three women in every hundred have their babies before the attendant has time to give the anesthetic and perform the episiotomy."

As we discussed the condition more seriously, I pointed out that the general rigidity of the birth canal has little to do with the physical condition of the woman, but varies according to her *mental* state. We went into the question of the neurology and the protective resistance and even spasm that could occur in a frightened woman. It was also realized that if a woman had a certain type of anesthesia she could be unconscious before the influence of fear was entirely absent, so that the perineum would remain tense.

Some forms of local anesthesia, such as epidural injections, undoubtedly assist in the relaxation of the perineum, and the professor of one large university hospital told me that since he had used that particular measure he found the necessity for episiotomy was not so general. In fact, using the epidural, he was now doing only 65 to 70 percent episiotomies rather than his routine of 100 percent with other forms of anesthesia.*

We discussed the position in which women were delivered, the details of the delivery of the child, and the behavior of the mother at that time. I was surprised to find that children were not received from the mother's body in the normal physiological direction, up and over the front of her body. Nature intended every mother to take her own baby and hold it up to herself as soon as it came into the world. I was able to demonstrate easily, on a blackboard, what a large number of unnecessary tears occur because of the baby being pulled straight out from the mother.

"But," I went on, "allowing for all these details of the study of the delivery of the child, there are still a number of factors which must come into it. One is the experience which enables you to know when it is necessary to do an episiotomy in order to prevent a tear."

What impressed me about this delightful conversation was how very little some of the senior men appeared to understand the detailed mechanism of this important part of labor. One oft-repeated notion was that no woman could possibly have a baby pass through the outlet of the birth canal without a terrible pain. They taught this and believed it, so much so that if a woman did have her baby without unbearable discomfort, she was looked upon as a pathologi-

---

* With or without an episiotomy, deadening the sensations of the perineum by injection lessens or eliminates the birth climax—the pleasurable sexual orgasm accompanying many nonmedicated births, described in *Natural Childbirth and the Christian Family* by Helen Wessel (New York: Harper & Row, 1983).

cal or abnormal person. In fact, when it occurred, students were usually asked to go in and talk to her about it.

I pointed out once more that, from my experience and that of many other obstetricians who followed the prenatal education accurately and delivered according to the procedures of natural childbirth, more than 90 percent of women did not desire or require any cutting to enlarge the outlet. Occasionally, if the *fourchette,* the little membrane that seems to guard the back of the outlet, bursts early, one must be alert to the possible need of an episiotomy.

But it is not fully realized what a tremendous impact episiotomy has on the minds of a large number of sensitive women. It is not a thing that is discussed freely. But owing to the fact that I have not been a gynecologist only, or just an obstetrician, but have had the privilege of being a general practitioner of women's ailments of mind and behavior as well as body, I have become aware of several matters of great interest and importance.

One is that, after episiotomy, quite a definite percentage of women have developed frigidity. I have met many who were perfectly happy in married life until after their first baby was born, when they suddenly felt a deprivation of their virginal perfection. Tumescence ceased to occur and desire became much less importunate. Both husbands and young wives, happy with their babies of six or eight months old, have been to see me to ask why it is that orgasm has deserted the wife. The husband feels that she no longer loves him, and she feels horrified that such a thing could happen when they had been so happy.

If carefully examined, the condition is usually found to be primarily a mixture of physical effects and a psychological sense of deprivation and injury. These young women have suffered birth trauma. This may be a hard thing for gynecologists to understand, for the episiotomy seems so simple, so effective, so free of danger. Yet many women have told me, "Ever since I found it was sore to sit down for a few days after my baby was born, I felt something had happened to me that could never come right again. I seemed to lose all pride in that part of my body and didn't know whether to be ashamed of myself, angry with the baby, or just apologetic to my husband."

"A dreadful state," one woman told me, "and when I went to see my doctor about it, all he said was, 'Don't be silly!' "

Even if the damage is only in the woman's mind—her self-image as a sexual being—the effect may be as irreparable. That part of her body which, deep down in her consciousness, has meant so much because of its effectiveness and perfection, is now no longer as presentable to her man-lover as it was previously. The most secret gift to her husband's love was tarnished by her baby's arrival.

I emphasize this because it is an example of the repercussions of interference with a physiological function and the normal laws of nature of which we are not always aware. We must bear in mind the possibility of emotional disturbances in a woman's mind, below the levels of rational thought, from events that are commonplace to us. I can't emphasize this enough.

When I got into the car to be driven back to the hotel at which I was staying, my mind turned to the women in the large Dutch hospitals, and in some of the Italian hospitals, and I thought how relatively unusual it is for the doctors there to interfere with a healthy, normal birth. I wondered whether there was a closer understanding of women and their thoughts and feelings in some countries than in others. Naturally I at once thought of the native tribes of the Central Congo, and of that wonderful old midwife in Buganda who came to see me with the local government medical officer. He assured me that to his knowledge she never had tears except in grossly abnormal cases. "How in the world does she do it?" I asked him, and he replied, "She is a child of nature and understands it from A to Z, and she has had fifteen babies herself!"

My visits to other hospitals seemed to be arranged as a salve to my injured obstetric conscience. In Cleveland, Cedar Rapids, Buffalo, Milwaukee, Seattle, New York, Denver, Santa Fe, and many other large towns I found groups or even whole hospitals that had turned away from the mechanistic orgy of sensate materialism. Here women were being educated and trained, made adequate in mind and body to carry out the programs required by the laws of nature. Everywhere I was told of decreased operative deliveries and a lowered rate of stillbirth and neonatal deaths. There was no maternal morbidity attributable to childbirth, very few blood transfusions were required, and childbirth was approached by women without fear or anxiety for its outcome. A father remarked how everyone at the hospital where his child was born had put him at ease. He described it as a hospital for human, friendly, family-centered care. Another father commented by saying, "I can't say enough about the most loving, kind, and wonderful care." That atmosphere was combined with obviously first-class obstetric work. Thus as I traveled from place to place I found one or the other approach to childbirth, but with the "natural" spreading rapidly.

We learned many things about the Americans that helped us to understand some of their motives and behaviors. When people ask me, "What do you think of Americans?" I say, "Which Americans? From what point of view? Give me a more definite question and I will tell you if I have any experience upon which to give an opinion." We found so little common to all the states, but there were some things that were invariable—the kindliness and thought for its visitors.

Finally my conversations ceased, but I had no desire to leave. There was much I did not want to lose and so many I would miss. And I was conscious of an aching fear that one gets for the safety of a friend in danger! I wanted to stand up and shout: "For goodness sake, look to your production plants! The repair depots will take care of themselves."

## CHAPTER 20

# In Conclusion

As this imperfect collection of observations is concluded, it may well be asked of me, "Why have you written this book?" There is no more exacting task and no occupation more thankless than the public expression of heretical views. It has been many years since I published my first series of observations and outlined the theory and practice of natural childbirth. That teaching has borne much fruit, and so I write more fully, hoping, not without justification, that more of my medical brethren may be persuaded to give this method fair and prolonged trial. I am not prompted by missionary zeal that seeks to proselytize the obstetric world, but only to invite attention to bare and irrefutable facts.

It is primarily to the youth of our profession that I appeal: to those who have just qualified and to those who are about to qualify. It is for you to join in the battle against pain. Each one of you has it within his or her power to observe carefully the phenomena of labor; each one of you has the birthright of investigation. Do not accept the conservative teaching of generations past without careful examination. For the most part, such teaching will stand scrutiny and will be proved correct in general principle. But from time to time you will be amazed at the inadequacy of the evidence upon which accepted principles are borne. Be critical of culture; look long and carefully before you accept its tenets; take notice of the subtle ways and means by which youth is robbed of its power and its instinctive genius. Be accurate in your deductions, and delve deeply into the details of each succeeding problem. Analyze your observations, and do not be slow to ask: "Why?" Develop an inquiring mind; seek guidance and advice while you have around you those competent and willing to help you. There is no reason to be humble in your questioning, and certainly no justification for aggression in your differing. Learn from your mistakes, for if you seek the truth honestly, the errors that you make will be of service in your search. As you scramble from one pitfall to the next, you will gain strength and experience. The borderlands of the realm of knowledge are shrouded in a mist that is not penetrated by the earliest efforts of the beginner. As each person gains a greater foothold within those realms, so the mist clears, until he or she finds the vista of unending possibility, the existence of which had not previously been envisaged. There is no such thing as knowing all. Cowper wrote:

> Knowledge is proud that he has learned so much,
> Wisdom is humble that he knows no more.

If, therefore, you feel humble because of your limited accomplishments, recognize that in humility alone lies the true urge and goad to further progress. Let your practice be founded upon the judgment of the intelligent, and your reputation upon the honest opinion of those who are in the best position to judge. Above all, your own personal satisfaction will raise you to a different plane; your work will be in a different cause; you will not be numbered among the "Gehazis who seek only money."[1] Your belief is not in today, but rather in tomorrow and those distant tomorrows which will bring nearer to man his ultimate knowledge. Your faith is in the law of nature; your science is to be an adjuvant and not an impediment in its implementation.

But medicine is a science of opinion, and opinions differ, not only in diagnosis and treatment but in philosophy and ideals. In obstetrics you must form your own philosophy without fear, and observe with equanimity the ideals of those about you.

The privilege of attending women in childbirth is far greater than you are taught to realize. The public applauds the genius of skilled surgeons; famous physicians are beloved and respected for their healing power; great gynecologists are both surgeons and physicians within a limited field. Their lives are given up to the noble work of succoring the sick, curing the diseased, and mending the broken.

The casualties of living are the first call of the medical profession. But obstetricians do not work among casualties; their work is primarily among the supremely healthy members of the community. They watch over and improve original models from the great factories of human life; their responsibility is to improve the stock and render it fit to meet the new demands that modern communal existence makes upon each succeeding generation. The health of mothers and their babies should be the first consideration of an obstetrician.

You must make your choice now, and to your innermost self lay down the principles upon which your future will unfold. There are many paths leading to the rock of a physician's calling. Along the well-worn roads thousands pass, blindly following the lead of orthodoxy, pushing and jostling in a throng that steadily advances with the years to a comfortable plateau called Mediocrity. Here people gird themselves with mental and material armor, and search the descent to old age for respectable nooks and crannies where they may rest and watch the sun go down. It is possible to decorate a well-selected niche with an accolade, so that those who pass by may whisper to their friends, "Behold!"

There are also the untrodden paths that require not only youth, but freedom and fortitude. Those of you who seek a new truth must blaze a trail of your own. The jewels of our science lie off the beaten track. Press on in danger; with the risk of failure you have the urge to persevere. You will clamber among landmarks accepted by your forebears as immutable. Accept nothing, for under each established fact is the foundation of a new future. Gold is hidden in the solid vein of quartz. Climb alone up the precipice that leads to no plateau, but only to high peaks from which you can look down and see the truth you have uncovered on your way. You need no social armor in your isolation, need seek no comfortable haven of rest: sharpen your ax, respike your shoes, and struggle on, conscious always of the vision of youth, guided by the hand of experience to a greater reward than public recognition.

Pioneers pass on unheard and unlamented until the trail they blazed is followed by a few who have believed. At the end they are discovered where their life's work finished, mourned only by the wildflowers of the wilderness they loved.

# Epilogue: Pioneers Pass On

## by Jessica Dick-Read

*Childbirth Without Fear* has had an indelible impact upon the world as far back as 1933, when the subject first appeared in England under the title *Natural Childbirth*. In 1942 *The Revelation of Childbirth* brought a "gleam" of sanity to a country locked in the deadly combat of World War II. With so many dying in warfare, Dick's work brought promise of a happier rebirth.

In 1944, born of "The House of Harper," *Childbirth Without Fear* was offered to the women of America, still in a period when our very future as a human race was so sadly blurred by man's inhumanity to man. Dick's poignant message gave courage to those women who believed they were being denied their right—the right to fulfill their proudly cherished heritage of giving birth in surroundings of kindness, dignity, and peace.

The war ended, and with its passing women the world over heard that "call from out of the wilderness," and responded. Now, mainly through Dick's freeing childbirth from ugly and ignorant concepts, once again women everywhere can give birth more wisely, with their personal dignity restored.

To all potential mothers I can but simply say, he was *great*. I am proud not only to have been a beloved wife but also to have been at his side as, in the face of many conflicts, he introduced many through his teaching and guidance to the loveliness and truth that is childbirth.

To me, *Childbirth Without Fear* still remains Dick's "living" work. Some have asked whether he died a disappointed man. No, he certainly did not, though he was very tired due to the strain imposed by many tours and his determination, in writings and lectures, to exert all efforts in behalf of safer, kinder obstetrics. But he strongly believed that a light was beginning to glimmer among many of his profession who were at least attempting to put into practice the efficacy of natural childbirth. From my heart I say that I know that, though he never lived to see the full flowering of his great work, he died content in the knowledge of having tendered and nourished a "late" budding.

During mid-1955 Dick suffered his first fairly serious heart attack, and another during a tour in Europe the following year. But he continued his work, and came ahead to the United States and Canada in late 1957 for a lecture tour. A third heart attack occurred on this tour, while he was lecturing in Toronto in 1958.

Ironically, it was not a heart attack, as we feared might happen, that took his life. In January of 1959 a different kind of attack, a cerebral hemorrhage, occurred. After a few days' rest Dick again made one of his vital recoveries, and, quite truly, one could not believe that he had suffered in any way. But the second attack of that kind came soon after Easter. Dick was hospitalized for observation, in his old hospital, the London, in Whitechapel. Fortunately, his illness was short lived. When the end was considered by his doctor to be but a matter of hours, Dick looked up at me and said, "Home, Lovey."

With all speed I made arrangements to get him back to our home in Norfolk, and he lived for another nine days, happy, conscious, and content in the knowledge of being among those who loved him so. Toward the end his speech was gone, but through his eyes he continued to register and express that wonderful humanity and intelligence which I am unable to find words to define. His passing was peaceful, and as in 1942 when he held his beloved mother's hand as she crossed the threshold, I held his, and so the link remains unbroken.

# Notes

## Part I Natural Childbirth in Perspective

*CHAPTER 1.* THE CHILD WITHIN

1. Ashley Montagu, *Touching: The Human Significance of the Skin* (New York: Columbia University, 1971).
2. Harry Harlow, "Love in Infant Monkeys," *Scientific American* (June 1959).
3. Otto Rank, *The Trauma of Birth* (New York: Harper Torch Books, 1934).
4. Frank Lake, *Clinical Theology* (London: Darton, Longman and Todd, 1966).
5. See Arthur Janov, *The Primal Scream* (New York: Putnam, 1970); A. Janov and M. Holden, *The Primal Man* (New York: Thomas Crowell, 1975); and A. Janov, *Prisoners of Pain* (New York: Doubleday, 1980).
6. S. Mednick, "Longitudinal Studies of Danish Males from Birth to Adulthood," *Psychology Today,* 4:49 (1971).
7. W. Pieper, *et al.,* "Personality Traits in Cesarean Normally Delivered Children," *Archives of General Psychiatry,* 2:466 (1962).
8. David Cheek, "Maladjustment Patterns Apparently Related to Imprinting at Birth," *American Journal of Clinical Hypnosis,* 18:75–82 (1975).
9. David B. Chamberlain, "Natal and Prenatal Memories: The Consciousness of Babes at and Before Birth," *Napsac News,* 7:4 (Winter 1982). A report presented at the second annual meeting of the Association for

Birth Psychology in New York City, March 8, 1981. P.O. Box 267, Marble Hill, Mo. 63764.

10. Frank Lake, *Tight Corners in Pastoral Counselling* (London: Darton, Longman and Todd, 1981), pp. 26, 27.

11. Linda Mathison, "Down the Tunnel—An Inquiry into Memories of the Very Young," *International Childbirth Education Association News,* 20:1 (1981).

12. Helen Wessel, "Birth Memories," *Bookmates International News* (March 1983), P.O. Box 9883, Fresno, Calif. 93795.

13. Frederick Leboyer, *Birth Without Violence* (New York: Knopf, 1975).

14. Lake, *Tight Corners in Pastoral Counselling,* p. 18.

15. Thomas Verney, with John Kelley, *The Secret Life of the Unborn Child* (New York: Summit Books, a division of Simon & Schuster, 1981), p. 75.

16. Stanislaus Grof, *Realms of the Human Unconscious* (New York: Viking, 1975).

17. Frank Lake, *Studies in Constrictive Confusion.* Published by the Christian Theology Association, St. Mary's House, Church Westcote, Oxford OX7 6SF, England, 1980.

18. Lake, *Tight Corners in Pastoral Counselling,* p. xv.

19. Richard Dryden, *Before Birth* (London: Heinemann, 1978).

20. Lake, *Tight Corners in Pastoral Counselling,* pp. xv, xvi.

21. *Ibid.,* p. 129.

22. Walter B. Cannon, *Bodily Changes in Pain, Hunger, Fear and Rage* (rev. ed. New York: Harper & Row, 1963).

23. Leni Schwartz, *The World of the Unborn* (New York: Richard Marek Publishers, 1980).

## CHAPTER 2. BIRTH WITH DIGNITY

1. Cannon, *Bodily Changes in Pain, Hunger, Fear and Rage.*

2. Janov, *Prisoners of Pain,* p. 86.

3. Marshall Klaus and John H. Kennell, *Parent-Infant Bonding* (rev. ed. St. Louis, Mo.: C. V. Mosby, 1980).

4. Margaret Mead, *Male and Female* (New York: Morrow, 1949), p. 238.

5. Helene Deutsch, *Psychology of Women* (New York: Grune & Stratton, 1945), p. 207.

6. Helen Wessel, *Natural Childbirth and the Christian Family* (4th rev. ed. New York: Harper & Row, 1983).

7. Robert Bradley, *Husband-Coached Childbirth* (rev. ed. New York: Harper & Row, 1980).

8. Victor G. Vaugham III, "Insight in Social Behavior," *Journal of the American Medical Association,* 198:1 (Oct. 3, 1966).

9. Ruth Watson Lubic, "Six Years of Progress: The Rise of the Birth Center Alternative," *The Nation's Health* (January 1982).

10. What follows is a brief summary of the Family Centered Maternity

Program in use by The Sierra Medical Group in which Dr. Harlan Ellis is a partner, in Visalia, California.

CHAPTER 3. A HEALTHY PREGNANCY

1. *Williams Obstetrics.* 15th ed. Jack Pritchard and Paul MacDonald, eds. (New York: Appleton-Century-Crofts, 1976), pp. 254, 255.
2. *The Womanly Art of Breastfeeding* (3rd ed. Franklin Park, Ill: La Leche League International, 1981).
3. Arnold Kegel, M.D., gynecologist at the University of Southern California, has perfected and promoted pubococcygeal exercises in the United States so extensively that they are often simply called "the Kegel."

CHAPTER 4. RELAXATION: THE KEY TO COMFORT IN LABOR

1. Edmund Jacobson, *Progressive Relaxation* (New York: McGraw-Hill, 1929; rev. 1974). See also *You Must Relax* (New York: McGraw-Hill, 1927; rev. 1962, 1976) and *How to Relax and Have Your Baby* (New York: McGraw-Hill, 1959).

CHAPTER 5. OVERCOMING DOUBTS AND PROBLEMS

1. See Sir Henry Head, "Certain Aspects of Pain," *British Medical Journal,* 1923. See also his *Studies in Neurology* (London: Hodder & Stoughton, 1920).
2. Janov, *Prisoners of Pain,* p. 145.
3. Juliet M. DeSa Souza, M.D., "Postural Exercise Turns Fetus in Breech Position," a report given at the World Congress of Gynecology and Obstetrics, reported in *Ob/Gyn News,* 12:1 (1978).
4. Claire M. Andrews, CNM, "Changing Fetal Position Through Maternal Posturing," *Birth Defects: Original Article Series,* 17:6, pp. 85–96.
5. Margot Edwards and Penny Simkin, *Obstetric Tests and Technology. A Consumer's Guide* (Seattle: The Pennypress, 1980).
6. *Journal of Obstetrics and Gynecology,* 76 (October 1969), pp. 877–880.
7. Steer and Moore, "The Course of Perinatal Mortality: A Review of Etiologic Factors in the Sloane Hospital 1888–1967," *Obstetrics and Gynecology* S, no. 1 (March 1962), p. 61.
8. H. M. Wallace, "Teenage Pregnancy," *American Journal of Obstetrics and Gynecology,* 92:8, pp. 1129.

CHAPTER 6. LABOR AND BIRTH

1. *Williams Obstetrics.* 15th ed., p. 163.
2. *Journal of the Israel Medical Association,* 87:2 (July 15, 1974), p. 102.
3. *Williams Obstetrics.* 15th ed., pp. 187, 188.
4. Roberto Caldeyra-Barcia, "The Influence of Maternal Position During the Second Stage of Labor," *Highlights of the Tenth Biennial Convention*

*of the International Childbirth Education Association, Inc.* (Seattle: The Pennypress, 1978), pp. 31ff.

*CHAPTER 7.* THE HUMAN POTENTIAL OF THE NEWBORN

1. Klaus and Kennell, *Parent-Infant Bonding.*
2. Margaret A. Ribble, *The Rights of Infants* (rev. ed. New York: Columbia University Press, 1965), pp. 4, 131–145.
3. Harlow, "Love in Infant Monkeys," *Scientific American,* op. cit.
4. Eckhard H. Hess, "Imprinting in Animals," *Scientific American* (March 1958).
5. Konrad Lorenz, *King Solomon's Ring* (New York: Thomas Crowell, 1952).
6. James Clark Moloney, "What Americans Can Learn from Healthy Primitives," *Unity,* 149:3 (September–October 1963).
7. Clarence Pfaffenberger, *Dog Behavior* (New York: Howell Book House, 1964), p. 125.
8. Clarence Pfaffenberger, John Paul Scott, and John I. Fuller, *Genetics and Social Behavior of the Dog* (Chicago: University of Chicago Press, 1966).
9. Mead, *Male and Female.*
10. Stephen A. Richardson and Alan F. Guttmacher, eds., *Childbearing: Its Social and Psychological Effects* (Baltimore: Williams and Wilkins, 1967), p. viii.
11. Norman Morris, *Meeting the Childbearing Needs of Families in a Changing World* (New York: Maternity Center Association, 1962), p. 14.
12. Vaugham III, "Insight in Social Behavior," *Journal of the American Medical Association,* op. cit.
13. Ibid.
14. James Clark Moloney, *The Battle for Mental Health* (New York: Philosophical Library, 1952).
15. Mead, *Male and Female.*
16. Ribble, *The Rights of Infants.*
17. Niko Tinbergen, *Animal Behavior* (New York: Life Nature Library, 1968), p. 29.
18. T. G. R. Bower, *A Primer of Infant Development* (San Francisco: W. H. Freeman, 1977).
19. Montagu, *Touching: The Human Significance of the Skin.*
20. Janov, *Prisoners of Pain,* p. 221.
21. Ashley Montagu, *Prenatal Influences* (Springfield, Ill.: Charles C. Thomas, 1962), and *Human Heredity* (Cleveland: World Publishing Co., 1963).
22. W. Coda Martin, *A Matter of Life* (New York: Devin-Adair, 1964).
23. See Nancy Rambusch, *Learning How to Learn* (New York: Helicon Press, 1965), p. 18.
24. Ribble, *The Rights of Infants.*

## Part II The Philosophy of Natural Childbirth

*CHAPTER 9.* THE INFLUENCE OF MEMORY

1. Sir Francis Galton, *Inquiries into Human Faculty and Its Development* (London: Macmillan, 1883).
2. Ivan Petrovich Pavlov, *Conditioned Reflexes: An Investigation of the Physiological Activity of the Cerebral Cortex* (London: Oxford University Press, 1928).
3. A more complete discussion of the Judeo-Christian concepts and biblical translations can be found in Helen Wessel's *Natural Childbirth and the Christian Family.*
4. The 1942 British edition, renamed *Childbirth Without Fear* in the 1944 American edition.

*CHAPTER 10.* THE NEUROMUSCULAR HARMONY OF LABOR AND BIRTH

1. The material in this chapter is compiled primarily from Grantly Dick-Read's explanation of the physiology of childbirth in his first book, *Natural Childbirth* (London: Heinemann, 1933).
2. See *Complications of Pregnancy* (New York: Appleton, 1923).
3. Charles Henry Felix Routh, *The Causes and Prevention of Infant Mortality* (London: J. Churchill, 1860).
4. Francis Hugh Adam Marshall, *Physiology of Reproduction* (London and New York: Longmans, Green, 1910; 3rd ed. 1952).
5. Albert Kuntz, *The Autonomic Nervous System* (Philadelphia: Lea & Febiger, 1929; 4th ed. 1953).
6. Beckwith Whitehouse and Henry Featherstone, *British Medical Journal* (1923), p. 406.
7. *Ibid.*
8. Cannon, *Bodily Changes in Pain, Hunger, Fear and Rage.*
9. Ibid.
10. Pavlov, *Conditioned Reflexes: An Investigation of the Physiological Activity of the Cerebral Cortex.*
11. Sir Charles Scott Sherrington, *The Integrative Action of the Nervous System,* 1906 (New Haven: Yale University Press, 2nd ed. 1948); *Reflex Activity of the Spinal Cord* (Oxford: Clarendon Press, 1932). See also Judith P. Swazey, *Reflexes and Motor Integration: Sherrington's Concept of Integrative Action* (Cambridge, Mass.: Harvard University Press, 1969).
12. George Washington Crile, *Man—An Adaptive Mechanism* (New York: Macmillan, 1916); *The Origin and Nature of the Emotions* (Philadelphia and London: W. B. Saunders, 1915); *A Physical Interpretation of Shock, Exhaustion, and Restoration, an Extension of the Kinetic Theory* (London: Frowde, 1921).
13. See John Baxter Langley, *Via Medica* (London: Hardwicke, 1867); *Brain,* 1903; *Journal of Physiology, 1908;* Cannon, *Bodily Changes in*

*Pain, Hunger, Fear and Rage;* Sherrington, *The Integrative Action of the Nervous System;* Sir Thomas McCall Anderson, *Lectures on Clinical Medicine* (London: Macmillan, 1877); and Langley and Anderson, *Journal of Physiology,* 19 (1893–94, 1895–96): 71–131, 327.

14. Sir Henry Head, *Studies in Neurology* (London: Hodder & Stoughton, 1920); "Certain Aspects of Pain," *British Medical Journal,* 1923; see also Kenneth W. Cross, *et al., Henry Head Centenary* (London: Macmillan; New York: St. Martin's Press, 1961).

## *CHAPTER 11.* THE RELIEF OF PAIN IN LABOR

1. John Baxter Langley and Sir Thomas McCall Anderson, editors of *Journal of Physiology,* 1893–94.
2. Sir Thomas Lewis, *Archives of Internal Medicine,* 49 (May 1932), p. 713.
3. Andrew Moynihan Claye, *The Evolution of Obstetric Analgesia* (London: Oxford University Press, 1939), p. 95.
4. Clifford B. Lull and Robert A. Hingson, *Control of Pain in Childbirth: Anesthesia, Analgesia, Amnesia,* 3rd ed. (Philadelphia: Lippincott, 1948). "Continuous Caudal Analgesia in Obstetrical Surgery and Diseases of Women," *British Medical Journal* (October 1949), p. 777.
5. Nicholson Eastman, *Obstetrical and Gynaecological Survey* (April 1951).

## Part III Autobiography of Grantly Dick-Read, Pioneer of Natural Childbirth

## *CHAPTER 14.* EARLY IMPRESSIONS

1. Arthur Everett Shipley was a famous biologist, zoologist, and naturalist; Charles Fox Gardiner is known for his work on the use of natural therapeutic agents in the prevention and cure of tuberculosis.
2. William Halse R. Rivers (1864–1922), author of *History of Melanesian Society,* 2 vols. (1914); specialist in experimental medical psychology.

## *CHAPTER 15.* PROPHET WITHOUT HONOR

1. See his *Studies in Neurology* and *Henry Head Centenary,* ed. Cross, *et al.*
2. (London: J. & A. Churchill Ltd., 1935).
3. Joseph B. De Lee, *The Principles and Practice of Obstetrics,* 7th ed. (Philadelphia: W. B. Saunders, 1938), pp. 339–340.

## *CHAPTER 18.* SOME MISUNDERSTANDINGS

1. See H. Thoms and F. W. Goodrich, Jr., "A Clinical Study of Natural Childbirth," *American Journal of Obstetrics and Gynecology,* 56 (1948), p. 875.
2. A. P. Nicolayev. "Les Bases théoriques de la psychoprophylaxis de la

douleur dans l'accouchement," *Revue de la Nouvelle Médécine*, 1 (1953), p. 61.

## CHAPTER 20. IN CONCLUSION

1. The story of Gehazi is found in the Bible in 2 Kings 5. He was the servant of Elisha who became leprous after deceiving Elisha in order to receive money and gifts from Naaman, who had just been healed of his leprosy.

# Recommended Reading

## Pregnancy and Childbirth

Robert Bradley, M.D. *Husband-Coached Childbirth*, 3rd ed. New York: Harper & Row, 1981.

Gail Sforza Brewer, with Thomas Brewer, M.D. *What Every Pregnant Woman Should Know: The Truth About Diets and Drugs in Pregnancy.* New York: Random House, 1977.

————, and Janice Presser Greene. *Right from the Start.* Emmaus, Pa.: Rodale, 1981.

Nancy Wainer Cohen and Lois J. Estner. *Silent Knife. Cesarean Prevention and Vaginal Birth after Cesarean.* South Hadley, Mass.: Bergin & Garvey, 1983.

Grantly Dick-Read, M.D. *The Practice of Natural Childbirth.* Edited by Helen Wessel and Harlan Ellis, M.D. New York: Harper & Row, 1976.

Margot Edwards and Penny Simkin. *Obstetric Tests and Technology: A Consumers Guide.* Seattle: The Pennypress, 1980.

Esther Hermon, Dorothy Fitzgerald, Tina Long, Frances Ventra. *Home Oriented Maternity Experience.* H.O.M.E., 511 New York Ave., Takoma Park, Md. 20012.

Mabel Lum Fitzhugh. *Preparation for Childbirth. Handbook for Use in Exercise Classes for Expectant Parents,* 7th ed. edited by Margaret A. Farley. Read Natural Childbirth Foundation Inc. 1300 South Eliseo Drive, Suite 102, Greenbrae, Calif. 94904.

Geraldine Lux Flanagan. *The First Nine Months of Life.* New York: Simon and Schuster, 1962.

Doris Haire. *The Pregnant Patient's Bill of Rights—The Pregnant Patient's Responsibilities.* ICEA Publications, Box 20048, Minneapolis, Minn. 55420.

Lester Hazell. *Birth Goes Home.* Seattle: Catalyst Publishing, 1974.

———. *Commonsense Childbirth.* New York: Putnam, 1969.

Edmund Jacobson, M.D. *How to Relax and Have Your Baby.* New York: McGraw-Hill, 1959.

Madeleine Kenefick. *Positively Pregnant.* Los Angeles: Pinnacle, 1981.

Sheila Kitzinger. *The Complete Book of Pregnancy and Childbirth.* New York: Random House, 1980.

Sheila Kitzinger, ed. *Episiotomy: Physical and Emotional Aspects.* London: National Childbirth Trust, 1978.

Marilyn Moran. *Birth and the Dialogue of Love.* New Nativity Press, P.O. Box 6223, Leawood, Kan. 66206, 1980.

Elizabeth Noble. *Essential Exercises for the Childbearing Year.* Boston: Houghton Mifflin, 1976.

David and Lee Stewart. *Compulsory Hospitalization or Freedom of Choice in Childbirth?* NAPSAC, Box 267, Marble Hill, Mo. 63764, 1979.

———. *Safe Alternatives in Childbirth.* 3rd ed. NAPSAC, Box 267, Marble Hill, Mo. 63764, 1978.

———. *The Five Standards for Safe Childbirth.* NAPSAC, Box 267, Marble Hill, Mo. 63764, 1981.

———. *21st Obstetrics Now!* 2nd ed. 2 vols. NAPSAC, Box 267, Marble Hill, Mo. 63764, 1978.

Deborah Tanzer. *Why Natural Childbirth?* Garden City, N.Y.: Doubleday, 1972.

Helen Wessel. *Natural Childbirth and the Christian Family,* 4th ed. New York: Harper & Row, 1983.

———. *Under the Apple Tree: Marrying, Birthing, Parenting.* Bookmates International, P.O. Box 9883, Fresno, Calif. 93795.

Gregory White, M.D. *Emergency Childbirth.* Police Training Foundation, Franklin Park, Ill. 1969.

Diony Young and Charles Mahan, M.D. *Unnecessary Cesareans—Ways to Avoid Them.* ICEA Publications, Box 20048, Minneapolis, Minn. 55420.

Joy Young. *Christian Home Birth.* P.O. Box 33512, Detroit, Mich. 48232.

## Related Subjects

Sandra VanDam Anderson and Penny Simkin. *Birth—Through Children's Eyes.* Seattle: The Pennypress, 1981.

Richard Applebaum, M.D. *Abreast of the Times.* New York: Harper & Row, 1973.

Susan Borg and Judith Lesker. *When Pregnancy Fails: Families Coping With Miscarriage, Stillbirth, and Infant Death.* Boston: Beacon, 1981.

Dorothy Patricia Brewster. *You Can Breastfeed Your Baby—Even in Special Situations.* Emmaus, Pa.: Rodale, 1979.

Elizabeth Davis. *A Guide to Midwifery: Heart and Hands.* Santa Fe, N.M.: John Muir Publications, 1981.

Ronald M. Deutsch. *The Key to Feminine Response in Marriage.* New York: Ballantine, 1968.

Jay and Marjie Hathaway. *Children at Birth.* New York: Academy Press, 1978.

Edmund Jacobson, M.D. *Progressive Relaxation.* 3rd ed. New York: McGraw-Hill, 1974.

———. *You Must Relax.* 3rd ed. New York: McGraw-Hill, 1976.

Arthur Janov. *Prisoners of Pain.* Garden City, N.Y.: Doubleday, 1980.

John and Sheila Kippley. *The Art of Natural Family Planning.* Rev. ed. Couple to Couple League, Box 11084, Columbus, Ohio 45211, 1979.

Sheila Kippley. *Breastfeeding and Natural Child Spacing: The Ecology of Natural Mothering.* Baltimore: Penguin, 1975.

Marshall H. Klaus and John H. Kennell. *Parent-Infant Bonding.* 2nd ed. New York: Mosby, 1982.

La Leche League. *The Womanly Art of Breastfeeding.* 3rd rev. ed. LLLI, Franklin Park, Ill., 1981.

Frank Lake. *Clinical Theology.* London: Darton, Longman and Todd, 1966.

———. *Tight Corners in Pastoral Theology.* London: Darton, Longman and Todd, 1982.

———. *Studies in Constrictive Confusion.* The Christian Theology Association, St. Mary's House, Church Westcote, Oxford OX7 6SF, England, 1980.

Robert Mendelsohn, M.D. *Confessions of a Medical Heretic.* Chicago: Contemporary Books, 1979.

———. *MALepractice.* Chicago: Contemporary Books, 1981.

Judith Miles. *Journal from an Obscure Place.* Minneapolis, Minn.: Dimension Books, 1978.

Ashley Montagu. *Touching: The Human Significance of the Skin.* New York: Columbia University Press, 1971.

Joseph Roetzer, M.D. *Family Planning the Natural Way.* Old Tappan, N.J.: Revell, 1981.

Penny Simkin. *Directory of Alternative Birth Services and Consumer Guide.* NAPSAC, Box 267, Marble Hill, Mo. 63764, 1982.

Tine Thevenin. *The Family Bed: An Age-Old Concept in Child Rearing.* Box 16004, Minneapolis, Minn. 55416.

Ingrid Trobisch. *The Joy of Being a Woman, and What a Man Can Do.* New York: Harper & Row, 1975.

Thomas Verney, with John Kelley. *The Secret Life of the Unborn Child.* New York and Toronto: Knopf and Random House of Canada, 1980.

Ed Wheat, M.D., and Gaye Wheat. *Intended for Pleasure.* Old Tappan, N.J.: Revell. 1977.

# Glossary

*Abruptio placenta.* A premature tearing away of the placenta from the wall of the uterus, before the baby is born.

*Afterbirth.* The placenta and membranes in which the baby developed, expelled after the birth of the baby.

*Amniotic fluid.* The colorless fluid in which the baby floats in the womb before birth, enclosed in the membranes.

*Analgesia.* Insensibility to pain without loss of consciousness.

*Anesthesia.* Partial or complete loss of sensation, with or without loss of consciousness, depending on type used.

*Anterior.* Before, in front of, toward the front.

*Birth canal.* The passageway through which the baby is born, the uterine opening and vagina.

*Caput.* Usually refers to the soft swelling of the presenting part of the baby's scalp.

*Centimeter.* A unit of linear measure. One finger width equals about two centimeters.

*Cervix.* The lower, narrower end of the uterus, often called the "neck" of the uterus, through which the baby leaves the uterus and enters the vagina during birth.

*Coccyx.* The end of the vertebral column, beyond the sacrum; the tailbone.

*Contraction.* The tightening of a muscle.

*Cyanosis.* The slightly bluish discoloration of the skin caused by lowered oxygen and increased carbon dioxide in the blood.

*Dilatation.* The gradual opening of the cervix.

*Dorsal.* Pertaining to the back.

*Dyspareunia.* Painful coitus.

*Dyspnea.* Difficult breathing usually accompanied by pain.

*Ejaculation.* The ejection of semen from the penis.

*Episiotomy.* A small, straight cut made in the tissues (perineum) at the opening of the vagina, to enlarge the passageway.

*Expulsion.* The second stage of labor, pushing the baby out.

*Fetus.* The developing baby from twelve weeks pregnancy until birth.

*Flaccid.* Describing completely relaxed, absent muscular tone.

*Fourchette.* A fold of mucus membrane at the lower end of the vaginal opening.

*Fundus.* The top of the uterus, furthest from the opening.

*Hemorrhage.* Excessive bleeding.

*Hypertrophy.* Increase in the size of an organ due to growth or normal functioning.

*Hyperventilation.* Too rapid breathing, causing a loss of carbon dioxide from the lungs, numbness of hands and fingers, trembling, racing of heart, muscle cramps, and fainting.

*Imprinting.* In humans, usually referred to as "human socialization."

*Internal os.* The opening of the cervix inside the uterus.

*Ischemia.* The obstruction of circulation of blood to a part of the body.

*Labor.* The rhythmical contractions of the uterine muscles that open the cervix and expel the baby, membranes, and placenta.

*Laceration.* Tearing of the skin or muscles.

*Lactation.* The secretion of milk.

*Lightening.* The settling of the baby lower into the abdomen in late pregnancy.

*Lochia.* The discharge from the birth canal during the first few weeks after giving birth.

*Lumbar.* Describing the area of the lower back.

*Meconium.* The dark bowel movement of all newborns.

*Membranes.* The "bag of waters," a sac of thin membranes in which the baby floats within the uterus during pregnancy.

*Multipara.* A woman giving birth to her second or subsequent babies.

*Neurasthenia.* Complaints of weakness, exhaustion, depression.

*Nociceptors.* The nerve endings that receive pain sensations.

*Occipito anterior.* Describing the condition in which the back of the baby's head faces the front of the mother's body during birth, its face downward.

*Occipito posterior.* Describing the condition in which the back of the baby's head faces the back of the mother's body during birth, its face upward.

*Occiput.* The back of the head.

*Ovary (pl. ovaries).* One of two almond-shaped female glands situated on each side of the uterus at the end of ligaments, close to the Fallopian tubes.

*Ovum.* The cell or "egg" discharged from an ovary and carried to the uterus through the Fallopian tube.

*Parturient.* Describing a woman in labor.

*Parturition.* The process of giving birth.

*Pelvic cavity.* The space within the pelvis.

*Pelvic floor.* The muscles and outer tissues supporting the contents of the pelvic cavity.

*Pelvis.* The basin-shaped ring of bones at the bottom of the trunk of the body, which support the spine and rest on the legs.

*Perineum.* The tissues between the anus and the vagina.

*Placenta.* The spongelike organ attached to the uterine wall of the mother, and to the baby by the umbilical cord. The baby receives its nourishment and expels its wastes by means of the placenta.

*Podalic version.* The turning of the fetus so that the feet are born first.

*Posterior.* Behind, in back of, toward the back.

*Postmature.* Describing a baby born after the normal length of pregnancy.

*Postnatal.* After the baby is born.

*Postpartum.* After the baby is born.

*Precipitate.* Describing a rapid birth, occurring unexpectedly.

*Premature.* Describing a baby born before the normal length of pregnancy, and usually weighing under 5 pounds 8 ounces.

*Prenatal.* Before birth.

*Primigravida.* A woman giving birth to her first baby.

*Puerperium.* The period of time following birth until the pelvic organs return to the nonpregnant condition, usually about six weeks.

*Sacrum.* The triangular bone at the base of the spine, attached to the bones of the pelvis and formed of five united vertebra, directly below which is the coccyx, or tailbone.

*Sperm, spermatozoa.* The mature male sexual cell, which fertilizes the egg of the female.

*Thoracic.* Pertaining to the chest area.

*Tumescence.* Condition of swelling, or being distended.

*Umbilical cord.* A tubelike structure connecting the baby to the placenta, 12 to 36 inches in length.

*Uterus.* The organ in the female pelvis in which a fetus can develop; the womb.

*Vagina.* The passage from the cervix to the vulva, about five inches in length.

*Vascularization.* The process in which new blood vessels develop in a structure, to increase the supply of blood.

*Vernix caseosa.* The whitish cheesy deposit covering the baby's skin at birth. If left undisturbed, it gradually is absorbed into the baby's skin.

*Vulva.* The external female genitals, composed of the inner and outer folds of tissue *(labia minora, labia majora),* clitoris, and vaginal opening.

# For Further Information

*Alternative Birth Crisis Coalition.* P.O. Box 48371, Chicago, Ill. 60648.

The ABCC was formed to help defend parents who want alternatives to childbirth, as well as the practitioners who provide them, in the face of medical and professional pressures against alternative birthing. Its president is Marian Tompson (a founding mother of the La Leche League and its president for over twenty-five years).

*American Academy of Husband-Coached Childbirth.* P.O. Box 5224, Sherman Oaks, Calif. 91403.

The AAHCC (Bradley Method) was founded by Jay and Marjie Hathaway to promote Dr. Robert Bradley's program of natural childbirth, encouraging husband participation. The Bradley Method is based on the philosophy of Dr. Grantly Dick-Read and is in harmony with the principles of *Childbirth Without Fear*. The AAHCC offers teacher training and affiliation.

*American College of Home Obstetrics.* 644 North Michigan Ave., Suite 610, Chicago, Ill. 60611.

ACHO collects and publishes data on the safety and advantages of home birth, gathering data from member physicians for publication, and helping to provide encouragement and a united stand on the safety of home birth.

*American College of Nurse-Midwifery.* 1000 Vermont Ave. NW, Washington, D.C., 20005.

The ACNM is the certifying agency for nurse-midwives. It establishes curricula and standards for nurse-midwifery programs, emphasizing excellence in preparation for its practitioners, with a focus on the childrearing family's human dignity and worth.

*Apple Tree Family Ministries.* P.O. Box 9883, Fresno, Calif. 93795. Apple Tree Family Ministries (ATFM) was founded by Helen Wessel in response to the requests of many readers of *Natural Childbirth and the Christian Family* (Harper & Row) for material that could be used to teach natural childbirth and other aspects of family life in churches. Among those requesting material was Kathy Nesper, at whose instigation the program was begun and who was appointed director. Harlan Ellis, M.D., co-editor of the fourth and fifth editions of *Childbirth Without Fear,* is one of the ATFM consultants. The program is based upon the book *Under the Apple Tree: Marrying, Birthing, Parenting* and several supplemental guidebooks. Apple Tree Family Ministries offers leader certification in several areas, including childbirth education. Write for further information.

*Birth and Life Bookstore.* P.O. Box 70625, Seattle, Wash. 98107. An extensive selection of books and pamphlets relating to birth and various aspects of family life is available by mail order from Birth and Life, and orders are filled promptly. Lynn Moen, president, was formerly manager of the ICEA bookstore. A sample copy of Birth and Life's newsletter, *Imprints,* is available on request.

*Cesarean Birth Alliance.* 10 Summit Drive, Manhasset, N.Y. 11030.
*Cesarean/Support, Education and Concern (C/SEC).* 132 Adams Street, Room 6, Newton, Mass. 02158.
These two organizations were formed for the purpose of providing support for those desiring a vaginal birth after a cesarean (VBAC) and for those who must have a cesarean section.

*International Childbirth Education Association.* P.O. Box 20048, Minneapolis, Minn. 55420.
A valuable resource agency for those who want information concerning childbirth education, the ICEA is a federation of independent childbirth education groups and instructors worldwide, sponsoring numerous regional conferences and a biennial convention. It also makes available a wide range of books, pamphlets, films, and teaching aids on childbirth education.

*La Leche League International.* 9616 Minneapolis Ave., Franklin Park, Ill. 60131.
Any woman who plans to breastfeed can benefit from contacting LLL. It is especially helpful to those in circumstances where breastfeeding is not popular. Now more than twenty-five years old, LLL is recognized as the pioneer organization largely responsible for the resurgence of interest in breastfeeding. Local groups are active around the

world and can usually be located through physicians, local newspapers, telephone listings, childbirth educators, or hospitals, or by writing or phoning the international office (312-455-7730). Numerous publications, monthly meetings, as well as regional and national conferences, make LLL a valuable resource worldwide.

*NAPSAC International (International Association of Parents and Professionals for Safe Alternatives in Childbirth).* P.O. Box 267, Marble Hill, Mo. 63764.

NAPSAC is dedicated to implementing family-centered childbirth programs and to promoting natural childbirth, midwifery, home birth, breastfeeding, and nutrition as the five factors for a safe birth. Its dynamic founders, David and Lee Stewart, have a number of outstanding publications available on childbirth alternatives, including a quarterly newsletter.

*Pennypress.* 1100 23rd Ave. East, Seattle, Wash. 98112.

The Pennypress puts out many excellent leaflets, pamphlets, and small books on childbirth and related subjects. Its founder and editor is Penny Simkin.

*Read Natural Childbirth Foundation Inc.* 1300 So. Eliseo Drive, Suite 102, Greenbrae, Calif. 94904.

This nonprofit educational organization was founded to promote the philosophies and techniques of Dr. Grantly Dick-Read and to preserve his life work as it relates to childbirth. They have produced an award-winning film dedicated to Dr. Dick-Read called *A Time to Be Born,* which gives a total picture of all the stages of labor and birth in the complete absence of technological interference.

*The APRS Federal Monitor.* P.O. Box 6358, Alexandria, Va. 22306.

Published by the Alliance for Perinatal Research and Services Inc., this publication keeps subscribers informed about state and federal activities affecting the health of women and children, with a special emphasis on childbearing.

HELEN WESSEL graduated from Sioux Falls College in 1961 with a major in English literature. She has also studied Greek and Hebrew, and has done graduate work in sociology and psychology at the University of Minnesota. Like Dr. Ellis, she discovered Grantly Dick-Read's book *Childbirth Without Fear* in the early fifties, after the traumatic birth of her third child. Applying the principles she learned, she gave birth to three more children naturally, and began to promote the principles of natural childbirth to others.

In 1963 her first book, *Natural Childbirth and the Christian Family,* was published by Harper & Row, a thesis demonstrating that the Church's teaching on the "curse of Eve" is in error, not supported by original Greek and Hebrew texts. The book has become a classic in its field, with the fourth edition published by Harper & Row in 1983. She has written a sequel, *Under the Apple Tree: Marrying, Birthing, Parenting.*

Mrs. Wessel was president of the International Childbirth Education Association from 1964 to 1966, and is a consultant to that organization. She is one of the founders of the La Leche League and CEA of Greater Minneapolis/St. Paul. In 1972 she edited (with Dr. Ellis) the fourth edition of *Childbirth Without Fear.* In 1978 she founded the Apple Tree Family Ministries, an organization to promote the principles of natural family planning, natural childbirth, and breastfeeding among churches. She and her husband reside in San Diego.

HARLAN F. ELLIS, M.D., received his medical degree from the California College of Osteopathic Physicians and Surgeons in 1952. When he first began to practice obstetrics in the Los Angeles area, he did as he had been taught; but by 1955 he had discovered Grantly Dick-Read's book *Childbirth Without Fear,* and began applying its principles with his patients. By 1958 he was regularly including husbands both during the training and at the birth. In 1961 he received a research grant for the topic of newborn potential, and became convinced of the necessity of immediate newborn-parent bonding.

In 1962 he received his M.D. from the University of California at Irvine and was board certified in California in Obstetrics/Gynecology in 1963. In 1965 he was accepted as a Fellow in the

American College of Obstetrics and Gynecology. From 1958 to 1968 he taught at the Los Angeles County Hospital, and at the same time was Assistant Clinical Professor of Obstetrics and Gynecology at the University of California in Irvine, as well as maintaining his own practice.

In 1968 he moved from the Los Angeles area, as his natural childbirth practice had grown so large he thought living in a less populated area would provide more time for his own large family. He established a practice in Visalia, a moderately sized town in central California, where he has set up a model natural childbirth program at the Visalia Community Hospital with the cooperation of several other physicians.

# Index